Inside XSLT

Contents At a Glance

Inside XSLT

Steven Holzner

www.newriders.com
201 West 103rd Street, Indianapolis, Indiana 46290
An Imprint of Pearson Education
Boston • Indianapolis • London • Munich • New York • San Francisco

Inside XSLT

FIRST EDITION: July 2001

International Standard Book Number: 0-7357-1136-4

Library of Congress Catalog Card Number: 2001087698

05 04 03 02   7 6 5 4 3 2 1

Interpretation of the printing code: The rightmost double-digit number is the year of the book's printing; the rightmost single-digit number is the number of the book's printing. For example, the printing code 02-1 shows that the first printing of the book occurred in 2002.

Composed in Bembo and MCPdigital by New Riders Publishing

Printed in the United States of America

Trademarks

All terms mentioned in this book that are known to be trademarks or service marks have been appropriately capitalized. New Riders Publishing cannot attest to the accuracy of this information. Use of a term in this book should not be regarded as affecting the validity of any trademark or service mark.

W3C®—Massachusetts Institute of Technology (MIT), Institut National de Recherche en Informatique et en Automatique (INRIA), Keio University (Keio)

Warning and Disclaimer

This book is designed to provide information about XSLT. Every effort has been made to make this book as complete and as accurate as possible, but no warranty or fitness is implied.

The information is provided on an as-is basis. The authors and New Riders Publishing shall have neither liability nor responsibility to any person or entity with respect to any loss or damages arising from the information contained in this book or from the use of the discs or programs that may accompany it.

Publisher
David Dwyer

Associate Publisher
Al Valvano

Executive Editor
Stephanie Wall

Managing Editor
Gina Kanouse

Acquisitions Editor
Ann Quinn

Product Marketing Manager
Stephanie Layton

Publicity Manager
Susan Nixon

Senior Editor
Lori Lyons

Copy Editor
Margo Catts

Proofreader
Katherine Shull

Indexer
Joy Dean Lee

Manufacturing Coordinator
Jim Conway

Book Designer
Louisa Klucznik

Cover Designer
Aren Howell

Composition
Scan Communications Group, Inc.

❖

To Nancy, as always, and forever.
And to Tamsen, Dan, Claire.
And my parents, who never read my books,
but enjoy stacking them on shelves.

❖

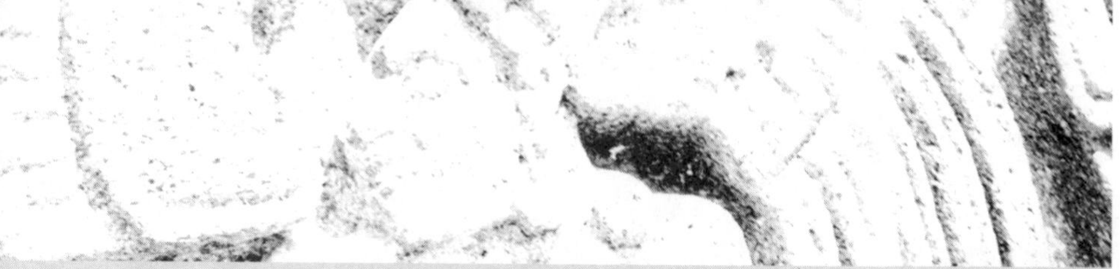

Table of Contents

About the Author

Steven Holzner is an award-winning author who has been writing about XML topics, such as XSLT, as long as they've been around. He's written 67 books, all on programming topics, and selling well over a million copies. His books have been translated into 16 languages around the world and include a good number of industry bestsellers. He's a former contributing editor of *PC Magazine*, graduated from MIT, and received his Ph.D. at Cornell. He's been on the faculty of both MIT and Cornell, and also teaches corporate seminars around the country.

About the Technical Reviewers

These reviewers contributed their considerable hands-on expertise to the entire development process for *Inside XSLT*. As the book was being written, these dedicated professionals reviewed all the material for technical content, organization, and flow. Their feedback was critical to ensuring that *Inside XSLT* fits our reader's need for the highest quality technical information.

Jason A. Buss is a programmer/analyst, developing single-source publishing solutions for a leading aircraft manufacturer in the Midwest. He is married with four children (not including himself). In his spare time, he enjoys playing with his children, upgrading and working with his home PC (he is currently developing his mastery with FreeBSD), reading, playing guitar, and enjoying live music. He can be admired, lauded, cursed, or otherwise reached at `jabuss@worldnet.att.net`.

Darrin Bishop is a consultant for Levi, Ray and Shoup, Inc., an information technology firm located in the Midwest. He is currently the product architect for a large project that is leveraging XML technologies. The product architect role includes managing the architectural design and researching technologies and technical issues to support the project. Darrin's past projects include a real-estate title Web application, a pension product, and various support applications. His current technical focus is using HTTP and XML to bridge disparate systems.

Acknowledgments

A book like the one you're holding is the work of a great many people, not just the author. The people at New Riders have been great, and I'd like to thank Stephanie Wall, Executive Editor extraordinaire; Lori Lyons and Margo Catts, Editors, who kept things moving along; and finally, the Technical Reviewers, Jason Buss and Darrin Bishop, who did a great job of checking everything. Thanks, everyone, for all your much-appreciated hard work.

Tell Us What You Think

As the reader of this book, you are the most important critic and commentator. We value your opinion and want to know what we're doing right, what we could do better, what areas you'd like to see us publish in, and any other words of wisdom you're willing to pass our way.

As the Executive Editor for the Web Development team at New Riders Publishing, I welcome your comments. You can fax, email, or write me directly to let me know what you did or didn't like about this book—as well as what we can do to make our books stronger.

Please note that I cannot help you with technical problems related to the topic of this book, and that due to the high volume of mail I receive, I might not be able to reply to every message.

When you write, please be sure to include this book's title and author as well as your name and phone or fax number. I will carefully review your comments and share them with the author and editors who worked on the book.

Fax: 317-581-4663

Email: `stephanie.wall@newriders.com`

Mail: Stephanie Wall
Executive Editor
New Riders Publishing
201 West 103rd Street
Indianapolis, IN 46290 USA

Introduction

Welcome to *Inside XSLT*, the book on Extensible Stylesheet Language Transformations. This book is designed to be as comprehensive—and as accessible—as it is possible for a single book on XSLT to be. XSLT is all about transforming XML documents into other XML documents, or other kinds of documents entirely, and it's become an extremely popular topic. I've written this book to be the most complete one available on XSLT, and I believe it provides more coverage of XSLT than any other book you can buy. This is an exploding field, and a complex one—I've tried to put in the hard work so you won't have to.

Many XSLT books concentrate simply on XML-to-HTML transformations, but we're going to go much farther than that. XML-to-XML transformations are becoming very important, and will soon be more important than XML-to-HTML transformations as different dialects of XML applications increase.

In fact, in this book, we'll push the envelope, seeing XSLT transformations from XML to XML, to HTML, to XHTML, to RTF (rich-text format documents), to plain text, to JavaScript, to SQL-based databases, and to XSL-FO (Extensible Stylesheet Language Formatting Object documents).

To cover XSLT completely, this book describes all the available XSLT elements, one by one, as well as all their attributes. It also covers every XSLT and XPath function that you can use in XSLT stylesheets.

And you're going to see *hundreds* of working examples. That's the best way to see how XSLT works—there's no question. If I fail to explain something in the text, you can always look at the accompanying example, because there's a working, *complete* example for nearly every point in this book.

All these examples are there to run; I use the most popular XSLT processors available, all of which you can download for free from the Internet: Xalan, XT, Saxon, Oracle's XSLT processor, even the one built into the Microsoft Internet Explorer. I'll cover where to get all this software on the Internet, and how to use it, throughout this book.

Like writing XML, XSLT is not some ordinary and monotonous task: It inspires artistry, devotion, passion, exaltation and eccentricity—not to mention exasperation and frustration. I'll try to be true to that spirit and capture as much of the excitement and power of XSLT in this book as I can.

What's Inside?

This book is designed to give you as much of the whole XSLT story as one book can hold. You'll not only see the full XSLT syntax—from the most basic to the most advanced—but also dig into many of the ways in which XSLT is used today.

There are hundreds of real-world topics covered in this book, such as performing XSLT transformations on Web servers, connecting to databases, and using browsers to perform transformations on the fly.

Here's a sample of some of the topics in this book. Note that each of these topics have many subtopics (too many to list here):

- The XSLT 1.0 Recommendation
- The XSLT 1.1 Working Draft
- The XSLT 2.0 Requirements
- The XPATH 1.0 Recommendation
- The XPath 2.0 requirements
- The XSL 1.0 Candidate Recommendation
- Using the Xalan, Saxon, XT, and Oracle XSLT processors
- Creating XML, HTML, RTF, and text output
- Recursive template processing
- Default template rules
- Handling whitespace
- Disabling output escaping
- Selecting which template to apply
- Creating match patterns
- Using predicates in match patterns
- Matching Elements, Children, Element Descendants, Attributes, and so on
- Matching by ID
- XPath abbreviated syntax
- If conditions
- For-each constructs
- Making conditional "choice" decisions
- Simple element sorting
- Handling multiple selections
- Nested templates

- Stylesheet parameters
- Simplified stylesheets
- Writing stylesheets for the Internet Explorer
- Creating stylesheet rules
- Using extension elements
- Using extension functions
- Creating literal result elements
- Using attribute value templates
- Stripping whitespace
- Creating new elements, attributes, comments, and more
- XSLT modes (context-specific formatting)
- Result tree fragments
- XPath data formats
- XPath expressions
- All the XSLT and XPath functions
- Creating attribute sets
- Calling named templates
- Keys, single and multiple
- Creating multiple output documents
- Using Oracle, Saxon, XML4Java, XT in Java code with API calls
- Using JavaScript for XSLT in the Internet Explorer
- The XSL-FO Formatting Objects
- The XSL-FO Formatting Properties
- Server-side XSLT transformations with Java Server Pages (JSP), Active Server Pages (ASP), and Java servlets.

This book fully covers the official XSLT specifications, as created by the World Wide Web Consortium (W3C: the XSLT 1.0 recommendation, the XSLT 1.1 working draft, and the XSLT 2.0 requirements—for more on what these terms mean, see Chapter 1). As I discuss in Chapter 1, the W3C has announced that the XSLT 1.1 working draft is not going to become an official recommendation, because they're pressing on with XSLT 2.0. (XSLT 2.0 is now in the requirements stage, which comes before the working draft stage.) However, because the contents of the XSLT 1.1 working draft will be absorbed into XSLT 2.0—and because many XSLT processors will implement what's known of XSLT 1.1—I cover the XSLT 1.1 working draft completely in this book as well, making it clear when we're dealing with XSLT 1.1 working draft-only material.

You must specify the XSLT version you're using when you write an XSLT stylesheet. Because version 1.1 is never going to go past the working draft stage or be officially released, I set the version to 1.0 in the examples in this book, except during discussions of XSLT 1.1 working draft-only material, in which case I explicitly set the version to 1.1.

There is also an enormous amount of material on XSLT available on the Internet today, so I also fill this book with the URLs of dozens of those resources, including all the software that we'll use in this book, which is free to download. (However, there's a hazard here that I should mention—URLs change frequently on the Internet, so don't be surprised if some of these URLs have changed by the time you look for them.)

One of the resources available online is the complete code listings for this book. You can find them on the New Riders site, `www.newriders.com`.

Who This Book Is For

This book is designed for just about anyone that wants to learn XSLT and how it's used today in the real world. The only assumption that I make is that you have some knowledge of how to create documents using both XML and HTML. The companion volume to this book is New Riders' *Inside XML*, and I encourage you to pick up that book if you need to come up to speed on XML (and because I wrote it). You don't have to be any great expert, but knowledge of these topics will be helpful. That's really all the preparation you need.

If you want to follow along with the examples in this book using the XSLT processors you can download for free online, you should also have Java installed on your system (it's free), and I'll discuss this fully in Chapter 1.

At What Level This Book Is Written

This book is written at several different levels, from basic to advanced, because the XSLT spectrum is so broad. I try to cover as much XSLT as possible, so just about everything is here, from the introductory to advanced level. As mentioned, I assume that you have some knowledge of both XML and HTML.

I'm not going to assume that you have any programming knowledge except in one chapter, Chapter 10, which is specifically designed to take advantage of what you can do with XSLT processors using Java. If you want to work through that chapter, you should have some Java programming experience.

Because there are so many uses of XSLT available today, this book uses several different software packages; all the packages I use are free to download from the Internet, and I tell you where to find them.

Conventions Used

You should be aware of a few conventions that I use in this book. Most importantly, when I add new sections of code, I mark them this way to point out the actual lines I'm discussing so they stand out:

```
<xsl:template match="PLANET">
    <xsl:value-of select="NAME"/>
    <xsl:if test="position()!=last()">, </xsl:if>
    <xsl:if test="position()=last()-1">and </xsl:if>
    <xsl:if test="position()=last()">.</xsl:if>
</xsl:template>
```

Also, note that the code listings that are numbered are in the code that you can download for this book at www.newriders.com. Downloading this code will save you a lot of time if you want to run or modify the examples in the book.

Where there's something worth noting or some additional information that adds something to the discussion, I'll add a sidebar. That looks like this:

Setting the Initial Page Number

Here's another tip: To set the initial page number of a page sequence, you can use the <fo:page-sequence> element's initial-page-number property. This enables you, for example, to format chapters separately, starting each with the correct page number.

Now you're ready to go. If you have comments, I encourage you to write to me, care of New Riders. This book is designed to be the new standard in XSLT coverage, truly more complete and more accessible than ever before. Please do keep in touch with me with ways to improve it and keep it on the forefront. If you think the book lacks anything, let me know—I'll add it, because I want to make sure this book stays on top.

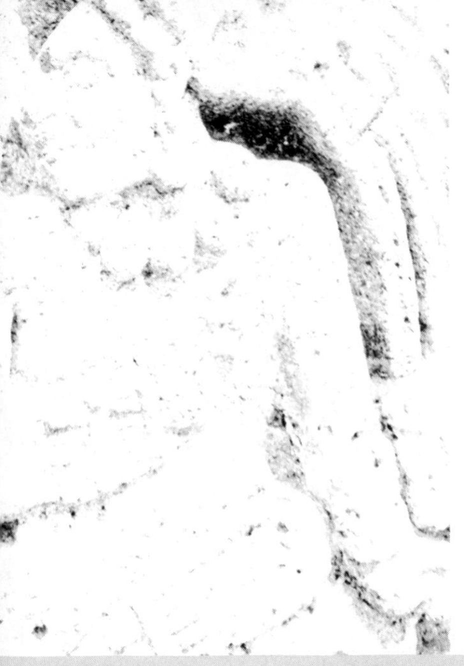

1 Essential XSLT

WELCOME TO THE WORLD OF EXTENSIBLE STYLESHEET Language Transformations, XSLT. This book is your guided tour to that world, which is large and expanding in unpredictable ways every minute. In this book, we're going to make that world your world. There's a lot of territory to cover, because these days XSLT is getting into the most amazing places, and in the most amazing ways. And you're going to see all of it at work in this book.

XSLT is all about handling and formatting the contents of XML documents (the companion volume to this book is *Inside XML*, New Riders, 2000). XML has become a very hot topic, and now it's XSLT's turn. XML enables you to structure the data in documents, and XSLT enables you to work with the contents of XML documents—manipulating the content and creating other documents, such as when you sort an XML employee records database or store that data in an HTML document, as well as format that data in a detailed way.

You can work with the contents of XML documents by writing your own programs that interface to XML parser applications, but that involves writing your own code. With XSLT, on the other hand, you can perform the same kinds of tasks, and there's no programming required. Rather than write your own Java, Visual Basic, or C++ to handle the contents of XML documents, you just use XSLT to specify what you want to do, and an XSLT processor does the rest. That's what XSLT is all about, and it's become the next big thing in the XML world.

XSL = XSLT + XSL-FO

XSLT itself is actually part of a larger specification, Extensible Stylesheet Language, or XSL. XSL is all about specifying the exact format, down to the millimeter, of documents. The formatting part of XSL, which is a far larger specification than XSLT is based on special formatting objects, and this part of XSL is often called XSL-FO (or XSL:FO, or XSLFO). XSL-FO is an involved topic, because styling your documents with formatting objects can be an intricate process. In fact, XSLT was originally added to XSL to make it easier to transform XML documents into documents that are based on XSL-FO formatting objects.

This book is all about XSLT, but it also provides an introduction to XSL-FO, including how to use XSLT to transform documents to XSL-FO form; after all, XSLT was first introduced to make working with XSL-FO easier. To get started, this chapter examines both XSLT and XSL-FO in overview.

A Little Background

XSL itself is a creation of the World Wide Web Consortium (W3C, `www.w3.org`), a coalition of groups originally founded by Tim Berners-Lee. The W3C is the body that releases the specifications, such as those for XSL, that are used in this book. They make XML and XSL what they are.

W3C and Style Languages

You can read about the history of W3C's work with style languages at `www.w3.org/Style/History`. It's interesting to see how much work has gone on—and how much style languages have changed over the years.

The W3C originally developed the grandfather of XML, SGML (Standard Generalized Markup Language), in the 1980s, but it was too complex to find much use, and in fact, XML (like HTML) is a simplified version of SGML. The W3C also created a style language called DSSSL (for Document Style Semantics and Specification Language) for use with SGML, and in the same way that XML was derived from SGML, XSL is based on the original DSSSL. As the W3C says: "The model used by XSL for rendering documents on the screen builds upon many years of work on a complex ISO-standard style language called the Document Style Semantics and Specification Language (DSSSL)."

However, the original part of XSL—that is, XSL-FO—has not proven easy enough to find widespread use yet either, so XSLT was introduced to make it easier to convert XML documents to XSL-FO form. As it turns out,

XSLT is what has really taken off, because it provides a complete transformation language that enables you to work with the contents of XML documents without writing programming code, transforming those documents into another XML document, HTML, or other text-based formats. The big success story here, surprising even the W3C, is XSLT.

XSLT—XSL Transformations

XSLT lets you work with the contents of XML documents directly. For example, you might have a huge XML document that holds all baseball statistics for the most recent baseball season, but you might be interested only in the statistics for pitchers. To extract the data on pitchers, you can write your own program in Java, Visual Basic, or C++ that works with XML *parsers*. Parsers are special software packages that read XML documents and pass all the data in the document, piece by piece, to your own code. You can then write a new XML document, pitchers.xml, that contains only data about pitchers.

That way of doing things works, but it involves quite a bit of programming, as well as the investment of a lot of time and testing. XSLT was invented to solve problems such as this. XSLT can be read by XSLT processors, which work on XML documents for you—all you have to do is create an XSLT stylesheet that specifies the rules you want to apply to transform one document into another. No programming is needed—and that's what makes it attractive to many people, even experienced programmers. For the baseball example, all you'd have to do is write an XSLT stylesheet that specifies what you want to do, and let the XSLT processor do the rest.

Besides transforming one XML document into another XML document, you can also transform XML documents into other types of documents, such as HTML documents, rich text (RTF) documents, documents that use XSL-FO, and others. You can also transform XML documents into other XML-based languages, such as MathML, MusicML, VML, XHTML, and more—all without programming.

In many ways, XSLT can function like a database language such as SQL (Structured Query Language, the famous database-access language), because it enables you to extract the data you want from XML documents, much like applying an SQL statement to a database. Some people even think of XSLT as the SQL of the Web, and if you're familiar with SQL, that gives you some idea of the boundless horizons available to XSLT. For example, using an XSLT stylesheet, you can extract a subset of data from an XML document, create an entire table of contents for a long document, find all elements that match a specific test—such as customers in a particular zip code—and so on. And you can do it all in one step!

XSL-FO: XSL Formatting Objects

The other part of XSL is XSL-FO, which is the formatting language part of XSL, and you'll get a taste of XSL-FO in this book. You can use XSL-FO to specify how the data in XML documents is to be presented, down to the margin sizes, fonts, alignments, header and footer size, and page width. When you're formatting an XML document, there are hundreds of items to think about, and accordingly, XSL-FO is much bigger than XSLT.

On the other hand, because of its very complexity, XSL-FO is not very popular yet, certainly not compared to XSLT. There's not much software that supports XSL-FO at this point, and none that implements anywhere near the complete standard. Just as the most common use of XSLT is to transform XML to HTML, the most common use of XSL-FO is to convert XML to formatted PDF (Portable Data Format), the format used by the Adobe Acrobat. You'll see an example of that at the end of this chapter, as well as in Chapter 11.

The W3C Specifications

W3C releases the specifications for both XML and XSL, and those specifications are what we'll be working with in this book. W3C specifications are not called standards because by international agreement, standards are created only by government-approved bodies. Instead, the W3C starts by releasing the *requirements* for a new specification. The requirements are goals, and list a sort of preview of what the specification will be all about, but the specification isn't written at that point. Next, the W3C releases specifications first as *working drafts*, which anyone may comment on, then as *candidate recommendations*, which are still subject to review, and then finally as *recommendations*, which are final.

The following list includes the XSLT-related W3C specifications that we'll be using in this book and where you can find them:

- **The complete XSL candidate recommendation** `www.w3.org/TR/xsl/`. This is the big document that specifies all there is to XSL.
- **The XSL Transformations 1.0 recommendation** `www.w3.org/TR/xslt`. XSLT's function is to transform the contents of XML documents into other documents, and it's what's made XSL so popular.
- **The XSLT 1.1 working draft** `www.w3.org/TR/xslt11`. This is the XSLT 1.1 working draft, which will not be upgraded into a recommendation—the W3C plans to add the XSLT 1.1 functionality to XSLT 2.0.
- **The XSLT 2.0 requirements** `www.w3.org/TR/xslt20req`. W3C has released the set of goals for XSLT 2.0, including more support for XML schemas.

- **The XPath 1.0 specification** `www.w3.org/TR/xpath`. You use XPath to locate and point to specific sections and elements in XML documents so that you can work with them.
- **The XPath 2.0 requirements** `www.w3.org/TR/xpath20req`. XPath is being updated to offer more support for XSLT 2.0.

XSLT Versions

The specifications for XSLT have been considerably more active than the specifications for XSL as a whole. The XSLT 1.0 recommendation was made final November 16, 1999, and that's the version that forms the backbone of XSLT today.

Next came the XSLT 1.1 working draft, and although it was originally intended to go on and become a new recommendation, some people in the W3C started working on XSLT 2.0; after a while, the W3C decided to *cancel* the XSLT 1.1 recommendation. This means that the XSLT 1.1 working draft is not going to go any further—it'll always stay in working draft form and will not become a recommendation. In other words, there will be no official version 1.1 of XSLT.

However, the W3C also says that it plans to integrate much of what was done in the XSLT 1.1 working draft into XSLT 2.0, and for that reason, I'll take a look at the XSLT 1.1 working draft in this book. I'll be sure to label material as "XSLT 1.1 working draft only" when we're discussing something new that was introduced in the XSLT 1.1 working draft.

Here are the changes from XSLT 1.0 that were made in the XSLT 1.1 working draft; note that this list is included just for reference, because most of this material probably won't mean anything to you yet:

- The result tree fragment data type, supported in XSLT 1.0, was eliminated.
- The output method no longer has complete freedom to add namespace nodes, because a process of namespace fixup is applied automatically.
- Support for XML Base was added.
- Multiple output documents are now supported with the `<xsl:document>` element.
- The `<xsl:apply-imports>` element is now allowed to have parameters.
- Extension functions can now be defined using the `<xsl:script>` function.
- Extension functions are now allowed to return *external objects*, which do not correspond to any of the XPath data types.

This book covers the XSLT 1.0 recommendation, as well as the XSLT 1.1 working draft. In fact, the W3C has raced ahead and has released the requirements for XSLT 2.0, and we'll also cover what's known of XSLT 2.0 in this book. The following list gives you an overview of the goals for XSLT 2.0:

- Add more support for the use of XML Schema-typed content with XSLT.
- Simplify manipulation of string content.
- Make it easier to use XSLT.
- Improve internationalization support.
- Maintain backward compatibility with XSLT 1.0.
- Support improved processor efficiency.

Although XSLT 2.0 won't be out for quite a while yet, I'll cover all that's known about it so far when we discuss pertinent topics. For example, the W3C's successor for HTML is the XML-based XHTML. In XSLT 1.0 the XSLT 1.1 working draft, there is no special support for XML to XHTML transformations, so we'll have to create that transformation from scratch. However, that support is coming in XSLT 2.0, and I'll mention that fact when we discuss XHTML.

That provides us with an overview, and sets the stage. Now it's time to get to work. XSL is designed to work on XML documents, so I'm going to review the structure of XML documents first. You'll be working on XML documents, but XSL stylesheets themselves are actually XML documents as well, which is something you have to keep in mind as you write them. This book assumes that you have some knowledge of both XML and HTML. (As mentioned earlier, this book is the companion volume to New Rider's *Inside XML.*)

XML Documents

It's going to be important for you to know how XML documents work, so use this section to ensure that you're up to speed. Here's an example XML document that I'll take a look at:

```
<?xml version="1.0" encoding="UTF-8"?>
<DOCUMENT>
    <GREETING>
        Hello From XML
    </GREETING>
    <MESSAGE>
        Welcome to the wild and woolly world of XML.
    </MESSAGE>
</DOCUMENT>
```

Here's how this document works: I start with the XML *processing instruction* `<?xml version="1.0" encoding="UTF-8"?>` (all XML processing instructions start with <? and end with ?>), which indicates that I'm using XML version 1.0, the only version currently defined, and UTF-8 character encoding, which means that I'm using an eight-bit condensed version of Unicode:

```
<?xml version="1.0" encoding="UTF-8"?>
<DOCUMENT>
    <GREETING>
        Hello From XML
    </GREETING>
    <MESSAGE>
        Welcome to the wild and woolly world of XML.
    </MESSAGE>
</DOCUMENT>
```

Next, I create a new *tag* named `<DOCUMENT>`. You can use any name, not just DOCUMENT, for a tag, as long as the name starts with a letter or underscore (_), and the following characters consist of letters, digits, underscores, dots (.), or hyphens (-), but no spaces. In XML, tags always start with < and end with >.

XML documents are made up of XML *elements*, and you create XML elements with an opening tag, such as `<DOCUMENT>`, followed by any element content (if any), such as text or other elements, and ending with the matching closing tag that starts with </, such as `</DOCUMENT>`. You enclose the entire document, except for processing instructions, in one element, called the *root element*, and that's the `<DOCUMENT>` element here:

```
<?xml version="1.0" encoding="UTF-8"?>
<DOCUMENT>
    .
    .
    .
</DOCUMENT>
```

Now I'll add a new element, `<GREETING>`, that encloses text content (in this case, "Hello From XML") within this XML document as follows:

```
<?xml version="1.0" encoding="UTF-8"?>
<DOCUMENT>
    <GREETING>
        Hello From XML
    </GREETING>
    .
    .
    .
</DOCUMENT>
```

Next, I can add a new element as well, <MESSAGE>, which also encloses text content, like this:

```
<?xml version="1.0" encoding="UTF-8"?>
<DOCUMENT>
    <GREETING>
        Hello From XML
    </GREETING>
    <MESSAGE>
        Welcome to the wild and woolly world of XML.
    </MESSAGE>
</DOCUMENT>
```

Now the <DOCUMENT> root element contains two elements—<GREETING> and <MESSAGE>. And each of the <GREETING> and <MESSAGE> elements themselves hold text. In this way, I've created a new XML document.

There's more to the story, however—XML documents can also be *well-formed* and *valid*.

Well-Formed XML Documents

To be well-formed, an XML document must follow the syntax rules set up for XML by the W3C in the XML 1.0 recommendation (which you can find at www.w3.org/TR/REC-xml). Informally, "well-formed" means mostly that the document must contain one or more elements, and one element, the *root element*, must contain all the other elements. Also, each element must nest inside any enclosing elements properly. For example, the following document is not well formed, because the </GREETING> closing tag comes after the opening <MESSAGE> tag for the next element:

```
<?xml version="1.0" encoding="UTF-8"?>
<DOCUMENT>
    <GREETING>
        Hello From XML
    <MESSAGE>
    </GREETING>
        Welcome to the wild and woolly world of XML.
    </MESSAGE>
</DOCUMENT>
```

Valid XML Documents

Most XML browsers will check your document to see whether it is well-formed. Some of them can also check whether it's valid. An XML document is valid if a *Document Type Declaration* (DTD) or XML *schema* is associated with it, and if the document complies with that DTD or schema. That is, the

DTD or schema specifies a set of rules for the document's own internal consistency, and if the browser can confirm that the document follows those rules, the document is valid.

XML schemas are gaining popularity, and much more support for schemas is coming in XSLT 2.0 (in fact, supporting XML schemas is the motivating force behind XSLT 2.0), but DTDs are still the most commonly used tools for ensuring validity. DTDs can be stored in a separate file, or they can be stored in the document itself, in a `<!DOCTYPE>` element. This example adds a `<!DOCTYPE>` element to the example XML document we developed:

```
<?xml version="1.0" encoding="UTF-8"?>
<?xml-stylesheet type="text/css" href="first.css"?>
<!DOCTYPE DOCUMENT [
    <!ELEMENT DOCUMENT (GREETING, MESSAGE)>
    <!ELEMENT GREETING (#PCDATA)>
    <!ELEMENT MESSAGE (#PCDATA)>
]>
<DOCUMENT>
    <GREETING>
        Hello From XML
    </GREETING>
    <MESSAGE>
        Welcome to the wild and woolly world of XML.
    </MESSAGE>
</DOCUMENT>
```

This book does not cover DTDs (see *Inside XML* for all the details on DTDs), but what this DTD says is that you can have `<GREETING>` and `<MESSAGE>` elements inside a `<DOCUMENT>` element, that the `<DOCUMENT>` element is the root element, and that the `<GREETING>` and `<MESSAGE>` elements can hold text.

You can have all kinds of hierarchies in XML documents, where one element encloses another, down to many levels deep. You can also give elements *attributes*, like this: `<CIRCLE COLOR="blue">`, where the COLOR attribute holds the value "blue." You can use such attributes to store additional data about elements. You can also include *comments* in XML documents that explain more about specific elements by enclosing comment text inside `<!--` and `-->`.

Here's an example of an XML document, planets.xml, that puts these features to work by storing data about the planets Mercury, Venus, and Earth, such as their mass, length of their day, density, distance from the sun, and so on. This document is used throughout the book, because it includes most of the XML features you'll work with in a short, compact form:

Listing 1.1 ***planets.xml***

```
<?xml version="1.0"?>
<PLANETS>
    <PLANET>
        <NAME>Mercury</NAME>
        <MASS UNITS="(Earth = 1)">.0553</MASS>
        <DAY UNITS="days">58.65</DAY>
        <RADIUS UNITS="miles">1516</RADIUS>
        <DENSITY UNITS="(Earth = 1)">.983</DENSITY>
        <DISTANCE UNITS="million miles">43.4</DISTANCE><!--At perihelion-->
    </PLANET>

    <PLANET>
        <NAME>Venus</NAME>
        <MASS UNITS="(Earth = 1)">.815</MASS>
        <DAY UNITS="days">116.75</DAY>
        <RADIUS UNITS="miles">3716</RADIUS>
        <DENSITY UNITS="(Earth = 1)">.943</DENSITY>
        <DISTANCE UNITS="million miles">66.8</DISTANCE><!--At perihelion-->
    </PLANET>

    <PLANET>
        <NAME>Earth</NAME>
        <MASS UNITS="(Earth = 1)">1</MASS>
        <DAY UNITS="days">1</DAY>
        <RADIUS UNITS="miles">2107</RADIUS>
        <DENSITY UNITS="(Earth = 1)">1</DENSITY>
        <DISTANCE UNITS="million miles">128.4</DISTANCE><!--At perihelion-->
    </PLANET>
</PLANETS>
```

You also need to understand a few XML definitions in this book:

- **CDATA.** Simple character data (that is, text that does not include any markup).
- **ID.** A proper XML name, which must be unique (that is, not shared by any other attribute of the ID type).
- **IDREF.** Will hold the value of an ID attribute of some element, usually another element that the current element is related to.
- **IDREFS.** Multiple IDs of elements separated by whitespace.
- **NAME Character.** A letter, digit, period, hyphen, underscore, or colon.
- **NAME.** An XML name, which must start with a letter, an underscore, or a colon, optionally followed by additional name characters.
- **NAMES.** A list of names, separated by whitespace.

- **NMTOKEN.** A token made up of one or more letters, digits, hyphens, underscores, colons, and periods.
- **NMTOKENS.** Multiple proper XML names in a list, separated by whitespace.
- **NOTATION.** A notation name (which must be declared in the DTD).
- **PCDATA.** Parsed character data. PCDATA does not include any markup, and any entity references have been expanded already in PCDATA.

That gives us an overview of XML documents, including what a well-formed and valid document is. If you don't feel you're up to speed on XML documents, read another book on the subject, such as *Inside XML*. You might also look at some of the XML resources on the Web:

- `http://www.w3c.org/xml`. The World Wide Web Consortium's main XML site, the starting point for all things XML.
- `http://www.w3.org/XML/1999/XML-in-10-points`. "XML In 10 Points" (actually only seven); an XML overview.
- `http://www.w3.org/TR/REC-xml`. This is the official W3C recommendation for XML 1.0, the current (and only) version. Not terribly easy to read.
- `http://www.w3.org/TR/xml-stylesheet/`. All about using stylesheets and XML.
- `http://www.w3.org/TR/REC-xml-names/`. All about XML namespaces.
- `http://www.w3.org/XML/Activity.html`. An overview of current XML activity at W3C.
- `http://www.w3.org/TR/xmlschema-0/`, `http://www.w3.org/TR/xmlschema-1/`, and `http://www.w3.org/TR/xmlschema-2/`. XML schemas, the alternative to DTDs.
- `http://www.w3.org/TR/xlink/`. The XLinks specification.
- `http://www.w3.org/TR/xptr`. The XPointers specification.
- `http://www.w3.org/TR/xhtml1/`. The XHTML 1.0 specification.
- `http://www.w3.org/TR/xhtml11/`. The XHTML 1.1 specification.
- `http://www.w3.org/DOM/`. The W3C Document Object Model, DOM.

So, now you've created XML documents—how can you take a look at them?

What Does XML Look Like in a Browser?

You can use a browser such as the Microsoft Internet Explorer, version 5 or later, to display raw XML documents directly. For example, if I saved the XML document we just created in a document named greeting.xml, and opened that document in the Internet Explorer, you'd see something like Figure 1.1.

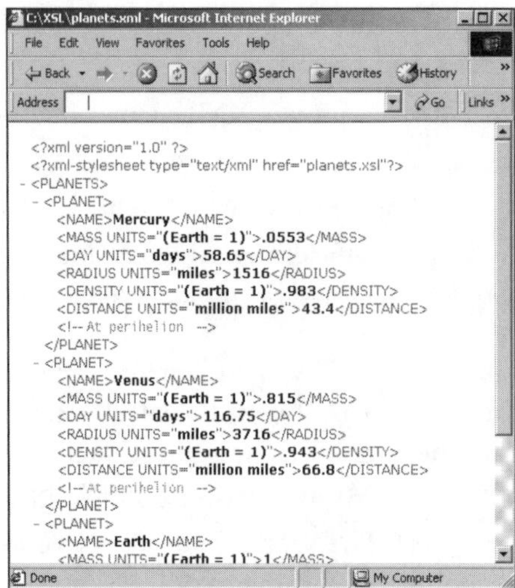

Figure 1.1 An XML document in the Internet Explorer.

You can see the complete XML document in Figure 1.1. There's no particular formatting at all; the XML document appears in the Internet Explorer just as it does when you might print it out on a printer. (In fact, the Internet Explorer default stylesheet for XML documents was used for the screen shown in Figure 1.1. The stylesheet converts XML into Dynamic HTML, which the Internet Explorer knows how to use.) But what if you want to present the data in a different way? For example, what if you want to present the data in planets.xml in an HTML document as an HTML table?

This is where XSLT transformations enter the picture. We'll take a look at them first in this chapter. At the end of this chapter, we'll take a look at the other side of XSL, XSL-FO.

XSLT Transformations

XSLT is a powerful language for manipulating the data in XML documents. For example, using an XSLT stylesheet, I'll be able to take the data in planets.xml and format that data into an HTML table. *Stylesheets* contain the rules you've set up to transform an XML document, and much of this book focuses on writing stylesheets and helping you understand how they work. Here's what the XSLT stylesheet planets.xsl, that transforms the data in planets.xml into an HTML table, looks like (we'll dissect it in Chapter 2):

Listing 1.2 ***planets.xsl***

```
<?xml version="1.0"?>
<xsl:stylesheet version="1.0"
xmlns:xsl="http://www.w3.org/1999/XSL/Transform">

    <xsl:template match="/PLANETS">
        <HTML>
            <HEAD>
                <TITLE>
                    The Planets Table
                </TITLE>
            </HEAD>
            <BODY>
                <H1>
                    The Planets Table
                </H1>
                <TABLE BORDER="2">
                    <TR>
                        <TD>Name</TD>
                        <TD>Mass</TD>
                        <TD>Radius</TD>
                        <TD>Day</TD>
                    </TR>
                    <xsl:apply-templates/>
                </TABLE>
            </BODY>
        </HTML>
    </xsl:template>

    <xsl:template match="PLANET">
       <TR>
          <TD><xsl:value-of select="NAME"/></TD>
          <TD><xsl:apply-templates select="MASS"/></TD>
          <TD><xsl:apply-templates select="RADIUS"/></TD>
          <TD><xsl:apply-templates select="DAY"/></TD>
       </TR>
   </xsl:template>

    <xsl:template match="MASS">
        <xsl:value-of select="."/>
        <xsl:text> </xsl:text>
        <xsl:value-of select="@UNITS"/>
    </xsl:template>

    <xsl:template match="RADIUS">
        <xsl:value-of select="."/>
        <xsl:text> </xsl:text>
        <xsl:value-of select="@UNITS"/>
    </xsl:template>
```

continues ▶

Listing 1.2 **Continued**

```
    <xsl:template match="DAY">
        <xsl:value-of select="."/>
        <xsl:text> </xsl:text>
        <xsl:value-of select="@UNITS"/>
    </xsl:template>

</xsl:stylesheet>
```

You can see that this XSLT stylesheet has the look of an XML document—and for good reason, because that's exactly what it is. All XSLT stylesheets are also XML documents, and as such should be well-formed XML. You'll see these two documents—planets.xml (as given in Listing 1.1) and its associated stylesheet, planets.xsl (as given in Listing 1.2)—throughout the book as we perform XSLT transformations in many different ways.

How do you connect this stylesheet to the XML document planets.xml? As we'll see in the next chapter, one way to do that is with an `<?xml-stylesheet?>` XML processing instruction. This processing instruction uses two attributes. The first attribute is `type`, which you set to "text/xml" to indicate that you're using an XSLT stylesheet. (To use the other type of stylesheets, cascading stylesheets [CSS]—which are usually used with HTML—you'd use "text/css".) The second attribute is `href`, which you set to the URI (recall that XML uses Uniform Resource Identifiers, URIs, rather than URLs) of the stylesheet:

```
<?xml version="1.0"?>
<?xml-stylesheet type="text/xml" href="planets.xsl"?>
<PLANETS>

    <PLANET>
        <NAME>Mercury</NAME>
        <MASS UNITS="(Earth = 1)">.0553</MASS>
        <DAY UNITS="days">58.65</DAY>
        <RADIUS UNITS="miles">1516</RADIUS>
        <DENSITY UNITS="(Earth = 1)">.983</DENSITY>
        <DISTANCE UNITS="million miles">43.4</DISTANCE><!--At perihelion-->
    </PLANET>
        .
        .
        .
```

Now I can use an XSLT *processor* to apply planets.xsl to planets.xml and create a new document, planets.html. The XSLT processor creates planets.html, and you can see that new HTML document in Figure 1.2.

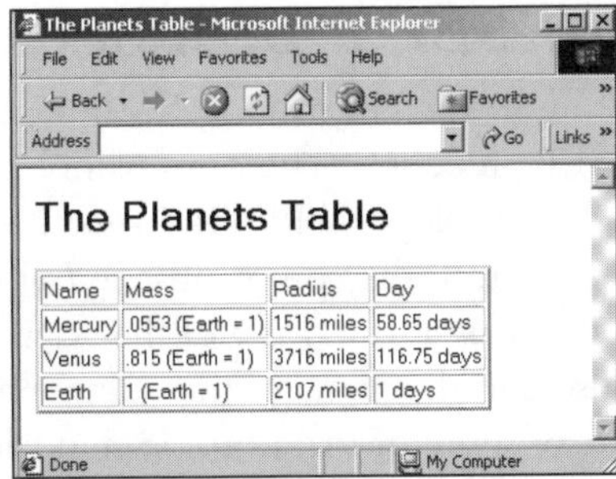

Figure 1.2 An HTML document created by an XSLT processor.

As you see in Figure 1.2, the XSLT processor read the data in planets.xml, applied the rules put into planets.xsl, and created an HTML table in planets.html. That's the first example of an XSLT transformation.

What actually happened here? You've seen the XML document, planets.xml, and the XSLT stylesheet, planets.xsl. But how did they combine to create planets.html?

Making an XSLT Transformation Happen

You use an XSLT processor to bring about an XSLT transformation, such as transforming planets.xml into planets.html. You can use XSLT in three ways to transform XML documents:

- **With standalone programs called XSLT Processors.** There are several programs, usually based on Java, that will perform XSLT transformations; we'll see a number of them in this chapter.
- **In the client.** A client program, such as a browser, can perform the transformation, reading in the stylesheet you specify with the `<?xml-stylesheet?>` processing instruction. The Internet Explorer can handle transformations this way to some extent.
- **In the server.** A server program, such as a Java servlet, can use a stylesheet to transform a document automatically and send it to the client.

We'll see all three ways of performing XSLT transformation in this book. In fact, you're going to see an overview of all these different ways of doing things right here in this chapter.

Using Standalone XSLT Processors

One of the most common ways of making XSLT transformations happen is to use standalone XSLT processors. There are plenty of such processors around, although not all can handle all possible XSLT stylesheets. To use an XSLT processor, you just run it from the command line (which means in a DOS window in Windows), giving it the name of the XML source document, the XSLT stylesheet to use, and the name of the document you want to create.

Here's a starter list of some of the available standalone XSLT processors available online, in alphabetical order—most (but not all) are free:

- **4XSLT** `http://Fourthought.com/4Suite/4XSLT`. A Python XSLT processor.
- **EZ/X** `http://www.activated.com/products/products.html`. A Java package for both XML parsing and XSLT processing.
- **iXSLT** `http://www.infoteria.com/en/contents/download/index.html`. A command-line XSLT processor.
- **Koala XSL Engine** `http://www.inria.fr/koala/XML/xslProcessor`. A Java XSLT processor using the Simple API for XML (SAX 1.0) and the Document Object Model (DOM 1.0) API.
- **LotusXSL** `http://www.alphaworks.ibm.com/tech/LotusXSL`. IBM's LotusXSL implements an XSLT processor in Java, and can interface to APIs that conform to the Document Object Model (DOM) Level 1 Specification. A famous XSLT processor, but it now appears to be superceded by Xalan 2.0.
- **MDC-XSL** `http://mdc-xsl.sourceforge.net`. An XSLT processor in C++ that can be used as a standalone program.
- **Microsoft XML Parser** `http://msdn.microsoft.com/downloads/webtechnology/xml/msxml.asp`. This is the Microsoft XML parser, a high-performance parser that is available as a COM component, and can be used to implement XSLT support in applications.
- **Sablotron** `http://www.gingerall.com/charlie-bin/get/webGA/act/sablotron.act`. Sablotron is a fast, compact and portable XSLT processor. Currently supports a subset of the XSLT recommendation. You can use it with C or Perl.
- **SAXON** `http://users.iclway.co.uk/mhkay/saxon/index.html`. An XSLT processor that fully implements XSLT 1.0 and XPath 1.0, as well as a number of extensions to these specifications. Note that this release has some support for the XSLT 1.1 working draft as well.
- **Transformiix** `http://www.mozilla.org`. Transformiix is Mozilla's XSLT component, now implemented to some extent in Netscape 6.0.

- **Unicorn XSLT processor (UXT)** `http://www.unicorn-enterprises.com`. This XSLT processor supports XSLT Transformations, and is written in C++.
- **Xalan C++** `http://xml.apache.org/xalan-c/index.html`. Implementation of the W3C Recommendations for XSLT and the XML Path Language (XPath). The C++ version of the famous Apache Xalan processor.
- **Xalan Java** `http://xml.apache.org/xalan-j/index.html`. Java Implementation of the W3C Recommendations for XSLT and the XML Path Language (XPath). The Java version of the famous Apache Xalan processor. Also includes extension functions for SQL access to databases via JDBC, and much more.
- **xesalt** `http://www.inlogix.de/products.html`. This XSLT processor is available as a Web server module (for both Apache and IIS Web servers), Netscape 4.x plug-in, and command line processor.
- **XML parser for C** `http://technet.oracle.com/tech/xml/parser_c2`. Oracle's XSLT processor. Supports the XSLT 1.0 Recommendation, created for use with C.
- **XML parser for Java** `http://technet.oracle.com/tech/xml/parser_java2`. Oracle's XSLT processor. Supports the XSLT 1.0 Recommendation, created for use with Java.
- **XML parser for PL/SQL** `http://technet.oracle.com/tech/xml/parser_plsql`. Oracle's XSLT processor. Supports the XSLT 1.0 Recommendation, created for use with PL/SQL.
- **XML::XSLT** `http://xmlxslt.sourceforge.net`. This is an XSLT parser written in Perl. It implements parts of the XSLT Recommendation.
- **Xport** `http://www.timelux.lu`. An XSLT transformation processor, available as a COM object.
- **XSL:P** http://`www.clc-marketing.com/xslp/download.html`. An up-to-date XSLT processor.
- **XT** `http://www.jclark.com/xml/xt.html`. XT is a well-known implementation in Java of the XSLT Recommendation.

The following sections examine four of these XSLT processors in more detail: XT, Saxon, Oracle's XSLT processor, and Xalan. All these programs are available for free online, and can implement the XSLT examples shown in this book. If you want to follow the examples in this book, it will be useful to pick up one or more of these standalone XSLT processors (probably the best known and most widely used is Xalan). To make XSLT transformations happen, I'll use these XSLT processors throughout the book.

These processors are all Java-based, so you'll need Java installed on your system. If you don't already have Java, you can get it for free at Sun's Java site. The most recent edition, Java 2 version 1.3, is available at `http://java.sun.com/j2se/1.3`, as of this writing. All you have to do is download Java for your operating system and follow the installation instructions on the download pages.

Although you need Java to run these XSLT processors, don't panic if you're not a programmer—no programming is required. Although Chapter 10 does go into some Java programming to show you how to create XSLT transformations in code, all these processors—XT, Saxon, Oracle's XSLT processor, and Xalan—can be run from the command line.

If you are running Windows, there's an even easier way to use XT and Saxon—they both come packaged as an .exe file (xt.exe and saxon.exe) that you can run directly in Windows, and you won't need Java at all. This way of doing things is covered as well.

Using a Java XSLT Processor

To use a Java-based XSLT processor, you download it and unzip it, and it's ready to go. You should read the posted directions, of course, but typically there are just two steps to take.

First, you must let Java know how to find the XSLT processor, which is stored in a Java Archive, or JAR, file. To tell Java to search the JAR file, you set the `classpath` environment variable to the path of the JAR file. For example, in any version of Windows, you start by opening a DOS window. Then you can execute a line such as the following, which sets the `classpath` variable to the Oracle XSLT processor's JAR file, xmlparserv2.jar, which in this case is stored in the directory c:\oraclexml\lib:

```
C:\>set classpath=c:\oraclexml\lib\xmlparserv2.jar
```

Now you're ready to take the second step, which is to run the XSLT processor. This involves executing the Java *class* that supports the XSLT processor. For the Oracle XSLT processor, this is oracle.xml.parser.v2.oraxsl. In Windows, for example, you could change to the directory that held the planets.xml and planets.xsl files, and execute oracle.xml.parser.v2.oraxsl using Java this way:

```
C:\planets>java oracle.xml.parser.v2.oraxsl planets.xml planets.xsl planets.html
```

This will transform planets.xml to planets.html using planets.xsl. Note that this example assumes that java.exe, which is what runs Java, is in your Windows path. If java.exe is not in your path, you can specifically give its location, which is the Java bin directory, such as c:\jdk1.3\bin (JDK stands for Java Development Kit, and Java 2 version 1.3 installs itself in the c:\jdk1.3 directory by default) as follows:

```
C:\planets>c:\jdk1.3\bin\java oracle.xml.parser.v2.oraxsl
➥planets.xml planets.xsl planets.html
```

In fact, you can combine the two steps (setting the `classpath` and running the XSLT processor) into one if you use `-cp` with Java to indicate what `classpath` to use:

```
C:\planets>c:\jdk1.3\bin\java -cp c:\oraclexml\lib\xmlparserv2.jar
➥oracle.xml.parser.v2.oraxsl planets.xml planets.xsl planets.html
```

These are all fairly long command lines, and at first you might feel that this is a complex way of doing things. However, there's a reason that most XSLT processors are written in Java: Java is supported on many platforms, from the Macintosh to UNIX, which means that the XSLT processor can run on all those platforms as well.

Of course, this is all a lot easier if you're running Windows and use the precompiled version of either XT (which is xt.exe) or Saxon (saxon.exe). For example, here's how to use xt.exe in Windows to perform the same transformation (this example assumes that xt.exe is in your path):

```
C:\planets>xt planets.xml planets.xsl planets.html
```

That's the process in overview; now I'll take a look at each of the four XSLT processors (XT, Saxon, Oracle's XSLT processor, and Xalan) in depth, showing exactly how to use each one. First, note two things: XML and XSL software changes very quickly, so by the time you read this, some of it might already be out of date; and although all these XSLT processors are supposed to support all standard XSLT, they give different results on some occasions.

James Clark's XT

You can get James Clark's XT at `www.jclark.com/xml/xt.html`. Besides XT itself, you'll also need an XML *parser*, which XT will use to read your XML document. The XT download also comes with sax.jar, which holds James Clark's XML parser, or you can use James Clark's XP parser, which you can get at `www.jclark.com/xml/xp/index.html`, for this purpose.

My own preference is to use the Apache Project's Xerces XML parser, which is available at `http://xml.apache.org`. (As of this writing, the current version, Xerces 1.3.0, is available at `http://xml.apache.org/dist/xerces-j/` in zipped format for UNIX as Xerces-J-bin.1.3.0.tar.gz and Windows as Xerces-J-bin.1.3.0.zip.)

XT itself is a Java application, and included in the XT download is the JAR file you'll need, xt.jar. To use xerces.jar and xt.jar, you must include them both in your classpath, as shown in the following example for Windows (modify the locations of these files as needed):

```
C:\>set classpath=C:\xerces-1_3_0\xerces.jar;C:\xt\xt.jar
```

Then you can use the XT transformation class, com.jclark.xsl.sax.Driver.class. You supply the name of the parser you want to use, which in this case is org.apache.xerces.parsers.SAXParser in xerces.jar, by setting the com.jclark.xsl.sax.parser variable to that name on the command line. For example, here's how I use XT to transform planets.xml, using planets.xsl, into planets.html in Windows (assuming that c:\planets is the directory that holds planets.xml and planets.xsl, and that java.exe is in your path):

```
C:\planets>java -Dcom.jclark.xsl.sax.parser=org.apache.xerces.parsers.SAXParser
➥com.jclark.xsl.sax.Driver planets.xml planets.xsl planets.html
```

That line is quite a mouthful, so it might provide some relief to know that XT is also packaged as a Win32 executable program, xt.exe. To use xt.exe, however, you need the Microsoft Java Virtual Machine (VM) installed (which is included with the Internet Explorer). Here's an example in Windows that performs the same transformation as the preceding command, assuming xt.exe is in your path:

```
C:\planets>xt planets.xml planets.xsl planets.html
```

If xt.exe is not in your path, you can specify its location directly, like this if xt.exe is in c:\xt:

```
C:\planets>c:\xt\xt planets.xml planets.xsl planets.html
```

Saxon

Saxon by Michael Kay is one of the earliest XSLT processors, and you can get it for free at http://users.iclway.co.uk/mhkay/saxon/. All you have to do is download saxon.zip and unzip it, which creates the Java JAR file you need, saxon.jar.

To perform XSLT transformations, you first make sure that saxon.jar is in your classpath. For example, in Windows, assuming that saxon.jar is in c:\saxon, you can set the classpath variable this way:

```
C:\>set classpath=c:\saxon\saxon.jar
```

Now you can use com.icl.saxon.StyleSheet.class, the Saxon XSLT class, like this to perform an XSLT transformation:

```
C:\planets>java com.icl.saxon.StyleSheet planets.xml planets.xsl
```

By default, Saxon sends the resulting output to the screen, which is not what you want if you want to create the file planets.html. To create planets.html, you can use the UNIX or DOS > pipe symbol like this, which sends Saxon's output to that file:

```
C:\planets>java com.icl.saxon.StyleSheet planets.xml planets.xsl > planets.html
```

If you're running Windows, you can also use instant Saxon, which is a Win32 executable program named saxon.exe. You can download saxon.exe from `http://users.iclway.co.uk/mhkay/saxon/`, and run it in Windows like this (the `-o planets.html` part specifies the name of the output file here):

```
C:\planets>saxon -o planets.html planets.xml planets.xsl
```

Oracle XSLT

Oracle corporation also has a free XSLT processor, which you can get from `http://technet.oracle.com/tech/xml/`. You have to go through a lengthy registration process to get it, though. As of this writing, you click the XDK for Java link at `http://technet.oracle.com/tech/xml/` to get the XSLT processor.

When you unzip the download from Oracle, the JAR file you need (as of this writing) is named xmlparserv2.jar. You can put it in your `classpath` in Windows as follows:

```
C:\>set classpath=c:\oraclexml\lib\xmlparserv2.jar
```

The actual Java class you need is oracle.xml.parser.v2.oraxsl, and you can use it like this to transform planets.xml into planets.html using planets.xsl:

```
C:\planets>java oracle.xml.parser.v2.oraxsl planets.xml planets.xsl planets.html
```

Xalan

Probably the most widely used standalone XSLT processor is Xalan, from the Apache Project (Apache is a type of Web server in widespread use). You can get the Java version of Xalan at `http://xml.apache.org/xalan-j/index.html`. Just click the zipped file you want, currently xalan-j_2_0_0.zip for Windows or xalan-j_2_0_0.tar.gz for UNIX.

When you unzip the downloaded file, you get both xalan.jar, the XSLT processor, and xerces.jar, the XML parser you need. You can include both these JAR files in your classpath like this in Windows (modify the paths here as appropriate for your system):

```
C:\>set classpath=c:\xalan-j_2_0_0\bin\xalan.jar;c:\xalan-j_2_0_0\bin\xerces.jar
```

To then use planets.xsl to transform planets.xml into planets.html, execute the Java class you need, org.apache.xalan.xslt.Process, as follows:

```
C:\planets>java org.apache.xalan.xslt.Process
➥-IN planets.xml -XSL planets.xsl -OUT planets.html
```

Note that you use `-IN` to specify the name of the input file, `-OUT` to specify the name of the output file, and `-XSL` to specify the name of the XSLT stylesheet. Xalan is the XSLT processor we'll use most frequently, so here are some more details. The following list includes all the tokens you can use with the org.apache.xalan.xslt.Process class, as printed out by Xalan itself:

- `-CR` (Use carriage returns only on output—default is CR/LF)
- `-DIAG` (Output timing diagnostics)
- `-EDUMP [optional]FileName` (Do stackdump on error)
- `-HTML` (Use HTML formatter)
- `-IN inputXMLURL`
- `-INDENT` (Number of spaces to indent each level in output tree—default is 0)
- `-LF` (Use linefeeds only on output—default is CR/LF)
- `-OUT outputFileName`
- `-PARAM name value` (Set a stylesheet parameter)
- `-Q` (Quiet mode)
- `-QC` (Quiet Pattern Conflicts Warnings)
- `-TEXT` (Use simple text formatter)
- `-TG` (Trace each result tree generation event)
- `-TS` (Trace each selection event)
- `-TT` (Trace the templates as they are being called)
- `-TTC` (Trace the template children as they are being processed)
- `-V` (Version info)
- `-VALIDATE` (Validate the XML and XSL input—validation is off by default)
- `-XML` (Use XML formatter and add XML header)
- `-XSL XSLTransformationURL`

You'll see all these processors in this book, but as mentioned, probably the one I'll use most is Xalan. (The reason I use Xalan most often is because it has become the most popular XSTL processor and is the most widespread use). Of course, you can use any XSLT processor, as long as it conforms to the W3C XSLT specification.

That completes your look at standalone XSLT processors. There's another way to transform XML documents without a standalone program—you can use a client program, such as a browser, to transform documents.

Using Browsers to Transform XML Documents

Both the Microsoft Internet Explorer and Netscape Navigator include some support for XSLT. Of the two, the Internet Explorer's support is far more developed, and I'll use version 5.5 of that browser here. You can read about the Internet Explorer XSLT support at `http://msdn.microsoft.com/xml/XSLGuide/`.

Internet Explorer 5.5 and earlier does not support exact XSLT syntax by default, so we'll have to make a few modifications to planets.xml and planets.xsl. (You'll learn more about this in the next chapter. There are downloads you can install for updated XSLT support.) In fact, just as this book goes to print, Internet Explorer 6.0 has become available. When I installed and tested it, it does appear to support standard XSLT syntax (except you still must use the type "text/xsl" for stylesheets like this: `<?xml-stylesheet type="text/xsl" href="planets.xsl"?>` instead of "text/xml". If you still use IE 5.5 or earlier, you'll have to make the changes outlined here and in the next chapter. If you want to avoid all that, I suggest you upgrade to IE 6.0—it looks like that browser supports full XSLT syntax.

To use planets.xml with IE (including version 6.0), I have to convert the `type` attribute in the `<?xml-stylesheet?>` processing instruction from "text/xml" to "text/xsl" (this assumes that planets.xsl is in the same directory as planets.xml, as specified by the `href` attribute):

Listing 1.3 **Microsoft Internet Explorer Version of planets.xml**

```
<?xml version="1.0"?>
<?xml-stylesheet type="text/xsl" href="planets.xsl"?>
<PLANETS>

    <PLANET>
        <NAME>Mercury</NAME>
        <MASS UNITS="(Earth = 1)">.0553</MASS>
        <DAY UNITS="days">58.65</DAY>
        <RADIUS UNITS="miles">1516</RADIUS>
        <DENSITY UNITS="(Earth = 1)">.983</DENSITY>
        <DISTANCE UNITS="million miles">43.4</DISTANCE><!--At perihelion-->
    </PLANET>

    <PLANET>
        <NAME>Venus</NAME>
        <MASS UNITS="(Earth = 1)">.815</MASS>
        <DAY UNITS="days">116.75</DAY>

        <RADIUS UNITS="miles">3716</RADIUS>
        <DENSITY UNITS="(Earth = 1)">.943</DENSITY>
```

continues ▸

Listing 1.3 **Continued**

```
        <DISTANCE UNITS="million miles">66.8</DISTANCE><!--At perihelion-->
    </PLANET>

    <PLANET>
        <NAME>Earth</NAME>
        <MASS UNITS="(Earth = 1)">1</MASS>
        <DAY UNITS="days">1</DAY>
        <RADIUS UNITS="miles">2107</RADIUS>
        <DENSITY UNITS="(Earth = 1)">1</DENSITY>
        <DISTANCE UNITS="million miles">128.4</DISTANCE><!--At perihelion-->
    </PLANET>

</PLANETS>
```

Now you must also convert the stylesheet planets.xsl for use in IE if you're using version 5.5 or earlier (but not version 6.0 or later—the only change you have to make is setting the `type` attribute in the `<?xml-stylesheet?>` processing instruction from "text/xml" to "text/xsl"). You'll see how to make this conversion in the next chapter; here's the new version of planets.xsl that you use:

Listing 1.4 **Microsoft Internet Explorer Version of planets.xsl**

```
<?xml version="1.0"?>
<xsl:stylesheet xmlns:xsl="http://www.w3.org/TR/WD-xsl">

    <xsl:template match="/">
        <HTML>
            <HEAD>
                <TITLE>
                    The Planets Table
                </TITLE>
            </HEAD>
            <BODY>
                <H1>
                    The Planets Table
                </H1>
                <TABLE BORDER="2">
                    <TR>
                        <TD>Name</TD>
                        <TD>Mass</TD>
                        <TD>Radius</TD>
                        <TD>Day</TD>
                    </TR>
                    <xsl:apply-templates/>
                </TABLE>
            </BODY>
```

```
        </HTML>
    </xsl:template>

    <xsl:template match="PLANETS">
        <xsl:apply-templates/>
    </xsl:template>

    <xsl:template match="PLANET">
       <TR>
          <TD><xsl:value-of select="NAME"/></TD>
          <TD><xsl:apply-templates select="MASS"/></TD>
          <TD><xsl:apply-templates select="RADIUS"/></TD>
          <TD><xsl:apply-templates select="DAY"/></TD>
       </TR>
   </xsl:template>

    <xsl:template match="MASS">
        <xsl:value-of select="."/>
        <xsl:value-of select="@UNITS"/>
    </xsl:template>

    <xsl:template match="RADIUS">
        <xsl:value-of select="."/>
        <xsl:value-of select="@UNITS"/>
    </xsl:template>

    <xsl:template match="DAY">
        <xsl:value-of select="."/>
        <xsl:value-of select="@UNITS"/>
    </xsl:template>

</xsl:stylesheet>
```

Now you can open planets.xml in the Internet Explorer directly, as you see in Figure 1.3.

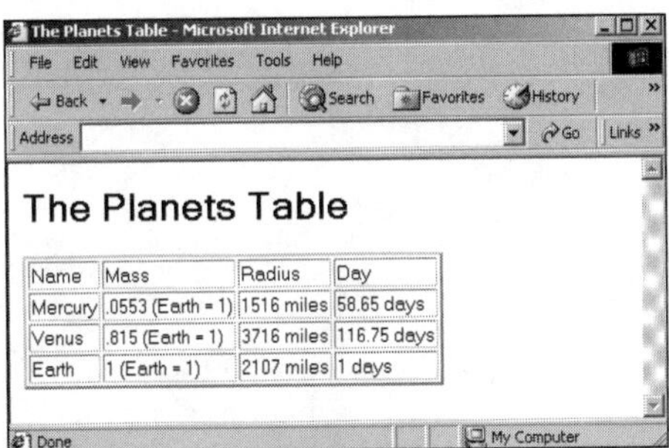

Figure 1.3 Performing an XSLT transformation in the Internet Explorer.

Although you can use XSLT with the Internet Explorer in this way, you need to modify your stylesheet to match what the Internet Explorer requires. Because the Internet Explorer does not currently support true XSLT when you open XML documents by navigating to them, I won't be using that browser to perform XSLT transformations in this book unless specifically noted. I'll use XSLT processors like Saxon and Xalan to perform transformations, and when the result is HTML, take a look at that result in the Internet Explorer.

Interestingly, there *is* a way to perform true XSLT transformations in the Internet Explorer without making any special modifications to XML or XSL documents, even if you don't download and install the latest MSXML parser (as discussed in Chapter 2)—rather than navigate to an XML document, however, you must access the XSLT processor in the Internet Explorer, MSXML3, directly, using JavaScript.

Using XSLT and JavaScript in the Internet Explorer

The XSLT processor in the Internet Explorer 5.5 is part of the MSXML3 XML parser, and if you access MSXML3 directly, using JavaScript, you don't have to modify the original planets.xml and planets.xsl (Listings 1.1 and 1.2) as you saw in the previous section. You'll see how this works in Chapter 10, but here's a Web page, xslt.html, that uses JavaScript and MSXML3 to transform planets.xml using planets.xsl and displays the results (note that you can adapt this document to use your own XML and XSLT documents without writing any JavaScript; just replace the names planets.xml and planets.xsl with the names of your XML and XSL documents):

Listing 1.5 **Microsoft Internet Explorer JavaScript Transformation**

```
<HTML>
    <HEAD>
        <TITLE>XSLT Using JavaScript</TITLE>

        <SCRIPT LANGUAGE="JavaScript">
        <!--

        function xslt()
        {
            var XMLDocument = new ActiveXObject('MSXML2.DOMDocument.3.0');
            var XSLDocument = new ActiveXObject('MSXML2.DOMDocument.3.0');
            var HTMLtarget = document.all['targetDIV'];

            XMLDocument.validateOnParse = true;
            XMLDocument.load('planets.xml');
```

```
            if (XMLDocument.parseError.errorCode != 0) {
                HTMLtarget.innerHTML = "Error!"
                return false;
            }

            XSLDocument.validateOnParse = true;
            XSLDocument.load('planets.xsl');
            if (XSLDocument.parseError.errorCode != 0) {
                HTMLtarget.innerHTML = "Error!"
                return false;
            }

            HTMLtarget.innerHTML = XMLDocument.transformNode(XSLDocument);
            return true;
        }

        //-->
        </SCRIPT>
    </HEAD>

    <BODY onload="xslt()">
        <DIV ID="targetDIV">
        </DIV>
    </BODY>
</HTML>
```

This Web page produces the same result you see in Figure 1.3, and it does so by loading planets.xml and planets.xsl directly and applying the MSXML3 parser to them. These files, planets.xml and planets.xsl, are the same as we've seen throughout this chapter, without the modifications necessary in the previous topic, where we navigated to planets.xml directly using the Internet Explorer. See Chapter 10 for more information.

Using VBScript

You can also use the Internet Explorer's other scripting language, VBScript, to achieve the same results if you're more comfortable with VBScript.

XSLT Transformations on Web Servers

You can also perform XSLT transformations on a Web server so that an XML document is transformed before the Web server sends it to a browser. The most common transformation here is to transform an XML document to HTML, but XML-to-XML transformations on the server are becoming more and more common.

Unlike the other XSLT transformations we've seen so far in this chapter, if you want to perform XSLT transformations on a Web server, you'll usually need to do some programming. There are three common ways to perform XSLT transformations on Web servers: using Java servlets, Java Server Pages (JSP), and Active Server Pages (ASP). Chapter 10 explores all three in greater detail. Some XSLT processors can be set up to be used on Web servers—here's a starter list:

- **AXSL** `www.javalobby.org/axsl.html`. AXSL is a server-side tool that converts XML to HTML using XSLT.
- **Microsoft XML Parser** `http://msdn.microsoft.com/downloads/webtechnology/xml/msxml.asp`. MSXML3 provides server-safe HTTP access for use with ASP.
- **mod_xslt** `http://modxslt.userworld.com`. A simple Apache Web server module that uses XSLT to deliver XML-based content. Uses the Sablotron processor to do the XSLT processing.
- **PXSLServlet** `www.pault.com/Pxsl`. This servlet can be used to convert XML to HTML with XSLT. It also enables you to read from and write to a SQL database (JDBC).
- **xesalt** `www.inlogix.de/products.html`. This XSLT processor is available as a module for both Apache and IIS Web servers.
- **XML Enabler** `www.alphaworks.ibm.com/tech/xmlenabler`. The XML Enabler enables you to send requests to a servlet and when the servlet responds, the XML Enabler can format the data using different XSLT stylesheets.
- **XT** can be used as a Java servlet. It requires a servlet engine that implements at least version 2.1 of the Java Servlet API. The Java servlet class is com.jclark.xsl.sax.XSLServlet.

The following example shows JSP used to invoke Xalan on the Web server. Xalan converts planets.xml to planets.html, using the planets.xsl stylesheet. The code then reads in planets.html and sends it back to the browser from the Web server:

```
<%@ page errorPage="error.jsp" language="java"
    contentType="text/html" import="org.apache.xalan.xslt.*;java.io.*" %>

<%
    try
    {
        XSLTProcessor processor = XSLTProcessorFactory.getProcessor();
        processor.process(new XSLTInputSource("planets.xml"),
            new XSLTInputSource("planets.xsl"),
            new XSLTResultTarget("planets.html"));
```

```
        }
        catch(Exception e) {}

        FileReader filereader = new FileReader("planets.html");
        BufferedReader bufferedreader = new BufferedReader(filereader);
        String instring;

        while((instring = bufferedreader.readLine()) != null) { %>
            <%= instring %>
<%      }
        filereader.close();
%>
```

You can see the results in Figure 1.4, which shows planets.html as sent to the Internet Explorer from a Web server running JSP. Chapter 10 provides more information about using Java servlets, JSP, and ASP for server-side XSLT transformations.

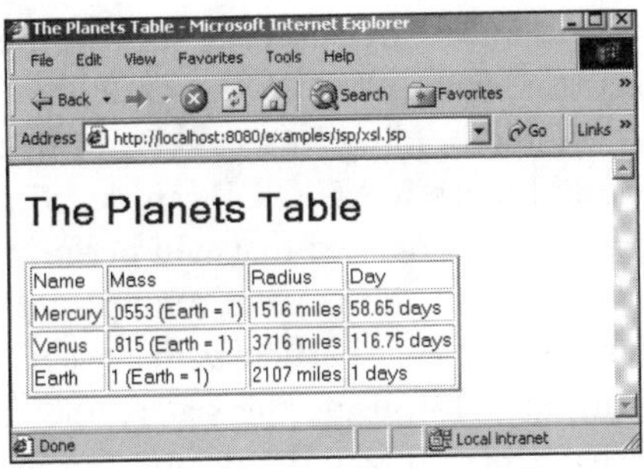

Figure 1.4 Transforming XML on the Web server.

Up to this point, you've seen how to perform XSLT transformations using standalone XSLT processors in the Internet Explorer browser and on Web servers. However, the only transformation we've done so far is to transform XML into HTML. Although that's the most popular transformation, XML to XML transformations are becoming increasingly popular.

XML-to-XML Transformations

XML-to-XML transformations are sometimes thought of as SQL for the Internet, because they enable you to use what amount to database queries on XML documents. Here's an example of what I mean. The planets.xml file we've been using has a lot of data about each planet, as you see here:

```
<?xml version="1.0"?>
<PLANETS>
    <PLANET>
        <NAME>Mercury</NAME>
```

```
        <MASS UNITS="(Earth = 1)">.0553</MASS>
        <DAY UNITS="days">58.65</DAY>
        <RADIUS UNITS="miles">1516</RADIUS>
        <DENSITY UNITS="(Earth = 1)">.983</DENSITY>
        <DISTANCE UNITS="million miles">43.4</DISTANCE><!--At perihelion-->
    </PLANET>

    <PLANET>
        <NAME>Venus</NAME>
        <MASS UNITS="(Earth = 1)">.815</MASS>
        <DAY UNITS="days">116.75</DAY>
        <RADIUS UNITS="miles">3716</RADIUS>
        <DENSITY UNITS="(Earth = 1)">.943</DENSITY>
        <DISTANCE UNITS="million miles">66.8</DISTANCE><!--At perihelion-->
    </PLANET>
        .
        .
        .
```

What if you just want a subset of that data, such as the name and mass of each planet? In database terms, planets.xml represents a table of data, and you want to create a new table holding just a subset of that data. That's what SQL can do in databases, and that's what XSLT can do with XML documents.

Here's a new version of planets.xsl that will perform the transformation we want, selecting only the name and mass of each planet, and sending that data to the output document. Note in particular that we're performing an XML-to-XML transformation, so I'm using the `<xsl:output>` element with the `method` attribute set to "xml" (in fact, the default output type is usually XML, but if an XSLT processor sees a `<html>` tag, it usually defaults to HTML):

Listing 1.6 **Selecting Name and Mass Only**

```
<?xml version="1.0"?>
<xsl:stylesheet version="1.0"
xmlns:xsl="http://www.w3.org/1999/XSL/Transform">

<xsl:strip-space elements="*"/>
<xsl:output method="xml" indent="yes"/>

<xsl:template match="/">
    <xsl:apply-templates/>
</xsl:template>

    <xsl:template match="PLANETS">
        <xsl:apply-templates/>
    </xsl:template>
```

```
    <xsl:template match="PLANET">
       <xsl:copy>
          <xsl:apply-templates/>
       </xsl:copy>
   </xsl:template>

    <xsl:template match="MASS">
        <xsl:copy>
        <xsl:value-of select="."/>
        <xsl:value-of select="@UNITS"/>
        </xsl:copy>
    </xsl:template>

    <xsl:template match="RADIUS">
    </xsl:template>

    <xsl:template match="DAY">
    </xsl:template>

    <xsl:template match="DENSITY">
    </xsl:template>

    <xsl:template match="DISTANCE">
    </xsl:template>

</xsl:stylesheet>
```

I'll apply this new version of planets.xsl to planets.xml using Xalan to create a new XML document, new.xml:

```
C:\planets>java org.apache.xalan.xslt.Process -IN planets.xml -XSL planets.xsl -OUT new.xml
```

Here's what the resulting XML document, new.xml, looks like:

```
<?xml version="1.0" encoding="UTF-8"?>
<PLANET>
    <NAME>Mercury</NAME>
    <MASS>.0553(Earth = 1)</MASS>
</PLANET>
<PLANET>
    <NAME>Venus</NAME>
    <MASS>.815(Earth = 1)</MASS>
</PLANET>
<PLANET>
    <NAME>Earth</NAME>
    <MASS>1(Earth = 1)</MASS>
</PLANET>
```

Note that this looks much like the original planets.xml, except that each `<PLANET>` element contains only `<NAME>` and `<MASS>` elements. In this way, we've been able to get a subset of the data in the original XML document.

You can make any number of other types of XML-to-XML transformations, of course. You can process the data in an XML document to create entirely new XML documents. For example, you can take an XML document full of student names and scores and create a new document that shows average scores. XSLT supports many built-in functions that enable you to work with data in this way, and you'll see those functions in Chapter 8.

In addition, many programs use XML to exchange data online, and they usually format their XML documents differently, so another popular use of XML-to-XML transformations on the Internet is to transform XML from the format used by one program to that used by another.

XML-to-XHTML Transformations

Although many books concentrate on XML-to-HTML transformations, the truth is that the W3C isn't overwhelmingly happy about that. They've been trying to phase out HTML (and they're the ones who standardized it originally) in favor of their new specification, XHTML, which is an XML-compliant revision of HTML. XHTML documents are also well-formed valid XML documents, so transforming from XML to XHTML is really transforming from XML to a special kind of XML.

Although the W3C is really pushing XHTML, it's not in widespread use yet. For that reason, I'll stick to HTML in this book, but because the W3C says you should use XHTML, I'll take a brief look at that here and in Chapter 6. If you want to learn more about XHTML, take a look at the W3C XHTML 1.0 recommendation at `www.w3.org/TR/xhtml1/`, as well as the XHTML 1.1 recommendation at `www.w3.org/TR/xhtml11/`.

Although the W3C says you should be converting from XML to XHTML rather than HTML, I've never seen a working example on the W3C site. The examples that they do present do not, in fact, produce valid XHTML documents. However, support for XML-to-XHTML transformations is supposed to be built into XSLT 2.0, so presumably that's coming.

I'll take a closer look at this type of transformation in Chapter 6, but here's a working version of planets.xsl that will create a valid XHTML version of planets.html. Note that this time you need to use the `doctype-public` attribute in the `<xsl:output>` element, and although that is correct XSLT, not all XSLT processors can handle it:

Listing 1.7 XML-to-XHTML Transformation

```
<?xml version="1.0"?>
<xsl:stylesheet version="1.0"
xmlns:xsl="http://www.w3.org/1999/XSL/Transform">
<xsl:output method="xml" doctype-system
="http://www.w3.org/TR/xhtml1/DTD/xhtml1-transitional.dtd"
    doctype-public="-//W3C//DTD XHTML 1.0 Transitional//EN" indent="yes"/>

    <xsl:template match="/PLANETS">
        <html>
            <head>
                <title>
                    The Planets Table
                </title>
            </head>
            <body>
                <h1>
                    The Planets Table
                </h1>
                <table>
                    <tr>
                        <td>Name</td>
                        <td>Mass</td>
                        <td>Radius</td>
                        <td>Day</td>
                    </tr>
                    <xsl:apply-templates/>
                </table>
            </body>
        </html>
    </xsl:template>

    <xsl:template match="PLANET">
       <tr>
          <td><xsl:value-of select="NAME"/></td>
          <td><xsl:apply-templates select="MASS"/></td>
          <td><xsl:apply-templates select="RADIUS"/></td>
          <td><xsl:apply-templates select="DAY"/></td>
       </tr>
   </xsl:template>

    <xsl:template match="MASS">
        <xsl:value-of select="."/>
        <xsl:text> </xsl:text>
        <xsl:value-of select="@UNITS"/>
    </xsl:template>

    <xsl:template match="RADIUS">
        <xsl:value-of select="."/>
```

continues ▸

Listing 1.7 **Continued**

```
        <xsl:text> </xsl:text>
        <xsl:value-of select="@UNITS"/>
    </xsl:template>

    <xsl:template match="DAY">
        <xsl:value-of select="."/>
        <xsl:text> </xsl:text>
        <xsl:value-of select="@UNITS"/>
    </xsl:template>

</xsl:stylesheet>
```

I'll convert planets.xml into a valid XHTML document, planets.html, using this new version of planets.xsl and the XT XSLT processor. First, I set the classpath as needed:

```
C:\>set classpath=c:xerces\xerces-1_3_0\xerces.jar;c:\xt\xt.jar;
```

Then I perform the transformation:

```
C:\planets>java -Dcom.jclark.xsl.sax.parser=org.apache.xerces.parsers.SAXParser
➥com.jclark.xsl.sax.Driver planets.xml planets.xsl planets.html
```

Here's the resulting XHTML file, planets.html:

```
<?xml version="1.0" encoding="UTF-8"?>
<!DOCTYPE html PUBLIC "-//W3C//DTD XHTML 1.0
Transitional//EN"
    "http://www.w3.org/TR/xhtml1/DTD/xhtml1-transitional.dtd">
<html>
    <head>
        <title>
            The Planets Table
        </title>
    </head>

    <body>
        <h1>
            The Planets Table
        </h1>

        <table>
            <tr>
                <td>Name</td>
                <td>Mass</td>
                <td>Radius</td>
                <td>Day</td>
```

```
            </tr>

            <tr>
                <td>Mercury</td>
                <td>.0553 (Earth = 1)</td>
                <td>1516 miles</td>
                <td>58.65 days</td>
            </tr>

            <tr>
                <td>Venus</td>
                <td>.815 (Earth = 1)</td>
                <td>3716 miles</td>
                <td>116.75 days</td>
            </tr>

            <tr>
                <td>Earth</td>
                <td>1 (Earth = 1)</td>
                <td>2107 miles</td>
                <td>1 days</td>
            </tr>
        </table>
    </body>
</html>
```

This document, planets.html, does indeed validate as well-formed and valid transitional XHTML 1.0 (the kind of XHTML in most popular use) according to the W3C HTML and XHTML validation program. The HTML/XHTML validator tool can be found online at `http://validator.w3.org/file-upload.html`. Chapter 6 provides more information on XML-to-XHTML transformations.

So far, you've gotten a good overview of how XSLT works at this point, performing XML-to-HTML, XML, and XHTML transformations. You'll also see XML-to-RTF (Rich Text Format text), to plain text, to XSL-FO, to JavaScript, to SQL-based databases, as well as other types of XSLT transformations in this book. In addition, there's a lot more material available to you on XSLT that you should know about, and we'll now take a look at what kinds of XSLT resources you can find online.

XSLT Resources

You can find a great deal of material on XSLT online, and it's worth knowing what's out there. Note that all the following URLs are subject to change without notice—these lists are only as up to date as the people that maintain these sites allow them to be, and things can change frequently.

XSLT Specifications, Tutorials, and Examples

The starting place for XSLT resources, of course, is W3C itself. Here are the URLs for the W3C specifications that are used in this book:

- `www.w3.org/Style/XSL/`. The main W3C XSL page.
- `www.w3.org/TR/xslt`. The XSLT 1.0 specification.
- `www.w3.org/TR/xslt11`. The XSLT 1.1 working draft, which makes it easier to extend XSLT, and adds support for the W3C XBase recommendation.
- `www.w3.org/TR/xslt20req`. The XSLT 2.0 requirements, which offer a preview of XSLT 2.0, including more support for XML schemas.
- `www.w3.org/TR/xsl/`. XSL Formatting objects.
- `www.w3.org/Style/2000/xsl-charter.html`. Goals of the XSL committee.
- `www.w3.org/TR/xpath`. The XPath 1.0 recommendation.
- `www.w3.org/TR/xpath20req`. The XPath 2.0 requirements, which offer a preview of XPath 2.0, which includes more support for XSLT 2.0.
- `http://lists.w3.org/Archives/Public/www-xml-stylesheet-comments/`. The W3C list on XML stylesheets.

Many XSLT tutorials and examples are available from other sources as well; here's a starter list:

- `http://http.cs.berkeley.edu/~wilensky/CS294/xsl-examples.html`. A number of XSLT examples.
- `http://msdn.microsoft.com/xml/reference/xsl/Examples.asp`. XSLT pattern examples used in matching elements.
- `http://msdn.microsoft.com/xml/XSLGuide/xsl-overview.asp`. Getting started with XSLT.
- `www.lists.ic.ac.uk/hypermail/xml-dev/xml-dev-Nov-1999/0371.html`. PowerPoint XSLT tutorial.
- `www.mulberrytech.com/xsl/xsl-list/`. An open list dedicated to discussing XSL.
- `www.nwalsh.com/docs/tutorials/xsl/xsl/slides.html`. XSLT tutorial.
- `www.oasis-open.org/cover/xsl.html`. Coverage of what's going on in XSLT.
- `www.w3.org/Style/Activity`. Good page listing what's going on at W3C on stylesheets.
- `www.xml101.com/xsl/`. Good set of tutorials on XSLT.

- `www.xslinfo.com`. Good collection of XSLT resources, collected by James Tauber.
- `www.zvon.org/xxl/XSLTutorial/Books/Book1/bookInOne.html`. Tutorials on XSLT, XPath, XML, WML, and others.

I know of only one Usenet group on XSLT, however, and it's run by Microsoft—`microsoft.public.xsl`. Others will appear in time. You might also want to check out an XSL mailing list—it's at `www.mulberrytech.com/xsl/xsl-list`.

Besides W3C specifications, tutorials, and examples, you'll also find plenty of editors that you can use to create XSLT stylesheets online.

XSLT Editors

To create the XML and XSL documents used in this book, all you need is a text editor of some kind, such as vi, emacs, pico, Windows Notepad or Windows WordPad. By default, XML and XSL documents are supposed to be written in Unicode, although in practice you can write them in ASCII, and nearly all of them are written that way so far. Just make sure that when you write a document, you save it in your editor's plain text format.

> **Using WordPad**
> Windows text editors such as WordPad have an annoying habit of appending the extension .txt to a filename if they don't understand the extension you've given the file. That's not actually a problem with .xml and .xsl files, because WordPad understands the extensions .xml and .xsl, but if you try to save documents that you create while working with this book with extensions that WordPad doesn't recognize, it'll add the extension .txt at the end. To avoid that, place the name of the file in quotation marks when you save it, as in "file.abc".

However, it can be a lot easier to use an actual XML editor, which is designed explicitly for the job of handling XML documents. Here's a list of some programs you can use to edit XML documents:

- **Adobe FrameMaker** `www.adobe.com`. Adobe includes great, but expensive, XML support in FrameMaker.
- **XML Pro** `www.vervet.com/`. Costly but powerful XML editor.
- **XML Writer**, on disk, XMLWriter `http://xmlwriter.net/`. Color syntax highlighting, nice interface.
- **XML Notepad** `msdn.microsoft.com/xml/notepad/intro.asp`. Microsoft's free XML editor—a little obscure to use.

- **eNotepad** `www.edisys.com/Products/eNotepad/enotepad.asp`. A WordPad replacement that does well with XML and has a good user interface.
- **XMetal from SoftQuad** www.`xmetal.com`. An expensive but very powerful XML editor, and many authors' editor of choice.
- **XML Spy** `www.xmlspy.com/`. A good user interface and easy to use.
- **Arbortext's Epic** `www.arbortext.com/`. A powerful editor, expensive, and customizable.

You can see XML Spy at work in Figure 1.5, XML Writer in Figure 1.6, and XML Notepad in Figure 1.7.

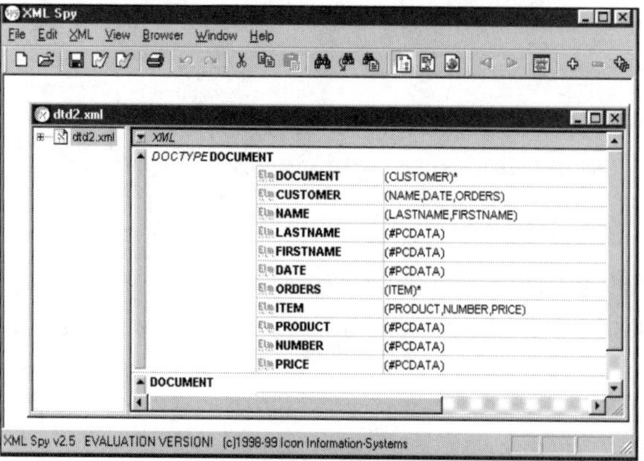

Figure 1.5 XML Spy editing XML.

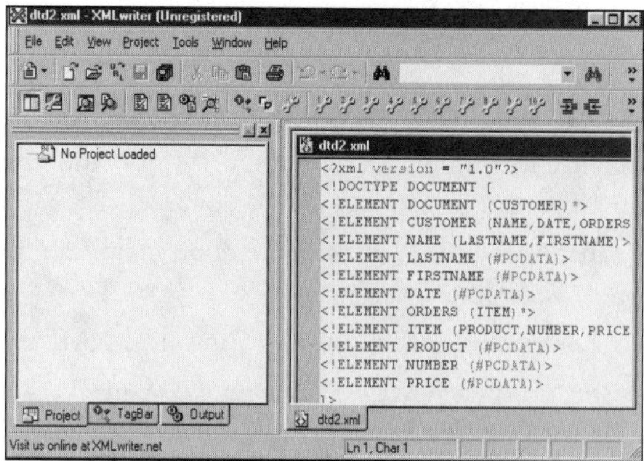

Figure 1.6 XML Writer editing XML.

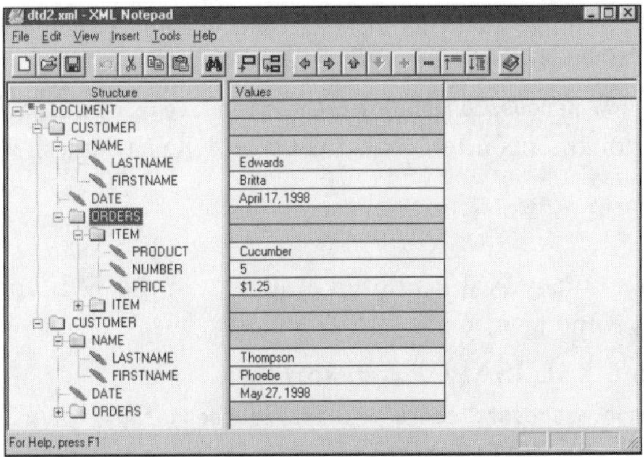

Figure 1.7 XML Notepad editing XML.

In fact, some dedicated XSLT editors are available. Here's a starter list:

- `http://lists.w3.org/Archives/Public/xsl-editors/`. A W3C list discussing XSL editors.
- **IBM XSL Editor** `www.alphaworks.ibm.com/tech/xsleditor`. Java XSLT stylesheet editor that provides a visual interface for writing stylesheets and writing select-and-match expressions. Currently, you must have Java 2 version 1.1 (not 1.2 or 1.3) installed, however.
- **Stylus** `www.exceloncorp.com/products/excelon_stylus.html`. Stylus includes an XSLT stylesheet editor.
- **Visual XML Transformation Tool** `www.alphaworks.ibm.com/aw.nsf/techmain/visualxmltools`. Visual XML Transformation Tool generates XSLT for transforming source documents into target documents for you.
- **Whitehill Composer** `www.whitehill.com/products/prod4.html`. A drag-and-drop, WYSIWYG XSLT generator of XSLT stylesheets.
- **XL-Styler** `www.seeburger.de/xml`. Includes syntax highlighting, tag completion, HTML preview, and more.
- **XML Cooktop** `http://xmleverywhere.com/cooktop/`. This one is just out, and it looks like a good one, it lets you develop and test XSLT stylesheets.
- **XML Spy** `www.xmlspy.com/`. XML Spy is an XML editor you can also use to edit XSLT.
- **XML Style Wizard** `www.infoteria.com/en/contents/download`. A tool for generating XSLT files. The wizard creates an XSLT file by examining XML data and asking the user questions.

- **xslide** `www.mulberrytech.com/xsl/xslide`. Supports an XSLT editing mode for Emacs.
- **XSpLit** `www.percussion.com/xmlzone/technology.htm`. Enables you to split HTML documents into XML DTDs and XSLT stylesheets.

XSLT Utilities

There are also many XSLT utilities available on the Web, and the following list includes some favorites:

- **Microsoft XSL ISAPI Extension** `http://msdn.microsoft.com/downloads/webtechnology/xml/xslisapi.asp`. The Microsoft XSL ISAPI Extension simplifies the task of performing server-side XSLT transformations.
- **Microsoft XSL-to-XSLT Converter** `http://msdn.microsoft.com/downloads/webtechnology/xml/xsltconv.asp`. Converts XSL into XSLT.
- **XSL Lint** `www.nwalsh.com/xsl/xslint`. XSL Lint is a syntax checker for XSLT that detects many types of errors.
- **XSL Trace** `www.alphaworks.ibm.com/tech/xsltrace`. This product enables a user to visually step through XSLT.
- **XSLT Compiler** `www.sun.com/xml/developers/xsltc`. Converts XSLT files into Java classes for transforming XML files.
- **XSLT test tool** `www.netcrucible.com/xslt/xslt-tool.htm`. This tool enables you to run XSLT with various popular processors so that you can make sure your transforms work well on all systems. It also enables you to call Microsoft's MSXML3 from the command-line like any other XSLT processor.
- **XSLTC** `www3.cybercities.com/x/xsltc`. Compiles XSLT stylesheets into C++ code. It's based on Transformiix, Mozilla's XSLT processor.
- **XSLTracer** `www.zvon.org/xxl/XSLTracer/Output/introduction.html`. XSLTracer is a Perl tool that shows how the processing of XML files with XSLT stylesheet works.

That completes your overview of XSLT in this chapter, the foundation chapter. As you can see, there's a tremendous amount of material here, waiting to be put to work in this book. The rest of this chapter provides an overview of XSL-FO.

XSL Formatting Objects: XSL-FO

The most popular part of XSL is the XSLT transformation part that you've already seen in this chapter. The other, and far larger, part is the XSL Formatting Objects part, XSL-FO.

Using XSL-FO, you can specify down to the millimeter how an XML document should be formatted and displayed. You specify everything for your documents: the text font, position, alignment, color, flow, indexing, margin size, and more. It's sort of like writing a word processor by hand, and the complexity of XSL-FO makes some people reluctant to use it. You'll learn more about what XSL-FO has to offer and how to use it in Chapters 11 and 12.

XSL-FO Resources

Some XSL-FO resources are available to you on the Web, but far fewer than those for XSLT. Here are the main ones:

- `www.w3.org/TR/xsl`. The main XSL candidate recommendation, which also includes XSL-FO.
- `http://lists.w3.org/Archives/Public/www-xsl-fo/`. A W3C list for comments on XSL-FO.

Just as there are XSLT processors out there for you to use, there are also XSL-FO processors. None comes close to implementing the whole standard, however. Here's a starter list of XSL-FO processors:

- **FOP** `http://xml.apache.org/fop`. A Java application that reads an XSL formatting object tree (which you create with an XML parser) and creates a PDF document.
- **PassiveTeX** `http://users.ox.ac.uk/~rahtz/passivetex`. A TeX package that formats XSL-FO output to PDF. Makes use of David Carlisle's xmltex XML parser.
- **SAXESS Wave** `www.saxess.com/wave/index.html`. An XML-to-Shockwave/Flash converter.
- **TeXML** `www.alphaworks.ibm.com/tech/texml`. Converts XML documents into TeX.
- **Unicorn Formatting Objects (UFO)** `www.unicorn-enterprises.com`. XSL Formatting Objects processor written in C++. It can generate output in PostScript, PDF, and other formats supported by TeX DVI drivers.
- **XEP** `http://www.renderx.com/FO2PDF.html`. A Java XSL-FO processor that converts XSL formatting objects to PDF or PostScript.

In this book, I'll use fop (formatting objects processor), which is probably the most widely used XSL-FO processor. This Java-based XSL-FO processor takes an XML document that is written to use the XSL-FO formatting objects and translates it to PDF format, which you can examine with Adobe Acrobat. Although XSLT transformations are often made to HTML, that won't work for XSL-FO, because in that case, you specify every aspect of the presentation format down to the last detail, which means that PDF format is much more appropriate.

Formatting an XML Document

To format planets.xml into planets.pdf, we can use the XSL-FO formatting objects that are introduced in Chapter 12. For example, here's how we might display the name of the first planet, Mercury, using XSL-FO formatting objects such as `flow` and `block`:

```
<fo:page-sequence master-name="page">
    <fo:flow flow-name="xsl-region-body">
<fo:block font-family="sans-serif" line-height="48pt"
            font-size="36pt" font-weight="bold">
            Mercury
        </fo:block>
            .
            .
            .
```

However, writing an entire document using the XSL formatting objects is not an easy task for any but short documents. W3C foresaw that difficulty, and that's one of the main reasons they introduced the transformation language, XSLT. In particular, you can write a stylesheet and use XSLT to transform an XML document so that it uses the XSL formatting objects.

In practice, using stylesheets is almost invariably the way such transformations are done, and it's the way we'll do things in Chapters 11 and 12. All you have to do is supply an XSLT stylesheet that can be used to convert your document to use formatting objects. In this way, an XSLT processor can do all the work for you, transforming a document from a form you're comfortable working with to formatting object form, which you can then feed to a program that can handle formatting objects and display the formatted result.

To make all this self-evident, here's an example using the XML document we've already seen in this chapter, planets.xml:

```
<?xml version="1.0"?>
<PLANETS>
    <PLANET>
        <NAME>Mercury</NAME>
```

```
        <MASS UNITS="(Earth = 1)">.0553</MASS>
        <DAY UNITS="days">58.65</DAY>
        <RADIUS UNITS="miles">1516</RADIUS>
        <DENSITY UNITS="(Earth = 1)">.983</DENSITY>
        <DISTANCE UNITS="million miles">43.4</DISTANCE><!--At perihelion-->
    </PLANET>

    <PLANET>
        <NAME>Venus</NAME>
        <MASS UNITS="(Earth = 1)">.815</MASS>
        <DAY UNITS="days">116.75</DAY>
        <RADIUS UNITS="miles">3716</RADIUS>
        <DENSITY UNITS="(Earth = 1)">.943</DENSITY>
        <DISTANCE UNITS="million miles">66.8</DISTANCE><!--At perihelion-->
    </PLANET>

    <PLANET>
        <NAME>Earth</NAME>
        <MASS UNITS="(Earth = 1)">1</MASS>
        <DAY UNITS="days">1</DAY>
        <RADIUS UNITS="miles">2107</RADIUS>
        <DENSITY UNITS="(Earth = 1)">1</DENSITY>
        <DISTANCE UNITS="million miles">128.4</DISTANCE><!--At perihelion-->
    </PLANET>
</PLANETS>
```

In this example, I'll use an XSLT stylesheet—which you'll see how to create in Chapter 11—to transform planets.xml so that it uses formatting objects. Then I'll use the FOP processor to turn the new document into a PDF file. I'll also take a look at the formatted document as it appears in Adobe Acrobat.

The XSLT Stylesheet

Here's what that stylesheet, planetsPDF.xsl, looks like. This stylesheet takes the data in planets.xml and formats it in a PDF file, planets.pdf. In this case, I'll use a large font for text—36 point:

Listing 1.8 **XML to XSL-FO Transformation**

```
<?xml version='1.0'?>
<xsl:stylesheet xmlns:xsl="http://www.w3.org/1999/XSL/Transform"
    xmlns:fo="http://www.w3.org/1999/XSL/Format"
    version='1.0'>

    <xsl:template match="PLANETS">
        <fo:root xmlns:fo="http://www.w3.org/1999/XSL/Format">
            <fo:layout-master-set>
                <fo:simple-page-master master-name="page"
```

continues ▸

Listing 1.8 **Continued**

```
                page-height="400mm" page-width="300mm"
                margin-top="10mm" margin-bottom="10mm"
                margin-left="20mm" margin-right="20mm">

                <fo:region-body
                    margin-top="0mm" margin-bottom="10mm"
                    margin-left="0mm" margin-right="0mm"/>

                <fo:region-after extent="10mm"/>
            </fo:simple-page-master>
        </fo:layout-master-set>

        <fo:page-sequence master-name="page">
            <fo:flow flow-name="xsl-region-body">
                <xsl:apply-templates/>
            </fo:flow>
        </fo:page-sequence>
    </fo:root>
</xsl:template>

<xsl:template match="PLANET/NAME">
    <fo:block font-weight="bold" font-size="36pt"
        line-height="48pt" font-family="sans-serif">
        Name:
        <xsl:apply-templates/>
    </fo:block>
</xsl:template>

<xsl:template match="PLANET/MASS">
    <fo:block font-size="36pt" line-height="48pt"
        font-family="sans-serif">
        Mass (Earth = 1):
        <xsl:apply-templates/>
    </fo:block>
</xsl:template>

<xsl:template match="PLANET/DAY">
    <fo:block font-size="36pt" line-height="48pt" font-family="sans-serif">
        Day (Earth = 1):
        <xsl:apply-templates/>
    </fo:block>
</xsl:template>

<xsl:template match="PLANET/RADIUS">
    <fo:block font-size="36pt" line-height="48pt" font-family="sans-serif">
        Radius (in miles):
        <xsl:apply-templates/>
    </fo:block>
</xsl:template>
```

```
    <xsl:template match="PLANET/DENSITY">
        <fo:block font-size="36pt" line-height="48pt" font-family="sans-serif">
            Density (Earth = 1):
            <xsl:apply-templates/>
        </fo:block>
    </xsl:template>

    <xsl:template match="PLANET/DISTANCE">
        <fo:block font-size="36pt" line-height="48pt" font-family="sans-serif">
            Distance (million miles):
            <xsl:apply-templates/>
        </fo:block>
    </xsl:template>
</xsl:stylesheet>
```

Transforming a Document into Formatting Object Form

To transform planets.xml into a document that uses formatting objects, which I'll call planets.fo, all I have to do is apply the stylesheet planetsPDF.xsl. You can do that using the XSLT techniques you already saw in this chapter.

For example, to use Xalan to create planets.fo, you first set the `classpath` something like this in Windows:

```
C:\>set classpath=c:\xalan\xalan-j_2_0_0\bin\xalan.jar;
c:\xalan\xalan-j_2_0_0\bin\xerces.jar
```

Then you apply planetsPDF.xsl to planets.xml to produce planets.fo:

```
C:\planets>java org.apache.xalan.xslt.Process
➥-IN planets.xml -XSL planetsPDF.xsl -OUT planets.fo
```

The document planets.fo uses the XSL formatting objects to specify how the document should be formatted. Here's what planets.fo looks like:

Listing 1.9 **planets.fo**

```
<?xml version="1.0" encoding="UTF-8"?>
<fo:root xmlns:fo="http://www.w3.org/1999/XSL/Format">

<fo:layout-master-set>
<fo:simple-page-master margin-right="20mm" margin-left="20mm"
        margin-bottom="10mm" margin-top="10mm"
        page-width="300mm" page-height="400mm" master-name="page">
<fo:region-body margin-right="0mm" margin-left="0mm"
          margin-bottom="10mm" margin-top="0mm"/>
```

continues ▸

Listing 1.9 **Continued**

```
        <fo:region-after extent="10mm"/>
    </fo:simple-page-master>
</fo:layout-master-set>

<fo:page-sequence master-name="page">
    <fo:flow flow-name="xsl-region-body">
<fo:block font-family="sans-serif" line-height="48pt"
            font-size="36pt" font-weight="bold">
            Name:
            Mercury
        </fo:block>
        <fo:block font-family="sans-serif" line-height="48pt"
            font-size="36pt">
            Mass (Earth = 1):
            .0553
        </fo:block>
        <fo:block font-family="sans-serif" line-height="48pt"
            font-size="36pt">
            Day (Earth = 1):
            58.65
        </fo:block>
        <fo:block font-family="sans-serif" line-height="48pt"
            font-size="36pt">
            Radius (in miles):
            1516
        </fo:block>
        <fo:block font-family="sans-serif" line-height="48pt"
            font-size="36pt">
            Density (Earth = 1):
            .983
        </fo:block>
        <fo:block font-family="sans-serif" line-height="48pt"
            font-size="36pt">
            Distance (million miles):
            43.4
        </fo:block>

<fo:block font-family="sans-serif" line-height="48pt"
            font-size="36pt" font-weight="bold">
            Name:
            Venus
        </fo:block>
        <fo:block font-family="sans-serif" line-height="48pt"
            font-size="36pt">
            Mass (Earth = 1):
            .815
        </fo:block>
        <fo:block font-family="sans-serif" line-height="48pt"
            font-size="36pt">
            Day (Earth = 1):
            116.75
```

```
        </fo:block>
        <fo:block font-family="sans-serif" line-height="48pt"
            font-size="36pt">
            Radius (in miles):
            3716
        </fo:block>
        <fo:block font-family="sans-serif" line-height="48pt"
            font-size="36pt">
            Density (Earth = 1):
            .943
        </fo:block>
        <fo:block font-family="sans-serif" line-height="48pt"
            font-size="36pt">
            Distance (million miles):
            66.8
        </fo:block>

<fo:block font-family="sans-serif" line-height="48pt"
            font-size="36pt" font-weight="bold">
            Name:
            Earth
        </fo:block>
        <fo:block font-family="sans-serif" line-height="48pt"
            font-size="36pt">
            Mass (Earth = 1):
            1
        </fo:block>
        <fo:block font-family="sans-serif" line-height="48pt"
            font-size="36pt">
            Day (Earth = 1):
            1</fo:block>
        <fo:block font-family="sans-serif" line-height="48pt"
            font-size="36pt">
            Radius (in miles):
            2107
        </fo:block>
        <fo:block font-family="sans-serif" line-height="48pt"
            font-size="36pt">
            Density (Earth = 1):
            1</fo:block>
        <fo:block font-family="sans-serif" line-height="48pt"
            font-size="36pt">
            Distance (million miles):
            128.4
        </fo:block>
    </fo:flow>
</fo:page-sequence>

</fo:root>
```

OK, now we've created planets.fo. How can we use it to create a formatted PDF file?

Creating a Formatted Document

To process planets.fo and create a formatted document, I'll use James Tauber's fop, which has now been donated to the Apache XML Project.

The main fop page is `http://xml.apache.org/fop`, and currently, you can download fop from `http://xml.apache.org/fop/download.html`. The fop package, including documentation, comes zipped, so you have to unzip it. It's implemented as a Java JAR file, fop.jar, and I'll use fop version 0.15 here.

You can use fop from the command line with a Java class that at this writing is org.apache.fop.apps.CommandLine. You need to provide the XML parser you want to use, and I'll use the Xerces Java parser in xerces.jar (which comes with Xalan). Here's how I use fop to convert planets.fo to planets.pdf with Java in Windows; in this case, I'm specifying the `classpath` with the `-cp` switch to include xerces.jar, as well as two necessary JAR files that come with the fop download—fop.jar and w3c.jar. (This example assumes that fop.jar, xerces.jar, and w3c.jar are all in C:\planets—if not, you can specify their full paths.)

```
C:\planets>java -cp fop.jar;xerces.jar;w3c.jar
➥org.apache.fop.apps.CommandLine planets.fo planets.pdf
```

You can use the Adobe Acrobat PDF reader to see the resulting file, planets.pdf, as shown in Figure 1.8. (You can get Acrobat PDF Reader for free at `www.adobe.com/products/acrobat/readermain.html`.) The planets.xml document appears in that figure formatted as specified in the planetsPDF.xsl stylesheet.

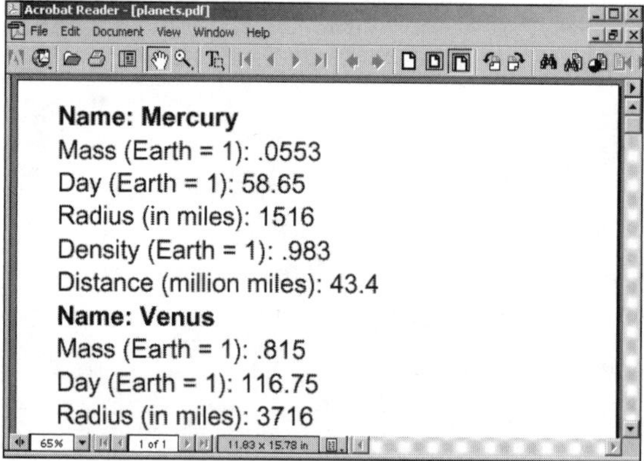

Figure 1.8 A PDF document created with formatting objects.

The PDF format is a good one for formatting object output, although it has some limitations—for example, it can't handle dynamic tables that can expand or collapse at the click of a mouse, or interactive multiple-target links, both of which are part of the formatting objects specification. Although there is little support in any major browser for XSL-FO today, it will most likely be supported in browsers one day.

That completes your overview. In this book, you're going to see all there is to XSLT, and you'll also get an introduction to XSL-FO. Now it's time to dig into XSLT, starting with the next chapter.

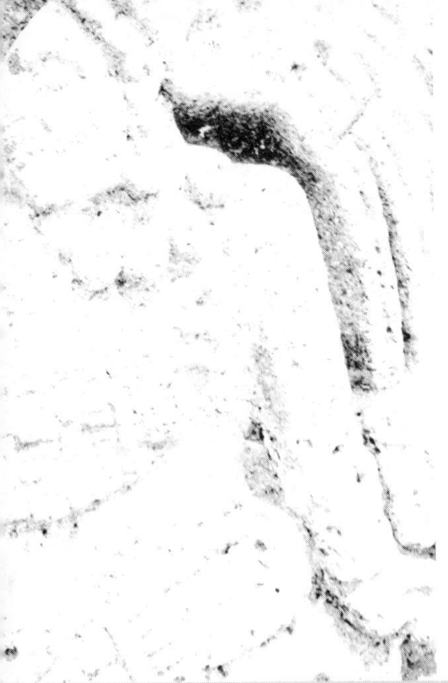

2

Creating and Using Stylesheets

IN THE PREVIOUS CHAPTER, WE GOT STARTED with XSLT in overview. In this chapter, we're going to start working with it in detail. We're going to see how to think of documents in XSLT terms, how to structure an XSLT stylesheet, and how to embed stylesheets in documents. This chapter gives an introduction to how to create stylesheet templates, which are the very heart of XSLT stylesheets. Templates implement the actual rules you want to apply to your data, and we'll work with templates in more depth in the next chapter.

This chapter begins our systematic work with stylesheets, and without question, the place to start is to see what an XML document looks like from a stylesheet's point of view.

Trees and Nodes

When you're working with XSLT, you no longer think in terms of documents, but rather in terms of trees. A tree represents the data in a document as a set of nodes—elements, attributes, comments, and so on are all treated as nodes—in a hierarchy, and in XSLT, the tree structure follows the W3C XPath recommendation (`www.w3.org/TR/xpath`). In this chapter, I'll go through what's happening conceptually with trees and nodes, and in Chapters 3 and 4, I'll give a formal introduction to XPath and how it relates to XSLT. You use XPath expressions to locate data in XML documents, and those expressions are written in terms of trees and nodes.

In fact, the XSLT recommendation does not require conforming XSLT processors to have anything to do with documents; formally, XSLT transformations accept a source tree as input, and produce a result tree as output. Most XSLT processors do, however, add support so that you can work with documents.

From the XSLT point of view, then, documents are trees built of nodes; XSLT recognizes seven types of nodes:

- **The root node.** This is the very start of the document. This node represents the entire document to the XSLT processor. Important: Don't get the root *node* mixed up with the root *element*, which is also called the document element (more on this later in this chapter).
- **Attribute node.** Holds the value of an attribute after entity references have been expanded and surrounding whitespace has been trimmed.
- **Comment node.** Holds the text of a comment, not including <!-- and -->.
- **Element node.** Consists of the part of the document bounded by a start and matching end tag, or a single empty element tag, such as `<br/>`.
- **Namespace node.** Represents a namespace declaration—and note that it is added to each element to which it applies.
- **Processing instruction node.** Holds the text of the processing instruction, which does not include <? and ?>. The XML declaration, `<?xml version="1.0"?>`, by the way, is *not* a processing instruction, even though it looks like one. XSLT processors strip it out automatically.
- **Text node.** Text nodes hold sequences of characters—that is, PCDATA text. Text nodes are normalized by default in XSLT, which means that adjacent text nodes are merged.

As you'll see in Chapter 7, you use XPath expressions to work with trees and nodes. An XPath expression returns a single node that matches the expression; or, if more than one node matches the expression, the expression returns a *node set*. XPath was designed to enable you to navigate through trees, and understanding XPath is a large part of understanding XSLT.

Here's an important point to keep in mind: The root node of an XSLT tree represents the entire document. It is *not* the same as the root element. For example, take a look at the following document; in XSLT terms, the root node represents the whole document, and the root element is `<library>`:

```
<?xml version="1.0"?>
<library>
   <book>
```

```
        <title>
            Earthquakes for Lunch
        </title>
        <title>
            Volcanoes for Dinner
        </title>
    </book>
</library>
```

The term *root element* comes from the XML recommendation, and because it's easy to confuse with the XSLT *root node*, which comes from the XPath recommendation, some XSLT authors call the root element the *document element*. This overlap in nomenclature is definitely unfortunate.

In addition, you should know that XSLT processors *normalize* text nodes. That is, they merge any two adjacent text nodes into one large text node to make it easier to work with the tree structure of a document. This means, for example, that there will never be more than one text node between two adjacent element nodes, as long as there was only text between the element nodes to start with.

In XSLT, nodes can have *names*, as well as *child nodes* and *parent nodes*. In other words, element nodes, attribute nodes, namespace nodes, and processing instruction nodes can have names; every element node and the root node can have children; and all nodes except the root node have parents.

For example, here's how the XML document we just saw looks to an XSLT processor as a tree of nodes:

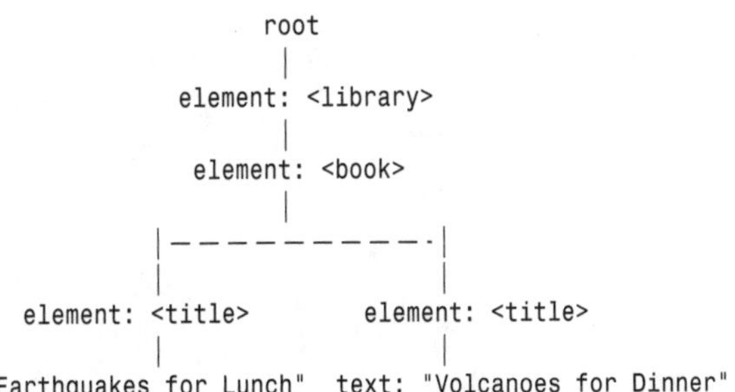

As you can see, the root node is at the very top of the tree, followed by the root element's node, corresponding to the `<library>` element. This is followed by the `<book>` node, which has two `<title>` node children. These two `<title>` nodes are *grandchildren* of the `<library>` element. The parents, grandparents, and great-grandparents of a node, all the way back to and including the root node, are that element's *ancestors*. The nodes that are descended from a node (its children, grandchildren, great-grandchildren, and so on) are called its *descendants*. Nodes on the same level are called *siblings*.

This kind of tree model can represent every well-formed XML document. In fact, XSLT is not limited to working with well-formed documents. In well-formed documents, there must be one element that contains all the others, but the XSLT recommendation does not require this. In XSLT, the root node can have any children that an element can have, such as multiple elements or text nodes. In this way, XSLT can work with *document fragments*, not simply well-formed documents.

Result Tree Fragments

Besides working with input tree fragments, processors can include a special data type in XSLT 1.0 called a *result tree fragment* in their output. The result tree fragment data type has been eliminated in the XSLT 1.1 working draft, however (see Chapter 7), which means it will probably not be part of XSLT 2.0.

Actually, the tree diagram shown earlier does not represent the whole picture from an XSLT processor's point of view. I've left out one type of node that causes a great deal of confusion: text nodes that contain only whitespace. Because this causes so much confusion in XSLT, it's worth taking a look at now.

Whitespace

The example XML document we've been working on so far is nicely indented to show the hierarchical structure of its elements, like this:

```
<?xml version="1.0"?>
<library>
   <book>
        <title>
            Earthquakes for Lunch
        </title>
        <title>
            Volcanoes for Dinner
        </title>
   </book>
</library>
```

However, from an XSLT point of view, the whitespace I've used to indent elements in this example actually represents text nodes. This means that by default, those spaces will be copied to the output document. Understanding how this works is a major source of confusion in XSLT, so I'll take a quick look at it here, and take a look at how to handle whitespace in detail in the next chapter.

In XSLT, there are four whitespace characters: spaces, carriage returns, line feeds, and tabs. These characters are all treated as whitespace. That means that from an XSLT processor's point of view, the input document looks like this:

```
<?xml version="1.0"?>
<library>↵
....<book>↵
........<title>↵
............Earthquakes for Lunch↵
........</title>↵
........<title>↵
............Volcanoes for Dinner↵
........</title>↵
....</book>↵
</library>
```

All the whitespace between the elements is treated as whitespace text nodes in XSLT. That means that there are five whitespace text nodes we have to add to our diagram: one before the `<book>` element, one after the `<book>` element, as well as one before, after, and in between the `<title>` elements:

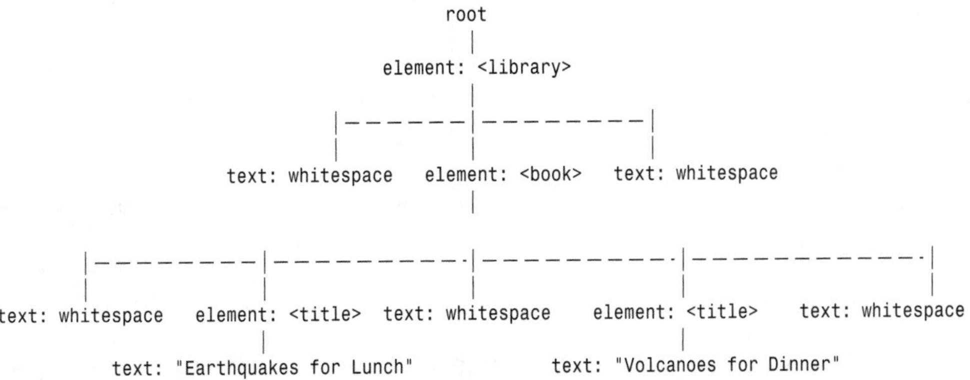

Whitespace nodes such as these are text nodes that contain nothing but whitespace. Because XSLT processors preserve this whitespace by default, you should not be surprised when it shows up in result documents. This extra whitespace is usually not a problem in HTML, XML, and XHTML documents, and I'll eliminate it in the result documents here in the text to make sure the indenting indicates the correct document structure. We'll see how XSLT processors can strip whitespace nodes from documents, as well as how XSLT processors can indent result documents. Note that text nodes that contain characters other than whitespace are not considered whitespace nodes, and so will never be stripped from a document.

Another thing to note is that attributes are themselves treated as nodes. Although attribute nodes are *not* considered child nodes of the elements in which they appear, the element is considered their parent node. (This is different from the XML DOM model, in which attributes both are not children and do not have parents.) If I add an attribute to an element like this:

```
<?xml version="1.0"?>
<library>
   <book>
        <title>
            Earthquakes for Lunch
        </title>
        <title pub_date="2001">

            Volcanoes for Dinner
        </title>
   </book>
</library>
```

Then here's how this attribute appears in the document tree:

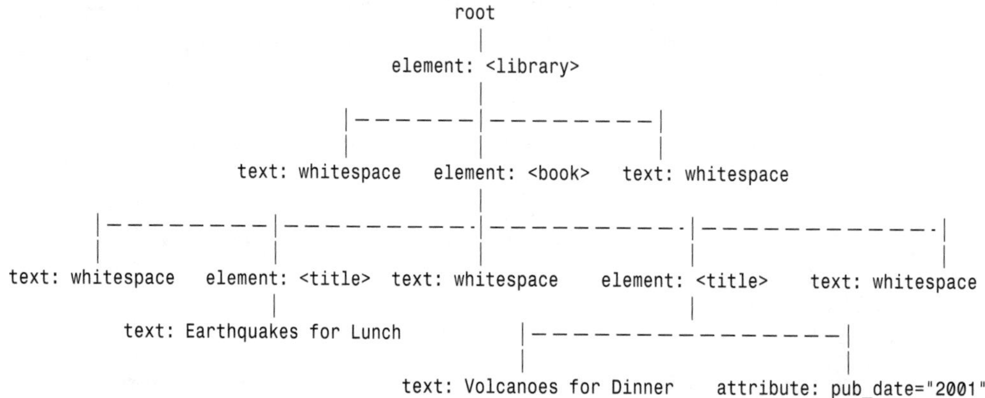

Each node has a number of set properties associated with it in XSLT, and the following list includes the kinds of properties that the writers of XSLT processors keep track of for each node:

- **name**. The name of the node.
- **string-value**. The text of the node.
- **base-URI**. The node's base URI (the XML version of an URL).
- **child**. A list of child nodes; null if there are no children.
- **parent**. The node's parent node.
- **has-attribute**. Specifies an element node's attributes if it has any.
- **has-namespace**. Specifies an element node's namespace nodes.

There's another consideration to take into account when working with trees: XSLT processors are built on top of XML parsers, and the rules for XML parsers and XSLT processors are slightly different, which can lead to problems. This issue can become important in some cases, so the following section discusses it briefly.

The Information Set Model Versus the XSLT Tree Model

XML parsers pass on only certain information, as dictated by the core XML Information Set specification, which you can find at `www.w3.org/TR/xml-infoset` (see New Rider's *Inside XML* for more information on XML Information Sets), whereas XSLT processors adhere to the XSLT tree model. These models, and what they consider important, are different, which can lead to problems.

For example, two XML items that are part of the core information set but are not available in XSLT: notations and skipped entity references (entity references that the XML parser has chosen not to expand). In practice, this means that even if the XML parser passes on information about these items, the XSLT processor can't do anything with it. However, notations are rarely used, and very few XML parsers generate skipped entity references, so this is not a significant problem.

On the other hand, XML parsers *can* strip comments out of XML documents, which is something you should know about, because the XSLT model is supposed to include them.

In addition, DTD information is *not* passed on from the XML parser to the XSLT processor (perhaps because W3C is planning more widespread use of XML schemas in XSLT 2.0, although there's still no official mechanism to connect XML schemas with XML documents yet). That's not usually a problem, because it's up to the XML parser to validate the XML document, except in one case: when an attribute is declared of type `ID`. In XML, you can declare an attribute with any name to be of type `ID`, so the XSLT processor has no idea which attributes are of this type unless the processor has access to the DTD. This is important when you're using stylesheets that are embedded in XML documents, because then the XSLT processor needs to be able to know which element in the document holds the stylesheet you want to use to transform the document. In this case, some XSLT processors, like Saxon, exceed the XSLT recommendation and scan the DTD, if there is one, to see which attributes are of type `ID`.

There are a few more items that you also might want to know about. For example, the XSLT processing model makes namespace prefixes available in the input tree, but it gives you very little control over them in the output tree, where they are handled automatically. Also, the XSLT processing model defines a base URI for every node in a tree, which is the URI of the external entity from which the node was derived. (In the XSLT 1.1 working draft, that's been extended to support the XML, that's been extended to support the XML Base specification, as you'll see near the end of this chapter.) However, in the XML information set, base URIs are considered peripheral, which means that the XML parser may not pass that information on to the XSL processor.

All in all, you should know that XSLT processors use XML parsers to read XML documents, and that the junction between those packages is not a seamless one. If you find you're missing some necessary information in an XSLT transformation, that's something to bear in mind. In fact, the differences between the XML infoset and XSLT tree model is one of the areas that XSLT 2.0 is supposed to address. Among other things, XSLT 2.0 is supposed to make it easier to recover ID and key information from the source document, as well as to recover information from the source document's XML declaration, such as XML version and encoding.

Working with XSLT Elements

To build XSLT stylesheets, you need to be familiar with XSLT elements such as `<xsl:template>` and `<xsl:stylesheet>`. These elements support many attributes, and W3C has some formal definitions of the type of data you can assign to those attributes, so here are a few XSLT definitions you need to know:

- `NCNameChar`. A letter, digit, period, hyphen, or underscore.
- `NCName`. A letter or an underscore optionally followed by `NCNameChars`. That is, an XML name that doesn't contain any colons. (See Chapter 1 for the definition of XML names.)
- `QName`. A qualified name. It's made up of a prefix (which must be an `NCName`), followed by a colon, followed by a local part (which must also be an `NCName`).
- `NameTest`. A name (such as "book") or a generic name with wildcards (such as "book*" or "*").

Now it's time to begin creating XSLT stylesheets, starting with the element you use to connect stylesheets to XML documents, `<?xsl:stylesheet?>`.

The *<?xsl:stylesheet?>* Processing Instruction

When you have an XSL stylesheet you want to apply to an XML document, you need some way of connecting that stylesheet to the document, and that's often done with the `<?xsl:stylesheet?>` processing instruction. This instruction has several possible attributes:

- `href` (mandatory). The URI of the stylesheet. May be a full URI, or may be of the fragment form `#new_style`. Set to a URI.
- `type` (mandatory). The MIME type of the stylesheet. Typically "text/xml" or "application/xml". For the Internet Explorer, use "text/xsl". Set to a valid MIME type.
- `title` (optional). Use a title to distinguish between several `<?xsl:stylesheet?>` elements. Some XML parsers enable you to specify which one to use. Set to a string value.
- `media` (optional). Description of the output medium, such as "print" or "aural". Set to one of the values listed in the W3C HTML 4.0 specification.
- `charset` (optional). Sets the character encoding. Note that XSLT stylesheets set their own encoding, because they are XML documents, so this attribute has no real use. Set to a character encoding such as "UTF-8".
- `alternate` (optional). Set to "yes" to indicate this is an alternate stylesheet, or "no" to indicate it is the preferred stylesheet.

The `<?xsl:stylesheet?>` processing instruction is added in the XML document, not the XSL stylesheet, and shows XSLT processors which stylesheet to use with this document.

In practice, `<?xsl:stylesheet?>` is used mostly with browsers, because with standalone processors, you usually give the name of the stylesheet document directly, as when you use the Oracle XSLT processor this way:

```
C:\planets>java oracle.xml.parser.v2.oraxsl planets.xml planets.xsl planets.html
```

In fact, it may surprise you to learn that `<?xsl:stylesheet?>` is not part of the XSLT recommendation. This processing instruction has its own recommendation just for itself, which you can find at `www.w3c.org/TR/xml-stylesheet`. Among other things, this means that XSLT processors are not obliged to support this processing instruction, and most standalone processors do not.

Here's an example. In Chapter 1, you saw planets.xml, a well-formed XML document that holds data about three planets: Mercury, Venus, and the Earth. You can use the `<?xml-stylesheet?>` processing instruction in planets.xml to indicate what XSLT stylesheet to use, where you set the `type` attribute to "text/xml" (W3C also allows "application/xml", and the Internet Explorer requires "text/xsl") and the `href` attribute to the URI of the XSLT stylesheet, such as planets.xsl:

Listing 2.1 **planets.xml**

```
<?xml version="1.0"?>
<?xml-stylesheet type="text/xml" href="planets.xsl"?>
<PLANETS>

    <PLANET>
        <NAME>Mercury</NAME>
        <MASS UNITS="(Earth = 1)">.0553</MASS>
        <DAY UNITS="days">58.65</DAY>
        <RADIUS UNITS="miles">1516</RADIUS>
        <DENSITY UNITS="(Earth = 1)">.983</DENSITY>
        <DISTANCE UNITS="million miles">43.4</DISTANCE><!--At perihelion-->
    </PLANET>

    <PLANET>
        <NAME>Venus</NAME>
        <MASS UNITS="(Earth = 1)">.815</MASS>
        <DAY UNITS="days">116.75</DAY>
        <RADIUS UNITS="miles">3716</RADIUS>
        <DENSITY UNITS="(Earth = 1)">.943</DENSITY>
        <DISTANCE UNITS="million miles">66.8</DISTANCE><!--At perihelion-->
    </PLANET>

    <PLANET>
        <NAME>Earth</NAME>
        <MASS UNITS="(Earth = 1)">1</MASS>
        <DAY UNITS="days">1</DAY>
        <RADIUS UNITS="miles">2107</RADIUS>
        <DENSITY UNITS="(Earth = 1)">1</DENSITY>
        <DISTANCE UNITS="million miles">128.4</DISTANCE><!--At perihelion-->
    </PLANET>

</PLANETS>
```

That's how to use the `<?xml-stylesheet?>` element; now it's time to start working on writing the stylesheet itself. I'll do that by creating planets.xsl.

The *<xsl:stylesheet>* Element

XSL stylesheets begin with the XML declaration because they are well-formed XML documents, so planets.xsl starts with this same declaration:

```
<?xml version="1.0"?>
    .
    .
    .
```

The XML declaration is stripped off by the XSLT processor immediately, however, and won't figure in our XSLT discussion. The first element of an XSL stylesheet that is pure XSL is the `<xsl:stylesheet>` element (not to be confused with the `<?xml-stylesheet?>` processing instruction, which goes in the XML document). Some people have objected to the name of this element, because it's usually used in XSLT transformations, so W3C also allows you to refer to this element as `<xsl:transform>`.

Here's how you use this element:

```
<?xml version="1.0"?>
<xsl:stylesheet version="1.0"
xmlns:xsl="http://www.w3.org/1999/XSL/Transform">
    .
    .
    .
```

The following list includes the attributes of `<xsl:stylesheet>`:

- `id` (optional). Used to identify the stylesheet. Set to an XML name.
- `version` (mandatory). Sets the version of XSLT needed to work with the stylesheet. This value is normally set to "1.0" currently. You can also set this value to "1.1"; although, because XSLT 1.1 is not going to go past the working draft stage, this will probably not be a "legal" value as far as W3C is concerned.
- `extension-element-prefixes` (optional). Defines the extensions in the stylesheet used to identify extension elements. Set to a whitespace-separated list of `NCNames`.
- `exclude-result-prefixes` (optional). Specifies the namespaces in the stylesheet that should not be copied to the output (unless they are intentionally used in the output document). Set to a whitespace-separated list of `NCNames`.

The content of this element can consist of any of the following top-level XSL elements: `<xsl:attribute-set>`, `<xsl:decimal-format>`, `<xsl:import>`, `<xsl:include>`, `<xsl:key>`, `<xsl:namespace-alias>`, `<xsl:output>`, `<xsl:param>`, `<xsl:preserve-space>`, `<xsl:strip-space>`, `<xsl:template>`, or `<xsl:variable>`. XSLT 1.1 added `<xsl:script>` to this list.

Note that the `id` attribute of this element can be used when you want to refer to a particular stylesheet (and note that you should have an XSLT processor that also reads DTDs or XML schemas in this case).

The `version` attribute is mandatory, and currently can be set to "1.0". You can also set this value to "1.1" for the XSLT 1.1 working draft; however, because XSLT 1.1 is not going past the working draft stage, "1.1" will probably not be considered a legal value for this attribute in the long run. I'm going to set the `version` attribute to "1.0" in this book, because that's the current W3C XSLT recommendation, and version 1.1 is not going to progress beyond working draft stage. As mentioned in Chapter 1, the W3C has also released the requirements for XSLT 2.0, so that will be the next version.

XSLT Processors and Forward Compatibility

If the XSLT version is not one that the XSLT processor recognizes, W3C says the processor must assume any new elements are part of the new XSLT version and not just quit, which is what W3C calls *forward compatibility*. Any elements the processor does not recognize must not be rejected unless the stylesheet tries to instantiate that element and finds no `<xsl:fallback>` child element (see Chapter 5). The upshot is that you can set the XSLT version to 2.0, even in XSLT processors that were written for XSLT 1.0, and there should be no problem unless you use XSLT 2.0-specific features. (An exception here seems to be MSXML3, which currently does generate errors if you set the version to values other than 1.0.)

The XSL Namespace

Note that XSLT elements such as `<xsl:stylesheet>` use the namespace prefix `xsl`, which, now that XSLT has been standardized, is always set to "http://www.w3.org/1999/XSL/Transform". That namespace is usually set with the `xmlns` attribute (which is not an XSL attribute, but rather an attribute of any XML element), in the stylesheet's root element, `<xsl:stylesheet>`:

```
<xsl:stylesheet version="1.0" xmlns:xsl="http://www.w3.org/1999/XSL/Transform">
    .
    .
    .
```

XSL stylesheets use their own namespace this way to avoid conflict with the other elements you use in your stylesheet. For example, you might want to indicate what stylesheet was used to transform a document, in which case you might create your own `<stylesheet>` element—which is no problem, because it won't conflict with the XSL element `<xsl:stylesheet>`.

The namespace prefix customarily used in XSLT stylesheets for XSLT elements is `xsl`. You can, in fact, use any namespace prefix you want for XSLT elements (or even none at all), but `xsl` is used almost universally because that's the namespace used throughout the XSLT recommendation.

More on Namespaces

For more on namespaces, see the companion New Riders book, *Inside XML*, which has an in-depth treatment and plenty of examples.

In practice, this means that all XSLT elements we'll be using start with the namespace prefix `xsl`, as in `<xsl:stylesheet>`. That, then, is how you start an XSLT stylesheet, with the `<xsl:stylesheet>` element. (There is one exception: "simplified" stylesheets omit this element, as you'll see later in this chapter).

Like any other XML application, XSLT has a well-defined set of rules for what makes an XSLT stylesheet valid. The W3C even defines a pseudo-DTD for XSLT, listing all the syntax rules, and you can find that DTD in Appendix A, which is a good resource if you're ever at a loss to understand some part of XSLT syntax. As Appendix A shows, the `<xsl:stylesheet>` element can legally contain several other XSLT elements, and those elements are called *top-level elements*.

Handling Default Namespaces

The question of namespaces can be tricky. For example, some people assign a default namespace to the whole `<xsl:stylesheet>` element as in `<xsl:stylesheet version="1.0" xmlns:xsl="http://www.w3.org/1999/XSL/Transform" xmlns="mydefault">`, and then expect `<xsl:template match="mysymbol">` to match `mysymbol` in the "mydefault" namespace of the source document. It won't, though. Handling default namespaces such as this is one of the issues that XSLT 2.0 is supposed to address.

Top-Level Stylesheet Elements

XSL defines a number of top-level elements that can be direct child elements of `<xsl:stylesheet>`:

- `<xsl:attribute-set>`
- `<xsl:decimal-format>`
- `<xsl:import>`
- `<xsl:include>`
- `<xsl:key>`
- `<xsl:namespace-alias>`

- <xsl:output>
- <xsl:param>
- <xsl:preserve-space>
- <xsl:strip-space>
- <xsl:template>
- <xsl:variable>

The XSLT 1.1 working draft adds one more top-level element:

- <xsl:script>

You'll see all these official top-level XSLT elements in this book.

Note that in addition to all these top-level elements, you can also use normal XML comments throughout, because XSLT stylesheets are also XML documents:

```
<?xml version="1.0"?>
<xsl:stylesheet version="1.0"
xmlns:xsl="http://www.w3.org/1999/XSL/Transform">

    <!-- This template matches all PLANETS elements -->

    <xsl:template match="/PLANETS">
        <HTML>
            <HEAD>
            .
            .
            .
```

In addition to the official top-level elements, several XSLT processors define their own top-level elements, and those elements use namespaces that are not the same as the XSL namespace. What these *implementer-defined top-level elements* do is up to the creator of the XSLT processor.

You can also define your own top-level elements, called *user-defined top-level elements*. These elements must have a different namespace from XSL and implementer-defined top-level elements. The XSLT processor ignores user-defined top-level elements, but because you can gain access to the whole document yourself with the `document` function (which you'll see in Chapter 8), you can make use of these elements yourself.

Of all the top-level elements, the most popular is the `<xsl:template>` element:

```
<?xml version="1.0">
<xsl:stylesheet version="1.0" xmlns:xsl="http://www.w3.org/1999/XSL/Transform">

    <xsl:template>
    .
    .
    .
```

```
</xsl:template>
.
.
.
```

Creating and using templates is the very heart of XSLT, and I'll take a look at that element next, as we continue writing planets.xsl.

The *<xsl:template>* Element

XSL templates enable you to specify how you want your transformation to work. Each `<sxl:template>` element is set up to match one node (which may contain other nodes) or a number of nodes in the source document, and to specify exactly how that node should be transformed.

The following list describes the attributes of `<xsl:template>`:

- `match` (optional). Specifies a pattern that matches nodes to be processed. Set to a valid pattern.
- `name` (optional). Holds the name of the template, which enables it to be called. If you do not use this attribute, you must use the `match` attribute. Set to a `QName`.
- `priority` (optional). A positive or negative integer or real number that sets the priority of this template. Used when more than one template matches the same node. Set to a number.
- `mode` (optional). If you use `<xsl:apply-templates>` on a set of nodes, the only templates used have a matching mode. Set to a `QName`.

Each such `<xsl:template>` element is called a *rule*. In general, the `<xsl:template>` element can contain zero or more `<xsl:param>` elements (which you'll see in Chapter 9), followed by the *template body*, which specifies how you want the transformation to take place.

Template Bodies

Templates have very specific rules. They can contain `<xsl:param>` elements, followed by a template body, which can contain `PCDATA`, XSLT instructions, extension elements, and literal result elements.

XSLT Instructions

A number of XSLT elements, called *instructions*, may appear in a template body:

- `<xsl:apply-imports>`
- `<xsl:apply-templates>`

- `<xsl:attribute>`
- `<xsl:call-template>`
- `<xsl:choose>`
- `<xsl:comment>`
- `<xsl:copy>`
- `<xsl:copy-of>`
- `<xsl:element>`
- `<xsl:fallback>`
- `<xsl:for-each>`
- `<xsl:if>`
- `<xsl:message>`
- `<xsl:number>`
- `<xsl:processing-instruction>`
- `<xsl:text>`
- `<xsl:value-of>`
- `<xsl:variable>`

No other XSLT element may appear directly in a template body. As you'll see in Chapter 9, the `<xsl:param>` element may appear in a template before the template body, but it is not called an XSLT instruction. In addition, other XSLT elements, such as `<xsl:sort>`, `<xsl:otherwise>`, `<xsl:with-param>`, can appear in templates, but only at specific locations, so W3C doesn't call them instructions. You'll see how to use each of these instructions throughout this book.

Extension Elements

Extension elements are covered in Chapter 5; these elements are defined by the user or the XSLT processor, and extend XSLT. Many XSLT processors have defined their own extensions, and that's one of the reasons W3C has introduced the XSLT 1.1 working draft, where the extension mechanism is more regulated. Presumably, this functionality will be incorporated into XSLT 2.0.

Literal Result Elements

If an element in a template body is not an XSL instruction or an extension element, then the XSLT processor must treat it as a literal result element. This means that an element must be treated literally and copied to the result tree (that is, copied to the output node tree created by the XSLT processor).

For example, in the following template body, the <TD> element is a literal result element, which will be copied to the output document:

```
<xsl:template match="RADIUS">
    <TD>RADIUS</TD>
</xsl:template>
```

Literal result elements may themselves have content, which is then treated as another template body and parsed by the XSLT processor. You'll see how this works later in this chapter.

Literal result elements may also have attributes, which are interpreted by the XSLT processor. For example, you can use the `version` attribute to specify that all XSLT elements inside a literal result element must be XSLT version 1.0 elements, as follows:

```
<xsl:template match="RADIUS">
    <TD xsl:version="1.0">RADIUS</TD>
</xsl:template>
```

The following list includes all the possible literal result element attributes (note that they're all optional):

- Attribute Value Templates (optional). Any XPath expressions in curly braces are evaluated, and the string value of the result is copied to an attribute in the result tree. Set to an attribute value template (see Chapter 3).
- `xsl:exclude-result-prefixes` (optional). Specifies which namespaces are not to be copied to the result tree. Set to a whitespace-separated list of namespace prefixes.
- `xsl:extension-element-prefixes` (optional). Makes the XSLT processor treat child elements of the literal result element in the listed namespaces as extension elements rather than literal result elements.
- `xsl:use-attribute-sets` (optional). The attributes in the listed attribute sets are added to the literal result element and copied to the result tree. Set to a list of `QNames` that identify named `<xsl:attribute-set>` elements.
- `xsl:version` (optional). Sets the version of XSL elements enclosed in the literal result element. Set to a number.

Now it's time to put this information to work.

Matching Elements in Templates

To indicate what node or nodes you want to work on in a template, XSLT supports various ways of matching or selecting nodes. You set the `match` attribute of `<xsl:template>` to a *pattern* that matches the name of the node or nodes you want to work with. Chapter 3, which is on templates, shows you how to create patterns. For example, the pattern "/" stands for the root node. The pattern "*" matches any element node. The pattern "PLANET" matches all <PLANET> element nodes, and so on.

To get started, I'll create a short example that replaces the root node—and therefore the whole document—with an HTML page. The first thing I do is create a template with the <xsl:template> element, setting the match attribute to the pattern to match "/":

```
<?xml version="1.0">
<xsl:stylesheet version="1.0" xmlns:xsl="http://www.w3.org/1999/XSL/Transform">
    <xsl:template match="/">
    .
    .
    .
    </xsl:template>
</xsl:stylesheet>
```

When the root node is matched, the template is applied to that node. In this case, I want to replace the root node with an HTML document, so I just include that HTML document directly as the content of the <xsl:template> element:

Listing 2.2 **A Trivial Transformation**

```
<?xml version="1.0"?>
<xsl:stylesheet version="1.0" xmlns:xsl="http://www.w3.org/1999/XSL/Transform">

    <xsl:template match="/">
        <HTML>
            <HEAD>
                <TITLE>
                    A trivial transformation
                </TITLE>
            </HEAD>
            <BODY>
                This transformation has replaced
                the entire document.
            </BODY>
        </HTML>
    </xsl:template>

</xsl:stylesheet>
```

And that's all it takes; by using the <xsl:template> element, I've set up a rule in the stylesheet. When the XSL processor reads the document, the first node it sees is the root node. This rule matches that root node, so the XSL processor copies the literals to the result tree that will give us the HTML doc and replace it with the HTML document, producing the following result:

```
<HTML>

    <HEAD>
        <TITLE>
            A trivial transformation
        </TITLE>
    </HEAD>
    <BODY>
        This transformation has replaced
        the entire document.
    </BODY>
</HTML>
```

This example illustrates a first, rudimentary transformation. So far, it has created only a simple stylesheet with one `<xsl:template>` element, and that element contains only a literal result element. All this example has done is to replace the whole XML document with an HTML document, which is not too exciting. Next, we'll see how recursive processing works with the `<xsl:apply-templates>` element.

The *<xsl:apply-templates>* Element

In the basic template we've already written, the root node has been matched with the expression "/" and replaced with a literal result element. However, when you match the root node, you usually have the whole rest of the document to work on, and we'll do that with the `<xsl:apply-templates>` element.

The following list includes the attributes of the `<xsl:apply-templates>` element:

- `select` (optional). Node-set to be processed. If omitted, all children of the node are processed automatically. Set to an expression.
- `mode` (optional). Sets the processing mode. Template rules with a matching mode are applied to this node. Set to a `QName`.

The `<xsl:apply-templates>` element can contain zero or more `<xsl:sort>` elements, or zero or more `<xsl:with-param>` elements.

In the following example, the template matches the root node, and replaces it with the `<HTML>` literal result element:

```
<?xml version="1.0">
<xsl:stylesheet version="1.0" xmlns:xsl="http://www.w3.org/1999/XSL/Transform">
    <xsl:template match="/">
        <HTML>
        </HTML>
```

```
    </xsl:template>
        .
        .
        .
```

On the other hand, we've only matched the root node, and the planets.xml data tree has a number of nodes under the root node:

```
<?xml version="1.0"?>
<?xml-stylesheet type="text/xml" href="planets.xsl"?>
<PLANETS>

    <PLANET>
        <NAME>Mercury</NAME>
        <MASS UNITS="(Earth = 1)">.0553</MASS>
        <DAY UNITS="days">58.65</DAY>
        <RADIUS UNITS="miles">1516</RADIUS>
        <DENSITY UNITS="(Earth = 1)">.983</DENSITY>
        <DISTANCE UNITS="million miles">43.4</DISTANCE><!--At perihelion-->
    </PLANET>
        .
        .
        .
```

To process more than just the root node, you can use `<xsl:apply-templates>` by adding that element like this:

```
<?xml version="1.0">
<xsl:stylesheet version="1.0" xmlns:xsl="http://www.w3.org/1999/XSL/Transform">

    <xsl:template match="/">
        <HTML>
            <xsl:apply-templates/>
        </HTML>
    </xsl:template>
        .
        .
        .
```

This element makes the XSLT processor look at any child nodes of the root node and try to find any template that matches those nodes. For example, you might want to replace all `<PLANET>` elements with `<P>Planet</P>`. The `<PLANET>` elements are children of the `<PLANETS>` element, so I add a new template for `<PLANETS>` first, just telling the XSLT processor to keep searching for child nodes:

```
<?xml version="1.0">
<xsl:stylesheet version="1.0" xmlns:xsl="http://www.w3.org/1999/XSL/Transform">

    <xsl:template match="/">
        <HTML>
            <xsl:apply-templates/>
```

```
    </HTML>
  </xsl:template>

  <xsl:template match="PLANETS">
        <xsl:apply-templates/>
  </xsl:template>
      .
      .
      .
```

Now I can add another template for the next level down, which includes the <PLANET> elements. In this case, I'll just replace each <PLANET> element with the literal result element <P>Planet</P>:

Listing 2.3 **Using *<xsl:apply-templates/>***

```
<?xml version="1.0"?>
<xsl:stylesheet version="1.0" xmlns:xsl="http://www.w3.org/1999/XSL/Transform">

    <xsl:template match="/">
        <HTML>
            <xsl:apply-templates/>
        </HTML>
    </xsl:template>

    <xsl:template match="PLANETS">
            <xsl:apply-templates/>
    </xsl:template>

    <xsl:template match="PLANET">
        <P>
            Planet
        </P>
    </xsl:template>

</xsl:stylesheet>
```

Here's the result of this stylesheet:

```
<HTML>
    <P>
        Planet
    </P>
    <P>
        Planet
    </P>
    <P>
       Planet
    </P>
</HTML>
```

As you can see, there is nothing left of the `<PLANETS>` element at all. All that's left is the three literal result elements `<P>Planet</P>` that were substituted for the three `<PLANET>` elements.

> **Omitting the `select` Attribute**
> If you omit the `select` attribute, then only the child nodes of the current node are processed, which does not include attribute or namespace nodes, because they are not considered children. If you want to process those kinds of nodes, you'll have to use the `select` attribute, as you'll see in Chapter 3.

This is all very interesting, but not too useful. It would be far better, for example, to be able to access the actual value of each element (such as the name of each planet) and make use of that data. And, of course, you can.

Accessing Node Values

You can access the value of a node with the `<xsl:value-of>` element. This element has two possible attributes:

- `select` (mandatory). The value that will be output. Set to an expression.
- `disable-output-escaping` (optional). Indicates that characters such as ">" should be sent to the output as is, without being changed to ">". Set to "yes" or "no".

The `<xsl:value-of>` element is always empty.

You can use the `select` attribute to indicate which node you want to get the value. For example, you might want to get the value of the `<NAME>` node in each `<PLANET>` element, which is the text enclosed in that node. You can do that like this:

Listing 2.4 **Using *<xsl:value-of>***

```
<?xml version="1.0">
<xsl:stylesheet version="1.0" xmlns:xsl="http://www.w3.org/1999/XSL/Transform">

    <xsl:template match="/">
        <HTML>
            <xsl:apply-templates/>
        </HTML>
    </xsl:template>

    <xsl:template match="PLANETS">
        <xsl:apply-templates/>
    </xsl:template>

    <xsl:template match="PLANET">
```

```
        <P>
            <xsl:value-of select="NAME"/>
        </P>
    </xsl:template>

</xsl:stylesheet>
```

The value of a node that contains text is just that text, so here is the result of applying this stylesheet to planets.xml:

```
<HTML>
    <P>Mercury</P>
    <P>Venus</P>
    <P>Earth</P>
</HTML>
```

Disable-Output-Escaping Attribute

Chapter 3 goes into more detail on the disable-output-escaping attribute of the `<xsl:value-of>` element.

Suppose that you want to do something a little more advanced, such as transforming the data in planets.xml into an HTML table in the new file planets.html, as you saw in Chapter 1, and which you can see in Figure 2.1. You can do that now with `<xsl:value-of>`.

It's important to consider one issue here. There is no formal restriction on the order of the `<MASS>`, `<RADIUS>`, `<DAY>` and `<DISTANCE>` elements in planets.xml, but it's important that these elements be processed in a particular order to match the headings of the table. For that reason, I will use the `<xsl:value-of>` elements in the order that the HTML table needs them.

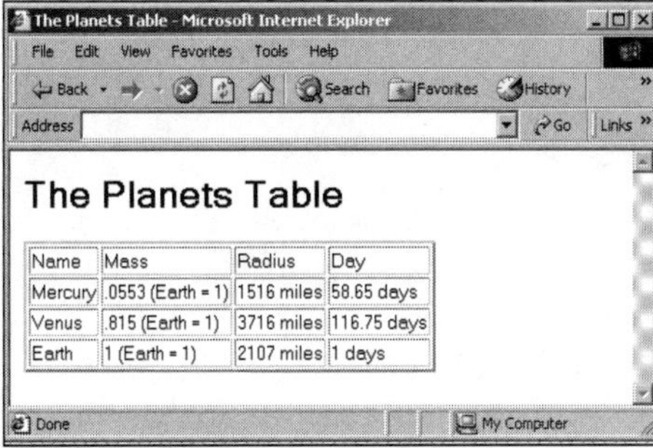

Figure 2.1 Planets.html in the Internet Explorer.

To create the HTML table you see in Figure 2.1, then, I'll first match the <PLANETS> element, and then replace it with the HTML needed to create the HTML table itself. The <PLANETS> element is a child element of the root node, and because you can refer to the root node as "/", you can refer to the <PLANETS> element directly as "/PLANETS", without having to first use a template for the root node. This is an example of an XPath expression, and you'll see many more of them in Chapter 4.

Here's how I start the HTML table by matching the <PLANETS> element directly as "/PLANETS"—note that I use <xsl:apply-templates> to apply templates to any child nodes of <PLANETS>:

```
<?xml version="1.0"?>
<xsl:stylesheet version="1.0"
xmlns:xsl="http://www.w3.org/1999/XSL/Transform">

    <xsl:template match="/PLANETS">
        <HTML>
            <HEAD>
                <TITLE>
                    The Planets Table
                </TITLE>
            </HEAD>
            <BODY>
                <H1>
                    The Planets Table
                </H1>
                <TABLE BORDER="2">
                    <TR>
                        <TD>Name</TD>
                        <TD>Mass</TD>
                        <TD>Radius</TD>
                        <TD>Day</TD>
                    </TR>
                    <xsl:apply-templates/>
                </TABLE>
            </BODY>
        </HTML>
    </xsl:template>
          .
          .
          .
```

Each <PLANET> child node has a <NAME>, <MASS>, <RADIUS>, and <DAY> child node, and I want to process them in that order so that they are added to the HTML table to match the table's headings. To specify the order in which they should be processed, I'll put the <xsl:value-of> elements in that order:

Listing 2.5 **planets.xsl**

```
<?xml version="1.0"?>
<xsl:stylesheet version="1.0" xmlns:xsl="http://www.w3.org/1999/XSL/Transform">

    <xsl:template match="/PLANETS">
        <HTML>
            <HEAD>
                <TITLE>
                    The Planets Table
                </TITLE>
            </HEAD>
            <BODY>
                <H1>
                    The Planets Table
                </H1>
                <TABLE BORDER="2">
                    <TR>
                        <TD>Name</TD>
                        <TD>Mass</TD>
                        <TD>Radius</TD>
                        <TD>Day</TD>
                    </TR>
                    <xsl:apply-templates/>
                </TABLE>
            </BODY>
        </HTML>
    </xsl:template>

    <xsl:template match="PLANET">
       <TR>
          <TD><xsl:value-of select="NAME"/></TD>
          <TD><xsl:value-of select="MASS"/></TD>
          <TD><xsl:value-of select="RADIUS"/></TD>
          <TD><xsl:value-of select="DAY"/></TD>
       </TR>
   </xsl:template>
</xsl:stylesheet>
```

That's all you need; here's the result:

```
<HTML>
    <HEAD>
        <TITLE>
            The Planets Table
        </TITLE>
    </HEAD>

    <BODY>
        <H1>
```

```
            The Planets Table
        </H1>

        <TABLE BORDER="2">
            <TR>
                <TD>Name</TD>
                <TD>Mass</TD>
                <TD>Radius</TD>
                <TD>Day</TD>
            </TR>
            <TR>
                <TD>Mercury</TD>
                <TD>.0553</TD>
                <TD>1516</TD>
                <TD>58.65</TD>
            </TR>
            <TR>
                <TD>Venus</TD>
                <TD>.815</TD>
                <TD>3716</TD>
                <TD>116.75</TD>
            </TR>
            <TR>
                <TD>Earth</TD>
                <TD>1</TD>
                <TD>2107</TD>
               <TD>1</TD>
           </TR>
        </TABLE>
    </BODY>
</HTML>
```

This is almost what we want. If you look at Figure 2.2, you'll see that this HTML file doesn't list the value of the UNITS attribute that each element (except the <NAME> attribute) has in planets.xml:

```
<?xml version="1.0"?>
<?xml-stylesheet type="text/xml" href="planets.xsl"?>
<PLANETS>

    <PLANET>
        <NAME>Mercury</NAME>
        <MASS UNITS="(Earth = 1)">.0553</MASS>
        <DAY UNITS="days">58.65</DAY>
        <RADIUS UNITS="miles">1516</RADIUS>
        <DENSITY UNITS="(Earth = 1)">.983</DENSITY>
        <DISTANCE UNITS="million miles">43.4</DISTANCE><!--At perihelion-->
    </PLANET>
        .
        .
        .
```

Chapter 3, which works with templates in more detail, shows how to extract the value of the attributes from XML elements.

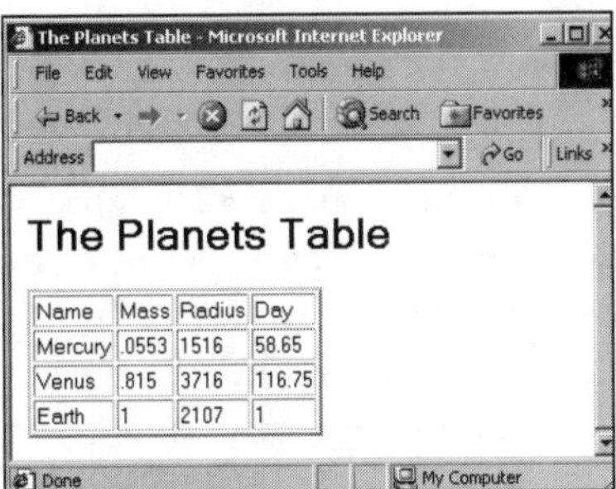

Figure 2.2 Planets.html without attributes in the Internet Explorer.

In the meantime, before you start working with templates in detail, you need to understand a lot more about stylesheets in general. For example, the XSLT 1.1 working draft included support for the XML Base recommendation, which means it will also appear in XSLT 2.0.

XML Base Support

One of the additions to the XSLT 1.1 working draft was support for the W3C XML Base specification. As of this writing, the XML Base specification is in Proposed Recommendation form (dated 20 December 2000), and you can find the current version of this document at `www.w3.org/TR/xmlbase/`.

This specification enables you to provide a base URI for XML and XSL documents, just like the HTML `<BASE>` element. (In fact, the HTML `<BASE>` element is the reason XBase exists—W3C is committed to giving XML all the power HTML 4.0 linking has, and then build on that.) As you recall, one of the properties of XSL elements is their base URI, and now you can use XML Base to set that URI. However, no XSLT processors that I know of support XML Base yet.

You can find full coverage of XML Base in *Inside XML*. Here's how it works in overview: You can use the `xml:base` attribute in an XML document to set the document's base URI. The other URIs in the document are then resolved using that value as a base. Note that `xml:base` uses the `xml` namespace; the `xml` namespace is predefined in XML as `"http://www.w3.org/XML/1998/namespace"`. The following example uses XML links (that is, XLinks, as also covered in *Inside XML*):

```
<?xml version="1.0"?>
<MOVIE_REVIEW xmlns:xlink = "http://www.w3.org/1999/xlink"
    xml:base="http://www.starpowder.com/"
    xlink:type = "simple"
    xlink:show = "new"
```

```
    xlink:href = "reviews.xml">
    Mr. Blandings Builds His Dream House
</MOVIE_REVIEW>
```

Using the value assigned to the `xml:base` attribute, the URI in this example's `xlink:href` attribute, "reviews.xml", is resolved to the full URI "http://www.starpowder.com/reviews.xml". In this way, you can use `xml:base` to provide a base URI for a document or a specific element.

In the XSLT 1.1 working draft, every node has an associated URI called its base URI, which is used for resolving attribute values that represent relative URIs into absolute URIs. Here's how you determine the base URI:

- The base URI for a root node is the URI of the document.
- The base URI for an element node is the base URI specified by an `xml:base` attribute in the element (if one exists), or the base URI of the element's parent element in the document or external entity (if one exists), or the base URI of the document entity or external entity that contains the element.
- The base URI for a processing instruction node is the URI that would apply to a URI reference in the content of the processing instruction. According to the XML Base specification, the base URI for a URI reference appearing in the content of a processing instruction is the base URI of the parent element of the processing instruction (if one exists), within the document entity or external entity, or the base URI of the document entity or external entity containing the processing instruction.
- The base URI for a text node, a comment node, or an attribute node is the base URI of the parent of the node.
- The base URI for a namespace node, however, is implementation-dependent.

Setting the base URI of documents and elements can be useful if you have an extensive set of documents to work with. If you reorganize that document set, you need to reset only the base URI as appropriate, not all individual URIs. As I said, however, no XSLT processors that I know of have any support for XML Base yet.

Choosing Output Methods

Another important aspect of writing stylesheets is picking the output method: XML, HTML, text (that is, any kind of text-based document that is not XML or HTML), and so on. In other words, the output method determines the type of document you're creating. By default, the output method is XML, although most processors create HTML documents if they see a `<HTML>` element. (Some processors also do this if the extension of the document file you're creating is .html.)

Chapter 6 discusses how this works in depth, but I'll look at this topic in overview now. Unless you are sure that the default output type rules of your XSLT processor are doing what they should, it's often advisable to set the output type explicitly to match the kind of output document you want, using the `<xsl:output>` element. The output type can determine, for example, whether the XSLT processor writes the XML processing instruction, `<?xml version="1.0"?>`, at the beginning of the document, and it can determine the MIME type (such as "text/xml" or "text/html") of documents sent back from an XSLT processor on a Web server to a browser. In addition, if you set the output type to HTML, most XSLT processors recognize that not all elements in HTML need closing as well as opening tags, and so on.

Chapter 6 is about converting from XML to other document types, but I'll take a look at `<xsl-output>` in overview here because it's important to understand when working with stylesheets in general. The following list includes the attributes of `<xsl-output>`:

- `cdata-section-elements` (optional). Sets the names of those elements whose content you want output as CDATA sections. Set to a whitespace-separated list of `QNames`.
- `doctype-public` (optional). Specifies the public identifier to be used in the `<!DOCTYPE>` declaration in the output. Set to a string value.
- `doctype-system` (optional). Specifies the system identifier to be used in the `<!DOCTYPE>` declaration in the output. Set to a string value.
- `encoding` (optional). Sets the character encoding. Set to a string value.
- `indent` (optional). Specifies whether the output should be indented to show its nesting structure. Set to "yes" or "no".
- `media-type` (optional). Sets the MIME type of the output. Set to a string value.
- `method` (optional). Sets the output format. Set to "xml", "html", "text", or a valid `QName`.
- `omit-xml-declaration` (optional). Specifies whether the XML declaration should be included in the output. Set to "yes" or "no".
- `standalone` (optional). Specifies whether a standalone declaration should be included in the output and sets its value if so. Set to "yes" or "no".
- `version` (optional). Sets the version of the output. Set to a valid `NMToken`.

The most-used attribute of this element is `method`, because that's what you use to set the output tree type you want. The three most common settings are "html", "xml", and "text".

Output Method: HTML

The planets.xsl stylesheet we've been working with doesn't use the `<xsl:output>` element; it turns out that I've been relying on the default output rules with that stylesheet. By default, the output type is XML, unless the XSLT processor sees an `<HTML>` or `<html>` tag. (Note that this is not a formal requirement, just a convention, so you can't expect all XSLT processors to honor it.) I've used the <HTML> tag in planets.xsl like this:

```
<?xml version="1.0"?>
<xsl:stylesheet version="1.0"
xmlns:xsl="http://www.w3.org/1999/XSL/Transform">

    <xsl:template match="/PLANETS">
        <HTML>
            <HEAD>
                <TITLE>
                    The Planets Table
                </TITLE>
            </HEAD>
        .
        .
        .
```

However, if you remove this tag:

```
<?xml version="1.0"?>
<xsl:stylesheet version="1.0"
xmlns:xsl="http://www.w3.org/1999/XSL/Transform">

    <xsl:template match="/PLANETS">

            <HEAD>
                <TITLE>
                    The Planets Table
                </TITLE>
            </HEAD>
        .
        .
        .
```

Then this is the kind of output you'll get from James Clark's XT. Note the XML processing instruction at the beginning:

```
<?xml version="1.0" encoding="utf-8"?>
    <HEAD>
        <TITLE>
```

```
        The Planets Table
    </TITLE>
</HEAD>
    .
    .
    .
```

On the other hand, you can explicitly specify the output type as HTML with the `<xsl:output>` element, even without using the `<HTML>` element:

```
<?xml version="1.0"?>
<xsl:stylesheet version="1.0"
xmlns:xsl="http://www.w3.org/1999/XSL/Transform">
    <xsl:output method="html"/>

    <xsl:template match="/PLANETS">
            <HEAD>
                <TITLE>
                    The Planets Table
                </TITLE>
            </HEAD>
        .
        .
        .
```

Here's the output from XT in this case—just an HTML fragment, no XML processing instruction:

```
<HEAD>
    <TITLE>
        The Planets Table
    </TITLE>
</HEAD>
    .
    .
    .
```

Automatic <meta> Elements Added to HTML

If you do use the `<xml:output method="html"/>` element explicitly, some XSLT processors, such as Saxon, add a `<meta>` element to the output document's `<head>` element something like this: `<meta http-equiv="Content-Type" content="text/html; charset=utf-8">`.

In general, XSLT processors are supposed to realize that certain elements, such as `<br>`, `<img>`, `<frame>`, and so on are empty in HTML. Also, spaces and other characters in URI attribute values are converted as specified in the HTML specification (a space becomes "%20" and so on), processing instructions are terminated with > rather than ?>, and the fact that standalone attributes are not assigned a value is recognized.

Output Method: XML

In this section I'm going to use an example that you'll see more about in Chapter 6. I'm going to look ahead and use the <xsl:copy> element, which you'll see in Chapter 3, to create a stylesheet that just makes a copy of any XML document.

I use the match pattern "*", which, as mentioned earlier, matches any element, and use the <xsl:copy> element to copy the current element to the output document. This is what the new stylesheet, which just copies the source document to the result document, looks like:

```
<?xml version="1.0"?>
<xsl:stylesheet version="1.0"
xmlns:xsl="http://www.w3.org/1999/XSL/Transform">
    <xsl:template match="*">
        <xsl:copy>
            <xsl:apply-templates/>
        </xsl:copy>
    </xsl:template>
</xsl:stylesheet>
```

Because this stylesheet is for copying any XML document to a new XML document—even XHTML documents, which are XML documents that use the <html> tag—I explicitly indicate that the output method is XML here. If I didn't do this, copied XHTML documents would not start with the XML declaration:

```
<?xml version="1.0"?>
<xsl:stylesheet version="1.0"
xmlns:xsl="http://www.w3.org/1999/XSL/Transform">
    <xsl:output method="xml"/>
    <xsl:template match="*">
        <xsl:copy>
            <xsl:apply-templates/>
        </xsl:copy>
    </xsl:template>
</xsl:stylesheet>
```

This example copies only elements to the result document, not text nodes, comments, or attributes. You'll see a more complete version of this same stylesheet in Chapter 4.

Remember that XML is the default output method, unless your input document contains an <HTML> or <html> tag. However, even if you are transforming from one XML document to another, it's often useful to use the <xsl:output> element to specify, for example, the character encoding (the default is usually UTF-8, the eight-bit Unicode subset), or whether the output document should be indented (which is covered in Chapter 3).

Working with XML Fragments

You can even work on XML fragments, not just entire XML documents. In that case, you can set the `omit-xml-declaration` attribute to "yes" to omit the XML declaration at the beginning of the output tree, as discussed in Chapter 6.

When you use the XML output method, the output tree is well-formed XML (but there is no requirement that it be valid). There is no requirement that it be a well-formed XML document; it could be an XML external general parsed entity. The content of the output can contain character data, CDATA sections, entity references, processing instructions, comments, and elements. The output must also conform to the XML namespaces declaration.

Output Method: Text

The text output method is not just for creating plain text; it's used for any non-XML, non-HTML text-based format. For example, you can use it to create Rich Text Format (RTF) documents. Rich Text Format uses embedded text-based codes to specify the format of documents, and you can place those text-based codes in documents yourself if you use the text output method.

Here's an example stylesheet (that you'll see in Chapter 6) that converts planets.xml into planets.rtf:

Listing 2.6 **RTF Stylesheet**

```
<?xml version="1.0"?>
<xsl:stylesheet version="1.0"
xmlns:xsl="http://www.w3.org/1999/XSL/Transform">
    <xsl:output method="text"/>
    <xsl:strip-space elements="*"/>
<xsl:template match="/PLANETS">{\rtf1\ansi\deff0{\fonttbl{\f0\fnil\fcharset0
Courier New;}}
\viewkind4\uc1\pard\lang1033\b\f0\fs36 The Planets Table\par
\b0\fs20
Name\tab Mass\tab Rad.\tab Day\par
<xsl:apply-templates/>
\par
}</xsl:template>
<xsl:template match="PLANET">
<xsl:value-of select="NAME"/>
\tab
<xsl:value-of select="MASS"/>
\tab
<xsl:value-of select="RADIUS"/>
\tab
<xsl:value-of select="DAY"/>
\tab
\par
</xsl:template>
</xsl:stylesheet>
```

You can see the resulting RTF document, planets.rtf, in Figure 2.3 in Microsoft Word 2000.

Note that I've set the output method to text with <xsl:output method="text"/>:

```
<?xml version="1.0"?>
<xsl:stylesheet version="1.0"
xmlns:xsl="http://www.w3.org/1999/XSL/Transform">
    <xsl:output method="text"/>
    <xsl:template
match="/PLANETS">{\rtf1\ansi\deff0{\fonttbl{\f0\fnil\fcharset0 Courier New;}}
\viewkind4\uc1\pard\lang1033\b\f0\fs36 The Planets Table\par
        .
        .
        .
```

You might also note that I've started the RTF codes immediately after the <xsl:template> element. I've done that because RTF documents must start with RTF codes from the very beginning; if I had begun inserting RTF codes on the next line, like this:

```
<?xml version="1.0"?>
<xsl:stylesheet version="1.0"
xmlns:xsl="http://www.w3.org/1999/XSL/Transform">
    <xsl:output method="text"/>
    <xsl:template match="/PLANETS">
{\rtf1\ansi\deff0{\fonttbl{\f0\fnil\fcharset0 Courier New;}}
\viewkind4\uc1\pard\lang1033\b\f0\fs36 The Planets Table\par
        .
        .
        .
```

then the RTF output file would have started with a newline character, which would throw off the RTF application like Microsoft Word. You'll learn more on RTF and other formats in Chapter 6.

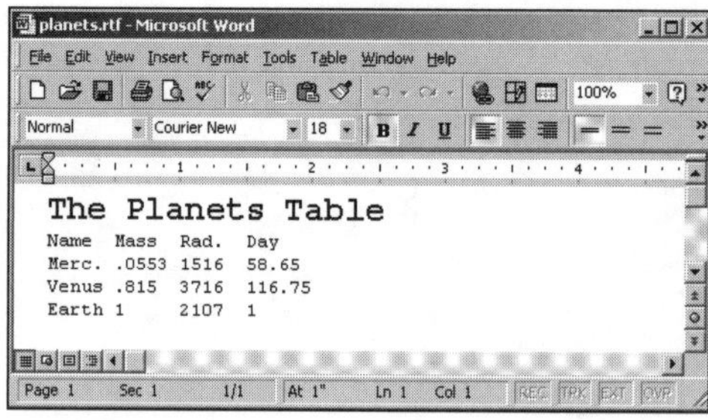

Figure 2.3 Planets.rtf in Microsoft Word.

Simplified Stylesheets

As you can see from the material covered so far, it can take some thought to create XSLT stylesheets. The W3C has tried to make things easier by introducing *simplified stylesheets*, where you don't need to—and in fact cannot—include the `<xsl:stylesheet>` element or any other top-level elements.

In fact, a simplified stylesheet is simply the result document with a few non-top-level XSL elements in it. W3C calls this a "literal result element as stylesheet."

In Listing 2.7, I'll transform planets.xml into planets.html, but this time I'll do it with a simplified stylesheet. In simplified stylesheets, you can't use top-level elements such as `<xsl:template>`, which allow recursive processing of all elements in the source document. So here, I'll look ahead a little and use the `<xsl:for-each>` element (covered in Chapter 5), which is not a top-level element, but which enables you to loop over a number of nodes at once.

I'll also need some way of matching all `<PLANET>` elements in the source document, and you might not think that's possible without several levels of templates—for example, one for the root node, then one to match the next level down, which is the `<PLANETS>` root element, and then another level down for the `<PLANET>` elements themselves. In fact, using XPath, you can use the expression `"//PLANET"` to match *any* `<PLANET>` element node that is descended from the root node (see Chapter 4). This means that I can write the simplified stylesheet as follows:

Listing 2.7 **Simplified Stylesheet**

```
<HTML xmlns:xsl="http://www.w3.org/1999/XSL/Transform" xsl:version="1.0">
    <HEAD>
        <TITLE>
           The Planets Table
        </TITLE>
    </HEAD>
    <BODY>
        <H1>
           The Planets Table
        </H1>
        <TABLE BORDER="2">
           <TR>
                <TD>Name</TD>
                <TD>Mass</TD>
                <TD>Radius</TD>
                <TD>Day</TD>
           </TR>
```

continues ▸

Listing 2.7 **Continued**

```
            <xsl:for-each select="//PLANET">
                <TR>
                    <TD><xsl:value-of select="NAME"/></TD>
                    <TD><xsl:value-of select="MASS"/></TD>
                    <TD><xsl:value-of select="RADIUS"/></TD>
                    <TD><xsl:value-of select="DAY"/></TD>
                </TR>
            </xsl:for-each>
        </TABLE>
    </BODY>
</HTML>
```

This version works just as the previous version of planets.xsl did, and without any top-level elements at all. Simplified stylesheets such as this one were introduced to help HTML authors make the transition to XSL, but the fact is that they're only of limited utility. As you can see, you still need to know how to use XSL elements, and the fact that you can't use `<xsl:template>` has only made the job more difficult here. But you should know that simplified stylesheets exist, and they're part of the XSLT specification.

Default Handling without an `<xsl:stylesheet>` Element

If an XSLT processor can't find the `<xsl:stylesheet>` element in a stylesheet, it's supposed to treat the stylesheet as a simplified stylesheet.

Embedded Stylesheets

The XSLT recommendation also supports *embedded stylesheets* (following the use of embedded stylesheets and style elements in HTML), but like simplified stylesheets, they're not in widespread use.

Not all XSLT processors can handle embedded stylesheets, but some, such as Saxon, do. Here's an example. In this case, I'll include the entire stylesheet element from planets.xsl in planets.xml to create a new document, embedded.xml. This new document will have all the data and the entire stylesheet in it. Note that to be well-formed XML, embedded.xml must have only one root element, so I'll make the stylesheet (that is, the `<xsl:stylesheet>` element) a child element of the `<PLANETS>` root element.

To indicate which element is to be treated as the embedded stylesheet, I'll give the `<xsl:stylesheet>` element the ID "stylesheet" by setting an attribute named `id` to that name:

```
<xsl:stylesheet version="1.0" id="stylesheet"
mlns:xsl="http://www.w3.org/1999/XSL/Transform">
```

I also assign that name, "stylesheet", to the `href` attribute of the `<?xml-stylesheet?>` element at the beginning of the document:

```
<?xml-stylesheet type="text/xml" href="#stylesheet"?>
```

Now the XSLT processor knows which element I want to use as the stylesheet—the element with the ID "stylesheet". However, which element is that? XML elements are made ID-type elements in XML DTDs or schemas, and as you recall, DTD and schema information is not as yet passed on to the XSLT processor.

Some XSLT processors, such as Saxon, read a DTD, if present, to determine which attributes are of type ID, so I can include a DTD in embedded.xml:

Listing 2.8 **planets.xml with an Embedded Stylesheet**

```
<?xml version="1.0"?>
<?xml-stylesheet type="text/xml" href="#stylesheet"?>
<!DOCTYPE PLANETS [
<!ELEMENT PLANET (CUSTOMER)*>
<!ELEMENT CUSTOMER (NAME,MASS,RADIUS,DAY)>
<!ELEMENT NAME (#PCDATA)>
<!ELEMENT MASS (#PCDATA)>
<!ELEMENT RADIUS (#PCDATA)>
<!ELEMENT DAY (#PCDATA)>
<!ELEMENT xsl:stylesheet (xsl:template)*>
<!ELEMENT xsl:template (#PCDATA)>
<!ATTLIST xsl:stylesheet
    id ID #REQUIRED
    version CDATA #IMPLIED>
]>
<PLANETS>
    <PLANET>
        <NAME>Mercury</NAME>
        <MASS UNITS="(Earth = 1)">.0553</MASS>
        <DAY UNITS="days">58.65</DAY>
        <RADIUS UNITS="miles">1516</RADIUS>
        <DENSITY UNITS="(Earth = 1)">.983</DENSITY>
        <DISTANCE UNITS="million miles">43.4</DISTANCE><!—At perihelion—>
    </PLANET>

    <PLANET>
        <NAME>Venus</NAME>
        <MASS UNITS="(Earth = 1)">.815</MASS>
        <DAY UNITS="days">116.75</DAY>
        <RADIUS UNITS="miles">3716</RADIUS>
        <DENSITY UNITS="(Earth = 1)">.943</DENSITY>
        <DISTANCE UNITS="million miles">66.8</DISTANCE><!—At perihelion—>
    </PLANET>
```

continues ▶

Listing 2.8 **Continued**

```
    <PLANET>
        <NAME>Earth</NAME>
        <MASS UNITS="(Earth = 1)">1</MASS>
        <DAY UNITS="days">1</DAY>
        <RADIUS UNITS="miles">2107</RADIUS>
        <DENSITY UNITS="(Earth = 1)">1</DENSITY>
        <DISTANCE UNITS="million miles">128.4</DISTANCE><!--At perihelion-->
    </PLANET>
<xsl:stylesheet version="1.0" id="stylesheet"
xmlns:xsl="http://www.w3.org/1999/XSL/Transform">

    <xsl:template match="/PLANETS">
        <HTML>
            <HEAD>
                <TITLE>
                    The Planets Table
                </TITLE>
            </HEAD>
            <BODY>
                <H1>
                    The Planets Table
                </H1>
                <TABLE BORDER="2">
                    <TR>
                        <TD>Name</TD>
                        <TD>Mass</TD>
                        <TD>Radius</TD>
                        <TD>Day</TD>
                    </TR>
                    <xsl:apply-templates/>
                </TABLE>
            </BODY>
        </HTML>
    </xsl:template>

    <xsl:template match="PLANET">
       <TR>
          <TD><xsl:value-of select="NAME"/></TD>
          <TD><xsl:value-of select="MASS"/></TD>
          <TD><xsl:value-of select="RADIUS"/></TD>
          <TD><xsl:value-of select="DAY"/></TD>
       </TR>
   </xsl:template>

    <xsl:template match="xsl:stylesheet"></xsl:template>

</xsl:stylesheet>

</PLANETS>
```

You should note one final thing: Now that I've included the entire stylesheet in embedded.xml in the `<xsl:stylesheet>` element, I have to supply a stylesheet template for the `<xsl:stylesheet>` element. (If I didn't, the text in the stylesheet's text nodes would be copied to the result document as discussed in Chapter 3 in the section on default rules for templates). I leave that element empty by placing the following line at the end of the stylesheet in embedded.xml so nothing is copied from the stylesheet itself to the result document:

```
<xsl:template match="xsl:stylesheet"></xsl:template>
```

Now, in Saxon, I can use embedded.xml to create planets.html. In Windows, you use `-a` to indicate to Saxon that you're using an embedded stylesheet:

```
C:\planets>saxon -a embedded.xml > planets.html
```

The *<xsl:include>* Element

Another way to insert stylesheets inside other documents is to use the `<xsl:include>` element. This element enables you to include the contents of a file at a particular place in a stylesheet. This element has only one attribute:

- `href` (mandatory). The URI of the stylesheet you want to include.

This element is empty and has no content.

Here's an example. In this case, I'll put part of the stylesheet in planets.xsl into a new document, rules.xml. Then I can include rules.xml in planets.xsl:

Listing 2.9 **Including a Stylesheet**

```
<?xml version="1.0"?>
<xsl:stylesheet version="1.0"
xmlns:xsl="http://www.w3.org/1999/XSL/Transform">

    <xsl:include href="rules.xsl"/>

    <xsl:template match="/PLANETS">
        <HTML>
            <HEAD>
                <TITLE>
                    The Planets Table
                </TITLE>
            </HEAD>
            <BODY>
                <H1>
```

continues ▸

Listing 2.9 **Continued**

```
                The Planets Table
            </H1>
            <TABLE BORDER="2">
                <TD>Name</TD>
                <TD>Mass</TD>
                <TD>Radius</TD>
                <TD>Day</TD>
                <xsl:apply-templates/>
            </TABLE>
        </BODY>
    </HTML>
</xsl:template>

</xsl:stylesheet>
```

Here's what rules.xsl looks like. Note that it's a full XSL document with the XML declaration and the `<xsl:stylesheet>` element:

Listing 2.10 **rules.xsl**

```
<?xml version="1.0"?>
<xsl:stylesheet version="1.0"
xmlns:xsl="http://www.w3.org/1999/XSL/Transform">

    <xsl:template match="PLANET">
       <TR>
          <TD><xsl:value-of select="NAME"/></TD>
          <TD><xsl:value-of select="MASS"/></TD>
          <TD><xsl:value-of select="RADIUS"/></TD>
          <TD><xsl:value-of select="DAY"/></TD>
       </TR>
   </xsl:template>

</xsl:stylesheet>
```

And that's all it takes. Besides using `<xsl:include>` to insert stylesheets or stylesheet fragments, you can also use `<xsl:import>`.

Upcoming in XSLT 2.0

One of the issues that XSLT 2.0 is specifically supposed to address is that included documents are supposed to be able to use their own stylesheets. For example, if you include a document written in the XML language MathML, that included document should be able to use its own stylesheet.

The *<xsl:import>* Element

Like `<xsl:include>`, `<xsl:import>` enables you to insert a stylesheet or stylesheet fragment in another stylesheet. And like `<xsl:include>`, `<xsl:import>` has only one attribute:

- `href` (mandatory). The URI of the stylesheet you want to include.

Also like `<xsl:include>`, `<xsl:import>` is empty and has no content. So what's the difference between `<xsl:include>` and `<xsl:import>`? The difference lies in *import precedence.*

Import precedence gives the XSLT processor a way to settle any conflicts that may arise when, for example, two rules match the same node. The precedence of an imported stylesheet or stylesheet fragment is lower than the precedence of the stylesheet that's importing it. And if you import several stylesheets or stylesheet fragments, the first one has lower precedence than the one imported next, which has lower precedence than the one imported after it, and so on.

Otherwise, though, importing a stylesheet or stylesheet fragment looks much like including it, although you use `<xsl:import>` rather than `<xsl:include>`:

Listing 2.11 **Importing a Stylesheet**

```
<?xml version="1.0"?>
<xsl:stylesheet version="1.0"
xmlns:xsl="http://www.w3.org/1999/XSL/Transform">

    <xsl:import href="rules.xsl"/>

    <xsl:template match="/PLANETS">
        <HTML>
            <HEAD>
                <TITLE>
                    The Planets Table
                </TITLE>
            </HEAD>
            <BODY>
                <H1>
                    The Planets Table
                </H1>
                <TABLE BORDER="2">
                    <TD>Name</TD>
                    <TD>Mass</TD>
                    <TD>Radius</TD>
                    <TD>Day</TD>
                    <xsl:apply-templates/>
                </TABLE>
            </BODY>
```

continues ▸

Listing 2.11 **Continued**

```
        </HTML>
    </xsl:template>

</xsl:stylesheet>
```

The *<xsl:apply-imports>* Element

If you import a stylesheet with a template for, say, the `<PLANET>` element, and then define your own `<PLANET>` element, the imported version is overridden. How do you access the overridden version? You can use the `<xsl:apply-imports>` element.

In XSLT 1.0, this element has no attributes, and takes no content. In the XSLT 1.1 working draft, the `<xsl:apply-imports>` element can handle parameters, so this element may contain zero or more `<xsl:with-param>` elements (see Chapter 9 for the details on parameters).

As an example, I'll modify the `<xsl:import>` example we just saw. In this case, I'll add another column to the HTML table this example produces, labeled DATA, and I'll do that by overriding the `<PLANET>` template in rules.xsl with a new `<PLANET>` template in planets.xsl. The new template simply adds a new column to the table and then uses the old `<PLANET>` template for the rest of the data. I'll access the old template with `<xsl:apply-imports>`:

Listing 2.12 **Using *<xsl:apply-imports>***

```
<?xml version="1.0"?>
<xsl:stylesheet version="1.0"
xmlns:xsl="http://www.w3.org/1999/XSL/Transform">

    <xsl:import href="rules.xsl"/>

    <xsl:template match="/PLANETS">
        <HTML>
            <HEAD>
                <TITLE>
                    The Planets Table
                </TITLE>
            </HEAD>
            <BODY>
                <H1>
                    The Planets Table
                </H1>
                <TABLE BORDER="2">
```

```
                <TR>
                    <TD>Date</TD>
                    <TD>Name</TD>
                    <TD>Mass</TD>
                    <TD>Radius</TD>
                    <TD>Day</TD>
                <xsl:apply-templates/>
                </TR>
            </TABLE>
        </BODY>
    </HTML>
</xsl:template>

<xsl:template match="PLANET">
    <TR>
        <TD>4/1/2002</TD>
        <xsl:apply-imports/>
    </TR>
</xsl:template>

</xsl:stylesheet>
```

Here's what the new version of rules.xsl looks like:

Listing 2.13 **New Version of rules.xsl**

```
<?xml version="1.0"?>
<xsl:stylesheet version="1.0"
xmlns:xsl="http://www.w3.org/1999/XSL/Transform">

    <xsl:template match="PLANET">
          <TD><xsl:value-of select="NAME"/></TD>
          <TD><xsl:value-of select="MASS"/></TD>
          <TD><xsl:value-of select="RADIUS"/></TD>
          <TD><xsl:value-of select="DAY"/></TD>
   </xsl:template>

</xsl:stylesheet>
```

You can see the results in Figure 2.4. I've used one template to build on another, which is the closest you'll get in XSLT to object-oriented inheritance.

In the XSLT 1.1 working draft, you can also use stylesheet parameters with `<xsl:apply-imports>`, which means you can use `<xsl:with-param>` elements as the content of `<xsl:apply-imports>`. You'll get all the details on parameters and `<xsl:with-param>` in Chapter 9.

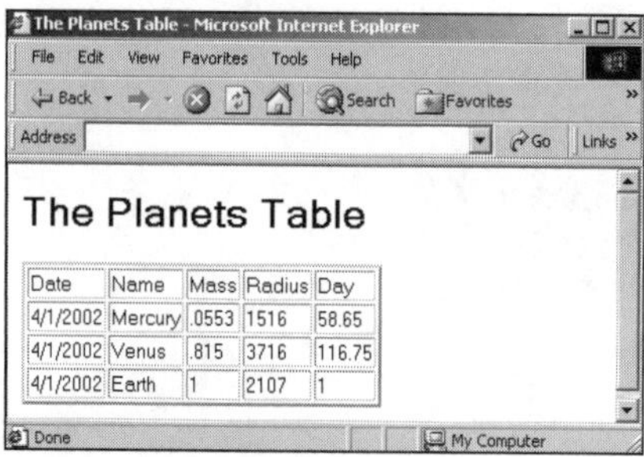

Figure 2.4 Using `<xsl:apply-imports>`.

Using Internet Explorer to Transform XML Documents

There's one more topic to discuss during this overview of stylesheets, and that's how to use stylesheets in the Internet Explorer. As we saw in Chapter 1, you can use JavaScript to read in XML and XSL documents, and use the MSXML3 parser to perform the transformation. (For more information on this, see Chapter 10. You can also read about the Internet Explorer support at `http://msdn.microsoft.com/xml/XSLGuide/`).

However, if you want to open an XML document directly in Internet Explorer by navigating to it (for example, by typing its URI into the Address box), you're relying on the browser to use the `<?xml-stylesheet?>` and `<xsl:stylesheet>` elements itself, which means you need to make a few changes if you're using IE 5.5 or earlier.

Internet Explorer 6.0 and Getting and Installing the MSXML Parser

Note: IE 6.0 is just out as this book goes to press, and it does support full XSLT syntax (except that you still must use the type "text/xsl" for stylesheets like this: `<?xml-stylesheet type="text/xsl" href="planets.xsl"?>` instead of "text/xml"). If you're using IE 5.5 or earlier, you can also download and install the latest version of the MSXML parser directly from Microsoft, replacing the earlier one used by the Internet Explorer. When you do, you don't need to make the modifications listed in this section. For more information, see `http://msdn.microsoft.com/xml/general/xmlparser.asp`. The download is currently at `http://msdn.microsoft.com/downloads/default.asp?URL=/code/sample.asp?url=/msdn-files/027/000/541/msdncompositedoc.xml`. (Note, however, that Microsoft seems to reorganize its site every fifteen minutes or so.) If you're using IE 5.5 or earlier, I urge you to download MSXML so that you won't have to modify all your XSLT stylesheets to use them in IE, or upgrade to version 6.0 or later.

It's necessary to modify both planets.xml and planets.xsl for IE version 5.5 or earlier. To use planets.xml with IE, you convert the `type` attribute in the `<?xml-stylesheet?>` processing instruction from "text/xml" to "text/xsl":

Listing 2.14 **Internet Explorer Version of planets.xml**

```
<?xml version="1.0"?>
<?xml-stylesheet type="text/xsl" href="planets.xsl"?>
<PLANETS>

    <PLANET>
        <NAME>Mercury</NAME>
        <MASS UNITS="(Earth = 1)">.0553</MASS>
        <DAY UNITS="days">58.65</DAY>
        <RADIUS UNITS="miles">1516</RADIUS>
        <DENSITY UNITS="(Earth = 1)">.983</DENSITY>
        <DISTANCE UNITS="million miles">43.4</DISTANCE><!--At perihelion-->
    </PLANET>

    <PLANET>
        <NAME>Venus</NAME>
        <MASS UNITS="(Earth = 1)">.815</MASS>
        <DAY UNITS="days">116.75</DAY>
        <RADIUS UNITS="miles">3716</RADIUS>
        <DENSITY UNITS="(Earth = 1)">.943</DENSITY>
        <DISTANCE UNITS="million miles">66.8</DISTANCE><!--At perihelion-->
    </PLANET>

    <PLANET>
        <NAME>Earth</NAME>
        <MASS UNITS="(Earth = 1)">1</MASS>
        <DAY UNITS="days">1</DAY>
        <RADIUS UNITS="miles">2107</RADIUS>
        <DENSITY UNITS="(Earth = 1)">1</DENSITY>
        <DISTANCE UNITS="million miles">128.4</DISTANCE><!--At perihelion-->
    </PLANET>

</PLANETS>
```

You must also convert the stylesheet planets.xsl for use in IE version 5.5 or earlier. A major difference between the W3C XSL recommendation and the XSL implementation in IE is that version 5.5 or earlier does not implement any default XSL rules—see Chapter 3 (note that IE version 6.0, just out as this book goes to press, does not have this problem). That means for IE version 5.5 or earlier, I have to include an XSL rule for the root node of the document, which you specify with "/". I also have to use a different XSL namespace in the stylesheet, "http://www.w3.org/TR/WD-xsl", and omit the `version` attribute in the `<xsl:stylesheet>` element:

Listing 2.15 **Internet Explorer Version of planets.xsl**

```
<?xml version="1.0"?>
<xsl:stylesheet xmlns:xsl="http://www.w3.org/TR/WD-xsl">

    <xsl:template match="/">
        <HTML>
            <HEAD>
                <TITLE>
                    The Planets Table
                </TITLE>
            </HEAD>
            <BODY>
                <H1>
                    The Planets Table
                </H1>
                <TABLE BORDER="2">
                    <TR>
                        <TD>Name</TD>
                        <TD>Mass</TD>
                        <TD>Radius</TD>
                        <TD>Day</TD>
                    </TR>
                    <xsl:apply-templates/>
                </TABLE>
            </BODY>
        </HTML>
    </xsl:template>

    <xsl:template match="PLANETS">
        <xsl:apply-templates/>
    </xsl:template>

    <xsl:template match="PLANET">
       <TR>
          <TD><xsl:value-of select="NAME"/></TD>
          <TD><xsl:value-of select="MASS"/></TD>
          <TD><xsl:value-of select="RADIUS"/></TD>
          <TD><xsl:value-of select="DAY"/></TD>
       </TR>
   </xsl:template>

</xsl:stylesheet>
```

And that's it! Now we've successfully implemented planets.xml and planets.xsl for direct viewing in the Internet Explorer. Those are the changes you must make to use this browser when you navigate to XSL-styled XML documents directly.

That completes this overview of working with stylesheets in XSL. The next chapter looks at the heart of stylesheets—templates—in more detail.

3

Creating and Using Templates

THIS CHAPTER IS ALL ABOUT CREATING and using templates, which are at the heart of XSLT stylesheets. Each template creates a rule that the XSLT processor tries to apply to the source document.

Chapter 2 took a look at stylesheets in overview, and introduced basic templates so that the stylesheet examples would actually do something. In this chapter, you're going to work with templates in depth, and in the next chapter you'll see what kinds of expressions you can use to create match patterns in templates so that they match the nodes you want. XSLT match patterns are a subset of the full XPath language, and are complex enough to merit their own chapter.

This chapter first reviews how basic templates work, and then moves on to topics such as default template rules, selecting which template to use, handling attributes, making shallow and deep copies of elements, terminating template processing, and a great deal more.

Creating a Template

In Chapter 2, I created a basic template to match the nodes in planets.xml and convert that document to HTML. You create templates with `<xsl:template>` elements in your stylesheets, which specify the rules for the transformations you want to apply. We created a template that matched the `<PLANETS>` root element by matching the *pattern* "/PLANETS", which stands for all <PLANETS> elements that are children of the root node, as follows:

```
<?xml version="1.0"?>
<xsl:stylesheet version="1.0"
xmlns:xsl="http://www.w3.org/1999/XSL/Transform">

    <xsl:template match="/PLANETS">
        .
        .
        .
    </xsl:template>
        .
        .
        .
</xsl:stylesheet>
```

When the XSLT processor finds a node that matches your template's pattern, that node becomes the *context* node for the template, which means that all operations are performed with respect to that node. You can refer to the current node as "." which is an XPath expression. You'll see more XPath expressions in this chapter and in Chapter 7.

Upcoming in XSLT 2.0

XSLT 1.0 has trouble matching elements or attributes whose values have been set to null. That's one of the topics that XSLT 2.0 is supposed to address.

Inside this template, put the HTML markup that starts the table you want to create; this kind of direct markup insertion is called a *literal result element.* When the processor encounters a literal, it copies it to the result tree:

```
<?xml version="1.0"?>
<xsl:stylesheet version="1.0"
xmlns:xsl="http://www.w3.org/1999/XSL/Transform">

    <xsl:template match="/PLANETS">
        <HTML>
            <HEAD>
                <TITLE>
                    The Planets Table
                </TITLE>
            </HEAD>
            <BODY>
                <H1>
                    The Planets Table
                </H1>
                <TABLE BORDER="2">
                    <TR>
```

```
                    <TD>Name</TD>
                    <TD>Mass</TD>
                    <TD>Radius</TD>
                    <TD>Day</TD>
                </TR>
            </TABLE>
        </BODY>
    </HTML>
</xsl:template>
    .
    .
    .
</xsl:stylesheet>
```

However, this rule processes only the <PLANETS> element, not any of its <PLANET> children, which contain the actual data. By the default template rules, the <PLANET> elements would also be processed if I set up a template to match them. That's not good enough, however, because I want to insert the result of processing the <PLANET> elements in a specific place in the HTML I'm creating. To do that, I need to use the <xsl:apply-templates> element.

Processing Child Nodes

You use the <xsl:apply-templates> element to tell the XSLT processor it should process any matching templates for child nodes of the context node. The <xsl:apply-templates> element enables you to indicate exactly when the processing of child nodes should be finished, and that's crucial if you want to insert their data into the HTML table at the correct point.

One important point often causes confusion: The <xsl:apply-templates> element applies templates to only the child nodes of the context or selected node or node set, by default. That seems innocuous enough, but what many people forget is that attributes are *not* considered child nodes of elements, and for that matter, neither are namespace declarations. That means you have to take an extra step or two if you want to process attributes as well as elements, as you'll see in this chapter.

In the following example, you place the <xsl:apply-templates> element at the point where you want to insert the data from the <PLANET> elements into the HTML table. I'll also add a new template to handle the <PLANET> elements:

```
<?xml version="1.0"?>
<xsl:stylesheet version="1.0"
xmlns:xsl="http://www.w3.org/1999/XSL/Transform">

    <xsl:template match="/PLANETS">
        <HTML>
```

```
            <HEAD>
                <TITLE>
                    The Planets Table
                </TITLE>
            </HEAD>
            <BODY>
                <H1>
                    The Planets Table
                </H1>
                <TABLE BORDER="2">
                    <TR>
                        <TD>Name</TD>
                        <TD>Mass</TD>
                        <TD>Radius</TD>
                        <TD>Day</TD>
                    </TR>
                    <xsl:apply-templates/>
                </TABLE>
            </BODY>
        </HTML>
    </xsl:template>

    <xsl:template match="PLANET">
        .
        .
        .
   </xsl:template>
</xsl:stylesheet>
```

In the new template that handles <PLANET> elements, I have to recover the data in each <PLANET> element, which means I have to recover the values in the child elements of the <PLANET> element, such as <MASS>, <DAY>, and so on:

```
<?xml version="1.0"?>
<?xml-stylesheet type="text/xml" href="planets.xsl"?>
<PLANETS>

    <PLANET>
        <NAME>Mercury</NAME>
        <MASS UNITS="(Earth = 1)">.0553</MASS>
        <DAY UNITS="days">58.65</DAY>
        <RADIUS UNITS="miles">1516</RADIUS>
        <DENSITY UNITS="(Earth = 1)">.983</DENSITY>
        <DISTANCE UNITS="million miles">43.4</DISTANCE><!--At perihelion-->
    </PLANET>
        .
        .
        .
```

You can do that with the <xsl:value-of> element.

Accessing Node Values

The <xsl:value-of> element writes the string value of an expression to the result document; in particular, you can use it to return the value of a node, which, for an element, is the element's enclosed text.

You can assign the <xsl:value-of> element's select attribute an XPath expression that specifies a node or node set. When you're in the template that matches <PLANET> elements, you can use the XPath expression "child::MASS" to refer to the <MASS> child element. As you'll see in Chapter 4, you can abbreviate XPath expressions in a number of ways, and in particular, "child::MASS" can also be written simply as "MASS". That means you can recover the data from the child elements such as <MASS>, <DAY>, and so on in this way:

Listing 3.1 **Full Version of planets.xsl**

```
<?xml version="1.0"?>
<xsl:stylesheet version="1.0"
xmlns:xsl="http://www.w3.org/1999/XSL/Transform">

    <xsl:template match="/PLANETS">
        <HTML>
            <HEAD>
                <TITLE>
                    The Planets Table
                </TITLE>
            </HEAD>
            <BODY>
                <H1>
                    The Planets Table
                </H1>
                <TABLE BORDER="2">
                    <TR>
                        <TD>Name</TD>
                        <TD>Mass</TD>
                        <TD>Radius</TD>
                        <TD>Day</TD>
                    </TR>
                    <xsl:apply-templates/>
                </TABLE>
            </BODY>
        </HTML>
    </xsl:template>

    <xsl:template match="PLANET">
       <TR>
```

continues ▸

Listing 3.1 **Continued**

```
            <TD><xsl:value-of select="NAME"/></TD>
            <TD><xsl:value-of select="MASS"/></TD>
            <TD><xsl:value-of select="RADIUS"/></TD>
            <TD><xsl:value-of select="DAY"/></TD>
        </TR>
    </xsl:template>
</xsl:stylesheet>
```

Creating Match Patterns

As you might expect from the discussion on how "child::MASS" can be abbreviated as "MASS", and the use of patterns such as "/", "/PLANETS", and so on, it's going to take a little work to get thoroughly familiar with creating match patterns—Chapter 4 is devoted to doing that.

Match patterns are a subset of the full XPath language, and you use them in <xsl:template>, <xsl:key>, and <xsl:number>. In particular, you can set the match attribute of <xsl:template> and <xsl:key>, and the count and from attributes of <xsl:number> to a pattern. The following list includes a few examples of match patterns; you'll see many more in Chapter 4 during the detailed discussion on using Xpath to select nodes and attributes:

- "/" Matches the root node
- "*" Matches element nodes (not all nodes, which is a common mistake to make)
- "PLANET" Matches <PLANET> elements
- "PLANET/MASS" Matches all <MASS> elements that are children of a <PLANET> element
- "//PLANET" Matches all <PLANET> elements descending from the root node
- "." Matches the current node (technically, this is not a match pattern, but an XPath expression, as you'll see in Chapter 7)

You can also use patterns in the select attribute of the <xsl:apply-templates>, <xsl:value-of>, <xsl:for-each>, <xsl:copy-of>, and <xsl:sort> elements; in fact, the select attribute of these elements can hold full XPath expressions and is not limited to just match patterns. The select attribute of <xsl:value-of> indicates for which child node you want the value, as follows:

```
<xsl:template match="PLANET">
        <TR>
            <TD><xsl:value-of select="NAME"/></TD>
            <TD><xsl:value-of select="MASS"/></TD>
```

```
            <TD><xsl:value-of select="RADIUS"/></TD>
            <TD><xsl:value-of select="DAY"/></TD>
        </TR>
    </xsl:template>
```

Now it's time to use the `select` attribute of `<xsl:apply-templates>` because doing so enables you to specify what template to use at what time.

Selecting Which Template to Apply

Up to this point, I've used only the default version of `<xsl:apply-templates>`, like this:

```
<TABLE BORDER="2">
    <TR>
        <TD>Name</TD>
        <TD>Mass</TD>
        <TD>Radius</TD>
        <TD>Day</TD>
    </TR>
    <xsl:apply-templates/>
</TABLE>
```

Using `<xsl:apply-templates/>` alone simply makes the XSLT processor search for all templates that match the child nodes of the context node, and that's the default usage. However, sometimes that's not good enough, because you may want to apply templates in a specific order, or otherwise choose what templates to apply, and you do that with the `select` attribute of the `<xsl:apply-templates/>`.

For example, so far we've only recovered the value of each `<MASS>`, `<DAY>`, and `<RADIUS>` element using `<xsl:value-of>`:

```
<?xml version="1.0"?>
<xsl:stylesheet version="1.0"
xmlns:xsl="http://www.w3.org/1999/XSL/Transform">

    <xsl:template match="/PLANETS">
        <HTML>
            <HEAD>
                <TITLE>
                    The Planets Table
                </TITLE>
            </HEAD>
            <BODY>
                <H1>
                    The Planets Table
                </H1>
                <TABLE BORDER="2">
```

```
                    <TR>
                        <TD>Name</TD>
                        <TD>Mass</TD>
                        <TD>Radius</TD>
                        <TD>Day</TD>
                    </TR>
                    <xsl:apply-templates/>
                </TABLE>
            </BODY>
        </HTML>
    </xsl:template>

    <xsl:template match="PLANET">
       <TR>
          <TD><xsl:value-of select="NAME"/></TD>
          <TD><xsl:value-of select="MASS"/></TD>
          <TD><xsl:value-of select="RADIUS"/></TD>
          <TD><xsl:value-of select="DAY"/></TD>
       </TR>
   </xsl:template>
</xsl:stylesheet>
```

This just gets the raw string value of each node and places it into the HTML table. On the other hand, you might want to do more processing for each element—for example, you might also want to get the value of the `UNITS` attributes in each element and display those values as well:

```
<?xml version="1.0"?>
<?xml-stylesheet type="text/xml" href="planets.xsl"?>
<PLANETS>

    <PLANET>
        <NAME>Mercury</NAME>
        <MASS UNITS="(Earth = 1)">.0553</MASS>
        <DAY UNITS="days">58.65</DAY>
        <RADIUS UNITS="miles">1516</RADIUS>
        <DENSITY UNITS="(Earth = 1)">.983</DENSITY>
        <DISTANCE UNITS="million miles">43.4</DISTANCE><!--At perihelion-->
    </PLANET>
          .
          .
          .
```

To do that, you can't just use `<xsl:value-of>` because it would return the node value only as text, not as attribute values. Instead, you have to create a new set of templates, one for each of the elements that you are interested in: `<MASS>`, `<RADIUS>`, and `<DAY>`. The `<NAME>` element doesn't have any attributes, so no template is needed there—you need only the node value. Each of these new templates needs to get the value of the element, as well as the value of the `UNITS` attribute.

To make sure that these new templates are applied in the correct order to match the headings in the HTML table, I'll list each of these new templates explicitly, selecting them one by one with the `select` attribute:

```
<?xml version="1.0"?>
<xsl:stylesheet version="1.0"
xmlns:xsl="http://www.w3.org/1999/XSL/Transform">

    <xsl:template match="/PLANETS">
        <HTML>
            <HEAD>
                <TITLE>
                    The Planets Table
                </TITLE>
            </HEAD>
            <BODY>
                <H1>
                    The Planets Table
                </H1>
                <TABLE BORDER="2">
                    <TD>Name</TD>
                    <TD>Mass</TD>
                    <TD>Radius</TD>
                    <TD>Day</TD>
                    <xsl:apply-templates/>
                </TABLE>
            </BODY>
        </HTML>
    </xsl:template>

    <xsl:template match="PLANET">
       <TR>
          <TD><xsl:value-of select="NAME"/></TD>
          <TD><xsl:apply-templates select="MASS"/></TD>
          <TD><xsl:apply-templates select="RADIUS"/></TD>
          <TD><xsl:apply-templates select="DAY"/></TD>
       </TR>
   </xsl:template>
</xsl:stylesheet>
```

Using Named Templates

In addition to selecting templates this way, you can also call *named templates* by name. You'll see how that works in Chapter 9.

Now that you're applying a new template for each of the `<MASS>`, `<RADIUS>`, and `<DAY>` elements—not just getting the node's string value with `<xsl:value-of>`—

you can do more processing on each of these elements, such as reading the values of their UNITS attributes. I'll start by getting the string value of each of the <MASS>, <RADIUS>, and <DAY> elements. Now that we have a template for each of these element nodes, and each node is the context node in its template, instead of referring to the element node by name, we now refer to it as the context node with the XPath expression ".":

Listing 3.2 **Match Version of planets.xsl**

```
<?xml version="1.0"?>
<xsl:stylesheet version="1.0"
xmlns:xsl="http://www.w3.org/1999/XSL/Transform">

    <xsl:template match="/PLANETS">
        <HTML>
            <HEAD>
                <TITLE>
                    The Planets Table
                </TITLE>
            </HEAD>
            <BODY>
                <H1>
                    The Planets Table
                </H1>
                <TABLE BORDER="2">
                    <TD>Name</TD>
                    <TD>Mass</TD>
                    <TD>Radius</TD>
                    <TD>Day</TD>
                    <xsl:apply-templates/>
                </TABLE>
            </BODY>
        </HTML>
    </xsl:template>

    <xsl:template match="PLANET">
       <TR>
          <TD><xsl:value-of select="NAME"/></TD>
          <TD><xsl:apply-templates select="MASS"/></TD>
          <TD><xsl:apply-templates select="RADIUS"/></TD>
          <TD><xsl:apply-templates select="DAY"/></TD>
       </TR>
   </xsl:template>

    <xsl:template match="MASS">
        <xsl:value-of select="."/>
    </xsl:template>

    <xsl:template match="RADIUS">
        <xsl:value-of select="."/>
```

```
    </xsl:template>

    <xsl:template match="DAY">
        <xsl:value-of select="."/>
    </xsl:template>

</xsl:stylesheet>
```

That just reproduces what we've done before with the previous version of planets.xsl, which uses `<xsl:value-of select="MASS">`, `<xsl:value-of select="RADIUS">`, and so on—that is, it reads and displays the data in each `<MASS>`, `<RADIUS>`, and `<DAY>` element. However, now that you have an individual template for each of those elements, you can do more processing, such as reading the values of attributes.

Reading Attribute Values

To refer to an attribute value using XPath, you preface the attribute name with `@` like this: `"@src"`, `"@height"`, `"@width"`, and so on. To match any attribute, you can use the expression `"@*"`. To refer to the `UNITS` attribute in each `<MASS>`, `<RADIUS>`, and `<DAY>` element, you can use the expression `"@UNITS"`. That means you can recover and display the units used for each measurement in planets.xml this way:

Listing 3.3 **Reading Attribute Values**

```
<?xml version="1.0"?>
<xsl:stylesheet version="1.0"
xmlns:xsl="http://www.w3.org/1999/XSL/Transform">

    <xsl:template match="/PLANETS">
        <HTML>
            <HEAD>
                <TITLE>
                    The Planets Table
                </TITLE>
            </HEAD>
            <BODY>
                <H1>
                    The Planets Table
                </H1>
                <TABLE BORDER="2">
                    <TD>Name</TD>
                    <TD>Mass</TD>
                    <TD>Radius</TD>
                    <TD>Day</TD>
```

continues ▸

Listing 3.3 **Continued**

```
                <xsl:apply-templates/>
            </TABLE>
        </BODY>
    </HTML>
</xsl:template>

<xsl:template match="PLANET">
   <TR>
      <TD><xsl:value-of select="NAME"/></TD>
      <TD><xsl:apply-templates select="MASS"/></TD>
      <TD><xsl:apply-templates select="RADIUS"/></TD>
      <TD><xsl:apply-templates select="DAY"/></TD>
   </TR>
</xsl:template>

<xsl:template match="MASS">
    <xsl:value-of select="."/>
    <xsl:value-of select="@UNITS"/>
</xsl:template>

<xsl:template match="RADIUS">
    <xsl:value-of select="."/>
    <xsl:value-of select="@UNITS"/>
</xsl:template>

<xsl:template match="DAY">
    <xsl:value-of select="."/>
    <xsl:value-of select="@UNITS"/>
</xsl:template>

</xsl:stylesheet>
```

You can see the results in Figure 3.1. As you see, you've now recovered the string value of the `UNITS` attribute and displayed it.

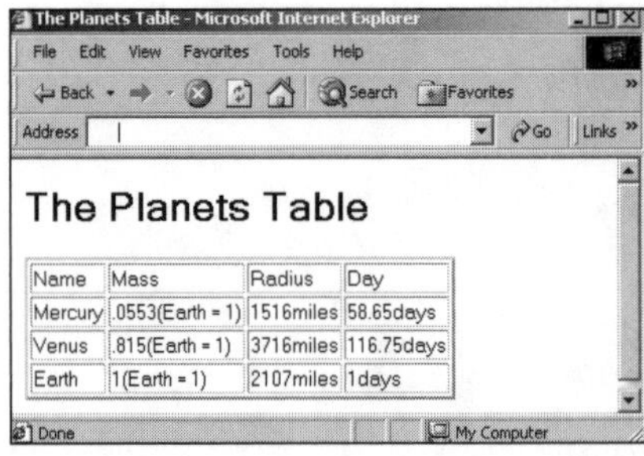

Figure 3.1 Displaying attribute values, first attempt.

Figure 3.1 isn't quite perfect, however—note that there is no space between each value in the table and the associated unit of measure. The XSLT processor simply placed the text in the result tree without any whitespace between text nodes. Although this is exactly what the XSLT recommendation requires, you want table entries such as "1516 miles", not "1516miles." How can you get that extra space?

The *<xsl:text>* Element

Handling spaces is always something of an involved topic in XSLT, and I'll spend a little time on it in this chapter. Inserting a single space, " ", isn't difficult if you use the `<xsl:text>` element, which you use to insert literal text directly into the output tree. This element only has one attribute:

- `disable-output-escaping`. Set to "yes" to make sure characters such as < and > are output literally rather than as < and >. The default is "no."

This element can contain only a text node.

You create text nodes with the `<xsl:text>` element, allowing you to do things such as replace whole elements with text on the fly. One reason to use `<xsl:text>` is to preserve whitespace, as in the following example, where I'll use `<xsl:text>` to insert spaces:

Listing 3.4 **Adding Spaces in a Stylesheet**

```
<?xml version="1.0"?>
<xsl:stylesheet version="1.0"
xmlns:xsl="http://www.w3.org/1999/XSL/Transform">

    <xsl:template match="/PLANETS">
        <HTML>
            <HEAD>
                <TITLE>
                    The Planets Table
                </TITLE>
            </HEAD>
            <BODY>
                <H1>
                    The Planets Table
                </H1>
                <TABLE>
                    <TD>Name</TD>
                    <TD>Mass</TD>
                    <TD>Radius</TD>
                    <TD>Day</TD>
```

continues ▸

Listing 3.4 **Continued**

```
                <xsl:apply-templates/>
            </TABLE>
        </BODY>
    </HTML>
</xsl:template>

<xsl:template match="PLANET">
   <TR>
    <TD><xsl:value-of select="NAME"/></TD>
    <TD><xsl:apply-templates select="MASS"/></TD>
    <TD><xsl:apply-templates select="RADIUS"/></TD>
   </TR>
</xsl:template>

<xsl:template match="MASS">
  <xsl:value-of select="."/>
  <xsl:text> </xsl:text>
  <xsl:value-of select="@UNITS"/>
</xsl:template>

<xsl:template match="RADIUS">
  <xsl:value-of select="."/>
  <xsl:text> </xsl:text>
  <xsl:value-of select="@UNITS"/>
</xsl:template>

<xsl:template match="DAY">
  <xsl:value-of select="."/>
  <xsl:text> </xsl:text>
  <xsl:value-of select="@UNITS"/>
</xsl:template>

</xsl:stylesheet>
```

You can see the new result in Figure 3.2, where you can see the spaces inserted between the numeric values and their units.

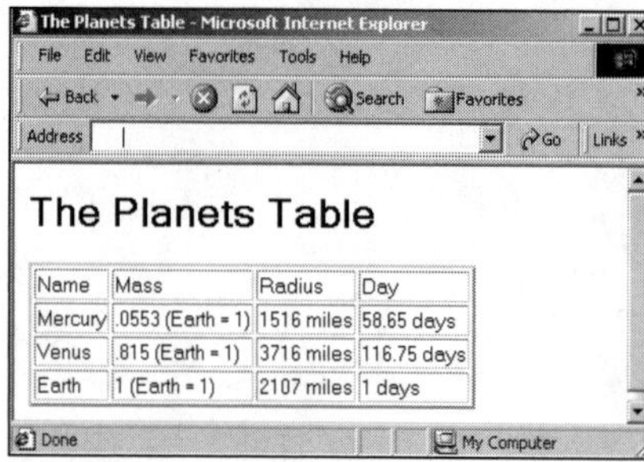

Figure 3.2 Displaying attribute values, second attempt.

As you can see, the <xsl:text> element is a useful one. However, there's one thing you should know: By default, <xsl:text> elements escape characters that could be part of markup. For example, <xsl:text>Here is a greater-than sign: ></xsl:text> gets written as "Here is a greater-than sign: >," not "Here is a greater-than sign: >." And if you try to use a < inside an <xsl:text> element, XSLT processors think that you're trying to enclose an element inside an <xsl:text> element, which is illegal. So how do you send sensitive characters such as < and > to the output if you really need to? You can do that by *disabling output escaping.*

Upcoming in XSLT 2.0

One of the issues that XSLT 2.0 is supposed to address is how to make it easier to import unparsed text of the kind you've seen here from other files.

Disabling Output Escaping

You can use <xsl:text> when you want characters such as < and & to appear in your output document, rather than < and &. To do that, set the <xsl:text> element's disable-output-escaping attribute to "yes" (the default is "no"). Here's an example where I write the text "<PLANET/>" to the output document directly, using <xsl:text>:

```
<?xml version="1.0"?>
<xsl:stylesheet version="1.0"
xmlns:xsl="http://www.w3.org/1999/XSL/Transform">

<xsl:template match="PLANETS">
    <HTML>
        <HEAD>
            <TITLE>
                Planets
            </TITLE>
        </HEAD>
        <BODY>
            <xsl:apply-templates select="PLANET"/>
        </BODY>
    </HTML>
</xsl:template>

<xsl:template match="PLANET">
    <xsl:text disable-output-escaping = "yes">
        &lt;PLANET/&gt;
    </xsl:text>
</xsl:template>

</xsl:stylesheet>
```

Here is the result:

```
<HTML>

    <HEAD>
        <TITLE>
            Planets
        </TITLE>
    </HEAD>

    <BODY>
      <PLANET/>
      <PLANET/>
      <PLANET/>
  </BODY>

</HTML>
```

It wasn't necessary to output `<PLANET/>` using `<xsl:text>`, of course; I could have placed that element directly into a literal result element. But what about cases where the XSLT processor won't recognize an element you need in your output as a true element? For example, in transitional XHTML documents, you need the element `<!DOCTYPE html PUBLIC "-//W3C//DTD XHTML 1.0 Transitional//EN">`, but XSLT processors complain that this is not well-formed XML. How can you place this element into the output?

You could try placing this element into a `<![CDATA[ ]]>` section, as you'll see in Chapter 6, and try to treat it as simple character data, but XSLT processors still invariably escape the < as < and > as >.

The proper way to add a `<!DOCTYPE>` element to the output is actually with the `doctype-public` attribute of the `<xsl:output>` element as you'll see in Chapter 6, but as an example for demonstration purposes, I'll disable output escaping in `<xsl:text>` here to do the same thing (this is *not* the recommended way of creating `<!DOCTYPE>` elements in output documents). Here's how it looks:

```
<?xml version="1.0"?>
<xsl:stylesheet version="1.0"
xmlns:xsl="http://www.w3.org/1999/XSL/Transform">
    <xsl:output method="xml"/>

    <xsl:template match="/PLANETS">
        <xsl:text disable-output-escaping="yes">
            &lt;!DOCTYPE html PUBLIC "-//W3C//DTD XHTML 1.0 Transitional//EN"&gt;
        </xsl:text>
        <HTML>
            <HEAD>
                <TITLE>
                    The Planets Table
```

```
                </TITLE>
            </HEAD>
            <BODY>
                <H1>
                    The Planets Table
                </H1>
                <TABLE BORDER="2">
                    <TD>Name</TD>
                    <TD>Mass</TD>
                    <TD>Radius</TD>
                    <TD>Day</TD>
                    <xsl:apply-templates/>
                </TABLE>
            </BODY>
        </HTML>
    </xsl:template>

    <xsl:template match="PLANET">
       <TR>
          <TD><xsl:value-of select="NAME"/></TD>
          <TD><xsl:apply-templates select="MASS"/></TD>
          <TD><xsl:apply-templates select="RADIUS"/></TD>
          <TD><xsl:apply-templates select="DAY"/></TD>
       </TR>
   </xsl:template>

    <xsl:template match="MASS">
        <xsl:value-of select="."/>
        <xsl:text> </xsl:text>
        <xsl:value-of select="@UNITS"/>
    </xsl:template>

    <xsl:template match="RADIUS">
        <xsl:value-of select="."/>
        <xsl:text> </xsl:text>
        <xsl:value-of select="@UNITS"/>
    </xsl:template>

    <xsl:template match="DAY">
        <xsl:value-of select="."/>
        <xsl:text> </xsl:text>
        <xsl:value-of select="@UNITS"/>
    </xsl:template>

</xsl:stylesheet>
```

And here's the result:

```
<?xml version="1.0" encoding="UTF-8"?>
<!DOCTYPE html PUBLIC "-//W3C//DTD XHTML 1.0 Transitional//EN">
    <HTML>
        <HEAD>
```

```
        <TITLE>
            The Planets Table
        </TITLE>
    </HEAD>

    <BODY>
        <H1>
            The Planets Table
            .
            .
            .
```

You'll see other uses for <xsl:text> throughout this book, including during the discussion of whitespace later in this chapter.

Writing Attribute Values

There are several ways to write attribute values to output documents in XSLT, and the most powerful one is to create attributes from scratch with the <xsl:attribute> element you'll see in Chapter 6. However, you can also use attribute value templates for many purposes, and I'll take a look at them in this chapter.

For example, suppose that you want to convert the text in the elements such as <MASS>, <DAY>, and <NAME> to attributes of <PLANET> elements, converting planets.xml to this form:

```
<?xml version="1.0" encoding="UTF-8"?>
<PLANETS>
    <PLANET DAY="58.65 days" RADIUS="1516 miles"
        MASS=".0553 (Earth = 1)" NAME="Mercury"/>
    <PLANET DAY="116.75 days" RADIUS="3716 miles"
        MASS=".815 (Earth = 1)" NAME="Venus"/>
    <PLANET DAY="1 days" RADIUS="2107 miles"
        MASS="1 (Earth = 1)" NAME="Earth"/>
</PLANETS>
```

To create the transformation, you can't just use expressions such as the following, where I take the values of the <NAME>, <MASS>, and <DAY> elements and try to make them into attribute values:

```
<xsl:template match="PLANET">
    <PLANET NAME="<xsl:value-of select="NAME"/>"
        MASS="<xsl:value-of select="MASS"/>"
        DAY="<xsl:value-of select="DAY"/>"
    />
```

This doesn't work, because you can't use < inside attribute values as I have in the preceding example. XLST provides multiple ways to do that, however. One way is to use attribute value templates.

Attribute Value Templates

The name *attribute value template* has nothing to do with templates as we've been using them—that is, to create stylesheet rules. Instead, using an attribute value template just means that the value of an attribute can be set at execution time.

In this case, you can set an attribute to the value of an XPath expression (this topic is covered more thoroughly in Chapter 4) if you enclose that expression in curly braces, { and }. For example, to set the `NAME` attribute to the string value of a `<DESCRIPTION>` element that is a child of the context node, you could assign that value like this: `NAME={DESCRIPTION}`.

Here's the correct XSLT to use to assign the values from the `<NAME>`, `<MASS>`, `<RADIUS>`, and `<DAY>` elements to attributes with the same names in the `<PLANET>` element:

Listing 3.5 **Using Attribute Value Templates**

```
<?xml version="1.0"?>
<xsl:stylesheet version="1.0"
xmlns:xsl="http://www.w3.org/1999/XSL/Transform">
<xsl:output method="xml"/>

<xsl:template match="PLANETS">
    <xsl:copy>
        <xsl:apply-templates select="PLANET"/>
    </xsl:copy>
</xsl:template>

<xsl:template match="PLANET">
    <PLANET NAME="{NAME}"
        MASS="{MASS}"
        RADIUS="{RADIUS}"
        DAY="{DAY}"
    />
</xsl:template>

</xsl:stylesheet>
```

That's all it takes; now look at the resulting document where the values in various elements have been converted to attributes:

```
<?xml version="1.0" encoding="UTF-8"?>
<PLANETS>
    <PLANET DAY="58.65 " RADIUS="1516 " MASS=".0553 " NAME="Mercury"/>
    <PLANET DAY="116.75 " RADIUS="3716 " MASS=".815 " NAME="Venus"/>
    <PLANET DAY="1 " RADIUS="2107 " MASS="1 " NAME="Earth"/>
</PLANETS>
```

Suppose now that you also want to include the units for each measurement. Each <MASS>, <NAME>, and <RADIUS> element includes a UNITS attribute that gives the units of the measurement,—it's possible to recover those values. The context node is a <PLANET> element, because that's what the template is set up to match, so you can refer to the child <MASS>, <NAME>, and <RADIUS> elements as "MASS", "NAME", and "RADIUS". To address the UNITS attribute of these elements, you can use the syntax "MASS/@UNITS", "NAME/@UNITS", and "RADIUS/@UNITS", as follows:

```
<?xml version="1.0"?>
<xsl:stylesheet version="1.0"
xmlns:xsl="http://www.w3.org/1999/XSL/Transform">
<xsl:output method="xml"/>

<xsl:template match="PLANETS">
    <xsl:copy>
        <xsl:apply-templates select="PLANET"/>
    </xsl:copy>
</xsl:template>

<xsl:template match="PLANET">
    <PLANET NAME="{NAME}"
        MASS="{MASS} {MASS/@UNITS}"
        RADIUS="{RADIUS} {RADIUS/@UNITS}"
        DAY="{DAY} {DAY/@UNITS}"
    />
</xsl:template>

</xsl:stylesheet>
```

And here's the result, complete with the units for each measurement:

```
<?xml version="1.0" encoding="UTF-8"?>
<PLANETS>
    <PLANET DAY="58.65 days" RADIUS="1516 miles"
        MASS=".0553 (Earth = 1)" NAME="Mercury"/>
    <PLANET DAY="116.75 days" RADIUS="3716 miles"
        MASS=".815 (Earth = 1)" NAME="Venus"/>
    <PLANET DAY="1 days" RADIUS="2107 miles"
        MASS="1 (Earth = 1)" NAME="Earth"/>
</PLANETS>
```

Note that you cannot nest "{" and "}" in attribute value templates, and if you have an expression that uses "{" and "}", such as "function printHello {cout << 'Hello';}", you must double the curly braces so that the XSLT processor knows to ignore them: "function printHello {{cout << 'Hello';}}".

Attribute value templates always work with the context node. You cannot, however, use attribute value templates anywhere you want in a stylesheet, which causes much confusion for XSLT developers. You can use attribute value templates in only the following places:

- Literal result elements.
- Extension elements (see Chapter 5).
- `<xsl:attribute>`. You can use the `name` and `namespace` attributes here (see Chapter 6).
- `<xsl:element>`. You can use the `name` and `namespace` attributes here (see Chapter 6).
- `<xsl:number>`. You can use the `format`, `lang`, `letter-value`, `grouping-separator`, and `grouping-size` attributes here (see Chapter 4).
- `<xsl:processing-instruction>`. You can use the `name attribute` here (see Chapter 6).
- `<xsl:sort>`. You can use the `lang`, `data-type`, `order`, and `case-order` attributes here (see Chapter 5).

Chapter 6 has more on this topic, where you learn how to create attributes (and new elements) from scratch. And you'll see more on the XPath expressions you can use in attribute value templates in Chapter 7.

Handling Whitespace

Whitespace gives XSLT authors a lot of trouble at first. Chapter 2 explained that pure whitespace nodes are text nodes that contain only whitespace (spaces, carriage returns, line feeds, and tabs). These nodes are copied by default when they come from the source document.

Note that you can also have whitespace nodes in your *stylesheets* as well:

```
<xsl:template match="PLANETS">
    <xsl:copy>
        <xsl:apply-templates select="PLANET"/>
    </xsl:copy>
</xsl:template>
```

In this case, I'm using spaces to indent the stylesheet elements, as well as carriage returns to spread things out. Pure whitespace nodes such as these are *not* copied from the stylesheet to the output document. Note, however, that the whitespace in the following `<TITLE>` element *is* copied to the output, because it's not a pure whitespace node (it also contains the text "The Planets Table"):

```
    <xsl:template match="/PLANETS">
        <HTML>
            <HEAD>
```

```
            <TITLE>
                The Planets Table
            </TITLE>
            .
            .
            .
```

If you want to eliminate this whitespace and retain the indented format, you can use empty `<xsl:text>` elements so the whitespace becomes pure whitespace nodes:

```
<xsl:template match="/PLANETS">
    <HTML>
        <HEAD>
            <TITLE>
                <xsl:text/>The Planets Table<xsl:text/>
            </TITLE>
            .
            .
            .
```

Pure whitespace nodes are not copied from the stylesheet to the output document unless they are inside an `<xsl:text>` element, or an enclosing element has the `xml:space` attribute set to "preserve" (for more on `xml:space`, see *Inside XML*).

On the other hand, by default, XSLT preserves whitespace text nodes in the source document and copies them to the result document. Use the copying stylesheet we've already seen, which copies all elements from the source document to the result document:

```
<?xml version="1.0"?>
<xsl:stylesheet version="1.0"
xmlns:xsl="http://www.w3.org/1999/XSL/Transform">
    <xsl:output method="xml"/>
    <xsl:template match="*">
        <xsl:copy>
            <xsl:apply-templates/>
        </xsl:copy>
    </xsl:template>
</xsl:stylesheet>
```

and apply this stylesheet to planets.xml, all the whitespace I've used in planets.xml is copied over to the result document as well:

```
<?xml version="1.0"?>
<?xml-stylesheet type="text/xml" href="planets.xsl"?>
<PLANETS>

    <PLANET>
        <NAME>Mercury</NAME>
        <MASS UNITS="(Earth = 1)">.0553</MASS>
```

```
        <DAY UNITS="days">58.65</DAY>
        <RADIUS UNITS="miles">1516</RADIUS>
        <DENSITY UNITS="(Earth = 1)">.983</DENSITY>
        <DISTANCE UNITS="million miles">43.4</DISTANCE><!--At perihelion-->
    </PLANET>
        .
        .
        .
```

However, there are times you want to remove the whitespace used to format input documents, and you can do that with the `<xsl:strip-space>` element.

The *<xsl:strip-space>* and *<xsl:preserve-space>* Elements

The `<xsl:strip-space>` element causes the XSLT processor to strip all pure whitespace nodes (also called "expendable" whitespace nodes) from the input document. A pure whitespace node consists of only whitespace characters, without any other type of text. This element has only one attribute:

- `elements` (mandatory). Specifies the elements from which to strip the whitespace. Set to a whitespace-separated list of NameTests (which are names or generic names with wildcards).

This element contains no content.

For example, to strip all whitespace nodes from planets.xml, I could use `<xsl:strip-space elements="*"/>` like this:

```
<?xml version="1.0"?>
<xsl:stylesheet version="1.0"
xmlns:xsl="http://www.w3.org/1999/XSL/Transform">
    <xsl:strip-space elements="*"/>
    <xsl:output method="xml"/>
    <xsl:template match="*">
        <xsl:copy>
            <xsl:apply-templates/>
        </xsl:copy>
    </xsl:template>
</xsl:stylesheet>
```

Here's the result document when I apply this stylesheet to planets.xml. Note that all whitespace has been stripped out, including all newline characters:

```
<?xml version="1.0" encoding="utf-8"?><PLANETS><PLANET><NAME>Mercury</NAME>
<MASS>.0553
</MASS><DAY>58.65</DAY><RADIUS>1516</RADIUS><DENSITY>.983</DENSITY>
<DISTANCE>43.4</DISTANCE></PLANET><PLANET><NAME>Venus</NAME><MASS>.815</MASS>
<DAY>116.75</DAY><RADIUS>3716</RADIUS><DENSITY>.943</DENSITY><DISTANCE>66.8</DISTANCE>
</PLANET><PLANET><NAME>Earth</NAME><MASS>1</MASS><DAY>1</DAY><RADIUS>2107</RADIUS>
<DENSITY>1</DENSITY><DISTANCE>128.4</DISTANCE></PLANET></PLANETS>
```

Notice that only pure whitespace nodes are removed this way. For example, the text content of the element `<TITLE>Volcanoes for Dinner</TITLE>` does not include any pure whitespace text nodes, so the text, "Volcanoes for Dinner", would be preserved in the output document, including the spaces. This would be true even if the text contained multiple adjacent spaces, as in "Volcanoes   for   Dinner".

There may be times you might not want to remove *all* the whitespace nodes throughout a document, and you can use the `<xsl:preserve-space>` element to indicate in which elements you want to preserve whitespace nodes. This element has the same attribute as `<xsl:strip-space>`:

- `elements` (mandatory). Specifies the elements in which to preserve the whitespace. Set to a whitespace-separated list of `NameTests` (which are names or generic names with wildcards).

In fact, `<xsl:preserve-space>` is the default for all elements in XSLT. If you've used `<xsl:strip-space>`, you can still indicate in which element or elements you want whitespace nodes preserved by setting the `elements` attribute in `<xsl:preserve-space>` to a list of that element or elements, as follows:

```
<?xml version="1.0"?>
<xsl:stylesheet version="1.0"
xmlns:xsl="http://www.w3.org/1999/XSL/Transform">
    <xsl:strip-space elements="*"/>
    <xsl:preserve-space elements="MASS RADIUS"/>
    <xsl:output method="xml"/>
    <xsl:template match="*">
        <xsl:copy>
            <xsl:apply-templates/>
        </xsl:copy>
    </xsl:template>
</xsl:stylesheet>
```

All this discussion of stripping and preserving whitespace may make you a little nervous when it comes to formatting output documents with indentation spaces, but there is an easy way: You can use the `indent` attribute of the `<xsl:output>` element to automatically indent the result document.

Automatic Indenting

The `<xsl:output>` element supports an attribute called `indent`, which you can set to "yes" or "no", and which indicates to the XSLT processor whether you want the result document indented. Usually, indenting the result document doesn't matter very much, because that document is targeted to an application that doesn't care about indenting, as in the XML-to-XML and -HTML examples you've seen. However, there are times when you'd like to view the result document as straight text, and in such cases, indenting that document to show its hierarchical structure can help.

How an XSLT processor uses the indent variable varies by processor, because it's not specified by W3C, so you have to experiment to get the results you want. Say, for example, that you have a version of planets.xml without any indentation at all, like the following:

```
<?xml version="1.0"?>
<?xml-stylesheet type="text/xml" href="planets.xsl"?>
<PLANETS>

<PLANET>
<NAME>Mercury</NAME>
<MASS UNITS="(Earth = 1)">.0553</MASS>
<DAY UNITS="days">58.65</DAY>
<RADIUS UNITS="miles">1516</RADIUS>
<DENSITY UNITS="(Earth = 1)">.983</DENSITY>
<DISTANCE UNITS="million miles">43.4</DISTANCE><!--At perihelion-->
</PLANET>

<PLANET>
<NAME>Venus</NAME>
<MASS UNITS="(Earth = 1)">.815</MASS>
<DAY UNITS="days">116.75</DAY>
<RADIUS UNITS="miles">3716</RADIUS>
<DENSITY UNITS="(Earth = 1)">.943</DENSITY>
<DISTANCE UNITS="million miles">66.8</DISTANCE><!--At perihelion-->
</PLANET>

<PLANET>
<NAME>Earth</NAME>
<MASS UNITS="(Earth = 1)">1</MASS>
<DAY UNITS="days">1</DAY>
<RADIUS UNITS="miles">2107</RADIUS>
<DENSITY UNITS="(Earth = 1)">1</DENSITY>
<DISTANCE UNITS="million miles">128.4</DISTANCE><!--At perihelion-->
</PLANET>

</PLANETS>
```

You can use the `<xsl:output indent="yes"/>` element to instruct the XSLT processor to indent this document when you convert it to HTML:

Listing 3.6 **Indenting Stylesheet**

```
<?xml version="1.0"?>
<xsl:stylesheet version="1.0"
xmlns:xsl="http://www.w3.org/1999/XSL/Transform">
    <xsl:output indent="yes"/>

    <xsl:template match="/PLANETS">
<HTML>
<HEAD>
<TITLE>
          The Planets Table
      </TITLE>
</HEAD>
<BODY>
<H1>
          The Planets Table
      </H1>
<TABLE BORDER="2">
<TD>Name</TD>
<TD>Mass</TD>
<TD>Radius</TD>
<TD>Day</TD>
<xsl:apply-templates/>
</TABLE>
</BODY>
</HTML>
</xsl:template>

<xsl:template match="PLANET">
<TR>
<TD><xsl:value-of select="NAME"/></TD>
<TD><xsl:value-of select="MASS"/></TD>
<TD><xsl:value-of select="RADIUS"/></TD>
<TD><xsl:value-of select="DAY"/></TD>
</TR>
</xsl:template>

</xsl:stylesheet>
```

Here's the result, using Saxon (which is particularly good at indenting), indented as desired:

```
<HTML>
   <HEAD>
      <meta http-equiv="Content-Type" content="text/html; charset=utf-8">

      <TITLE>
         The Planets Table
```

```
    </TITLE>
  </HEAD>
  <BODY>
    <H1>
      The Planets Table

    </H1>
    <TABLE BORDER="2">
      <TD>Name</TD>
      <TD>Mass</TD>
      <TD>Radius</TD>
      <TD>Day</TD>


      <TR>
        <TD>Mercury</TD>
        <TD>.0553</TD>
        <TD>1516</TD>
        <TD>58.65</TD>
      </TR>


      <TR>
        <TD>Venus</TD>
        <TD>.815</TD>
        <TD>3716</TD>
        <TD>116.75</TD>
      </TR>


      <TR>
        <TD>Earth</TD>
        <TD>1</TD>
        <TD>2107</TD>
        <TD>1</TD>
      </TR>

    </TABLE>
  </BODY>
</HTML>
```

As you can see, handling whitespace takes a little bit of thought in XSLT, but it's easier if you know what's going on.

Indenting Documents in this Book

How your XSLT processor indents documents is processor-dependent. When displaying documents in this book, I'll indent them for readability, even if the actual document has not been indented by the XSLT processor.

Default Template Rules

Take a look at the following XSLT stylesheet; it has rules that match the root node, <PLANETS> nodes, and <PLANET> nodes:

```
<?xml version="1.0"?>
<xsl:stylesheet version="1.0"
xmlns:xsl="http://www.w3.org/1999/XSL/Transform">

    <xsl:template match="/">
        <HTML>
            <xsl:apply-templates/>
        </HTML>
    </xsl:template>

    <xsl:template match="PLANETS">
        <xsl:apply-templates/>
    </xsl:template>

    <xsl:template match="PLANET">
        <P>
            <xsl:value-of select="NAME"/>
        </P>
    </xsl:template>

</xsl:stylesheet>
```

Note the rule for the <PLANETS> element; that rule simply uses <xsl:apply-templates> to apply templates to all its child nodes. However, there is a *default rule* in template processing that if you don't supply a rule for an element, <apply-templates/> is called automatically. So, the following stylesheet—where I've omitted the rule for <PLANETS—is the same as the preceding one:

```
<?xml version="1.0"?>
<xsl:stylesheet version="1.0"
xmlns:xsl="http://www.w3.org/1999/XSL/Transform">

    <xsl:template match="/">
        <HTML>
            <xsl:apply-templates/>
        </HTML>
    </xsl:template>

    <xsl:template match="PLANET">
        <P>
            <xsl:value-of select="NAME"/>
        </P>
    </xsl:template>

</xsl:stylesheet>
```

In this case, I've taken advantage of the default template rules. Here are the default rules for each kind of node, which are put into effect if you don't explicitly give a rule for the node:

- **Root node.** Call `<xsl:apply-templates/>` by default.
- **Element nodes.** Call `<xsl:apply-templates/>` by default.
- **Attribute nodes**. Copy the attribute value to the result document. But copy it as *text*, not as an attribute.
- **Text nodes.** Copy the text to the result document.
- **Comment nodes.** Do no XSLT processing; nothing is copied.
- **Processing instruction nodes.** Do no XSLT processing; nothing is copied.
- **Namespace nodes.** Do no XSLT processing; nothing is copied.

The most important default rule applies to elements, and can be expressed as follows:

```
<xsl:template match="*">
    <xsl:apply-templates/>
</xsl:template>
```

This rule is there simply to make sure that every element, from the root on down, is processed with `<xsl:apply-templates/>` if you don't supply some other rule. If you do supply another rule, it overrides the corresponding default rule.

The default rule for text nodes can be expressed as follows, where the XSLT function `text` matches the text in the node, so that the text of the text node is added to the output document:

```
<xsl:template match="text()">
    <xsl:value-of select="."/>
</xsl:template>
```

The same kind of default rule applies to attributes, which are added to the output document with a default rule like this, where the expression `"@*"` matches any attribute:

```
<xsl:template match="@*">
    <xsl:value-of select="."/>
</xsl:template>
```

By default, processing instructions are not inserted in the output document, so their default rule can be expressed simply as follows using the XSLT function processing-instruction, which matches processing instructions (as you'll see in Chapter 8):

```
<xsl:template match="processing-instruction()"/>
```

And the same goes for comments, whose default rule can be expressed as follows using the XSLT function `comment`, which you'll also see in Chapter 8:

```
<xsl:template match="comment()"/>
```

The upshot of the default rules is that if you don't supply any rules at all, all the parsed character data in the input document is inserted in the output document. Here's what a XSLT stylesheet with no explicit rules looks like:

```
<?xml version="1.0"?>
<xsl:stylesheet version="1.0"
xmlns:xsl="http://www.w3.org/1999/XSL/Transform">
</xsl:stylesheet>
```

And here's the result of applying this stylesheet to planets.xml. Note that the default rule for attributes has not been applied, because they are not children of other nodes:

```
<?xml version="1.0" encoding="UTF-8"?>

    Mercury
    .0553
    58.65
    1516
    .983
    43.4

    Venus
    .815
    116.75
    3716
    .943
    66.8

    Earth
    1
    1
    2107
    1
    128.4
```

The Internet Explorer and Default Rules

One of the problems of working with XSLT in the Internet Explorer 5.5 or earlier is that the browser does not supply any default rules. You have to supply all the rules yourself, unless you've installed the MSXML3 processor in replace mode (see Chapter 2 for the details) or you've upgraded to Internet Explorer 6.0.

In addition, whitespace nodes are preserved from the source document, so by default, you can also say this is a template rule: `<xsl:output preserve-space="*"/>`.

Deleting Content

If your rule for a node does nothing—that is, it's empty—the content of the matched node is not copied to the output document. In this way, you can selectively remove content from the source document when you write the output document.

Imagine that you wanted to remove all data about the various planets in planets.xml except for their names and masses. Here's a stylesheet that does the trick:

Listing 3.7 **Deleting Content**

```
<?xml version="1.0"?>
<xsl:stylesheet version="1.0"
xmlns:xsl="http://www.w3.org/1999/XSL/Transform">
<xsl:strip-space elements="*"/>
<xsl:output method="xml" indent="yes"/>

<xsl:template match="/">
        <xsl:apply-templates/>
</xsl:template>

    <xsl:template match="PLANETS">
        <xsl:apply-templates/>
    </xsl:template>

    <xsl:template match="PLANET">
       <xsl:copy>
          <xsl:apply-templates/>
       </xsl:copy>
   </xsl:template>

    <xsl:template match="NAME">
       <xsl:copy>
          <xsl:apply-templates/>
       </xsl:copy>
   </xsl:template>

    <xsl:template match="MASS">
        <xsl:copy>
        <xsl:value-of select="."/>
        <xsl:value-of select="@UNITS"/>
        </xsl:copy>
    </xsl:template>
```

continues ▸

Listing 3.7 **Continued**

```
    <xsl:template match="RADIUS">
    </xsl:template>

    <xsl:template match="DAY">
    </xsl:template>

    <xsl:template match="DENSITY">
    </xsl:template>

    <xsl:template match="DISTANCE">
    </xsl:template>
</xsl:stylesheet>
```

And here's the result document (note that all that I've preserved are the <NAME> and <MASS> elements):

```
<?xml version="1.0" encoding="UTF-8"?>
<PLANET>
    <NAME>Mercury</NAME>
    <MASS>.0553(Earth = 1)</MASS>
</PLANET>

<PLANET>
    <NAME>Venus</NAME>
    <MASS>.815(Earth = 1)</MASS>
</PLANET>

<PLANET>
    <NAME>Earth</NAME>
    <MASS>1(Earth = 1)</MASS>
</PLANET>
```

In this way, you can filter XML documents, creating new XML documents with just the data you want.

Template Conflict Resolution

Another important aspect of template use is *conflict resolution*. If two templates match the same node or node set, XSLT relies on the priority of the two templates to determine which template to apply.

Each template has a default priority based on the `select` attribute value. Generally, the more specific the match or expression (such as `"PLANET"` versus `"*"`) is, the higher its priority. Chapter 4 looks at how the processor determines priorities and how the processor deals with templates that have the same priority.

You can also set the priority of a template with the `priority` attribute. Here's an example; in this case, a rule created with the element `<xsl:template`

`priority="1"/>` has lower priority than one created with the `<xsl:template priority="2"/>` element:

Listing 3.8 **Setting Template Priority**

```
<?xml version="1.0"?>
<xsl:stylesheet version="1.0"
xmlns:xsl="http://www.w3.org/1999/XSL/Transform">

    <xsl:template match="/PLANETS">
        <HTML>
            <HEAD>
                <TITLE>
                    The Planets Table
                </TITLE>
            </HEAD>
            <BODY>
                <H1>
                    The Planets Table
                </H1>
                <TABLE BORDER="2">
                    <TR>
                        <TD>Name</TD>
                        <TD>Mass</TD>
                        <TD>Radius</TD>
                        <TD>Day</TD>
                    </TR>
                    <xsl:apply-templates/>
                </TABLE>
            </BODY>
        </HTML>
    </xsl:template>

    <xsl:template match="PLANET">
       <TR>
          <TD><xsl:value-of select="NAME"/></TD>
          <TD><xsl:apply-templates select="MASS"/></TD>
          <TD><xsl:apply-templates select="RADIUS"/></TD>
          <TD><xsl:apply-templates select="DAY"/></TD>
       </TR>
   </xsl:template>

    <xsl:template match="MASS" priority="2">
        <xsl:value-of select="."/>
        (<I>Very</I> heavy)
    </xsl:template>

    <xsl:template match="MASS" priority="1">
        <xsl:value-of select="."/>
    </xsl:template>
```

continues ▸

Listing 3.8 **Continued**

```
    <xsl:template match="RADIUS">
        <xsl:value-of select="."/>
        <xsl:text> </xsl:text>
        <xsl:value-of select="@UNITS"/>
    </xsl:template>

    <xsl:template match="DAY">
        <xsl:value-of select="."/>
        <xsl:text> </xsl:text>
        <xsl:value-of select="@UNITS"/>
    </xsl:template>

</xsl:stylesheet>
```

The XSLT processor selects the template with the higher priority, and that template adds the text `"(<I>Very</I> heavy)"` after each mass measurement. Here's the result, where you can see the template with the higher priority was used:

```
<HTML>

    <HEAD>
        <TITLE>
            The Planets Table
        </TITLE>
    </HEAD>

    <BODY>
        <H1>
            The Planets Table
        </H1>

        <TABLE BORDER="2">
            <TR>
                <TD>Name</TD>
                <TD>Mass</TD>
                <TD>Radius</TD>
                <TD>Day</TD>
            </TR>

           <TR>
               <TD>Mercury</TD>
               <TD>.0553(<I>Very</I> heavy)</TD>
               <TD>1516 miles</TD>
               <TD>58.65 days</TD>
           </TR>

           <TR>
               <TD>Venus</TD>
```

```
            <TD>.815(<I>Very</I> heavy)</TD>
            <TD>3716 miles</TD>
            <TD>116.75 days</TD>
        </TR>

        <TR>
            <TD>Earth</TD>
            <TD>1(<I>Very</I> heavy)</TD>
            <TD>2107 miles</TD>
            <TD>1 days</TD>
        </TR>

      </TABLE>
  </BODY>
</HTML>
```

Upcoming in XSLT 2.0

The question of template priority is one that XSLT 2.0 is supposed to address. In particular, W3C is considering adding a new element, hypothetically named `<xsl:next-match/>`, that will enable you to select the *second* best match to a template.

Here's another useful thing to know about priority: If two templates match the same node and no priority has been assigned these templates, the XSLT processor will choose the template that is a more specific match. For example, a match to `"PLANET"` is preferred over a match to the generic `"*"`.

The *<xsl:copy>* Element

The `<xsl:copy>` element enables you to copy a node from the source tree to the output tree. Note that this is a *shallow* copy, however, which does not copy any of the node's descendents or attributes.

This element has one attribute:

- `use-attribute-sets`. Specifies the names of attribute sets to be applied to a created element. Set to a whitespace-separated list of `QNames`. You can use the attribute only when the context node is an element; see Chapter 6 for the details on attribute sets.

This element can contain a template body, which is used only when the node to copy is a root node or an element. Note that using `<xsl:copy>` does nothing when used on the root node, because the root of the output document is created automatically.

Here's an example; this stylesheet first appeared in Chapter 2, and all it does is copy all elements from the source document to the result document:

Listing 3.9 **Element-Copying Stylesheet**

```
<?xml version="1.0"?>
<xsl:stylesheet version="1.0"
xmlns:xsl="http://www.w3.org/1999/XSL/Transform">
    <xsl:output method="xml"/>

    <xsl:template match="*">
        <xsl:copy>
            <xsl:apply-templates/>
        </xsl:copy>
    </xsl:template>
</xsl:stylesheet>
```

However, `<xsl:copy>` does *not* copy attributes, so here's the result when this stylesheet is used on planets.xml:

```
<?xml version="1.0" encoding="UTF-8"?>
<PLANETS>

    <PLANET>
        <NAME>Mercury</NAME>
        <MASS>.0553</MASS>
        <DAY>58.65</DAY>
        <RADIUS>1516</RADIUS>
        <DENSITY>.983</DENSITY>
        <DISTANCE>43.4</DISTANCE>
    </PLANET>

    <PLANET>
        <NAME>Venus</NAME>
        <MASS>.815</MASS>
        <DAY>116.75</DAY>
        <RADIUS>3716</RADIUS>
        <DENSITY>.943</DENSITY>
        <DISTANCE>66.8</DISTANCE>
    </PLANET>

    <PLANET>
        <NAME>Earth</NAME>
        <MASS>1</MASS>
        <DAY>1</DAY>
        <RADIUS>2107</RADIUS>
        <DENSITY>1</DENSITY>
```

```
        <DISTANCE>128.4</DISTANCE>
    </PLANET>

</PLANETS>
```

Copying attributes, too, is a little more difficult, because you have to specifically find a way to apply `<xsl:copy>` to each element's attributes. That can be done, for example, with `<xsl:for-each>`, which is shown in Chapter 5:

Listing 3.10 **Copying Attributes**

```
<?xml version="1.0"?>
<xsl:stylesheet version="1.0"
xmlns:xsl="http://www.w3.org/1999/XSL/Transform">
    <xsl:output method="xml"/>

    <xsl:template match="*">
        <xsl:copy>
            <xsl:for-each select="@*">
                <xsl:copy/>
            </xsl:for-each>
            <xsl:apply-templates/>
        </xsl:copy>
    </xsl:template>
</xsl:stylesheet>
```

Here's the result—note that this time, the attributes are intact:

```
<?xml version="1.0" encoding="UTF-8"?>
<PLANETS>

    <PLANET>
        <NAME>Mercury</NAME>
        <MASS UNITS="(Earth = 1)">.0553</MASS>
        <DAY UNITS="days">58.65</DAY>
        <RADIUS UNITS="miles">1516</RADIUS>
        <DENSITY UNITS="(Earth = 1)">.983</DENSITY>
        <DISTANCE UNITS="million miles">43.4</DISTANCE>
    </PLANET>

    <PLANET>
        <NAME>Venus</NAME>
        <MASS UNITS="(Earth = 1)">.815</MASS>
        <DAY UNITS="days">116.75</DAY>
        <RADIUS UNITS="miles">3716</RADIUS>
        <DENSITY UNITS="(Earth = 1)">.943</DENSITY>
        <DISTANCE UNITS="million miles">66.8</DISTANCE>
    </PLANET>
```

```
    <PLANET>
        <NAME>Earth</NAME>
        <MASS UNITS="(Earth = 1)">1</MASS>
        <DAY UNITS="days">1</DAY>
        <RADIUS UNITS="miles">2107</RADIUS>
        <DENSITY UNITS="(Earth = 1)">1</DENSITY>
        <DISTANCE UNITS="million miles">128.4</DISTANCE>
    </PLANET>

</PLANETS>
```

However, there's an easier way of making sure that you copy all the children, attributes, and other descendents of nodes: You can use `<xsl:copy-of>` rather than `<xsl:copy>`.

Making Deep Copies

You'll see a way of using `<xsl:copy>` to make a deep copy of a document in Chapter 4, which describes the node function and explains how to call the same template recursively.

The *<xsl:copy-of>* Element

The `<xsl:copy-of>` element enables you to make a *deep* copy of nodes, which means that not just the node, but all attributes and descendents are copied as well. This element has one attribute:

- `select` (mandatory). The node or node set you want copied.

This element is empty, and takes no content.

Here's an example that shows how this works; in this case, I'll replace the `<xsl:for-each>` element in Listing 3.10 with an `<xsl:copy-of>` element that specifically selects all attributes of the context element to copy:

Listing 3.11 **Using *<copy-of>***

```
<?xml version="1.0"?>
<xsl:stylesheet version="1.0"
xmlns:xsl="http://www.w3.org/1999/XSL/Transform">
    <xsl:output method="xml"/>

    <xsl:template match="*">
        <xsl:copy>
```

```
            <xsl:copy-of select="@*"/>
            <xsl:apply-templates/>
        </xsl:copy>
    </xsl:template>
</xsl:stylesheet>
```

This works as the previous example did, copying all elements and attributes. On the other hand, I don't need to modify the previous example in Listing 3.10 at all; I can simply use `<xsl:copy-of>` to copy the entire document by matching the root node and copying all descendents of that node like this:

```
<?xml version="1.0"?>
<xsl:stylesheet version="1.0"
xmlns:xsl="http://www.w3.org/1999/XSL/Transform">
    <xsl:output method="xml"/>
    <xsl:template match="/">
        <xsl:copy-of select="*"/>
    </xsl:template>
</xsl:stylesheet>
```

You can also use `<xsl:copy-of>` to copy particular nodes and their descendents instead of matching the wildcard "*". For example, the following rule copies all `<MASS>` elements and their descendents:

```
<xsl:template match="MASS">
        <xsl:copy-of select="."/>
    </xsl:template>
```

For that matter, I can replace a `<MASS>` element with a `<DAY>` element like this:

```
     <xsl:template match="MASS">
        <xsl:copy-of select="DAY"/>
    </xsl:template>
```

The *<xsl:message>* Element

You can use the `<xsl:message>` element to cause the XSLT processor to display a message, and, optionally, quit processing a stylesheet. The `<xsl:message>` element has one attribute:

- `terminate` (optional). Set to "yes" to terminate processing. The default is "no".

Where the message is actually sent depends on the XSLT processor. For Java-based XSLT processors, the message is usually sent to the Java error output stream, which corresponds to the screen if you invoke the XSLT processor on the command line. Other XSLT processors may display messages in pop-up windows, or in Web pages sent to browsers.

Here's an example. In this case, I'll terminate XSLT processing when the XSLT processor tries to transform a `<DAY>` element in planets.xml, displaying the message `"Sorry, DAY information is classified."`:

Listing 3.12 **Using *<xsl:message>***

```
<?xml version="1.0"?>
<xsl:stylesheet version="1.0"
xmlns:xsl="http://www.w3.org/1999/XSL/Transform">

    <xsl:template match="/PLANETS">
        <HTML>
            <HEAD>
                <TITLE>
                    The Planets Table
                </TITLE>
            </HEAD>
            <BODY>
                <H1>
                    The Planets Table
                </H1>
                <TABLE BORDER="2">
                    <TD>Name</TD>
                    <TD>Mass</TD>
                    <TD>Radius</TD>
                    <TD>Day</TD>
                    <xsl:apply-templates/>
                </TABLE>
            </BODY>
        </HTML>
    </xsl:template>

    <xsl:template match="PLANET">
       <TR>
          <TD><xsl:value-of select="NAME"/></TD>
          <TD><xsl:apply-templates select="MASS"/></TD>
          <TD><xsl:apply-templates select="RADIUS"/></TD>
          <TD><xsl:apply-templates select="DAY"/></TD>
       </TR>
   </xsl:template>

    <xsl:template match="MASS">
        <xsl:value-of select="."/>
        <xsl:text> </xsl:text>
        <xsl:value-of select="@UNITS"/>
    </xsl:template>
```

```
    <xsl:template match="RADIUS">
        <xsl:value-of select="."/>
        <xsl:text> </xsl:text>
        <xsl:value-of select="@UNITS"/>
    </xsl:template>

    <xsl:template match="DAY">
        <xsl:message terminate="yes">
            Sorry, DAY information is classified.
        </xsl:message terminate="yes">
    </xsl:template>

</xsl:stylesheet>
```

Here are the results when you use this stylesheet with Xalan:

```
C:\planets>java org.apache.xalan.xslt.Process -IN planets.xml -XSL message.xsl -OUT
➥planets.html
file:///C:/XSL/messages/message.xsl; Line 49; Column 38; Sorry, DAY information
➥is classified.
XSLT Error (javax.xml.transform.TransformerException): Stylesheet directed termination
```

Using `<xsl:message>`, you can display information about what's going on during stylesheet processing, which is good not only for displaying errors and warnings, but also to debug stylesheets.

More template topics are coming up throughout the book, such as calling named templates and using template parameters. In the next chapter, I'll take a look at a large and important topic: how to create the match patterns you use to specify what node or nodes you want to work with in XSLT. I've already touched on how to create and use match patterns, but it's time to take a systematic look at match patterns.

4 Creating Match Patterns

EVERYTHING YOU'VE DONE IN THIS BOOK SO far has been fairly straightforward, except for one thing: match patterns, which have been a little mysterious. We've used various match patterns, such as "/PLANETS" in `<xsl:template>` elements, without offering a lot of systematic explanation on how these patterns really work, as in this case:

```
<xsl:template match="/PLANETS">
    <HTML>
        <HEAD>
            <TITLE>
                The Planets Table
            </TITLE>
        </HEAD>
        <BODY>
        .
        .
        .
        </BODY>
    </HTML>
</xsl:template>
```

This chapter is going to provide all you need to know to create match patterns in XSLT. You use match patterns in the `<xsl:template>`, `<xsl:key>`, and `<xsl:number>` elements; we've been working with `<xsl:template>` from the beginning of the book, and you're going to see `<xsl:key>` in Chapter 9 and `<xsl:number>` in Chapter 5. In particular, you use the `match` attribute of `<xsl:template>` and `<xsl:key>`, and the `count` and `from` attributes of `<xsl:number>`, to match patterns.

You also can use match patterns in the `select` attribute of elements, such as `<xsl:apply-templates>`, `<xsl:value-of>`, `<xsl:for-each>`, and `<xsl:copy-of>`. Here's one important thing you need to know, however: The `select` attribute of these elements is more powerful than the `match`, `count`, and `from` attributes of `<xsl:template>`, `<xsl:key>`, and `<xsl:number>`, because you can use full XPath expressions, not just match patterns in `select`.

Match patterns are a *subset* of XPath expressions—that is, all match patterns are valid XPath expressions, but not all XPath expressions are match patterns. The only XPath expressions that can be patterns are those that return a node set (even a node set with one node) and that use paths that specify only child or attribute nodes.

Match patterns are defined in the XSLT recommendation itself, whereas XPath expressions are defined in the XPath recommendation (`www.w3.org/TR/xpath`); however, the two are compatible because all match patterns are also XPath expressions.

Creating Full XPath Expressions

Chapter 7, "Using and Understanding XPath," shows how to create full XPath expressions. You can use full XPath expressions in XSLT in the following places: in the `select` attribute of the `<xsl:apply-templates>`, `<xsl:value-of>`, `<xsl:for-each>`, `<xsl:param>`, `<xsl:variable>`, `<xsl:wit-param>`, `<xsl:copy-of>`, and `<xsl:sort>` elements; in attribute value templates; in the `test` attribute of `<xsl:if>` and `<xsl:when>` elements; in the `value` attribute of `<xsl:number>`; and in the predicates of match patterns.

To make things just a little more confusing, it turns out that you actually *can* use XPath expressions in a special, optional part (and only this part) of match patterns: the *predicate*. As you're going to see in this chapter, predicates are XPath expressions that evaluate to either true/false values or numbers, which you enclose in brackets, `[` and `]`. For example, the pattern `PLANET[NAME="Venus"]` matches the `<PLANET>` children of the context node that have `<NAME>` children with text equal to "Venus." The expressions inside the `[` and `]` are true XPath expressions with some restrictions that you'll see in this chapter.

There is no question that writing match patterns takes some experience, so I include many examples in this chapter.

Microsoft and Nonstandard Match Patterns

Microsoft supports match patterns with its MSXML3 XML processor, but there's one thing you should know: Microsoft also supports a great deal of non-standard, non-W3C syntax in its match patterns. I'm going to stick to the official, W3C, version in this chapter, and if you happen to read Microsoft documentation on match patterns, keep in mind that much of what you read is Microsoft-only.

Matching the Root Node

As you've already seen, you can match the root node with the match pattern "/" like this:

```
<xsl:template match="/">
    <HTML>
        <xsl:apply-templates/>
    </HTML>
</xsl:template>
```

Matching Elements

You can match elements simply by giving their names, as you've also seen. The following template matches <PLANETS> elements:

```
<xsl:template match="PLANETS">
  <HTML>
    <xsl:apply-templates/>
  </HTML>
</xsl:template>
```

Matching Children

You can use the / step operator to separate element names when you want to refer to a child of a particular node. For example, say that you want to create a rule that applies to only those <NAME> elements that are children of <PLANET> elements. In that case, you can match the expression "PLANET/NAME". Here's a rule that surrounds the text of such elements in a <H3> HTML element:

```
<xsl:template match="PLANET/NAME">
    <H3>
        <xsl:value-of select="."/>
    </H3>
</xsl:template>
```

You also can use the * character as a wildcard, standing for any element. (* can match only elements, although note that the pattern @* can match any attribute.) For example, the following rule applies to all <NAME> elements that are *grandchildren* of <PLANET> elements:

```
<xsl:template match="PLANET/*/NAME">
    <H3>
        <xsl:value-of select="."/>
    </H3>
</xsl:template>
```

Matching Element Descendants

In the preceding section, I used the expression "PLANET/NAME" to match all <NAME> elements that are direct children of <PLANET> elements, and the expression "PLANET/*/NAME" to match all <NAME> elements that are grandchildren of <PLANET> elements. However, there's an easier way to perform both matches: just use the expression "PLANET//NAME", which matches all <NAME> elements that are inside <PLANET> elements, no matter how many levels deep (the matched elements are called *descendants* of the <PLANET> element). In other words, "PLANET//NAME" matches "PLANET/NAME", "PLANET/*/NAME", "PLANET/*/*/NAME", and so on:

```
<xsl:template match="PLANETS//NAME">
    <H3>
        <xsl:value-of select="."/>
    </H3>
</xsl:template>
```

Matching Attributes

As Chapter 3, "Creating and Using Templates," showed, you can match attributes if you preface their names with an @. You've already worked with the UNITS attribute that most of the children of <PLANET> elements support:

```
<PLANET>
        <NAME>Earth</NAME>
        <MASS UNITS="(Earth = 1)">1</MASS>
        <DAY UNITS="days">1</DAY>
        <RADIUS UNITS="miles">2107</RADIUS>
        <DENSITY UNITS="(Earth = 1)">1</DENSITY>
        <DISTANCE UNITS="million miles">128.4</DISTANCE><!--At perihelion-->
</PLANET>
```

To recover the units and display them as well as the values for the mass and so on, you can match the UNITS attribute with @UNITS, as follows:

Listing 4.1 **Matching Attributes**

```
<?xml version="1.0"?>
<xsl:stylesheet version="1.0"
xmlns:xsl="http://www.w3.org/1999/XSL/Transform">

    <xsl:template match="/PLANETS">
        <HTML>
            <HEAD>
```

```
            .
            .
            .
            </HEAD>

            <BODY>
            .
            .
            .
            </BODY>
        </HTML>
    </xsl:template>

    <xsl:template match="PLANET">
       <TR>
          <TD><xsl:value-of select="NAME"/></TD>
          <TD><xsl:apply-templates select="MASS"/></TD>
          <TD><xsl:apply-templates select="RADIUS"/></TD>
       </TR>
   </xsl:template>

    <xsl:template match="MASS">
        <xsl:value-of select="."/>
        <xsl:text> </xsl:text>
        <xsl:value-of select="@UNITS"/>
    </xsl:template>

    <xsl:template match="RADIUS">
        <xsl:value-of select="."/>
        <xsl:text> </xsl:text>
        <xsl:value-of select="@UNITS"/>
    </xsl:template>

    <xsl:template match="DAY">
        <xsl:value-of select="."/>
        <xsl:text> </xsl:text>
        <xsl:value-of select="@UNITS"/>
    </xsl:template>

</xsl:stylesheet>
```

Now the resulting HTML table includes not only values, but also their units of measurement:

```
<HTML>
    <HEAD>
        <TITLE>
            The Planets Table
        </TITLE>
```

```
    </HEAD>

    <BODY>
        <H1>
            The Planets Table
        </H1>

        <TABLE>
            <TR>
             .
             .
             .
            <TR>
                <TD>Mercury</TD>
                <TD>.0553 (Earth = 1)</TD>
                <TD>1516 miles</TD>
            </TR>

            <TR>
                <TD>Venus</TD>
                <TD>.815 (Earth = 1)</TD>
                <TD>3716 miles</TD>
            </TR>
             .
             .
             .
        </TABLE>
    </BODY>
</HTML>
```

You also can use the `@*` wildcard to select all attributes of an element. For example, `"PLANET/@*"` selects all attributes of `<PLANET>` elements.

Formally Defining Match Patterns

You also can find the definition of match patterns in the W3C XSLT Recommendation. Match patterns are defined in terms of XPath expressions this way:

> "The syntax for patterns is a subset of the syntax for [XPath] expressions. In particular, location paths that meet certain restrictions can be used as patterns. An expression that is also a pattern always evaluates to an object of type node-set. A node matches a pattern if the node is a member of the result of evaluating the pattern as an expression with respect to some possible context; the possible contexts are those whose context node is the node being matched or one of its ancestors."

The most important sentence in the preceding paragraph is the last one. The idea is that a node X matches a pattern if and only if there is a node that is either X or an ancestor of X, such that when you apply the pattern as an XPath expression to that node, the resulting node set includes X.

So what does that actually *mean*? It means that if you want to see whether a pattern matches a node, first apply it to the node itself as an XPath expression, then apply it to all its ancestor nodes in succession, back to the root node. If any node set that results from doing this includes the node itself, the node matches the pattern. Working this way makes sense because match patterns are written to apply to the current node or children of the current node.

Consequences of the Formal Definition of Match Patterns

Defining patterns in terms of XPath expressions this way is relatively straightforward, but now and again there are consequences that aren't obvious at first. For example, although the `node()` function is defined to match any node, when you use it as a pattern, `"node()"`, it's really an abbreviation for `"child::node()"`, as you'll see later in this chapter. Among other things, that means that the pattern `"node()"` can only match child nodes—it will never match the root node. You should also note that there are no patterns that can match namespace-declaration nodes.

The W3C gives the formal definition of match patterns using Extended Backus-Naur Form (EBNF) notation, which is the same notation that the XML specification is written in. You can find an explanation of this grammar at `www.w3.org/TR/REC-xml`, Section 6. I include the formal definition for patterns here only for the sake of reference. (This whole chapter is devoted to unraveling what this formal definition says and making it clear.) The following list includes the EBNF notations used here:

- `::=` means "is defined as"
- `+` means "one or more"
- `*` means "zero or more"
- `|` means "or"
- `-` means "not"
- `?` means "optional"

The following is the actual, formal W3C definition of match patterns; when an item is quoted with single quotation marks, such as `'child'` or `'::'`, that item is meant to appear in the pattern literally (such as "child::NAME"), as are items called *Literals*:

```
Pattern  ::= LocationPathPattern | Pattern '|' LocationPathPattern

LocationPathPattern ::=  '/' RelativePathPattern?
    | IdKeyPattern ('/' | '//') RelativePathPattern)?
    | '//'? RelativePathPattern

IdKeyPattern ::=  'id' '(' Literal ')'  | 'key' '(' Literal ',' Literal ')'

RelativePathPattern ::=  StepPattern | RelativePathPattern '/' StepPattern
    | RelativePathPattern '//'     StepPattern

StepPattern ::=  ChildOrAttributeAxisSpecifier NodeTest Predicate*

ChildOrAttributeAxisSpecifier ::=  AbbreviatedAxisSpecifier
    | ('child' | 'attribute') '::'
```

The definitions for *NodeText* and *Predicate* come from the XPath specification as follows (Expr stands for an XPath expression, and NCName and QName were defined at the beginning of Chapter 2, "Creating and Using Stylesheets"):

```
NodeTest ::= NameTest ¦ NodeType '(' ')' | 'processing-instruction' '(' Literal ')'

Predicate ::= '[' PredicateExpr ']'

PredicateExpr ::= Expr

AbbreviatedAxisSpecifier ::= '@'?

NameTest ::= '*' | NCName ':' '*' | QName

NodeType ::= 'comment' | 'text' | 'processing-instruction' | 'node'
```

As you can see, this is all more or less as clear as mud. Now it's time to start deciphering. First, a *pattern* consists of one or more *location path patterns.* A location path pattern, in turn, consists of one or more *step patterns*, separated by / or //, or one or more step patterns in conjunction with the id or key functions (which match elements that have specific IDs or keys).

Step patterns are the *building blocks* of patterns, and you can use multiple steps in a single path, separating them by / or //, as in the pattern "PLANET/*/NAME", which has three steps: "PLANET", "*", and "NAME". If you start the pattern itself with /, it's called *absolute*, because you're specifying the pattern from the root node (like "/PLANETS/PLANET" or "//PLANET"); otherwise, it's called *relative*, and it's applied starting with the context node (like "PLANET").

Next, a step pattern is made up of an *axis*, a *node test*, and zero or more *predicates*. For example, in the expression child::PLANET[position() = 5], child is the name of the axis, `PLANET` is the node test, and `[position() = 5]` is a predicate. (Predicates are always enclosed in `[` and `]`.) You can create patterns with one or more step patterns, such as `/child::PLANET/child::NAME`, which matches `<NAME>` elements that are children of a `<PLANET>` parent.

To understand patterns, then, you have to understand step patterns, because patterns are made up of one or more step patterns in expressions such as `"step-pattern1/step-pattern2/step-pattern3..."`. And to understand step patterns, you have to understand their three parts—axes, node tests, and predicates—which I'll take a look at in the following sections.

Part 1 of Step Patterns: Pattern Axes

Axes make up the first part of step patterns. For example, in the step pattern `child::NAME`, which refers to a `<NAME>` element that is a child of the context node, `child` is called the axis. Patterns support two axes (XPath, on the other hand, supports no less than 13 different axes—see Chapter 7):

- The `attribute` axis holds the attributes of the context node.
- The `child` axis holds the children of the context node. The `child` axis is the default axis if one is not explicitly set.

You can use axes to specify a location step or path as in the following example, where I use the `child` axis to indicate that I want to match the child nodes of the context node, which is a `<PLANET>` element:

```
<xsl:template match="PLANET">
    <HTML>
        <CENTER>
            <xsl:value-of select="child::NAME"/>
        </CENTER>
        <CENTER>
            <xsl:value-of select="child::MASS"/>
        </CENTER>
        <CENTER>
            <xsl:value-of select="child::DAY"/>
        </CENTER>
    </HTML>
</xsl:template>
```

Look at the following examples that use axes:

- `child::PLANET`. Returns the `<PLANET>` element children of the context node.
- `child::*`. Returns all element children (`*` matches only elements) of the context node.

- `attribute::UNIT`. Returns the `UNITS` attribute of the context node.
- `child::*/child::PLANET`. Returns all `<PLANET>` grandchildren of the context node.

Although these examples make it seem that you can use only the child and attribute axes, in practice this is not quite so. When it comes to specifying children, the `child` axis is a little limited, because you must specify every level that you want to match, such as `"child::PLANETS/child::PLANET/child::MASS"`, which matches a `<MASS>` element that is a child of a `<PLANET>` element that is a child of the `<PLANETS>` element. If you want to match all `<MASS>` elements that appear anywhere in the `<PLANETS>` element, whether they are children, grandchildren, great-grandchildren, and so on, it looks as if there's no way to do that in one pattern. In XPath, you can do that with an expression like `"child::PLANETS/descendant::MASS"`, but you can't use the descendant axis in patterns. However, remember that you *can* use the `//` operator, which amounts to the same thing. For example, the pattern `"child::PLANETS//child::MASS"` matches all `<MASS>` elements anywhere inside the `<PLANETS>` element. (In fact, this is a minor inconsistency in the specification.)

The next example shows how I might put this pattern to work, replacing the text in all `<MASS>` elements, no matter where they are inside the `<PLANETS>` element, with the text `"Very heavy!"`. To copy over all the other nodes in planets.xml to the XML result document, I also set up a rule that matches any node using the `node` node test, which you'll see later. Note that although the pattern that matches any node also matches all the `<MASS>` elements, the `"child::PLANETS//child::MASS"` pattern is a much more specific match, which (as discussed in Chapter 3) means the XSLT processor gives it higher priority for `<MASS>` elements:

Listing 4.2 **Matching *<MASS>* Elements**

```
<?xml version="1.0"?>
<xsl:stylesheet version="1.0"
xmlns:xsl="http://www.w3.org/1999/XSL/Transform">
<xsl:output method="xml"/>

    <xsl:template match="@*|node()">
        <xsl:copy>
          <xsl:apply-templates select="@*|node()"/>
        </xsl:copy>
    </xsl:template>
```

```
    <xsl:template match="child::PLANETS//child::MASS">
        <MASS>
            Very heavy!
        </MASS>
    </xsl:template>

</xsl:stylesheet>
```

And here's the resulting XML document:

```
<?xml version="1.0" encoding="UTF-8"?>
<?xml-stylesheet type="text/xml" href="planets.xsl"?>
<PLANETS>

    <PLANET>
        <NAME>Mercury</NAME>
        <MASS>
            Very heavy!
        </MASS>
        <DAY UNITS="days">58.65</DAY>
        <RADIUS UNITS="miles">1516</RADIUS>
        <DENSITY UNITS="(Earth = 1)">.983</DENSITY>
        <DISTANCE UNITS="million miles">43.4</DISTANCE><!--At perihelion-->
    </PLANET>

    <PLANET>
        <NAME>Venus</NAME>
        <MASS>
            Very heavy!
        </MASS>
        <DAY UNITS="days">116.75</DAY>
        <RADIUS UNITS="miles">3716</RADIUS>
        <DENSITY UNITS="(Earth = 1)">.943</DENSITY>
        <DISTANCE UNITS="million miles">66.8</DISTANCE><!--At perihelion-->
    </PLANET>

    <PLANET>
        <NAME>Earth</NAME>
        <MASS>
            Very heavy!
        </MASS>
        <DAY UNITS="days">1</DAY>
        <RADIUS UNITS="miles">2107</RADIUS>
        <DENSITY UNITS="(Earth = 1)">1</DENSITY>
        <DISTANCE UNITS="million miles">128.4</DISTANCE><!--At perihelion-->
    </PLANET>

</PLANETS>
```

You can also take advantage of a number of abbreviations when specifying axes in patterns. These abbreviations are almost invariably used when you're specifying axes in patterns.

Abbreviated Syntax

There are two rules for abbreviating axes in patterns:

- `child::childname` can be abbreviated as `childname`.
- `attribute::childname` can be abbreviated as `@childname`.

The following list includes some examples of patterns using abbreviated syntax—you'll see a lot more at the end of the chapter:

- `PLANET`. Matches the `<PLANET>` element children of the context node.
- `*`. Matches all element children of the context node.
- `@UNITS`. Matches the `UNITS` attribute of the context node.
- `@*`. Matches all the attributes of the context node.
- `*/PLANET`. Matches all `<PLANET>` grandchildren of the context node.
- `//PLANET`. Matches all `<PLANET>` descendants of the document root.
- `PLANETS//PLANET`. Matches all `<PLANET>` element descendants of the `<PLANETS>` element children of the context node.
- `//PLANET/NAME`. Matches all the `<NAME>` elements that are children of a `<PLANET>` parent.
- `PLANET[NAME]`. Matches the `<PLANET>` children of the context node that have `<NAME>` children.

In a pattern such as `"child::PLANET"`, `"child"` is the axis and `"PLANET"` is the *node test*, which is the second part of step patterns.

Part 2 of Step Patterns: Node Tests

The second part of a step pattern is made up of node tests. You can use names of nodes as node tests, or the wild card `*` to select element nodes as well as node types. For example, the expression `child::*/child::NAME` selects all `<NAME>` elements that are grandchildren of the context node.

In addition to node names and the wild card character, you also can use the following node tests:

- The `comment()` node test selects comment nodes.
- The `node()` node test selects any type of node.

- The `processing-instruction()` node test selects a processing instruction node. You can specify the name of the processing instruction to select in the parentheses.
- The `text()` node test selects a text node.

The following sections examine these node tests and provide examples to help you understand how they're used.

Matching Comments

You can match the text of comments with the pattern `comment()`. You shouldn't store data that should go into the output document in comments in the input document, of course. However, you might want to convert comments from the `<!--comment-->` form into something another markup language might use, such as a `<COMMENT>` element.

In the following example, I will extract comments from planet.xml and include them in the resulting output.

```
<PLANET>
    <NAME>Venus</NAME>
    <MASS UNITS="(Earth = 1)">.815</MASS>
    <DAY UNITS="days">116.75</DAY>
    <RADIUS UNITS="miles">3716</RADIUS>
    <DENSITY UNITS="(Earth = 1)">.943</DENSITY>
    <DISTANCE UNITS="million miles">66.8</DISTANCE><!--At perihelion-->
</PLANET>
```

To extract comments and put them into `<COMMENT>` elements, I'll include a rule just for comments:

Listing 4.3 **Matching Comments**

```
<?xml version="1.0"?>
<xsl:stylesheet version="1.0"
xmlns:xsl="http://www.w3.org/1999/XSL/Transform">

    <xsl:template match="PLANETS">
        <HTML>
            <xsl:apply-templates/>
        </HTML>
    </xsl:template>

<xsl:template match="comment()">
    <COMMENT>
        <xsl:value-of select="."/>
    </COMMENT>
</xsl:template>

</xsl:stylesheet>
```

Here's the result for Venus, where I've transformed the comment into a `<COMMENT>` element:

```
Venus
.815
116.75
3716
.943
66.8<COMMENT>At perihelion</COMMENT>
```

Note that here the text for the other elements in the `<PLANET>` element is also inserted into the output document, because the default rule for each element is to include its text in the output document. Because I haven't provided a rule for elements, their text is simply included in the output document.

Matching Nodes with *node()*

In a pattern, the `node` node test matches any node except the root node—remember, it is really `child::node()`. Say that you want to use `<xsl:copy> to` write a stylesheet that copies any XML document. (Chapter 3 used `<xsl:copy-of>` for this purpose.) I might start off as the following example shows. In this case, the template I'm using uses the OR operator, which you'll see later in this chapter, to match any element or any attribute (this template actually selects itself to keep on copying many levels deep):

```
<?xml version="1.0"?>
<xsl:stylesheet version="1.0"
xmlns:xsl="http://www.w3.org/1999/XSL/Transform">
<xsl:output method="xml"/>

    <xsl:template match="@*|*">
        <xsl:copy>
            <xsl:apply-templates select="@*|*"/>
        </xsl:copy>
    </xsl:template>

</xsl:stylesheet>
```

However, here's the result—notice that this version, which matches only elements and attributes (`@*|*`), doesn't copy whitespace nodes or text nodes:

```
<?xml version="1.0" encoding="UTF-8"?>
<PLANETS><PLANET><NAME/><MASS UNITS="(Earth = 1)"/><DAY UNITS="days"/><RADIUS
UNITS="miles"/><DENSITY UNITS="(Earth = 1)"/><DISTANCE UNITS="million miles"/>
</PLANET><PLANET><NAME/><MASS UNITS="(Earth = 1)"/><DAY UNITS="days"/><RADIUS
UNITS="miles"/><DENSITY UNITS="(Earth = 1)"/><DISTANCE UNITS="million miles"/>
</PLANET><PLANET><NAME/><MASS UNITS="(Earth = 1)"/><DAY UNITS="days"/><RADIUS
UNITS="miles"/><DENSITY UNITS="(Earth = 1)"/><DISTANCE UNITS="million miles"/>
</PLANET></PLANETS>
```

This is clearly incomplete. If I match to the pattern "@*|node()" rather than "@*|*", on the other hand, the new template rule will match all nodes except the root node (which is created in the result tree automatically), so it copies whitespace as well as text:

Listing 4.4 **A Copying Stylesheet**

```
<?xml version="1.0"?>
<xsl:stylesheet version="1.0"
xmlns:xsl="http://www.w3.org/1999/XSL/Transform">
<xsl:output method="xml"/>

  <xsl:template match="@*|node()">
    <xsl:copy>
      <xsl:apply-templates select="@*|node()"/>
    </xsl:copy>
  </xsl:template>

</xsl:stylesheet>
```

And here's the new result:

```
<?xml version="1.0" encoding="UTF-8"?>
<?xml-stylesheet type="text/xml" href="planets.xsl"?>
<PLANETS>

    <PLANET>
        <NAME>Mercury</NAME>
        <MASS UNITS="(Earth = 1)">.0553</MASS>
        <DAY UNITS="days">58.65</DAY>
        <RADIUS UNITS="miles">1516</RADIUS>
        <DENSITY UNITS="(Earth = 1)">.983</DENSITY>
        <DISTANCE UNITS="million miles">43.4</DISTANCE><!--At perihelion-->
    </PLANET>

    <PLANET>
        <NAME>Venus</NAME>
        <MASS UNITS="(Earth = 1)">.815</MASS>
        <DAY UNITS="days">116.75</DAY>
        <RADIUS UNITS="miles">3716</RADIUS>
        <DENSITY UNITS="(Earth = 1)">.943</DENSITY>
        <DISTANCE UNITS="million miles">66.8</DISTANCE><!--At perihelion-->
    </PLANET>
        .
        .
        .
```

Matching Text Nodes with *text()*

You can match the text in a node with the pattern `"text()"`. There's usually not much reason to ever use the `text` node test. XSLT includes a default rule that if no other rules match the text node, the text in that node is inserted into the output document. If you were to make that default rule explicit, it might look like this:

```
<xsl:template match="text()">
    <xsl:value-of select="."/>
</xsl:template>
```

You can override this rule by not sending the text in text nodes to the output document, like this:

```
<xsl:template match="text()">
</xsl:template>
```

One reason to use the `text` node test is when you want to match nodes with specific text. Used inside the predicate, as in `"NAME[text() = 'Venus']"`, `<NAME>` elements where the enclosed name is `"Venus"` are matched. (Note that you have to be careful about nesting quotation marks so the XSLT processor won't get confused; for example, this won't work: `"NAME[text() = "Venus"]"`.) Another reason to use the `text` node test is when you want to apply some test to text nodes using the XPath string functions (which you'll see later in this chapter). For example, I'll match the text node `"Earth"` in `<NAME>Earth</NAME>` with the pattern `"text()[starts-with(., 'E')]"`.

Stripping out comments

Earlier, you saw that the pattern `"@*|node()"` (which uses the OR operator, |, as you'll see discussed later) matches everything in planets.xml, including comments. If you want to strip out the comments, you can copy matching to a pattern such as `"@*|*|text()"`, which preserves only elements, attributes, and text nodes.

Matching Processing Instructions

You can use the pattern `processing-instruction()` to match processing instructions:

```
<xsl:template match="/processing-instruction()">
    <I>
        Found a processing instruction.
    </I>
</xsl:template>
```

You can also specify what processing instruction you want to match by giving the name of the processing instruction (excluding the `<?` and `?>`) as in the following case, where I match the processing instruction `<?xml-include?>`:

```
<xsl:template match="/processing-instruction(xml-include)">
    <I>
        Found an xml-include processing instruction.
    </I>
</xsl:template>
```

Distinction Between Root Nodes and Root Elements

One of the major reasons that there is a distinction between the root node at the very beginning of the document and the root element is so you have access to the processing instructions and other nodes in the document's prologue.

That takes care of the node tests that are possible in step patterns. The third and last part of step patterns is predicates.

Part 3 of Step Patterns: Predicates

Predicates, the third part of step patterns, contain XPath expressions. You can use the `[]` operator to enclose a predicate and test whether a certain condition is true.

For example, you can test

- The value of an attribute in a given string.
- The value of an element.
- Whether an element encloses a particular child, attribute, or other element.
- The position of a node in the node tree.

You'll work with XPath expressions in more detail in Chapter 7, but we'll get an introduction to them here because you can use them in pattern predicates.

XPath expressions are more involved than match patterns. If you run into trouble creating them, one thing that's good to know is that the Xalan package has a handy example program, ApplyXPath.java, that enables you to apply an XPath expression to a document and see what the results would be. For example, if I apply the XPath expression `"PLANET/NAME"` to planets.xml, the following example shows what the result looks like, displaying the values of all `<NAME>` elements that are children of `<PLANET>` elements (the opening and closing `<output>` tag is added by ApplyXPath):

```
C:\>java ApplyXPath planets.xml PLANET/NAME
<output>
<NAME>Mercury</NAME>
```

```
<NAME>Venus</NAME>
<NAME>Earth</NAME>
</output>
```

If the value of a predicate is numeric, it represents a *position test*. For example, NAME[1] matches the first <NAME> child of the context node. W3C position tests, and position tests in Xalan, Oracle, XT, Saxon, and MSXML3 (the Microsoft XML processor invoked using JavaScript, which you saw in Chapter 1 and will see more on in Chapter 10, "Using XSLT Processor APIs") are 1-based, so the first child is child 1. Position tests in XML documents that use XSL stylesheets, and are loaded into the current version of Internet Explorer (version 5.5 and in newly released version 6.0), are 0-based (and you can use only a very restricted form of XPath expressions in predicates) and so, in consequence, is much of the XSL documentation on the Microsoft site. Otherwise, the value of a predicate must be true or false, called a *Boolean test*. For example, the predicate `[@UNITS = "million miles"]` matches elements that have `UNITS` attributes with the value `"million miles"`.

Predicates are full XPath expressions, although predicates used in patterns have two restrictions:

- When a pattern is used in a `match` attribute, the predicate must not contain any reference to XSL variables (which you'll see in Chapter 9). This restriction does not apply to predicates used in `<xsl:number>` elements.
- Patterns may not use the XPath `current` function in predicates. This function returns the current node, and its use is restricted so processing is implementation-independent and does not depend on the current processing state.

The pattern in the following example matches <PLANET> elements that have child <NAME> elements:

```
<xsl:template match = "PLANET[NAME]">
    .
    .
    .
</xsl:template>
```

This pattern matches *any* element that has a <NAME> child element:

```
<xsl:template match = "*[NAME]">
    .
    .
    .
</xsl:template>
```

Now I've given the <PLANET> elements in planets.xml a new attribute, COLOR, which holds the planet's color:

```
<?xml version="1.0"?>
<?xml-stylesheet type="text/xml" href="planets.xsl"?>
<PLANETS>

  <PLANET COLOR="RED">
    <NAME>Mercury</NAME>
    <MASS UNITS="(Earth = 1)">.0553</MASS>
    <DAY UNITS="days">58.65</DAY>
    <RADIUS UNITS="miles">1516</RADIUS>
    <DENSITY UNITS="(Earth = 1)">.983</DENSITY>
    <DISTANCE UNITS="million miles">43.4</DISTANCE><!--At perihelion-->
  </PLANET>

  <PLANET COLOR="WHITE">
    <NAME>Venus</NAME>
    <MASS UNITS="(Earth = 1)">.815</MASS>
    <DAY UNITS="days">116.75</DAY>
    <RADIUS UNITS="miles">3716</RADIUS>
    <DENSITY UNITS="(Earth = 1)">.943</DENSITY>
    <DISTANCE UNITS="million miles">66.8</DISTANCE><!--At perihelion-->
  </PLANET>

  <PLANET COLOR="BLUE">
    <NAME>Earth</NAME>
    <MASS UNITS="(Earth = 1)">1</MASS>
    <DAY UNITS="days">1</DAY>
    <RADIUS UNITS="miles">2107</RADIUS>
    <DENSITY UNITS="(Earth = 1)">1</DENSITY>
    <DISTANCE UNITS="million miles">128.4</DISTANCE><!--At perihelion-->
  </PLANET>

</PLANETS>
```

The following expression matches <PLANET> elements that have COLOR attributes:

```
<xsl:template match="PLANET[@COLOR]">
    .
    .
    .
</xsl:template>
```

What if you wanted to match planets whose COLOR attribute was "BLUE"? You can do that with the = operator as shown in Listing 4.5.

Listing 4.5 **Using the = Operator**

```
<?xml version="1.0"?>
<xsl:stylesheet version="1.0"
xmlns:xsl="http://www.w3.org/1999/XSL/Transform">

    <xsl:template match="PLANETS">
        <HTML>
            <xsl:apply-templates/>
        </HTML>
    </xsl:template>

    <xsl:template match="PLANET[@COLOR = 'BLUE']">
            The <xsl:value-of select="NAME"/> is blue.
    </xsl:template>

    <xsl:template match="text()">
    </xsl:template>

</xsl:stylesheet>
```

The stylesheet shown in Listing 4.5 filters out all planets whose color is blue and omits the others by turning off the default rule for text nodes. Here's the result:

```
<HTML>
   The Earth is blue.
</HTML>
```

Creating Predicates

Predicates are true XPath expressions, and XPath is much more of a true language than patterns; for example, XPath expressions can return not only lists of nodes, but also Boolean, string, and numeric values. XPath expressions are not restricted to working with the current node or child nodes, because you can work with parent nodes, ancestor nodes, and more.

Chapter 7 gives its full attention to XPath, but it's worth getting an introduction to the subject during this discussion about patterns, because the predicate part of a pattern is its most powerful part. There are all kinds of expressions that you can work with in predicates; the following list includes some possible types, which are explored in the next sections:

- Node-sets
- Booleans
- Numbers
- Strings

Predicates: Node Sets

As its name implies, a node set is simply a set of nodes (and it may contain only a single node). The expression `child::PLANET` returns a node set of all `<PLANET>` elements. The expression `child::PLANET/child::NAME` returns a node list of all `<NAME>` elements that are children of `<PLANET>` elements. To select a node or nodes from a node set, you can use the following functions that work on node sets in predicates.

- `last()`. Returns the number of nodes in a node set.
- `position()`. Returns the position of the context node in the context node set (starting with 1).
- `count(`*`node-set`*`)`. Returns the number of nodes in a node set. Omitting *`node-set`* makes this function use the context node.
- `id(string `*`ID`*`)`. Returns a node set containing the element whose ID matches the string passed to the function, or an empty node set if no element has the specified ID. You can list multiple IDs separated by white space, and this function returns a node set of the elements with those IDs.
- `local-name(`*`node-set`*`)`. Returns the local name of the first node in the node set. Omitting *`node-set`* makes this function use the context node.
- `namespace-uri(`*`node-set`*`)`. Returns the URI of the namespace of the first node in the node set. Omitting *`node-set`* makes this function use the context node.
- `name(`*`node-set`*`)`. Returns the full, qualified name of the first node in the node set. Omitting *`node-set`* makes this function use the context node.

Here's an example; in this case, I number the elements in the output document using the `position()` function:

Listing 4.6 **Using the *position* Function**

```
<?xml version="1.0"?>
<xsl:stylesheet version="1.0"
xmlns:xsl="http://www.w3.org/1999/XSL/Transform">

    <xsl:template match="PLANETS">
        <HTML>
            <HEAD>
                <TITLE>
                    The Planets
                </TITLE>
            </HEAD>
            <BODY>
                <xsl:apply-templates select="PLANET"/>
```

continues ▸

Listing 4.6 **Continued**

```
            </BODY>
        </HTML>
    </xsl:template>

    <xsl:template match="PLANET">
        <P>
            <xsl:value-of select="position()"/>.
            <xsl:text> </xsl:text>
            <xsl:value-of select="NAME"/>
        </P>
    </xsl:template>

</xsl:stylesheet>
```

Here's the result, where you can see that the planets are numbered:

```
<HTML>
    <HEAD>
        <TITLE>
            The Planets
        </TITLE>
    </HEAD>

    <BODY>
        <P>
            1. Mercury
        </P>
        <P>
            2. Venus
        </P>
        <P>
            3. Earth
        </P>
    </BODY>
</HTML>
```

You can also use functions that operate on node sets in predicates, as I do here: `PLANET[position() = last()]`, which selects the last `<PLANET>` child of the context node.

Predicates: Booleans

You can also use Boolean values in XPath expressions. Numbers are considered false if they're zero, and true otherwise. An empty string, "", is also considered false, and all other strings are considered true.

You can use the following XPath logical operators to produce Boolean true/false results:

- != means "is not equal to"
- < means "is less than" (use < in XML or XSL documents)
- <= means "is less than or equal to" (use <= in XML or XSL documents)
- = means "is equal to" (C, C++, Java, JavaScript programmers take note: this operator is one = sign, not two).
- > means "is greater than"
- >= means "is greater than or equal to"

Using the < Character

Note in particular that you shouldn't use < directly in XML or XSL documents, so you should use the entity reference < instead.

You can also use the keywords and and or to connect Boolean clauses with a logical And or Or operation, and you can use not to flip the logical sense of an expression, from true to false, or false to true.

In the following example, I identify Earth's <PLANET> element and place the strings "Earth", "needs", "no", and "introduction" in the table rather than Earth's numeric data. I identify which planet is Earth with the predicate "[NAME='Earth']", which checks the value of the <NAME> element, which in turn is its enclosed text. I also provide a template for the other planets, matching the predicate "[NAME!='Earth']":

Listing 4.7 **Finding Planet Earth**

```
<?xml version="1.0"?>
<xsl:stylesheet version="1.0"
xmlns:xsl="http://www.w3.org/1999/XSL/Transform">

    <xsl:template match="/PLANETS">
        <HTML>
            <HEAD>
                <TITLE>
                    The Planets Table
                </TITLE>
            </HEAD>
            <BODY>
                <H1>
                    The Planets Table
                </H1>
                <TABLE BORDER="2">
                    <TR>
```

continues ▶

Listing 4.7 **Continued**

```
                    <TD>Name</TD>
                    <TD>Mass</TD>
                    <TD>Radius</TD>
                    <TD>Day</TD>
                </TR>
                <xsl:apply-templates/>
            </TABLE>
        </BODY>
    </HTML>
</xsl:template>


<xsl:template match="PLANET[NAME='Earth']">
    <TR>
       <TD>Earth</TD>
       <TD>needs</TD>
       <TD>no</TD>
       <TD>introduction.</TD>
    </TR>
</xsl:template>


<xsl:template match="PLANET[NAME!='Earth']">
    <TR>
       <TD><xsl:value-of select="NAME"/></TD>
       <TD><xsl:apply-templates select="MASS"/></TD>
       <TD><xsl:apply-templates select="RADIUS"/></TD>
       <TD><xsl:apply-templates select="DAY"/></TD>
    </TR>
</xsl:template>

<xsl:template match="MASS">
    <xsl:value-of select="."/>
    <xsl:text> </xsl:text>
    <xsl:value-of select="@UNITS"/>
</xsl:template>

<xsl:template match="RADIUS">
    <xsl:value-of select="."/>
    <xsl:text> </xsl:text>
    <xsl:value-of select="@UNITS"/>
</xsl:template>

<xsl:template match="DAY">
    <xsl:value-of select="."/>
    <xsl:text> </xsl:text>
    <xsl:value-of select="@UNITS"/>
</xsl:template>

</xsl:stylesheet>
```

Here's the result:

```
<HTML>
    <HEAD>
        <TITLE>
            The Planets Table
        </TITLE>
    </HEAD>

    <BODY>
        <H1>
            The Planets Table
        </H1>

        <TABLE BORDER="2">
            <TR>
                <TD>Name</TD>
                <TD>Mass</TD>
                <TD>Radius</TD>
                <TD>Day</TD>
            </TR>
            .
            .
            .
            <TR>
                <TD>Earth</TD>
                <TD>needs</TD>
                <TD>no</TD>
                <TD>introduction.</TD>
            </TR>
        </TABLE>
    </BODY>
</HTML>
```

You can see this result in Figure 4.1.

The following example uses the logical operator `>`. This rule applies to all `<PLANET>` elements after position 5:

```
<xsl:template match="PLANET[position() > 5]">
    <xsl:value-of select="."/>
</xsl:template>
```

There is also a `true` function that always returns a value of true, and a `false` function that always returns a value of false. You can also use the `not` function to reverse the logical sense of an expression, as in the following case, where I'm selecting all but the last `<PLANET>` element:

```
<xsl:template match="PLANET[not(position() = last())]">
    <xsl:value-of select="."/>
</xsl:template>
```

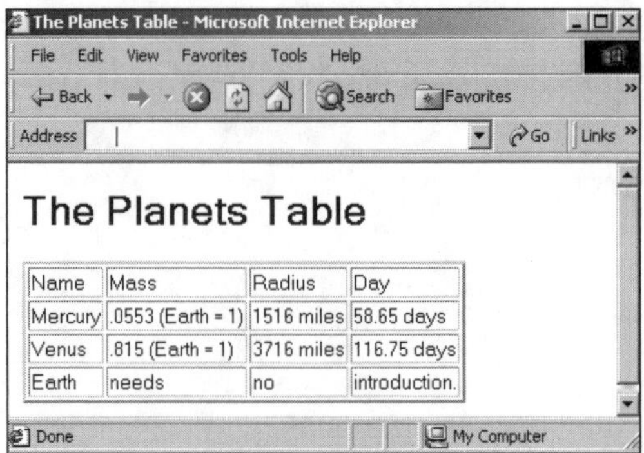

Figure 4.1 Using XPath predicates.

Finally, the lang function returns true or false depending on whether the language of the context node (which is given by xml:lang attributes) is the same as the language you pass to this function.

Predicates: Numbers

In XPath, numbers actually are stored in double floating point format. (Technically speaking, all XPath numbers are stored in 64-bit IEEE 754 floating-point double format.) All numbers are stored as doubles, even integers such as 5, as in the example you just saw:

```
<xsl:template match="PLANET[position() > 5]">
    <xsl:value-of select="."/>
</xsl:template>
```

You can use several operators on numbers:

- + addition
- - subtraction
- * multiplication
- div division (the / character, which stands for division in other languages, is already heavily used in XML, XSL, and XPath)
- mod returns the modulus of two numbers (the remainder after dividing the first by the second).

For example, the element `<xsl:value-of select="180 + 420"/>` inserts the string "600" into the output document. The following example selects all planets whose day (measured in Earth days) divided by its mass (where the mass of the earth = 1) is greater than 100:

```
<xsl:template match="PLANETS">
    <HTML>
        <BODY>
            <xsl:apply-templates select="PLANET[DAY div MASS > 100]"/>
        </BODY>
    </HTML>
</xsl:template>
```

XPath also supports these functions that operate on numbers:

- `ceiling()`. Returns the smallest integer larger than the number you pass it.
- `floor()`. Returns the largest integer smaller than the number you pass it.
- `round()`. Rounds the number you pass it to the nearest integer.
- `sum()`. Returns the sum of the numbers you pass it.

For example, here's how you can find the average mass of the planets in planets.xml:

Listing 4.8 **Finding Average Planetary Mass**

```
<?xml version="1.0"?>
<xsl:stylesheet version="1.0"
xmlns:xsl="http://www.w3.org/1999/XSL/Transform">
<xsl:output method="xml"/>

<xsl:template match="PLANETS">
    <HTML>
        <BODY>
            The average planetary mass is:
<xsl:value-of select="sum(child::PLANET/child::MASS) div count(child::PLANET)"/>
        </BODY>
    </HTML>
</xsl:template>

</xsl:stylesheet>
```

Strings

In XPath, strings are made up of Unicode characters, as you'd expect. A number of functions are specially designed to work on strings:

- `string(object object1)`. Converts an object into a string.
- `starts-with(string string1, string string2)`. Returns true if the first string starts with the second string.
- `contains(string string1, string string2)`. Returns true if the first string contains the second one.
- `substring(string string1, number offset, number length)`. Returns *length* characters from the string, starting at *offset*.
- `substring-before(string string1, string string2)`. Returns the part of *string1* up to the first occurrence of *string2*.
- `substring-after(string string1, string string2)`. Returns the part of *string1* after the first occurrence of *string2*.
- `string-length(string string1)`. Returns the number of characters in *string1*.
- `normalize-space(string string1)`. Returns *string1* after leading and trailing whitespace is stripped and multiple consecutive whitespace is replaced with a single space.
- `translate(string string1,string string2,string string3)`. Returns *string1* with all occurrences of the characters in *string2* replaced by the matching characters in *string3*.
- `concat(string string1, string string2,...)`. Returns all strings concatenated (that is, joined) together.

And there's another string function you should know about that is actually part of XSLT, not XPath:

- `format-number(number number1, string string2, string string3)`. Returns a string holding the formatted string version of *number1*, using *string2* as a formatting string (you create formatting strings as you would for Java's `java.text.DecimalFormat` method) and *string3* as the optional locale string.

In the following example, I match text nodes whose text starts with 'E' to match the Earth, and add the text '(the World)' to the description of Earth, making it 'Earth (the World)'. To do that, I use the predicate `"text()[starts-with(., 'E')]"`:

Listing 4.9 **Using the *starts-with* Function**

```
<?xml version="1.0"?>
<xsl:stylesheet version="1.0"
xmlns:xsl="http://www.w3.org/1999/XSL/Transform">

    <xsl:template match="/PLANETS">
        <HTML>
            <HEAD>
        .
        .
        .
            </BODY>
        </HTML>
    </xsl:template>

    <xsl:template match="PLANET">
       <TR>
          <TD><xsl:apply-templates select="NAME"/></TD>
          <TD><xsl:apply-templates select="MASS"/></TD>
          <TD><xsl:apply-templates select="RADIUS"/></TD>
          <TD><xsl:apply-templates select="DAY"/></TD>
       </TR>
   </xsl:template>

    <xsl:template match="text()[starts-with(., 'E')]">
        <xsl:text>(the World)</xsl:text>
    </xsl:template>

    <xsl:template match="NAME">
        <xsl:value-of select="."/>
        <xsl:text> </xsl:text>
        <xsl:value-of select="@UNITS"/>
        <xsl:apply-templates/>
    </xsl:template>
        .
        .
        .
    <xsl:template match="DAY">
        <xsl:value-of select="."/>
        <xsl:text> </xsl:text>
        <xsl:value-of select="@UNITS"/>
    </xsl:template>

</xsl:stylesheet>
```

And here's the result—note that the caption for Earth has become "Earth (the World)":

```
<HTML>
    <HEAD>
        <TITLE>
            The Planets Table
        </TITLE>
    </HEAD>

    <BODY>
        <H1>
            The Planets Table
        </H1>

        <TABLE BORDER="2">
            <TR>
                <TD>Name</TD>
                <TD>Mass</TD>
                <TD>Radius</TD>
                <TD>Day</TD>
            </TR>
            .
            .
            .
            <TR>
                <TD>Earth (the World)</TD>
                <TD>1 (Earth = 1)</TD>
                <TD>2107 miles</TD>
                <TD>1 days</TD>
            </TR>
        </TABLE>
    </BODY>
</HTML>
```

You can see this document in Figure 4.2.

Predicates: Result Tree Fragments

XSLT 1.0 adds *result tree fragments* to the data types supported by XPath. Result tree fragments are tree fragments that you could assign to XSLT variables, and aren't put to much use. About all you can do with them is evaluate their string value. Support for them was removed in the XSLT 1.1 working draft, so presumably, they'll no longer be in use in XSLT 2.0.

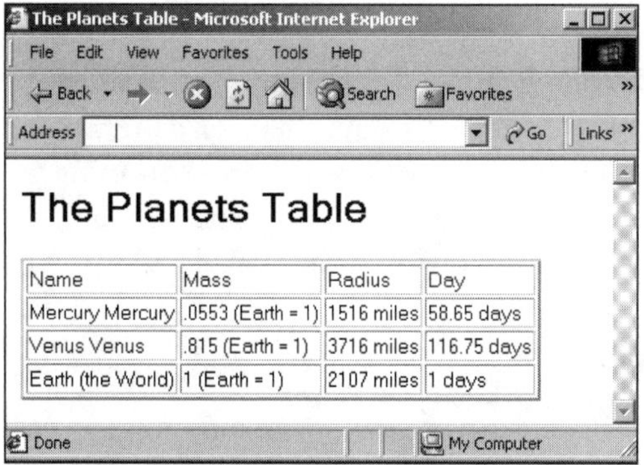

Name	Mass	Radius	Day
Mercury Mercury	.0553 (Earth = 1)	1516 miles	58.65 days
Venus Venus	.815 (Earth = 1)	3716 miles	116.75 days
Earth (the World)	1 (Earth = 1)	2107 miles	1 days

Figure 4.2 Using text predicates.

Abbreviated Syntax for Predicates

You can abbreviate predicate expressions by omitting `"position() ="` if you like. For example, `[position() = 3]` becomes `[3]`, `[position() = last()]` becomes `[last()]`, and so on. Using the abbreviated syntax makes XPath expressions in predicates much easier to use. Here are some examples:

- `PLANET[2]`. Returns the second `<PLANET>` child of the context node.
- `PLANET[last()]`. Returns the last `<PLANET>` child of the context node.
- `/PLANETS/PLANET[2]/NAME[1]`. Returns the first `<NAME>` element of the second `<PLANET>` element of the `<PLANETS>` element.
- `PLANET[5][@UNITS = "million miles"]`. Returns the fifth `<PLANET>` child of the context node, only if that child has a `UNITS` attribute with value `"million miles"`. Can also be written as `PLANET[@UNITS = "million miles"][5]`.

That completes this look at the three parts of step patterns: axes, node tests, and predicates. They are the building blocks of match patterns. The best way to learn how to create patterns is by example, and many examples are coming up. First, though, it's important to cover one or two quick topics. As you may recall from the discussion of the formal definition of a match pattern, you can create patterns that match elements by ID or by key in addition to using step patterns.

Matching by ID

In addition to making patterns out of step patterns that specify an axis, node test, and predicate, you can also use the `id()` pattern to match elements that have a specific ID value. To use this pattern, you must give elements an ID attribute, and you must declare that attribute of type ID, as you can do in a DTD or schema. The following example rule adds the text of all elements that have the ID "favorite":

```
<xsl:template match = "id('favorite')">
    <H3><xsl:value-of select="."/></H3>
</xsl:template>
```

Here's what a DTD for planets.xml might look like that declares an ID and sets it to "favorite":

```
<?xml version="1.0"?>
<?xml-stylesheet type="text/xml" href="#stylesheet"?>
<!DOCTYPE PLANETS [
<!ELEMENT PLANET (CUSTOMER)*>
<!ELEMENT CUSTOMER (NAME,MASS,RADIUS,DAY)>
<!ELEMENT NAME (#PCDATA)>
<!ELEMENT MASS (#PCDATA)>
<!ELEMENT RADIUS (#PCDATA)>
<!ELEMENT DAY (#PCDATA)>
<!ATTLIST PLANET
    id ID #REQUIRED>
]>
<PLANETS>
    <PLANET id="favorite">
        <NAME>Mercury</NAME>
        <MASS UNITS="(Earth = 1)">.0553</MASS>
        <DAY UNITS="days">58.65</DAY>
        <RADIUS UNITS="miles">1516</RADIUS>
        <DENSITY UNITS="(Earth = 1)">.983</DENSITY>
        <DISTANCE UNITS="million miles">43.4</DISTANCE><!--At perihelion-->
    </PLANET>
        .
        .
        .
```

Some XSLT processors don't match by ID because they don't read DDS or XML schema. (This is one of the issues that XSLT 2.0 is supposed to address—how to make ID information available.) However, there's another option: you can match by *key*.

Possible Support for IDREFs

In addition to making it easier to work with IDs, W3C is even considering adding support for IDREFs in XSLT 2.0. In particular, given an ID, the XSLT processor could provide you with a list of all elements that have an IDREF or IDREFS attribute that refers to that ID. (Note that currently, however, you can do the same thing using `<xsl:key>` and the "key()" pattern.)

Matching by Key

Keys give you an easy way to identify elements, and you can match specific keys with the pattern `"key()"`. Chapter 9 discusses how to use keys in detail, but I'll include a quick example here.

You use the `<xsl:key>` element to create a key. This element is a top-level element, so it appears outside templates and as a child element of `<xsl:stylesheet>`. In the following example, I use a key to match planets whose `COLOR` attribute is set to "BLUE", which means Earth:

```
<?xml version="1.0"?>
<?xml-stylesheet type="text/xml" href="planets.xsl"?>
<PLANETS>
        .
        .
        .
    <PLANET COLOR="BLUE">
        <NAME>Earth</NAME>
        <MASS UNITS="(Earth = 1)">1</MASS>
        <DAY UNITS="days">1</DAY>
        <RADIUS UNITS="miles">2107</RADIUS>
        <DENSITY UNITS="(Earth = 1)">1</DENSITY>
        <DISTANCE UNITS="million miles">128.4</DISTANCE><!--At perihelion-->
    </PLANET>

</PLANETS>
```

Now I can create a key named `COLOR` that matches `<PLANET>` elements by checking their `COLOR` attribute:

```
<?xml version="1.0"?>
<xsl:stylesheet version="1.0"
xmlns:xsl="http://www.w3.org/1999/XSL/Transform">

    <xsl:key name="COLOR" match="PLANET" use="@COLOR"/>
        .
        .
        .
```

Now I can use the pattern `"key()"` to match `<PLANET>` elements with the `COLOR` attribute set to "BLUE" as follows:

```
<?xml version="1.0"?>
<xsl:stylesheet version="1.0"
xmlns:xsl="http://www.w3.org/1999/XSL/Transform">

    <xsl:key name="COLOR" match="PLANET" use="@COLOR"/>

    <xsl:template match="/PLANETS">
        <HTML>
            <HEAD>
                <TITLE>
                    The Planets Table
                </TITLE>
            </HEAD>
            <BODY>
                <H1>
                    The Planets Table
                </H1>
                <TABLE BORDER="2">
                    <TR>
                        <TD>Name</TD>
                        <TD>Mass</TD>
                        <TD>Radius</TD>
                        <TD>Day</TD>
                    </TR>
                    <xsl:apply-templates select="key('COLOR', 'BLUE')"/>
                </TABLE>
            </BODY>
        </HTML>
    </xsl:template>
        .
        .
        .
```

And here's the result—as you can see, Earth was the only planet that matched the pattern I used:

```
<HTML>
    <HEAD>
        <TITLE>
            The Planets Table
        </TITLE>
    </HEAD>

    <BODY>
        <H1>
            The Planets Table
        </H1>

        <TABLE BORDER="2">
            <TR>
```

```
                <TD>Name</TD>
                <TD>Mass</TD>
                <TD>Radius</TD>
                <TD>Day</TD>
            </TR>

            <TR>
                <TD>Earth</TD>
                <TD>1 (Earth = 1)</TD>
                <TD>2107 miles</TD>
                <TD>1 days</TD>
            </TR>
        </TABLE>
    </BODY>
</HTML>
```

Using the Or Operator

Using the Or operator, |, you can match to a number of possible patterns, which is very useful when your documents get a little more involved. In the following example, I want to display <NAME> and <MASS> elements in bold, which I do with the HTML <B> tag. To match either <NAME> *or* <MASS> elements, I'll use the Or operator in a new rule:

```
<?xml version="1.0"?>
<xsl:stylesheet version="1.0"
xmlns:xsl="http://www.w3.org/1999/XSL/Transform">

    <xsl:template match="/PLANETS">
        <HTML>
            <HEAD>
            .
            .
            .
            </BODY>
        </HTML>
    </xsl:template>

    <xsl:template match="PLANET">
       <TR>
          <TD><xsl:apply-templates select="NAME"/></TD>
          <TD><xsl:apply-templates select="MASS"/></TD>
          <TD><xsl:apply-templates select="RADIUS"/></TD>
          <TD><xsl:apply-templates select="DAY"/></TD>
       </TR>
   </xsl:template>

    <xsl:template match="NAME | MASS">
        <B>
            <xsl:apply-templates/>
```

```
        </B>
    </xsl:template>

    <xsl:template match="RADIUS">
        <xsl:value-of select="."/>
        <xsl:text> </xsl:text>
        <xsl:value-of select="@UNITS"/>
    </xsl:template>

    <xsl:template match="DAY">
        <xsl:value-of select="."/>
        <xsl:text> </xsl:text>
        <xsl:value-of select="@UNITS"/>
    </xsl:template>

</xsl:stylesheet>
```

Here are the results; note that the name and mass values are both enclosed in <B> elements:

```
<HTML>
    <HEAD>
        <TITLE>
            The Planets Table
        </TITLE>
    </HEAD>

    <BODY>
        .
        .
        .
            <TR>
                <TD><B>Mercury</B></TD>
                <TD><B>.0553</B></TD>
                <TD>1516 miles</TD>
                <TD>58.65 days</TD>
            </TR>

            <TR>
                <TD><B>Venus</B></TD>
                <TD><B>.815</B></TD>
                <TD>3716 miles</TD>
                <TD>116.75 days</TD>
            </TR>

            <TR>
                <TD><B>Earth</B></TD>
                <TD><B>1</B></TD>
                <TD>2107 miles</TD>
                <TD>1 days</TD>
```

```
            </TR>
        </TABLE>
    </BODY>
</HTML>
```

You can use any valid pattern with the `|` operator, such as expressions like `"PLANET | PLANET//NAME"`, and you can use multiple `|` operators, like `"NAME | MASS | DAY"`, and so on.

Pattern Examples

The best way to understand patterns is by example. Suppose that you want to transform planets.xml into planets.html, but retain only the first planet, Mercury. You can do that with the predicate `[position() < 2]`, because the first planet's position is 1, the next is 2, and so on. Note, however, that < is invariably a sensitive character for XSLT processors, because it's what you use to start markup; rather than <, you should use `<.;`. And note that you have to strip the other elements out of planets.xml by supplying an empty template for them, which I can do with the predicate `[position() >= 2]`:

Listing 4.10 **Retaining Only Mercury**

```
<?xml version="1.0"?>
<xsl:stylesheet version="1.0"
xmlns:xsl="http://www.w3.org/1999/XSL/Transform">

    <xsl:template match="/PLANETS">
        <HTML>
            <HEAD>
                <TITLE>
                    The Planets Table
                </TITLE>
            </HEAD>
            <BODY>
                <H1>
                    The Planets Table
                </H1>
                <TABLE BORDER="2">
                    <TR>
                        <TD>Name</TD>
                        <TD>Mass</TD>
                        <TD>Radius</TD>
                        <TD>Day</TD>
                    </TR>
                    <xsl:apply-templates/>
                </TABLE>
            </BODY>
        </HTML>
```

continues ▸

Listing 4.10 **Continued**

```
    </xsl:template>

    <xsl:template match="PLANET[position() &lt.; 2]">
        <TR>
            <TD><xsl:value-of select="NAME"/></TD>
            <TD><xsl:apply-templates select="MASS"/></TD>
            <TD><xsl:apply-templates select="RADIUS"/></TD>
            <TD><xsl:apply-templates select="DAY"/></TD>
        </TR>
    </xsl:template>

    <xsl:template match="PLANET[position() >= 2]">
    </xsl:template>
<xsl:template match="MASS">
        <xsl:value-of select="."/>
        <xsl:text> </xsl:text>
        <xsl:value-of select="@UNITS"/>
    </xsl:template>

    <xsl:template match="RADIUS">
        <xsl:value-of select="."/>
        <xsl:text> </xsl:text>
        <xsl:value-of select="@UNITS"/>
    </xsl:template>

    <xsl:template match="DAY">
        <xsl:value-of select="."/>
        <xsl:text> </xsl:text>
        <xsl:value-of select="@UNITS"/>
    </xsl:template>

</xsl:stylesheet>
```

Here's the resulting document—note that only the first planet, Mercury, was retained:

```
<HTML>
    <HEAD>
        <TITLE>
            The Planets Table
        </TITLE>
    </HEAD>

    <BODY>
        <H1>
            The Planets Table
        </H1>
```

```
        <TABLE BORDER="2">
            <TR>
                <TD>Name</TD>
                <TD>Mass</TD>
                <TD>Radius</TD>
                <TD>Day</TD>
            </TR>

            <TR>
                <TD>Mercury</TD>
                <TD>.0553 (Earth = 1)</TD>
                <TD>1516 miles</TD>
                <TD>58.65 days</TD>
            </TR>
        </TABLE>
    </BODY>
</HTML>
```

In the following example, `COLOR` and `POPULATED` attributes have been added to Earth's `<PLANET>` element:

```
    <PLANET COLOR="blue" POPULATED="yes">
        <NAME>Earth</NAME>
        <MASS UNITS="(Earth = 1)">1</MASS>
        <DAY UNITS="days">1</DAY>
        <RADIUS UNITS="miles">2107</RADIUS>
        <DENSITY UNITS="(Earth = 1)">1</DENSITY>
        <DISTANCE UNITS="million miles">128.4</DISTANCE><!--At perihelion-->
    </PLANET>
```

How can you select only elements that have both `COLOR` and `POPULATED` attributes? You can use the predicate `"[@COLOR and @POPULATED]"`. To strip out the other elements so the default rules don't place their text into the result document, you can use a predicate such as `"[not(@COLOR) or not(@POPULATED)]"`, as shown in Listing 4.11.

Listing 4.11 **Selecting Only Elements That Have Both *COLOR* and *POPULATED* Attributes**

```
<?xml version="1.0"?>
<xsl:stylesheet version="1.0"
xmlns:xsl="http://www.w3.org/1999/XSL/Transform">

    <xsl:template match="/PLANETS">
        <HTML>
            <HEAD>
                <TITLE>
                    Colorful, Populated Planets
                </TITLE>
            </HEAD>
```

continues ▸

Listing 4.11 **Continued**

```
            <BODY>
                <H1>
                    Colorful, Populated Planets
                </H1>
                <TABLE BORDER="2">
                    <TR>
                        <TD>Name</TD>
                        <TD>Mass</TD>
                        <TD>Radius</TD>
                        <TD>Day</TD>
                    </TR>
                    <xsl:apply-templates/>
                </TABLE>
            </BODY>
        </HTML>
    </xsl:template>

    <xsl:template match="PLANET[@COLOR and @POPULATED]">
       <TR>
          <TD><xsl:value-of select="NAME"/></TD>
          <TD><xsl:apply-templates select="MASS"/></TD>
          <TD><xsl:apply-templates select="RADIUS"/></TD>
          <TD><xsl:apply-templates select="DAY"/></TD>
       </TR>
    </xsl:template>

    <xsl:template match="PLANET[not(@COLOR) or not(@POPULATED)]">
    </xsl:template>

    <xsl:template match="MASS">
        <xsl:value-of select="."/>
        <xsl:text> </xsl:text>
        <xsl:value-of select="@UNITS"/>
    </xsl:template>

    <xsl:template match="RADIUS">
        <xsl:value-of select="."/>
        <xsl:text> </xsl:text>
        <xsl:value-of select="@UNITS"/>
    </xsl:template>

    <xsl:template match="DAY">
        <xsl:value-of select="."/>
        <xsl:text> </xsl:text>
        <xsl:value-of select="@UNITS"/>
    </xsl:template>

</xsl:stylesheet>
```

And here's the result:

```
<HTML>
    <HEAD>
        <TITLE>
            Colorful, Populated Planets
        </TITLE>
    </HEAD>

    <BODY>
        <H1>
            Colorful, Populated Planets
        </H1>

        <TABLE BORDER="2">
            <TR>
                <TD>Name</TD>
                <TD>Mass</TD>
                <TD>Radius</TD>
                <TD>Day</TD>
            </TR>

            <TR>
                <TD>Earth</TD>
                <TD>1 (Earth = 1)</TD>
                <TD>2107 miles</TD>
                <TD>1 days</TD
            </TR>
        </TABLE>
    </BODY>
</HTML>
```

You can see this document in Figure 4.3.

In the following example, I copy planets.xml to a new XML document, and change the text in Venus's `<NAME>` element to `"The Planet of Love"`. To do that, I start by copying all nodes and attributes to the result document:

```
<?xml version="1.0"?>
<xsl:stylesheet version="1.0"
xmlns:xsl="http://www.w3.org/1999/XSL/Transform">
<xsl:output method="xml"/>

  <xsl:template match="@*|node()">
    <xsl:copy>
      <xsl:apply-templates select="@*|node()"/>
    </xsl:copy>
  </xsl:template>
        .
        .
        .
```

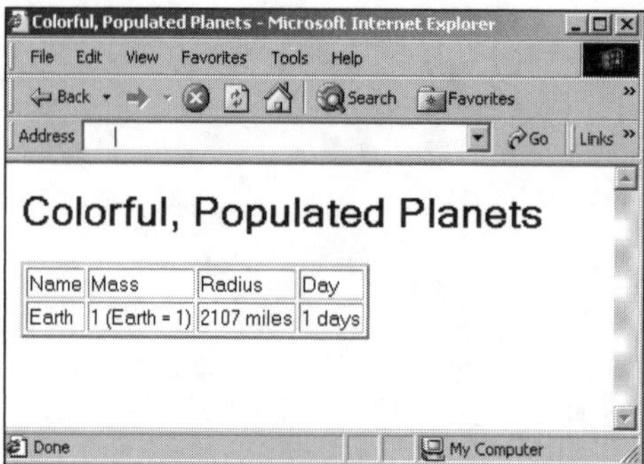

Figure 4.3 Using XPath predicates to check attributes.

Now I'll add a new rule that matches <NAME> elements that have the text "Venus" with the pattern "NAME[text() = 'Venus']". Even though <NAME> elements match both rules in this stylesheet, the rule with the pattern "NAME[text() = 'Venus']" is a more specific match, so the XSLT processor uses it for Venus's <NAME> element:

```
<?xml version="1.0"?>
<xsl:stylesheet version="1.0"
xmlns:xsl="http://www.w3.org/1999/XSL/Transform">
<xsl:output method="xml"/>

  <xsl:template match="@*|node()">
    <xsl:copy>
      <xsl:apply-templates select="@*|node()"/>
    </xsl:copy>
  </xsl:template>

    <xsl:template match="NAME[text() = 'Venus']">
        <NAME>
            The Planet of Love
        </NAME>
    </xsl:template>

</xsl:stylesheet>
```

And here's the result:

```
<?xml version="1.0" encoding="utf-8"?>
<?xml-stylesheet type="text/xml" href="planets.xsl"?>
<PLANETS>

    <PLANET>
        <NAME>Mercury</NAME>
        <MASS UNITS="(Earth = 1)">.0553</MASS>
        <DAY UNITS="days">58.65</DAY>
        <RADIUS UNITS="miles">1516</RADIUS>
        <DENSITY UNITS="(Earth = 1)">.983</DENSITY>
        <DISTANCE UNITS="million miles">43.4</DISTANCE><!--At perihelion-->
    </PLANET>

    <PLANET>
        <NAME>
            The Planet of Love
        </NAME>
        <MASS UNITS="(Earth = 1)">.815</MASS>
        <DAY UNITS="days">116.75</DAY>
        <RADIUS UNITS="miles">3716</RADIUS>
        <DENSITY UNITS="(Earth = 1)">.943</DENSITY>
        <DISTANCE UNITS="million miles">66.8</DISTANCE><!--At perihelion-->
    </PLANET>

    <PLANET>
        <NAME>Earth</NAME>
        <MASS UNITS="(Earth = 1)">1</MASS>
        <DAY UNITS="days">1</DAY>
        <RADIUS UNITS="miles">2107</RADIUS>
        <DENSITY UNITS="(Earth = 1)">1</DENSITY>
        <DISTANCE UNITS="million miles">128.4</DISTANCE><!--At perihelion-->
    </PLANET>

</PLANETS>
```

In fact, in XPath expressions, you can refer to the context node as ".", and the default value of a node is its text, so the following rule works exactly the same way:

```
<?xml version="1.0"?>
<xsl:stylesheet version="1.0"
xmlns:xsl="http://www.w3.org/1999/XSL/Transform">
<xsl:output method="xml"/>

  <xsl:template match="@*|node()">
    <xsl:copy>
      <xsl:apply-templates select="@*|node()"/>
```

```
    </xsl:copy>
  </xsl:template>

    <xsl:template match="NAME[. = 'Venus']">
        <NAME>
            The Planet of Love
        </NAME>
    </xsl:template>

</xsl:stylesheet>
```

It's worth packing in as many examples as possible—you can never have too many match pattern or XPath examples. The following is a good collection of match pattern examples:

- `PLANET` matches the `<PLANET>` element children of the context node.
- `/PLANETS` matches the root element (`PLANETS`) of this document.
- `*` matches all element children of the context node.
- `PLANET[3]` matches the third `<PLANET>` child of the context node.
- `PLANET[last()]` matches the last `<PLANET>` child of the context node.
- `PLANET[NAME]` matches the `<PLANET>` children of the context node that have `<NAME>` children.
- `PLANET[DISTANCE]/NAME` matches all `<NAME>` elements of `<PLANET>` elements that contain at least one `<DISTANCE>` element.
- `PLANET[DISTANCE]/PLANET[DAY]` matches all `<PLANET>` elements of `<PLANET>` elements where the `<PLANET>` element contains at least one `<DISTANCE>` element, and the `<PLANET>` element has at least one `<DAY>` element.
- `PLANETS[PLANET/DAY]` matches all `<PLANETS>` elements that have `<PLANET>` elements with at least one `<DAY>` element.
- `PLANET[DISTANCE][NAME]` matches all `<PLANET>` elements that have `<DISTANCE>` and `<NAME>` elements.
- `PLANETS/PLANET[last()]` matches the last `<PLANET>` in each `<PLANETS>` element.
- `*/PLANET` matches all `<PLANET>` grandchildren of the context node.
- `/PLANETS/PLANET[3]/NAME[2]` matches the second `<NAME>` element of the third `<PLANET>` element of the `<PLANETS>` element.
- `//PLANET` matches all the `<PLANET>` descendants of the document root.
- `PLANETS//PLANET` matches the `<PLANET>` element descendants of the `<PLANETS>` element children of the context node.
- `//PLANET/NAME` matches all the `<NAME>` elements that are children of a `<PLANET>` parent.

- PLANETS//PLANET/DISTANCE//PERIHELION matches <PERIHELION> elements anywhere inside a <PLANET> element's <DISTANCE> element, anywhere inside a <PLANETS> element.
- @UNITS matches the UNITS attribute of the context node.
- @* matches all the attributes of the context node.
- *[@UNITS] matches all elements with the UNITS attribute.
- DENSITY/@UNITS matches the UNITS attribute in <DENSITY> elements.
- PLANET[not(@COLOR) or not(@SIZE)] matches <PLANET> elements that do not have both COLOR and SIZE attributes.
- PLANETS[@STAR="Sun"]//DENSITY matches any <DENSITY> element with a <PLANETS> ancestor element that has a STAR attribute set to "Sun".
- PLANET[NAME="Venus"] matches the <PLANET> children of the context node that have <NAME> children with text equal to "Venus".
- PLANET[NAME[1] = "Venus"] matches all <PLANET> elements where the text in the first <NAME> element is "Venus".
- DAY[@UNITS != "million miles"] matches all <PLANET> elements where the UNITS attribute is not "million miles".
- PLANET[@UNITS = "days"] matches all <PLANET> children of the context node that have a UNITS attribute with value "days".
- PLANET[6][@UNITS = "days"] matches the sixth <PLANET> child of the context node, only if that child has a UNITS attribute with value "days". Can also be written as PLANET[@UNITS = "days"][6].
- PLANET[@COLOR and @UNITS] matches all the <PLANET> children of the context node that have both a COLOR attribute and a UNITS attribute.
- *[1][NAME] matches any <NAME> element that is the first child of its parent.
- *[position() < 5] matches the first five children of the context node.
- *[position() < 5][@UNIT] matches the first five children of the context node with a UNITS attribute.
- text() matches all text node children of the context node.
- text()[starts-with(., "In the course of human events")] matches all text nodes that are children of the context node and start with "In the course of human events".
- /PLANETS[@UNITS = "million miles"] matches all PLANETS where the value of the UNITS attribute is equal to "million miles".
- PLANET[/PLANETS/@UNITS = @REFERENCE] matches all <PLANET> elements where the value of the REFERENCE attribute is the same as the value of the UNITS attribute of the PLANETS element at the root of the document.

- PLANET/* matches all element children of PLANET elements.
- PLANET/*/DAY matches all DAY elements that are grandchildren of PLANET elements that are children of the context node.
- */* matches the grandchildren elements of the current element.
- astrophysics:PLANET matches the PLANET element in the "astrophysics" namespace.
- astrophysics:* matches any elements in the "astrophysics" namespace.
- PLANET[DAY and DENSITY] matches all <PLANET> elements that have at least one <DAY> and one <DENSITY> element.
- PLANET[(DAY or DENSITY) and MASS] matches all <PLANET> elements that have at least one <DAY> or <DENSITY> element, and also have at least one <MASS> element.
- PLANET[DAY and not(DISTANCE)] matches all <PLANET> elements that have at least one <DAY> element and no <DISTANCE> elements.
- PLANET[MASS = /STANDARD/REFERENCE/MASS] matches all <PLANET> elements where the <MASS> element's value is the same as the value of the /<STANDARD>/<REFERENCE>/<MASS> element.

That completes this coverage of match patterns for the moment; you'll see related material in Chapter 7 on XPath expressions. Chapter 5 starts looking at ways of working with the data in XML documents by sorting that data and using it to make choices based on data values.

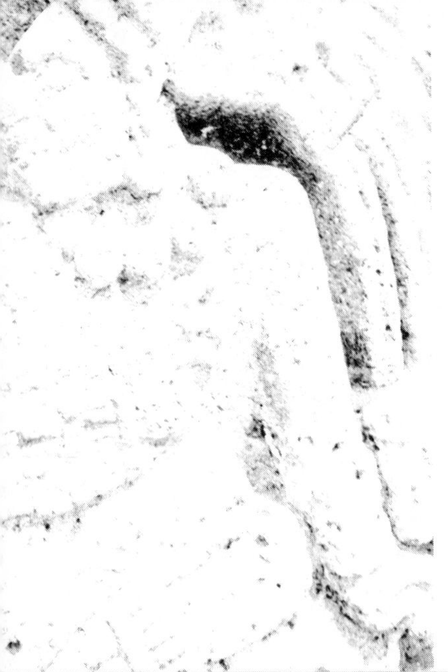

5 Making Choices and Sorting Data

THIS CHAPTER IS ALL ABOUT MAKING CHOICES, sorting, and handling the data in XML documents in various ways. Here, you'll see the `<xsl:if>`, `<xsl:choose>`, `<xsl:when>`, `<xsl:otherwise>`, `<xsl:for-each>`, and `<xsl:sort>` elements. You can use these elements to handle your data, making choices on how transformations should proceed depending on the value of that data.

However, these elements don't offer anything like the precision that a programming language does. For that reason, I also introduce XSLT *extensions* in this chapter, including the XSLT 1.1 working draft `<xsl:script>` element. This element was intended to make it easy to use Java or JavaScript with an XSLT processor. (It's not necessary to understand Java or JavaScript to read this book, but if you know these languages, it's good to know that some XSLT processors offer you the chance to use them while transforming XML.) Something like this element will surely appear in XSLT 2.0. With extensions, you can extend the XSLT specification by adding new elements and functions of your own or some vendor's design to XSLT.

You'll also see how to number elements in documents in this chapter, what to do if your XSLT processor doesn't support a particular extension, and more. I begin with the most frequently used of the elements you'll see in this chapter: `<xsl:if>`.

The <xsl:if> Element

You use `<xsl:if>` to make tests and take different actions depending on the result of the test. It's much like the `if` statement in programming languages. The `<xsl:if>` element has one attribute:

- `test` (mandatory). Set to a Boolean (true/false) condition that you want tested.

This element encloses a template body.

Here's how it works: You enclose a template body inside the `<xsl:if>` element, which tests some expression. If that expression evaluates to true, the template body is used, but if the expression evaluates to false, the template body is ignored:

```
<xsl:if test="expression">
    <!--template body-->
</xsl:if>
```

You can test any XPath expression. Use the following rules for converting them to true/false in the `<xsl:if>` element:

- If the expression evaluates to a node set, it's treated as true if the node set contains at least one node.
- If the expression is a string, it's considered true if the string is not empty.
- If the expression is a result tree fragment, it's treated as true if it contains any nodes.
- If the expression evaluated to a number, it's considered true if it's non-zero.

The `<xsl:if>` element is much like the `if-then` statement in programming languages. However, there is no `<xsl:else>` statement that supports `if-then-else` statements—you need to use `<xsl:choose>` instead.

Here's an example. In this case, I list the planets in planets.xml one after the other, and add an HTML horizontal rule, `<HR>`, element after the last element—but only after the last element. I can do that with `<xsl:if>` this way:

Listing 5.1 **Using <xsl:if>**

```
<?xml version="1.0"?>
<xsl:stylesheet version="1.0" xmlns:xsl="http://www.w3.org/1999/XSL/Transform">

<xsl:template match="PLANETS">
    <HTML>
        <HEAD>
            <TITLE>
                Planets
```

```
            </TITLE>
        </HEAD>
        <BODY>
            <xsl:apply-templates select="PLANET"/>
        </BODY>
    </HTML>
</xsl:template>

<xsl:template match="PLANET">
    <P>
    <xsl:value-of select="NAME"/>
    is planet number <xsl:value-of select="position()"/> from the sun.
    </P>
    <xsl:if test="position() = last()"><HR/></xsl:if>
</xsl:template>

</xsl:stylesheet>
```

Here is the result; as you can see, the <HR> element appears after only the last planet has been listed:

```
<HTML>
    <HEAD>
        <TITLE>
            Planets
        </TITLE>
    </HEAD>

    <BODY>
        <P>
            Mercury is planet number 1 from the sun.
        </P>
        <P>
            Venus is planet number 2 from the sun.
        </P>
        <P>
            Earth is planet number 3 from the sun.
        </P>
        <HR>
    </BODY>
</HTML>
```

Here's another example. This is an XML-to-XML transformation, and in it, I list the planets from planets.xml. However, I don't want to have the output simply say, "The first three planets are: Mercury Venus Earth", but rather "The first three planets are: Mercury, Venus, and Earth." I can add the correct punctuation using the `position` function to determine which element we're working on, and use `<xsl:if>` to check the position:

Listing 5.2 **Second Example Using *<xsl:if>***

```
<?xml version="1.0"?>
<xsl:stylesheet version="1.0"
xmlns:xsl="http://www.w3.org/1999/XSL/Transform">
<xsl:output method="xml"/>
<xsl:template match="PLANETS">
<DOCUMENT>
    <TITLE>
        The Planets
    </TITLE>
    <PLANETS>
        The first three planets are: <xsl:apply-templates select="PLANET"/>
    </PLANETS>
</DOCUMENT>
</xsl:template>

<xsl:template match="PLANET">
    <xsl:value-of select="NAME"/>
    <xsl:if test="position()!=last()">, </xsl:if>
    <xsl:if test="position()=last()-1">and </xsl:if>
    <xsl:if test="position()=last()">.</xsl:if>
</xsl:template>

</xsl:stylesheet>
```

Here's the result:

```
<?xml version="1.0" encoding="UTF-8"?>
<DOCUMENT>

    <TITLE>
        The Planets
    </TITLE>

    <PLANETS>
        The first three planets are: Mercury, Venus, and Earth.
    </PLANETS>

</DOCUMENT>
```

As you can see, I've been able to add the correct punctuation using `<xsl:if>` to determine where we are in the document.

You can also use `<xsl:if>` for detecting errors during transformations. For example, if a `<NAME>` element is in planets.xml, you can display a message using `<xsl:if>`:

Listing 5.3 **Detecting Errors with *<xsl:if>***

```
<?xml version="1.0"?>
<xsl:stylesheet version="1.0"
xmlns:xsl="http://www.w3.org/1999/XSL/Transform">

<xsl:output method = "xml"/>
<xsl:template match="PLANETS">
<DOCUMENT>
    <TITLE>
        The Planets
    </TITLE>
    <PLANETS>
        The first three planets are: <xsl:apply-templates select="PLANET"/>
    </PLANETS>
</DOCUMENT>
</xsl:template>

<xsl:template match="PLANET">
    <xsl:if test="NAME[not(text())]">
        <xsl:message terminate="yes">
            Each planet must have a name!
        </xsl:message>
    </xsl:if>
    <xsl:value-of select="NAME"/>
    <xsl:if test="position()!=last()">, </xsl:if>
    <xsl:if test="position()=last()-1">and </xsl:if>
    <xsl:if test="position()=last()">.</xsl:if>
</xsl:template>

</xsl:stylesheet>
```

To give this a try, I start by making sure one of the <NAME> elements is empty:

```
<?xml version="1.0"?>
<?xml-stylesheet type="text/xml" href="planets.xsl"?>
<PLANETS>

    <PLANET>
        <NAME>Mercury</NAME>
        <MASS UNITS="(Earth = 1)">.0553</MASS>
        <DAY UNITS="days">58.65</DAY>
        <RADIUS UNITS="miles">1516</RADIUS>
        <DENSITY UNITS="(Earth = 1)">.983</DENSITY>
        <DISTANCE UNITS="million miles">43.4</DISTANCE><!--At perihelion-->
    </PLANET>

    <PLANET>
        <NAME></NAME>
```

```
        <MASS UNITS="(Earth = 1)">.815</MASS>
        <DAY UNITS="days">116.75</DAY>
        <RADIUS UNITS="miles">3716</RADIUS>
        <DENSITY UNITS="(Earth = 1)">.943</DENSITY>
        <DISTANCE UNITS="million miles">66.8</DISTANCE><!--At perihelion-->
    </PLANET>
        .
        .
        .
```

And here's what happens when I use Xalan on this example:

```
C:\planets>java org.apache.xalan.xslt.Process -IN planets.xml -XSL errors.xsl -OUT new.xml
➥file:///C:/XSL/w.xsl; Line 18; Column 38; Each planet must have a name!

XSLT Error (javax.xml.transform.TransformerException): Stylesheet directed termination
```

If you're familiar with the `if` construct in programming languages, you know that where there's an `if` statement, there's usually an `else` statement that can be executed if the condition for the `if` statement turns out to be false. There is no `<xsl:else>` element in XSLT, however. You can use `<xsl:choose>` if you want to specify alternate paths for XSLT processing.

The *<xsl:choose>*, *<xsl:when>*, and *<xsl:otherwise>* Elements

The `<xsl:choose>` element is something like the Java `switch` statement, which enables you to compare a test value against several possible matches.

The `<xsl:choose>` element has no attributes. It contains one or more `<xsl:when>` elements, and, optionally, one `<xsl:otherwise>` element, which must come last if you use it.

Here's how it works; you enclose `<xsl:when>` elements, each of which has a true/false test, in an `<xsl:choose>` element. The template body in the first `<xsl:when>` element whose test evaluates as true is used, and all the others are not. The last element inside the `<xsl:choose>` element may be an `<xsl:otherwise>` element, and the template body inside this element is used if none of the tests in the preceeding `<xsl:when>` elements evaluate to true:

```
<xsl:choose>
    <xsl:when test="expression1">
        <!--template-body 1-->
    </xsl:when>
    <xsl:when test="expression2>
        <!--template-body 2-->
    </xsl:when>
    <xsl:when test="expression3">
        <!--template-body 3-->
```

```
    </xsl:when>
    <xsl:otherwise>
        <!--template-body 4-->
    </xsl:otherwise>
</xsl:choose>
```

In the preceding section, it took three `<xsl:if>` elements to perform this transformation properly:

```
<?xml version="1.0"?>
<xsl:stylesheet version="1.0"
xmlns:xsl="http://www.w3.org/1999/XSL/Transform">
<xsl:output method="xml/>
<xsl:template match="PLANETS">
<DOCUMENT>
    <TITLE>
        The Planets
    </TITLE>
    <PLANETS>
        The first three planets are: <xsl:apply-templates select="PLANET"/>
    </PLANETS>
</DOCUMENT>
</xsl:template>

<xsl:template match="PLANET">
    <xsl:if test="NAME[not(text())]">
        <xsl:message terminate="yes">
            Each planet must have a name!
        </xsl:message>
    </xsl:if>
    <xsl:value-of select="NAME"/>
    <xsl:if test="position()!=last()">, </xsl:if>
    <xsl:if test="position()=last()-1">and </xsl:if>
    <xsl:if test="position()=last()">.</xsl:if>
</xsl:template>

</xsl:stylesheet>
```

Now I'll do the same thing with a single `<xsl:choose>` element:

```
<?xml version="1.0"?>
<xsl:stylesheet version="1.0" xmlns:xsl="http://www.w3.org/1999/XSL/Transform">
<xml:output method="xml"/>
<xsl:output method="xml"/>

<xsl:template match="PLANETS">
<DOCUMENT>
    <TITLE>
        The Planets
    </TITLE>
    <PLANETS>
        The first three planets are: <xsl:apply-templates select="PLANET"/>
    </PLANETS>
</DOCUMENT>
```

```
</xsl:template>

<xsl:template match="PLANET">
    <xsl:if test="NAME[not(text())]">
        <xsl:message terminate="yes">
            Each planet must have a name!
        </xsl:message>
    </xsl:if>
    <xsl:value-of select="NAME"/>
    <xsl:choose>
        .
        .
        .
    </xsl:choose>
</xsl:template>

</xsl:stylesheet>
```

We'll need to test where we are in the document by enclosing several <xsl:when> elements. This element has only one attribute:

- test (mandatory). Set to a Boolean (true/false) condition that you want tested.

The <xsl:when> element contains a template body.

You set the test attribute of <xsl:when> to a true/false expression that specifies whether the enclosed template body is used or ignored. For example, here's how I add <xsl:when> elements with the appropriate punctuation for any of the planets that are not the last one:

```
<?xml version="1.0"?>
<xsl:stylesheet version="1.0" xmlns:xsl="http://www.w3.org/1999/XSL/Transform">
<xsl:output method="xml"/>
<xsl:template match="PLANETS">
<DOCUMENT>
    <TITLE>
        The Planets
    </TITLE>
    <PLANETS>
        The first three planets are: <xsl:apply-templates select="PLANET"/>
    </PLANETS>
</DOCUMENT>
</xsl:template>

<xsl:template match="PLANET">
    <xsl:if test="NAME[not(text())]">
        <xsl:message terminate="yes">
            Each planet must have a name!
        </xsl:message>
    </xsl:if>
    <xsl:value-of select="NAME"/>
```

```
    <xsl:choose>
        <xsl:when test="position()!=last()">, </xsl:when>
        <xsl:when test="position()=last()-1">and </xsl:when>
        .
        .
        .
    </xsl:choose>
</xsl:template>

</xsl:stylesheet>
```

These two <xsl:when> elements match all <PLANET> elements except the last one, so an <xsl:otherwise> element can be used for the last <PLANET> element. The template body in this element is used if no <xsl:when> element in the <xsl:choose> element had a test that evaluated as true.

The <xsl:otherwise> element has no attributes, and contains a template body. Here's how I put it to work in this example:

Listing 5.4 **Using *<xsl:choose>***

```
<?xml version="1.0"?>
<xsl:stylesheet version="1.0"
xmlns:xsl="http://www.w3.org/1999/XSL/Transform">
<xsl:output method="xml"/>

<xsl:template match="PLANETS">
<DOCUMENT>
    <TITLE>
        The Planets
    </TITLE>
    <PLANETS>
        The first three planets are: <xsl:apply-templates select="PLANET"/>
    </PLANETS>
</DOCUMENT>
</xsl:template>

<xsl:template match="PLANET">
    <xsl:if test="NAME[not(text())]">
        <xsl:message terminate="yes">
            Each planet must have a name!
        </xsl:message>
    </xsl:if>
    <xsl:value-of select="NAME"/>
    <xsl:choose>
        <xsl:when test="position()!=last()">, </xsl:when>
        <xsl:when test="position()=last()-1">and </xsl:when>
        <xsl:otherwise>.</xsl:otherwise>
    </xsl:choose>
</xsl:template>

</xsl:stylesheet>
```

And that's it; this code produces the same result as when we used `<xsl:if>` to check the position of the `<PLANET>` elements:

```
<?xml version="1.0" encoding="UTF-8"?>
<DOCUMENT>

    <TITLE>
        The Planets
    </TITLE>

    <PLANETS>
        The first three planets are: Mercury, Venus, and Earth.
    </PLANETS>

</DOCUMENT>
```

Here's another XML-to-XML example. In this case, I convert planets.xml to a new XML document, preserving only the name of each planet, and adding a description:

```
<?xml version="1.0" encoding="UTF-8"?>
<DOCUMENT>

    <TITLE>
        The Planets
    </TITLE>

    <PLANETS>
        <PLANET>
            <NAME>Mercury</NAME>
            <DESCRIPTION>Hottest</DESCRIPTION>
        </PLANET>
        <PLANET>
            <NAME>Venus</NAME>
            <DESCRIPTION>Hot</DESCRIPTION>
        </PLANET>
        <PLANET>
            <NAME>Earth</NAME>
            <DESCRIPTION>OK</DESCRIPTION>
        </PLANET>
    </PLANETS>

</DOCUMENT>
```

I can implement this transformation by checking the value of each `<NAME>` element, which is its enclosed text (note that string matches like this are case-sensitive in XSLT):

Listing 5.5 **Second *<xsl:choose>* Example**

```
<?xml version="1.0"?>
<xsl:stylesheet version="1.0"
xmlns:xsl="http://www.w3.org/1999/XSL/Transform">

<xsl:output method="xml"/>
<xsl:template match="PLANETS">
<DOCUMENT>
    <TITLE>
        The Planets
    </TITLE>
    <PLANETS>
        <xsl:apply-templates select="PLANET"/>
    </PLANETS>
</DOCUMENT>
</xsl:template>

<xsl:template match="PLANET">
    <xsl:if test="NAME[not(text())]">
        <xsl:message terminate="yes">
            Each planet must have a name!
        </xsl:message>
    </xsl:if>
    <PLANET>
        <NAME>
            <xsl:value-of select="NAME"/>
        </NAME>
        <DESCRIPTION>
            <xsl:choose>
                <xsl:when test="NAME='Mercury'">Hottest</xsl:when>
                <xsl:when test="NAME='Venus'">Hot</xsl:when>
                <xsl:when test="NAME='Earth'">OK</xsl:when>
            </xsl:choose>
        </DESCRIPTION>
    </PLANET>
</xsl:template>

</xsl:stylesheet>
```

That's all it takes.

Now, suppose that I want to add COLOR attributes to each <PLANET> element:

```
<?xml version="1.0"?>
<?xml-stylesheet type="text/xml" href="planets.xsl"?>
<PLANETS>

  <PLANET COLOR="RED">
    <NAME>Mercury</NAME>
    <MASS UNITS="(Earth = 1)">.0553</MASS>
```

```
    <DAY UNITS="days">58.65</DAY>
    <RADIUS UNITS="miles">1516</RADIUS>
    <DENSITY UNITS="(Earth = 1)">.983</DENSITY>
    <DISTANCE UNITS="million miles">43.4</DISTANCE><!--At perihelion-->
  </PLANET>

  <PLANET COLOR="WHITE">
    <NAME>Venus</NAME>
    <MASS UNITS="(Earth = 1)">.815</MASS>
    <DAY UNITS="days">116.75</DAY>
    <RADIUS UNITS="miles">3716</RADIUS>
    <DENSITY UNITS="(Earth = 1)">.943</DENSITY>
    <DISTANCE UNITS="million miles">66.8</DISTANCE><!--At perihelion-->
  </PLANET>

  <PLANET COLOR="BLUE">
    <NAME>Earth</NAME>
    <MASS UNITS="(Earth = 1)">1</MASS>
    <DAY UNITS="days">1</DAY>
    <RADIUS UNITS="miles">2107</RADIUS>
    <DENSITY UNITS="(Earth = 1)">1</DENSITY>
    <DISTANCE UNITS="million miles">128.4</DISTANCE><!--At perihelion-->
  </PLANET>

</PLANETS>
```

We could display the names of the various planets, formatted in different ways, by using HTML `<B>`, `<I>`, and `<U>` tags, depending on the value of the `COLOR` attribute, with an `<xsl:choose>` element, as follows:

Listing 5.6 **Formatting Using *<xsl:choose>***

```
<?xml version="1.0"?>
<xsl:stylesheet version="1.0"
xmlns:xsl="http://www.w3.org/1999/XSL/Transform">

<xsl:template match="PLANETS">
    <HTML>
        <HEAD>
            <TITLE>
                Planets
            </TITLE>
        </HEAD>
        <BODY>
            <xsl:apply-templates select="PLANET"/>
        </BODY>
    </HTML>
</xsl:template>

<xsl:template match="PLANET">
```

```
    <xsl:choose>
        <xsl:when test="@COLOR = 'RED'">
            <B>
                <xsl:value-of select="NAME"/>
            </B>
        </xsl:when>
        <xsl:when test="@COLOR = 'WHITE'">
            <I>
                <xsl:value-of select="NAME"/>
            </I>
        </xsl:when>
        <xsl:when test="@COLOR = 'BLUE'">
            <U>
                <xsl:value-of select="NAME"/>
            </U>
        </xsl:when>
        <xsl:otherwise>
             <PRE>
                 <xsl:value-of select="."/>
             </PRE>
        </xsl:otherwise>
    </xsl:choose>
</xsl:template>

</xsl:stylesheet>
```

Here is the result document:

```
<HTML>

    <HEAD>
        <TITLE>
            Planets
        </TITLE>
    </HEAD>

    <BODY>
        <B>Mercury</B>
        <I>Venus</I>
        <U>Earth</U>
    </BODY>

</HTML>
```

You've seen that you can use `<xsl:if>` to test single conditions and `<xsl:choose>` to test multiple conditions, and these elements mirror what's available in most programming languages. In addition to conditional statements such as these, most programming languages also include looping statements, and XSLT contains something similar: the `<xsl:for-each>` element.

The *<xsl:for-each>* Element

The `<xsl:for-each>` element enables you to loop over a template body, over and over, for all elements of a node set. Technically speaking, it works on a node set returned by an XPath expression, and performs the same operation on each node in the set. Each time you loop over the template body, it's applied to the next node from the node set, making it easy to handle multiple nodes.

> **`<xsl:for-each>` Versus `<xsl:apply-templates>`**
>
> You might have noticed that this description is a lot like the one for the `<xsl:apply-templates>` element, and I'll compare `<xsl:for-each>` and `<xsl:apply-templates>` in a few pages.

The `<xsl:for-each>` element has one attribute:

- `select` (mandatory). Set to an XPath expression that returns the node set through which you want to loop.

This element encloses zero or more `<xsl:sort>` elements, followed by a template body. You'll learn how to use `<xsl:sort>` later in this chapter.

In the enclosed template body, the `position` function returns the current node position in a node set, and `last` returns the number of nodes in a set. If you don't use `<xsl:sort>`, nodes are processed in document order (the order in which they are listed in the document); if you do use `<xsl:sort>`, the node set is sorted first as you specify with the `<xsl:sort>` element.

Say that you want to format all the names of planets inside HTML `<P>` elements; you can do that as follows:

```
<xsl:template match="PLANET">
    <P>
        <xsl:value-of select="NAME"/>
    </P>
</xsl:template>
```

However, what if some planets had two names, like this:

```
<PLANET>
    <NAME>Mercury</NAME>
    <NAME>Closest planet to the sun</NAME>
    <MASS UNITS="(Earth = 1)">.0553</MASS>
    <DAY UNITS="days">58.65</DAY>
    <RADIUS UNITS="miles">1516</RADIUS>
    <DENSITY UNITS="(Earth = 1)">.983</DENSITY>
    <DISTANCE UNITS="million miles">43.4</DISTANCE><!—At perihelion—>
</PLANET>
```

This is a problem, because the `<xsl:value-of>` element's `select` attribute by itself selects only the first `<NAME>` element; to loop over all possible matches, you can use the `<xsl:for-each>` element this way instead:

Listing 5.7 **Using *<xsl:for-each>***

```
<?xml version="1.0"?>
<xsl:stylesheet version="1.0"
xmlns:xsl="http://www.w3.org/1999/XSL/Transform">

    <xsl:template match="PLANETS">
        <HTML>
            <xsl:apply-templates/>
        </HTML>
    </xsl:template>

<xsl:template match="PLANET">
    <xsl:for-each select="NAME">
        <P>
            <xsl:value-of select="."/>
        </P>
    </xsl:for-each>
</xsl:template>

</xsl:stylesheet>
```

This style sheet catches all `<NAME>` elements, places their values in a `<P>` element, and adds them to the output document this way:

```
<HTML>

    <P>Mercury</P>
    <P>Closest planet to the sun</P>
    <P>Venus</P>
    <P>Earth</P>

</HTML>
```

Here's another example, which first appeared in Chapter 3, "Creating and Using Templates," where `<xsl: for-each>` was used to loop over all attributes in an element:

```
<?xml version="1.0"?>
<xsl:stylesheet version="1.0"
xmlns:xsl="http://www.w3.org/1999/XSL/Transform">
    <xsl:output method="xml"/>

    <xsl:template match="*">
        <xsl:copy>
            <xsl:for-each select="@*">
                <xsl:copy/>
```

```
            </xsl:for-each>
            <xsl:apply-templates/>
        </xsl:copy>
    </xsl:template>
</xsl:stylesheet>
```

This next example appeared in Chapter 2, "Creating and Using Stylesheets." It's a simplified stylesheet, where you can't use any top-level elements, which means that you can't use <xsl:template> or <xsl:apply-templates>, but you can loop over nodes with <xsl:for-each>:

```
<HTML xmlns:xsl="http://www.w3.org/1999/XSL/Transform" xsl:version="1.0">
    <HEAD>
        <TITLE>
            The Planets Table
        </TITLE>
    </HEAD>
    <BODY>
        <H1>
            The Planets Table
        </H1>
        <TABLE BORDER="2">
            <TR>
                <TD>Name</TD>
                <TD>Mass</TD>
                <TD>Radius</TD>
                <TD>Day</TD>
            </TR>
            <xsl:for-each select="//PLANET">
                <TR>
                    <TD><xsl:value-of select="NAME"/></TD>
                    <TD><xsl:value-of select="MASS"/></TD>
                    <TD><xsl:value-of select="RADIUS"/></TD>
                    <TD><xsl:value-of select="DAY"/></TD>
                </TR>
            </xsl:for-each>
        </TABLE>
    </BODY>
</HTML>
```

This simplified stylesheet formats planets.xml into planets.html just as well as a template that uses <xsl:apply-templates>, which brings up an interesting question: When do you use <xsl:for-each> to loop over nodes, and when do you use <xsl:apply-templates>?

In general, it's good to use <xsl:apply-templates> when the organization of child nodes is unknown, and you want to apply different templates to different kinds of children, no matter how many levels deep their organization extends. On the other hand, if child nodes have a regular, well-defined organization, you can set up an <xsl:for-each> that handles them all.

The `<xsl:for-each>` element functions a lot like `<xsl:apply-templates>`; you can even nest templates with `<xsl:for-each>` as you can with successive `<xsl:apply-templates>` elements. In the following example, I loop over each `<PLANET>` element, and then loop over all elements contained in the `<PLANET>` element, listing their data in `<DATA>` elements this way:

Listing 5.8 **Second *<xsl:for-each>* Example**

```
<?xml version="1.0"?>
<xsl:stylesheet version="1.0"
xmlns:xsl="http://www.w3.org/1999/XSL/Transform">
    <xsl:output method="xml"/>

    <xsl:template match="PLANETS">
        <PLANETS>
            <xsl:for-each select="PLANET">
                <PLANET>
                    <xsl:for-each select="*">
                        <DATA>
                            <xsl:value-of select="."/>
                        </DATA>
                    </xsl:for-each>
                </PLANET>
            </xsl:for-each>
        </PLANETS>
    </xsl:template>
</xsl:stylesheet>
```

And here's the result:

```
<?xml version="1.0" encoding="UTF-8"?>
<PLANETS>
    <PLANET>
        <DATA>Mercury</DATA>
        <DATA>.0553</DATA>
        <DATA>58.65</DATA>
        <DATA>1516</DATA>
        <DATA>.983</DATA>
        <DATA>43.4</DATA>
    </PLANET>
    <PLANET>
        <DATA>Venus</DATA>
        <DATA>.815</DATA>
        <DATA>116.75</DATA>
        <DATA>3716</DATA>
        <DATA>.943</DATA>
        <DATA>66.8</DATA>
```

```
    </PLANET>
    <PLANET>
        <DATA>Earth</DATA>
        <DATA>1</DATA>
        <DATA>1</DATA>
        <DATA>2107</DATA>
        <DATA>1</DATA>
        <DATA>128.4</DATA>
    </PLANET>
</PLANETS>
```

Sorting Elements

You can use `<xsl:sort>` to sort nodes. This element sets the order of node processing for `<xsl:apply-templates>` and `<xsl:for-each>`. The following list includes the attributes of `<xsl:sort>`:

- `select` (optional). Sets to an XPath expression that returns a node set to sort. The default is "string(.)".
- `order` (optional). Sets the sort order; set to "ascending" or "descending".
- `case-order` (optional). Determines whether upper-case letters come before lower-case letters. Set to "upper-first" or "lower-first".
- `lang` (optional). Sets the language whose sorting conventions are to be used. Set to a language code valid in the xml:lang attribute.
- `data-type` (optional). Sets whether the sort should be alphabetical or numerical. Set to "text", "number", or a QName.

This element takes no content. You use it inside `<xsl:apply-templates>` or `<xsl:for-each>` elements to sort the node sets on which those elements work.

In the following example, I just sort the `<PLANET>` elements in planets.xml in ascending alphabetical order based on their names, using `<xsl:for-each>` in a simplified stylesheet:

Listing 5.9 **Sorting Data**

```
<HTML xmlns:xsl="http://www.w3.org/1999/XSL/Transform" xsl:version="1.0">
    <HEAD>
        <TITLE>
            The Sorted Planets Table
        </TITLE>
    </HEAD>
    <BODY>
        <H1>
            The Sorted Planets Table
```

```
        </H1>
        <TABLE BORDER="2">
           <TR>
                <TD>Name</TD>
                <TD>Mass</TD>
                <TD>Radius</TD>
                <TD>Day</TD>
           </TR>
           <xsl:for-each select="//PLANET">
                <xsl:sort/>
                <TR>
                    <TD><xsl:value-of select="NAME"/></TD>
                    <TD><xsl:value-of select="MASS"/></TD>
                    <TD><xsl:value-of select="RADIUS"/></TD>
                    <TD><xsl:value-of select="DAY"/></TD>
                </TR>
            </xsl:for-each>
        </TABLE>
    </BODY>
</HTML>
```

And here's the result. Note that the planets are indeed sorted as Earth, Mercury, and then Venus:

```
<HTML>
    <HEAD>
        <TITLE>
           The Sorted Planets Table
        </TITLE>
    </HEAD>

    <BODY>
        <H1>
           The Sorted Planets Table
        </H1>

        <TABLE BORDER="2">
            <TR>
                <TD>Name</TD>
                <TD>Mass</TD>
                <TD>Radius</TD>
                <TD>Day</TD>
            </TR>
            <TR>
                <TD>Earth</TD>
                <TD>1</TD>
                <TD>2107</TD>
                <TD>1</TD>
            </TR>
            <TR>
                <TD>Mercury</TD>
```

```
                <TD>.0553</TD>
                <TD>1516</TD>
                <TD>58.65</TD>
            </TR>
            <TR>
                <TD>Venus</TD>
                <TD>.815</TD>
                <TD>3716</TD>
                <TD>116.75</TD>
            </TR>
        </TABLE>
    </BODY>
</HTML>
```

You can see this result in Figure 5.1.

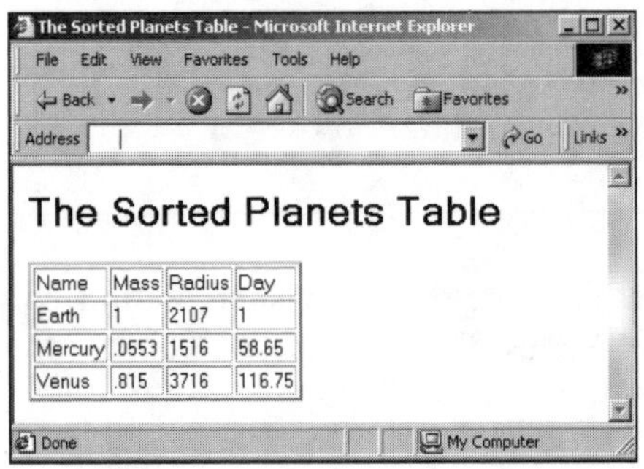

Figure 5.1 Sorting using a simplified template.

You use the `select` attribute to specify what to sort on. For example, here's how I sort the planets based on density:

Listing 5.10 **Sorting Planets Based on Density**

```
<?xml version="1.0"?>
<xsl:stylesheet version="1.0"
xmlns:xsl="http://www.w3.org/1999/XSL/Transform">

    <xsl:template match="PLANETS">
        <HTML>
            <HEAD>
                <TITLE>
                    Planets
                </TITLE>
            </HEAD>
```

```
            <BODY>
                <H1>Planets sorted by density</H1>
                <TABLE>
                    <TR>
                        <TD>Planet</TD>
                        <TD>Mass</TD>
                        <TD>Day</TD>
                        <TD>Density</TD>
                    </TR>
                    <xsl:apply-templates>
                        <xsl:sort select="DENSITY"/>
                    </xsl:apply-templates>
                </TABLE>
            </BODY>
        </HTML>
    </xsl:template>

    <xsl:template match="PLANET">
        <TR>
            <TD><xsl:apply-templates select="NAME"/></TD>
            <TD><xsl:apply-templates select="MASS"/></TD>
            <TD><xsl:apply-templates select="DAY"/></TD>
            <TD><xsl:apply-templates select="DENSITY"/></TD>
        </TR>
    </xsl:template>

</xsl:stylesheet>
```

Here are the results of this transformation:

```
<HTML>
    <HEAD>
        <TITLE>
            Planets
        </TITLE>
    </HEAD>

    <BODY>
        <H1>
            Planets sorted by density
        </H1>
        <TABLE>
            </TR>
                <TD>Planet</TD>
                <TD>Mass</TD>
                <TD>Day</TD>
                <TD>Density</TD>
            </TR>
```

```
            <TR>
                <TD>Venus</TD>
                <TD>.815</TD>
                <TD>116.75</TD>
                <TD>.943</TD>
            </TR>

            <TR>
                <TD>Mercury</TD>
                <TD>.0553</TD>
                <TD>58.65</TD>
                <TD>.983</TD>
            </TR>

            <TR>
                <TD>Earth</TD>
                <TD>1</TD>
                <TD>1</TD>
                <TD>1</TD>
            </TR>
        </TABLE>
    </BODY>
</HTML>
```

By default, `<xsl:sort>` performs an alphabetic sort, which means that "10" comes before "2". You can perform a true numeric sort by setting the data-type attribute to "number" like this:

```
<xsl:sort data-type="number" select="DENSITY"/>
```

You can create descending sorts by setting the `<xsl:sort>` element's `order` attribute to "descending". You can also sort on attribute values like this:

```
<xsl:apply-templates select="PLANETS">
    <xsl:sort select="@SIZE"/>
</xsl:apply-templates>
```

Coming up in XSLT 2.0

One of the big issues in XSLT 2.0 is support for XML schemas, and just as you can sort on strings or numbers now, the W3C is planning to let you sort on any data type specified in a document's schema in XSLT 2.0.

Using Multiple Sort Criteria

It's also worth noting that you can use multiple sort criteria in your sorting operations. To do so, simply use multiple `<xsl:sort>` elements. The first `<xsl:sort>` element sorts on the major criterion, the next element can sort on the next major criterion, and so on. For example, here's how you could sort on distance first, then on planet density (which will order planets that were at the same distance from the sun by density) inside an `<xsl:apply-templates>` element:

```
<xsl:apply-templates>
    <xsl:sort select="DISTANCE"/>
    <xsl:sort select="DENSITY"/>
</xsl:apply-templates>
```

That completes this discussion of sorting; next I'll turn to an allied topic: numbering.

The *<xsl:number>* Element

You use `<xsl:number>` to assign a number in a sequence to a node in the result document. For example, you can number paragraphs in a contract or stanzas in a poem. You can even number parts of a document down to multiple levels, such as "Paragraph 3.2.5.1." and so on.

Here are the `<xsl:number>` element's attributes:

- `level` (optional). Determines how sequence numbers are assigned. Set to "single", "multiple", or "any". The default is "single".
- `count` (optional). Determines which nodes are to be counted. Set to a pattern.
- `from` (optional). Determines the point at which counting starts. Set to a pattern.
- `value` (optional). A number to be formatted.
- format (optional). Determines the output format. Set to an attribute value template that returns a format string.
- `lang` (optional). Determines the language whose conventions to use for numbering. Set to a language code that you can use with the `xml:lang` attribute.
- `letter-value` (optional). Enables you to distinguish between different numbering schemes. Set to "alphabetical" or "traditional".
- `grouping-separator` (optional). A character used to separate groups of digits, such as a comma. Set to an attribute value template that returns a single character.
- `grouping-size` (optional). Number of digits in each group—determines where the grouping separator should be used. Set to an attribute value template that returns a number.

A Tip for Numbering

As you can see from this list of attributes, there's quite an array of options when it comes to numbering schemes. In fact, numbering operations can become quite complex, so here's a tip: if the numbering becomes too difficult and convoluted, I just produce the result document without numbering, then use a second stylesheet that applies the numbering.

There are three main ways of applying numbering, depending on how you set the level attribute: "single", "multiple", or "any". The following sections look at each of these schemes in turn, starting with single numbering, which is the default.

Single-Level Numbering

Single-level numbering is simple numbering, where you're just numbering sibling nodes on the same level. This is the default type of numbering. Here's an example where I'm using single numbering to number the planets in planets.xml:

Listing 5.11 **Single-Level Numbering**

```
<?xml version="1.0"?>
<xsl:stylesheet version="1.0"
xmlns:xsl="http://www.w3.org/1999/XSL/Transform">

    <xsl:template match="/PLANETS">
        <HTML>
            <HEAD>
                <TITLE>
                    The Planets Table
                </TITLE>
            </HEAD>
            <BODY>
                <H1>
                    The Planets Table
                </H1>
                <TABLE BORDER="2">
                    <TR>
                        <TD>Name</TD>
                        <TD>Mass</TD>
                        <TD>Radius</TD>
                        <TD>Day</TD>
                    </TR>
                    <xsl:apply-templates/>
                </TABLE>
            </BODY>
        </HTML>
    </xsl:template>
```

```
    <xsl:template match="PLANET">
       <TR>
          <TD><xsl:number/>. <xsl:value-of select="NAME"/></TD>
          <TD><xsl:apply-templates select="MASS"/></TD>
          <TD><xsl:apply-templates select="RADIUS"/></TD>
          <TD><xsl:apply-templates select="DAY"/></TD>
       </TR>
   </xsl:template>

    <xsl:template match="MASS">
        <xsl:value-of select="."/>
        <xsl:text> </xsl:text>
        <xsl:value-of select="@UNITS"/>
    </xsl:template>
        .
        .
        .
    <xsl:template match="DAY">
        <xsl:value-of select="."/>
        <xsl:text> </xsl:text>
        <xsl:value-of select="@UNITS"/>
    </xsl:template>

</xsl:stylesheet>
```

And here's the result:

```
<HTML>
    <HEAD>
        <TITLE>
            The Planets Table
         </TITLE>
    </HEAD>

    <BODY>
        <H1>
            The Planets Table
        </H1>

        <TABLE BORDER="2">
            <TR>
                <TD>Name</TD>
                <TD>Mass</TD>
                <TD>Radius</TD>
                <TD>Day</TD>
            </TR>

            <TR>
                <TD>1. Mercury</TD>
                <TD>.0553 (Earth = 1)</TD>
```

```
            <TD>1516 miles</TD>
            <TD>58.65 days</TD>
        </TR>

        <TR>
            <TD>2. Venus</TD>
            <TD>.815 (Earth = 1)</TD>
            <TD>3716 miles</TD>
            <TD>116.75 days</TD>
        </TR>

        <TR>
            <TD>3. Earth</TD>
            <TD>1 (Earth = 1)</TD>
            <TD>2107 miles</TD>
            <TD>1 days</TD>
        </TR>
    </TABLE>
  </BODY>
</HTML>
```

You can see this result in Figure 5.2.

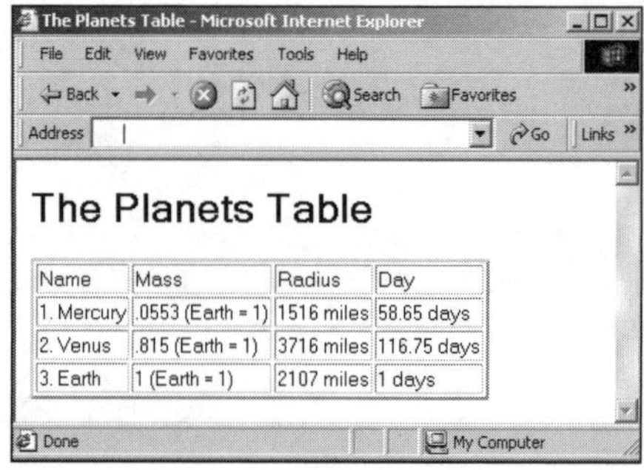

Figure 5.2 Single numbering of elements.

By default, numbering uses digits, but there are other options. For example, if I had used `<xsl:number format="a"/>`, the planets would have been assigned a., b., and c.:

```
<HTML>
  <HEAD>
    <TITLE>
      The Planets Table
    </TITLE>
  </HEAD>
```

```
<BODY>
    <H1>
        The Planets Table
    </H1>

    <TABLE BORDER="2">
        <TR>
            <TD>Name</TD>
            <TD>Mass</TD>
            <TD>Radius</TD>
            <TD>Day</TD>
        </TR>

        <TR>
            <TD>a. Mercury</TD>
            <TD>.0553 (Earth = 1)</TD>
            <TD>1516 miles</TD>
            <TD>58.65 days</TD>
        </TR>

        <TR>
            <TD>b. Venus</TD>
            <TD>.815 (Earth = 1)</TD>
            <TD>3716 miles</TD>
            <TD>116.75 days</TD>
        </TR>
    .
    .
    .
```

Here are the possible tokens you can use in the `format` attribute and what kinds of numbering they produce:

- 1 generates 1, 2, 3...
- 01 generates 01, 02, 03...
- Other Unicode digits in other numbering systems follow the same two preceding rules.
- a generates a, b, c...aa, ab...
- A generates A, B, C...AA, AB...
- i generates i, ii, iii, iv...ix, x, xi, xii...
- I generates I, II, III, IV...IX, X, XI, XII...

Any-Level Numbering

Sometimes, you might want to just count nodes of a specific type, no matter at what level they appear in the document. For example, you might have multiple <NAME> elements that appear at different places in a document's hierarchy, and you might simply want to treat the document as a stream of data, counting <NAME> elements as you encounter them.

Here's how it might look if you had <NAME> elements at different levels in planets.xml:

```
<?xml version="1.0"?>
<?xml-stylesheet type="text/xml" href="planets.xsl"?>
<PLANETS>
    <TITLE>
        <NAME>Planets Table</NAME>
    </TITLE>
    <PLANET>
        <NAME>Mercury</NAME>
        <MASS UNITS="(Earth = 1)">.0553</MASS>
        <DAY UNITS="days">58.65</DAY>
        <RADIUS UNITS="miles">1516</RADIUS>
        <DENSITY UNITS="(Earth = 1)">.983</DENSITY>
        <DISTANCE UNITS="million miles">43.4</DISTANCE><!--At perihelion-->
    </PLANET>

    <PLANET>
        <NAME>Venus</NAME>
        <MASS UNITS="(Earth = 1)">.815</MASS>
        <DAY UNITS="days">116.75</DAY>
        <RADIUS UNITS="miles">3716</RADIUS>
        <DENSITY UNITS="(Earth = 1)">.943</DENSITY>
        <DISTANCE UNITS="million miles">66.8</DISTANCE><!--At perihelion-->
    </PLANET>
        .
        .
        .
```

To count the total number of <NAME> elements, I can set the `level` attribute to "any" in a stylesheet:

Listing 5.12 **Any-Level Numbering**

```
<?xml version="1.0"?>
<xsl:stylesheet version="1.0"
xmlns:xsl="http://www.w3.org/1999/XSL/Transform">

    <xsl:template match="/PLANETS">
        <HTML>
            <HEAD>
                <TITLE>
                    The Planets Table
```

```
            </TITLE>
        </HEAD>
        <BODY>
            <H1>
                The Planets Table
            </H1>
            <xsl:apply-templates select="TITLE"/>
            <TABLE BORDER="2">
                <TR>
                    <TD>Name</TD>
                    <TD>Mass</TD>
                    <TD>Radius</TD>
                    <TD>Day</TD>
                </TR>
                <xsl:apply-templates select="PLANET"/>
            </TABLE>
        </BODY>
    </HTML>
</xsl:template>

<xsl:template match="PLANET">
   <TR>
      <TD><xsl:apply-templates select="NAME"/></TD>
      <TD><xsl:apply-templates select="MASS"/></TD>
      <TD><xsl:apply-templates select="RADIUS"/></TD>
      <TD><xsl:apply-templates select="DAY"/></TD>
   </TR>
</xsl:template>

<xsl:template match="TITLE">
    <xsl:apply-templates/>
</xsl:template>

<xsl:template match="NAME">
    <xsl:number level="any" count="NAME"/>. <xsl:value-of select="."/>
</xsl:template>

<xsl:template match="MASS">
    <xsl:value-of select="."/>
    <xsl:text> </xsl:text>
    <xsl:value-of select="@UNITS"/>
</xsl:template>
    .
    .
    .
<xsl:template match="DAY">
    <xsl:value-of select="."/>
    <xsl:text> </xsl:text>
    <xsl:value-of select="@UNITS"/>
</xsl:template>

</xsl:stylesheet>
```

And here's the result—note that the text from each <NAME> element, no matter where it appears in the document, is numbered:

```
<HTML>
    <HEAD>
        <TITLE>
            The Planets Table
        </TITLE>
    </HEAD>

    <BODY>
        <H1>
            The Planets Table
        </H1>
        1. Planets Table
       <TABLE BORDER="2">
           <TR>
               <TD>Name</TD>
               <TD>Mass</TD>
               <TD>Radius</TD>
               <TD>Day</TD>
           </TR>

           <TR>
               <TD>2. Mercury</TD>
               <TD>.0553 (Earth = 1)</TD>
               <TD>1516 miles</TD>
               <TD>58.65 days</TD>
           </TR>

           <TR>
               <TD>3. Venus</TD>
               <TD>.815 (Earth = 1)</TD>
               <TD>3716 miles</TD>
               <TD>116.75 days</TD>
           </TR>

           <TR>
               <TD>4. Earth</TD>
               <TD>1 (Earth = 1)</TD>
               <TD>2107 miles</TD>
               <TD>1 days</TD>
           </TR>

        </TABLE>
    </BODY>
</HTML>
```

You can also use the `from` attribute to indicate from which ancestor node to start counting; for example, if you set the ancestor node to a `<PLANET>` element as follows:

```
<xsl:number level="any" count="NAME" from="PLANET"/>
```

then the XSLT processor would count back only until it finds a `<PLANET>` ancestor, and start numbering from that point in the document.

Multiple-Level Numbering

The `<xsl:number>` element also supports multi-level numbering, such as 3.1.2.5 and so on. To use multiple-level numbering, you set the level attribute to "multiple". You can also indicate what type of nodes you want to number with the `count` attribute, setting it to a pattern, such as "PART|CHAPTER|PARAGRAPH". When processing `<xsl:number>` elements, the XSLT processor numbers nodes to match the document hierarchy.

In this example, I number every level in the element hierarchy of planets.xml, setting the `count` attribute to "*" to match all elements. I can also indicate the format I want to use for numbering with the `format` attribute. With multi-level numbering, you set the `format` attribute to indicate the numbering you want to use for various levels, as in "1.1.1." to number the top-level nodes 1., 2., and so on, the next level down 1.1., 1.2., and so on, and the next level down 1.2.1., 1.2.2., and so on. Here's what the stylesheet in this example looks like:

Listing 5.13 **Multiple-Level Numbering**

```
<?xml version="1.0"?>
<xsl:stylesheet version="1.0"
xmlns:xsl="http://www.w3.org/1999/XSL/Transform">
<xsl:output method="xml"/>

  <xsl:template match="node()">
    <xsl:copy>
      <xsl:number format="1.1.1. " level="multiple" count="*"/>
      <xsl:apply-templates select="node()"/>
    </xsl:copy>
  </xsl:template>

</xsl:stylesheet>
```

And here's the result of transforming planets.xml into a new XML document with all element levels numbered to show the document hierarchy:

```
<?xml version="1.0" encoding="utf-8"?>
<?xml-stylesheet type="text/xml" href="planets.xsl"?>
<PLANETS>1.

    <PLANET>1.1.
        <NAME>1.1.1. Mercury</NAME>
        <MASS>1.1.2. .0553</MASS>
        <DAY>1.1.3. 58.65</DAY>
        <RADIUS>1.1.4. 1516</RADIUS>
        <DENSITY>1.1.5. .983</DENSITY>
        <DISTANCE>1.1.6. 43.4</DISTANCE><!--At perihelion-->
    </PLANET>

    <PLANET>1.2.
        <NAME>1.2.1. Venus</NAME>
        <MASS>1.2.2. .815</MASS>
        <DAY>1.2.3. 116.75</DAY>
        <RADIUS>1.2.4. 3716</RADIUS>
        <DENSITY>1.2.5. .943</DENSITY>
        <DISTANCE>1.2.6. 66.8</DISTANCE><!--At perihelion-->
    </PLANET>

    <PLANET>1.3.
        <NAME>1.3.1. Earth</NAME>
        <MASS>1.3.2. 1</MASS>
        <DAY>1.3.3. 1</DAY>
        <RADIUS>1.3.4. 2107</RADIUS>
        <DENSITY>1.3.5. 1</DENSITY>
        <DISTANCE>1.3.6. 128.4</DISTANCE><!--At perihelion-->
    </PLANET>

</PLANETS>
```

That completes this look at document numbering; the final topic in this chapter is XSLT *extensibility*, and I'll turn to that now.

XSLT Extensibility

Despite the apparent complexity of XSLT, it's limited in many ways compared to programming languages, and one of the first things that XSLT processors did was to start introducing *extensions* to XSLT. For example, Saxon introduced the `<saxon:while>` element that implements a programming-style `while` loop in XSLT. Xalan introduced elements such as `<redirect:write>` to support multiple output documents. And Microsoft's

MSXML3 processor enables you to write functions in scripting languages such as JavaScript and then call them to execute the code in them.

One can imagine W3C viewing this trend with trepidation. Their job, after all, is to standardize how languages such as XSLT work, but manufacturers were introducing their own, non-standard extensions in the form of new elements and functions all the time. On the other hand, W3C couldn't anticipate all new elements and functions, so instead they started working on standardizing ways of connecting extension functions and elements to XSLT. Extensions must use some general rules:

- Extensions must use namespaces to avoid clashes with XSL elements.
- It must be possible for an XSLT processor to realize where an extension has been used, and fail in a well-defined way if the extension fails.
- It must be possible for a stylesheet to test whether a certain extension is available and fall back if not.

Upcoming in XSLT 2.0

It's easy to imagine W3C chafing even under these general rules, and in fact, one of the possibilities that the XSLT 2.0 committee is going to investigate is whether to implement all extensions in "pure" XSLT, without resorting to any external programming languages at all.

The W3C has allowed two kinds of extensions, mostly because they were already *de facto*: extension functions and extension elements. Although they are popular, this is a somewhat gray area, because different manufacturers have introduced different ways of implementing these kinds of extensions.

In XSLT 1.0, you can test whether an extension function is available with the `function-available` function, and you can test whether an extension element is available with the `element-available` function.

XSLT 2.0 is going to define a standard mechanism for connecting XSLT to extension elements, and it presumably will be much more elaborate than what's available now.

It's time to see all this in action. I'm going to take a look at both extension functions and extension elements in the following sections, starting with extension functions.

The EXSLT Initiative

Now that the extension mechanisms in the XSLT 1.1 working draft have been deferred to XSLT 2.0, various other efforts to standardize XSLT extensions have become more important. For example, take a look at EXSLT at `www.exslt.org`. EXSLT is an open community initiative working to standardize extensions to XSLT.

Extension Functions

In XSLT 1.0, W3C defined the way to differentiate extension functions from built-in functions by requiring that namespace-qualified names be used to reference extension functions, as in `starpowder:calculate()`. XSLT 1.0 also provided the `function-available()` function to test for the availability of a function by name.

The XSLT 1.1 working draft put some additional restrictions on extension functions:

- Extension functions *must* work like built-in functions.
- Language bindings *must* be provided for Java and ECMAScript.
- It *must* be *possible* to extend the mechanism naturally to support other languages in the future.
- A processor *should not* be *required* to implement the portable extension function binding for any particular language.
- A processor that implements extension functions for any language whose binding is provided by the XSLT specification *must* conform for those languages.
- Extension function implementations *must* be allowed both inline as well as externally.
- It *must* be possible to pass arguments of all XPath datatypes to extension functions.
- It *must* be possible for extension functions to return all XPath datatypes as a result.
- Extension functions *must* be able to construct and return node-sets of XML fragments.
- It *must* be possible to include or import extension functions from another stylesheet.
- A processor *should* fail with error if selection of extension function implementation is ambiguous.
- A processor *should* convert arguments in a way consistent with the built-in functions.
- It *should* be possible to return an object of *any* host-language type from the extension function.
- It *should* be possible to pass an object of *any* host-language type to an extension function.
- It *should* be possible to support invoking overloaded functions in Java.

Until recently, XSLT processors were free to define the way they implemented extension functions. For example, in Saxon and Xalan, you can run Java code directly if you define a namespace that specifies a Java class as the final part of its URI, as I do here, where I define a `Date` namespace that corresponds to the Java `Date` class:

```
<?xml version="1.0"?>
<xsl:stylesheet version="1.0"
xmlns:xsl="http://www.w3.org/1999/XSL/Transform"
xmlns:Date="http://www.saxon.com/java/java.util.Date">
        .
        .
        .
```

Now I can use Java `Date` functions such as `toString` and `new` to embed the current date in an `<H1>` HTML header in the output as follows:

Listing 5.14 **Using the Java *Date* Function**

```
<?xml version="1.0"?>
<xsl:stylesheet version="1.0"
xmlns:xsl="http://www.w3.org/1999/XSL/Transform"
xmlns:Date="http://www.saxon.com/java/java.util.Date">

    <xsl:template match="/PLANETS">
        <HTML>
            <HEAD>
                <TITLE>
                    The Planets Table
                </TITLE>
            </HEAD>
            <BODY>
                <H1>
                    The Planets Table
                </H1>
                <BR/>
                <H1>
                    <xsl:value-of select="Date:toString(Date:new())"/>
                </H1>
                <TABLE BORDER="2">
                    <TD>Name</TD>
                    <TD>Mass</TD>
                    <TD>Radius</TD>
                    <TD>Day</TD>
                    <xsl:apply-templates/>
                </TABLE>
            </BODY>
        </HTML>
```

continues ▸

Listing 5.14 **Continued**

```
    </xsl:template>

    <xsl:template match="PLANET">
       <TR>
          <TD><xsl:value-of select="NAME"/></TD>
          <TD><xsl:apply-templates select="MASS"/></TD>
          <TD><xsl:apply-templates select="RADIUS"/></TD>
          <TD><xsl:apply-templates select="DAY"/></TD>
       </TR>
   </xsl:template>

    <xsl:template match="MASS">
        <xsl:value-of select="."/>
    </xsl:template>

    <xsl:template match="RADIUS">
        <xsl:value-of select="."/>
    </xsl:template>

    <xsl:template match="DAY">
        <xsl:value-of select="."/>
    </xsl:template>

</xsl:stylesheet>
```

You can see the results of this stylesheet in Figure 5.3.

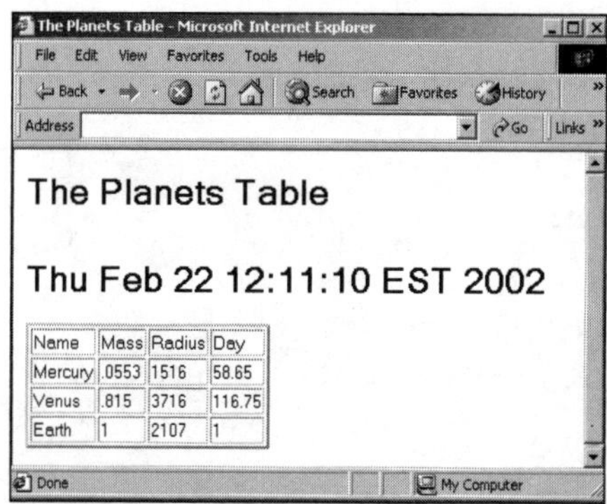

Figure 5.3 Using an extension function.

This certainly works, and it's a great way to interface Java to XSLT. However, the XSLT 1.1 working draft introduced the `<xsl:script>` element, and it's likely it will be a part of XSLT 2.0 as well.

The *<xsl:script>* Element

The `<xsl:script>` element was defined in the XSLT 1.1 working draft, and it gives you a well-defined way to connect extension functions to XSLT stylesheets. This element is a top-level element, and has the following attributes:

- `implements-prefix` (optional). Sets the name of the extension function namespace this element implements. Set to an NCNAME.
- `language` (optional). Sets the language used by the extension function. Set to "ecmascript" (the standardized form of JavaScript), "javascript", "java", or a QNAME that is not an NCNAME.
- `src` (optional). Provides the URI where the extension function is implemented. For example, this can be a Java class.
- `archive` (optional). Specifies archives that should be loaded before running the extension function, if any. Set to a whitespace-separated list of URIs.

This element contains character data (Microsoft uses a CDATA section) that implements the extension function or functions.

So how do you connect a function defined in an `<xsl:script>` element to your XSLT stylesheet? You first create the `<xsl:script>` element as a top-level element in your stylesheet, then place the functions you want to define in that element. Here's an example where I'm defining two JavaScript functions, `makeMoney` and `makeMoreMoney`, in an `<xsl:script>` element that implements the extension namespace "starpowder":

```
<xsl:script implements-prefix="starpowder" language="javascript">
    function makeMoney(e)
    {
    .
    .
    .
    }

    function makeMoreMoney(e)
    {
    .
    .
    .
    }
</xsl:script>
```

It can also be a good idea, depending on your XSLT processor, to enclose scripts like this in a CDATA section:

```
<xsl:script implements-prefix="starpowder" language="javascript">
    <![CDATA[
        function makeMoney(e)
        {
        .
        .
        .
        }

    function makeMoreMoney(e)
    {
    .
    .
    .
    }
    ]]>
</xsl:script>
```

Now you can use the “starpowder” namespace to indicate that you’re calling an extension function, as follows:

```
<CASH>
    <xsl:value-of select="starpowder:makeMoney(1000000)"/>
</CASH>
```

That’s all it takes (if your XSLT processor is compliant). If you want to specify Java class rather than a script, you can use the `src` attribute to specify the Java class you want to use:

```
<xsl:script implements-prefix="starpowder" src="java:com.MakeMoney"
language="java">
</xsl:script>
```

Working with External Resources

You can also use the `src` attribute if you have an archive of JavaScript routines, as in this example: src="archives.js".

No XSLT processor that I know of implements the `<xsl:script>` element yet except the Microsoft MSXML3 processor. You can find information on how you can use scripts to write extension functions for use in the Internet Explorer on the Microsoft site (currently, that page is at `http://msdn.microsoft.com/xml/xslguide/script-overview.asp`, but Microsoft seems to reorganize its site every two days or so).

The next example shows how to use `<xsl:script>` with the Internet Explorer. In this example, I write a JavaScript function to convert the planetary radius measurements in planets.xml, which are in miles, to kilometers, and display those measurements in kilometers.

As discussed in "Using Internet Explorer to Transform XML Documents," in Chapter 2, you need to make some modifications to browse an XML document that uses an XSL stylesheet in Internet Explorer version 5.5 or earlier (unless you've installed the newest MSXML parser or use version 6.0, just out, except that you must still use "text/xsl"). To start, use the MIME type "text/xsl", not "text/xml", for an XSL stylesheet. I'll also give the URI for the stylesheet, kilometers.xsl, as follows:

Listing 5.15 **planets.xml Set to Use kilometers.xsl in Internet Explorer**

```
<?xml version="1.0"?>
<?xml-stylesheet type="text/xsl" href="kilometers.xsl"?>
<PLANETS>

    <PLANET>
        <NAME>Mercury</NAME>
        <MASS UNITS="(Earth = 1)">.0553</MASS>
        <DAY UNITS="days">58.65</DAY>
        <RADIUS UNITS="miles">1516</RADIUS>
        <DENSITY UNITS="(Earth = 1)">.983</DENSITY>
        <DISTANCE UNITS="million miles">43.4</DISTANCE><!--At perihelion-->
    </PLANET>

    <PLANET>
        <NAME>Venus</NAME>
        <MASS UNITS="(Earth = 1)">.815</MASS>
        <DAY UNITS="days">116.75</DAY>
        <RADIUS UNITS="miles">3716</RADIUS>
        <DENSITY UNITS="(Earth = 1)">.943</DENSITY>
        <DISTANCE UNITS="million miles">66.8</DISTANCE><!--At perihelion-->
    </PLANET>
        .
        .
        .
```

To convert for use in IE 5.5 or earlier in the stylesheet, kilometers.xsl, I use the XSL namespace that the IE uses, and add the `<xsl:script>` element, indicating that the scripts I'll write will be in JavaScript. Note, however, that the Internet Explorer's `<xsl:script>` element does not support the `implements-prefix` attribute, so I can't connect the functions I define to a namespace:

```
<xsl:stylesheet xmlns:xsl="http://www.w3.org/TR/WD-xsl">

    <xsl:script language="javascript">
        .
        .
        .
```

```
    </xsl:script>
        .
        .
        .
```

The Internet Explorer requires that you enclose your code in a CDATA section. Here, I define the function `milesToKilometers`. This function is passed a node, and reads the text in the node with the text property, then uses the JavaScript `parseInt` function to convert the text to a number of miles. I multiply the number of miles by 1.6 to convert miles to kilometers, and return that result:

```
<xsl:stylesheet xmlns:xsl="http://www.w3.org/TR/WD-xsl">

    <xsl:script language="javascript">
        <![CDATA[

            function milesToKilometers(e)
            {
                miles = parseInt(e.text);
                return miles * 1.6;
            }

        ]]>
    </xsl:script>
        .
        .
        .
```

Because you can't associate a namespace with an extension function in the Internet Explorer yet, you use the Microsoft-only element `<xsl:eval>` to call extension functions. Here's how that looks in the stylesheet kilometers.xsl, where I'm passing the `milesToKilometers` function the current `<RADIUS>` node so it will convert miles to kilometers. Because IE 5.5 or earlier does not support default rules (although version 6.0—just out as this book goes to press—does, so you won't have to make this change), I can provide a rule for the root node as well for IE 5.5 or earlier:

Listing 5.16 **kilometers.xsl**

```
<xsl:stylesheet xmlns:xsl="http://www.w3.org/TR/WD-xsl">

    <xsl:script language="javascript">
        <![CDATA[

            function milesToKilometers(e)
            {
                miles = parseInt(e.text);
                return miles * 1.6;
            }
```

```
    ]]>
  </xsl:script>

  <xsl:template match="/">
      <HTML>
          <HEAD>
              <TITLE>
                  The Planets Table
              </TITLE>
          </HEAD>
          <BODY>
              <H1>
                  The Planets Table
              </H1>
              <TABLE BORDER="2">
                  <TR>
                      <TD>Name</TD>
                      <TD>Mass</TD>
                      <TD>Radius</TD>
                      <TD>Day</TD>
                  </TR>
                  <xsl:apply-templates/>
              </TABLE>
          </BODY>
      </HTML>
  </xsl:template>

  <xsl:template match="PLANETS">
      <xsl:apply-templates/>
  </xsl:template>

  <xsl:template match="PLANET">
     <TR>
        <TD><xsl:value-of select="NAME"/></TD>
        <TD><xsl:value-of select="MASS"/></TD>
        <TD><xsl:apply-templates match="RADIUS"/></TD>
        <TD><xsl:value-of select="DAY"/></TD>
     </TR>
 </xsl:template>

  <xsl:template match="RADIUS">
      <xsl:eval>milesToKilometers(this)</xsl:eval>
  </xsl:template>

</xsl:stylesheet>
```

And that's it; you can see the results of this transformation in Figure 5.4.

In time, vendors will provide more and more built-in extension functions. How can you determine whether a given extension function is available? You can use the `function-available` function.

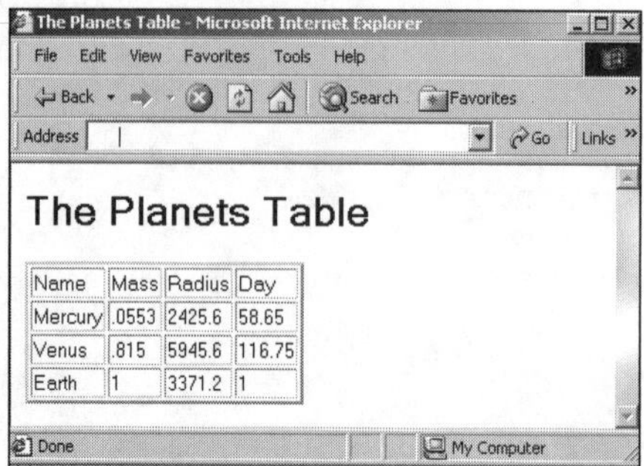

Figure 5.4 Using an extension function in the Internet Explorer.

Using the *function-available* Function

You use the XSLT 1.0 function named `function-available` to test whether a function is available. In the following example I want to use the extension function `starpowder:calculate` to do some math, and if it's not available, I send the text "Sorry, can't do math today." to the result document (although you could, of course, also quit processing and display an error message with the `<xsl:message>` element):

```
<xsl:choose xmlns:starpowder="http://www.starpowder.com">
    <xsl:when test="function-available('starpowder:calculate')">
        <xsl:value-of select="starpowder:calculate('2+2')"/>
    </xsl:when>
    <xsl:otherwise>
        <xsl:text>Sorry, can't do math today.</xsl:text>
    </xsl:otherwise>
</xsl:choose>
```

External Objects

The support for extension functions in the XSLT 1.1 working draft introduced a new data type. This new data type is called an *external object*. An XSLT variable, which is covered in Chapter 9, may be assigned an external object rather than one of the four XPath data-types supported in XSLT (string, number, Boolean, node set). An external object represents an object that is created by an external programming language and returned by an extension function and that is not convertible to one of the four XPath data types. The data type "external object" was added to XSLT to give you a safe "wrapper" for such data. No one implements external objects yet, but that's coming.

Extension Elements

Extension elements are just what they sound like—elements that have been added to XSLT by the user or vendor. The XSLT 1.1 working draft set up some rules for extension elements, and XSLT 2.0 is supposed to go into a lot more depth on them. In the XSLT 1.1 working draft, the rules were that extension elements must be elements that are user-defined or vendor-defined, but are not top-level elements. And they must belong to a namespace that has been defined as an extension namespace.

You define an extension namespace by using the `extension-element-prefixes` attribute in an `<xsl:stylesheet>` element or an `xsl:extension-element-prefixes` attribute in a literal result element or extension element.

Here's an example. Xalan enables you to create multiple output documents with its `<redirect:write>` extension element. To use this extension element, I can add a `file` attribute to the document element in planets.xml, giving the name of a file to which output should be sent, redirected.xml:

```
<?xml version="1.0"?>
<?xml-stylesheet type="text/xml" href="planets.xsl"?>
<PLANETS file="redirected.xml">

    <PLANET>
        <NAME>Mercury</NAME>
        <MASS UNITS="(Earth = 1)">.0553</MASS>
        <DAY UNITS="days">58.65</DAY>
        <RADIUS UNITS="miles">1516</RADIUS>
        <DENSITY UNITS="(Earth = 1)">.983</DENSITY>
        <DISTANCE UNITS="million miles">43.4</DISTANCE><!--At perihelion-->
    </PLANET>
        .
        .
        .
```

Now, in the XSLT stylesheet, which I'll call redirect.xsl, I define the "redirect" namespace so that it corresponds to the Java class that supports it in Xalan: org.apache.xalan.lib.Redirect. I'll also set the `extension-element-prefixes` attribute of `<xsl:stylesheet>` to the "redirect" namespace:

```
<xsl:stylesheet xmlns:xsl="http://www.w3.org/1999/XSL/Transform"
    version="1.0"
    xmlns:lxslt="http://xml.apache.org/xslt"
```

```
    xmlns:redirect="org.apache.xalan.lib.Redirect"
    extension-element-prefixes="redirect">
        .
        .
        .
```

At this point, I'm free to use the `<redirect:write>` extension element to write output to a new file (as opposed to the one specified on the command line). For example, to send the formatted contents of the `<PLANETS>` element to another file, I can get the filename to create from the `file` attribute of <PLANETS> and write to that new file as follows:

```
<xsl:stylesheet xmlns:xsl="http://www.w3.org/1999/XSL/Transform"
    version="1.0"
    xmlns:lxslt="http://xml.apache.org/xslt"
    xmlns:redirect="org.apache.xalan.lib.Redirect"
    extension-element-prefixes="redirect">

  <lxslt:component prefix="redirect" elements="write open close" functions="">
    <lxslt:script lang="javaclass" src="org.apache.xalan.lib.Redirect"/>
  </lxslt:component>

  <xsl:output method="xml"/>

  <xsl:template match="/">
      <xsl:apply-templates/>
  </xsl:template>

  <xsl:template match="PLANETS">
    <redirect:write select="@file">
      <PLANETS>
        <xsl:apply-templates/>
      </PLANETS>
    </redirect:write>
  </xsl:template>

  <xsl:template match="@*|node()">
    <xsl:copy>
      <xsl:apply-templates select="@*|node()"/>
    </xsl:copy>
  </xsl:template>

</xsl:stylesheet>
```

That's all it takes; here's how that might look, using Xalan in Windows:

```
C:planets>java org.apache.xalan.xslt.Process -IN planets.xml
➥-XSL redirect.xsl -OUT new.xml
```

This creates the file redirected.xml, which looks like this:

```
<?xml version="1.0" encoding="UTF-8"?>
<PLANETS>

    <PLANET>
        <NAME>Mercury</NAME>
        <MASS UNITS="(Earth = 1)">.0553</MASS>
        <DAY UNITS="days">58.65</DAY>
        <RADIUS UNITS="miles">1516</RADIUS>
        <DENSITY UNITS="(Earth = 1)">.983</DENSITY>
        <DISTANCE UNITS="million miles">43.4</DISTANCE>
    </PLANET>

    <PLANET>
        <NAME>Venus</NAME>
        <MASS UNITS="(Earth = 1)">.815</MASS>
        <DAY UNITS="days">116.75</DAY>
        <RADIUS UNITS="miles">3716</RADIUS>
        <DENSITY UNITS="(Earth = 1)">.943</DENSITY>
        <DISTANCE UNITS="million miles">66.8</DISTANCE>
    </PLANET>
        .
        .
        .
```

Using the *element-available* Function

You can use the XSLT 1.0 function `element-available` to test whether an element is available. Here's an example where I check for an element named `<starpowder:calculate>`:

```
<xsl:choose xmlns:starpowder="http://www.starpowder.com">
    <xsl:when test="element-available('starpowder:calculate')">
        <starpowder:calculate xsl:extension-element-prefixes="starpowder"/>
    </xsl:when>
    <xsl:otherwise>
        <xsl:text>Sorry, can't do math today.</xsl:text>
    </xsl:otherwise>
</xsl:choose>
```

There's another way to handle the case where an extension element isn't available: You can use the `<xsl:fallback>` element.

The *<xsl:fallback>* Element

You use the XSLT 1.0 `<xsl:fallback>` element to indicate what to do if an extension element is not available. This element is enclosed in the extension element and is used if the extension element isn't available.

The <xsl:fallback> element has no attributes, and encloses a template body.

In the following example, I create a fallback element inside the <redirect:write> element from the previous example. The <xsl:fallback> element will terminate processing with a message if the <redirect:write> element isn't available:

```
<xsl:stylesheet xmlns:xsl="http://www.w3.org/1999/XSL/Transform"
    version="1.0"
    xmlns:lxslt="http://xml.apache.org/xslt"
    xmlns:redirect="org.apache.xalan.lib.Redirect"
    extension-element-prefixes="redirect">

  <lxslt:component prefix="redirect" elements="write open close" functions="">
    <lxslt:script lang="javaclass" src="org.apache.xalan.lib.Redirect"/>
  </lxslt:component>

  <xsl:output method="xml"/>

  <xsl:template match="/">
      <xsl:apply-templates/>
  </xsl:template>

  <xsl:template match="PLANETS">
    <redirect:write select="@file">
      <PLANETS>
        <xsl:apply-templates/>
      </PLANETS>
      <xsl:fallback>
          <xsl:message terminate="yes">
              <xsl:text>Could not create multiple output documents.</xsl:text>
          </xsl:message>
      </xsl:fallback>
    </redirect:write>
  </xsl:template>

  <xsl:template match="@*|node()">
    <xsl:copy>
      <xsl:apply-templates select="@*|node()"/>
    </xsl:copy>
  </xsl:template>

</xsl:stylesheet>
```

And that's it for this introduction to working with the data in XML documents. In the next chapter, I'll dig deeper into this topic to examine how to modify document contents, as well as how to create new elements, attributes, and processing instructions.

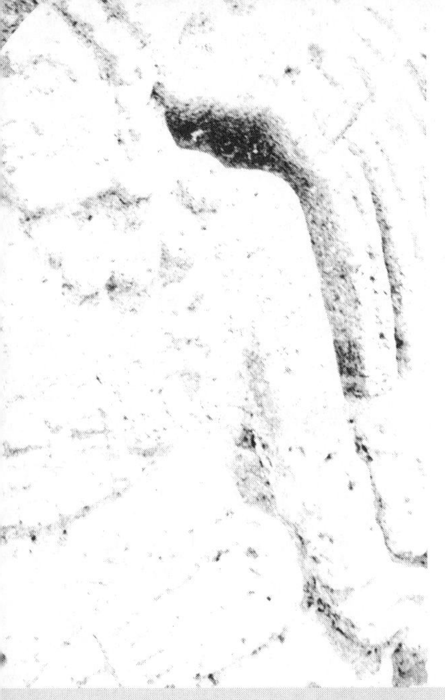

6

Transforming from XML to XML, HTML, XHTML, RTF, and Modifying Document Content

YOUR COMPANY'S ONLINE MARKETING SITE IS POWERED by XML-based Commerce One software, which uses the Java Message Service (JMS) for secure communications over the Internet. You've been so successful that you've just taken over your rival. Unfortunately, your former rival uses another XML-based product for its online marketing site, RosettaNet. How can you translate between a Commerce One xCBL purchase order written in XML into a RosettaNet purchase order—also written in XML, but using an entirely different dialect?

You use XSLT, of course. XML-to-XML transformations like this are becoming more and more common. In fact, more and more companies are using JMS for secure communications over the Internet, and because JMS runs in Java, it's perfect to interface to Java-based XSLT processors such as Xalan or Saxon.

You've been transforming XML to HTML, XML, and plain text already in this book, but this chapter looks at the process in more depth. You'll also see a new type of transformation in this chapter: XML to JavaScript. In Chapter 10, you'll see XML-to-SQL-based database transformations, and in Chapter 11, you'll also see XML-to-XSL-FO transformations.

A great deal of XSLT is not just about substituting one element for another, but about completely reorganizing an XML document's content.

For example, you might want to reorganize planets.xml in terms of planet density, using XSLT to create a new XML document this way:

```
<?xml version="1.0" encoding="UTF-8"?>
<DATA>

    <DENSITY>
        <VALUE>.983</VALUE>
        <NAME>Mercury</NAME>
        <MASS>.0553</MASS>
        <DAY>58.65</DAY>
        <RADIUS>1516</RADIUS>
    </DENSITY>

    <DENSITY>
        <VALUE>.943</VALUE>
        <NAME>Venus</NAME>
        <MASS>.815</MASS>
        <DAY>116.75</DAY>
        <RADIUS>3716</RADIUS>
    </DENSITY>

    <DENSITY>
        <VALUE>1</VALUE>
        <NAME>Earth</NAME>
        <MASS>1</MASS>
        <DAY>1</DAY>
        <RADIUS>2107</RADIUS>
    </DENSITY>

</DATA>
```

In fact, this chapter includes a transformation that changes the content in planets.xml completely, leaving only a little HTML and some JavaScript to display a few buttons in a Web browser.

So far in this book, you've only created new elements using literal result elements—that is, by treating the new elements as text and embedding them into a stylesheet. But as you'll see in this chapter, it's not always possible to know the names of the new elements you want to create. You can cobble together elements created on the fly, treating them as raw text, but that's fairly crude because it treats markup as text. In this chapter, you'll start using the XSLT `<xsl:element>`, `<xsl:attribute>`, `<xsl:processing-instruction>`, and `<xsl:comment>` elements to create new elements, attributes, processing instructions, and comments at run time. A thorough knowledge of these elements is essential when you start reorganizing XML content.

You'll also see how to use XSLT *modes* for multiple transformation passes on a document, and how to apply only one of multiple matching templates.

Much of this chapter explores the possibilities of the `<xsl:output>` element, and I'll start with that element to provide some overview.

The *<xsl:output>* Element

You first saw the `<xsl:output>` element in Chapter 2, and you use this element primarily to set the type of the result document. That type can determine, for example, whether the XSLT processor will write the XML processing instruction, `<?xml version="1.0"?>`, at the beginning of the document, and it can determine the MIME type (such as "text/xml" or "text/html") of documents sent back from an XSLT processor on a Web server to a browser. In addition, if you set the output type to HTML, most XSLT processors recognize that not all elements in HTML need closing as well as opening tags, and so on.

The following list includes the attributes of `<xsl-output>`:

- `cdata-section-elements` (optional). Sets the names of those elements whose content should be output as CDATA sections. Set to a whitespace-separated list of QNames.
- `doctype-public` (optional). Specifies the public identifier to be used in the <!DOCTYPE> declaration in the output. Set to a string value.
- `doctype-system` (optional). Specifies the system identifier to be used in the <!DOCTYPE> declaration in the output. Set to a string value.
- `encoding` (optional). Sets the character encoding. Set to a string value.
- `indent` (optional). Specifies whether the output should be indented to show its nesting structure. Set to "yes" or "no".
- `media-type` (optional). Sets the MIME type of the output. Set to a string value.
- `method` (optional). Sets the output format. Set to "xml", "html", "text", or a valid QName.
- `omit-xml-declaration` (optional) Specifies whether the XML declaration should be included in the output. Set to "yes" or "no".
- `standalone` (optional). Specifies whether an XML standalone declaration should be included in the output and sets its value if so. Set to "yes" or "no".
- `version` (optional). Sets the version of the output. Set to a valid NMToken.

The most-used attribute of this element is `method`, because that's what you set to the output tree type you want. Officially, the default output method is HTML if all three of the following conditions are satisfied:

- The root node of the result tree has an element child.
- The name of the document element of the result tree has a local part "html" (in any combination of upper- and lowercase) and a null namespace URI.
- Any text nodes before the first element child of the root node contain only whitespace characters.

If all three of these conditions are met, then the output method is set to HTML by default. Otherwise, the default output method is XML.

You shouldn't rely on default settings for `method`, however, but rather assign this attribute a value. The three common settings for the `method` attribute are "html", "xml", and "text", and I'll take a look at them in the following sections.

Output Method: HTML

The XSLT processor is supposed to take certain actions if the output method is HTML. For example, for this output method, the `version` attribute indicates the version of the HTML. The default value is 4.0.

This method should not add an end-tag for empty elements. (For HTML 4.0, the empty elements are `<AREA>`, `<BASE>`, `<BASEFONT>`, `<BR>`, `<COL>`, `<FRAME>`, `<HR>`, `<IMG>`, `<INPUT>`, `<ISINDEX>`, `<LINK>`, `<META>`, and `<PARAM>`.) The HTML output method should recognize the names of HTML elements regardless of case.

Also, according to W3C, the HTML output method should not add escaping for the content of `<SCRIPT>` or `<STYLE>` elements. For example, the following literal result element:

```
<SCRIPT>
    if (x &lt; y) {...}
</SCRIPT>
```

or this one, which uses a CDATA section:

```
<SCRIPT>
    <![CDATA[if (x < y) {...}]]>
</SCRIPT>
```

should be transformed to:

```
<SCRIPT>
    if (x < y) {...}
</SCRIPT>
```

The HTML output method should also not escape "<" characters that appear in attribute values.

When you set the output method to HTML, the processor may pay attention to the `indent` attribute. If this attribute has the value "yes", then the XSLT processor can add (or remove) whitespace to indent the result, as long as it doesn't affect how a browser would display the result document. The default value is "yes" for the HTML output method.

As you'd expect, the HTML output method should terminate processing instructions with > rather than ?>. And it should support standalone attributes, as HTML does. For example, this tag:

```
<TD NOWRAP="NOWRAP">
```

should be transformed to:

```
<TD NOWRAP>
```

In addition, you can set the `media-type` attribute for this method; default value is "text/html". The HTML method should not escape a & character that appears in an attribute value immediately followed by a curly brace. Also, the `encoding` attribute specifies the encoding to be used. If there is a `<HEAD>` element, this output method should add a `<META>` element right after the `<HEAD>` tag specifying the character encoding as follows:

```
<HEAD>
    <META http-equiv="Content-Type" content="text/html; charset=utf-8">
        .
        .
        .
```

You can also use the `doctype-public` or `doctype-system` attributes to output a document type declaration immediately before the first element, as you'll see when we transform XML to XHTML.

Those are the rules for HTML output. Here's an example of an XML to HTML example with a little pizzazz. In this case, the stylesheet will actually write JavaScript code to show how to use XSLT to create JavaScript. In particular, we'll read in planets.xml and create a new HTML document that displays three buttons, each with the name of one of the three planets in planets.xml. When the user clicks a button, the page will display the corresponding planet's mass.

All you need is two `<xsl:for-each>` elements, one to loop over all three planets and create an HTML button for each, and one to loop over the planets and create a JavaScript function for each. I'll use the planet's name as the name of the corresponding JavaScript function; when that function is called, it'll display the corresponding planet's mass. Note that to build the required JavaScript, all you have to do is to use the `<xsl:value-of>` element to get the names and masses of the planets. I'm also using two new XSLT elements you'll see later in this chapter—`<xsl:element>` and `<xsl:attribute-set>`—to create a new element and give it a set of attributes:

Listing 6.1 A Transformation to JavaScript

```
<?xml version="1.0"?>
<xsl:stylesheet version="1.0"
xmlns:xsl="http://www.w3.org/1999/XSL/Transform">
<xsl:output method="html"/>

    <xsl:template match="/PLANETS">
<HTML>

    <HEAD>
        <TITLE>
            The Mass Page
         </TITLE>

        <SCRIPT LANGUAGE='javascript'>

        <xsl:for-each select="PLANET">
        <xsl:text>
            function </xsl:text><xsl:value-of select="NAME"/><xsl:text>()
            {
                display.innerHTML = 'The mass of </xsl:text>
                <xsl:value-of select="NAME"/>
                <xsl:text> equals </xsl:text>
                <xsl:value-of select="MASS"/>
                <xsl:text> Earth masses.'</xsl:text>
            }
        </xsl:for-each>

        </SCRIPT>
     </HEAD>

    <BODY>
        <CENTER>
            <H1>The Mass Page</H1>
        </CENTER>
        <xsl:for-each select="PLANET">
            <P/>
            <xsl:element name="input" use-attribute-sets="attribs"/>
        </xsl:for-each>
        <P/>
        <P/>
        <DIV ID='display'></DIV>
    </BODY>

</HTML>
    </xsl:template>

    <xsl:attribute-set name="attribs">
    <xsl:attribute name="type">BUTTON</xsl:attribute>
```

```
    <xsl:attribute name="value"><xsl:value-of select="NAME"/></xsl:attribute>
    <xsl:attribute name="onclick"><xsl:value-of select="NAME"/>()</xsl:attribute>
    </xsl:attribute-set>

</xsl:stylesheet>
```

Here's the result, including a `<SCRIPT>` element for the new JavaScript:

Listing 6.2 **JavaScript-Enabled Result Document**

```
<HTML>
    <HEAD>
        <TITLE>
            The Mass Page
        </TITLE>

        <SCRIPT LANGUAGE="javascript">
            function Mercury()
            {
display.innerHTML =
                    'The mass of Mercury equals .0553 Earth masses.'
            }

            function Venus()
            {
                display.innerHTML = 'The mass of Venus equals .815 Earth masses.'
            }

            function Earth()
            {
                display.innerHTML = 'The mass of Earth equals 1 Earth masses.'
            }
        </SCRIPT>

    </HEAD>

    <BODY>
        <CENTER>
            <H1>The Mass Page</H1>
        </CENTER>

        <P></P>
        <input type="BUTTON" value="Mercury" onclick="Mercury()">
        <P></P>
        <input type="BUTTON" value="Venus" onclick="Venus()">
        <P></P>
        <input type="BUTTON" value="Earth" onclick="Earth()">
```

continues ▸

Listing 6.2 **Continued**

```
        <P></P>
        <P></P>
        <DIV ID="display"></DIV>

    </BODY>
</HTML>
```

As you can see, I've written JavaScript using XSLT to loop over the various planets. You can see this HTML document in Figure 6.1; when the user clicks a button, the corresponding planet's mass is displayed.

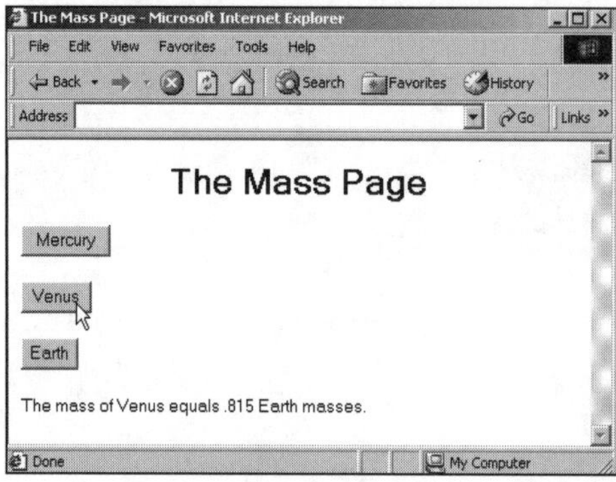

Figure 6.1 Transforming XML into HTML with JavaScript.

Output Method: XML

Formally, when you use the XML output method, the XSLT processor creates a well-formed XML external general parsed entity. If the root node of the result tree has a single element node child and no text node children, then the entity should also be a well-formed XML document entity.

Using the XML output method, the `version` attribute sets the version of XML to be used for output. Note that if the XSLT processor does not support this version of XML, it is supposed to use a version of XML that it does support. The default value is 1.0.

The `encoding` attribute sets the encoding to use for the result document. XSLT processors are required to support at least the values "UTF-8" and "UTF-16" here. For other values, if the XSLT processor does not support the specified encoding it may signal an error; if it does not signal an error it should use UTF-8 or UTF-16 instead. The XSLT processor must not use an encoding that has not been approved by the W3C (in `www.w3.org/TR/REC-xml`). If no encoding attribute is specified, then the XSLT processor should default to "UTF-8" or "UTF-16".

Handling Unknown Characters

If the result document contains a character that cannot be represented in the encoding that the XSLT processor is using for output, then the character may be output as a character reference. If that's not possible, the XSLT processor should generate an error.

As with the HTML output method, if the `indent` attribute is set to "yes", then the XML output method may add or remove whitespace in addition to the whitespace in the result tree in order to indent the result nicely. The default value is "no". Note that if the whitespace is stripped, the resulting XML document's infoset should be the same as if whitespace had never been added or removed to indent the document.

Indenting Mixed-Content Documents

It's usually not a good idea to set indent to "yes" with XML documents that include elements with mixed content, because that confuses the XSLT processor.

You can use the `cdata-section-elements` attribute to specify a whitespace-separated list of element names whose content should be treated as CDATA sections. For instance, if you set the `cdata-section-elements` attribute to "DATA":

```
<xsl:output cdata-section-elements="DATA"/>
```

then this literal result element:

```
<DATA>&lt;DOCUMENT></DATA>
```

would be transformed into:

```
<DATA><![CDATA[<DOCUMENT>]]></DATA>
```

In addition, the XML output method should output an XML declaration in the result document unless the `omit-xml-declaration` attribute has been set to "yes". In general, the XML declaration that is put into the result document usually includes the XML version (which is mandatory) and encoding information (although technically, encoding information is optional in XML documents). If the `standalone` attribute is specified, the result document should include a standalone document declaration with the same value as the value of the `standalone` attribute.

If you use the `doctype-system` attribute, the XSLT processor should create a document type declaration just before the first element. In this case, the name following <!DOCTYPE is the name of the root element. Note that if you also use the `doctype-public` attribute, the XSLT processor outputs "PUBLIC", followed by the public identifier and then the system identifier. If you don't use the `doctype-public` attribute, then it should output "SYSTEM", followed by the system identifier. Theoretically, the `doctype-public` attribute should be ignored unless the `doctype-system` attribute is also specified, although that's not the way most XSLT processors seem to work. You'll see how to use both `doctype-public` and `doctype-system` in this chapter when we convert XML to XHTML.

Finally, the default value for the `media-type` attribute is "text/xml" for the XML output method.

You've already seen many XML-to-XML transformations in this book. For example, from Chapter 4, the following transformation just copies one XML document to another. Note that the output method is set to XML:

```
<?xml version="1.0"?>
<xsl:stylesheet version="1.0"
xmlns:xsl="http://www.w3.org/1999/XSL/Transform">
<xsl:output method="xml"/>

  <xsl:template match="@*|node()">
    <xsl:copy>
      <xsl:apply-templates select="@*|node()"/>
    </xsl:copy>
  </xsl:template>

</xsl:stylesheet>
```

You saw this example in the beginning of the chapter, where planets.xml was reorganized based on planet density:

```
<?xml version="1.0" encoding="UTF-8"?>
<DATA>

    <DENSITY>
        <VALUE>.983</VALUE>
        <NAME>Mercury</NAME>
        <MASS>.0553</MASS>
        <DAY>58.65</DAY>
        <RADIUS>1516</RADIUS>
```

```
    </DENSITY>

    <DENSITY>
        <VALUE>.943</VALUE>
        <NAME>Venus</NAME>
        <MASS>.815</MASS>
        <DAY>116.75</DAY>
        <RADIUS>3716</RADIUS>
    </DENSITY>

    <DENSITY>
        <VALUE>1</VALUE>
        <NAME>Earth</NAME>
        <MASS>1</MASS>
        <DAY>1</DAY>
        <RADIUS>2107</RADIUS>
    </DENSITY>

</DATA>
```

Here's the stylesheet that creates this transformation:

Listing 6.3 **Reorganizing planets.xml Based on Density**

```
<?xml version="1.0"?>
<xsl:stylesheet version="1.0"
xmlns:xsl="http://www.w3.org/1999/XSL/Transform">
<xsl:output method="xml" indent="yes"/>

    <xsl:template match="PLANETS">
        <DATA>
            <xsl:apply-templates/>
        </DATA>
    </xsl:template>

    <xsl:template match="PLANET">
        <DENSITY>
            <VALUE>
                <xsl:value-of select="DENSITY"/>
            </VALUE>
            <xsl:apply-templates/>
        </DENSITY>
    </xsl:template>

    <xsl:template match="NAME">
        <NAME>
            <xsl:value-of select="."/>
        </NAME>
    </xsl:template>
```

continues ▸

Listing 6.3 **Continued**

```
    <xsl:template match="MASS">
        <MASS>
        <xsl:value-of select="."/>
        </MASS>
    </xsl:template>

    <xsl:template match="RADIUS">
        <RADIUS>
        <xsl:value-of select="."/>
        </RADIUS>
    </xsl:template>

    <xsl:template match="DAY">
        <DAY>
        <xsl:value-of select="."/>
        </DAY>
    </xsl:template>

    <xsl:template match="DENSITY">
    </xsl:template>

    <xsl:template match="DISTANCE">
    </xsl:template>

</xsl:stylesheet>
```

You first saw the next example in Chapter 5. In this case, I just listed the planets from planets.xml, but didn't want to have the output simply say, "The first three planets are: Mercury Venus Earth", but rather, "The first three planets are: Mercury, Venus, and Earth." I used `<xsl:if>` elements to do that:

```
<?xml version="1.0"?>
<xsl:stylesheet version="1.0" xmlns:xsl="http://www.w3.org/1999/XSL/Transform">

<xsl:output method="xml"/>
<xsl:template match="PLANETS">
<DOCUMENT>
    <TITLE>
        The Planets
    </TITLE>
    <PLANETS>
        The first three planets are: <xsl:apply-templates select="PLANET"/>
    </PLANETS>
</DOCUMENT>
</xsl:template>
```

```
<xsl:template match="PLANET">
    <xsl:value-of select="NAME"/>
    <xsl:if test="position()!=last()">, </xsl:if>
    <xsl:if test="position()=last()-1">and </xsl:if>
    <xsl:if test="position()=last()">.</xsl:if>
</xsl:template>

</xsl:stylesheet>
```

And here's the result:

```
<?xml version="1.0" encoding="UTF-8"?>
<DOCUMENT>

    <TITLE>
        The Planets
    </TITLE>

    <PLANETS>
        The first three planets are: Mercury, Venus, and Earth.
    </PLANETS>

</DOCUMENT>
```

Although many books concentrate on XML-to-HTML transformations, it's important to realize that XML-to-XML transformations are becoming more and more common, which is why I'm focusing on them also.

Output Method: Text

This type of output represents pure text. In this case, the output document is simply the plain text of the document tree. That is, the XSLT processor creates the result tree by outputting the string value of every text node, without any escaping.

The default value for the `media-type` attribute is "text/plain". The `encoding` attribute sets the encoding that the XSLT processor uses to convert sequences of characters to sequences of bytes. Note that if the result document contains a character that cannot be represented in the encoding that the XSLT processor is using for output, the XSLT processor should generate an error.

The following example converts planets.xml into plain text using the text output method:

Listing 6.4 **A Transformation to Plain Text**

```
<?xml version="1.0"?>
<xsl:stylesheet version="1.0"
xmlns:xsl="http://www.w3.org/1999/XSL/Transform">

    <xsl:output method="text" indent="yes"/>

    <xsl:template match="PLANET">
          <xsl:value-of select="NAME"/>
          <xsl:text>'s mass is </xsl:text>
          <xsl:value-of select="MASS"/>
          <xsl:text> Earth masses. Its radius is </xsl:text>
          <xsl:value-of select="RADIUS"/>
          <xsl:text> miles. Its day is </xsl:text>
          <xsl:value-of select="DAY"/>
          <xsl:text> Earth days long.</xsl:text>
   </xsl:template>

</xsl:stylesheet>
```

And here's the result—just pure text, no markup, no escaped characters, no processing instructions:

```
Mercury's mass is .0553 Earth masses. Its radius is 1516 miles. Its day
is 58.65 Earth days long.

Venus's mass is .815 Earth masses. Its radius is 3716 miles. Its day
is 116.75 Earth days long.

Earth's mass is 1 Earth masses. Its radius is 2107 miles. Its day
is 1 Earth days long.
```

On the other hand, the text output method is not just for creating plain text; it's also used for any non-XML, non-HTML text-based format. As you saw in Chapter 2, you can use it to create Rich Text Format (RTF) documents. Rich Text Format uses embedded text-based codes to specify the format of documents, and you can place those text-based codes in documents yourself if you use the text output method.

You originally saw the following example stylesheet in Chapter 2, where it was used to translate planets.xml into RTF format, which you're better equipped to understand now. In this case, I'm converting planets.xml to planets.rtf by using RTF codes as literal result elements:

```
<?xml version="1.0"?>
<xsl:stylesheet version="1.0"
xmlns:xsl="http://www.w3.org/1999/XSL/Transform">
    <xsl:output method="text"/>
```

```
    <xsl:strip-space elements="*"/>
<xsl:template match="/PLANETS">{\rtf1\ansi\deff0{\fonttbl
{\f0\fnil\fcharset0 Courier New;}}
\viewkind4\uc1\pard\lang1033\b\f0\fs36 The Planets Table\par
\b0\fs20
Name\tab Mass\tab Rad.\tab Day\par
<xsl:apply-templates/>
\par
}</xsl:template>
<xsl:template match="PLANET">
<xsl:value-of select="NAME"/>
\tab
<xsl:value-of select="MASS"/>
\tab
<xsl:value-of select="RADIUS"/>
\tab
<xsl:value-of select="DAY"/>
\tab
\par
</xsl:template>
</xsl:stylesheet>
```

You can see the resulting RTF document, planets.rtf, in Figure 6.2 in Microsoft Word 2000.

Note that the output method here is text, not something like “rtf”:

```
<?xml version="1.0"?>
<xsl:stylesheet version="1.0"
xmlns:xsl="http://www.w3.org/1999/XSL/Transform">
    <xsl:output method="text"/>
```

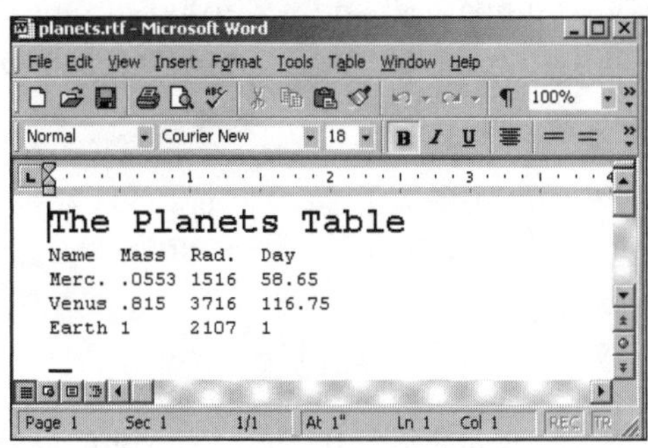

Figure 6.2 Planets.rtf in Microsoft Word.

```
<xsl:template match="/PLANETS">{\rtf1\ansi\deff0
{\fonttbl{\f0\fnil\fcharset0 Courier New;}}
\viewkind4\uc1\pard\lang1033\b\f0\fs36 The Planets Table\par
        .
        .
        .
```

Also note that I've placed the RTF codes immediately after the <xsl:template> element, because RTF documents must start with RTF codes from the very beginning; if I had begun inserting RTF codes on the next line, like this:

```
<?xml version="1.0"?>
<xsl:stylesheet version="1.0"
xmlns:xsl="http://www.w3.org/1999/XSL/Transform">
    <xsl:output method="text"/>

    <xsl:template match="/PLANETS">
{\rtf1\ansi\deff0{\fonttbl{\f0\fnil\fcharset0 Courier New;}}
\viewkind4\uc1\pard\lang1033\b\f0\fs36 The Planets Table\par
        .
        .
        .
```

then the RTF output file would have started with a newline character, which would throw off the RTF application (such as, possibly, Microsoft Word).

Outputting XHTML

W3C introduced XHTML to succeed HTML, but neither XSLT 1.0 nor the XSLT 1.1 working draft have any special support for XML-to-XHTML transformations. That support is supposed to be coming in XSLT 2.0. However, you can still create XHTML documents with XSLT processors.

> **More on XHTML**
> If you want to learn more about XHTML, take a look at *Inside XML*. Or you can go to the source: the W3C XHTML 1.0 recommendation at www.w3.org/TR/xhtml1/, as well as the XHTML 1.1 recommendation at www.w3.org/TR/xhtml11/.

In addition to making sure your document adheres to the rules for XHTML (such as no standalone attributes, quoting all attribute values, using lower-case characters for markup, making sure every start tag has a corresponding closing tag, making sure the document is well-formed XML, and so on), the main issue is to make sure that a <!DOCTYPE> element appears in the result document.

Here are the <!DOCTYPE> elements you use with the three types of XHTML 1.0—strict, transitional, and frameset (see *Inside XML* for information on how these versions are different):

```
<!DOCTYPE html
     PUBLIC "-//W3C//DTD XHTML 1.0 Strict//EN"
     "http://www.w3.org/TR/xhtml1/DTD/xhtml1-strict.dtd">

<!DOCTYPE html
     PUBLIC "-//W3C//DTD XHTML 1.0 Transitional//EN"
     "http://www.w3.org/TR/xhtml1/DTD/xhtml1-transitional.dtd">

<!DOCTYPE html
     PUBLIC "-//W3C//DTD XHTML 1.0 Frameset//EN"
     "http://www.w3.org/TR/xhtml1/DTD/xhtml1-frameset.dtd">
```

And here's the <!DOCTYPE> element for XHTML 1.1:

```
<!DOCTYPE html PUBLIC "-//W3C//DTD XHTML 1.1//EN"
     "http://www.w3.org/TR/xhtml11/DTD/xhtml11.dtd">
```

<!DOCTYPE> Elements and HTML 4.01

Strictly speaking, even HTML documents are supposed to start with a <!DOCTYPE> element. Officially, there are three forms of HTML 4.01: strict, transitional, and frameset. Here are the complete <!DOCTYPE> elements for those versions: `<!DOCTYPE HTML PUBLIC "-//W3C//DTD HTML 4.01//EN" "http://www.w3.org/TR/html4/strict.dtd">`, `<!DOCTYPE HTML PUBLIC "-//W3C//DTD HTML 4.01 Transitional//EN" "http://www.w3.org/TR/html4/loose.dtd">`, and `<!DOCTYPE HTML PUBLIC "-//W3C//DTD HTML 4.01 Frameset//EN" "http://www.w3.org/TR/html4/frameset.dtd">`. If you're producing rigidly correct HTML documents, consider adding this element to your documents. For more information, see www.w3.org/TR/html40/struct/global.html.

You can use the <xsl:output> element's doctype-system and doctype-public attributes to create a <!DOCTYPE> element if you set the output method to XML. Here's the <xsl:output> element that creates the <!DOCTYPE> element for transitional XHTML 1.0:

```
<xsl:output method="xml"
    doctype-system="http://www.w3.org/TR/xhtml1/DTD/xhtml1-transitional.dtd"
    doctype-public="-//W3C//DTD XHTML 1.0 Transitional//EN" indent="yes"/>
```

Here's the full stylesheet that uses this <xsl:output> element to convert planets.xml into a valid XHTML document, planets.html:

Listing 6.5 **Transforming planets.xml to XHTML**

```
<?xml version="1.0"?>
<xsl:stylesheet version="1.0"
xmlns:xsl="http://www.w3.org/1999/XSL/Transform">
<xsl:output method="xml"
    doctype-system="http://www.w3.org/TR/xhtml1/DTD/xhtml1-transitional.dtd"
    doctype-public="-//W3C//DTD XHTML 1.0 Transitional//EN" indent="yes"/>

    <xsl:template match="/PLANETS">
        <html>
            <head>
                <title>
                    The Planets Table
                </title>
            </head>
            <body>
                <h1>
                    The Planets Table
                </h1>
                <table>
                    <tr>
                        <td>Name</td>
                        <td>Mass</td>
                        <td>Radius</td>
                        <td>Day</td>
                    </tr>
                    <xsl:apply-templates/>
                </table>
            </body>
        </html>
    </xsl:template>

    <xsl:template match="PLANET">
       <tr>
          <td><xsl:value-of select="NAME"/></td>
          <td><xsl:apply-templates select="MASS"/></td>
          <td><xsl:apply-templates select="RADIUS"/></td>
          <td><xsl:apply-templates select="DAY"/></td>
       </tr>
   </xsl:template>

    <xsl:template match="MASS">
        <xsl:value-of select="."/>
        <xsl:text> </xsl:text>
        <xsl:value-of select="@UNITS"/>
    </xsl:template>

    <xsl:template match="RADIUS">
        <xsl:value-of select="."/>
        <xsl:text> </xsl:text>
        <xsl:value-of select="@UNITS"/>
```

```
    </xsl:template>

    <xsl:template match="DAY">
        <xsl:value-of select="."/>
        <xsl:text> </xsl:text>
        <xsl:value-of select="@UNITS"/>
    </xsl:template>

</xsl:stylesheet>
```

Here's the resulting XHTML file:

```
<?xml version="1.0" encoding="UTF-8"?>
<!DOCTYPE html PUBLIC "-//W3C//DTD XHTML 1.0 Transitional//EN"
    "http://www.w3.org/TR/xhtml1/DTD/xhtml1-transitional.dtd">
<html>
    <head>
        <title>
            The Planets Table
        </title>
    </head>

    <body>
        <h1>
            The Planets Table
        </h1>

        <table>
            <tr>
                <td>Name</td>
                <td>Mass</td>
                <td>Radius</td>
                <td>Day</td>
            </tr>

            <tr>
                <td>Mercury</td>
                <td>.0553 (Earth = 1)</td>
                <td>1516 miles</td>
                <td>58.65 days</td>
            </tr>

            <tr>
                <td>Venus</td>
                <td>.815 (Earth = 1)</td>
                <td>3716 miles</td>
                <td>116.75 days</td>
            </tr>

            <tr>
                <td>Earth</td>
```

```
                <td>1 (Earth = 1)</td>
                <td>2107 miles</td>
                <td>1 days</td>
            </tr>
        </table>
    </body>
</html>
```

This document, planets.html, validates as well-formed and valid transitional XHTML 1.0, according to the W3C HTML and XHTML validation program, which is at http://validator.w3.org/file-upload.html. Note that because XHTML documents are also well-formed XML documents, you use the XML output method, so this transformation is not too difficult; the only issue that takes a little thought is creating the <!DOCTYPE> element.

Altering Document Structure Based on Input

So far, the templates I've created have been based on somewhat rigid skeletons, specifying exactly what should go into the output document, and in what order. But you can use XSLT elements such as <xsl:element>, <xsl:attribute>, <xsl:text>, and so on to create new nodes on the fly, based on what you find in the input document.

You've already had a little experience in this area, because I used attribute value templates in Chapter 3. As you recall, you can use attribute value templates to set an attribute to the value of an XPath expression, if you enclose that expression in curly braces, { and }. For example, to set the NAME attribute to the string value of a <DESCRIPTION> element that is a child of the context node, you could assign that value like this: NAME={DESCRIPTION}. However, now it's time to dig deeper into the whole topic of creating new elements and attributes on the fly, starting with <xsl:element>.

The *<xsl:element>* Element: Creating New Elements at Run Time

You can create new elements with the <xsl:element> element, which is very useful if you need to determine a new element's name at run time.

This element has three attributes:

- name (mandatory). Name of the element you want to create. Set to an attribute value template that returns a QName.
- namespace (optional). The namespace URI of the new element. Set to an attribute value template returning a URI.

- `use-attribute-sets` (optional). Specifies the attribute sets containing the attributes for this element. Set to a whitespace-separated list of QNames.

The `<xsl:element>` element contains a template body.

For example, say that I want to store the names of the planets in `NAME` attributes rather than in a `<NAME>` element in planets.xml, like this:

```
<?xml version="1.0"?>
<?xml-stylesheet type="text/xml" href="planets.xsl"?>
<PLANETS>

  <PLANET NAME="Mercury">
      <MASS UNITS="(Earth = 1)">.0553</MASS>
      <DAY UNITS="days">58.65</DAY>
      <RADIUS UNITS="miles">1516</RADIUS>
      <DENSITY UNITS="(Earth = 1)">.983</DENSITY>
      <DISTANCE UNITS="million miles">43.4</DISTANCE><!--At perihelion-->
  </PLANET>
     .
     .
     .
```

Suppose now that I want to use the value of that attribute to create new element names in the result document such as `<Mercury>`, `<Venus>`, and `<Earth>`:

```
<?xml version="1.0" encoding="UTF-8"?>
<?xml-stylesheet type="text/xml" href="planets.xsl"?>
<PLANETS>

    <Mercury>
        <MASS UNITS="(Earth = 1)">.0553</MASS>
        <DAY UNITS="days">58.65</DAY>
        <RADIUS UNITS="miles">1516</RADIUS>
        <DENSITY UNITS="(Earth = 1)">.983</DENSITY>
        <DISTANCE UNITS="million miles">43.4</DISTANCE><!--At perihelion-->
    </Mercury>
        .
        .
        .
```

In this case, I don't know the name of the output element until run time, so I can't just use a literal result element. I could cobble together a new element, treating it as text this way, where I'm using the `<xsl:text>` element's `disable-output-escaping` attribute to output characters such as "<":

```
<?xml version="1.0"?>
<xsl:stylesheet version="1.0"
xmlns:xsl="http://www.w3.org/1999/XSL/Transform">
<xsl:output method="xml"/>
```

```
  <xsl:template match="@*¦node()">
    <xsl:copy>
      <xsl:apply-templates select="@*¦node()"/>
    </xsl:copy>
  </xsl:template>

  <xsl:template match="PLANET">
    <xsl:text disable-output-escaping="yes">&lt;</xsl:text>
    <xsl:value-of select="@NAME"/>
    <xsl:text disable-output-escaping="yes">&gt;</xsl:text>
    <xsl:apply-templates/>
    <xsl:text disable-output-escaping="yes">&lt;/</xsl:text>
    <xsl:value-of select="@NAME"/>
    <xsl:text disable-output-escaping="yes">&gt;</xsl:text>
  </xsl:template>

</xsl:stylesheet>
```

But this way is clumsy and it treats markup as simple text. On the other hand, I could create a new element using the name of a planet with `<xsl:element>`, getting the name of the new planet from the `name` attribute this way:

Listing 6.6 **Using *<xsl:element>***

```
<?xml version="1.0"?>
<xsl:stylesheet version="1.0"
xmlns:xsl="http://www.w3.org/1999/XSL/Transform">
<xsl:output method="xml"/>

  <xsl:template match="@*¦node()">
    <xsl:copy>
      <xsl:apply-templates select="@*¦node()"/>
    </xsl:copy>
  </xsl:template>

<xsl:template match="PLANET">
    <xsl:element name="{@NAME}">
        <xsl:apply-templates/>
    </xsl:element>
</xsl:template>

</xsl:stylesheet>
```

This is a lot cleaner and simpler. Here is the result, where I've created the new elements, each with the name of a different planet and created at run time:

```
<?xml version="1.0" encoding="UTF-8"?>
<?xml-stylesheet type="text/xml" href="planets.xsl"?>
<PLANETS>

    <Mercury>
        <MASS UNITS="(Earth = 1)">.0553</MASS>
        <DAY UNITS="days">58.65</DAY>
        <RADIUS UNITS="miles">1516</RADIUS>
        <DENSITY UNITS="(Earth = 1)">.983</DENSITY>
        <DISTANCE UNITS="million miles">43.4</DISTANCE><!--At perihelion-->
    </Mercury>

    <Venus>
        <MASS UNITS="(Earth = 1)">.815</MASS>
        <DAY UNITS="days">116.75</DAY>
        <RADIUS UNITS="miles">3716</RADIUS>
        <DENSITY UNITS="(Earth = 1)">.943</DENSITY>
        <DISTANCE UNITS="million miles">66.8</DISTANCE><!--At perihelion-->
    </Venus>

    <Earth>
        <MASS UNITS="(Earth = 1)">1</MASS>
        <DAY UNITS="days">1</DAY>
        <RADIUS UNITS="miles">2107</RADIUS>
        <DENSITY UNITS="(Earth = 1)">1</DENSITY>
        <DISTANCE UNITS="million miles">128.4</DISTANCE><!--At perihelion-->
    </Earth>

</PLANETS>
```

In this way, you can create new elements and name them when the XSLT transformation takes place.

The *<xsl:attribute>* Element: Creating New Attributes

Just as you can create new elements with `<xsl:element>` and set the element name and content at run time, you can use the `<xsl:attribute>` element to do the same for attributes.

This element has two attributes:

- `name` (mandatory). The name of the new attribute. Set to an attribute value template returning a QName.
- `namespace` (optional). The namespace of the new attribute. Set to a URI.

This element encloses a template body that sets the value of the attribute.

In the following example, I'm creating new <PLANET> elements with attributes corresponding to the various planet names, and values taken from the COLOR attribute in the original <PLANET> elements:

Listing 6.7 **Using *<xsl:attribute>***

```
<?xml version="1.0"?>
<xsl:stylesheet version="1.0"
xmlns:xsl="http://www.w3.org/1999/XSL/Transform">

<xsl:template match="PLANETS">
    <HTML>
        <HEAD>
            <TITLE>
                Planets
            </TITLE>
        </HEAD>
        <BODY>
            <xsl:apply-templates select="PLANET"/>
        </BODY>
    </HTML>
</xsl:template>

<xsl:template match="PLANET">
    <PLANET>
        <xsl:attribute name="{NAME}">
            <xsl:value-of select="@COLOR"/>
        </xsl:attribute>
    </PLANET>
</xsl:template>

</xsl:stylesheet>
```

As you can see in the following results, I've created new attributes on the fly, using the names of the planets:

```
<HTML>
    <HEAD>
        <TITLE>
            Planets
        </TITLE>
    </HEAD>

    <BODY>
        <PLANET Mercury="RED">
        </PLANET>
        <PLANET Venus="WHITE">
        </PLANET>
        <PLANET Earth="BLUE">
        </PLANET>
    </BODY>

</HTML>
```

The *<xsl:comment>* Element: Generating Comments

You can also create comments on the fly with the `<xsl:comment>` element. This element has no attributes and encloses a template body that sets the text of the comment.

In the following example, I'm creating comments that are to replace `<PLANET>` elements, and I'll include the name of the planet in the text of the comment:

Listing 6.8 **Using *<xsl:comment>***

```
<?xml version="1.0"?>
<xsl:stylesheet version="1.0"
xmlns:xsl="http://www.w3.org/1999/XSL/Transform">

<xsl:template match="PLANETS">
    <HTML>
        <HEAD>
            <TITLE>
                Planets
            </TITLE>
        </HEAD>
        <BODY>
            <xsl:apply-templates select="PLANET"/>
        </BODY>
    </HTML>
</xsl:template>

<xsl:template match="PLANET">
    <xsl:comment>This was the <xsl:value-of select="NAME"/> element</xsl:comment>

</xsl:template>

</xsl:stylesheet>
```

Here's the result:

```
<HTML>
    <HEAD>
        <TITLE>
            Planets
        </TITLE>
    </HEAD>

    <BODY>
        <!--This was the Mercury element-->
        <!--This was the Venus element-->
        <!--This was the Earth element-->
    </BODY>

</HTML>
```

The *<xsl:processing-instruction>* Element: Generating Processing Instructions

You can create new processing instructions with the `<xsl:processing-instruction>` element. This element has one attribute:

- `name` (mandatory). Sets the name of the processing instruction. Set to an attribute value template that returns an NCName.

In the following example, I've removed the `<?xml-stylesheet?>` instruction from the beginning of planets.xml:

```
<?xml version="1.0"?>

<PLANETS>

    <PLANET>
        <NAME>Mercury</NAME>
        <MASS UNITS="(Earth = 1)">.0553</MASS>
        <DAY UNITS="days">58.65</DAY>
        <RADIUS UNITS="miles">1516</RADIUS>
        <DENSITY UNITS="(Earth = 1)">.983</DENSITY>
        <DISTANCE UNITS="million miles">43.4</DISTANCE><!--At perihelion-->
    </PLANET>

    <PLANET>
        <NAME>Venus</NAME>
        <MASS UNITS="(Earth = 1)">.815</MASS>
        <DAY UNITS="days">116.75</DAY>
        <RADIUS UNITS="miles">3716</RADIUS>
        <DENSITY UNITS="(Earth = 1)">.943</DENSITY>
        <DISTANCE UNITS="million miles">66.8</DISTANCE><!--At perihelion-->
    </PLANET>
        .
        .
        .
```

To add that processing instruction again, you can use the `<xsl:processing-instruction>` element. The `type` and `href` items in a processing instruction such as `<?xml-stylesheet type="text/xml" href="planets.xsl"?>` are *not* actually attributes, so rather than set their values with `<xsl:attribute>`, you use simple text:

Listing 6.9 **Using *<xsl:processing-instruction>***

```
<?xml version="1.0"?>
<xsl:stylesheet version="1.0"
xmlns:xsl="http://www.w3.org/1999/XSL/Transform">
<xsl:output method="xml"/>

  <xsl:template match="/">
    <xsl:processing-instruction name="xml-stylesheet">
        <xsl:text>type="text/xml" href="planets.xsl"</xsl:text>
    </xsl:processing-instruction>
    <xsl:apply-templates/>
  </xsl:template>

  <xsl:template match="@*|node()">
    <xsl:copy>
      <xsl:apply-templates select="@*|node()"/>
    </xsl:copy>
  </xsl:template>

</xsl:stylesheet>
```

Here's the result, where you can see the `<?xml-stylesheet?>` processing instruction back in place:

```
<?xml version="1.0" encoding="UTF-8"?>
<?xml-stylesheet type="text/xml" href="planets.xsl"?>
<PLANETS>

    <PLANET>
        <NAME>Mercury</NAME>
        <MASS UNITS="(Earth = 1)">.0553</MASS>
        <DAY UNITS="days">58.65</DAY>
        <RADIUS UNITS="miles">1516</RADIUS>
        <DENSITY UNITS="(Earth = 1)">.983</DENSITY>
        <DISTANCE UNITS="million miles">43.4</DISTANCE><!--At perihelion-->
    </PLANET>

    <PLANET>
        <NAME>Venus</NAME>
        <MASS UNITS="(Earth = 1)">.815</MASS>
        <DAY UNITS="days">116.75</DAY>
        <RADIUS UNITS="miles">3716</RADIUS>
        <DENSITY UNITS="(Earth = 1)">.943</DENSITY>
        <DISTANCE UNITS="million miles">66.8</DISTANCE><!--At perihelion-->
    </PLANET>
        .
        .
        .
```

The *<xsl:document>* Element: Generating Multiple Output Documents

The XSLT 1.1 working draft introduced a new element, `<xsl:document>`, to support multiple output documents, and it's likely this element will be added to XSLT 2.0. It has the following attributes:

- `href` (mandatory). Indicates where the new document should be placed. Set to an absolute or relative URI, without a fragment identifier.
- `method` (optional). Sets the output method used to create the result document. Set to "xml", "html","text", or a QName that is not an NCName.
- `version` (optional). Sets the version of the output document. Set to an NMTOKEN.
- `encoding` (optional). Sets the encoding of the output document. Set to a string.
- `omit-xml-declaration` (optional). Set to "yes" or "no" to omit the XML declaration or not.
- `cdata-section-elements` (optional). Sets the names of those elements whose content you want output as CDATA sections. Set to a whitespace-separated list of QNames.
- `doctype-public` (optional). Specifies the public identifier to be used in the <!DOCTYPE> declaration in the output. Set to a string value.
- `doctype-system` (optional). Specifies the system identifier to be used in the <!DOCTYPE> declaration in the output. Set to a string value.
- `encoding` (optional). Sets the character encoding. Set to a string value.
- `indent` (optional). Specifies whether the output should be indented to show its nesting structure. Set to "yes" or "no".
- `media-type` (optional). Sets the MIME type of the output. Set to a string value.
- `standalone` (optional). Specifies whether a standalone declaration should be included in the output and sets its value if so. Set to "yes" or "no".

This element contains a template body.

In the following example, based on a simplified stylesheet, I create two frames in an HTML document, as well as the two HTML documents that are to be displayed in those frames, frame1.html and frame2.html. I create the first frame and the document that is to appear in it, frame1.html, this way, using `<xsl:document>` (note that here, I'm setting the `version` attribute to

"1.1" because we're using a feature that is only a part of the XSLT 1.1 working draft, but "1.1" will probably not be a legal `version` value in the long run; if `<xsl:document>` is part of XSLT 2.0, you should set the version to "2.0"):

```
<HTML xmlns:xsl="http://www.w3.org/1999/XSL/Transform" xsl:version="1.1">
    <HEAD>
        <TITLE>
            Two Frames
        </TITLE>
    </HEAD>

    <FRAMESET cols="50%, 50%">
        <FRAME src="frame1.html"/>

        <xsl:document href="frame1.html">
            <HTML>
                <HEAD>
                    <TITLE>
                        Frame 1
                    </TITLE>
                </HEAD>

                <BODY>
                    <H1>This is frame 1.</H1>
                </BODY>
            </HTML>
        </xsl:document>
        .
        .
        .
```

Then I can create the second frame and the document that is to appear in that frame, frame2.html, as follows:

Listing 6.10 **Using *<xsl:document>***

```
<HTML xmlns:xsl="http://www.w3.org/1999/XSL/Transform" xsl:version="1.1">
    <HEAD>
        <TITLE>
            Two Frames
        </TITLE>
    </HEAD>

    <FRAMESET cols="50%, 50%">

        <FRAME src="frame1.html"/>

        <xsl:document href="frame1.html">
            <HTML>
                <HEAD>
```

continues ▸

Listing 6.10 **Continued**

```
                <TITLE>
                    Frame 1
                </TITLE>
            </HEAD>

            <BODY>
                <H1>This is frame 1.</H1>
            </BODY>
        </HTML>
    </xsl:document>

    <FRAME src="frame2.html"/>

    <xsl:document href="frame2.html">
        <HTML>
            <HEAD>
                <TITLE>
                    Frame 2
                </TITLE>
            </HEAD>

            <BODY>
                <H1>This is frame 2.</H1>
            </BODY>
        </HTML>
    </xsl:document>

  </FRAMESET>

</HTML>
```

An XSLT 1.1-Only Example

Note that this is an XSLT 1.1 working draft-only example. No publicly-available XSLT processors (that I know of) handle the `<xsl:document>` element yet.

The *<xsl:namespace>* Element: Generating Namespace Declarations

Another new element is coming in XSLT 2.0: the `<xsl:namespace>` element. This element enables you to add namespace declarations to the result document. However, nothing more is known about this element at this time, so it's impossible to list any details here. Keep watching the W3C site for more information.

The *<xsl:attribute-set>* Element: Generating Attribute Sets

Sometimes when you create a new element, you want to add a number of attributes to that element all at once. There's an easy way to do that, because you can use the `<xsl:attribute-set>` element.

This element has two attributes:

- `name` (mandatory). The name of the attribute set. Set to a QName.
- `use-attribute-sets` (optional). The names of other attribute sets you want included in this one. Set to a whitespace-separated list of QNames.

The `<xsl:attribute-set>` element encloses `<xsl:attribute>` elements, one for each new attribute you want to create. When you use `<xsl:attribute-set>` to create a new set of attributes for an element, you give the attribute set a name. You can then assign that name to the `use-attribute-sets` attribute of the `<xsl:copy>`, `<xsl:element>`, `<xsl:for-each>` elements—and of even the `<xsl:attribute-set>` element itself—to use that attribute set when you create the new element.

You already saw one example that used attribute sets in the JavaScript-creating template earlier in this chapter. In that example, I used an attribute set to specify all the attributes in the planets' HTML buttons, then used that attribute set in an `<xsl:element>` element to create those buttons:

```
<BODY>
        <CENTER>
            <H1>The Mass Page</H1>
        </CENTER>
        <xsl:for-each select="PLANET">
            <P/>
            <xsl:element name="input" use-attribute-sets="attribs"/>
        </xsl:for-each>
        <P/>
        <P/>
        <DIV ID='display'></DIV>
    </BODY>

</HTML>
    </xsl:template>

    <xsl:attribute-set name="attribs">
    <xsl:attribute name="type">BUTTON</xsl:attribute>
    <xsl:attribute name="value"><xsl:value-of select="NAME"/></xsl:attribute>
    <xsl:attribute name="onclick"><xsl:value-of select="NAME"/>()</xsl:attribute>
    </xsl:attribute-set>
```

In the result document, this attribute set was added to every HTML button, like this:

```
<P></P>
<input type="BUTTON" value="Mercury" onclick="Mercury()">
<P></P>
<input type="BUTTON" value="Venus" onclick="Venus()">
<P></P>
<input type="BUTTON" value="Earth" onclick="Earth()">
```

In the following example, I use an attribute set to number the planets in planets.xml. I add two attributes to each `<PLANET>` element: `number` and `total`. The `number` attribute will hold the planet's number, starting from 1, and the `total` attribute will hold the total number of planets in planets.xml, which I can determine with the `count` function (which you'll see in Chapter 8):

Listing 6.11 **Using *<xsl:attribute-set>***

```
<xsl:stylesheet
 xmlns:xsl="http://www.w3.org/1999/XSL/Transform"
 version="1.0">

<xsl:output method="xml" indent="yes"/>

<xsl:template match="*">
    <xsl:copy>
        <xsl:apply-templates/>
    </xsl:copy>
</xsl:template>

<xsl:template match="PLANET">
    <xsl:copy use-attribute-sets="numbering">
        <xsl:apply-templates/>
    </xsl:copy>
</xsl:template>

<xsl:attribute-set name="numbering">
    <xsl:attribute name="number"><xsl:number/></xsl:attribute>
    <xsl:attribute name="total"><xsl:value-of select="count(//PLANET)"/></xsl:attribute>
</xsl:attribute-set>

</xsl:stylesheet>
```

Here's the result. Note that every `<PLANET>` element has both a `number` and `total` attribute:

```
<?xml version="1.0" encoding="UTF-8"?>
<PLANETS>

    <PLANET number="1" total="3">
        <NAME>Mercury</NAME>
        <MASS>.0553</MASS>
        <DAY>58.65</DAY>
        <RADIUS>1516</RADIUS>
        <DENSITY>.983</DENSITY>
        <DISTANCE>43.4</DISTANCE>
    </PLANET>

    <PLANET number="2" total="3">
        <NAME>Venus</NAME>
        <MASS>.815</MASS>
        <DAY>116.75</DAY>
        <RADIUS>3716</RADIUS>
        <DENSITY>.943</DENSITY>
        <DISTANCE>66.8</DISTANCE>
    </PLANET>

    <PLANET number="3" total="3">
        <NAME>Earth</NAME>
        <MASS>1</MASS>
        <DAY>1</DAY>
        <RADIUS>2107</RADIUS>
        <DENSITY>1</DENSITY>
        <DISTANCE>128.4</DISTANCE>
    </PLANET>

</PLANETS>
```

Omitting the XML Declaration and Generating XML Fragments

Many people new to XSLT find themselves frustrated by the XML declaration that always seems to appear at the tops of their result documents, especially if they don't realize that the default output method is XML. Of course, there's a way of getting rid of the XML declaration, and it's useful if you're creating well-formed XML fragments that are not necessarily complete documents. You just have to set the `omit-xml-declaration` attribute of the `<xsl:output>` element to "yes": `<xsl:output method="xml" omit-xml-declaration="yes"/>`.

In the following example, I just strip the XML declaration from a document, copying everything else. Note that the XML declaration is not a node, so there's no danger of it matching the copying template:

```
<?xml version="1.0"?>
<xsl:stylesheet version="1.0"
xmlns:xsl="http://www.w3.org/1999/XSL/Transform">
<xsl:output method="xml" omit-xml-declaration="yes"/>

  <xsl:template match="@*|node()">
    <xsl:copy>
      <xsl:apply-templates select="@*|node()"/>
    </xsl:copy>
  </xsl:template>

</xsl:stylesheet>
```

This stylesheet converts planets.xml:

```
<?xml version="1.0"?>
<PLANETS>

    <PLANET>
        <NAME>Mercury</NAME>
        <MASS UNITS="(Earth = 1)">.0553</MASS>
        <DAY UNITS="days">58.65</DAY>
        <RADIUS UNITS="miles">1516</RADIUS>
        <DENSITY UNITS="(Earth = 1)">.983</DENSITY>
        <DISTANCE UNITS="million miles">43.4</DISTANCE><!--At perihelion-->
    </PLANET>

    <PLANET>
        <NAME>Venus</NAME>
        <MASS UNITS="(Earth = 1)">.815</MASS>
        <DAY UNITS="days">116.75</DAY>
        <RADIUS UNITS="miles">3716</RADIUS>
        <DENSITY UNITS="(Earth = 1)">.943</DENSITY>
        <DISTANCE UNITS="million miles">66.8</DISTANCE><!--At perihelion-->
    </PLANET>
        .
        .
        .
```

to this new version, without the XML declaration:

```
<PLANETS>

    <PLANET>
        <NAME>Mercury</NAME>
        <MASS UNITS="(Earth = 1)">.0553</MASS>
        <DAY UNITS="days">58.65</DAY>
        <RADIUS UNITS="miles">1516</RADIUS>
```

```
        <DENSITY UNITS="(Earth = 1)">.983</DENSITY>
        <DISTANCE UNITS="million miles">43.4</DISTANCE><!--At perihelion-->
    </PLANET>

    <PLANET>
        <NAME>Venus</NAME>
        <MASS UNITS="(Earth = 1)">.815</MASS>
        <DAY UNITS="days">116.75</DAY>
        <RADIUS UNITS="miles">3716</RADIUS>
        <DENSITY UNITS="(Earth = 1)">.943</DENSITY>
        <DISTANCE UNITS="million miles">66.8</DISTANCE><!--At perihelion-->
    </PLANET>
        .
        .
        .
```

This is useful to know when you're generating XML fragments or doing other custom work. Note, however, that all complete XML documents, even custom ones written in various XML applications such as WML, require an XML declaration at the beginning.

Using *generate-id* to Create Unique Identifiers

It's important to consider another topic when you're substantially reorganizing documents: how to create identifiers in the result document that you can use to identify elements and so refer to them if needed. For example, imagine that you want to use an XSLT stylesheet to add a table of contents to a document and to make the entries in the table of contents hyperlinks so the user has only to click them to jump to the right section. In that case, you need some way of identifying elements in the result document, and the `generate-id` function is useful here.

In the following example, I add a hyperlinked table of contents to planets.html. To generate that table of contents, I use `<xsl:for-each>` to loop over all the planets. Each time through the loop, I create a hyperlink and use an attribute value template to create an `HREF` attribute that is set to a unique identifier for the current planet. Note that despite the name, the `generate-id` function generates only a string-based *identifier* for an element; it does not create ID *attributes*:

```
<?xml version="1.0"?>
<xsl:stylesheet version="1.0"
xmlns:xsl="http://www.w3.org/1999/XSL/Transform">

    <xsl:template match="/PLANETS">
        <HTML>
            <HEAD>
```

```
            <TITLE>
                The Planets Table
            </TITLE>
        </HEAD>
        <BODY>
            <H1>
                The Planets Table
            </H1>
            <xsl:for-each select="PLANET">
                <H2><A HREF="#{generate-id()}">
                    <xsl:value-of select="NAME"/></A>
                </H2>
                <P/>
            </xsl:for-each>
             .
             .
             .
```

This adds an identifier to each planet and creates the necessary hyperlinks. The `generate-id` function not only creates a new identifier for an element, but it also returns that identifier when you use `generate-id` on the element from then on. That's useful here, because it means I can create the hyperlink anchors in the planetary data HTML table, setting the anchor's `NAME` attribute to the identifier for each `<PLANET>` element in turn so that it becomes a hyperlink target:

Listing 6.12 **Using the *generate-id* Function**

```
<?xml version="1.0"?>
<xsl:stylesheet version="1.0"
xmlns:xsl="http://www.w3.org/1999/XSL/Transform">

    <xsl:template match="/PLANETS">
        <HTML>
            <HEAD>
                <TITLE>
                    The Planets Table
                </TITLE>
            </HEAD>
            <BODY>
                <H1>
                    The Planets Table
                </H1>
                <xsl:for-each select="PLANET">
                    <H2><A HREF="#{generate-id()}">
                        <xsl:value-of select="NAME"/></A>
                    </H2>
                    <P/>
```

```
                </xsl:for-each>

                <TABLE BORDER="2">
                    <TR>
                        <TD>Name</TD>
                        <TD>Mass</TD>
                        <TD>Radius</TD>
                        <TD>Day</TD>
                    </TR>
                    <xsl:apply-templates/>
                </TABLE>
            </BODY>
        </HTML>
    </xsl:template>

    <xsl:template match="PLANET">
       <TR>
          <TD><A NAME="{generate-id(.)}">
          <xsl:value-of select="NAME"/></A></TD>
          <TD><xsl:apply-templates select="MASS"/></TD>
          <TD><xsl:apply-templates select="RADIUS"/></TD>
          <TD><xsl:apply-templates select="DAY"/></TD>
       </TR>
   </xsl:template>

    <xsl:template match="MASS">
        <xsl:value-of select="."/>
        <xsl:text> </xsl:text>
        <xsl:value-of select="@UNITS"/>
    </xsl:template>

    <xsl:template match="RADIUS">
        <xsl:value-of select="."/>
        <xsl:text> </xsl:text>
        <xsl:value-of select="@UNITS"/>
    </xsl:template>

    <xsl:template match="DAY">
        <xsl:value-of select="."/>
        <xsl:text> </xsl:text>
        <xsl:value-of select="@UNITS"/>
    </xsl:template>

</xsl:stylesheet>
```

That's all it takes; now I've created hyperlinks that have an HREF attribute that is set to an identifier for a <PLANET> element, and I've used the same identifier to make each <PLANET> element a hyperlink target. When the user clicks a hyperlink in the table of contents, the browser scrolls to the corresponding planet's entry in the HTML table of data. (Note that the HTML table must be off the screen before most browsers scroll the display.) Each XSLT processor creates its own identifiers; here's the result if I use Xalan:

```
<HTML>
    <HEAD>
        <TITLE>
            The Planets Table
        </TITLE>
    </HEAD>

    <BODY>
        <H1>
            The Planets Table
        </H1>
        <H2>
        <A href="#N5">Mercury</A>
        </H2>
        <P></P>
        <H2>
        <A href="#N20">Venus</A>
        </H2>
        <P></P>
        <H2>
        <A href="#N3B">Earth</A>
        </H2>
        <P></P>

        <TABLE BORDER="2">
            <TR>
                <TD>Name</TD>
                <TD>Mass</TD>
                <TD>Radius</TD>
                <TD>Day</TD>
            </TR>

            <TR>
                <TD><A NAME="N5">Mercury</A>
                </TD><TD>.0553 (Earth = 1)</TD>
                <TD>1516 miles</TD>
                <TD>58.65 days</TD>
            </TR>

            <TR>
                <TD><A NAME="N20">Venus</A></TD>
                <TD>.815 (Earth = 1)</TD>
                <TD>3716 miles</TD>
                <TD>116.75 days</TD>
            </TR>
```

```
            <TR>
                <TD><A NAME="N3B">Earth</A></TD>
                <TD>1 (Earth = 1)</TD>
                <TD>2107 miles</TD>
                <TD>1 days</TD>
            </TR>

        </TABLE>
    </BODY>
</HTML>
```

You can see the result in Figure 6.3, including the hyperlinked table of contents. All the user has to do is click a hyperlink to the corresponding table entry.

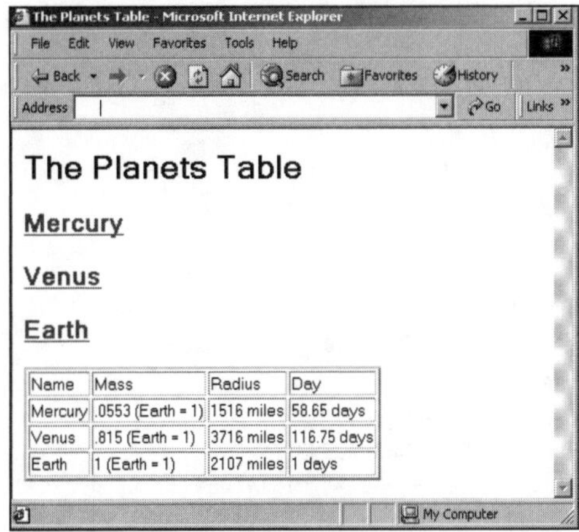

Figure 6.3 Using generated IDs in hyperlinks.

Creating CDATA Sections

In XML-to-XML transformations, you might want to output CDATA sections. XSLT makes it easy to do that with the `<xsl:output>` element's `cdata-section-elements` attribute. This attribute enables you to indicate which elements' content should be enclosed in a CDATA section. That's useful, for example, when you're creating script elements and want to deal with a browser that requires script code to be inside a CDATA section.

In the following example, I place the contents of the <NAME> and <MASS> elements in planets.xml in CDATA sections:

```
<?xml version="1.0"?>
<xsl:stylesheet version="1.0"
xmlns:xsl="http://www.w3.org/1999/XSL/Transform">
<xsl:output method="xml" cdata-section-elements="NAME MASS"/>

  <xsl:template match="@*|node()">
    <xsl:copy>
      <xsl:apply-templates select="@*|node()"/>
    </xsl:copy>
  </xsl:template>

</xsl:stylesheet>
```

And here's the result:

```
<?xml version="1.0" encoding="UTF-8"?>
<?xml-stylesheet type="text/xml" href="planets.xsl"?>
<PLANETS>

    <PLANET>
        <NAME><![CDATA[Mercury]]></NAME>
        <MASS UNITS="(Earth = 1)"><![CDATA[.0553]]></MASS>
        <DAY UNITS="days">58.65</DAY>
        <RADIUS UNITS="miles">1516</RADIUS>
        <DENSITY UNITS="(Earth = 1)">.983</DENSITY>
        <DISTANCE UNITS="million miles">43.4</DISTANCE><!--At perihelion-->
    </PLANET>

    <PLANET>
        <NAME><![CDATA[Venus]]></NAME>
        <MASS UNITS="(Earth = 1)"><![CDATA[.815]]></MASS>
        <DAY UNITS="days">116.75</DAY>
        <RADIUS UNITS="miles">3716</RADIUS>
        <DENSITY UNITS="(Earth = 1)">.943</DENSITY>
        <DISTANCE UNITS="million miles">66.8</DISTANCE><!--At perihelion-->
    </PLANET>
        .
        .
        .
```

Handling Source Versus Result CDATA

This technique generates CDATA sections in the result document; it does not treat any data in the *source document* as CDATA. For example, if you want to transform `<script>if x < y {...}</script>` into `<script><![CDATA[if x < y {...}]]></script>` because your browser requires script code to be in CDATA sections, the XSLT processor will have trouble with the unescaped < in "x < y". In this case, you must use `<script>if x < y {...}</script>` so the XSLT processor will generate `<script><![CDATA[if x < y {...}]]></script>`.

Setting Character Encoding

Now that we're doing more substantial rewrites of source documents, it's useful to know that you can set the character encoding of result documents with the `encoding` attribute of the `<xsl:output>` element. However, that's no guarantee that your XSLT processor supports the encoding you want to use, because XSLT processors are required to support only UTF-8 and UTF-16. On the other hand, if you use a character that is not supported in the character encoding you're using, the XSLT processor should either output the character as an entity reference or generate an error.

More on Character Encoding

For more on character encoding, see *Inside XML*. The only approved character encodings are specified in the XML 1.0 recommendation, www.w3.org/TR/REC-xml.

The `encoding` attribute in a document's XML declaration is optional; if it's not included, XML parsers are supposed to assume the encoding is UTF-8 by default. However, if you want to make the character encoding explicit or use another character encoding, you can specify that encoding as follows, where I'm specifying UTF-16:

```
<?xml version="1.0"?>
<xsl:stylesheet version="1.0"
xmlns:xsl="http://www.w3.org/1999/XSL/Transform">
<xsl:output method="xml" encoding="UTF-16"/>

  <xsl:template match="@*|node()">
    <xsl:copy>
      <xsl:apply-templates select="@*|node()"/>
    </xsl:copy>
  </xsl:template>

</xsl:stylesheet>
```

And here's what appears in the result document:

```
<?xml version="1.0" encoding="UTF-16"?>
<?xml-stylesheet type="text/xml" href="planets.xsl"?>
<PLANETS>

    <PLANET>
        <NAME>Mercury</NAME>
        <MASS UNITS="(Earth = 1)">.0553</MASS>
        <DAY UNITS="days">58.65</DAY>
        <RADIUS UNITS="miles">1516</RADIUS>
        <DENSITY UNITS="(Earth = 1)">.983</DENSITY>
        <DISTANCE UNITS="million miles">43.4</DISTANCE><!--At perihelion-->
    </PLANET>
```

```
    <PLANET>
        <NAME>Venus</NAME>
        <MASS UNITS="(Earth = 1)">.815</MASS>
        <DAY UNITS="days">116.75</DAY>
        <RADIUS UNITS="miles">3716</RADIUS>
        <DENSITY UNITS="(Earth = 1)">.943</DENSITY>
        <DISTANCE UNITS="million miles">66.8</DISTANCE><!--At perihelion-->
    </PLANET>
        .
        .
        .
```

Modes: Context-Specific Formatting

Sometimes, matching nodes can be an art. For example, a template that matches "*" also matches "PLANET". However, if you want <PLANET> elements handled differently than all other elements, you can set up a template that matches "PLANET"; the XSLT processor, knowing "PLANET" is a closer match to a <PLANET> element than "*", uses the "PLANET" match. On the other hand, sometimes things aren't so clear. For example, you may want "PLANETS" to match some <PLANET> elements, but not others. One way of making sure that happens is to use *modes*.

You can use the mode attribute of <xsl:apply-templates> to set a processing mode. When you set a mode, the only templates that match are those <xsl:template> elements that have their mode attribute set to the same mode. In this way, you can make templates match only one particular node, even if otherwise they would match many nodes. That's great, for example, if you want to handle some <PLANET> elements differently from others.

The following example shows how this works. In this case, I create a new processing mode for planets called "fancy" that displays planetary data in bold. However, I just want the Earth's planetary data to appear in bold, and not any of the other planets' data. That could be a problem, because all the data for the planets are stored in the same type of element—<PLANET>—so they're all matched by the pattern "PLANET". However, I can use modes to solve this problem. In particular, if the current planet is Earth, I can set the processing mode to "fancy":

```
<?xml version="1.0"?>
<xsl:stylesheet version="1.0"
xmlns:xsl="http://www.w3.org/1999/XSL/Transform">

    <xsl:template match="/PLANETS">
        <HTML>
```

```
        <HEAD>
            <TITLE>
                The Planets Table
            </TITLE>
        </HEAD>
        <BODY>
            <H1>
                The Planets Table
            </H1>
            <TABLE BORDER="2">
                <TR>
                    <TD>Name</TD>
                    <TD>Mass</TD>
                    <TD>Radius</TD>
                    <TD>Day</TD>
                </TR>
                <xsl:apply-templates/>
            </TABLE>
        </BODY>
    </HTML>
</xsl:template>

<xsl:template match="PLANET">
   <xsl:if test="NAME='Earth'">
   <TR>
      <TD><xsl:apply-templates select="NAME" mode="fancy"/></TD>
      <TD><xsl:apply-templates select="MASS" mode="fancy"/></TD>
      <TD><xsl:apply-templates select="RADIUS" mode="fancy"/></TD>
      <TD><xsl:apply-templates select="DAY" mode="fancy"/></TD>
   </TR>
   </xsl:if>
   <xsl:if test="NAME!='Earth'">
   <TR>
      <TD><xsl:apply-templates select="NAME"/></TD>
      <TD><xsl:apply-templates select="MASS"/></TD>
      <TD><xsl:apply-templates select="RADIUS"/></TD>
      <TD><xsl:apply-templates select="DAY"/></TD>
   </TR>
   </xsl:if>
</xsl:template>
      .
      .
      .
```

Then I set up the template rules I want, both for the fancy processing mode, which bolds its output, and no special processing mode:

Listing 6.13 **Using Modes**

```
<?xml version="1.0"?>
<xsl:stylesheet version="1.0"
xmlns:xsl="http://www.w3.org/1999/XSL/Transform">

    <xsl:template match="/PLANETS">
        <HTML>
            <HEAD>
                <TITLE>
                    The Fancy Planets Table
                </TITLE>
            </HEAD>
            <BODY>
                <H1>
                    The Fancy Planets Table
                </H1>
                <TABLE BORDER="2">
                    <TR>
                        <TD>Name</TD>
                        <TD>Mass</TD>
                        <TD>Radius</TD>
                        <TD>Day</TD>
                    </TR>
                    <xsl:apply-templates/>
                </TABLE>
            </BODY>
        </HTML>
    </xsl:template>

    <xsl:template match="PLANET">
       <xsl:if test="NAME='Earth'">
       <TR>
          <TD><xsl:apply-templates select="NAME" mode="fancy"/></TD>
          <TD><xsl:apply-templates select="MASS" mode="fancy"/></TD>
          <TD><xsl:apply-templates select="RADIUS" mode="fancy"/></TD>
          <TD><xsl:apply-templates select="DAY" mode="fancy"/></TD>
       </TR>
       </xsl:if>
       <xsl:if test="NAME!='Earth'">
       <TR>
          <TD><xsl:apply-templates select="NAME"/></TD>
          <TD><xsl:apply-templates select="MASS"/></TD>
          <TD><xsl:apply-templates select="RADIUS"/></TD>
          <TD><xsl:apply-templates select="DAY"/></TD>
       </TR>
       </xsl:if>
   </xsl:template>

    <xsl:template match="NAME">
        <xsl:value-of select="."/>
```

```
    </xsl:template>

    <xsl:template match="MASS">
        <xsl:value-of select="."/>
        <xsl:text> </xsl:text>
        <xsl:value-of select="@UNITS"/>
    </xsl:template>

    <xsl:template match="RADIUS">
        <xsl:value-of select="."/>
        <xsl:text> </xsl:text>
        <xsl:value-of select="@UNITS"/>
    </xsl:template>

    <xsl:template match="DAY">
        <xsl:value-of select="."/>
        <xsl:text> </xsl:text>
        <xsl:value-of select="@UNITS"/>
    </xsl:template>

    <xsl:template match="NAME" mode="fancy">
        <B><xsl:value-of select="."/></B>
    </xsl:template>

    <xsl:template match="MASS" mode="fancy">
        <B>
            <xsl:value-of select="."/>
            <xsl:text> </xsl:text>
            <xsl:value-of select="@UNITS"/>
        </B>
    </xsl:template>

    <xsl:template match="RADIUS" mode="fancy">
        <B>
            <xsl:value-of select="."/>
            <xsl:text> </xsl:text>
            <xsl:value-of select="@UNITS"/>
        </B>
    </xsl:template>

    <xsl:template match="DAY" mode="fancy">
        <B>
            <xsl:value-of select="."/>
            <xsl:text> </xsl:text>
            <xsl:value-of select="@UNITS"/>
        </B>
    </xsl:template>

</xsl:stylesheet>
```

Here's the result. Note that Earth's data, and only Earth's data, is made bold:

```
<HTML>
    <HEAD>
        <TITLE>
            The Fancy Planets Table
        </TITLE>
    </HEAD>

    <BODY>
        <H1>
            The Fancy Planets Table
        </H1>

        <TABLE BORDER="2">
            <TR>
                <TD>Name</TD>
                <TD>Mass</TD>
                <TD>Radius</TD>
                <TD>Day</TD>
            </TR>

            <TR>
                <TD>Mercury</TD>
                <TD>.0553 (Earth = 1)</TD>
                <TD>1516 miles</TD>
                <TD>58.65 days</TD>
            </TR>

            <TR>
                <TD>Venus</TD>
                <TD>.815 (Earth = 1)</TD>
                <TD>3716 miles</TD>
                <TD>116.75 days</TD>
            </TR>

            <TR>
                <TD><B>Earth</B></TD>
                <TD><B>1 (Earth = 1)</B></TD>
                <TD><B>2107 miles</B></TD>
                <TD><B>1 days</B></TD>
            </TR>

        </TABLE>
    </BODY>
</HTML>
```

You can see this result in Figure 6.4.

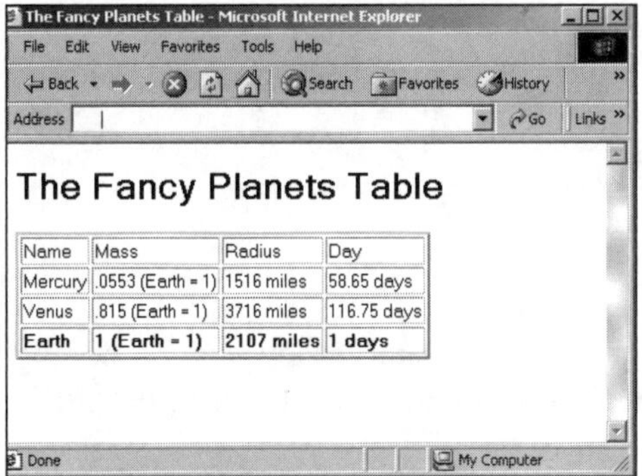

Figure 6.4 Using processing modes.

Modes are also very useful when you want to process the same document more than once, and the classic example is when you're creating a table of contents.

The following example shows how that works; in this case, I add a table of contents to planets.xml in a <TOC> element that has three <ENTRY> elements, one for each planet. Note that I have to use two templates that match <PLANET> elements here, one to create the table of contents and one to copy over all <PLANET> elements to the result document, so I use modes to keep them straight. I start by setting the mode to "toc" and using a template that supports that mode and creates the table of contents:

```
<?xml version="1.0"?>
<xsl:stylesheet version="1.0"
xmlns:xsl="http://www.w3.org/1999/XSL/Transform">
<xsl:output method="xml"/>

  <xsl:template match="PLANETS">
    <PLANETS>
        <TOC>
            <xsl:apply-templates mode="toc"/>
        </TOC>
        .
        .
        .
    </PLANETS>
  </xsl:template>
```

```
  <xsl:template match="PLANET" mode="toc">
    <ENTRY>
        <xsl:value-of select="NAME"/>
    </ENTRY>
  </xsl:template>
        .
        .
        .
```

Next, I apply a general template without any processing modes to all elements and attributes so I can copy them to the result document:

Listing 6.14 Creating a Table of Contents

```
<?xml version="1.0"?>
<xsl:stylesheet version="1.0"
xmlns:xsl="http://www.w3.org/1999/XSL/Transform">
<xsl:output method="xml"/>

  <xsl:template match="PLANETS">
    <PLANETS>
        <TOC>
            <xsl:apply-templates mode="toc"/>
        </TOC>
        <xsl:apply-templates select="@*|node()"/>
    </PLANETS>
  </xsl:template>

  <xsl:template match="PLANET" mode="toc">
    <ENTRY>
        <xsl:value-of select="NAME"/>
    </ENTRY>
  </xsl:template>

  <xsl:template match="@*|node()">
    <xsl:copy>
      <xsl:apply-templates select="@*|node()"/>
    </xsl:copy>
  </xsl:template>

</xsl:stylesheet>
```

And here's the result, showing planets.xml with a table of contents:

```
<?xml version="1.0" encoding="UTF-8"?>
<?xml-stylesheet type="text/xml" href="planets.xsl"?>
<PLANETS>
```

```
    <TOC>
        <ENTRY>Mercury</ENTRY>
        <ENTRY>Venus</ENTRY>
        <ENTRY>Earth</ENTRY>
    </TOC>

    <PLANET>
        <NAME>Mercury</NAME>
        <MASS UNITS="(Earth = 1)">.0553</MASS>
        <DAY UNITS="days">58.65</DAY>
        <RADIUS UNITS="miles">1516</RADIUS>
        <DENSITY UNITS="(Earth = 1)">.983</DENSITY>
        <DISTANCE UNITS="million miles">43.4</DISTANCE><!--At perihelion-->
    </PLANET>
        .
        .
        .
</PLANETS>
```

This chapter has covered a lot of ground, and in the next chapter I'm going to press on, taking a look at creating full XPath expressions. Although you got a taste of this topic when you saw match patterns created in Chapter 4, there's a great deal more coming up.

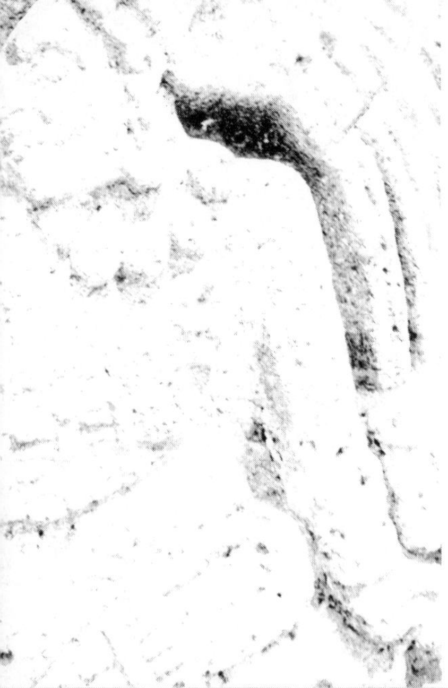

7
Using and Understanding XPath

CHAPTER 4 EXPLAINED HOW TO CONSTRUCT MATCH patterns, which you use with the match attribute of elements such as <xsl:template>. Those patterns are a *subset* of the full XPath language, and this chapter explores the full version of XPath.

XSLT actually has many more places to use XPath expressions than match patterns—you can use XPath expressions in the select attribute of the <xsl:apply-templates>, <xsl:value-of>, <xsl:for-each>, <xsl:param>, <xsl:variable>, <xsl:with-param>, <xsl:copy-of>, and <xsl:sort> elements, in attribute value templates, in the test attribute of <xsl:if> and <xsl:when> elements, the value attribute of <xsl:number>, and in the predicate of match patterns. There's no getting around it: you don't know XSLT unless you know XPath, and this chapter is all about using and creating XPath expressions.

In fact, you've been dealing with XPath expressions since Chapter 1, when you first saw the select attribute in <xsl:apply-templates> and <xsl:value-of>:

```
<?xml version="1.0"?>
<xsl:stylesheet version="1.0"
xmlns:xsl="http://www.w3.org/1999/XSL/Transform">

    <xsl:template match="/PLANETS">
        <HTML>
            <HEAD>
                <TITLE>
                    The Planets Table
                </TITLE>
```

```
            </HEAD>
            <BODY>
                <H1>
                    The Planets Table
                </H1>
                <TABLE BORDER="2">
                    <TR>
                        <TD>Name</TD>
                        <TD>Mass</TD>
                        <TD>Radius</TD>
                        <TD>Day</TD>
                    </TR>
                    <xsl:apply-templates/>
                </TABLE>
            </BODY>
        </HTML>
    </xsl:template>

    <xsl:template match="PLANET">
       <TR>
          <TD><xsl:value-of select="NAME"/></TD>
          <TD><xsl:apply-templates select="MASS"/></TD>
          <TD><xsl:apply-templates select="RADIUS"/></TD>
          <TD><xsl:apply-templates select="DAY"/></TD>
       </TR>
   </xsl:template>

    <xsl:template match="MASS">
        <xsl:value-of select="."/>
        <xsl:text> </xsl:text>
        <xsl:value-of select="@UNITS"/>
    </xsl:template>

    <xsl:template match="RADIUS">
        <xsl:value-of select="."/>
        <xsl:text> </xsl:text>
        <xsl:value-of select="@UNITS"/>
    </xsl:template>

    <xsl:template match="DAY">
        <xsl:value-of select="."/>
        <xsl:text> </xsl:text>
        <xsl:value-of select="@UNITS"/>
    </xsl:template>

</xsl:stylesheet>
```

Understanding XPath

Although we already know, for example, that you can assign "." to a `select` attribute to refer to the current node, "." is not a valid match pattern; it's an XPath abbreviation for `self::node()`. Match patterns are restricted to only two axes: `child` and `attribute`, but XPath has *thirteen* axes, including `self`. You'll see all those axes in this chapter, as well as an example of each at work.

Formally speaking, XPath enables you to refer to specific sections of XML documents; it's a language for addressing the various parts of such documents. XPath is what you use to indicate what part of a document you want to work with. W3C says of XPath:

> "The primary purpose of XPath is to address parts of an XML document. In support of this primary purpose, it also provides basic facilities for manipulation of strings, numbers and Booleans. XPath uses a compact, non-XML syntax to facilitate use of XPath within URIs and XML attribute values. XPath operates on the abstract, logical structure of an XML document, rather than its surface syntax. XPath gets its name from its use of a path notation as in URLs for navigating through the hierarchical structure of an XML document."

This quotation comes from the XPath 1.0 specification. Note that although the primary purpose of XPath is to address parts of XML documents, it also supports syntax to work with strings, numbers, and Boolean true/false values; that support is also very useful by itself, as you'll see.

Currently, XPath version 1.0 is the standard, but the requirements for XPath 2.0 have been released. There are no drafts of XPath 2.0 yet, just a list of what W3C plans to put into it. An overview at the end of this chapter looks at that list. You can find the primary XPath resources in two places:

- **The XPath 1.0 specification.** You use XPath to locate and point to specific sections and elements in XML documents so that you can work with them. `www.w3.org/TR/xpath`
- **The XPath 2.0 requirements**. XPath is being updated to offer more support for XSLT 2.0—primarily support for XML schemas. `www.w3.org/TR/xpath20req`

For more on XPath, see *Inside XML*. You might also want to take a look at these XPath tutorials:

- `www.zvon.org/xxl/XPathTutorial/General/examples.html`
- `www.pro-solutions.com/tutorials/xpath/`

The match patterns you've seen so far have returned node sets that you can loop over or match, but XPath is more general than that. In addition to node sets, XPath expressions can also return numbers, Boolean (true/false) values, and strings. Understanding XPath means understanding XPath expressions, and only one kind of XPath expression (although a very important kind) returns node sets that locate sections of a document. Other XPath expressions return other kinds of data, as you'll see.

The full syntax of XPath expressions is given in the XPath specification, and I include it here for reference. As it does for match patterns, W3C uses Extended Backus-Naur Form (EBNF) notation to give the formal definition of XPath expressions. (You can find an explanation of this grammar in `www.w3.org/TR/REC-xml`, section 6.) The following list includes the EBNF notations you need:

- ::= means "is defined as"
- + means "one or more"
- * means "zero or more"
- | means "or"
- - means "not"
- ? means "optional"

Also, note that when an item is quoted with single quotation marks, as in 'ancestor' or '::', that item is meant to appear in an expression literally (like "ancestor::PLANET"), as are items named `literals`. Here's the formal definition of an XPath expression (named `Expr` in this definition) in full:

```
Expr    ::=    OrExpr

OrExpr    ::=    AndExpr | OrExpr 'or' AndExpr

AndExpr    ::=    EqualityExpr  | AndExpr 'and' EqualityExpr

EqualityExpr    ::=    RelationalExpr  | EqualityExpr '=' RelationalExpr
     | EqualityExpr '!=' RelationalExpr

RelationalExpr    ::=    AdditiveExpr | RelationalExpr '<' AdditiveExpr
   | RelationalExpr '>' AdditiveExpr | RelationalExpr '<=' AdditiveExpr
   | RelationalExpr '>=' AdditiveExpr

AdditiveExpr    ::=    MultiplicativeExpr    | AdditiveExpr '+' MultiplicativeExpr
   | AdditiveExpr '-' MultiplicativeExpr
```

```
MultiplicativeExpr    ::=    UnaryExpr | MultiplicativeExpr MultiplyOperator UnaryExpr
   | MultiplicativeExpr 'div' UnaryExpr | MultiplicativeExpr 'mod' UnaryExpr

UnaryExpr    ::=    UnionExpr  | '-' UnaryExpr

MultiplyOperator    ::=    '*'

UnionExpr    ::=    PathExpr   | UnionExpr '|' PathExpr

PathExpr    ::=    LocationPath | FilterExpr
   | FilterExpr '/' RelativeLocationPath
   | FilterExpr '//' RelativeLocationPath

LocationPath    ::=    RelativeLocationPath  | AbsoluteLocationPath

AbsoluteLocationPath    ::=    '/' RelativeLocationPath?  | AbbreviatedAbsoluteLocationPath

RelativeLocationPath    ::=    Step   | RelativeLocationPath '/' Step
     | AbbreviatedRelativeLocationPath

AbbreviatedAbsoluteLocationPath    ::=    '//' RelativeLocationPath

AbbreviatedRelativeLocationPath    ::=    RelativeLocationPath '//' Step

Step    ::=    AxisSpecifier NodeTest Predicate*   | AbbreviatedStep

AxisSpecifier    ::=    AxisName '::'   | AbbreviatedAxisSpecifier

AxisName    ::=    'ancestor' | 'ancestor-or-self' | 'attribute' | 'child' | 'descendant'
   | 'descendant-or-self' | 'following' | 'following-sibling' | 'namespace' | 'parent'
   | 'preceding' | 'preceding-sibling' | 'self'

AbbreviatedAxisSpecifier    ::=    '@'?

NodeTest    ::=    NameTest  | NodeType '(' ')'   | 'processing-instruction' '(' Literal ')'

NameTest    ::=    '*' | NCName ':' '*' | QName

NodeType    ::=    'comment' | 'text' | 'processing-instruction' | 'node'

Predicate    ::=    '[' PredicateExpr ']'

PredicateExpr    ::=    Expr

FilterExpr    ::=    PrimaryExpr  | FilterExpr Predicate

PrimaryExpr    ::=    VariableReference | '(' Expr ')' | Literal    | Number | FunctionCall

VariableReference    ::=    '$' QName
```

```
Number    ::=   Digits ('.' Digits?)? | '.' Digits

Digits    ::=   [0-9]+

FunctionCall    ::=   FunctionName '(' ( Argument ( ',' Argument )* )? ')'

FunctionName    ::=   QName - NodeType

Argument    ::=   Expr

AbbreviatedStep    ::=   '.' | '..'
```

As you can see, there's a lot to this specification, including calls to XPath functions (which you'll see in the next chapter). The best way to understand XPath expressions is to organize them by the data types they can return.

XPath Data Types

There are four XPath data types, not just the node set type that match patterns must return:

- Node sets
- Booleans
- Numbers
- Strings

Result Tree Fragments

XSLT 1.0 also added *result tree fragments* to the XPath data types. As mentioned in Chapter 4, result tree fragments were just tree fragments that you could assign to XSLT variables. Support for them was removed in the XSLT 1.1 working draft, which means they probably won't be a part of XSLT 2.0. You can treat result tree fragments as data types by using `<xsl:variable>`, which we'll see in Chapter 9.

The following sections look at these various types in turn.

XPath Node Sets

As its name implies, a node set is simply a set of nodes. A node set may include a number of nodes, a single node, or be empty. Because the primary purpose of XPath is to locate sections of documents, XPath expressions that return node sets are the most popular type of expressions. For example, the XPath expression `child::PLANET` returns a node set of all `<PLANET>` elements that are children of the context node. The expression `child::PLANET/child::NAME` returns a node set of all `<NAME>` elements that are children of `<PLANET>`

elements of the context node. These kinds of XPath expressions are called *location paths* (W3C calls them "the most important construct" in XPath), and I'll devote a lot of this chapter to helping you understand location paths.

To select a node or nodes from a node set, or to handle those nodes, you can use the following XPath functions that work on node sets, which you first saw in Chapter 4 (and which you'll see in the next chapter in more detail):

- `count(node-set)`. This function returns the number of nodes in *node-set*. Note that if you omit *node-set*, this function uses the context node.
- `id(string ID)`. This function returns a node set of the element whose ID matches the string passed to the function, or an empty node set if no element has the specified ID. Also, note that you can specify multiple IDs separated by whitespace, and this function returns a node set of the elements with those IDs.
- `last()`. This function returns the number of the last node in a node set.
- `local-name(node-set)`. This function returns the local name of the first node in the node set. Omitting *node-set* makes this function use the context node.
- `name(node-set)`. This function returns the full, qualified name of the first node in the node set. Omitting *node-set* makes this function use the context node.
- `namespace-uri(node-set)`. This function returns the URI of the namespace of the first node in the node set. Omitting *node-set* makes this function use the context node.
- `position()`. This function returns the position of the context node in the context node set (starting with 1).

The following example, from Chapter 6, used the `count` function to return the number of nodes in a node set. In this case, the node set is made up of all the `<PLANET>` elements in planets.xml, and I get that node set with the location path "\\PLANET" (which, as a location path, is also an XPath expression):

```
<xsl:stylesheet
 xmlns:xsl="http://www.w3.org/1999/XSL/Transform"
 version="1.0">

<xsl:output method="xml" indent="yes"/>

<xsl:template match="*">
    <xsl:copy>
        <xsl:apply-templates/>
    </xsl:copy>
```

```
</xsl:template>

<xsl:template match="PLANET">
    <xsl:copy use-attribute-sets="numbering">
        <xsl:apply-templates/>
    </xsl:copy>
</xsl:template>

<xsl:attribute-set name="numbering">
    <xsl:attribute name="number"><xsl:number/></xsl:attribute>
    <xsl:attribute name="total"><xsl:value-of select="count(//PLANET)"/></xsl:attribute>
</xsl:attribute-set>

</xsl:stylesheet>
```

Here's the result; note that every `<PLANET>` element has both a `number` and `total` attribute, and the `total` attribute holds the total number of `<PLANET>` elements in the document:

```
<?xml version="1.0" encoding="UTF-8"?>
<PLANETS>

    <PLANET number="1" total="3">
        <NAME>Mercury</NAME>
        <MASS>.0553</MASS>
        <DAY>58.65</DAY>
        <RADIUS>1516</RADIUS>
        <DENSITY>.983</DENSITY>
        <DISTANCE>43.4</DISTANCE>
    </PLANET>

    <PLANET number="2" total="3">
        <NAME>Venus</NAME>
        <MASS>.815</MASS>
        <DAY>116.75</DAY>
        <RADIUS>3716</RADIUS>
        <DENSITY>.943</DENSITY>
        <DISTANCE>66.8</DISTANCE>
    </PLANET>

    <PLANET number="3" total="3">
        <NAME>Earth</NAME>
        <MASS>1</MASS>
        <DAY>1</DAY>
        <RADIUS>2107</RADIUS>
        <DENSITY>1</DENSITY>
        <DISTANCE>128.4</DISTANCE>
    </PLANET>

</PLANETS>
```

Among the node-set functions, note in particular the `name` and `local-name` functions. These give you a way of determining the name of the current element; for example, if the current element is `<DAY>`, `local-name` returns "DAY". To see how this can be useful, look at the following stylesheet, where I use tags such as `<PLANETS>`, `<PLANET>`, and `<DATA>` as literal result elements:

```
<?xml version="1.0"?>
<xsl:stylesheet version="1.0"
xmlns:xsl="http://www.w3.org/1999/XSL/Transform">
    <xsl:output method="xml"/>

    <xsl:template match="PLANETS">
        <PLANETS>
            <xsl:for-each select="PLANET">
                <PLANET>
                    <xsl:for-each select="*">
                        <DATA>
                            <xsl:value-of select="."/>
                        </DATA>
                    </xsl:for-each>
                </PLANET>
            </xsl:for-each>
        </PLANETS>
    </xsl:template>

</xsl:stylesheet>
```

However, this treats markup as simple text. I can use `<xsl:element>` to create new elements instead, using `local-name` to find the name of context nodes this way:

```
<?xml version="1.0"?>
<xsl:stylesheet version="1.0"
xmlns:xsl="http://www.w3.org/1999/XSL/Transform">
    <xsl:output method="xml"/>

    <xsl:template match="PLANETS">
        <xsl:element name="{local-name(.)}">
            <xsl:for-each select="PLANET">
                <xsl:element name="{local-name(.)}">
                    <xsl:for-each select="*">
                        <xsl:element name="DATA">
                            <xsl:value-of select="."/>
                        </xsl:element>
                    </xsl:for-each>
                </xsl:element>
            </xsl:for-each>
        </xsl:element>
    </xsl:template>

</xsl:stylesheet>
```

Some XSLT authors think of XPath expressions only in terms of expressions that return node sets. However, XPath expressions also return Booleans, numbers, or strings, and those results are used in such places as `<xsl:param>`, `<xsl:with-param>`, `<xsl:number>`, `<xsl:value-of>`, `<xsl:sort>`, attribute value templates, and the predicates of location paths. In the preceding example, I assigned the XPath expression `count(//PLANET)`, which returns a number, not a node set, to the `select` attribute of the `<xsl:value-of>` element, to insert a number into a document. I'll take a closer look at the numbers you can handle using XPath expressions next.

XPath Numbers

In XPath, numbers are stored in double floating point format. Formally defined, all XPath numbers are supposed to be stored in 64-bit IEEE 754 double floating point format, and all numbers are stored in double precision floating point format.

You can use the following XPath operators on numbers, as you first saw in Chapter 4 during the discussion of XPath predicates:

- + addition
- - subtraction
- * multiplication
- `div` division (The / character, which stands for division in other languages, is already used in XML and XPath.)
- `mod` finding the modulus of two numbers (the remainder after dividing the first by the second)

For example, the element `<xsl:value-of select="15 + 75"/>` inserts the string "90" into the output document. The following example selects all planets whose day (measured in Earth days) multiplied by its distance from the Sun (measured in millions of miles) is greater than 60,000:

```
<xsl:template match="PLANETS">
    <HTML>
        <BODY>
            <xsl:apply-templates select="PLANET[DAY * MASS > 60000]"/>
        </BODY>
    </HTML>
</xsl:template>
```

XPath also supports these functions that operate on numbers:

- `ceiling()`. This function returns the smallest integer larger than the number you pass it.

- `floor()`. This function returns the largest integer smaller than the number you pass it.
- `round()`. This function rounds the number you pass it to the nearest integer.
- `sum()`. This function returns the sum of the numbers you pass to it.

For example, here's an example that determines the average distance from the Sun (in million miles) of the planets in planets.xml:

```
<?xml version="1.0"?>
<xsl:stylesheet version="1.0"
xmlns:xsl="http://www.w3.org/1999/XSL/Transform">
<xsl:output method="xml"/>

<xsl:template match="PLANETS">
    <HTML>
        <BODY>
            The average planetary distance from the Sun is:
            <xsl:value-of select="sum(child::PLANET/child::DISTANCE) div
            ➥count(child::PLANET)"/>
        </BODY>
    </HTML>
</xsl:template>

</xsl:stylesheet>
```

XPath Strings

In XPath, strings are made up of Unicode characters by default. As you first saw in Chapter 4 during the discussion of XPath expressions in match predicates, a number of functions are specially designed to work on strings (you'll see them in more detail in the next chapter):

- `concat(string string1, string string2, ...)`. This function returns all strings concatenated together.
- `contains(string string1, string string2)`. This function returns true if the first string contains the second one.
- `format-number(number number1, string string2, string string3)`. This function returns a string holding the formatted string version of *`number1`*, using *`string2`* as a formatting string (you create formatting strings as you would for Java's `java.text.DecimalFormat` method), and *`string3`* as the optional locale string.
- `normalize-space(string string1)`. This function returns *`string1`* after leading and trailing whitespace is stripped and multiple consecutive whitespace is replaced with a single space.

- `starts-with(string string1, string string2)`. This function returns true if the first string starts with the second string.
- `string-length(string string1)`. This function returns the number of characters in *string1*.
- `substring(string string1, number offset, number length)`. This function returns *length* characters from the string, starting at *offset*.
- `substring-after(string string1, string string2)`. This function returns the part of *string1* after the first occurrence of *string2*.
- `substring-before(string string1, string string2)`. This function returns the part of *string1* up to the first occurrence of *string2*.
- `translate(string string1, string string2, string string3)`. This function returns *string1* with all occurrences of the characters in *string2* replaced by the matching characters in *string3*.

In the following example, I search all attributes for the word "miles", and if found, I add the text "You should switch to kilometers." in the result document:

Listing 7.1 **Searching Attributes for Text**

```
<?xml version="1.0"?>
<xsl:stylesheet version="1.0"
xmlns:xsl="http://www.w3.org/1999/XSL/Transform">

    <xsl:template match="/PLANETS">
        <HTML>
            <HEAD>
                <TITLE>
                    The Planets Table
                </TITLE>
            </HEAD>
            <BODY>
                <H1>
                    The Planets Table
                </H1>
                <TABLE BORDER="2">
                    <TR>
                        <TD>Name</TD>
                        <TD>Mass</TD>
                        <TD>Radius</TD>
                        <TD>Day</TD>
                        <TD>Distance</TD>
                    </TR>
                    <xsl:apply-templates/>
                </TABLE>
```

```
            </BODY>
        </HTML>
    </xsl:template>

    <xsl:template match="PLANET">
       <TR>
          <TD><xsl:value-of select="NAME"/></TD>
          <TD><xsl:apply-templates select="MASS"/></TD>
          <TD><xsl:apply-templates select="RADIUS"/></TD>
          <TD><xsl:apply-templates select="DAY"/></TD>
          <TD><xsl:apply-templates select="DISTANCE"/></TD>
       </TR>
   </xsl:template>

    <xsl:template match="MASS">
        <xsl:value-of select="."/>
        <xsl:text> </xsl:text>
        <xsl:value-of select="@UNITS"/>
    </xsl:template>

    <xsl:template match="RADIUS">
        <xsl:value-of select="."/>
        <xsl:text> </xsl:text>
        <xsl:value-of select="@UNITS"/>
    </xsl:template>

    <xsl:template match="DAY">
        <xsl:value-of select="."/>
        <xsl:text> </xsl:text>
        <xsl:value-of select="@UNITS"/>
    </xsl:template>

    <xsl:template match="DISTANCE">
        <xsl:value-of select="."/>
        <xsl:text> </xsl:text>
        <xsl:value-of select="@UNITS"/>
    </xsl:template>

    <xsl:template match="//*[contains(@UNITS, 'miles')]">
        <xsl:value-of select="."/>
        <xsl:text> </xsl:text>
        <xsl:text>You should switch to kilometers.</xsl:text>
    </xsl:template>

</xsl:stylesheet>
```

Here's the result document:

```
<HTML>
    <HEAD>
        <TITLE>
```

```
            The Planets Table
        </TITLE>
    </HEAD>

    <BODY>
        <H1>
            The Planets Table
        </H1>

        <TABLE BORDER="2">
            <TR>
                <TD>Name</TD>
                <TD>Mass</TD>
                <TD>Radius</TD>
                <TD>Day</TD>
                <TD>Distance</TD>
            </TR>

            <TR>
                <TD>Mercury</TD>
                <TD>.0553 (Earth = 1)</TD>
                <TD>1516 You should switch to kilometers.</TD>
                <TD>58.65 days</TD>
                <TD>43.4 You should switch to kilometers.</TD>
            </TR>

            <TR>
                <TD>Venus</TD>
                <TD>.815 (Earth = 1)</TD>
                <TD>3716 You should switch to kilometers.</TD>
                <TD>116.75 days</TD>
                <TD>66.8 You should switch to kilometers.</TD>
            </TR>

            <TR>
                <TD>Earth</TD>
                <TD>1 (Earth = 1)</TD>
                <TD>2107 You should switch to kilometers.</TD>
                <TD>1 days</TD>
                <TD>128.4 You should switch to kilometers.</TD>
            </TR>

        </TABLE>
    </BODY>
</HTML>
```

In addition to working with node sets, numbers, and strings, you can also work with Boolean true/false values.

XPath Booleans

XPath Boolean expressions evaluate to either true or false, and they're usually used only in predicates. Numbers are considered false if they're zero, and true otherwise. An empty string, "", is also considered false, and all other strings are considered true. Node sets are considered true if they're not empty.

You can use a number of logical operators to produce true/false results in XPath, as you saw in overview in Chapter 4:

- `!=` means "is not equal to"
- `<` means "is less than" (use < in XML documents)
- `<=` means "is less than or equal to" (use <= in XML documents)
- `=` means "is equal to" (C, C++, Java, JavaScript programmers take note: this operator is one = sign, not two)
- `>` means "is greater than"
- `>=` means "is greater than or equal to"

You can also use the keywords `and` or `or` to connect Boolean clauses with a logical `And` or `Or` operation, and the `not` function to reverse the logical sense of an expression, as in this case, where I'm selecting all `<PLANET>` elements that are not the first or last such element:

```
<xsl:template match="PLANET[not(position() = 1) and not(position() = last())]">
    <xsl:value-of select="."/>
</xsl:template>
```

Here's an example you first saw in Chapter 5 that uses the logical operator `not` and the operators `=` and `!=`:

```
<xsl:template match="PLANET">
    <xsl:if test="NAME[not(text())]">
        <xsl:message terminate="yes">
            Each planet must have a name!
        </xsl:message>
    </xsl:if>
    <xsl:value-of select="NAME"/>
    <xsl:choose>
        <xsl:when test="position()!=last()">, </xsl:when>
        <xsl:when test="position()=last()-1">and </xsl:when>
        <xsl:otherwise>.</xsl:otherwise>
    </xsl:choose>
</xsl:template>
```

In addition, there is a `true` function that always returns true, and a `false` function that always returns a value of false. There's also a `lang` function that you can use to check the language set in the document's `xml:lang` attribute;

this function returns a value of true if the language you pass it is the same as the language set in the document.

As you see, there are all kinds of XPath expressions, including ones that return nodes, numbers, strings, and Boolean values. The most important type of XPath expression is the *location path*; creating location paths is what XPath was originally designed for, and I'll spend the remainder of this chapter working with them.

Creating XPath Location Paths

You're already familiar with the XPath way of thinking of documents; for example, it's XPath that defines the seven types of document nodes:

- **The root node.** The very start of the document. This node represents the entire document in XPath.
- **Element nodes.** Represents an element in XPath trees, as bounded by a start and matching end tag, or a single empty element tag.
- **Attribute nodes.** The value of an attribute after entity references have been expanded and surrounding whitespace has been trimmed.
- **Comment nodes.** The text of a comment, not including <!-- and -->.
- **Namespace nodes.** A namespace declaration. In XPath, a namespace node is added to each element for each active namespace, including default ones.
- **Processing instruction nodes.** Includes the text of the processing instruction, which does not include <? and ?>.
- **Text nodes.** PCDATA text. Text nodes are normalized by default in XPath, which is to say that immediately adjacent text nodes are merged.

To specify a node or set of nodes in XPath, you use a location path. A location path, in turn, consists of one or more *location steps*—also called simply *steps*—separated by / or //. If you start the location path with /, the location path is called an *absolute location path*, because you're specifying the path from the root node; otherwise, the location path is *relative*, starting from the context *node*.

Location steps, the building blocks of location paths, are much like the step patterns that make up match patterns, which you saw in Chapter 4. In particular, a location step is made up of an *axis*, a *node test*, and zero or more *predicates*, as follows: `axis::nodetest[predicate]`. For example, in the expression `ancestor::NAME[position() > 100]`, `ancestor` is the name of the axis, `NAME` is the node test and `[position() > 100]` is the predicate. (The predicate itself holds a complete XPath expression—usually an expression that returns a Boolean value.) You can create location paths with one or more location steps, such as `/descendant::PLANET/child::NAME`, which selects all the `<NAME>` elements that have a `<PLANET>` parent.

XPath steps look like the step patterns you saw in Chapter 4 because the general form is the same—`axis::nodetest[predicate]`—but there's a lot more to cover here. For example, there are thirteen axes now, not just two.

Part 1 of XPath Location Steps: Axes

In the location path `ancestor::NAME`, which refers to a `<NAME>` element that is an ancestor of the context node, `ancestor` is the axis. XPath supports many different axes, and here's the complete list:

- The `ancestor` axis holds the ancestors of the context node; the ancestors of the context node are the parent of context node and the parent's parent and so forth, back to and including the root node.
- The `ancestor-or-self` axis holds the context node and the ancestors of the context node.
- The `attribute` axis holds the attributes of the context node.
- The `child` axis holds the children of the context node.
- The `descendant` axis holds the descendants of the context node. A descendant is a child or a child of a child and so on.
- The `descendant-or-self` axis contains the context node and the descendants of the context node.
- The `following` axis holds all nodes in the same document as the context node that come after the context node.
- The `following-sibling` axis holds all the following siblings of the context node. A sibling is a node on the same level as the context node.
- The `namespace` axis holds the namespace nodes of the context node.
- The `parent` axis holds the parent of the context node.
- The `preceding` axis contains all nodes that come before the context node.
- The `preceding-sibling` axis contains all the preceding siblings of the context node. A sibling is a node on the same level as the context node.
- The `self` axis contains the context node.

In the following example template I use the descendant axis to indicate that I want to match descendants of the context node, which include child nodes, grandchild nodes, great-grandchild nodes, and so on:

```
<xsl:template match="PLANET">
    <DATA>
        <NAME>
            <xsl:value-of select="descendant::NAME"/>
        </NAME>
        <MASS>
            <xsl:value-of select="descendant::MASS"/>
        </MASS>
        <DAY>
            <xsl:value-of select="descendant::DAY"/>
        </DAY>
    </DATA>
</xsl:template>
```

This chapter looks at each of these axes. In this example, descendant is the axis, and the element names NAME, MASS, and DAY are *node tests*.

Part 2 of XPath Location Steps: Node Tests

When constructing patterns, you can use names of nodes as node tests, or the wild card * to select any element node. For example, the expression child::*/child::NAME selects all <NAME> elements that are grandchildren of the context node. In addition to node names and the wild card character, you can also use these node tests in XPath, just as you can in match patterns:

- The comment() node test selects comment nodes.
- The node() node test selects any type of node.
- The processing-instruction() node test selects a processing instruction node. You specify the name of the processing instruction to select in the parentheses.
- The text() node test selects a text node.

For example, the following stylesheet finds all comments in a document, using the comment() node test, and creates a new comment, <!--Warning: comment found!-->, for each one:

Listing 7.2 **Matching Comments**

```
<?xml version="1.0"?>
<xsl:stylesheet version="1.0"
xmlns:xsl="http://www.w3.org/1999/XSL/Transform">
<xsl:output method="xml"/>

  <xsl:template match="/">

  <xsl:for-each select="descendant::comment()">
      <xsl:comment>Warning: comment found!</xsl:comment>
  </xsl:for-each>

  </xsl:template>

</xsl:stylesheet>
```

Here's the result document when you use this stylesheet on planets.xml:

```
<?xml version="1.0" encoding="UTF-8"?>
<!--Warning: comment found!-->
<!--Warning: comment found!-->
<!--Warning: comment found!-->
```

Part 3 of XPath Location Steps: Predicates

The predicate in an XPath location step itself contains an XPath expression enclosed in brackets, [and]. The contained XPath expression is treated as if it evaluated to true or false. If it evaluates to a string, XPath treats it as true if the string is not empty. If it evaluates to a node set, XPath treats it as true if the node set is not empty. If it evaluates to a number, the overall result is considered true if that number matches the context position—for example, `PLANET[3]` is true if and only if `PLANET[position() = 3]` is true.

The predicate contains XPath expressions of the kind you've seen throughout this chapter: rarely those that return node sets, mostly those that return strings, numbers, or Boolean values. For example, the location path `preceding-sibling::MASS[position() = 4]` selects the fourth previous `<MASS>` sibling element of the context node.

Using the XPath Axes

That's it for the three parts of location steps—the axis, node test, and predicate. You should be familiar with these to some extent from the work we've done with match patterns, but notice the axis I used in the previous example—the `preceding-sibling` axis. So far in this book, you've only seen the axes that match XSLT patterns—`child` and `attribute` axes—and now it's time to take a look at the new axes available in full XPath expressions, starting with the `ancestor` axis.

Using the *ancestor* Axis

The `ancestor` axis contains all the ancestors of the context node, including its parents, grandparents, great-grandparents, and so on. This axis always contains the root node—unless the context node is the root node.

Look at the following example, which shows how to use the `ancestor` axis to find the names (as stored in a `<NAME>` element) of all the ancestors of <MASS> elements:

Listing 7.3 **Using the *ancestor* Axis**

```
<?xml version="1.0"?>
<xsl:stylesheet version="1.0"
xmlns:xsl="http://www.w3.org/1999/XSL/Transform">
<xsl:output method="xml"/>

<xsl:template match="MASS">
    <xsl:for-each select="ancestor::*">
        <xsl:value-of select="./NAME"/>
    </xsl:for-each>
</xsl:template>

<xsl:template match="PLANET">
    <xsl:apply-templates select="MASS"/>
</xsl:template>

</xsl:stylesheet>
```

And here's the result when I use this stylesheet on planets.xml:

```
<?xml version="1.0" encoding="utf-8"?>
    Mercury
    Venus
    Earth
```

Using the *ancestor-or-self* Axis

The `ancestor-or-self` axis contains all the ancestors of the context node, as well as the context node itself. That means, among other things, that this axis always contains the root node.

In the following example, I've added an `AUTHOR` attributes set to "Steve" throughout this document:

Listing 7.4 **planets.xml with *AUTHOR* Attributes**

```
<?xml version="1.0"?>
<?xml-stylesheet type="text/xml" href="planets.xsl"?>
<PLANETS AUTHOR="Steve" >

    <PLANET AUTHOR="Steve" >
        <NAME>Mercury</NAME>
        <MASS AUTHOR="Steve" UNITS="(Earth = 1)">.0553</MASS>
        <DAY UNITS="days">58.65</DAY>
        <RADIUS UNITS="miles">1516</RADIUS>
        <DENSITY UNITS="(Earth = 1)">.983</DENSITY>
        <DISTANCE UNITS="million miles">43.4</DISTANCE><!--At perihelion-->
    </PLANET>

    <PLANET AUTHOR="Steve">
        <NAME>Venus</NAME>
        <MASS UNITS="(Earth = 1)">.815</MASS>
        <DAY UNITS="days">116.75</DAY>
        <RADIUS UNITS="miles">3716</RADIUS>
        <DENSITY UNITS="(Earth = 1)">.943</DENSITY>
        <DISTANCE UNITS="million miles">66.8</DISTANCE><!--At perihelion-->
    </PLANET>

    <PLANET>
        <NAME>Earth</NAME>
        <MASS UNITS="(Earth = 1)">1</MASS>
        <DAY UNITS="days">1</DAY>
        <RADIUS UNITS="miles">2107</RADIUS>
        <DENSITY UNITS="(Earth = 1)">1</DENSITY>
        <DISTANCE UNITS="million miles">128.4</DISTANCE><!--At perihelion-->
    </PLANET>

</PLANETS>
```

Now say that I want to list all ancestors of <MASS> elements, by name, that have an AUTHOR attribute—as well as the current <MASS> element, if it has an AUTHOR attribute. I can do that with the ancestor-or-self axis and the local-name function:

Listing 7.5 **Using the *ancestor-of-self* Axis**

```
<?xml version="1.0"?>
<xsl:stylesheet version="1.0"
xmlns:xsl="http://www.w3.org/1999/XSL/Transform">
<xsl:output method="xml"/>

<xsl:template match="MASS">
    <xsl:for-each select="ancestor-or-self::*[@AUTHOR]">
        <xsl:value-of select="local-name(.)"/>
        <xsl:text> </xsl:text>
    </xsl:for-each>
</xsl:template>

<xsl:template match="PLANET">
    <xsl:apply-templates select="MASS"/>
</xsl:template>

</xsl:stylesheet>
```

Here's the result, showing the matching ancestors of all three <MASS> elements, including the <MASS> element itself if it has an AUTHOR attribute:

```
<?xml version="1.0" encoding="UTF-8"?>

    PLANETS PLANET MASS
    PLANETS PLANET
    PLANETS
```

Using the *descendant* Axis

The descendant axis contains all the descendants of the context node. Note that this does not include any attributes or namespace nodes, because they are not considered child nodes.

The following example puts this axis to work; in this case, I want to add an annotation to Mercury's <PLANET> element: <INFO>Sorry, Mercury has blown up and is no longer available.</INFO>. To find Mercury, all I have to do is to check whether any descendant of a <PLANET> element has the string value "Mercury", which I do in an XPath expression inside a match predicate:

Listing 7.6 **Using the *descendant* Axis**

```
<?xml version="1.0"?>
<xsl:stylesheet version="1.0"
xmlns:xsl="http://www.w3.org/1999/XSL/Transform">
<xsl:output method="xml"/>

  <xsl:template match="PLANET[descendant::*='Mercury']">
    <xsl:copy>
      <xsl:apply-templates select="@*|node()"/>
      <INFO>Sorry, Mercury has blown up and is no longer available.</INFO>
    </xsl:copy>
  </xsl:template>

  <xsl:template match="@*|node()">
    <xsl:copy>
      <xsl:apply-templates select="@*|node()"/>
    </xsl:copy>
  </xsl:template>

</xsl:stylesheet>
```

Here's the result document, complete with the new <INFO> element, for Mercury only:

```
<?xml version="1.0" encoding="utf-8"?>
<?xml-stylesheet type="text/xml" href="planets.xsl"?>
<PLANETS>

    <PLANET>
        <NAME>Mercury</NAME>
        <MASS UNITS="(Earth = 1)">.0553</MASS>
        <DAY UNITS="days">58.65</DAY>
        <RADIUS UNITS="miles">1516</RADIUS>
        <DENSITY UNITS="(Earth = 1)">.983</DENSITY>
        <DISTANCE UNITS="million miles">43.4</DISTANCE><!--At perihelion-->
        <INFO>Sorry, Mercury has blown up and is no longer available.</INFO>
    </PLANET>

    <PLANET>
        <NAME>Venus</NAME>
        <MASS UNITS="(Earth = 1)">.815</MASS>
        <DAY UNITS="days">116.75</DAY>
        <RADIUS UNITS="miles">3716</RADIUS>
        <DENSITY UNITS="(Earth = 1)">.943</DENSITY>
        <DISTANCE UNITS="million miles">66.8</DISTANCE><!--At perihelion-->
    </PLANET>
        .
        .
        .
</PLANETS>
```

Using the *descendant-or-self* Axis

The `descendant-or-self` axis contains all the descendants of the context node, and the context node itself. Note, however, that it does not contain any attributes or namespace nodes.

The following example puts this axis to work. In this case, I write a simplified stylesheet (see Chapter 2 for more on simplified stylesheets) to process all elements by using descendants to produce the HTML table of planetary data you're already familiar with:

Listing 7.7 **Using the *descendant-or-self* Axis**

```
<HTML xmlns:xsl="http://www.w3.org/1999/XSL/Transform" xsl:version="1.0">
    <HEAD>
        <TITLE>
           The Planets Table
        </TITLE>
    </HEAD>
    <BODY>
        <H1>
           The Planets Table
        </H1>
        <TABLE BORDER="2">
           <TR>
                <TD>Name</TD>
                <TD>Mass</TD>
                <TD>Radius</TD>
                <TD>Day</TD>
           </TR>
           <xsl:for-each select="/descendant-or-self::node()/PLANET">
               <TR>
                   <TD><xsl:value-of select="NAME"/></TD>
                   <TD><xsl:value-of select="MASS"/></TD>
                   <TD><xsl:value-of select="RADIUS"/></TD>
                   <TD><xsl:value-of select="DAY"/></TD>
               </TR>
            </xsl:for-each>
        </TABLE>
    </BODY>
</HTML>
```

That's all it takes. I'm using a simplified stylesheet here to point out that using a descendant axis such as `descendant` or `descendant-or-self` enables you to work through all matching nodes automatically, much as an `<xsl:for-each>` or `<xsl:template>` element does.

Using the *following* Axis

The `following` axis contains all nodes that are after the context node in document order (in other words, in the order in which they appear in the document, starting at the beginning of the document), excluding any of the context node's descendants and also excluding attribute nodes and namespace nodes.

In this example I match each `<PLANET>` element and copy all the following elements to the result document:

Listing 7.8 **Using the *following* Axis**

```
<?xml version="1.0"?>
<xsl:stylesheet version="1.0"
xmlns:xsl="http://www.w3.org/1999/XSL/Transform">
<xsl:output method="xml"/>

<xsl:template match="PLANET">
    <xsl:for-each select="following::*">
        <xsl:copy-of select="."/>
    </xsl:for-each>
</xsl:template>

</xsl:stylesheet>
```

Here's what the result looks like. Note that when this template matches Mercury's `<PLANET>` element, it copies all the following elements, which are Venus, then all the descendants of Venus, then Earth, then all the descendants of Earth. Next, it matches Venus' `<PLANET>` element and copies all the following elements—that is, Earth, and all of Earth's descendants:

```
<?xml version="1.0" encoding="UTF-8"?>

    <PLANET>
        <NAME>Venus</NAME>
        <MASS UNITS="(Earth = 1)">.815</MASS>
        <DAY UNITS="days">116.75</DAY>
        <RADIUS UNITS="miles">3716</RADIUS>
        <DENSITY UNITS="(Earth = 1)">.943</DENSITY>
        <DISTANCE UNITS="million miles">66.8</DISTANCE><!--At perihelion-->
    </PLANET>
    <NAME>Venus</NAME>
    <MASS UNITS="(Earth = 1)">.815</MASS>
    <DAY UNITS="days">116.75</DAY>
    <RADIUS UNITS="miles">3716</RADIUS>
    <DENSITY UNITS="(Earth = 1)">.943</DENSITY>
```

```
<DISTANCE UNITS="million miles">66.8</DISTANCE>
<PLANET>
    <NAME>Earth</NAME>
    <MASS UNITS="(Earth = 1)">1</MASS>
    <DAY UNITS="days">1</DAY>
    <RADIUS UNITS="miles">2107</RADIUS>
    <DENSITY UNITS="(Earth = 1)">1</DENSITY>
    <DISTANCE UNITS="million miles">128.4</DISTANCE><!--At perihelion-->
</PLANET>
<NAME>Earth</NAME>
<MASS UNITS="(Earth = 1)">1</MASS>
<DAY UNITS="days">1</DAY>
<RADIUS UNITS="miles">2107</RADIUS>
<DENSITY UNITS="(Earth = 1)">1</DENSITY>
<DISTANCE UNITS="million miles">128.4</DISTANCE>
<PLANET>
    <NAME>Earth</NAME>
    <MASS UNITS="(Earth = 1)">1</MASS>
    <DAY UNITS="days">1</DAY>
    <RADIUS UNITS="miles">2107</RADIUS>
    <DENSITY UNITS="(Earth = 1)">1</DENSITY>
    <DISTANCE UNITS="million miles">128.4</DISTANCE><!--At perihelion-->
</PLANET>
<NAME>Earth</NAME>
<MASS UNITS="(Earth = 1)">1</MASS>
<DAY UNITS="days">1</DAY>
<RADIUS UNITS="miles">2107</RADIUS>
<DENSITY UNITS="(Earth = 1)">1</DENSITY>
<DISTANCE UNITS="million miles">128.4</DISTANCE>
```

On the other hand, if you use the `following-sibling` axis, then only the following siblings—that is, only `<PLANET>` elements—are copied to the result document, as you'll see in the next section.

Using the *following-sibling* Axis

The `following-sibling` axis contains all the following siblings of the context node.

For example, I can match each `<PLANET>` element and copy all the nodes in the `following-sibling` axis to the result document like this:

Listing 7.9 **Using the *following-sibling* Axis**

```
<?xml version="1.0"?>
<xsl:stylesheet version="1.0"
xmlns:xsl="http://www.w3.org/1999/XSL/Transform">
<xsl:output method="xml"/>

<xsl:template match="PLANET">
```

```
    <xsl:for-each select="following-sibling::*">
        <xsl:copy-of select="."/>
    </xsl:for-each>
</xsl:template>

</xsl:stylesheet>
```

This copies over the two siblings following Mercury first (Venus and Earth) then copies over the following sibling of Venus, which is Earth. Earth itself has no following siblings, so this is the result:

```
<?xml version="1.0" encoding="UTF-8"?>

    <PLANET>
        <NAME>Venus</NAME>
        <MASS UNITS="(Earth = 1)">.815</MASS>
        <DAY UNITS="days">116.75</DAY>
        <RADIUS UNITS="miles">3716</RADIUS>
        <DENSITY UNITS="(Earth = 1)">.943</DENSITY>
        <DISTANCE UNITS="million miles">66.8</DISTANCE><!--At perihelion-->
    </PLANET>
    <PLANET>
        <NAME>Earth</NAME>
        <MASS UNITS="(Earth = 1)">1</MASS>
        <DAY UNITS="days">1</DAY>
        <RADIUS UNITS="miles">2107</RADIUS>
        <DENSITY UNITS="(Earth = 1)">1</DENSITY>
        <DISTANCE UNITS="million miles">128.4</DISTANCE><!--At perihelion-->
    </PLANET>

    <PLANET>
        <NAME>Earth</NAME>
        <MASS UNITS="(Earth = 1)">1</MASS>
        <DAY UNITS="days">1</DAY>
        <RADIUS UNITS="miles">2107</RADIUS>
        <DENSITY UNITS="(Earth = 1)">1</DENSITY>
        <DISTANCE UNITS="million miles">128.4</DISTANCE><!--At perihelion-->
    </PLANET>
```

Using the *namespace* Axis

The `namespace` axis contains the namespace nodes of the context node. Note that the axis is empty unless the context node is an element. An element has a namespace node for

- Every attribute of the element whose name starts with "xmlns:".
- Every attribute of an ancestor element whose name starts "xmlns:" (unless, of course, the element itself or a nearer ancestor redeclares the namespace).
- An `xmlns` attribute, if the element, or some ancestor, has an `xmlns` attribute.

In the following example, I'm going to display the namespace of the <PLANETS> element in the result document, and I'm setting that namespace to "http://www.starpowder.com" in the source document:

Listing 7.10 **planets.xml with a Namespace Declaration**

```
<?xml version="1.0"?>
<?xml-stylesheet type="text/xml" href="planets.xsl"?>
<PLANETS xmlns="http://www.starpowder.com">

    <PLANET>
        <NAME>Mercury</NAME>
        <MASS UNITS="(Earth = 1)">.0553</MASS>
        <DAY UNITS="days">58.65</DAY>
        <RADIUS UNITS="miles">1516</RADIUS>
        <DENSITY UNITS="(Earth = 1)">.983</DENSITY>
        <DISTANCE UNITS="million miles">43.4</DISTANCE><!--At perihelion-->
    </PLANET>
        .
        .
        .
```

Here's the stylesheet, where I check the namespaces used in the <PLANETS> element:

Listing 7.11 **Using the *namespace* axis in planets.xml**

```
<?xml version="1.0"?>
<xsl:stylesheet version="1.0"
xmlns:xsl="http://www.w3.org/1999/XSL/Transform">
<xsl:output method="xml"/>

<xsl:template match="PLANETS">
    <xsl:value-of select="namespace::*"/>
</xsl:template>

</xsl:stylesheet>
```

And here's the result document (note that this result may vary by XSLT processor):

```
<?xml version="1.0" encoding="UTF-8"?>
http://www.starpowder.com
```

Using the *parent* Axis

The parent axis contains the parent (and just the parent) of the context node, if there is one.

Say that I want to change the content of Earth's <MASS> element to "The mass of Earth is set to 1." The following template does that by checking whether a <MASS> element's parent <PLANET> contains a <NAME> whose string value is "Earth":

Listing 7.12 **Using the *parent* Axis**

```
<?xml version="1.0"?>
<xsl:stylesheet version="1.0"
xmlns:xsl="http://www.w3.org/1999/XSL/Transform">
<xsl:output method="xml"/>

  <xsl:template match="@*|node()">
    <xsl:copy>
      <xsl:apply-templates select="@*|node()"/>
    </xsl:copy>
  </xsl:template>

  <xsl:template match="MASS[parent::node()/NAME='Earth']">
    <MASS>The mass of Earth is set to 1.</MASS>
  </xsl:template>

</xsl:stylesheet>
```

And here's the result:

```
<?xml version="1.0" encoding="utf-8"?>
<?xml-stylesheet type="text/xml" href="planets.xsl"?>
<PLANETS>

    <PLANET>
        <NAME>Mercury</NAME>
        <MASS UNITS="(Earth = 1)">.0553</MASS>
        <DAY UNITS="days">58.65</DAY>
        <RADIUS UNITS="miles">1516</RADIUS>
        <DENSITY UNITS="(Earth = 1)">.983</DENSITY>
        <DISTANCE UNITS="million miles">43.4</DISTANCE><!--At perihelion-->
    </PLANET>

    <PLANET>
        <NAME>Venus</NAME>
        <MASS UNITS="(Earth = 1)">.815</MASS>
        <DAY UNITS="days">116.75</DAY>
```

```
        <RADIUS UNITS="miles">3716</RADIUS>
        <DENSITY UNITS="(Earth = 1)">.943</DENSITY>
        <DISTANCE UNITS="million miles">66.8</DISTANCE><!--At perihelion-->
    </PLANET>

    <PLANET>
        <NAME>Earth</NAME>
        <MASS>The mass of Earth is set to 1.</MASS>
        <DAY UNITS="days">1</DAY>
        <RADIUS UNITS="miles">2107</RADIUS>
        <DENSITY UNITS="(Earth = 1)">1</DENSITY>
        <DISTANCE UNITS="million miles">128.4</DISTANCE><!--At perihelion-->
    </PLANET>

</PLANETS>
```

Using the *preceding* Axis

The `preceding` axis contains all nodes that are before the context node in document order, excluding any ancestors of the context node, and also excluding attribute nodes and namespace nodes.

For example, say that I want to set the content of the `<DISTANCE>` element to the text "This planet is farther from the Sun than Mercury." if the current planet is indeed farther from the Sun than Mercury. One way to do that is to see whether Mercury comes before the current planet in document order, using the `preceding` axis:

Listing 7.13 **Using the *preceding* Axis**

```
<?xml version="1.0"?>
<xsl:stylesheet version="1.0"
xmlns:xsl="http://www.w3.org/1999/XSL/Transform">
<xsl:output method="xml"/>

  <xsl:template match="DISTANCE[preceding::*/NAME='Mercury']">
    <DISTANCE>This planet is farther from the Sun than Mercury.</DISTANCE>
  </xsl:template>

  <xsl:template match="@*|node()">
    <xsl:copy>
      <xsl:apply-templates select="@*|node()"/>
    </xsl:copy>
  </xsl:template>

</xsl:stylesheet>
```

If the current planet does come after Mercury, I can insert the message in its <DISTANCE> element. Here's the result:

```
<?xml version="1.0" encoding="utf-8"?>
<?xml-stylesheet type="text/xml" href="planets.xsl"?>
<PLANETS>

    <PLANET>
        <NAME>Mercury</NAME>
        <MASS UNITS="(Earth = 1)">.0553</MASS>
        <DAY UNITS="days">58.65</DAY>
        <RADIUS UNITS="miles">1516</RADIUS>
        <DENSITY UNITS="(Earth = 1)">.983</DENSITY>
        <DISTANCE UNITS="million miles">43.4</DISTANCE>
        <!--At perihelion-->
    </PLANET>

    <PLANET>
        <NAME>Venus</NAME>
        <MASS UNITS="(Earth = 1)">.815</MASS>
        <DAY UNITS="days">116.75</DAY>
        <RADIUS UNITS="miles">3716</RADIUS>
        <DENSITY UNITS="(Earth = 1)">.943</DENSITY>
        <DISTANCE>This planet is farther from the Sun than Mercury.</DISTANCE>
        <!--At perihelion-->
    </PLANET>

    <PLANET>
        <NAME>Earth</NAME>
        <MASS UNITS="(Earth = 1)">1</MASS>
        <DAY UNITS="days">1</DAY>
        <RADIUS UNITS="miles">2107</RADIUS>
        <DENSITY UNITS="(Earth = 1)">1</DENSITY>
        <DISTANCE>This planet is farther from the Sun than Mercury.</DISTANCE>
        <!--At perihelion-->
    </PLANET>

</PLANETS>
```

Using the *preceding-sibling* Axis

The `preceding-sibling` axis contains all the preceding siblings of the context node. Note that if the context node is an attribute node or a namespace node, the `preceding-sibling` axis is empty.

For example, what if you wanted to write a template that would match only <DISTANCE> elements in Mercury's <PLANET> element? One way to do that is to check whether any siblings preceding the <DISTANCE> element are <NAME> elements whose string value is "Mercury". If you use the `preceding-sibling` axis, the search is restricted to the current <PLANET>

element, which means there's no chance of matching Mercury unless you're in the correct <PLANET> element:

Listing 7.14 Using the *preceding-sibling* Axis

```
<?xml version="1.0"?>
<xsl:stylesheet version="1.0"
xmlns:xsl="http://www.w3.org/1999/XSL/Transform">
<xsl:output method="xml"/>

  <xsl:template match="DISTANCE[preceding-sibling::*='Mercury']">
    <DISTANCE>This is the planet Mercury, closest to the Sun.</DISTANCE>
  </xsl:template>

  <xsl:template match="@*|node()">
    <xsl:copy>
      <xsl:apply-templates select="@*|node()"/>
    </xsl:copy>
  </xsl:template>

</xsl:stylesheet>
```

And here's the result:

```
<?xml version="1.0" encoding="utf-8"?>
<?xml-stylesheet type="text/xml" href="planets.xsl"?>
<PLANETS>

    <PLANET>
        <NAME>Mercury</NAME>
        <MASS UNITS="(Earth = 1)">.0553</MASS>
        <DAY UNITS="days">58.65</DAY>
        <RADIUS UNITS="miles">1516</RADIUS>
        <DENSITY UNITS="(Earth = 1)">.983</DENSITY>
        <DISTANCE>This is the planet Mercury, closest to the Sun.</DISTANCE>
        <!--At perihelion-->
    </PLANET>

    <PLANET>
        <NAME>Venus</NAME>
        <MASS UNITS="(Earth = 1)">.815</MASS>
        <DAY UNITS="days">116.75</DAY>
        <RADIUS UNITS="miles">3716</RADIUS>
        <DENSITY UNITS="(Earth = 1)">.943</DENSITY>
        <DISTANCE UNITS="million miles">66.8</DISTANCE><!--At perihelion-->
    </PLANET>

    <PLANET>
        <NAME>Earth</NAME>
```

```
    <MASS UNITS="(Earth = 1)">1</MASS>
    <DAY UNITS="days">1</DAY>
    <RADIUS UNITS="miles">2107</RADIUS>
    <DENSITY UNITS="(Earth = 1)">1</DENSITY>
    <DISTANCE UNITS="million miles">128.4</DISTANCE><!--At perihelion-->
  </PLANET>

</PLANETS>
```

Using the *self* Axis

The `self` axis contains just the context node. In fact, one of the XPath abbreviations that you'll see later is that you can abbreviate "self::node()" as ".".

This is a useful axis to know about, because as you recall from Chapter 4, if you omit the axis, the default is `child::`, and sometimes you want to refer to the current node instead. For example, `[self::PLANET]` is true only if the context node is a `<PLANET>` element.

In the following example, I combine the templates for `<NAME>` and `<MASS>` elements into one template. Because those elements are formatted differently, however, I need to tell them apart inside the same template, and I can do that by checking `self::NAME`, which returns a non-empty node set if the context node is a `<NAME>` element, and `self::MASS`, which returns a non-empty node set if the context node is a `<MASS>` element:

```
<xsl:template match="PLANET">
  <TR>
    <TD><xsl:apply-templates select="NAME"/></TD>
    <TD><xsl:apply-templates select="MASS"/></TD>
    <TD><xsl:apply-templates select="RADIUS"/></TD>
    <TD><xsl:apply-templates select="DAY"/></TD>
  </TR>
</xsl:template>

<xsl:template match="NAME | MASS">

    <xsl:if test="self::NAME">
        <xsl:value-of select="."/>
    </xsl:if>

    <xsl:if test="self::MASS">
        <xsl:value-of select="."/>
        <xsl:text> </xsl:text>
        <xsl:value-of select="@UNITS"/>
    </xsl:if>

</xsl:template>
    .
    .
    .
```

That completes our look at the new XPath axes. It's time to get to some examples.

Location Path Examples

You've seen a lot of location path theory, so how about some examples? The best way to learn this material is by example, so the following list includes a number of location path examples. (The abbreviated versions are next.)

- `child::PLANET`. Returns the `<PLANET>` element children of the context node.
- `child::text()`. Returns all text node children of the context node.
- `child::node()`. Returns all the children of the context node.
- `attribute::UNIT`. Returns the `UNIT` attribute of the context node.
- `descendant::PLANET`. Returns the `<PLANET>` element descendants of the context node.
- `ancestor::PLANET`. Returns all `<PLANET>` ancestors of the context node.
- `ancestor-or-self::PLANET`. Returns the `<PLANET>` ancestors of the context node. If the context node is a `<PLANET>` as well, also returns the context node.
- `descendant-or-self::PLANET`. Returns the `<PLANET>` element descendants of the context node. If the context node is a `<PLANET>` element as well, also returns the context node.
- `self::PLANET`. Returns the context node if the context node is a `<PLANET>` element.
- `child::PLANET/descendant::NAME`. Returns the `<NAME>` element descendants of the child `<PLANET>` elements of the context node.
- `child::*/child::PLANET`. Returns all `<PLANET>` grandchildren of the context node.
- `/`. Returns the root node.
- `/descendant::PLANET`. Returns all the `<PLANET>` elements in the document.
- `/descendant::PLANET/child::NAME`. Returns all the `<NAME>` elements that have a `<PLANET>` parent in the document.
- `child::PLANET[position() = 3]` . Returns the third `<PLANET>` child of the context node.
- `child::PLANET[position() = last()]`. Returns the last `<PLANET>` child of the context node.
- `/descendant::PLANET[position() = 3]` . Returns the third `<PLANET>` element in the document.

- `child::PLANETS/child::PLANET[position() = 4 ]/child::NAME[position() = 3]` . Returns the third <NAME> element of the fourth <PLANET> element of the <PLANETS> element.
- `child::PLANET[position() > 3]`. Returns all the <PLANET> children of the context node after the first three.
- `preceding-sibling::NAME[position() = 2]`. Returns the second previous <NAME> sibling element of the context node.
- `child::*[self::NAME or self::MASS]`. Returns both the <NAME> and <MASS> children of the context node.
- `child::*[self::NAME or self::MASS][position() = last()]`. Returns the last <NAME> or <MASS> child of the context node.

As you can see, some of this syntax is pretty involved, and a little lengthy to type. However, as with patterns, there is an abbreviated form of XPath syntax.

XPath Abbreviated Syntax

You can take advantage of a number of abbreviations in XPath syntax. Here are the rules:

- `self::node()` can be abbreviated as `.`
- `parent::node()` can be abbreviated as `..`
- `child::`*`childname`* can be abbreviated as *`childname`*
- `attribute::`*`childname`* can be abbreviated as `@`*`childname`*
- `/descendant-or-self::node()/` can be abbreviated as `//`

For example, the location path `.//PLANET` is short for `self::node()/descendant-or-self::node()/child::PLANET`. You can also abbreviate the predicate expression `[position() = 3]` as `[3]`, `[position() = last()]` as `[last()]`, and so on. Using the abbreviated syntax makes XPath location paths a lot easier to use. The following list includes some examples of location paths that use abbreviated syntax:

- `PLANET` returns the <PLANET> element children of the context node.
- `*` returns all element children of the context node.
- `text()` returns all text node children of the context node.
- `@UNITS` returns the `UNITS` attribute of the context node.
- `@*` returns all the attributes of the context node.
- `PLANET[3]` returns the third <PLANET> child of the context node.

- PLANET[last()] returns the last <PLANET> child of the context node.
- */PLANET returns all <PLANET> grandchildren of the context node.
- /PLANETS/PLANET[3]/NAME[2] returns the second <NAME> element of the third <PLANET> element of the <PLANETS> element.
- //PLANET returns all the <PLANET> descendants of the document root.
- PLANETS//PLANET returns the <PLANET> element descendants of the <PLANETS> element children of the context node.
- //PLANET/NAME returns all the <NAME> elements that have a <PLANET> parent.
- . returns the context node itself.
- .//PLANET returns the <PLANET> element descendants of the context node.
- .. returns the parent of the context node.
- ../@UNITS returns the UNITS attribute of the parent of the context node.
- .//.. returns all parents of a descendant of the context node, and the parent of the context node.
- PLANET[NAME] returns the <PLANET> children of the context node that have <NAME> children.
- PLANET[NAME="Venus"] returns the <PLANET> children of the context node that have <NAME> children with text equal to "Venus".
- PLANET[@UNITS = "days"] returns all <PLANET> children of the context node that have a UNITS attribute with value "days".
- PLANET[6][@UNITS = "days"] returns the sixth <PLANET> child of the context node, only if that child has a UNITS attribute with value "days". Can also be written as PLANET[@UNITS = "days"][6].
- PLANET[@COLOR and @UNITS] returns all the <PLANET> children of the context node that have both a COLOR attribute and a UNITS attribute.
- "//PLANET[not(.=preceding::PLANET)]" selects all <PLANET> elements that do not have the same value as any preceding <PLANET> element.
- *[1][self::NAME] matches any <NAME> element that is the first child of its parent.
- *[position() lt; 5][@UNITS] matches the first five children of the context node that have a UNITS attribute.

Checking XPath Expressions

The Xalan package has a handy example program, ApplyXPath.java, that enables you to apply an XPath expression to a document and see what the results would be, which is great for testing. To run this example, you need to compile ApplyXPath.java into ApplyXPath.class using the java.exe tool that comes with Java.

As an example, I'll apply the XPath expression "PLANET/NAME" to planets.xml using ApplyXPath.class. Here's the result, displaying all `<NAME>` elements that are children of `<PLANET>` elements (the `<output>` tags are added by ApplyXPath):

```
%java ApplyXPath planets.xml PLANET/NAME
<output>
<NAME>Mercury</NAME><NAME>Venus</NAME><NAME>Earth</NAME>
</output>
```

XPath 2.0

XPath is being updated to offer more support for XSLT 2.0 (see www.w3.org/TR/xpath20req). XPath 2.0 has the following goals:

- Simplify manipulation of XML schema-typed content.
- Simplify manipulation of string content.
- Support related XML standards.
- Improve ease of use.
- Improve interoperability.
- Improve international support.
- Maintain backward compatibility.
- Enable improved processor efficiency.

The following list provides an overview of the XPath 2.0 requirements. The big items on the agenda are XML schema support and support for regular expressions, which provide ways of handling string searches and manipulations. (For more on regular expressions, see www.perldoc.com/perl5.6/pod/perlre.html.) According to W3C, XPath 2.0

- Must support the W3C XML architecture by integrating well with the other standards in the XML family.
- Must express its data model in terms of the XML infoset.
- Must provide a common core syntax for XSLT 2.0 and XML Query language 1.0.
- Must support an explicit "for any" or "for all" comparison and equality syntax.
- Must extend the set of aggregation functions. (For example, XSLT users have frequently requested the addition of min() and max().)

- Should maintain backward compatibility with XPath 1.0.
- Should provide intersection and difference functions; that is, XPath 1.0 supports the union of two node sets, and that should be expanded to include intersection and difference functions.
- Should support a unary plus operator (because XML schema allows decimals to have a leading plus).
- Must improve ease of use.
- Must loosen restrictions on location steps.
- Must provide a conditional expression that takes three expressions: expression1 (Boolean operator) expression2, and expression3. It must evaluate to expression2 if expression1 is true and to expression3 if expression1 is false.
- Must define a consistent syntax for subexpressions that handle collections of items.
- Should support additional string functions. For example, W3C is considering adding support to string replacement, string padding, and string case conversions.
- Should support aggregation functions when applied to collections. For example, some XPath 1.0 users have wanted to apply an aggregate function, such as the `sum` function, to the values of expressions applied to node sets.
- Must support regular expressions for matching in strings using the regular expression notation as established in XML schema.
- Must add support for XML schema primitive datatypes. That is, in addition to the types supported by the XPath 1.0 data model—string, number, Boolean, and node-set—the XPath 2.0 data model must support XML schema primitive types.
- Must support the representations of floats and doubles supported by XML schema, which uses scientific notation.
- Must define an appropriate set of functions to enable users to work with XML schema primitive types.
- Should add a list data type to XPath (because XML schema allows the definition of simple types derived by a list).
- Must support accessing simple-typed value of elements and attributes. Because XML schemas introduce many new types, XPath 2.0 must support access to the native, simple-typed value of an element or attribute.

- Must define the behavior of operators for null arguments.
- Should be able to select elements or attributes based on an explicit XML schema type.
- Should be able to select elements or attributes based on XML schema type hierarchy.
- Should be able to select elements based on XML schema substitution groups.
- Should support lookups based on schema unique constraints and keys.

Although this is the end of the chapter, that's not all for XPath. This topic is continued in the next chapter, where you'll get a closer look at the functions available in XPath and those functions that are already built into XSLT.

8
Using the XSLT and XPath Functions

THIS CHAPTER EXPLORES THE FUNCTIONS AVAILABLE to you in XSLT, both the built-in XSLT functions and the XPath functions you can use. You've already seen a number of these functions, such as `id`, `generate-id`, `position`, `count`, and so on. In this chapter, you'll see all the available functions.

Some of the functions available are built into XSLT, and some from within XPath. Both XSLT and XPath are in the process of being upgraded to version 2.0, and at the end of this chapter I'll take a look at the future and what new functions will be appearing. (No new version 2.0 functions have been made public yet.)

The following functions are built into XSLT:

- `element-available()`
- `function-available()`
- `current()`
- `document()`
- `key()`
- `format-number()`
- `generate-id()`
- `system-property()`
- `unparsed-entity-uri()`

There are many functions from XPath that are also available to you. I'll organize these functions by the XPath data type on which they work. There are four such data types: node sets, strings, numbers, and Booleans. Here are the XPath functions that work on node sets:

- `count()`
- `id()`
- `last()`
- `local-name()`
- `name()`
- `namespace-uri()`
- `position()`

These are the XPath functions that work on strings:

- `concat()`
- `contains()`
- `normalize-space()`
- `starts-with()`
- `string()`
- `string-length()`
- `substring()`
- `substring-after()`
- `substring-before()`
- `translate()`

These XPath functions work on numbers:

- `ceiling()`
- `floor()`
- `number()`
- `round()`
- `sum()`

And these XPath functions work with Boolean values:

- `boolean()`
- `false()`

- `lang()`
- `not()`
- `true()`

You'll see all these functions at work in this chapter, starting with the functions that are built into XSLT. This is not necessarily a chapter to read straight through, but rather to keep in mind as a reference—all the functions are here, ready to look up and put to work.

The XSLT Functions

The following list includes, in overview, the functions built into XSLT:

- `current()`. Returns the current node—not the context node. The current node is the present node in loops such as `<xsl:for-each>`. You cannot use `current` in patterns.
- `document()`. Enables you to read in multiple documents.
- `element-available()`. Indicates whether an extension element is available.
- `format-number()`. Formats numbers for display.
- `function-available()`. Indicates whether an extension function is available.
- `generate-id()`. Causes the XSLT processor to assign and return an identifier to a node. When you call `generate-id` again on the same node, this function returns the previously assigned identifier.
- `key()`. Enables you to search by key.
- `system-property()`. Enables you to check three system properties: `xsl:version` (the version of XSLT supported by the XSLT processor), `xsl:vendor` (the name of the XSLT processor's vendor), and `xsl:vendor-url` (the URL of the XSLT processor's vendor).
- `unparsed-entity-uri()`. Gives you access to unparsed entities as declared in a DTD or schema using a URI.

The following sections explain all these functions in detail, with examples.

current()

The `current` function returns the current node—not the context node. The context node for a template is the node in the matched node set to which the template is being applied. The current node, on the other hand, is the present node in loops such as `<xsl:for-each>`. This function returns the current node as a node set with one node:

```
node-set current()
```

Note that you cannot use `current` in patterns because patterns are supposed to be processing-path independent, and the way XSLT processors may implement structures such as loops may vary.

To see how `current` works, look at the following example, in which I match `<PLANET>` elements with a template. I also put an `<xsl:for-each>` element inside the template, and apply the template only if the context node matched by the template is the same as the current node in the present iteration in the `<xsl:for-each>` element:

Listing 8.1 **Using the *current* Function**

```
<?xml version="1.0"?>
<xsl:stylesheet version="1.0"
xmlns:xsl="http://www.w3.org/1999/XSL/Transform">

    <xsl:template match="/PLANETS">
        <HTML>
        .
        .
        .
                <TABLE BORDER="2">
                    <TR>
                        <TD>Name</TD>
                        <TD>Mass</TD>
                        <TD>Radius</TD>
                        <TD>Day</TD>
                    </TR>
                    <xsl:apply-templates/>
                </TABLE>
            </BODY>
        </HTML>
    </xsl:template>

    <xsl:template match="PLANET">
       <xsl:for-each select="/PLANETS/*[.=current()]">
       <TR>
          <TD><xsl:value-of select="NAME"/></TD>
          <TD><xsl:apply-templates select="MASS"/></TD>
          <TD><xsl:apply-templates select="RADIUS"/></TD>
          <TD><xsl:apply-templates select="DAY"/></TD>
       </TR>
       </xsl:for-each>
```

```
  </xsl:template>

   <xsl:template match="MASS">
       <xsl:value-of select="."/>
       <xsl:text> </xsl:text>
       <xsl:value-of select="@UNITS"/>
   </xsl:template>
       .
       .
       .
   <xsl:template match="DAY">
       <xsl:value-of select="."/>
       <xsl:text> </xsl:text>
       <xsl:value-of select="@UNITS"/>
   </xsl:template>

</xsl:stylesheet>
```

The net result of this stylesheet is the same as if the `<xsl:for-each>` element were not there at all, because the body of the `<xsl:for-each>` element is applied only when the context node is the same as the current node.

document()

The `document` function is a particularly useful one, because it enables you to read multiple documents and process their contents. Here's how you use `document`:

```
node-set document(uri, base-uri?)
```

You pass this function the `uri` argument, which can be the URI of a document to read in, or a node set of nodes whose string values are URIs. You can also pass a second, optional, argument, `base-uri`, which is a node set, and the base URI of this node set is used to resolve any relative URIs found in the `uri` argument.

In the following example, I use an XSLT processor on one document, planets1.xml, but also read in a second, planets2.xml, and process that document as well. Here's planets1.xml:

Listing 8.2 **planets1.xml**

```
<?xml version="1.0"?>
<?xml-stylesheet type="text/xml" href="planets.xsl"?>
<PLANETS href="planets2.xml">
</PLANETS>
```

Here's planets2.xml, which has one planet in a <PLANET> element:

Listing 8.3 **planets2.xml**

```
<?xml version="1.0"?>
<PLANET>
    <NAME>Mercury</NAME>
    <MASS UNITS="(Earth = 1)">.0553</MASS>
    <DAY UNITS="days">58.65</DAY>
    <RADIUS UNITS="miles">1516</RADIUS>
    <DENSITY UNITS="(Earth = 1)">.983</DENSITY>
    <DISTANCE UNITS="million miles">43.4</DISTANCE><!--At perihelion-->
</PLANET>
```

And here's the stylesheet, planets.xsl, that I'll use on planets1.xml. This stylesheet has a template that matches the <PLANETS> element in planets1.xml, and in that template, I'll use <xsl:apply-templates> and the `document` function to read in planets2.xml:

Listing 8.4 **Using the *document* Function**

```
<?xml version="1.0"?>
<xsl:stylesheet version="1.0"
xmlns:xsl="http://www.w3.org/1999/XSL/Transform">

    <xsl:template match="/PLANETS">
        <HTML>
            <HEAD>
                <TITLE>
                    The Planets Table
                </TITLE>
            </HEAD>
            <BODY>
                <H1>
                    The Planets Table
                </H1>
                <TABLE BORDER="2">
                    <TR>
                        <TD>Name</TD>
                        <TD>Mass</TD>
                        <TD>Radius</TD>
                        <TD>Day</TD>
                    </TR>
                    <xsl:apply-templates select="document(@href)"/>
                </TABLE>
            </BODY>
        </HTML>
    </xsl:template>
```

```
    <xsl:template match="PLANET">
       <TR>
          <TD><xsl:value-of select="NAME"/></TD>
          <TD><xsl:apply-templates select="MASS"/></TD>
          <TD><xsl:apply-templates select="RADIUS"/></TD>
          <TD><xsl:apply-templates select="DAY"/></TD>
       </TR>
   </xsl:template>
          .
          .
          .
    <xsl:template match="DAY">
        <xsl:value-of select="."/>
        <xsl:text> </xsl:text>
        <xsl:value-of select="@UNITS"/>
    </xsl:template>

</xsl:stylesheet>
```

This stylesheet processes the data in planets1.xml and also reads in and processes planets2.xml as well; here is the full result—as you can see, the data for planets2.xml has been added as it should be:

```
<HTML>
    <HEAD>
        <TITLE>
            The Planets Table
        </TITLE>
    </HEAD>

    <BODY>
        <H1>
            The Planets Table
        </H1>

        <TABLE BORDER="2">
            <TR>
                <TD>Name</TD>
                <TD>Mass</TD>
                <TD>Radius</TD>
                <TD>Day</TD>
            </TR>
            <TR>
                <TD>Mercury</TD>
                <TD>.0553 (Earth = 1)</TD>
                <TD>1516 miles</TD>
                <TD>58.65 days</TD>
            </TR>
        </TABLE>
    </BODY>
</HTML>
```

The `document` function is useful because it enables you to read in additional documents at run time, such as copyright or disclaimer references, company letterhead, and so on.

element-available()

You can use the `element-available` function to determine whether a particular extension element is available. Here's how you use this function:

```
boolean element-available(element-name)
```

You pass this function the name of the element you're looking for, and it returns true if the element is available, false otherwise.

You saw this function in Chapter 5. In the `element-available` example in that chapter, I checked for an element named `<starpowder:calculate>` this way:

```
<xsl:choose xmlns:starpowder="http://www.starpowder.com">
    <xsl:when test="element-available('starpowder:calculate')">
        <starpowder:calculate xsl:extension-element-prefixes="starpowder"/>
    </xsl:when>
    <xsl:otherwise>
        <xsl:text>Sorry, can't do math today.</xsl:text>
    </xsl:otherwise>
</xsl:choose>
```

format-number()

As its name implies, you can use the `format-number` function to format numbers into strings. Here's how you use this function:

```
string format-number(number, format, name?)
```

This function returns the formatted number as a string. You pass it the `number` to format, a `format` string, and an optional `name` string. The `name` string is a QName that specifies a format as created by the `<xsl:decimal-format>` element (which you'll see at the end of this chapter).

You write the `format` string to follow the conventions of the Java `DecimalFormat` class.

The Java `DecimalFormat` Class

As of this writing, the documentation for the Java `DecimalFormat` class is available online at `http://java.sun.com/products/jdk/1.1/docs/api/java.text.DecimalFormat.html`.

Here are the parts of a format string:

- format-string:= subpattern (;subpattern)?
- subpattern:= prefix? integer (.fraction)?suffix?
- prefix:= [#x0..#xFFFD] - specialCharacters
- suffix:= [#x0..#xFFFD] - specialCharacters
- integer:= '#'* '0'* '0'
- fraction:= '0'* '#'*

Here are the special characters (`specialCharacters` above) that you can use in a subpattern (you can change these characters with the `<xsl:decimal-format>` element which you'll see at the end of this chapter):

- 0 A digit always appears at this place.
- # A digit, unless it is a redundant leading or trailing zero.
- . The decimal separator.
- , A grouping separator.
- ; Separates formats.
- - A minus sign.
- % Multiply by 100 and show as percentage.
- ? Multiply by 1000 and show as per mille.
- E Separates mantissa and exponent.
- ¤ The symbol for currency (#xA4).
- ' Used to quote special characters.

To see how this works, look at the following example, in which I format the values from planets.xml that are displayed in the HTML table:

Listing 8.5 **Formatting Numbers**

```
<?xml version="1.0"?>
<xsl:stylesheet version="1.0"
xmlns:xsl="http://www.w3.org/1999/XSL/Transform">

    <xsl:template match="/PLANETS">
        .
        .
        .
```

continues ▶

Listing 8.5 **Continued**

```
    </xsl:template>

    <xsl:template match="PLANET">
       <TR>
          <TD><xsl:value-of select="NAME"/></TD>
          <TD><xsl:apply-templates select="MASS"/></TD>
          <TD><xsl:apply-templates select="RADIUS"/></TD>
          <TD><xsl:apply-templates select="DAY"/></TD>
       </TR>
   </xsl:template>

    <xsl:template match="MASS">
        <xsl:value-of select="format-number(., '#.###')"/>
        <xsl:text> </xsl:text>
        <xsl:value-of select="@UNITS"/>
    </xsl:template>

    <xsl:template match="RADIUS">
        <xsl:value-of select="format-number(., '#,###')"/>
        <xsl:text> </xsl:text>
        <xsl:value-of select="@UNITS"/>
    </xsl:template>

    <xsl:template match="DAY">
        <xsl:value-of select="format-number(., '###.##')"/>
        <xsl:text> </xsl:text>
        <xsl:value-of select="@UNITS"/>
    </xsl:template>

</xsl:stylesheet>
```

Here's the result, where you can see the formatted numbers:

```
<HTML>
    <HEAD>
        <TITLE>
            The Formatted Planets Table
        </TITLE>
    </HEAD>

    <BODY>
        <H1>
            The Formatted Planets Table
        </H1>

        <TABLE BORDER="2">
            <TR>
                <TD>Name</TD>
```

```
                <TD>Mass</TD>
                <TD>Radius</TD>
                <TD>Day</TD>
            </TR>

            <TR>
                <TD>Mercury</TD>
                <TD>0.055 (Earth = 1)</TD>
                <TD>1,516 miles</TD>
                <TD>58.65 days</TD>
            </TR>

            <TR>
                <TD>Venus</TD>
                <TD>0.815 (Earth = 1)</TD>
                <TD>3,716 miles</TD>
                <TD>116.75 days</TD>
            </TR>

            <TR>
                <TD>Earth</TD>
                <TD>1 (Earth = 1)</TD>
                <TD>2,107 miles</TD>
                <TD>1 days</TD>
            </TR>
        </TABLE>
    </BODY>
</HTML>
```

You can see this result document in Figure 8.1. (MSXML3 and Saxon drop leading zeros, so 0.055 appears as .055, and so on.)

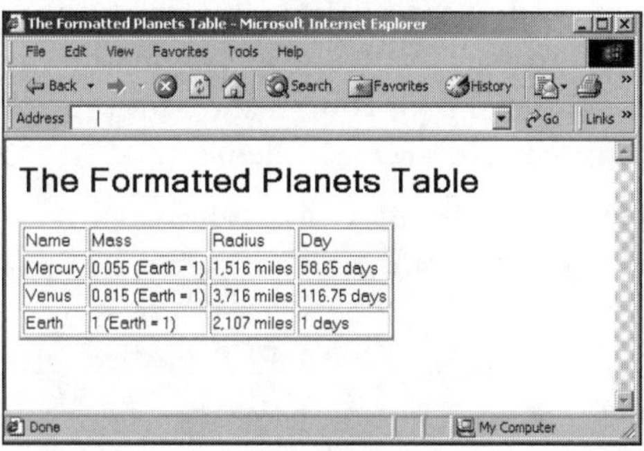

Figure 8.1 Formatting numbers using XSLT.

The following examples show how to put format strings to work. Note that you can use a semicolon (;) to separate patterns for positive and negative numbers:

- number: 4567, format string: "#,###", result: 4,567
- number: 4567.8, format string: "####.##", result: 4567.8
- number: 4567.8, format string: "#,##0.00", result: 4,567.80
- number: 456.789, format string: "#,##0.00", result: 456.79
- number: 4567890, format string: "#,##0.00", result: 4,567,890.00
- number: 4567, format string: "###0.0###", result: 4567.0
- number: .00045, format string: "##0.0###", result: 0.0005
- number: .45, format string: "#00%", result: 45%
- number: -4.56, format string: "#.00;(#.00)", result: (4.56)
- number: -45, format string: "#,##0.00", result: -45

function-available()

You use the XSLT 1.0 function `function-available` to test whether an extension function is available:

```
boolean function-available(function-name)
```

You pass this function the name of the function you're looking for, and it returns true if the function is available, and false otherwise.

You first saw the following example in Chapter 5. In this case, I want to use the extension function `starpowder:calculate` to do some math, and if it's not available, I want to send the text "Sorry, can't do math today." to the result document. (You could, of course, also quit processing and display an error message with the `<xsl:message>` element.)

```
<xsl:choose xmlns:starpowder="http://www.starpowder.com">
    <xsl:when test="function-available('starpowder:calculate')">
        <xsl:value-of select="starpowder:calculate('2+2')"/>
    </xsl:when>
    <xsl:otherwise>
        <xsl:text>Sorry, can't do math today.</xsl:text>
    </xsl:otherwise>
</xsl:choose>
```

generate-id()

The `generate-id` function causes the XSLT processor to assign an identifier (returned as a string) to a node. Here's how you use this function:

```
string generate-id(node)
```

You pass this function a node set containing just the node for which you want an identifier (any nodes after the first one are ignored), and this function returns a unique identifier for that node. If you pass this function the same node again, it returns the same identifier. Note that identifiers vary by XSLT processor.

The following example is from Chapter 6, but in this case I'm going to add a hyperlinked table of contents to planets.html. To generate that table of contents, I use `<xsl:for-each>` to loop over all the planets. Each time through the loop, I create a hyperlink and use an attribute value template to create an `HREF` attribute set to a unique identifier for the current planet:

```
<?xml version="1.0"?>
<xsl:stylesheet version="1.0"
xmlns:xsl="http://www.w3.org/1999/XSL/Transform">

    <xsl:template match="/PLANETS">
        <HTML>
            <HEAD>
                <TITLE>
                    The Planets Table
                </TITLE>
            </HEAD>
            <BODY>
                <H1>
                    The Planets Table
                </H1>
                <xsl:for-each select="PLANET">
                    <H2><A HREF="#{generate-id()}">
                        <xsl:value-of select="NAME"/></A>
                    </H2>
                    <P/>
                </xsl:for-each>
                    .
                    .
                    .
```

This adds an identifier to each planet and creates the necessary hyperlinks. I can create the hyperlink anchors in the planetary data HTML table, setting the anchor's `NAME` attribute to the identifier for each `<PLANET>` element in turn so that it becomes a hyperlink target:

```
<?xml version="1.0"?>
<xsl:stylesheet version="1.0"
xmlns:xsl="http://www.w3.org/1999/XSL/Transform">

    <xsl:template match="/PLANETS">
        <HTML>
        .
        .
        .
```

```
        </HTML>
    </xsl:template>

    <xsl:template match="PLANET">
        <TR>
           <TD><A NAME="{generate-id(.)}">
           <xsl:value-of select="NAME"/></A></TD>
           <TD><xsl:apply-templates select="MASS"/></TD>
           <TD><xsl:apply-templates select="RADIUS"/></TD>
           <TD><xsl:apply-templates select="DAY"/></TD>
        </TR>
   </xsl:template>

    <xsl:template match="MASS">
        <xsl:value-of select="."/>
        <xsl:text> </xsl:text>
        <xsl:value-of select="@UNITS"/>
    </xsl:template>
        .
        .
        .
    <xsl:template match="DAY">
        <xsl:value-of select="."/>
        <xsl:text> </xsl:text>
        <xsl:value-of select="@UNITS"/>
    </xsl:template>

</xsl:stylesheet>
```

That's all it takes; now I've created hyperlinks whose HREF attribute is set to an identifier for a <PLANET> element, and I made each <PLANET> element a hyperlink target using the same identifier.

When the user clicks a hyperlink in the table of contents, the browser scrolls to the corresponding planet's entry in the HTML table. Here's what the result document looks like if I use Xalan:

```
<HTML>
    <HEAD>
        <TITLE>
            The Planets Table
        </TITLE>
    </HEAD>

    <BODY>
        <H1>
            The Planets Table
        </H1>
        <H2>
        <A href="#N5">Mercury</A>
```

```
        </H2>
        <P></P>
        <H2>
        <A href="#N20">Venus</A>
        </H2>
        <P></P>
        <H2>
        <A href="#N3B">Earth</a>
        </H2>
        <P></P>

        <TABLE BORDER="2">
            <TR>
                <TD>Name</TD>
                <TD>Mass</TD>
                <TD>Radius</TD>
                <TD>Day</TD>
            </TR>

            <TR>
                <TD><A NAME="N5">Mercury</A>
                </TD><TD>.0553 (Earth = 1)</TD>
                <TD>1516 miles</TD>
                <TD>58.65 days</TD>
            </TR>

            <TR>
                <TD><A NAME="N20">Venus</A></TD>
                <TD>.815 (Earth = 1)</TD>
                <TD>3716 miles</TD>
                <TD>116.75 days</TD>
            </TR>

            <TR>
                <TD><A NAME="N3B">Earth</A></TD>
                <TD>1 (Earth = 1)</TD>
                <TD>2107 miles</TD>
                <TD>1 days</TD>
            </TR>

        </TABLE>
    </BODY>
</HTML>
```

key()

You use the key function to find nodes with a specific value for a named key; here's how you use this function:

```
node-set key(name, value)
```

You pass this function the name of the key as a string, and the required value for the key you want to match. This function returns a node set of nodes that match.

To create keys, you use the <xsl:key> element. You first saw the following example in Chapter 4; here, I use keys to match planets whose COLOR attribute is set to "BLUE":

```
<?xml version="1.0"?>
<?xml-stylesheet type="text/xml" href="planets.xsl"?>
<PLANETS>
        .
        .
        .
    <PLANET COLOR="BLUE">
        <NAME>Earth</NAME>
        <MASS UNITS="(Earth = 1)">1</MASS>
        <DAY UNITS="days">1</DAY>
        <RADIUS UNITS="miles">2107</RADIUS>
        <DENSITY UNITS="(Earth = 1)">1</DENSITY>
        <DISTANCE UNITS="million miles">128.4</DISTANCE><!--At perihelion-->
    </PLANET>

</PLANETS>
```

Now I can create a key, using <xsl:key>, named COLOR. This key matches <PLANET> elements and checks their COLOR attribute. Here's what that key, COLOR, looks like:

```
<?xml version="1.0"?>
<xsl:stylesheet version="1.0"
xmlns:xsl="http://www.w3.org/1999/XSL/Transform">

    <xsl:key name="COLOR" match="PLANET" use="@COLOR"/>
        .
        .
        .
```

At this point, I can use the pattern "key()" to match <PLANET> elements with the COLOR attribute set to "BLUE" this way:

```
<?xml version="1.0"?>
<xsl:stylesheet version="1.0"
xmlns:xsl="http://www.w3.org/1999/XSL/Transform">

    <xsl:key name="COLOR" match="PLANET" use="@COLOR"/>

    <xsl:template match="/PLANETS">
        <HTML>
        .
        .
        .
```

```
            <TABLE BORDER="2">
                <TR>
                    <TD>Name</TD>
                    <TD>Mass</TD>
                    <TD>Radius</TD>
                    <TD>Day</TD>
                </TR>
                <xsl:apply-templates select="key('COLOR', 'BLUE')"/>
            </TABLE>
        </BODY>
    </HTML>
</xsl:template>
    .
    .
    .
```

And here's the result—as you can see, Earth was the only planet that matched the pattern used:

```
<HTML>
    <HEAD>
        <TITLE>
            The Planets Table
        </TITLE>
    </HEAD>

    <BODY>
        <H1>
            The Planets Table
        </H1>

        <TABLE BORDER="2">
            <TR>
                <TD>Name</TD>
                <TD>Mass</TD>
                <TD>Radius</TD>
                <TD>Day</TD>
            </TR>

            <TR>
                <TD>Earth</TD>
                <TD>1 (Earth = 1)</TD>
                <TD>2107 miles</TD>
                <TD>1 days</TD>
            </TR>
        </TABLE>
    </BODY>
</HTML>
```

system-property()

The system-property function returns the value of several system properties as strings; here's how you use this function:

```
string system-property(property)
```

You can test the following possible system property values:

- xsl:version. Returns the XSLT version.
- xsl:vendor. Returns a string identifying the XSLT processor vendor
- xsl:vendor-url. Returns the XSLT processor vendor's URL.

Here's an example; you can test the XSLT version by calling system-property('xsl:version'):

```
<?xml version="1.0"?>
<xsl:stylesheet version="2.0"
xmlns:xsl="http://www.w3.org/1999/XSL/Transform">
        .
        .
        .
<xsl:if text="system-property('xsl:version')=2.0">
    <xsl:namespace name="starpowder"/>
</xsl:if>
        .
        .
        .
</xsl:stylesheet>
```

Checking the XSLT version this way is useful if you want to use features that have been introduced in recent versions.

unparsed-entity-uri()

The unparsed-entity-uri function gives you access to declarations of unparsed entities in the DTD or schema of the source document. An unparsed entity is typically binary data, such as an image file. (For more on unparsed entities, see *Inside XML.*) This is how you use this function:

```
string unparsed-entity-uri(name)
```

You pass the name of the unparsed entity to this function, and it returns the identifier for the entity. In the following example, I add a DTD to planets.xml and declare three unparsed entities corresponding to images of the planets—image1, image2, and image3—and I refer to those entities by adding an IMAGE attribute to each <PLANET> element:

Listing 8.6 **planets.xml with Unparsed Entities**

```
<?xml version="1.0"?>
<?xml-stylesheet type="text/xml" href="planets.xsl"?>
<!DOCTYPE PLANETS [
<!ELEMENT PLANET (CUSTOMER)*>
<!ELEMENT CUSTOMER (NAME,MASS,RADIUS,DAY)>
<!ELEMENT NAME (#PCDATA)>
<!ELEMENT MASS (#PCDATA)>
<!ELEMENT RADIUS (#PCDATA)>
<!ELEMENT DAY (#PCDATA)>
<!ENTITY image1 SYSTEM "http://starpowder.com/image1.gif" NDATA GIF>
<!ENTITY image2 SYSTEM "http://starpowder.com/image2.gif" NDATA GIF>
<!ENTITY image3 SYSTEM "http://starpowder.com/image3.gif" NDATA GIF>
]>
<PLANETS>

    <PLANET IMAGE="image1">
        <NAME>Mercury</NAME>
        <MASS UNITS="(Earth = 1)">.0553</MASS>
        <DAY UNITS="days">58.65</DAY>
        <RADIUS UNITS="miles">1516</RADIUS>
        <DENSITY UNITS="(Earth = 1)">.983</DENSITY>
        <DISTANCE UNITS="million miles">43.4</DISTANCE><!--At perihelion-->
    </PLANET>

    <PLANET IMAGE="image2">
        <NAME>Venus</NAME>
        <MASS UNITS="(Earth = 1)">.815</MASS>
        <DAY UNITS="days">116.75</DAY>
        <RADIUS UNITS="miles">3716</RADIUS>
        <DENSITY UNITS="(Earth = 1)">.943</DENSITY>
        <DISTANCE UNITS="million miles">66.8</DISTANCE><!--At perihelion-->
    </PLANET>

    <PLANET IMAGE="image3">
        <NAME>Earth</NAME>
        <MASS UNITS="(Earth = 1)">1</MASS>
        <DAY UNITS="days">1</DAY>
        <RADIUS UNITS="miles">2107</RADIUS>
        <DENSITY UNITS="(Earth = 1)">1</DENSITY>
        <DISTANCE UNITS="million miles">128.4</DISTANCE><!--At perihelion-->
    </PLANET>

</PLANETS>
```

(Note that some XSLT processors are built on XML parsers that check to see whether they can find the entity at the given URI, so if you're going to try out this example, substitute the URI of some real images.) Now I can retrieve the URI of the images by using `unparsed-entity-uri` in a stylesheet and create HTML `<IMG>` elements using this function in the result document:

Listing 8.7 **Using *unparsed-entity-uri***

```
<?xml version="1.0"?>
<xsl:stylesheet version="1.0"
xmlns:xsl="http://www.w3.org/1999/XSL/Transform">

    <xsl:template match="/PLANETS">
        <HTML>
        .
        .
        .
        </HTML>
    </xsl:template>

    <xsl:template match="PLANET">
       <TR>
          <TD><xsl:value-of select="NAME"/><IMG SRC="{unparsed-entity-uri(@IMAGE)}"/></TD>
          <TD><xsl:apply-templates select="MASS"/></TD>
          <TD><xsl:apply-templates select="RADIUS"/></TD>
          <TD><xsl:apply-templates select="DAY"/></TD>
       </TR>
   </xsl:template>

    <xsl:template match="MASS">
        <xsl:value-of select="."/>
        <xsl:text> </xsl:text>
        <xsl:value-of select="@UNITS"/>
    </xsl:template>
        .
        .
        .
    <xsl:template match="DAY">
        <xsl:value-of select="."/>
        <xsl:text> </xsl:text>
        <xsl:value-of select="@UNITS"/>
    </xsl:template>

</xsl:stylesheet>
```

And here's the result document:

```
<HTML>
    <HEAD>
        <TITLE>
            The Planets Table
        </TITLE>
    </HEAD>

    <BODY>
        <H1>
            The Planets Table
        </H1>

        <TABLE BORDER="2">
            <TR>
                <TD>Name</TD>
                <TD>Mass</TD>
                <TD>Radius</TD>
                <TD>Day</TD>
            </TR>

            <TR>
                <TD>Mercury<IMG SRC="http://starpowder.com/image1.gif"></TD>
                <TD>.0553 (Earth = 1)</TD>
                <TD>1516 miles</TD>
                <TD>58.65 days</TD>
            </TR>

            <TR>
                <TD>Venus<IMG SRC="http://starpowder.com/image2.gif"></TD>
                <TD>.815 (Earth = 1)</TD>
                <TD>3716 miles</TD>
                <TD>116.75 days</TD>
            </TR>

            <TR>
                <TD>Earth<IMG SRC="http://starpowder.com/image3.gif"></TD>
                <TD>1 (Earth = 1)</TD>
                <TD>2107 miles</TD>
                <TD>1 days</TD>
            </TR>

        </TABLE>
    </BODY>
</HTML>
```

That completes the XSLT functions. I'll turn to the XPath functions next, starting with those you use on node sets.

The XPath Node Set Functions

The following XPath functions work on node sets:

- `count(node-set)`. This function returns the number of nodes in a node set.
- `id(string ID)`. This function returns a node set of the element whose ID matches the string passed to the function, or an empty node set if no element matches.
- `last()`. This function returns the number of nodes in a node set.
- `local-name(node-set)`. This function returns the local name of the first node in the node set.
- `name(node-set)`. This function returns the qualified name of the first node in the node set.
- `namespace-uri(node-set)`. This function returns the URI of the namespace of the first node in the node set.
- `position()`. This function returns the position of the context node in the context node set, starting with 1.

count()

You use the `count` function to count the number of nodes in a node set.

```
number count(node-set)
```

You pass this function a node set, and it returns the number of nodes in the node set.

You first saw the following example in Chapter 6, where I used the `count` function to return the number of nodes in a node set. In this case, the node set is made up of all the `<PLANET>` elements in planets.xml, and I get that node set using the location path "//PLANET":

```
<xsl:stylesheet
 xmlns:xsl="http://www.w3.org/1999/XSL/Transform"
 version="1.0">

<xsl:output method="xml" indent="yes"/>

<xsl:template match="*">
    <xsl:copy>
        <xsl:apply-templates/>
    </xsl:copy>
</xsl:template>
```

```
<xsl:template match="PLANET">
    <xsl:copy use-attribute-sets="numbering">
        <xsl:apply-templates/>
    </xsl:copy>
</xsl:template>

<xsl:attribute-set name="numbering">
    <xsl:attribute name="number"><xsl:number/></xsl:attribute>
    <xsl:attribute name="total"><xsl:value-of select="count(//PLANET)"/></xsl:attribute>
</xsl:attribute-set>

</xsl:stylesheet>
```

Here's the result; note that every `<PLANET>` element has both a `number` and `total` attribute, and the `total` attribute holds the total number of `<PLANET>` elements, which was found with `count`:

```
<?xml version="1.0" encoding="UTF-8"?>
<PLANETS>

    <PLANET number="1" total="3">
        <NAME>Mercury</NAME>
        <MASS>.0553</MASS>
        <DAY>58.65</DAY>
        <RADIUS>1516</RADIUS>
        <DENSITY>.983</DENSITY>
        <DISTANCE>43.4</DISTANCE>
    </PLANET>

    <PLANET number="2" total="3">
        <NAME>Venus</NAME>
        <MASS>.815</MASS>
        <DAY>116.75</DAY>
        <RADIUS>3716</RADIUS>
        <DENSITY>.943</DENSITY>
        <DISTANCE>66.8</DISTANCE>
    </PLANET>

    <PLANET number="3" total="3">
        <NAME>Earth</NAME>
        <MASS>1</MASS>
        <DAY>1</DAY>
        <RADIUS>2107</RADIUS>
        <DENSITY>1</DENSITY>
        <DISTANCE>128.4</DISTANCE>
    </PLANET>

</PLANETS>
```

id()

The `id` function returns a node set where all the nodes have the same ID as that passed to this function. Here's how you use this function:

```
node-set id(id-value)
```

You pass this function an `ID value` and it returns the node set of nodes with that ID. Note that you can specify multiple IDs separated by whitespace, and this function returns a node set of the elements with those IDs.

The following example rule matches the text of all elements that have the ID "favorite":

```
<xsl:template match = "id('favorite')">
    <H3><xsl:value-of select="."/></H3>
</xsl:template>
```

Note also that you must declare ID values as such in a DTD or schema. A DTD for planets.xml that declares an ID named `id` and sets it to "favorite" might look like this:

```
<?xml version="1.0"?>
<?xml-stylesheet type="text/xml" href="stylesheet.xsl"?>
<!DOCTYPE PLANETS [
<!ELEMENT PLANET (CUSTOMER)*>
<!ELEMENT CUSTOMER (NAME,MASS,RADIUS,DAY)>
<!ELEMENT NAME (#PCDATA)>
<!ELEMENT MASS (#PCDATA)>
<!ELEMENT RADIUS (#PCDATA)>
<!ELEMENT DAY (#PCDATA)>
<!ATTLIST PLANET
    id ID #REQUIRED>
]>
<PLANETS>
    <PLANET id='favorite'>
        <NAME>Mercury</NAME>
        <MASS UNITS="(Earth = 1)">.0553</MASS>
        <DAY UNITS="days">58.65</DAY>
        <RADIUS UNITS="miles">1516</RADIUS>
        <DENSITY UNITS="(Earth = 1)">.983</DENSITY>
        <DISTANCE UNITS="million miles">43.4</DISTANCE><!--At perihelion-->
    </PLANET>
        .
        .
        .
```

Note that some XSLT processors don't match by ID because they don't read DTDs or XML schema. This is one of the issues that XSLT 2.0 is supposed to address—how to make ID information available.

last()

The `last` function returns the number of nodes in a node set, so its value is equal to the position of the last node. Here's how you use this function:

```
number last()
```

The following example from Chapter 5 listed the planets by name in a sentence in the result document. However, I didn't want to have the output simply say, "The first three planets are: Mercury Venus Earth", but rather "The first three planets are: Mercury, Venus, and Earth." I can add the correct punctuation using the `position` function to determine what element we're working on, and use `<xsl:if>` to check the position, like this:

```
<?xml version="1.0"?>
<xsl:stylesheet version="1.0" xmlns:xsl="http://www.w3.org/1999/XSL/Transform">
<xml:output method="xml"/>

<xsl:template match="PLANETS">
<DOCUMENT>
    <TITLE>
        The Planets
    </TITLE>
    <PLANETS>
        The first three planets are: <xsl:apply-templates select="PLANET"/>
    </PLANETS>
</DOCUMENT>
</xsl:template>

<xsl:template match="PLANET">
    <xsl:value-of select="NAME"/>
    <xsl:if test="position()!=last()">, </xsl:if>
    <xsl:if test="position()=last()-1">and </xsl:if>
    <xsl:if test="position()=last()">.</xsl:if>
</xsl:template>

</xsl:stylesheet>
```

Here's the result:

```
<?xml version="1.0" encoding="UTF-8"?>
<DOCUMENT>

    <TITLE>
        The Planets
    </TITLE>

    <PLANETS>
        The first three planets are: Mercury, Venus, and Earth.
    </PLANETS>

</DOCUMENT>
```

local-name()

The `local-name` function returns the local (unqualified) name of a node. Here's how you use this function:

```
string local-name(node-set?)
```

You pass this function a node set with one node in it, and the function returns the local name of the node. (If the node set has more than one node, only the first is used.) If you don't pass any nodes, this function returns the local name of the context node.

In the following example, I use `<xsl:element>` to create new elements and `local-name` to find the name of context nodes, as follows:

```
<?xml version="1.0"?>
<xsl:stylesheet version="1.0"
xmlns:xsl="http://www.w3.org/1999/XSL/Transform">
    <xsl:output method="xml"/>

    <xsl:template match="PLANETS">
        <xsl:element name="{local-name(.)}">
            <xsl:for-each select="PLANET">
                <xsl:element name="{local-name(.)}">
                    <xsl:for-each select="*">
                        <xsl:element name="DATA">
                            <xsl:value-of select="."/>
                        </xsl:element>
                    </xsl:for-each>
                </xsl:element>
            </xsl:for-each>
        </xsl:element>
    </xsl:template>

</xsl:stylesheet>
```

name()

The `name` function is like the `local-name` function, except that it returns the fully qualified name of the node. Here's how you use this function:

```
string name(node-set?)
```

namespace-uri()

The `namespace-uri` function returns a string containing the URI of the namespace in a node's expanded name. Usually, this is the URI in a namespace declaration as set with the `xmlns` or `xmlns:`*`prefix`* attributes. (See Inside

XML for more details.) Here's how you use this function—note that you can use this function only on elements or attributes; other nodes result in an empty string:

```
string namespace-uri(node-set?)
```

For example, I might add a namespace, "star", to planets.xml:

```
<?xml version="1.0"?>
<?xml-stylesheet type="text/xml" href="planets.xsl"?>
<star:PLANETS xmlns:star="http://starpowder.com">

    <star:PLANET>
        <star:NAME>Mercury</star:NAME>
        <star:MASS UNITS="(Earth = 1)">.0553</star:MASS>
        <star:DAY UNITS="days">58.65</star:DAY>
        <star:RADIUS UNITS="miles">1516</star:RADIUS>
        <star:DENSITY UNITS="(Earth = 1)">.983</star:DENSITY>
        <star:DISTANCE UNITS="million miles">43.4</star:DISTANCE><!--At perihelion-->
    </star:PLANET>

    <star:PLANET>
        <star:NAME>Venus</star:NAME>
        <star:MASS UNITS="(Earth = 1)">.815</star:MASS>
        <star:DAY UNITS="days">116.75</star:DAY>
        <star:RADIUS UNITS="miles">3716</star:RADIUS>
        <star:DENSITY UNITS="(Earth = 1)">.943</star:DENSITY>
        <star:DISTANCE UNITS="million miles">66.8</star:DISTANCE><!--At perihelion-->
    </star:PLANET>
        .
        .
        .
```

And I can find the URI of this namespace in a stylesheet with `namespace-uri`:

```
<?xml version="1.0"?>
<xsl:stylesheet version="1.0"
xmlns:xsl="http://www.w3.org/1999/XSL/Transform"
xmlns:star="http://www.starpowder.com">

<xsl:template match="/PLANETS">
    <xsl:value-of select="namespace-uri()"/>
</xsl:template>
        .
        .
        .
```

And here's the result:

```
<?xml version="1.0" encoding="UTF-8"?>
http://starpowder.com
```

position()

The `position` function returns the position of the context node:

```
number position()
```

You've seen the `position` function throughout the book. Here's the example you saw earlier in this chapter that uses both the `last` and `position` functions to create the sentence, "The first three planets are: Mercury,Venus, and Earth.":

```
<?xml version="1.0"?>
<xsl:stylesheet version="1.0" xmlns:xsl="http://www.w3.org/1999/XSL/Transform">
<xml:output method="xml"/>

<xsl:template match="PLANETS">
<DOCUMENT>
    <TITLE>
        The Planets
    </TITLE>
    <PLANETS>
        The first three planets are: <xsl:apply-templates select="PLANET"/>
    </PLANETS>
</DOCUMENT>
</xsl:template>

<xsl:template match="PLANET">
    <xsl:value-of select="NAME"/>
    <xsl:if test="position()!=last()">, </xsl:if>
    <xsl:if test="position()=last()-1">and </xsl:if>
    <xsl:if test="position()=last()">.</xsl:if>
</xsl:template>

</xsl:stylesheet>
```

And here's the result:

```
<?xml version="1.0" encoding="UTF-8"?>
<DOCUMENT>

    <TITLE>
        The Planets
    </TITLE>

    <PLANETS>
        The first three planets are: Mercury, Venus, and Earth.
    </PLANETS>

</DOCUMENT>
```

The XPath String Functions

The following XPath string functions are available in XSLT:

- `concat(string string1, string string2, ...)`. This function returns all strings you pass to it concatenated together.
- `contains(string string1, string string2)`. This function checks for the existence of the second string within the first string—returns true if found.
- `normalize-space(string string1)`. This function returns *string1* (or context node if no string1) after leading and trailing whitespace is stripped and multiple consecutive whitespace is replaced with a single space.
- `starts-with(string string1, string string2)`. This function returns true if the first string starts with the second string.
- `string-length(string string1)`. This function returns the number of characters in *string1*.
- `substring(string string1, number offset, number length)`. This function returns *length* characters from the string, starting at *offset*.
- `substring-after(string string1, string string2)`. This function returns the part of *string1* starting after the first occurrence of *string2*.
- `substring-before(string string1, string string2)`. This function returns the part of *string1* up to the first occurrence of *string2*.
- `translate(string string1, string string2, string string3)`. This function returns *string1* with all occurrences of the characters in *string2* replaced by the matching characters in *string3*.

I go through each of these string functions in the sections that follow.

concat()

The `concat` function concatenates as many strings together as you pass to it, returning the concatenated string:

```
concat(string string1, string string2, ...)
```

For an example, look at the version of planets.xsl developed earlier in this book that displayed element values and the values of the `UNITS` attributes and used templates in this way:

```
<xsl:template match="MASS">
        <xsl:value-of select="."/>
        <xsl:text> </xsl:text>
        <xsl:value-of select="@UNITS"/>
    </xsl:template>
```

This displays the string value, the context node, a space, and the string value of the UNITS attribute. However, you could make this a lot shorter with the concat function:

Listing 8.8 **Using the *concat* Function**

```
<?xml version="1.0"?>
<xsl:stylesheet version="1.0"
xmlns:xsl="http://www.w3.org/1999/XSL/Transform">

    <xsl:template match="/PLANETS">
        <HTML>
        .
        .
        .
        </HTML>
    </xsl:template>

    <xsl:template match="PLANET">
       <TR>
          <TD><xsl:value-of select="NAME"/></TD>
          <TD><xsl:apply-templates select="MASS"/></TD>
          <TD><xsl:apply-templates select="RADIUS"/></TD>
          <TD><xsl:apply-templates select="DAY"/></TD>
       </TR>
   </xsl:template>

    <xsl:template match="MASS">
        <xsl:value-of select="concat(., ' ', @UNITS)"/>
    </xsl:template>

    <xsl:template match="RADIUS">
        <xsl:value-of select="concat(., ' ', @UNITS)"/>
    </xsl:template>

    <xsl:template match="DAY">
        <xsl:value-of select="concat(., ' ', @UNITS)"/>
    </xsl:template>

</xsl:stylesheet>
```

contains()

The contains function checks to see whether one string is contained inside another, and returns a value of true if so, false otherwise. Here's how you use this function:

```
boolean contains(container-string, contained-string)
```

The following example is from Chapter 7; in this case, I want to search all attributes for the word "miles", and if found, add the text "You should switch to kilometers." in the result document:

```
<?xml version="1.0"?>
<xsl:stylesheet version="1.0"
xmlns:xsl="http://www.w3.org/1999/XSL/Transform">

    <xsl:template match="/PLANETS">
        <HTML>
        .
        .
        .
        </HTML>
    </xsl:template>

    <xsl:template match="PLANET">
       <TR>
          <TD><xsl:value-of select="NAME"/></TD>
          <TD><xsl:apply-templates select="MASS"/></TD>
          <TD><xsl:apply-templates select="RADIUS"/></TD>
          <TD><xsl:apply-templates select="DAY"/></TD>
          <TD><xsl:apply-templates select="DISTANCE"/></TD>
       </TR>
   </xsl:template>

    <xsl:template match="MASS">
        <xsl:value-of select="."/>
        <xsl:text> </xsl:text>
        <xsl:value-of select="@UNITS"/>
    </xsl:template>
        .
        .
        .
    <xsl:template match="DISTANCE">
        <xsl:value-of select="."/>
        <xsl:text> </xsl:text>
        <xsl:value-of select="@UNITS"/>
    </xsl:template>

    <xsl:template match="//*[contains(@UNITS, 'miles')]">
        <xsl:value-of select="."/>
        <xsl:text> </xsl:text>
        <xsl:text>You should switch to kilometers.</xsl:text>
    </xsl:template>

</xsl:stylesheet>
```

Here's the result document:

```
<HTML>
    <HEAD>
        <TITLE>
            The Planets Table
        </TITLE>
    </HEAD>

    <BODY>
        <H1>
            The Planets Table
        </H1>

        <TABLE BORDER="2">
            <TR>
                <TD>Name</TD>
                <TD>Mass</TD>
                <TD>Radius</TD>
                <TD>Day</TD>
                <TD>Distance</TD>
            </TR>

            <TR>
                <TD>Mercury</TD>
                <TD>.0553 (Earth = 1)</TD>
                <TD>1516 You should switch to kilometers.</TD>
                <TD>58.65 days</TD>
                <TD>43.4 You should switch to kilometers.</TD>
            </TR>

            <TR>
                <TD>Venus</TD>
                <TD>.815 (Earth = 1)</TD>
                <TD>3716 You should switch to kilometers.</TD>
                <TD>116.75 days</TD>
                <TD>66.8 You should switch to kilometers.</TD>
            </TR>

            <TR>
                <TD>Earth</TD>
                <TD>1 (Earth = 1)</TD>
                <TD>2107 You should switch to kilometers.</TD>
                <TD>1 days</TD>
                <TD>128.4 You should switch to kilometers.</TD>
            </TR>

        </TABLE>
    </BODY>
</HTML>
```

normalize-space()

The `normalize-space` function removes leading and trailing whitespace and condenses all internal adjacent whitespace into a single space, returning the resulting string. Here's how you use this function:

```
string normalize-space(string?)
```

In the following example, I add extra whitespace to the `UNITS` element in Mercury's `<MASS>` element:

```
<?xml version="1.0"?>
<?xml-stylesheet type="text/xml" href="planets.xsl"?>
<PLANETS>

    <PLANET>
        <NAME>Mercury</NAME>
        <MASS UNITS="  (Earth    =     1)    ">.0553</MASS>
        <DAY UNITS="days">58.65</DAY>
        <RADIUS UNITS="miles">1516</RADIUS>
        <DENSITY UNITS="(Earth = 1)">.983</DENSITY>
        <DISTANCE UNITS="million miles">43.4</DISTANCE><!--At perihelion-->
    </PLANET>
        .
        .
        .
```

I can remove the extra whitespace in the stylesheet with `normalize-space`:

```
<?xml version="1.0"?>
<xsl:stylesheet version="1.0"
xmlns:xsl="http://www.w3.org/1999/XSL/Transform">

    <xsl:template match="/PLANETS">
        <HTML>
        .
        .
        .
        </HTML>
    </xsl:template>

    <xsl:template match="PLANET">
       <TR>
          <TD><xsl:value-of select="NAME"/></TD>
          <TD><xsl:apply-templates select="MASS"/></TD>
          <TD><xsl:apply-templates select="RADIUS"/></TD>
          <TD><xsl:apply-templates select="DAY"/></TD>
       </TR>
   </xsl:template>
```

```
    <xsl:template match="MASS">
        <xsl:value-of select="."/>
        <xsl:text> </xsl:text>
        <xsl:value-of select="normalize-space(@UNITS)"/>
    </xsl:template>
        .
        .
        .
```

And here's the result—note that the extra whitespace has been removed:

```
<HTML>
    <HEAD>
        <TITLE>
            The Planets Table
        </TITLE>
    </HEAD>

    <BODY>
        <H1>
            The Planets Table
        </H1>
        <TABLE BORDER="2">
            <TR>
                <TD>Name</TD>
                <TD>Mass</TD>
                <TD>Radius</TD>
                <TD>Day</TD>
            </TR>

            <TR>
                <TD>Mercury</TD>
                <TD>.0553 (Earth = 1)</TD>
                <TD>1516 miles</TD>
                <TD>58.65 days</TD>
            </TR>
        .
        .
        .
```

starts-with()

As you can guess from its name, you use the `starts-with` function to test whether one string starts with another.

```
boolean starts-with(string-to-examine, possible-start-string)
```

This example from Chapter 4 used `starts-with` to match text nodes whose text starts with "E" in order to match the Earth, and added the text "(the World)" to the description of Earth, making it "Earth (the World)":

```
<?xml version="1.0"?>
<xsl:stylesheet version="1.0"
xmlns:xsl="http://www.w3.org/1999/XSL/Transform">

    <xsl:template match="/PLANETS">
        <HTML>
            <HEAD>
        .
        .
        .
            </BODY>
        </HTML>
    </xsl:template>

    <xsl:template match="PLANET">
       <TR>
          <TD><xsl:apply-templates select="NAME"/></TD>
          <TD><xsl:apply-templates select="MASS"/></TD>
          <TD><xsl:apply-templates select="RADIUS"/></TD>
          <TD><xsl:apply-templates select="DAY"/></TD>
       </TR>
   </xsl:template>

    <xsl:template match="text()[starts-with(., 'E')]">
        <xsl:text>(the World)</xsl:text>
    </xsl:template>

    <xsl:template match="NAME">
        <xsl:value-of select="."/>
        <xsl:text> </xsl:text>
        <xsl:value-of select="@UNITS"/>
        <xsl:apply-templates/>
    </xsl:template>
        .
        .
        .
    <xsl:template match="DAY">
        <xsl:value-of select="."/>
        <xsl:text> </xsl:text>
        <xsl:value-of select="@UNITS"/>
    </xsl:template>

</xsl:stylesheet>
```

And here's the result—note that the caption for Earth has become "Earth (the World)":

```
<HTML>
    <HEAD>
        <TITLE>
            The Planets Table
        </TITLE>
```

```
    </HEAD>

    <BODY>
        <H1>
            The Planets Table
        </H1>

        <TABLE BORDER="2">
            <TR>
                <TD>Name</TD>
                <TD>Mass</TD>
                <TD>Radius</TD>
                <TD>Day</TD>
            </TR>
            .
            .
            .
            <TR>
                <TD>Earth (the World)</TD>
                <TD>1 (Earth = 1)</TD>
                <TD>2107 miles</TD>
                <TD>1 days</TD>
            </TR>
        </TABLE>
    </BODY>
</HTML>
```

string()

The `string` function just converts the item you pass it to a string. Here's how you use this function:

```
string string(object?)
```

Usually, this function is not needed because these types of conversions are made automatically. In fact, I can think of only a few limited examples where you really need to use the `string` function. For one, imagine that for some reason you put three `<NAME>` elements into each `<PLANET>` element in planets.xml, and that you wanted to use only the first `<NAME>` element as the real name of the planet:

```
<?xml version="1.0"?>
<?xml-stylesheet type="text/xml" href="planets.xsl"?>
<PLANETS>

    <PLANET>
        <NAME>Mercury</NAME>
        <NAME>Venus</NAME>
        <NAME>Earth</NAME>
```

```
        <MASS UNITS="(Earth = 1)">.0553</MASS>
        <DAY UNITS="days">58.65</DAY>
        <RADIUS UNITS="miles">1516</RADIUS>
        <DENSITY UNITS="(Earth = 1)">.983</DENSITY>
        <DISTANCE UNITS="million miles">43.4</DISTANCE><!--At perihelion-->
    </PLANET>

    <PLANET>
        <NAME>Venus</NAME>
        <NAME>Earth</NAME>
        <NAME>Mercury</NAME>
        <NAME>Planet of Love.</NAME>
        <MASS UNITS="(Earth = 1)">.815</MASS>
        <DAY UNITS="days">116.75</DAY>
        <RADIUS UNITS="miles">3716</RADIUS>
        <DENSITY UNITS="(Earth = 1)">.943</DENSITY>
        <DISTANCE UNITS="million miles">66.8</DISTANCE><!--At perihelion-->
    </PLANET>

    <PLANET>
        <NAME>Earth</NAME>
        <NAME>Mercury</NAME>
        <NAME>Venus</NAME>
        <NAME>The planet you're standing on.</NAME>
        <MASS UNITS="(Earth = 1)">1</MASS>
        <DAY UNITS="days">1</DAY>
        <RADIUS UNITS="miles">2107</RADIUS>
        <DENSITY UNITS="(Earth = 1)">1</DENSITY>
        <DISTANCE UNITS="million miles">128.4</DISTANCE><!--At perihelion-->
    </PLANET>

</PLANETS>
```

Now imagine that you want to match a specific planet, such as Venus. This test doesn't work, because NAME returns a node set of all the context node's <NAME> children, and because every planet has a <NAME> element with the name Venus in it, this test is always true:

```
    <xsl:template match="PLANET">
    <xsl:if test="NAME='Venus'">
       <TR>
          <TD><xsl:value-of select="NAME"/></TD>
          <TD><xsl:apply-templates select="MASS"/></TD>
          <TD><xsl:apply-templates select="RADIUS"/></TD>
          <TD><xsl:apply-templates select="DAY"/></TD>
       </TR>
    </xsl:if>
   </xsl:template>
```

If you want to test just the first <NAME> element in each <PLANET> element, you can use the `string` function in the following way, because it returns a string, not a node set:

```
<?xml version="1.0"?>
<xsl:stylesheet version="1.0"
xmlns:xsl="http://www.w3.org/1999/XSL/Transform">

    <xsl:template match="/PLANETS">
        <HTML>
        .
        .
        .
        </HTML>
    </xsl:template>

    <xsl:template match="PLANET">
    <xsl:if test="string(NAME)='Venus'">
       <TR>
          <TD><xsl:value-of select="NAME"/></TD>
          <TD><xsl:apply-templates select="MASS"/></TD>
          <TD><xsl:apply-templates select="RADIUS"/></TD>
          <TD><xsl:apply-templates select="DAY"/></TD>
       </TR>
    </xsl:if>
   </xsl:template>

    <xsl:template match="MASS">
        <xsl:value-of select="."/>
        <xsl:text> </xsl:text>
        <xsl:value-of select="@UNITS"/>
    </xsl:template>
        .
        .
        .
    <xsl:template match="DAY">
        <xsl:value-of select="."/>
        <xsl:text> </xsl:text>
        <xsl:value-of select="@UNITS"/>
    </xsl:template>

</xsl:stylesheet>
```

Of course, it's easier to use `NAME[1]` if you want to just match the first <NAME> child of the context node.

string-length()

As you can guess, the `string-length` function returns the length of a string you pass to it. Here's how you use this function:

```
number string-length(string?)
```

In the following example, I use `string-length` to find the length of each planet's name:

```
<?xml version="1.0"?>
<xsl:stylesheet version="1.0"
xmlns:xsl="http://www.w3.org/1999/XSL/Transform">

    <xsl:template match="/PLANETS">
        <HTML>
            <HEAD>
                <TITLE>
                    Length of Planet Names
                </TITLE>
            </HEAD>
            <BODY>
                <H1>
                    Length of Planet Names
                </H1>
                    <xsl:apply-templates/>
            </BODY>
        </HTML>
    </xsl:template>

    <xsl:template match="PLANET">
          <xsl:value-of select="NAME"/> is <xsl:value-of select="string-length(NAME)"/>
          ➥characters long.
          <BR/>
   </xsl:template>

    <xsl:template match="*">
    </xsl:template>

</xsl:stylesheet>
```

And here's the result:

```
<HTML>
    <HEAD>
        <TITLE>
            Length of Planet Names
        </TITLE>
    </HEAD>

    <BODY>
        <H1>
            Length of Planet Names
        </H1>

        Mercury is 7 characters long.
        <BR>

        Venus is 5 characters long.
```

```
        <BR>

        Earth is 5 characters long.
        <BR>

    </BODY>
</HTML>
```

You can see this result document in Figure 8.2.

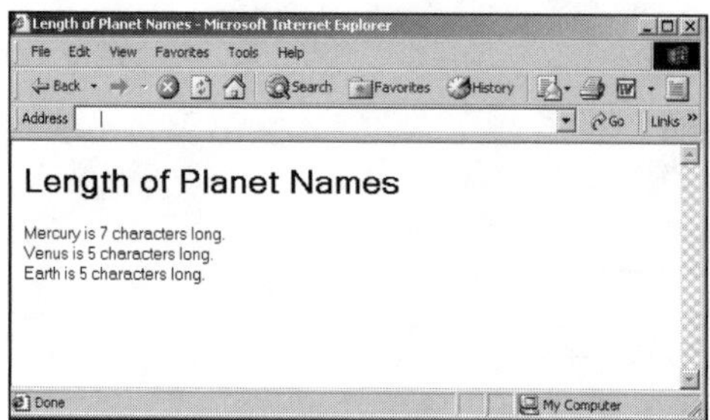

Figure 8.2 Checking the length of strings in XSLT.

substring()

The `substring` function returns a substring of a string. Here's how you use this function:

```
string substring(source-string, start-position, number-of-characters?)
```

You pass this function a `source-string`, a `start-position`, and, optionally, a `number-of-characters`. This function returns the substring of the source string starting at the starting position and continuing for the number of characters you've specified, or to the end of the string if you haven't specified a number of characters to return.

The substring function is one of a trio of substring functions: `substring-before`, which returns the string before a matched substring, `substring` itself, which returns substrings that you specify, and `substring-after`, which returns the substring after a match. The following example uses all three—in this case, I'll chop the name of the planet Mercury up into three substrings—"Mer", "c", and "ury"—and then concatenate them again. Here's how that works using these three functions—see the following two topics for more on `substring-before` and `substring_after`:

Listing 8.9 **Using *substring-before, substring,* and *substring-after***

```
<?xml version="1.0"?>
<xsl:stylesheet version="1.0"
xmlns:xsl="http://www.w3.org/1999/XSL/Transform">

    <xsl:template match="/PLANETS">
        <HTML>
            <HEAD>
                <TITLE>
                    Planetary Information
                </TITLE>
            </HEAD>
            <BODY>
                <H1>
                    Planetary Information
                </H1>
                    <xsl:apply-templates/>
            </BODY>
        </HTML>
    </xsl:template>

    <xsl:template match="PLANET">
        <xsl:if test="NAME='Mercury'">
          The first planet is
          <xsl:value-of
              select="concat(substring-before(NAME, 'c'),
              substring(NAME, 4, 1), substring-after(NAME, 'c'))"/>.
          <BR/>
        </xsl:if>
   </xsl:template>

    <xsl:template match="*">
    </xsl:template>

</xsl:stylesheet>
```

And here's the result document created by this transformation:

```
<HTML>
    <HEAD>
        <TITLE>
            Planetary Information
        </TITLE>
    </HEAD>
```

```
    <BODY>
        <H1>
            Planetary Information
        </H1>

        The first planet is Mercury.
        <BR>

    </BODY>
</HTML>
```

substring-after()

The `substring-after` function returns the substring following a matched string. You supply this function with a string, and a string to match inside the string, and it returns the substring following the match if there was a match, and an empty string otherwise. Here's how you use this function:

```
string substring-after(string, string-to-match)
```

See the `substring()` topic for an example that uses the `substring-before`, `substring`, and `substring-after` functions.

substring-before()

You supply `substring-before` with a string, and a string to match inside the string, and it returns the substring preceding the match if there was a match; otherwise, it returns an empty string. Here's how you use `substring-before`:

```
string substring-before(string, string-to-match)
```

See the `substring()` topic for an example that uses the `substring-before`, `substring`, and `substring-after` functions.

translate()

You use the `translate` function to *translate or replace specific* characters. (This function is much like the `tr` operator in Perl, if you're familiar with operators.) You supply two strings: one is a list of characters to match, and the other is a list of characters with which to replace the matched characters. Here's how you use this function:

```
string translate(string, from-characters, to-characters)
```

For example, if the third character in `from-characters` is found in `string`, the third character in `to-characters` is substituted for it in the result string.

In the following example, this use of `translate`

```
translate("steve-starpowder.com", "-", "@")
```

returns the result string "steve@starpowder.com".

Now in this example, I'm just converting a string to lower case:

```
translate("XSLT", "ABCDEFGHIJKLMNOPQRSTUVWXYZ", "abcdefghijklmnopqrstuvwxyz")
```

The XPath Number Functions

XPath supports the following functions that operate on numbers:

- `ceiling()`. Returns the smallest integer larger than the number you pass it.
- `floor()`. Returns the largest integer smaller than the number you pass it.
- `round()`. Rounds the number you pass it to the nearest integer.
- `sum()`. Returns the sum of the numbers you pass it.

The following sections provide examples for each of these functions.

ceiling()

The `ceiling` function returns the smallest integer that is still larger than the number you pass it; that is, it returns the next greater integer. Here's how you use this function:

```
number ceiling(number)
```

For example, this expression

```
ceiling(3.1415926535)
```

returns 4.

floor()

The `floor` function is the counterpart to the `ceiling` function. This function returns the largest integer that is still smaller than the number you pass it. In other words, this function returns the preceding integer. Here's how you use this function:

```
number floor(number)
```

In this example, I use `floor` to convert the length of planetary days to integers:

```
<?xml version="1.0"?>
<xsl:stylesheet version="1.0"
xmlns:xsl="http://www.w3.org/1999/XSL/Transform">

    <xsl:template match="/PLANETS">
        <HTML>
        .
        .
```

```
        </HTML>
    </xsl:template>

    <xsl:template match="PLANET">
       <TR>
          <TD><xsl:value-of select="NAME"/></TD>
          <TD><xsl:apply-templates select="MASS"/></TD>
          <TD><xsl:apply-templates select="RADIUS"/></TD>
          <TD><xsl:apply-templates select="DAY"/></TD>
       </TR>
   </xsl:template>

    <xsl:template match="MASS">
        <xsl:value-of select="."/>
        <xsl:text> </xsl:text>
        <xsl:value-of select="@UNITS"/>
    </xsl:template>

    <xsl:template match="RADIUS">
        <xsl:value-of select="."/>
        <xsl:text> </xsl:text>
        <xsl:value-of select="@UNITS"/>
    </xsl:template>

    <xsl:template match="DAY">
        <xsl:value-of select="floor(.)"/>
        <xsl:text> </xsl:text>
        <xsl:value-of select="@UNITS"/>
    </xsl:template>

</xsl:stylesheet>
```

And here's the result document:

```
<HTML>
    <HEAD>
        <TITLE>
            The Planets Table
        </TITLE>
    </HEAD>

    <BODY>
        <H1>
            The Planets Table
        </H1>

        <TABLE BORDER="2">
            <TR>
                <TD>Name</TD>
                <TD>Mass</TD>
                <TD>Radius</TD>
                <TD>Day</TD>
```

```
        </TR>

        <TR>
            <TD>Mercury</TD>
            <TD>.0553 (Earth = 1)</TD>
            <TD>1516 miles</TD>
            <TD>58 days</TD>
        </TR>

        <TR>
            <TD>Venus</TD>
            <TD>.815 (Earth = 1)</TD>
            <TD>3716 miles</TD>
            <TD>116 days</TD>
        </TR>

        <TR>
            <TD>Earth</TD>
            <TD>1 (Earth = 1)</TD>
            <TD>2107 miles</TD>
            <TD>1 days</TD>
        </TR>

    </TABLE>
  </BODY>
</HTML>
```

number()

The `number` function converts its argument to a number. Here's how you use this function:

```
number number(object?)
```

In this example, I'm passing `number` a string:

```
number("456.7")
```

This expression returns the number 456.7. If you try to convert something that `number` can't translate into a number, you get the XPath `NaN` (Not a Number) value. `NaN` is a legal value you can test for in XPath expressions.

round()

The `round` function rounds its value. Here's how you use this function:

```
number round(number)
```

For example, `round(3.1415926535)` returns 3, `round(4.5)` returns 5, and `round(-1.5)` returns -1.

sum()

The sum function sums the numeric values of a set of nodes and returns the result. Here's how you use this function:

```
number sum(node-set)
```

Look at this example from Chapter 4, which found the average mass of the planets in planets.xml:

```
<?xml version="1.0"?>
<xsl:stylesheet version="1.0"
xmlns:xsl="http://www.w3.org/1999/XSL/Transform">
<xsl:output method="xml"/>

<xsl:template match="PLANETS">
    <HTML>
        <BODY>
            The average planetary mass is:
            <xsl:value-of select="sum(child::PLANET/child::MASS) div
            ➥count(child::PLANET/child::MASS)"/>
        </BODY>
    </HTML>
</xsl:template>

</xsl:stylesheet>
```

The XPath Boolean Functions

XPath also supports the following set of Boolean functions:

- boolean(). Converts its argument to a Boolean value.
- false(). Returns a value of false.
- lang(). Tests whether the language set with the xml:lang attribute is the same as the language passed to this function.
- not(). Reverses the true.false value of its argument.
- true(). Returns a value of true.

boolean()

The boolean function converts its argument to a Boolean value. Here's how you use this function:

```
boolean boolean(object)
```

Here's what happens when you pass this function arguments of various XPath types:

- `number`. If the number is zero, the result is false; otherwise the result is true. NaN always returns false.
- `string`. If the string is not empty, the result is true, otherwise the result is false.
- `boolean`. Value not changed.
- `node set`. Empty node set is false, true otherwise.
- Result tree fragment in XSLT 1.0 always true.

false()

The `false` function returns a value of false. Here's how you use it:

```
boolean false()
```

XPath does not define any Boolean constants, so if you need to assign a value of false to a variable, you can use the `false` function. (You'll see variables in Chapter 9.)

lang()

The `lang` function tests whether the language of the context node (as defined by the `xml:lang` attribute) is the same as the language you pass to it. Here's how you use this function:

```
boolean lang(string)
```

You pass this function a string that corresponds to a language in the XML specification, such as "en" for English, "de" for German, and "jp" for Japanese.

In the following example I'm checking to make sure that the source document was written in English. I start by setting the `xml:lang` attribute in planets.xml to "English":

```
<?xml version="1.0"?>
<?xml-stylesheet type="text/xml" href="planets.xsl"?>
<PLANETS  xml:lang="en">

    <PLANET>
        <NAME>Mercury</NAME>
        <MASS UNITS="(Earth = 1)">.0553</MASS>
        <DAY UNITS="days">58.65</DAY>
        <RADIUS UNITS="miles">1516</RADIUS>
        <DENSITY UNITS="(Earth = 1)">.983</DENSITY>
```

```
        <DISTANCE UNITS="million miles">43.4</DISTANCE><!--At perihelion-->
    </PLANET>
        .
        .
        .
```

Now I test to make sure that the source document's language is indeed English before applying templates, as you see here:

```
<?xml version="1.0"?>
<xsl:stylesheet version="1.0"
xmlns:xsl="http://www.w3.org/1999/XSL/Transform">

    <xsl:template match="/PLANETS">
        <xsl:if test="lang('en')">
        <HTML>
            <HEAD>
                <TITLE>
                    The Planets Table
                </TITLE>
            </HEAD>
            <BODY>
                <H1>
                    The Planets Table
                </H1>
                <TABLE BORDER="2">
                    <TR>
                        <TD>Name</TD>
                        <TD>Mass</TD>
                        <TD>Radius</TD>
                        <TD>Day</TD>
                    </TR>
                    <xsl:apply-templates/>
                </TABLE>
            </BODY>
        </HTML>
        </xsl:if>
    </xsl:template>

    <xsl:template match="PLANET">
       <TR>
          <TD><xsl:value-of select="NAME"/></TD>
          <TD><xsl:apply-templates select="MASS"/></TD>
          <TD><xsl:apply-templates select="RADIUS"/></TD>
          <TD><xsl:apply-templates select="DAY"/></TD>
       </TR>
   </xsl:template>
        .
        .
        .
</xsl:stylesheet>
```

not()

The not function reverses the logical sense of its argument. If you pass it an argument whose logical value is true, this function returns false, and if you pass it a false argument, it returns true. Here's how you use this function:

```
boolean not(boolean)
```

In the following example, which you saw in Chapter 4, I want to select only elements that have both COLOR and POPULATED attributes. To do that, I use the match predicate "[@COLOR and @POPULATED]". To strip out the other elements so the default rules don't place their text into the result document, I use the predicate "[not(@COLOR) or not(@POPULATED)]":

```
<?xml version="1.0"?>
<xsl:stylesheet version="1.0"
xmlns:xsl="http://www.w3.org/1999/XSL/Transform">

    <xsl:template match="/PLANETS">
        <HTML>
            .
            .
            .
        </HTML>
    </xsl:template>

    <xsl:template match="PLANET[@COLOR and @POPULATED]">
        <TR>
            <TD><xsl:value-of select="NAME"/></TD>
            <TD><xsl:apply-templates select="MASS"/></TD>
            <TD><xsl:apply-templates select="RADIUS"/></TD>
            <TD><xsl:apply-templates select="DAY"/></TD>
        </TR>
    </xsl:template>

    <xsl:template match="PLANET[not(@COLOR) or not(@POPULATED)]">
    </xsl:template>

    <xsl:template match="MASS">
        <xsl:value-of select="."/>
        <xsl:text> </xsl:text>
        <xsl:value-of select="@UNITS"/>
    </xsl:template>

    <xsl:template match="RADIUS">
        <xsl:value-of select="."/>
        <xsl:text> </xsl:text>
        <xsl:value-of select="@UNITS"/>
    </xsl:template>
```

```
    <xsl:template match="DAY">
        <xsl:value-of select="."/>
        <xsl:text> </xsl:text>
        <xsl:value-of select="@UNITS"/>
    </xsl:template>

</xsl:stylesheet>
```

And here's the result:

```
<HTML>
    <HEAD>
        <TITLE>
            Colorful, Populated Planets
        </TITLE>
    </HEAD>

    <BODY>
        <H1>
            Colorful, Populated Planets
        </H1>

        <TABLE BORDER="2">
            <TR>
                <TD>Name</TD>
                <TD>Mass</TD>
                <TD>Radius</TD>
                <TD>Day</TD>
            </TR>

            <TR>
                <TD>Earth</TD>
                <TD>1 (Earth = 1)</TD>
                <TD>2107 miles</TD>
                <TD>1 days</TD
            </TR>
        </TABLE>
    </BODY>
</HTML>
```

true()

The `true` function returns a value of true. Here's how you use it:

```
boolean true()
```

XPath does not define any Boolean constants, so if you need to assign a value of true to a variable, you can use the `true` function. (You'll see variables in Chapter 9.)

The *<xsl:decimal-format>* Element: Creating Numeric Formats

Before finishing up with the XSLT and XPath functions, I'll take a look at a special XSLT element, `<xsl:decimal-format>`, whose sole purpose is to work with a particular function: `format-number`. In particular, you use this element to define characters and symbols that the `format-number` function should use. This element has several attributes:

- `name` (optional). Name of this decimal format. Set to a QName. If you don't supply a format, the default decimal format is used.
- `decimal-separator` (optional). Sets the character that is placed between the integer and fractional part of values. The default is ".". Set to a character.
- `grouping-separator` (optional). Sets the character that is placed between groups of digits. The default is ",". Set to a character.
- `infinity` (optional). Sets the string used to indicate positive infinity. The default is "Infinity". Set to a string.
- `minus-sign` (optional). Sets the character that represents a minus sign. The default is "-". Set to a character.
- `NaN` (optional). Sets the string used to represent the "Not a Number" value. The default is "NaN". Set to a string.
- `percent` (optional). Sets the character used to represent the percent sign. The default is "%". Set to a character.
- `per-mille` (optional). Sets the character used to represent per-mille, that is, per-thousand. The default is "‰". Set to a character.
- `zero-digit` (optional). Sets the character to be used in format strings to specify where you want a leading or trailing zero. The default is "0". Set to a character.
- `digit` (optional). Sets the character to be used in format strings where you want a digit. The default value is "0". Set to a character.
- `pattern-separator` (optional). Sets the character used to separate patterns for positive and negative numbers. The default is ";". Set to a character.

This element is a top-level element, and it's always empty. Using this element, you can set the formatting characters used by `format-number`. An `xsl:decimal-format` without a `name` attribute set becomes the default decimal format. It is an error to have more that one default `xsl:decimal-format` element or to have multiple `xsl:decimal-format` elements with the same name.

In the following example, I use European numeric formats to format the numbers in planets.xml—specifically, I use a comma rather than a decimal point to separate the integer from the fractional values, and a period rather than a comma to separate thousands. All I need to do is specify the new formatting with `<xsl:decimal-format>` and then put it to work in `format-number`:

```
<?xml version="1.0"?>
<xsl:stylesheet version="1.0"
xmlns:xsl="http://www.w3.org/1999/XSL/Transform">

    <xsl:decimal-format decimal-separator="," grouping-separator="."/>
    <xsl:template match="/PLANETS">
        <HTML>
            <HEAD>
                <TITLE>
                    The Formatted Planets Table
                </TITLE>
            </HEAD>
            <BODY>
                <H1>
                    The Formatted Planets Table
                </H1>
                <TABLE BORDER="2">
                    <TR>
                        <TD>Name</TD>
                        <TD>Mass</TD>
                        <TD>Radius</TD>
                        <TD>Day</TD>
                    </TR>
                    <xsl:apply-templates/>
                </TABLE>
            </BODY>
        </HTML>
    </xsl:template>

    <xsl:template match="PLANET">
       <TR>
          <TD><xsl:value-of select="NAME"/></TD>
          <TD><xsl:apply-templates select="MASS"/></TD>
          <TD><xsl:apply-templates select="RADIUS"/></TD>
          <TD><xsl:apply-templates select="DAY"/></TD>
       </TR>
   </xsl:template>

    <xsl:template match="MASS">
        <xsl:value-of select="format-number(., '#,###')"/>
        <xsl:text> </xsl:text>
        <xsl:value-of select="@UNITS"/>
    </xsl:template>
```

```
    <xsl:template match="RADIUS">
        <xsl:value-of select="format-number(., '#.###')"/>
        <xsl:text> </xsl:text>
        <xsl:value-of select="@UNITS"/>
    </xsl:template>

    <xsl:template match="DAY">
        <xsl:value-of select="format-number(., '###,##')"/>
        <xsl:text> </xsl:text>
        <xsl:value-of select="@UNITS"/>
    </xsl:template>

</xsl:stylesheet>
```

Here's the result document:

```
<HTML>
    <HEAD>
        <TITLE>
            The Formatted Planets Table
        </TITLE>
    </HEAD>

    <BODY>
        <H1>
            The Formatted Planets Table
        </H1>

        <TABLE BORDER="2">
            <TR>
                <TD>Name</TD>
                <TD>Mass</TD>
                <TD>Radius</TD>
                <TD>Day</TD>
            </TR>

            <TR>
                <TD>Mercury</TD>
                <TD>0,055 (Earth = 1)</TD>
                <TD>1.516 miles</TD>
                <TD>58,65 days</TD>
            </TR>

            <TR>
                <TD>Venus</TD>
                <TD>0,815 (Earth = 1)</TD>
                <TD>3.716 miles</TD>
                <TD>116,75 days</TD>
            </TR>

            <TR>
                <TD>Earth</TD>
```

```
                <TD>1 (Earth = 1)</TD>
                <TD>2.107 miles</TD>
                <TD>1 days</TD>
            </TR>

        </TABLE>
    </BODY>
</HTML>
```

You can see this result document in Figure 8.3.

And that's all it takes—now you can set the formatting options for the `format-number` function.

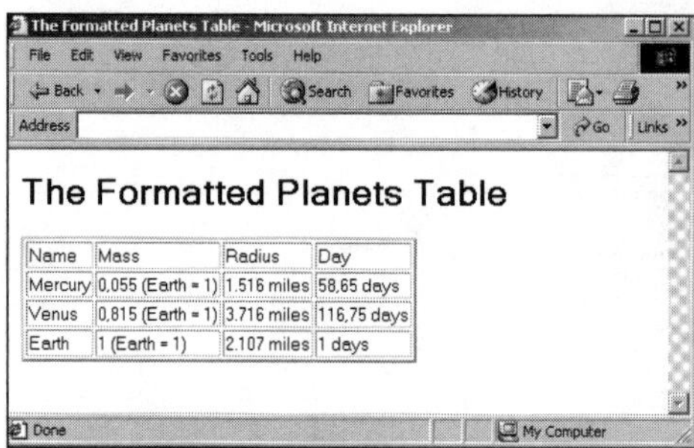

The Formatted Planets Table - Microsoft Internet Explorer
The Formatted Planets Table
Name | Mass | Radius | Day
Mercury | 0,055 (Earth = 1) | 1.516 miles | 58,65 days
Venus | 0,815 (Earth = 1) | 3.716 miles | 116,75 days
Earth | 1 (Earth = 1) | 2.107 miles | 1 days

Figure 8.3 Setting decimal formats.

New Functions in XSLT and XPath 2.0

There are some pretty big plans for functions in XSLT 2.0 and XPath 2.0. In particular, the following new functions are scheduled for XSLT 2.0:

- Could provide QName-aware functions to allow the namespace declarations that were in scope to be enforced.
- Must add date-formatting functions, to support XML schema.
- Should provide a function to make relative URIs absolute.
- Must simplify grouping. In XSLT 2.0, it must be possible to group nodes based on their string values.

The following changes are planned for functions in XPath 2.0:

- Must extend the set of aggregation functions, such as including `min` and `max`.
- Should provide intersection and difference functions for node sets.
- Should support additional string functions, such as functions for string replacement, string padding, and string case conversions.
- Should support aggregation functions when applied to collections such as node sets.
- Must define functions to work with XML schema primitive types.

That takes care of the functions available in XSLT and XPath for transformations. Chapter 9 explores variables, parameters, and other powerful topics.

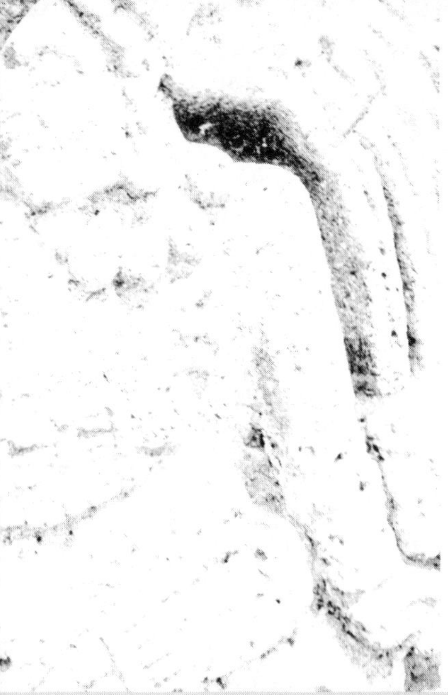

9

Named Templates, Parameters, and Variables

THIS CHAPTER LOOKS AT SOME POWERFUL FEATURES of XSLT, known as templates, stylesheet parameters, and variables. These topics are all related—you use parameters with named templates, and variables and parameters are practically the same, except for the way they're created.

When you give a template a name, you can specifically *call* it, using the `<xsl:call-template>` element. A template is applied when it is called, so rather than rely on the default processing of the stylesheet by the XSLT processor, you can determine when a template is applied, as well as which one is applied. For example, you might have multiple templates that would match the same node set, and want to select the template or templates you want to use. It's a little like using modes, but it gives you more control.

When you call a template, you can customize what it does through the use of *parameters*. For example, you may want the text in the text nodes created by the template to be in a specific language, such as English, German, or French, and so might create a new parameter named `language`. When you call a named template that you've set up to handle this parameter, you might set language to "en", "de", or "fr", then call the template with the help of the `<xsl:with-param>` element. In the named template itself, you declare the parameter used by the template, `language`, with the `<xsl:param>` element. After it's been declared, you are free to refer to the value in the `language` parameter as `$language` and use it in XPath expressions. We'll see numerous examples showing how this works in this chapter.

Variables are a lot like parameters, except that you create them differently. Also, parameters are generally used with named templates, whereas variables are used more generally, in any kind of XPath expression. As in programming languages, you can store values in variables in XSLT and then refer to them later. Note an important point, however: except in specific circumstances, you *cannot* change the value stored in a variable. (In fact, some XSLT authors believe it's a misnomer to call them variables.)

Variables are useful for holding values that take a lot of processing time to create but that are referred to many times in your stylesheet. Rather than re-create those values each time they're needed, you can store them in a variable and just refer to the value stored in the variable. As with parameters, you refer to the value in a variable by adding the prefix "$". For example, if you have a variable named `sandwich`, you can refer to the value stored in this variable as `$sandwich`. As with parameters, you can store data with any of the four XPath data types in variables. Variables are also useful for storing values that are changed later in a template. For example, "." usually refers to the context node for the template, but inside an `<xsl:for-each>` element, "." refers to the current node that the element is processing, not the context node for the whole template. To refer to the context node, you can store it in a variable named `contextnode` before entering the `<xsl:for-each>` loop, and then refer to it in the loop as `$contextnode`.

In addition to the four XPath data types, you'll also see a data type supported in XSLT 1.0, but not XSLT 1.1: result tree fragments. You create result tree fragments with the `<xsl:variable>` or `<xsl:with-param>`, and they can be convenient in some cases, as you'll see in this chapter.

Finally, you'll also see the <xsl:key> element in this chapter. You first saw this element briefly in Chapter 4, but it's time for a closer look here.

That's all the introduction you need; it's time to get to work, starting with variables.

The *<xsl:variable>* Element: Creating Variables

You use `<xsl:variable>` to create variables in XSLT. This element has the following attributes:

- `name` (mandatory). The name of the variable, set to a QName.
- `select` (optional). An XPath expression that specifies the value of the variable. If you omit this attribute, the value of the variable is specified by the contents of `<xsl:variable>`.

This element can either be a top-level element or be used inside a template body. This element can contain a template body; but if a body is present, you should not use the `select` attribute.

You create a variable by assigning its name to the `<xsl:variable>` element's `name` attribute, and its value to the `select` attribute, as in this case, where I'm creating a new variable named `number_books` and storing the value 255 in it:

```
<xsl:variable name="number_books" select="255"/>
        .
        .
        .
```

You can refer to the value in this variable by prefixing the variable's name with a $ like this:

```
<xsl:variable name="number_books" select="255"/>
<xsl:text>There are </xsl:text>
<xsl:value-of select="$number_books"/>
<xsl:text> books in my library </xsl:text>
```

Note that if you assign a literal to a variable, as in assigning the value "turkey" to the variable `sandwich`, you must enclose the literal in quotes (which must be different from the quotes you're using to enclose attribute values):

```
<xsl:variable name="sandwich" select="'turkey'"/>
```

In XSLT 1.0, you didn't have to use the `select` attribute—you could enclose data inside the `<xsl:variable>` itself this way:

```
<xsl:variable name="sandwich">turkey</xsl:variable>
```

Technically, however, when you omit the `select` attribute from `<xsl:variable>` or `<xsl:with-param>` and give those elements some contents, you are creating a *result tree fragment*, which is no longer legal in XSLT 1.1.

It's also worth noting that the name of the variable includes its prefix, if any, such as `star:PLANET`. If there is a prefix, it must correspond to an active namespace. Comparisons are made not by comparing prefixes but by checking the actual URI of the prefix, so `star:PLANET` could be the same as `nebula:PLANET` if the namspaces `star` and `nebula` correspond to the same URI.

Variable Scope

You can use `<xsl:variable>` as a top-level element or inside a template body to create variables. Variables created in top-level <xsl:variable> elements have *global scope*, whereas those created in template bodies have *local scope*. The *scope* of a variable indicates in what part of the stylesheet you can use it.

The scope of a global variable is the entire stylesheet, including imported or included stylesheets. That means it's available throughout the whole stylesheet, unless it is overridden by a local variable with the same name. You can even refer to a global variable before it's declared. However, you cannot have circular references. For example, if you declare *a* in terms of *b*, you cannot declare *b* in terms of *a*.

The scope of a local variable is limited to its following siblings, or descendants of following siblings. In particular, this means that if you declare a variable *inside* an element such as `<xsl:choose>`, `<xsl:if>`, or `<xsl:for-each>`, it won't be available outside that element.

You cannot usually change a variable's value, but you can override it with a more local version. That is, local variables can override global ones while the local variables are in scope. For example, say that I declare a variable named `movie`:

```
<xsl:variable name="movie" select="'Mr. Blandings Builds His Dream House'">

<!-- $movie = 'Mr. Blandings Builds His Dream House' here-->
        .
        .
        .
```

This is a top-level element, so `movie` is global. Even inside templates, `movie` still has its original value, if there is no local variable with the same name:

```
<xsl:variable name="movie" select="'Mr. Blandings Builds His Dream House'">

<!-- $movie = 'Mr. Blandings Builds His Dream House' here-->

<xsl:template match="entertainment">

    <!-- $movie = 'Mr. Blandings Builds His Dream House' here-->
        .
        .
        .
```

However, if you declare a local variable named `movie`, that new version overrides the global version in the template:

```
<xsl:variable name="movie" select="'Mr. Blandings Builds His Dream House'">

<!-- $movie = 'Mr. Blandings Builds His Dream House' here-->

<xsl:template match="entertainment">

    <!-- $movie = 'Mr. Blandings Builds His Dream House' here-->
```

```
    <xsl:variable name="movie" select="'Goldfinger'">

    <!-- $movie = 'Goldfinger' here-->
        .
        .
        .
```

In this case, we've overridden the global variable with a local one. But note that you can't declare the same variable again in the same template in an attempt to change its value:

```
<xsl:variable name="movie" select="'Mr. Blandings Builds His Dream House'">

<!-- $movie = 'Mr. Blandings Builds His Dream House' here-->

<xsl:template match="entertainment">

    <!-- $movie = 'Mr. Blandings Builds His Dream House' here-->

    <xsl:variable name="movie" select="'Goldfinger'">

    <!-- $movie = 'Goldfinger' here-->

    <xsl:variable name="movie" select="'Withnail and I'"><!-- Not allowed -->
        .
        .
        .
```

Outside the template, the local variable is invisible, and `movie` holds the global value:

```
<xsl:variable name="movie" select="'Mr. Blandings Builds His Dream House'">

<!-- $movie = 'Mr. Blandings Builds His Dream House' here-->

<xsl:template match="entertainment">

    <!-- $movie = 'Mr. Blandings Builds His Dream House' here-->

    <xsl:variable name="movie" select="'Goldfinger'">

    <!-- $movie = 'Goldfinger' here-->

    <xsl:variable name="movie" select="'Withnail and I'"><!-- Not allowed -->

</xsl:template>

<!-- $movie = 'Mr. Blandings Builds His Dream House' here-->
        .
        .
        .
```

Note that you can't redeclare a global variable either:

```
<xsl:variable name="movie" select="'Mr. Blandings Builds His Dream House'">

<!-- $movie = 'Mr. Blandings Builds His Dream House' here-->

<xsl:template match="entertainment">

    <!-- $movie = 'Mr. Blandings Builds His Dream House' here-->

    <xsl:variable name="movie" select="'Goldfinger'">

    <!-- $movie = 'Goldfinger' here-->

    <xsl:variable name="movie" select="'Withnail and I'"><!-- Not allowed -->

</xsl:template>

<!-- $movie = 'Mr. Blandings Builds His Dream House' here-->

<xsl:variable name="movie" select="'Goldfinger'"><!-- Not allowed -->
```

Despite all these restrictions, you *can* reset a variable's value each time through an `<xsl:for-each>` loop, as you'll see in the next section.

Variables at Work

Let's take a look at some examples that use variables. In this example, I assign a copyright notice to a variable, `copyright`, and then use that variable to add a `copyright` attribute to each element in planets.xml:

Listing 9.1 **Using a Variable**

```
<?xml version="1.0"?>
<xsl:stylesheet version="1.1"
xmlns:xsl="http://www.w3.org/1999/XSL/Transform">
    <xsl:output method="xml"/>

    <xsl:variable name="copyright" select="'(c)2002 Starpowder Inc.'"/>
    <xsl:template match="*">
        <xsl:copy>
            <xsl:attribute name="copyright">
                <xsl:value-of select="$copyright"/>
            </xsl:attribute>
            <xsl:apply-templates/>
        </xsl:copy>
    </xsl:template>
</xsl:stylesheet>
```

Here's the result document, complete with `copyright` attributes:

```
<?xml version="1.0" encoding="utf-8"?>
<PLANETS copyright="(c)2002 Starpowder Inc.">

    <PLANET copyright="(c)2002 Starpowder Inc.">
        <NAME copyright="(c)2002 Starpowder Inc.">Mercury</NAME>
        <MASS copyright="(c)2002 Starpowder Inc.">.0553</MASS>
        <DAY copyright="(c)2002 Starpowder Inc.">58.65</DAY>
        <RADIUS copyright="(c)2002 Starpowder Inc.">1516</RADIUS>
        <DENSITY copyright="(c)2002 Starpowder Inc.">.983</DENSITY>
        <DISTANCE copyright="(c)2002 Starpowder Inc.">43.4</DISTANCE>
    </PLANET>

    <PLANET copyright="(c)2002 Starpowder Inc.">
        <NAME copyright="(c)2002 Starpowder Inc.">Venus</NAME>
        <MASS copyright="(c)2002 Starpowder Inc.">.815</MASS>
        <DAY copyright="(c)2002 Starpowder Inc.">116.75</DAY>
        <RADIUS copyright="(c)2002 Starpowder Inc.">3716</RADIUS>
        <DENSITY copyright="(c)2002 Starpowder Inc.">.943</DENSITY>
        <DISTANCE copyright="(c)2002 Starpowder Inc.">66.8</DISTANCE>
    </PLANET>
        .
        .
        .
```

Here's another example. Variables are often useful for storing context-sensitive values, and I'll do so in an example I mentioned at the beginning of this chapter. In this case, I'll convert planets.xml to a new document with one element for each planet. Each of these new elements contains two `<SIBLINGPLANET>` elements, giving the sibling planets of the current planet—for example, Earth's siblings are Venus and Mercury:

```
<?xml version="1.0" encoding="utf-8"?>
<Mercury>
    <SIBLINGPLANET>
        Venus
    </SIBLINGPLANET>
    <SIBLINGPLANET>
        Earth
    </SIBLINGPLANET>
</Mercury>

<Venus>
    <SIBLINGPLANET>
        Mercury
    </SIBLINGPLANET>
    <SIBLINGPLANET>
        Earth
    </SIBLINGPLANET>
</Venus>
```

```
<Earth>
    <SIBLINGPLANET>
        Mercury
    </SIBLINGPLANET>
    <SIBLINGPLANET>
        Venus
    </SIBLINGPLANET>
</Earth>
```

To implement this example, I'll match each `<PLANET>` element in turn, and use an `<xsl:for-each>` loop to loop over all planets, creating `<SIBLINGPLANET>` elements for all planets that are not the context node. However, when I'm inside the `<xsl:for-each>` element, how do I know which planet is the context node that the template matched? Inside the `<xsl:for-each>` element, "." refers to the current node on which `<xsl:for-each>` is working, not the template's context node. To solve this problem, I can store the context node in a variable, which I name `contextnode`:

```
<?xml version="1.0"?>
<xsl:stylesheet version="1.1"
xmlns:xsl="http://www.w3.org/1999/XSL/Transform">
<xsl:output method="xml"/>

    <xsl:template match="PLANETS">

        <xsl:for-each select="PLANET">
            <xsl:element name="{NAME}">

                <xsl:variable name="contextnode" select="."/>
                .
                .
                .
```

Now I can refer to the template's context node as `$contextnode` in the `<xsl:for-each>` element when I'm checking to make sure the current element in the `<xsl:for-each>` loop isn't the context node:

Listing 9.2 **Using a Variable to Store Context-Sensitive Information**

```
<?xml version="1.0"?>
<xsl:stylesheet version="1.1"
xmlns:xsl="http://www.w3.org/1999/XSL/Transform">
<xsl:output method="xml"/>

    <xsl:template match="PLANETS">

        <xsl:for-each select="PLANET">
            <xsl:element name="{NAME}">
```

```
            <xsl:variable name="contextnode" select="."/>

            <xsl:for-each select="//PLANET">
                <xsl:if test=". != $contextnode">
                    <xsl:element name="SIBLINGPLANET">
                        <xsl:value-of select="NAME"/>
                    </xsl:element>
                </xsl:if>
            </xsl:for-each>

          </xsl:element>
        </xsl:for-each>

    </xsl:template>

</xsl:stylesheet>
```

And that's all it takes.

When the <xsl:variable> has a body, it creates a variable whose value is a result tree fragment. In the following example I use a result tree fragment to supply a default value for an attribute named COLOR if that attribute doesn't have a value already. In this case, I'm setting the default value to "blue":

```
<xsl:variable name="COLOR">
    <xsl:choose>
       <xsl:when test="@COLOR">
          <xsl:value-of select="@COLOR"/>
       </xsl:when>
       <xsl:otherwise>blue</xsl:otherwise>
    </xsl:choose>
</xsl:variable>
```

The string value of the result tree fragment (that is, either the value of the `COLOR` attribute or the default value, "blue") is assigned to the variable `$COLOR`. Now you can refer to the value of the variable, `$COLOR`, in XPath expressions rather than the attribute's value, `@COLOR`, and be confident that you'll always be working with a real color, even if the corresponding element doesn't have a `COLOR` attribute.

The following is another result tree fragment example; in this case, I store a literal result element in a variable, `START_HTML`:

```
<?xml version="1.0"?>
<xsl:stylesheet version="1.1"
xmlns:xsl="http://www.w3.org/1999/XSL/Transform">
    <xsl:output method="html"/>

<xsl:variable name="START_HTML">
    <HEAD>
```

```
        <TITLE>
            My page
        </TITLE>
    </HEAD>
</xsl:variable>
```

.
.
.

Now I can use this literal result element where ever I want:

```
<?xml version="1.0"?>
<xsl:stylesheet version="1.1"
xmlns:xsl="http://www.w3.org/1999/XSL/Transform">
    <xsl:output method="html"/>

<xsl:variable name="START_HTML">
    <HEAD>
        <TITLE>
            My page
        </TITLE>
    </HEAD>
</xsl:variable>

    <xsl:template match="PLANETS">

<HTML>
    <xsl:copy-of select="$START_HTML"/>
<BODY>
<H1>Welcome to my page</H1>
</BODY>
</HTML>
    </xsl:template>

</xsl:stylesheet>
```

And here's the result:

```
<HTML>
   <HEAD>
      <TITLE>
         My page
      </TITLE>
   </HEAD>
   <BODY>
      <H1>Welcome to my page</H1>
   </BODY>
</HTML>
```

However, now that result tree fragments are illegal in XSLT 1.1, this won't work anymore. So how do you store an entire literal result element in one easy-to-call package? You can create a *named template*.

The *<xsl:call-template>* Element: Using Named Templates

One of the attributes of the `<xsl:template>` element is `name`, which you use to give a name to the template. For example, if I have a literal result element consisting of two `<BR>` and two `<HR>` HTML elements that I use to create a vertical separator in HTML documents, as follows:

```
<BR/>
<HR/>
<BR/>
<HR/>
```

then I can create a template named "separator" with this literal result element this way:

```
<xsl:template name="separator">
    <BR/>
    <HR/>
    <BR/>
    <HR/>
</xsl:template>
```

This is a named template—all you have to do is assign a name to the `name` attribute of an `<xsl:template>` element, and you have a named template.

Note that this template is not set up to match anything in particular. To invoke this template, you must call it explicitly. So how do you do that?

You call named templates with the `<xsl:call-template>` element—it has just one attribute:

- `name` (mandatory). The name of the template to call; set to a QName.

The following example puts the template named "separator" to work. All I have to do is call that template when it's needed, as follows:

```
<?xml version="1.0"?>
<xsl:stylesheet version="1.1"
xmlns:xsl="http://www.w3.org/1999/XSL/Transform">

    <xsl:template match="/PLANETS">
        <HTML>
            <HEAD>
                <TITLE>
                    The Planets Table
                </TITLE>
            </HEAD>
            <BODY>
                <H1>
                    The Planets Table
                </H1>
                <xsl:call-template name="separator"/>
```

```
            <TABLE BORDER="2">
                <TR>
                    <TD>Name</TD>
                    <TD>Mass</TD>
                    <TD>Radius</TD>
                    <TD>Day</TD>
                </TR>
                <xsl:apply-templates/>
            </TABLE>
            <xsl:call-template name="separator"/>
        </BODY>
    </HTML>
</xsl:template>

<xsl:template match="PLANET">
   <TR>
      <TD><xsl:value-of select="NAME"/></TD>
      <TD><xsl:apply-templates select="MASS"/></TD>
      <TD><xsl:apply-templates select="RADIUS"/></TD>
      <TD><xsl:apply-templates select="DAY"/></TD>
   </TR>
</xsl:template>

<xsl:template match="MASS">
    <xsl:value-of select="."/>
    <xsl:text> </xsl:text>
    <xsl:value-of select="@UNITS"/>
</xsl:template>

<xsl:template match="RADIUS">
    <xsl:value-of select="."/>
    <xsl:text> </xsl:text>
    <xsl:value-of select="@UNITS"/>
</xsl:template>

<xsl:template match="DAY">
    <xsl:value-of select="."/>
    <xsl:text> </xsl:text>
    <xsl:value-of select="@UNITS"/>
</xsl:template>

<xsl:template name="separator">
    <BR/>
    <HR/>
    <BR/>
    <HR/>
</xsl:template>

</xsl:stylesheet>
```

Here's the result. Note that the <BR> and <HR> elements have been inserted as required:

```
<HTML>
    <HEAD>
        <TITLE>
            The Planets Table
        </TITLE>
    </HEAD>

    <BODY>
        <H1>
            The Planets Table
        </H1>
        <BR>
        <HR>
        <BR>
        <HR>
        <TABLE BORDER="2">
            <TR>
                <TD>Name</TD>
                <TD>Mass</TD>
                <TD>Radius</TD>
                <TD>Day</TD>
            </TR>

            <TR>
                <TD>Mercury</TD>
                <TD>.0553 (Earth = 1)</TD>
                <TD>1516 miles</TD>
                <TD>58.65 days</TD>
            </TR>

            <TR>
                 <TD>Venus</TD>
                 <TD>.815 (Earth = 1)</TD>
                 <TD>3716 miles</TD>
                 <TD>116.75 days</TD>
             </TR>

             <TR>
                 <TD>Earth</TD>
                 <TD>1 (Earth = 1)</TD>
                 <TD>2107 miles</TD>
                 <TD>1 days</TD>
             </TR>

         </TABLE>
        <BR>
        <HR>
        <BR>
        <HR>
    </BODY>
</HTML>
```

You can see this result document in Figure 9.1.

This answers the question of how you can refer to a literal result element by name for easy placement in the result document. However, this is pretty static—the literal result element is always the same. As it turns out, though, calling a named template is much like calling a subroutine in a programming language. Just as you can pass data to a subroutine, so you can pass data to named templates using *parameters*.

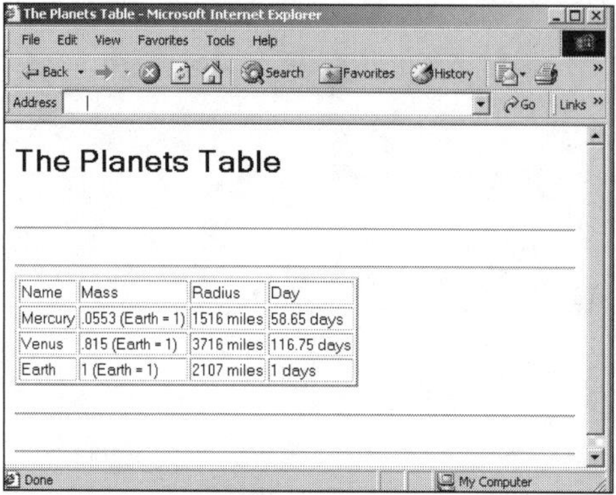

The Planets Table - Microsoft Internet Explorer
The Planets Table
Name | Mass | Radius | Day
Mercury | .0553 (Earth = 1) | 1516 miles | 58.65 days
Venus | .815 (Earth = 1) | 3716 miles | 116.75 days
Earth | 1 (Earth = 1) | 2107 miles | 1 days

Figure 9.1 Calling a named template.

The *<xsl:param>* and *<xsl:with-param>* Elements: Creating Parameters

Parameters are much like variables, except they're usually used with named templates. Parameters enable you to pass values into templates. You create parameters with the `<xsl:param>` element, which has two attributes:

- `name` (mandatory). The name of the variable, set to a QName.
- `select` (optional). The default value of the parameter. Set to an XPath expression.

Like `<xsl:variable>`, this element can either be a top-level element or be used inside a template body. Parameters created with top-level `<xsl:param>` elements are global parameters, and those created inside templates are local parameters. If you create a parameter inside a template body, the `<xsl:param>` element should come before any other child elements. This element also can contain an optional template body, which creates a result tree fragment, which is no longer allowed in XSLT 1.1. If this element does have a body, you should not use the `select` attribute.

After declaring a parameter with `<xsl:param>`, you can refer to its value in a template the same way as you would a variable: by prefixing its name with a "$".

When you call a named template with `<xsl:call-template>` or apply templates with `<xsl:apply-template>`, you can use the `<xsl:with-param>` element to set the value of the parameters used in the template. If the parameter itself was assigned a value with the `<xsl:param>` element's `select` element when it was declared, that value acts as a default value for the parameter. This default value is overridden if you specify a new value for the parameter with the `<xsl:with-param>` element.

The `<xsl:with-param>` element has two attributes:

- `name` (mandatory). The name of the variable; set to a QName.
- `select` (optional). An XPath expression that specifies the value of the parameter. If you omit this attribute, the value of the variable is specified by the contents of `<xsl:with-param>`.

This element could contain an optional template body, which created a result tree fragment, but that's no longer allowed in XSLT 1.1.

In the following example, I create a named template called "COLORS" that adds color to a planet's data in the HTML result document. This named template uses one parameter, `COLOR`, which you set to the color you want to use. Here's how it looks in practice, where I'm setting the `COLOR` parameter to various colors for the different planets, using `<xsl:with-param>` and calling the "COLORS" template:

Listing 9.3 **Using Stylesheet Parameters**

```
<xsl:stylesheet version="1.1"
xmlns:xsl="http://www.w3.org/1999/XSL/Transform">

    <xsl:template match="/PLANETS">
        <HTML>
        .
        .
        .
        </HTML>
    </xsl:template>
```

continues ▸

Listing 9.3 **Continued**

```
    <xsl:template match="PLANET">
        <xsl:if test="NAME='Mercury'">
            <xsl:call-template name="COLORS">
                <xsl:with-param name="COLOR" select="'RED'"/>
            </xsl:call-template>
        </xsl:if>
        <xsl:if test="NAME='Venus'">
            <xsl:call-template name="COLORS">
                <xsl:with-param name="COLOR" select="'GREEN'"/>
            </xsl:call-template>
        </xsl:if>
        <xsl:if test="NAME='Earth'">
            <xsl:call-template name="COLORS">
                <xsl:with-param name="COLOR" select="'BLUE'"/>
            </xsl:call-template>
        </xsl:if>
    </xsl:template>
        .
        .
        .
```

This calls the "COLORS" template with various different values in the `COLOR` parameter. I can make use of those colors when I format each planet's data. Note that I declare the `COLOR` parameter with `<xsl:param>` in the very beginning of the "COLORS" template, as follows:

```
<xsl:stylesheet version="1.1"
xmlns:xsl="http://www.w3.org/1999/XSL/Transform">

    <xsl:template match="/PLANETS">
        <HTML>
        .
        .
        .
        </HTML>
    </xsl:template>

    <xsl:template match="PLANET">
        <xsl:if test="NAME='Mercury'">
            <xsl:call-template name="COLORS">
                <xsl:with-param name="COLOR" select="'RED'"/>
            </xsl:call-template>
        </xsl:if>
        <xsl:if test="NAME='Venus'">
            <xsl:call-template name="COLORS">
                <xsl:with-param name="COLOR" select="'GREEN'"/>
            </xsl:call-template>
        </xsl:if>
        <xsl:if test="NAME='Earth'">
            <xsl:call-template name="COLORS">
```

```
                <xsl:with-param name="COLOR" select="'BLUE'"/>
            </xsl:call-template>
        </xsl:if>
    </xsl:template>

    <xsl:template name="COLORS">
        <xsl:param name="COLOR"/>
        <TR>
            <TD><FONT COLOR="{$COLOR}"><xsl:value-of select="NAME"/></FONT></TD>
            <TD><FONT COLOR="{$COLOR}"><xsl:apply-templates select="MASS"/></FONT></TD>
            <TD><FONT COLOR="{$COLOR}"><xsl:apply-templates select="RADIUS"/></FONT></TD>
            <TD><FONT COLOR="{$COLOR}"><xsl:apply-templates select="DAY"/></FONT></TD>
        </TR>
    </xsl:template>

    <xsl:template match="MASS">
        <xsl:value-of select="."/>
        <xsl:text> </xsl:text>
        <xsl:value-of select="@UNITS"/>
    </xsl:template>
        .
        .
        .

    <xsl:template match="DAY">
        <xsl:value-of select="."/>
        <xsl:text> </xsl:text>
        <xsl:value-of select="@UNITS"/>
    </xsl:template>

</xsl:stylesheet>
```

And here's the result:

```
<HTML>
    <HEAD>

        <TITLE>
            The Colorful Planets Table

        </TITLE>
    </HEAD>
    <BODY>
        <H1>
            The Colorful Planets Table

        </H1>
        <TABLE BORDER="2">
            <TR>
                <TD>Name</TD>
                <TD>Mass</TD>
                <TD>Radius</TD>
                <TD>Day</TD>
```

```
        </TR>

        <TR>
          <TD><FONT COLOR="RED">Mercury</FONT></TD>
          <TD><FONT COLOR="RED">.0553 (Earth = 1)</FONT></TD>
          <TD><FONT COLOR="RED">1516 miles</FONT></TD>
          <TD><FONT COLOR="RED">58.65 days</FONT></TD>
        </TR>

        <TR>
          <TD><FONT COLOR="GREEN">Venus</FONT></TD>
          <TD><FONT COLOR="GREEN">.815 (Earth = 1)</FONT></TD>
          <TD><FONT COLOR="GREEN">3716 miles</FONT></TD>
          <TD><FONT COLOR="GREEN">116.75 days</FONT></TD>
        </TR>

        <TR>
          <TD><FONT COLOR="BLUE">Earth</FONT></TD>
          <TD><FONT COLOR="BLUE">1 (Earth = 1)</FONT></TD>
          <TD><FONT COLOR="BLUE">2107 miles</FONT></TD>
          <TD><FONT COLOR="BLUE">1 days</FONT></TD>
        </TR>

      </TABLE>
    </BODY>
</HTML>
```

You can see this result document in Figure 9.2 (even if only in black and white).

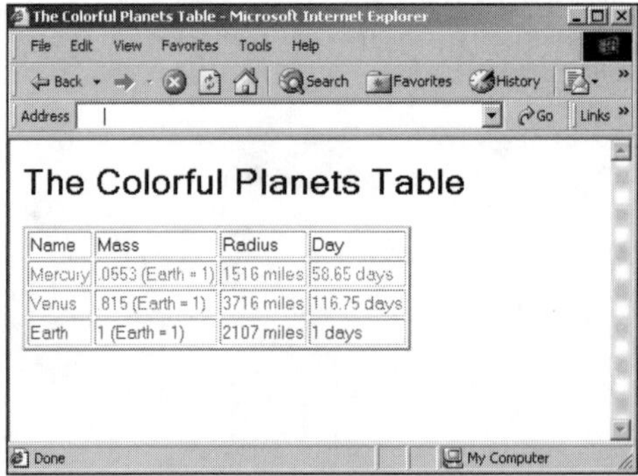

Figure 9.2 Calling a named template with parameters.

In the following example, I use parameters to localize the language used in a template. I create a new template called `localize` that uses a parameter named `language`. If `language` is set to "en" for English, the result document will be labeled "Planets"; if `language` is "de" for German, the result document will be labeled "Planeten"; and if "fr" for French, the result document will be labeled "Planètes".

Here's how I call the `localize` template, setting `language` to "fr":

```
<?xml version="1.0"?>
<xsl:stylesheet version="1.1"
xmlns:xsl="http://www.w3.org/1999/XSL/Transform">

    <xsl:template match="/PLANETS">
        <HTML>
            <HEAD>
                <TITLE>
                    <xsl:call-template name="localize">
                        <xsl:with-param name="language" select="'fr'"/>
                    </xsl:call-template>
                </TITLE>
            </HEAD>
            <BODY>
                <H1>
                    <xsl:call-template name="localize">
                        <xsl:with-param name="language" select="'fr'"/>
                    </xsl:call-template>
        .
        .
        .
```

And here's what the parameterized template "COLORS" looks like. Note that I declare the `COLOR` parameter in the template using an `<xsl:param>` element (and note that the HTML 4.01 character entity for the è in "Planètes" is è, which I use here):

```
<?xml version="1.0"?>
<xsl:stylesheet version="1.1"
xmlns:xsl="http://www.w3.org/1999/XSL/Transform">

    <xsl:template match="/PLANETS">
        <HTML>
            <HEAD>
                <TITLE>
                    <xsl:call-template name="localize">
                        <xsl:with-param name="language" select="'fr'"/>
                    </xsl:call-template>
                </TITLE>
            </HEAD>
            <BODY>
                <H1>
                    <xsl:call-template name="localize">
```

```
                    <xsl:with-param name="language" select="'fr'"/>
                </xsl:call-template>
            </H1>
            <TABLE BORDER="2">
                <TR>
                    <TD>Name</TD>
                    <TD>Mass</TD>
                    <TD>Radius</TD>
                    <TD>Day</TD>
                </TR>
                <xsl:apply-templates/>
            </TABLE>
        </BODY>
    </HTML>
</xsl:template>

<xsl:template name="localize">
    <xsl:param name="language"/>
    <xsl:if test="$language='en'">
        <xsl:text>Planets</xsl:text>
    </xsl:if>
    <xsl:if test="$language='de'">
        <xsl:text>Planten</xsl:text>
    </xsl:if>
    <xsl:if test="$language='fr'">
        <xsl:text>Plan&#232;tes</xsl:text>
    </xsl:if>
</xsl:template>
    .
    .
    .
```

And here's the resulting localized document:

```
<HTML>
   <HEAD>
      <TITLE>Plan&egrave;tes</TITLE>
   </HEAD>
   <BODY>
      <H1>Plan&egrave;tes</H1>
      <TABLE BORDER="2">
         <TR>
            <TD>Name</TD>
            <TD>Mass</TD>
            <TD>Radius</TD>
            <TD>Day</TD>
         </TR>
            .
            .
            .
```

You can see this result document in Figure 9.3.

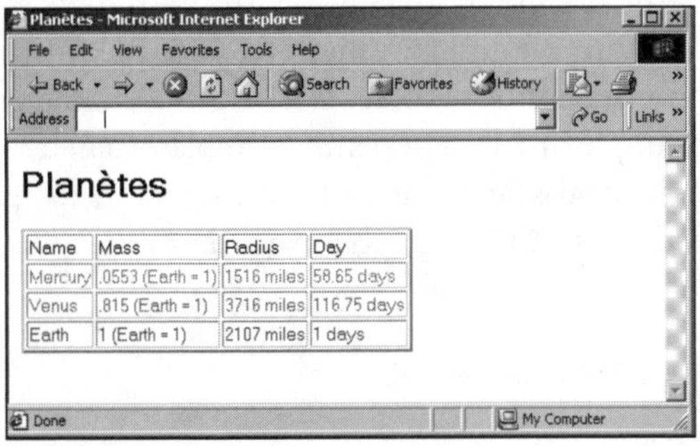

Figure 9.3 Calling a named template with parameters to set languages.

Calling a template is much like calling a function of the kind you saw in Chapter 8, and the capability to pass data using parameters enhances the similarity. However, in the absence of an assignment operator of the kind supported by programming languages, it seems that you can't assign a value returned from a named template to a variable—but you can, if you're clever. In fact, you can also do something else that you can do with functions: call them *recursively*.

Calling Templates Recursively

This topic is mostly for programmers, because I make XSLT act like a programming language here. One of the things I do here is make a named template call *itself*, which is called *recursion*. The classic example of recursion is to write a factorial program—for example, 6 factorial, written 6!, is equal to 6 * 5 * 4 * 3 * 2 * 1, or 720.

To implement recursion in a true programming language, you write a function named `factorial` that you call with the value 6: `factorial(6)`. The factorial of 6 is `6 * factorial(5)`, so all this function needs to do is to multiply the results of calling itself with a value of 5—that is, `factorial(5)`—by 6. On the other hand, `factorial(5)` is just `5 * factorial(4)`, so the function can call itself again to find out what `factorial(4)` is. This process continues all the way down to `factorial(1)`, and we know that 1! is just 1, so `factorial(1)` returns 1. From that point, control returns through all the previous stages, giving us 1 * 2 * 3 * 4 * 5 * 6, or 720, which is 6!

This sounds like a pretty tall order to implement in a style language such as XSLT. However, it can be done—in XSLT 1.0, anyway. The key is to realize that you can store the return value of a called template in a variable if you call the template inside the `<xsl:variable>` element that declares the variable. For example, if I have a named template called `factorial` and want to compute 6!, I can pass it a value of 6 using `<xsl:with-param>` and assign the string value of the result to a variable named `result`, which I then display:

```
<?xml version="1.0"?>
<xsl:stylesheet version="1.0"
xmlns:xsl="http://www.w3.org/1999/XSL/Transform">

    <xsl:template match="/">
        <xsl:variable name="result">
            <xsl:call-template name="factorial">
                <xsl:with-param name="value" select="6"/>
            </xsl:call-template>
        </xsl:variable>
        6! = <xsl:value-of select="$result"/>
    </xsl:template>
            .
            .
            .
```

The following example shows how you can implement the `factorial` template so that it calls itself to compute the factorial. In a programming language, I could write each stage of the recursion as `n! = n * factorial( n - 1)`, but there's no assignment operator here, so when I calculate `factorial( n - 1)` I store its value in a new variable, `temp`, and write each stage to return the value `n * $temp` instead:

```
<?xml version="1.0"?>
<xsl:stylesheet version="1.0"
xmlns:xsl="http://www.w3.org/1999/XSL/Transform">

    <xsl:template match="/">
        <xsl:variable name="result">
            <xsl:call-template name="factorial">
                <xsl:with-param name="value" select="6"/>
            </xsl:call-template>
        </xsl:variable>
        6! = <xsl:value-of select="$result"/>
    </xsl:template>

    <xsl:template name="factorial">
        <xsl:param name="value"/>
        <xsl:choose>
            <xsl:when test="$value=1">
                <xsl:value-of select="1"/>
```

```
            </xsl:when>
            <xsl:otherwise>
                <xsl:variable name="temp">
                    <xsl:call-template name="factorial">
                        <xsl:with-param name="value" select="$value - 1"/>
                    </xsl:call-template>
                </xsl:variable>
            <xsl:value-of select="$temp * $value"/>
        </xsl:otherwise>
    </xsl:choose>
</xsl:template>

</xsl:stylesheet>
```

Here's the result document:

```
<?xml version="1.0" encoding="utf-8"?>
6! = 720
```

As you see, it can be done, at least in XSLT 1.0, which allows the result tree fragments I've used here.

Default Template Values

As I mentioned earlier, if you give a parameter a value when you declare it, that value can be overridden if you specify a different value in an `<xsl:with-param>` element. However, if you don't specify a different value, the original value acts like a default value.

The following example adapts the earlier "COLORS" example. That template has a parameter named `COLOR`, but I can call this template without setting `COLOR` to any particular value:

```
<xsl:template match="PLANET">
        <xsl:if test="NAME='Mercury'">
            <xsl:call-template name="COLORS">
                <xsl:with-param name="COLOR" select="'RED'"/>
            </xsl:call-template>
        </xsl:if>
        <xsl:if test="NAME='Venus'">
            <xsl:call-template name="COLORS">
                <xsl:with-param name="COLOR" select="'GREEN'"/>
            </xsl:call-template>
        </xsl:if>
        <xsl:if test="NAME='Earth'">
            <xsl:call-template name="COLORS">
            </xsl:call-template>
        </xsl:if>
    </xsl:template>
```

In this case, the COLOR parameter defaults to the value I've given it in the <xsl:param> element in the "COLORS" template, "blue":

```
<xsl:template match="PLANET">
    <xsl:if test="NAME='Mercury'">
        <xsl:call-template name="COLORS">
            <xsl:with-param name="COLOR" select="'RED'"/>
        </xsl:call-template>
    </xsl:if>
    <xsl:if test="NAME='Venus'">
        <xsl:call-template name="COLORS">
            <xsl:with-param name="COLOR" select="'GREEN'"/>
        </xsl:call-template>
    </xsl:if>
    <xsl:if test="NAME='Earth'">
        <xsl:call-template name="COLORS">
        </xsl:call-template>
    </xsl:if>
</xsl:template>

<xsl:template name="COLORS">
    <xsl:param name="COLOR" select="'blue'"/>
    <TR>
        <TD><FONT COLOR="{$COLOR}"><xsl:value-of select="NAME"/></FONT></TD>
        <TD><FONT COLOR="{$COLOR}"><xsl:apply-templates select="MASS"/></FONT></TD>
        <TD><FONT COLOR="{$COLOR}"><xsl:apply-templates select="RADIUS"/></FONT></TD>
        <TD><FONT COLOR="{$COLOR}"><xsl:apply-templates select="DAY"/></FONT></TD>
    </TR>
</xsl:template>
```

Specifying Template Values on the Command Line

In addition to using <xsl:param> and <xsl:with-param>, you can also set the values of stylesheet parameters on the command line with many XSLT processors. How you set this is processor-specific.

For example, the following example shows how you assign param1 the value value1 on the command line using Oracle's XSLT processor in Windows. Note that when you set parameter values on the command line, you still need to declare them with <xsl:param> in your stylesheet:

```
C:\>java oracle.xml.parser.v2.oraxsl -p param1='value1' planets.xml planets.xsl output.xml
```

Here's how you'd do the same thing with Saxon:

```
C:\>saxon source.xml stylesheet.xsl param1=value1 > output.xml
```

and with Xalan:

```
C:\>java org.apache.xalan.xslt.Process -IN planets.xml
```

```
➥    -XSL planets.xsl -OUT output.xml -PARAM parma1 value1
```

and XT:

```
C:\XSL>java -Dcom.jclark.xsl.sax.parser=org.apache.xerces.parsers.SAXParser com.
➥jclark.xsl.sax.Driver planets.xml planets.xsl output.xml param1=value1
```

The *<xsl:key>* Element: Matching by Key

You use the `<xsl:key>` element when you want to create a key and match nodes using that key. The `<xsl:key>` element has the following attributes:

- `name` (mandatory). The name of the key; set to a QName.
- `match` (mandatory). Set to a match pattern to match the nodes to which this key applies.
- `use` (mandatory). Set to an expression used to determine the value of the key.

Keys give you an easy way to identify elements, and you can match specific keys with the pattern "key()". Chapter 4 gave you an introduction to single-valued keys. In that example, I used a key to match planets whose `COLOR` attribute was set to "BLUE", which in that case was the Earth:

```
<?xml version="1.0"?>
<?xml-stylesheet type="text/xml" href="planets.xsl"?>
<PLANETS>
        .
        .
        .
    <PLANET COLOR="BLUE">
        <NAME>Earth</NAME>
        <MASS UNITS="(Earth = 1)">1</MASS>
        <DAY UNITS="days">1</DAY>
        <RADIUS UNITS="miles">2107</RADIUS>
        <DENSITY UNITS="(Earth = 1)">1</DENSITY>
        <DISTANCE UNITS="million miles">128.4</DISTANCE><!--At perihelion-->
    </PLANET>

</PLANETS>
```

I created a key named `COLOR` that matches `<PLANET>` elements by checking their `COLOR` attribute. That key, `COLOR`, looks like this:

```
<?xml version="1.0"?>
<xsl:stylesheet version="1.1"
xmlns:xsl="http://www.w3.org/1999/XSL/Transform">

    <xsl:key name="COLOR" match="PLANET" use="@COLOR"/>
        .
        .
        .
```

Then I used the pattern “key()” to match <PLANET> elements with the COLOR attribute set to “BLUE” this way:

```
<?xml version="1.0"?>
<xsl:stylesheet version="1.1"
xmlns:xsl="http://www.w3.org/1999/XSL/Transform">

    <xsl:key name="COLOR" match="PLANET" use="@COLOR"/>

    <xsl:template match="/PLANETS">
        <HTML>
            <HEAD>
                <TITLE>
                    The Planets Table
                </TITLE>
            </HEAD>
            <BODY>
                <H1>
                    The Planets Table
                </H1>
                <TABLE BORDER="2">
                    <TR>
                        <TD>Name</TD>
                        <TD>Mass</TD>
                        <TD>Radius</TD>
                        <TD>Day</TD>
                    </TR>
                    <xsl:apply-templates select="key('COLOR', 'BLUE')"/>
                </TABLE>
            </BODY>
        </HTML>
    </xsl:template>
        .
        .
        .
```

And here’s the result—as you can see, Earth was the only planet that matched the pattern:

```
<HTML>
    <HEAD>
        <TITLE>
            The Planets Table
        </TITLE>
    </HEAD>

    <BODY>
        <H1>
            The Planets Table
        </H1>

        <TABLE BORDER="2">
            <TR>
```

```
                <TD>Name</TD>
                <TD>Mass</TD>
                <TD>Radius</TD>
                <TD>Day</TD>
            </TR>

            <TR>
                <TD>Earth</TD>
                <TD>1 (Earth = 1)</TD>
                <TD>2107 miles</TD>
                <TD>1 days</TD>
            </TR>
        </TABLE>
    </BODY>
</HTML>
```

However, there's more possible here. For example, multiple nodes can match a key, which means that the pattern using that key will return a node set. For example, say all planets had the same value for the COLOR attribute, "unknown":

```
<?xml version="1.0"?>
<?xml-stylesheet type="text/xml" href="planets.xsl"?>
<PLANETS>

    <PLANET COLOR="UNKNOWN">
        <NAME>Mercury</NAME>
        <MASS UNITS="(Earth = 1)">.0553</MASS>
        <DAY UNITS="days">58.65</DAY>
        <RADIUS UNITS="miles">1516</RADIUS>
        <DENSITY UNITS="(Earth = 1)">.983</DENSITY>
        <DISTANCE UNITS="million miles">43.4</DISTANCE><!--At perihelion-->
    </PLANET>

    <PLANET COLOR="UNKNOWN">
        <NAME>Venus</NAME>
        <MASS UNITS="(Earth = 1)">.815</MASS>
        <DAY UNITS="days">116.75</DAY>
        <RADIUS UNITS="miles">3716</RADIUS>
        <DENSITY UNITS="(Earth = 1)">.943</DENSITY>
        <DISTANCE UNITS="million miles">66.8</DISTANCE><!--At perihelion-->
    </PLANET>

    <PLANET COLOR="UNKNOWN">
        <NAME>Earth</NAME>
        <MASS UNITS="(Earth = 1)">1</MASS>
        <DAY UNITS="days">1</DAY>
        <RADIUS UNITS="miles">2107</RADIUS>
        <DENSITY UNITS="(Earth = 1)">1</DENSITY>
        <DISTANCE UNITS="million miles">128.4</DISTANCE><!--At perihelion-->
    </PLANET>

</PLANETS>
```

Now when you create the COLOR this way: `<xsl:key name="COLOR" match="PLANET" use="@COLOR"/>` and match to it with this pattern: "key('COLOR', 'BLUE')", then you match all three planets:

```
<HTML>
    <HEAD>
        <TITLE>
            The Planets Table
        </TITLE>
    </HEAD>
    <BODY>
        <H1>
            The Planets Table
        </H1>
        <TABLE BORDER="2">
            <TR>
                <TD>Name</TD>
                <TD>Mass</TD>
                <TD>Radius</TD>
                <TD>Day</TD>
            </TR>

            <TR>
                <TD>Mercury</TD>
                <TD>.0553 (Earth = 1)</TD>
                <TD>1516 miles</TD>
                <TD>58.65 days</TD>
            </TR>

            <TR>
                <TD>Venus</TD>
                <TD>.815 (Earth = 1)</TD>
                <TD>3716 miles</TD>
                <TD>116.75 days</TD>
            </TR>

            <TR>
                <TD>Earth</TD>
                <TD>1 (Earth = 1)</TD>
                <TD>2107 miles</TD>
                <TD>1 days</TD>
            </TR>
        </TABLE>

    </BODY>
</HTML>
```

In addition to using a key that matches several nodes, a node can also match several values for one key. For example, you might set up a key to use the <NAME> element inside a <PLANET> element. But what if each <PLANET> element had more than one <NAME> element, as in this example:

```
<?xml version="1.0"?>
<?xml-stylesheet type="text/xml" href="planets.xsl"?>
<PLANETS>

    <PLANET>
        <NAME>Mercury</NAME>
        <NAME>Sister Planet</NAME>
        <MASS UNITS="(Earth = 1)">.0553</MASS>
        <DAY UNITS="days">58.65</DAY>
        <RADIUS UNITS="miles">1516</RADIUS>
        <DENSITY UNITS="(Earth = 1)">.983</DENSITY>
        <DISTANCE UNITS="million miles">43.4</DISTANCE><!--At perihelion-->
    </PLANET>

    <PLANET>
        <NAME>Venus</NAME>
        <NAME>Sister Planet</NAME>
        <MASS UNITS="(Earth = 1)">.815</MASS>
        <DAY UNITS="days">116.75</DAY>
        <RADIUS UNITS="miles">3716</RADIUS>
        <DENSITY UNITS="(Earth = 1)">.943</DENSITY>
        <DISTANCE UNITS="million miles">66.8</DISTANCE><!--At perihelion-->
    </PLANET>

    <PLANET>
        <NAME>Earth</NAME>
        <MASS UNITS="(Earth = 1)">1</MASS>
        <DAY UNITS="days">1</DAY>
        <RADIUS UNITS="miles">2107</RADIUS>
        <DENSITY UNITS="(Earth = 1)">1</DENSITY>
        <DISTANCE UNITS="million miles">128.4</DISTANCE><!--At perihelion-->
    </PLANET>

</PLANETS>
```

In this case, each <NAME> element is checked for a match to the key. For example, say that I wanted to match <NAME> elements with the text "Sister Planet". Here's the stylesheet:

```
<?xml version="1.0"?>
<xsl:stylesheet version="1.1"
xmlns:xsl="http://www.w3.org/1999/XSL/Transform">
```

```
    <xsl:key name="NAME" match="PLANET" use="NAME"/>

    <xsl:template match="/PLANETS">
        <HTML>
            <HEAD>
                <TITLE>
                    The Planets Table
                </TITLE>
            </HEAD>
            <BODY>
                <H1>
                    The Planets Table
                </H1>
                <TABLE BORDER="2">
                    <TR>
                        <TD>Name</TD>
                        <TD>Mass</TD>
                        <TD>Radius</TD>
                        <TD>Day</TD>
                    </TR>
                    <xsl:apply-templates select="key('NAME', 'Sister Planet')"/>
                </TABLE>
            </BODY>
        </HTML>
    </xsl:template>

    <xsl:template match="PLANET">
       <TR>
          <TD><xsl:value-of select="NAME"/></TD>
          <TD><xsl:apply-templates select="MASS"/></TD>
          <TD><xsl:apply-templates select="RADIUS"/></TD>
          <TD><xsl:apply-templates select="DAY"/></TD>
       </TR>
   </xsl:template>

    <xsl:template match="MASS">
        <xsl:value-of select="."/>
        <xsl:text> </xsl:text>
        <xsl:value-of select="@UNITS"/>
    </xsl:template>
        .
        .
        .
    <xsl:template match="DAY">
        <xsl:value-of select="."/>
        <xsl:text> </xsl:text>
        <xsl:value-of select="@UNITS"/>
    </xsl:template>

</xsl:stylesheet>
```

And here's the result document:

```
<HTML>
    <HEAD>
        <TITLE>
            The Planets Table
        </TITLE>
    </HEAD>

    <BODY>
        <H1>
            The Planets Table
        </H1>

        <TABLE BORDER="2">
            <TR>
                <TD>Name</TD>
                <TD>Mass</TD>
                <TD>Radius</TD>
                <TD>Day</TD>
            </TR>

            <TR>
                <TD>Mercury</TD>
                <TD>.0553 (Earth = 1)</TD>
                <TD>1516 miles</TD>
                <TD>58.65 days</TD>
            </TR>

            <TR>
                <TD>Venus</TD>
                <TD>.815 (Earth = 1)</TD>
                <TD>3716 miles</TD>
                <TD>116.75 days</TD>
            </TR>
        </TABLE>

    </BODY>
</HTML>
```

The *<xsl:document>* Element: Generating Multiple Result Documents

A common thing to want to do is create multiple result documents during a transformation. For example, you might want to create a report indicating how the transformation went, or split an input document up into multiple result documents (such as splitting a novel into chapters). Or, you might want to create a result document set that is meant to be used together (such as when you create an HTML frameset document) along with two documents to be displayed in the frames.

Creating multiple result documents is such a common thing to do that nearly all XSLT processors enable you to do it, even in XSLT 1.0, where there's no special support for this task. XSLT processors add new extension elements to do this. For example, Xalan includes a `<write>` element that enables you to write to a new result document. To use this element, you create a new namespace prefix—I'll use "xalan" here—for the namespace Xalan uses for this element, "com.lotus.xsl.extensions.Redirect", and indicate that this new prefix is an extension element prefix:

```
<?xml version="1.0"?>
<xsl:stylesheet version="1.1"
    xmlns:xsl="http://www.w3.org/1999/XSL/Transform"
    xmlns:xalan="com.lotus.xsl.extensions.Redirect"
    extension-element-prefixes="xalan">
        .
        .
        .
```

Now I can use the `<xalan:write>` element's `file` attribute to write to a new file:

```
<?xml version="1.0"?>
<xsl:stylesheet version="1.1"
    xmlns:xsl="http://www.w3.org/1999/XSL/Transform"
    xmlns:xalan="com.lotus.xsl.extensions.Redirect"
    extension-element-prefixes="xalan">
        .
        .
        .
<xalan:write file="newdoc.txt">
    <xsl:text>Here's some text.</xsl:text>
</xalan:write>
```

In Saxon, you use the `<output>` element; I use the prefix "saxon" for this element, which corresponds to the URI "http://icl.com/saxon":

```
<?xml version="1.0"?>
<xsl:stylesheet version="1.1"
    xmlns:xsl="http://www.w3.org/1999/XSL/Transform"
    xmlns:saxon="http://icl.com/saxon"
    extension-element-prefixes="saxon">
        .
        .
        .
<saxon:output file="newdoc.txt">
    <xsl:text>Here's some text.</xsl:text>
</saxon:output>
```

You can also do the same thing in XT; in this case, you use the namespace "http://www.jclark.com/xt" with the `<document>` element and use the `href` attribute to specify the name of the new file:

```
<?xml version="1.0"?>
<xsl:stylesheet version="1.1"
    xmlns:xsl="http://www.w3.org/1999/XSL/Transform"
    xmlns:xt="http://www.jclark.com/xt"
    extension-element-prefixes="xt">
        .
        .
        .
<xt:document href="newdoc.txt">
    <xsl:text>Here's some text.</xsl:text>
</xt:document>
```

All this makes for quite a jungle of standards, because everyone has created their own implementations. For this reason, XSLT 1.1 introduced a new element, `<xsl:document>`, to support multiple result documents. This element has the following attributes:

- `href` (mandatory). Indicates where the new document should be placed. You set this to an absolute or relative URI, without a fragment identifier.
- `method` (optional). Sets the output method used to create the result document. Set to "xml", "html", "text", or a QName that is not an NCName.
- `version` (optional). Sets the version of the output document. Set to an NMTOKEN.
- `encoding` (optional) Sets the encoding of the output document. Set to a string.
- `omit-xml-declaration` (optional). Set to "yes" or "no" to omit the XML declaration or not.
- `cdata-section-elements` (optional). Sets the names of those elements whose content you want output as CDATA sections. Set to a whitespace-separated list of QNames.
- `doctype-public` (optional). Specifies the public identifier to be used in the `<!DOCTYPE>` declaration in the output. Set to a string value.
- `doctype-system` (optional). Specifies the system identifier to be used in the `<!DOCTYPE>` declaration in the output. Set to a string value.
- `encoding` (optional). Sets the character encoding. Set to a string value.
- `indent` (optional). Specifies whether the output should be indented to show its nesting structure. Set to "yes" or "no".

- `media-type` (optional). Sets the MIME type of the output. Set to a string value.
- `standalone` (optional). Specifies whether a standalone declaration should be included in the output and sets its value if so. Set to "yes" or "no".

This element contains a template body.

The following example is based on a simplified stylesheet. In this case, I create two frames in an HTML document, as well as the two HTML documents that are to be displayed in those frames (frame1.html and frame2.html). I create the first frame and the document that will appear in it as follows:

```
<HTML>
    <HEAD>
        <TITLE>
            Two Frames
        </TITLE>
    </HEAD>

    <FRAMESET cols="50%, 50%">
        <FRAME src="frame1.html"/>

        <xsl:document href="frame1.html">
            <HTML>
                <HEAD>
                    <TITLE>
                        Frame 1
                    </TITLE>
                </HEAD>

                <BODY>
                    <H1>This is frame 1.</H1>
                </BODY>
            </HTML>
        </xsl:document>
        .
        .
        .
```

Then I can create the second frame and the document that will appear in that frame in this way:

```
<HTML>
    <HEAD>
        <TITLE>
            Two Frames
        </TITLE>
    </HEAD>

    <FRAMESET cols="50%, 50%">
```

```
        <FRAME src="frame1.html"/>

        <xsl:document href="frame1.html">
            <HTML>
                <HEAD>
                    <TITLE>
                        Frame 1
                    </TITLE>
                </HEAD>

                <BODY>
                    <H1>This is frame 1.</H1>
                </BODY>
            </HTML>
        </xsl:document>

        <FRAME src="frame2.html"/>

        <xsl:document href="frame2.html">
            <HTML>
                <HEAD>
                    <TITLE>
                        Frame 2
                    </TITLE>
                </HEAD>

                <BODY>
                    <H1>This is frame 2.</H1>
                </BODY>
            </HTML>
        </xsl:document>

    </FRAMESET>

</HTML>
```

Note, however, that this is an XSLT 1.1-only example.

As I'm writing this, one XSLT processor seems to have implemented `<xsl:document>`: Saxon version 6.2.1 and later, which has changed its `<saxon:output>` element to `<xsl:document>`. That's the only XSLT processor I know of, however, that handles this element so far.

The *<xsl:namespace-alias>* Element: Generating Stylesheets

One of the primary uses for XSLT is to transform stylesheets into other stylesheets, although that might not be obvious at first. For example, you might want to flesh out long rules that need to be customized just before processing documents. And as you know, XSLT was originally introduced to help create formatting object stylesheets in the first place.

However, this raises an issue: If you process a stylesheet full of elements such as `<xsl:template>` and `<xsl:apply-templates>` that you want to appear in the result document—because the result document is itself a stylesheet—how is XSLT to know how to differentiate those literal result elements from the XSLT elements it should be processing?

This is where the `<xsl:namespace-alias>` element comes in, because this element enables you to use a new namespace for elements in the source document and convert that namespace back to the correct one in the result document. This element has two attributes:

- `stylesheet-prefix` (mandatory). The namespace prefix used in the stylesheet. Set to an NCName or "#default".
- `result-prefix` (mandatory.) The prefix whose URI to which you want the namespace to be assigned in the result document. Set to an NCName or "#default".

The following example shows what I mean. Imagine that this is the stylesheet you want to generate:

```
<?xml version="1.0" encoding="UTF-8"?>
<xsl:stylesheet
    xmlns:xsl="http://www.w3.org/1999/XSL/Transform" version="1.1">
    <xsl:template match="PLANET">
        <TR>
            <TD>
                <xsl:value-of select="NAME"/>
            </TD>
            <TD>
                <xsl:apply-templates select="MASS"/>
            </TD>
            <TD>
                <xsl:apply-templates select="RADIUS"/>
            </TD>
            <TD>
                <xsl:apply-templates select="DAY"/>
            </TD>
        </TR>
    </xsl:template>
</xsl:stylesheet>
```

Note that this stylesheet is full of XSLT elements with the "xsl" prefix, so if you try to create it using an XSLT transformation, the XSLT processor will try to execute those elements. To avoid that, I give these elements a new namespace prefix, "xslt". Here's how that looks in the stylesheet that produces the preceding stylesheet. Note that this stylesheet just matches the root element of the source document so that it can start working; it doesn't actually use the source document for any other purpose:

Listing 9.4 **Using *<xsl:namespace-alias>***

```
<xsl:stylesheet version="1.1"
    xmlns:xsl="http://www.w3.org/1999/XSL/Transform"
    xmlns:xslt="http://xslt">

<xsl:template match="/">
   <xslt:stylesheet version="1.1">
    <xslt:template match="PLANET">
       <TR>
          <TD><xslt:value-of select="NAME"/></TD>
          <TD><xslt:apply-templates select="MASS"/></TD>
          <TD><xslt:apply-templates select="RADIUS"/></TD>
          <TD><xslt:apply-templates select="DAY"/></TD>
       </TR>
   </xslt:template>
   </xslt:stylesheet>
</xsl:template>
        .
        .
        .
</xsl:stylesheet>
```

Here, I'm using the namespace "http://xslt" for the "xslt" prefix, but can change that to the correct XSLT namespace, "http://www.w3.org/1999/XSL/Transform", in the output document if I use the `<xsl:namespace-alias>` element:

```
<xsl:stylesheet version="1.1"
    xmlns:xsl="http://www.w3.org/1999/XSL/Transform"
    xmlns:xslt="http://xslt">

<xsl:template match="/">
   <xslt:stylesheet version="1.1">
    <xslt:template match="PLANET">
       <TR>
          <TD><xslt:value-of select="NAME"/></TD>
          <TD><xslt:apply-templates select="MASS"/></TD>
          <TD><xslt:apply-templates select="RADIUS"/></TD>
          <TD><xslt:apply-templates select="DAY"/></TD>
       </TR>
   </xslt:template>
   </xslt:stylesheet>
```

```
</xsl:template>

<xsl:namespace-alias stylesheet-prefix="xslt" result-prefix="xsl"/>

</xsl:stylesheet>
```

Here's the result. Note that it still uses the namespace prefix "xslt", but that namespace now corresponds to the correct XSLT namespace:

```
<?xml version="1.0" encoding="UTF-8"?>
<xslt:stylesheet
    xmlns:xslt="http://www.w3.org/1999/XSL/Transform" version="1.1">
    <xslt:template match="PLANET">
        <TR>
            <TD>
                <xslt:value-of select="NAME"/>
            </TD>
            <TD>
                <xslt:apply-templates select="MASS"/>
            </TD>
            <TD>
                <xslt:apply-templates select="RADIUS"/>
            </TD>
            <TD>
                <xslt:apply-templates select="DAY"/>
            </TD>
        </TR>
    </xslt:template>
</xslt:stylesheet>
```

And that's it for this chapter. The next chapter takes a look at using XSLT in code.

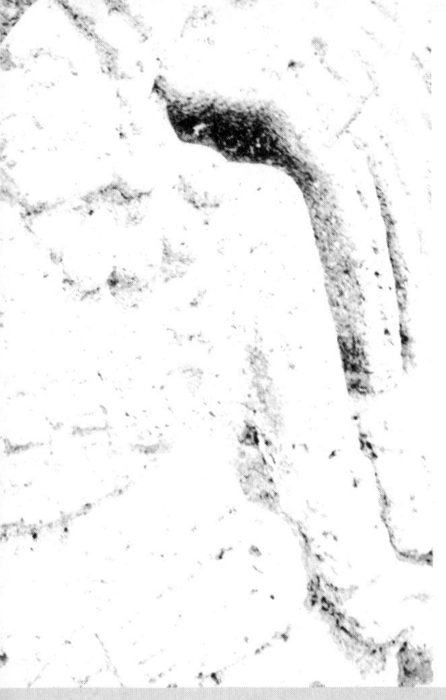

10 Using XSLT Processor APIs

As you've seen throughout this book, you don't need to do any programming to use XSLT. However, the XSLT processors we've been using so far—Xalan, Saxon, XT, Oracle, and MSXML—are all designed so you can work with them via program code if you prefer. I'll take a look at how to use these XSLT processors in code here. Feel free to skip this chapter if you're not a programmer or don't intend to become one. However, if you don't take advantage of the programming interface, you're missing a lot, including supporting XSLT on Web servers. This chapter also shows you how to transform XML into an SQL-based database.

I use Java and JavaScript in this chapter to interface to the various XSLT processor Application Programming Interfaces (APIs). If you're not familiar with these languages, you might take a look at *Inside XML*—it has a chapter introducing Java and another introducing JavaScript, covering all that you need to know here. You can use other languages, such as C++, or Visual Basic, with various XSLT processors, but Java has been the overwhelming choice of programmers so far, and JavaScript is useful for handling transformations in the Internet Explorer. In addition, the XSLT processors you've used are specifically designed to interface with Java, although the MSXML processor can also be used as a COM object for programming. As mentioned, the MSXML processor in the Internet Explorer can be used with JavaScript, and you saw an example of that as early as Chapter 1. And as promised in Chapter 1, I'll take a look at that example in more detail here.

XSLT Software Changes Very Rapidly!

Please note! XSLT software changes *very rapidly*, often monthly, so by the time you read this, parts of it might not apply. There's no way around this, and it's something you have to be aware of. All the examples in this chapter have been checked exhaustively by at least three people—me and at least two tech editors, all working independently—and all examples work as of this writing. If something is not working for you, check things such as the Java `classpath`, of course, but then also check your XSLT processor's documentation to see what might have changed.

XSLT and JavaScript in the Internet Explorer

Whether you like Microsoft or not, there's no denying that it is putting more and more XSLT power into the Internet Explorer (for more information, see `http://msdn.microsoft.com/xml/general/xmlparser.asp`), and so it bears examination here. I introduced an example creating XSLT transformations in the Internet Explorer using JavaScript in Chapter 1, and I take a closer look at it here. As you recall from Chapter 2, IE 5.5 or earlier can handle true XSLT transformations if you do them in JavaScript (and the new IE 6.0, just out, can handle straight XSLT syntax just by browsing to XML documents).

In this case, I use the MSXML processor and JavaScript to transform planets.xml using planets.xsl. To store these two documents, I create two new objects, `XMLDocument` and `XSLDocument`, using the `ActiveXObject` class and the `DOMDocument` class of the MSXML processor in a function named `xslt`. (This function runs as soon as the page loads because I set the `<BODY>` element's `onload` attribute to "xslt()".) I also create an object corresponding to the `<DIV>` element that displays the results of the transformation, as follows:

```
<HTML>
    <HEAD>
        <TITLE>XSLT Using JavaScript</TITLE>

        <SCRIPT LANGUAGE="JavaScript">

        function xslt()
        {
            var XMLDocument = new ActiveXObject('MSXML2.DOMDocument.3.0');
            var XSLDocument = new ActiveXObject('MSXML2.DOMDocument.3.0');
            var HTMLtarget = document.all['targetDIV'];
        .
        .
        .
```

Both planets.xml and planets.xsl are XML documents, and the MSXML processor can act as a validating XML parser if you set the `validateOnParse` property to `true`. To load planets.xml and planets.xsl into the `XMLDocument` and `XSLDocument` objects, you use the `load` method. I also check for errors by examining the parsing error code this way:

```
<HTML>
    <HEAD>
        <TITLE>XSLT Using JavaScript</TITLE>

        <SCRIPT LANGUAGE="JavaScript">

        function xslt()
        {
            var XMLDocument = new ActiveXObject('MSXML2.DOMDocument.3.0');
            var XSLDocument = new ActiveXObject('MSXML2.DOMDocument.3.0');
            var HTMLtarget = document.all['targetDIV'];

            XMLDocument.validateOnParse = true;
            XMLDocument.load('planets.xml');
            if (XMLDocument.parseError.errorCode != 0) {
                HTMLtarget.innerHTML = "Error!"
                return false;
            }

            XSLDocument.validateOnParse = true;
            XSLDocument.load('planets.xsl');
            if (XSLDocument.parseError.errorCode != 0) {
                HTMLtarget.innerHTML = "Error!"
                return false;
            }
        .
        .
        .
```

Now that both planets.xml and planets.xsl have been loaded, you can use the `XMLDocument` object's `transformNode` method to perform the transformation. Look at how I use `XSLDocument` to transform `XMLDocument`, and display the result in the target `<DIV>` element:

```
<HTML>
    <HEAD>
        <TITLE>XSLT Using JavaScript</TITLE>

        <SCRIPT LANGUAGE="JavaScript">

        function xslt()
        {
            var XMLDocument = new ActiveXObject('MSXML2.DOMDocument.3.0');
            var XSLDocument = new ActiveXObject('MSXML2.DOMDocument.3.0');
            var HTMLtarget = document.all['targetDIV'];
        .
        .
        .
           HTMLtarget.innerHTML = XMLDocument.transformNode(XSLDocument);
```

```
        return true;
    }

    </SCRIPT>
</HEAD>

<BODY onload="xslt()">
    <DIV ID="targetDIV">
    </DIV>
</BODY>
</HTML>
```

You can see the results in Figure 10.1.

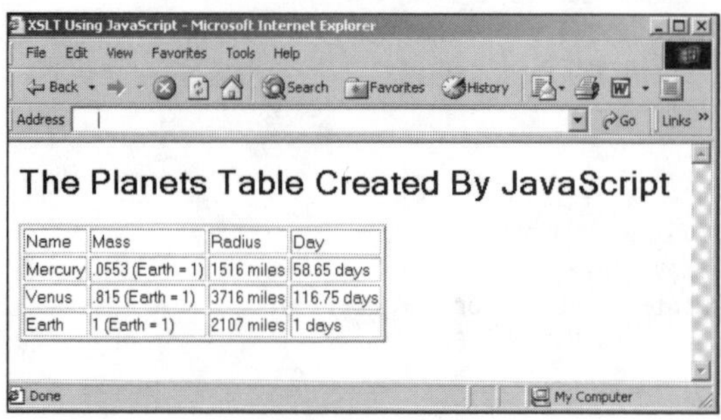

Figure 10.1 Using JavaScript to transform a document.

Handling Parsing Errors

Now that we're using JavaScript to load XML and XSL documents and work on them, it's useful to know how to report parsing errors. In the preceding example, I reported errors by displaying the message "Error!" in the target `<DIV>` element of the HTML document, but that's not too helpful. How can I get more information?

In the following example, I create a deliberate parsing error by changing the first `<PLANET>` tag in planets.xml to a `<PLANETS>` tag:

```
<?xml version="1.0"?>
<?xml-stylesheet type="text/xml" href="planets.xsl"?>
<PLANETS>

    <PLANETS>
```

```
    <NAME>Mercury</NAME>
    <MASS UNITS="(Earth = 1)">.0553</MASS>
    <DAY UNITS="days">58.65</DAY>
    <RADIUS UNITS="miles">1516</RADIUS>
    <DENSITY UNITS="(Earth = 1)">.983</DENSITY>
    <DISTANCE UNITS="million miles">43.4</DISTANCE><!--At perihelion-->
</PLANET>
    .
    .
    .
```

I have set the `XMLDocument` object's `validateOnParse` property to `true` (the default is `false`, which means no validation is performed) so the MSXML processor is sure to catch this parsing error. The `XMLDocument` object contains a `parseError` object, and if the `parseError` object's `errorCode` property is not zero, an error has occurred. Rather than just display the message "Error!" in this case, however, I decipher that error to get more details in a new function named `getError`, which returns a string explaining the error's position and nature.

To get this additional information, I use the `parseError` object's `url`, `line`, `linepos`, and `reason` properties to pinpoint the file that caused the problem, the line and position of the error, and the error's description:

Listing 10.1 **Creating an XSLT Transformation and Displaying Parse Errors**

```
<HTML>
    <HEAD>
        <TITLE>XSLT Using JavaScript</TITLE>

        <SCRIPT LANGUAGE="JavaScript">

        function xslt()
        {
            var XMLDocument = new ActiveXObject('MSXML2.DOMDocument.3.0');
            var XSLDocument = new ActiveXObject('MSXML2.DOMDocument.3.0');
            var HTMLtarget = document.all['targetDIV'];

            XMLDocument.validateOnParse = true;
            XMLDocument.load('planets.xml');
            if (XMLDocument.parseError.errorCode != 0) {
                HTMLtarget.innerHTML = getError(XMLDocument)
                return false;
            }

            XSLDocument.validateOnParse = true;
            XSLDocument.load('planets.xsl');
            if (XSLDocument.parseError.errorCode != 0) {
                HTMLtarget.innerHTML = getError(XSLDocument)
```

continues ▸

Listing 10.1 **Continued**

```
            return false;
        }

        HTMLtarget.innerHTML = XMLDocument.transformNode(XSLDocument);

        return true;
    }

    function getError(errorObject)
    {
        var Error = new String;
        Error = "Error. " + errorObject.parseError.url + "<BR>"
            + "Line: " + errorObject.parseError.line + "<BR>"
            + "Character: " + errorObject.parseError.linepos + "<BR>"
            + "Description: " + errorObject.parseError.reason;
        return Error;
    }

    </SCRIPT>
  </HEAD>

  <BODY onload="xslt()">
    <DIV ID="targetDIV">
    </DIV>
  </BODY>
</HTML>
```

You can see the results in Figure 10.2, where you see the file that caused the error, the location of the error, and the MSXML processor's explanation of the error. If you're going to handle XSLT transformations in the Internet Explorer when dealing with people browsing to your documents casually, handling parse errors such as this one is crucial.

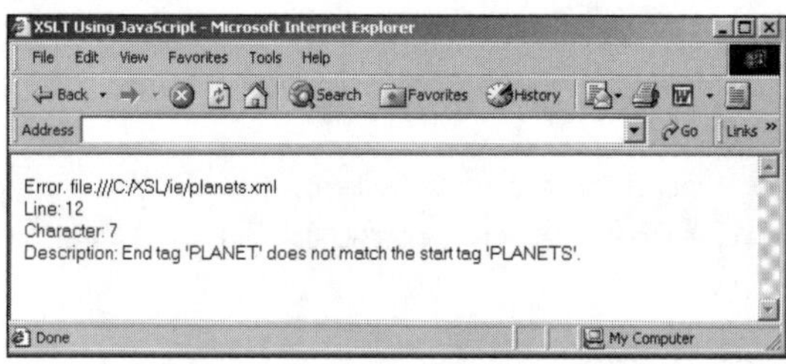

Figure 10.2 Handling a parsing error.

So far, I've only transformed an entire document using the MSXML processor, but there's considerably more control available to you here. For example, in the next section, I use XSLT in the Internet Explorer to enable the user to sort the HTML table that displays planetary data just by clicking buttons. And I do that by accessing the individual nodes inside the stylesheet.

Internet Explorer and Dynamic Styles

To indicate how much control you can exercise over XSLT transformations using the MSXML processor, I'll let the user dynamically sort the Planets table in this example. You can see the general idea in Figure 10.3. All the user has to do is to click a button to resort the table by name, mass, radius, or day.

To sort the table, I use a stylesheet that puts the `<xsl:sort>` element to work, as you'd expect. Here's how I perform the default sort, by planet name:

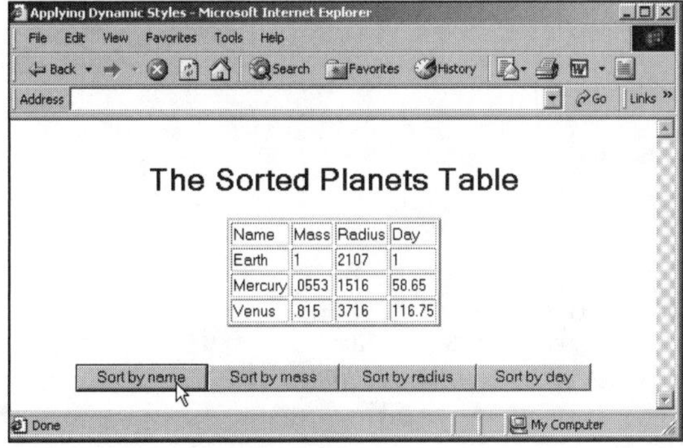

Figure 10.3 Supporting dynamic XSLT transformations.

Listing 10.2 **Applying Dynamic XSLT Transformations**

```
<?xml version="1.0" encoding="iso-8859-1" ?>
<xsl:stylesheet xmlns:xsl="http://www.w3.org/1999/XSL/Transform" version="1.1">

    <xsl:template match="/">
        <HTML>
            <HEAD>
```

continues ▸

Listing 10.2 **Continued**

```
            <TITLE>
                The Sorted Planets Table
            </TITLE>
        </HEAD>
        <BODY>
            <H1>
                The Sorted Planets Table
            </H1>
            <TABLE BORDER="2">
                <TR>
                    <TD>Name</TD>
                    <TD>Mass</TD>
                    <TD>Radius</TD>
                    <TD>Day</TD>
                </TR>
                <xsl:apply-templates select="/PLANETS/PLANET">
                    <xsl:sort select="NAME" order="ascending"/>
                </xsl:apply-templates>
            </TABLE>
        </BODY>
    </HTML>
</xsl:template>

<xsl:template match="PLANET">
   <TR>
      <TD><xsl:value-of select="NAME"/></TD>
      <TD><xsl:value-of select="MASS"/></TD>
      <TD><xsl:value-of select="RADIUS"/></TD>
      <TD><xsl:value-of select="DAY"/></TD>
   </TR>
</xsl:template>

</xsl:stylesheet>
```

This stylesheet sorts the planets in ascending alphabetic order, based on their names. That's fine if that's all you want to do, but it's possible to do more: you can let the user sort on other criteria as well. To do that, select the `<xsl:sort>` element's `select` attribute in this stylesheet and use JavaScript to change it dynamically from "NAME" to "MASS", "RADIUS", or whatever the user has asked for, then perform the XSLT transformation again. When the transformation is performed again, the new table appears, showing the new sort order.

As the first step in writing the HTML page that makes this possible, I load in planets.xml and the stylesheet I want to use, and perform the default sort, which is by planet name:

```
<HTML>
    <HEAD>
        <TITLE>
            Applying Dynamic Styles
        </TITLE>

        <SCRIPT LANGUAGE="JavaScript">
            var XMLDocument;
            var XSLDocument;
            var HTMLtarget;

            function initialize()
            {
                XMLDocument = new ActiveXObject('MSXML2.DOMDocument.3.0');
                XSLDocument = new ActiveXObject('MSXML2.DOMDocument.3.0');
                HTMLtarget = document.all['targetDIV'];

                XMLDocument.validateOnParse = true;
                XMLDocument.load('planets.xml');
                if (XMLDocument.parseError.errorCode != 0) {
                    HTMLtarget.innerHTML = "Error!"
                    return false;
                }

                XSLDocument.validateOnParse = true;
                XSLDocument.load('planets.xsl');
                if (XSLDocument.parseError.errorCode != 0) {
                    HTMLtarget.innerHTML = "Error!"
                    return false;
                }
                HTMLtarget.innerHTML = XMLDocument.transformNode(XSLDocument);
            }
                .
                .
                .
```

You've seen this part before. However, the user can also click a button to sort by mass, radius, and so on. To sort the table again, I write a function named `sort` and pass to it the name of the node (such as "MASS") to sort on when the user clicks a button. This is how the various buttons you saw in Figure 10.3 are created:

```
<INPUT TYPE="BUTTON" ONCLICK="sort('NAME')" VALUE="Sort by name"></INPUT>
<INPUT TYPE="BUTTON" ONCLICK="sort('MASS')" VALUE="Sort by mass"></INPUT>
<INPUT TYPE="BUTTON" ONCLICK="sort('RADIUS')" VALUE="Sort by radius"></INPUT>
<INPUT TYPE="BUTTON" ONCLICK="sort('DAY')" VALUE="Sort by day"></INPUT>
```

In the `sort` function, then, I want to perform a new sort, based on the name of the node passed to us. To perform the new sort, I change the select attribute of the <xsl:sort> element to the new node name to sort on. This is what the select attribute looks like now:

```
<xsl:apply-templates select="/PLANETS/PLANET">
                        <xsl:sort select="NAME" order="ascending"/>
                    </xsl:apply-templates>
```

I can access that node in the stylesheet, now stored in the XSLDocument object, by passing an XPath expression to that object's selectSingleNode method. The selectSingleNode method returns a node object, and I can change the text value of that node with the node object's nodeValue property. In this case, I just set the select attribute to the new node name to sort on:

```
<HTML>
    <HEAD>
        <TITLE>
            Applying Dynamic Styles
        </TITLE>

        <SCRIPT LANGUAGE="JavaScript">
            .
            .
            .
            function initialize()
            {
            .
            .
            .
            }

            function sort(sortNode)
            {
                (XSLDocument.selectSingleNode("//xsl:sort/@select")).nodeValue = sortNode;
            .
            .
            .
            }
        </SCRIPT>
            .
            .
            .
```

Now all that's left to do is to perform the transformation again, and display the results:

```
    </HEAD>
<HTML>
    <HEAD>
        <TITLE>
            Applying Dynamic Styles
```

```
        </TITLE>
        <SCRIPT LANGUAGE="JavaScript">
            .
            .
            .
            function initialize()
            {
            .
            .
            .
            }

            function sort(sortNode)
            {
                (XSLDocument.selectSingleNode("//xsl:sort/@select")).nodeValue = sortNode;
                HTMLtarget.innerHTML = XMLDocument.transformNode(XSLDocument);
            }
        </SCRIPT>
    </HEAD>
```

And that's all it takes. You can see the results in Figure 10.3. When the user clicks a button, the table is sorted again on the node value he or she has selected (bear in mind that this is an alphabetic sort; to sort by numeric values, see the discussion of `<xsl:sort>` in Chapter 5) and the table is re-displayed in the new sort order. Here's the whole HTML page:

Listing 10.3 **Applying Dynamic XSLT Transformations**

```
<HTML>
    <HEAD>
        <TITLE>
            Applying Dynamic Styles
        </TITLE>

        <SCRIPT LANGUAGE="JavaScript">
            var XMLDocument;
            var XSLDocument;
            var HTMLtarget;

            function initialize()
            {
                XMLDocument = new ActiveXObject('MSXML2.DOMDocument.3.0');
                XSLDocument = new ActiveXObject('MSXML2.DOMDocument.3.0');
                HTMLtarget = document.all['targetDIV'];

                XMLDocument.validateOnParse = true;
                XMLDocument.load('planets.xml');
                if (XMLDocument.parseError.errorCode != 0) {
```

continues ▶

Listing 10.3 **Continued**

```
                HTMLtarget.innerHTML = "Error!"
                return false;
            }

            XSLDocument.validateOnParse = true;
            XSLDocument.load('planets.xsl');
            if (XSLDocument.parseError.errorCode != 0) {
                HTMLtarget.innerHTML = "Error!"
                return false;
            }
            HTMLtarget.innerHTML = XMLDocument.transformNode(XSLDocument);
        }

        function sort(sortNode)
        {
            (XSLDocument.selectSingleNode("//xsl:sort/@select")).nodeValue = sortNode;
            HTMLtarget.innerHTML = XMLDocument.transformNode(XSLDocument);
        }
    </SCRIPT>
</HEAD>

<BODY ONLOAD="initialize()">
    <CENTER>

        <DIV ID="targetDIV"></div>
        <BR>
        <BR>

        <INPUT TYPE="BUTTON" ONCLICK="sort('NAME')" VALUE="Sort by name"></INPUT>
        <INPUT TYPE="BUTTON" ONCLICK="sort('MASS')" VALUE="Sort by mass"></INPUT>
        <INPUT TYPE="BUTTON" ONCLICK="sort('RADIUS')" VALUE="Sort by radius"></INPUT>
        <INPUT TYPE="BUTTON" ONCLICK="sort('DAY')" VALUE="Sort by day"></INPUT>

    </CENTER>
</BODY>
</HTML>
```

In fact, there's more than one way to load XML and XSL documents into objects in the Internet Explorer. I've been using the `ActiveXObject` class to create the `XMLDocument` and `XSLDocument` objects, but you could also create them directly, referring to the ActiveX objects that host XML documents by class ID as stored in the Windows Registry. In the following example I do that to load planets.xml and planets.xsl into `XMLDocument` and `XSLDocument`:

```
XMLDocument = document.all['XMLdoc'];
XSLDocument = document.all['XSLdoc'];
XMLDocument.load('planets.xml');
XSLDocument.load('planets.xsl');
    .
    .
    .
<OBJECT ID="XMLdoc" WIDTH="0" HEIGHT="0"
    CLASSID="clsid:f5078f32-c551-11d3-89b9-0000f81fe221">
</OBJECT>

<OBJECT ID="XSLdoc" WIDTH="0" HEIGHT="0"
    CLASSID="clsid:f5078f32-c551-11d3-89b9-0000f81fe221">
</OBJECT>
```

This technique is not as robust as using the `ActiveXObject` class, because the class IDs may vary with Internet Explorer version. (These class IDs are for Internet Explorer 5.5.) However, there's another way to load XML and XSL documents into the Internet Explorer as well: you can use *XML islands*.

Internet Explorer and XML Data Islands

The Internet Explorer supports a special tag, `<XML>`, that you can use to create XML islands. An XML island can enclose either straight XML or a reference to an XML document. For more on XML islands and how to create them, see Chapter 7 in *Inside XML*.

XML islands make it easy to load XML and XSL documents, so they're worth taking a look at here. In the following example, I create two XML islands, `sourceDocument` and `stylesheet`, and load planets.xml and planets.xsl just by referring to them with the `src` attribute:

```
<HTML>
    <HEAD>
        <TITLE>
            The Planets Table
        </TITLE>

        <XML id="sourceDocument" src="planets.xml"></XML>
        <XML id="stylesheet" src="planets.xsl"></XML>
        .
        .
        .
```

Now all I have to do to perform the XSLT transformation is use the `transformNode` method as before, and assign the results to a target `<DIV>` element to display those results:

Listing 10.4 **Loading XML and XSL Documents Using XML Islands**

```
<HTML>
    <HEAD>
        <TITLE>
            The Planets Table
        </TITLE>

        <XML id="sourceDocument" src="planets.xml"></XML>
        <XML id="stylesheet" src="planets.xsl"></XML>

        <SCRIPT FOR="window" EVENT="onload">
            targetDIV.innerHTML = sourceDocument.transformNode(stylesheet.XMLDocument);
        </SCRIPT>

    </HEAD>

    <BODY>
        <CENTER>
            <DIV id="targetDIV"></DIV>
        </CENTER>
    </BODY>
</HTML>
```

That's all it takes. Note that by default, the Internet Explorer 5.5 and earlier uses the older XSLT processor, as discussed in Chapter 2 (unless you've specifically installed the MSXML3 processor in replace mode, or IE 6.0, also in Chapter 2). If you're using IE 5.5 or earlier, you have to use an old-style Internet Explorer stylesheet, relying on no default rules and using the old XSL namespace, as in this example:

Listing 10.5 **Old-style Internet Explorer Stylesheet**

```
<?xml version="1.0"?>
<xsl:stylesheet version="1.1" xmlns:xsl="http://www.w3.org/TR/WD-xsl">

    <xsl:template match="/">
        <HTML>
            <HEAD>
                <TITLE>
                    The Planets Table
                </TITLE>
```

```
            </HEAD>
            <BODY>
                <H1>
                    The Planets Table
                </H1>
                <TABLE BORDER="2">
                    <TR>
                        <TD>Name</TD>
                        <TD>Mass</TD>
                        <TD>Radius</TD>
                        <TD>Day</TD>
                    </TR>
                    <xsl:apply-templates/>
                </TABLE>
            </BODY>
        </HTML>
    </xsl:template>

    <xsl:template match="PLANETS">
        <xsl:apply-templates/>
    </xsl:template>

    <xsl:template match="PLANET">
       <TR>
          <TD><xsl:value-of select="NAME"/></TD>
          <TD><xsl:value-of select="MASS"/></TD>
          <TD><xsl:value-of select="RADIUS"/></TD>
          <TD><xsl:value-of select="DAY"/></TD>
       </TR>
   </xsl:template>

</xsl:stylesheet>
```

As you can see, there's plenty you can do with JavaScript and XSLT in the Internet Explorer. For more information, see the Microsoft XSLT Developer's guide which is currently at `http://msdn.microsoft.com/library/default.asp?URL=/library/psdk/xmlsdk/xslp8tlx.htm`.

It's time to turn to interfacing XSLT to Java, starting by calling Java directly from XSLT processors.

Calling Java Directly from XSLT Processors

As discussed in Chapter 5, until recently, XSLT processors have been free to define the way they implement extension functions, and one of those ways includes calling Java functions directly. For example, in Saxon and Xalan, you can run Java code if you define a namespace that specifies a Java class as the final part of its URI as follows, where I'm defining a `Date` namespace that corresponds to the Java `Date` class:

```
<?xml version="1.0"?>
<xsl:stylesheet version="1.1"
xmlns:xsl="http://www.w3.org/1999/XSL/Transform"
xmlns:Date="http://www.saxon.com/java/java.util.Date">
        .
        .
        .
```

As you saw in Chapter 5, this means that you can use Java `Date` functions such as `toString` and `new` to embed the current date in an `<H1>` HTML header in the output this way:

Listing 10.6 **Using the Java *Date* Function**

```
<?xml version="1.0"?>
<xsl:stylesheet version="1.1"
xmlns:xsl="http://www.w3.org/1999/XSL/Transform"
xmlns:Date="http://www.saxon.com/java/java.util.Date">

    <xsl:template match="/PLANETS">
        <HTML>
            <HEAD>
                <TITLE>
                    The Planets Table
                </TITLE>
            </HEAD>
            <BODY>
                <H1>
                    The Planets Table
                </H1>
                <BR/>
                <H1>
                    <xsl:value-of select="Date:toString(Date:new())"/>
                </H1>
                <TABLE BORDER="2">
                    <TD>Name</TD>
                    <TD>Mass</TD>
                    <TD>Radius</TD>
                    <TD>Day</TD>
                    <xsl:apply-templates/>
                </TABLE>
            </BODY>
        </HTML>
    </xsl:template>
```

```
    <xsl:template match="PLANET">
       <TR>
          <TD><xsl:value-of select="NAME"/></TD>
          <TD><xsl:apply-templates select="MASS"/></TD>
          <TD><xsl:apply-templates select="RADIUS"/></TD>
          <TD><xsl:apply-templates select="DAY"/></TD>
       </TR>
   </xsl:template>

    <xsl:template match="MASS">
        <xsl:value-of select="."/>
    </xsl:template>

    <xsl:template match="RADIUS">
        <xsl:value-of select="."/>
    </xsl:template>

    <xsl:template match="DAY">
        <xsl:value-of select="."/>
    </xsl:template>

</xsl:stylesheet>
```

This certainly works, but it's a limited way to do things, and it relies on nonstandard extensions. Unless you're doing only a few simple calls, it's usually far better to start off with Java and interface to the XSLT processor instead.

The Xalan, Saxon, XT, and Oracle XSLT processors all define an API that you can use to call them from Java. All you have to do is make sure the correct JAR files are in the Java `classpath`. You've already seen how to use JAR files and classpaths from as far back as Chapter 1; now it's time to start writing some Java, not just running predefined classes from the command line. The code is available for download at `http://www.newriders.com/books/title.cfm?isbn=0735711364`, so if you are not a Java programmer you can follow along.

Interfacing to XSLT Java APIs

All Java-based XSLT processors define an extensive interface—an API—to connect to Java. Typically, you use the API to create Java objects and call methods, as you'll see in this chapter. However, all XSLT processors define their APIs differently, and they're usually extensive, because each processor is free to create its own class and method hierarchies.

In the following sections, I work through the process of creating XSLT transformations from Java with Xalan, Saxon, XT, and the Oracle XSLT processor.

You should refer to the documentation that comes with these processors to see what other kinds of capabilities are available. Note that the APIs of most of these processors could themselves fill a book, so the discussion of these processors is, of necessity, only an overview.

Naming Java Files

Writing Java files is one instance where the name of the file *does* matter, unlike the other examples in this book. As discussed in *Inside XML*, Java insists that the name of a file must match the name of the public class in the file. For that reason, I include the name of the file you should use for each listing in the heading that appears right before the listing. For example, "Listing 10.7, xalanjava.java, Interfacing Xalan to Java", means that you should save the code in the listing as xalanjava.java before trying to use it with Java (to make it easier, I use lowercase for all Java public classes and filenames). Note also that if you download the book's code, this example is named `10-07.java`, and you should rename it to `xalanjava.java` before using it. I also add the name you should use to store the file in a comment at the beginning of each Java file.

Interfacing Xalan to Java

Xalan is actually one of the easier XSLT processors to interface to Java, despite its size. To show how this works, I create a new Java class, `xalanjava`, which you can call like this to perform an XSLT transformation:

```
C:\>java xalanjava planets.xml planets.xsl planets.html
```

To create an XSLT transformation, I start by creating an object of the `TransformerFactory` class in the `xalanjava` class:

```
import javax.xml.transform.Transformer;
import javax.xml.transform.TransformerFactory;
import javax.xml.transform.stream.StreamSource;
import javax.xml.transform.stream.StreamResult;
import javax.xml.transform.TransformerException;
import javax.xml.transform.TransformerConfigurationException;
import java.io.FileOutputStream;
import java.io.FileNotFoundException;
import java.io.IOException;

public class xalanjava
{
    public static void main(String[] args)
        throws TransformerException, TransformerConfigurationException,
        FileNotFoundException, IOException
    {
        TransformerFactory tFactory = TransformerFactory.newInstance();
        .
        .
        .
```

The names of the XML document, XSL document, and result document have been passed to us as `args[0]`, `args[1]`, and `args[2]`, respectively. The next step is to load the XSL document into the new `TransformerFactory` object I've created. To do that, I create a `StreamSource` object and pass that object to the `TransformerFactory` object's `newTransformer` method to create a new `Transformer` object:

```
import javax.xml.transform.Transformer;
        .
        .
        .
public class xalanjava
{
    public static void main(String[] args)
        throws TransformerException, TransformerConfigurationException,
        FileNotFoundException, IOException
    {
        TransformerFactory tFactory = TransformerFactory.newInstance();

        Transformer transformer = tFactory.newTransformer(new StreamSource(args[1]));
        .
        .
        .
```

This `transformer` object, `transformer`, performs the XSLT transformation. To make the transformation happen, you use the `transformer` object's `transform` method, passing it a `StreamSource` object corresponding to the XML document, and a `StreamResult` object corresponding to the result document:

```
import javax.xml.transform.Transformer;
        .
        .
        .
public class xalanjava
{
    public static void main(String[] args)
        throws TransformerException, TransformerConfigurationException,
        FileNotFoundException, IOException
    {
        .
        .
        .
transformer.transform(new StreamSource(args[0]),
            new StreamResult(new FileOutputStream(args[2])));
    }
}
```

Here's the full Java file, xalanjava.java:

Listing 10.7 **xalanjava.java, Interfacing Xalan to Java**

```
import javax.xml.transform.Transformer;
import javax.xml.transform.TransformerFactory;
import javax.xml.transform.stream.StreamSource;
import javax.xml.transform.stream.StreamResult;
import javax.xml.transform.TransformerException;
import javax.xml.transform.TransformerConfigurationException;
import java.io.FileOutputStream;
import java.io.FileNotFoundException;
import java.io.IOException;

public class xalanjava
{
    public static void main(String[] args)
        throws TransformerException, TransformerConfigurationException,
        FileNotFoundException, IOException
    {
        TransformerFactory tFactory = TransformerFactory.newInstance();

        Transformer transformer = tFactory.newTransformer(new StreamSource(args[1]));

transformer.transform(new StreamSource(args[0]),
            new StreamResult(new FileOutputStream(args[2])));
    }
}
```

To compile xalanjava.java into xalanjava.class and run that class, you set the `classpath` to include Xalan and the XML parser you usually use with Xalan, Xerces (for more on Xerces, including where to get it, see Chapter 1), in something like this in Windows (as always, update these paths to match your system):

```
C:\>set classpath=.;c:\xalan\xalan.jar;c:\xalan\xerces.jar
```

Then you compile xalanjava.java with the Java compiler, javac, as follows:

```
C:\>javac xalanjava.java
```

This assumes that javac.exe is in your path so that you can simply invoke it on the command line directly. (The Java compiler, javac.exe, is usually in the Java bin directory, so if it's not in your path, you could also call it something like this: `C:\>c:\jdk1.3\bin\javac xalanjava.java`—see *Inside XML* for more information on Java code.) The Java compiler creates xalanjava.class, and you use that file to perform the transformation:

```
C:\>java xalanjava planets.xml planets.xsl planets.html
```

This creates planets.html from planets.xml and planets.xsl—and this time, I did it with my own Java class.

Using Sun's JAXP Package for XSLT

Sun, the creator of Java, has a Java package for XML processing named JAXP, which you can download at `http://java.sun.com/xml`. JAXP can also perform XSLT transformations. However, I'm not covering JAXP separately in this chapter, because JAXP (currently, at least) uses Xalan for all its transformations, and it comes with xalan.jar. That means that you can use the preceding example, Listing 10.7, unchanged with the Java JAXP package.

Interfacing Saxon to Java

The Saxon processor also defines an API for use with Java, but, of course, the details differ from Xalan. Here, I create a new Java class, saxonjava, to show how to create transformations using the Saxon API, version 6.0.2. You start by creating a new XSLT `Processor` object by calling the `Processor` class's `newInstance` method in the file saxonjava.java:

```
import java.io.*;
import org.xml.sax.*;
import org.w3c.dom.*;
import com.icl.saxon.trax.*;

public class saxonjava
{

    public static void main(String args[])
        throws ProcessorException, ProcessorFactoryException,
        TransformException, SAXException, IOException
    {
        Processor processor = Processor.newInstance("xslt");
        .
        .
        .
```

Next, you must create a `Templates` object based on the XSL stylesheet you want to use, whose name is stored in `args[1]`. You can use the `InputSource` class as follows:

```
import java.io.*;
        .
        .
        .
public class saxonjava
{
```

```
    public static void main(String args[])
        throws ProcessorException, ProcessorFactoryException,
        TransformException, SAXException, IOException
    {
        Processor processor = Processor.newInstance("xslt");

        Templates templates = processor.process(new InputSource(args[1]));
        .
        .
        .
    }
}
```

Using the new `Templates` object, you can create a `Transformer` object, which does the actual work:

```
import java.io.*;
        .
        .
        .
public class saxonjava
{

    public static void main(String args[])
        throws ProcessorException, ProcessorFactoryException,
        TransformException, SAXException, IOException
    {
        Processor processor = Processor.newInstance("xslt");

        Templates templates = processor.process(new InputSource(args[1]));

        Transformer transformer = templates.newTransformer();
        .
        .
        .
    }
}
```

Finally, you can perform the XSLT transformation using the `transformer` object's `transform` method this way, writing the result out to the result document using a `FileWriter` object:

Listing 10.8 **saxonjava.java, Interfacing Saxon to Java**

```
import java.io.*;
import org.xml.sax.*;
import org.w3c.dom.*;
import com.icl.saxon.trax.*;

public class saxonjava
{
```

```
    public static void main(String args[])
        throws ProcessorException, ProcessorFactoryException,
        TransformException, SAXException, IOException
    {
        Processor processor = Processor.newInstance("xslt");

        Templates templates = processor.process(new InputSource(args[1]));

        Transformer transformer = templates.newTransformer();

        transformer.transform(new InputSource(args[0]),
            new Result(new FileWriter(args[2])));
    }
}
```

To compile and use this new class, saxonjava, you set the `classpath` to include saxon.jar, something like this:

```
C:\>set classpath=.;c:\saxon\saxon.jar
```

Then you use the Java compiler, javac, to create saxonjava.class.

Like many API-based XSLT processors, Saxon expects to be passed URLs of the documents you want to work with, so I'll do that here:

```
C:\>java saxonjava http://www.starpowder.com/planets.xml
➥http://www.starpowder.com/planets.xsl planets.html
```

This creates planets.html as before. Note that if your documents are local, you can use a file URL instead. For example, in Windows, if the XML document is at `c:\XSL\saxonjava\planets.xml` and the XSL document is at `c:\XSL\saxonjava\planets.xsl`, you might use this command line:

```
C:\>java saxonjava file:///XSL/saxonjava/planets.xml
➥file:///XSL/saxonjava/planets.xsl planets.html
```

Converting from filenames to URLs

If you prefer to use local filenames on the command line rather than URLs, you can convert those filenames to URLs in your code. To do that, you need the filename's full path to pass to the Java `URL` class, and you can get that path with the `File` class's `getAbsolutePath` method like this: `File file = new File(filename); String fullpath = file.getAbsolutePath();`.

This example used Saxon 6.0.2, which is still listed as the stable version of Saxon on the Saxon site, but as I write this, the book is in tech review and there's a new, not fully tested, version available, Saxon 6.2.2. (There was no Saxon version 6.1.x.) In that newer version, it looks as if Saxon is going back to the same API model that Xalan uses, and code targeted at version 6.0.2 won't work with version 6.2.2 (surprise!). Here's what saxonjava.java would look like for version 6.2.2—make sure you include the new saxon.jar in your `classpath` when using this code (which is identical to xalanjava.java, shown earlier, except for the class name, `saxonjava`), and note that you don't have to supply file URLs, just filenames, when running it, as with xalanjava.java:

```
import javax.xml.transform.Transformer;
import javax.xml.transform.TransformerFactory;
import javax.xml.transform.stream.StreamSource;
import javax.xml.transform.stream.StreamResult;
import javax.xml.transform.TransformerException;
import javax.xml.transform.TransformerConfigurationException;
import java.io.FileOutputStream;
import java.io.FileNotFoundException;
import java.io.IOException;

public class saxonjava
{
    public static void main(String[] args)
        throws TransformerException, TransformerConfigurationException,
        FileNotFoundException, IOException
    {
        TransformerFactory tFactory = TransformerFactory.newInstance();

        Transformer transformer = tFactory.newTransformer(new StreamSource(args[1]));

transformer.transform(new StreamSource(args[0]),
            new StreamResult(new FileOutputStream(args[2])));
    }
}
```

Interfacing the Oracle XSLT Processor to Java

It takes a little more effort to perform an XSLT transformation using the Oracle XSLT processor's API. Here I show how it works in a new example, oraclejava.java.

First in oraclejava.java, you must read in the documents you want to work with, using a `DOMParser` object:

```
import org.w3c.dom.*;
import java.util.*;
import java.io.*;
import java.net.*;
```

```
import oracle.xml.parser.v2.*;

public class oraclejava
{
    public static void main (String args[]) throws Exception
    {
        DOMParser parser;

        try
        {
            parser = new DOMParser();
            parser.setPreserveWhitespace(true);
        .
        .
        .
```

Next, you convert the URLs of the XML source and XSLT stylesheet documents into Java `URL` objects, using the `parser` object's `parse` method to read those documents in. Then I use the parser's `getDocument` method to retrieve and store the XML and XSLT documents in `XMLDocument` objects:

```
public class oraclejava
{
    public static void main (String args[]) throws Exception
    {
        DOMParser parser;

        XMLDocument xmldoc, xsldoc;
        URL xslURL;
        URL xmlURL;

        try
        {
            parser = new DOMParser();
            parser.setPreserveWhitespace(true);

            xmlURL = new URL(args[0]);
            parser.parse(xmlURL);
            xmldoc = parser.getDocument();

            xslURL = new URL(args[1]);
            parser.parse(xslURL);
            xsldoc = parser.getDocument();
        .
        .
        .
```

At this point, planets.xml and planets.xsl are both in `XMLDocument` objects. To perform the transformation, I need an `XSLStylesheet` object and an `XSLProcessor` object built for the XSLT stylesheet. The actual XSLT transformation is made with the `parser` object's `processXSL` method, which returns a document fragment:

```
public class oraclejava
{
    public static void main (String args[]) throws Exception
    {
        DOMParser parser;
        .
        .
        .
            xslURL = new URL(args[1]);
            parser.parse(xslURL);
            xsldoc = parser.getDocument();

            XSLStylesheet xslstylesheet = new XSLStylesheet(xsldoc, xslURL);

            XSLProcessor processor = new XSLProcessor();

            DocumentFragment docfragment = processor.processXSL(xslstylesheet, xmldoc);
            .
            .
            .
```

That completes the transformation. Now the trick is to convert this document fragment into an XML document that can be written to disk. I do that by creating a new XML document, `newdoc`, and making the document fragment into the new document's root:

```
import org.w3c.dom.*;
        .
        .
        .
public class oraclejava
{
    public static void main (String args[]) throws Exception
    {
        DOMParser parser;
        XMLDocument xmldoc, xsldoc, newdoc;
        URL xslURL;
        URL xmlURL;

        try
        {
            .
            .
            .
```

```
        DocumentFragment docfragment = processor.processXSL(xslstylesheet, xmldoc);

        newdoc = new XMLDocument();

        Element rootElement = newdoc.createElement("root");
        newdoc.appendChild(rootElement);

        rootElement.appendChild(docfragment);
        .
        .
        .
```

All that remains is to store the new XML document to disk, using the name given to us as `args[2]`. I do that with a `FileOutputStream` object; here's the full code:

Listing 10.9 oraclejava.java, Interfacing the Oracle XSLT Processor to Java

```
import org.w3c.dom.*;
import java.util.*;
import java.io.*;
import java.net.*;
import oracle.xml.parser.v2.*;

public class oraclejava
{
    public static void main (String args[]) throws Exception
    {
        DOMParser parser;
        XMLDocument xmldoc, xsldoc, newdoc;
        URL xslURL;
        URL xmlURL;

        try
        {
            parser = new DOMParser();
            parser.setPreserveWhitespace(true);

            xmlURL = new URL(args[0]);
            parser.parse(xmlURL);
            xmldoc = parser.getDocument();

            xslURL = new URL(args[1]);
            parser.parse(xslURL);
            xsldoc = parser.getDocument();

            XSLStylesheet xslstylesheet = new XSLStylesheet(xsldoc, xslURL);

            XSLProcessor processor = new XSLProcessor();
```

continues ▸

Listing 10.9 **Continued**

```
            DocumentFragment docfragment = processor.processXSL(xslstylesheet, xmldoc);

            newdoc = new XMLDocument();

            Element rootElement = newdoc.createElement("root");
            newdoc.appendChild(rootElement);

            rootElement.appendChild(docfragment);

            OutputStream out = new FileOutputStream(args[2]);
            newdoc.print(out);
            out.close();
        }
        catch (Exception e){}
    }
}
```

And that completes oraclejava.java. To compile this example, set the `classpath` to include the Oracle XSLT processor's XSLT processor, xmlparserv2.jar:

```
C:\>set classpath=.;c:\oraclexml\lib\xmlparserv2.jar
```

Then compile oraclejava.java as I already did with other Java files, using the Java compiler, javac. To perform XSLT transformations, you supply the URLs of the documents you want to work with (you can use file URLs here, as before, if the documents are local):

```
C:\>java oraclejava http://starpowder.com/planets.xml
➥http://starpowder.com/planets.xsl planets.html
```

Interfacing XT to Java

You can also interface the XT processor to Java. The XT API is designed to interface easily with the classes defined in Sun's Project X TR2, which supports XML handling. You need the file xml.jar from Sun, which you can get by downloading Sun's Project X TR2. You need to be a member of Sun's developer site, `http://developer.java.sun.com`, to get xml.jar. Fortunately, becoming a member is free, but you have to fill out a number of forms at `http://developer.java.sun.com`.

You need xml.jar for the `com.sun.xml.tree.XmlDocument` class. This class supports XML documents, and I start this new example, xtjava.java, by creating a new `XmlDocument` object for the source document, the XSLT stylesheet, and the result document:

```
import java.io.IOException;
import java.io.OutputStream;
import java.io.FileOutputStream;
import org.xml.sax.SAXException;
import com.sun.xml.tree.XmlDocument;
import com.jclark.xsl.dom.Transform;
import com.jclark.xsl.dom.TransformEngine;
import com.jclark.xsl.dom.TransformException;
import com.jclark.xsl.dom.XSLTransformEngine;

class xtjava
{
    public static void main(String[] args)
        throws IOException, SAXException, TransformException
    {

        XmlDocument XMLdoc = new XmlDocument().createXmlDocument(args[0]);
        XmlDocument XSLdoc = new XmlDocument().createXmlDocument(args[1]);
        XmlDocument newdoc = new XmlDocument();
        .
        .
        .
```

Next, I create an `XSLTranformationEngine` object, and use this object's `createTransform` method to create a new `Transform` object based on the XSLT stylesheet:

```
import java.io.IOException;
        .
        .
        .
class xtjava
{
    public static void main(String[] args)
        throws IOException, SAXException, TransformException
    {

        XmlDocument doc = new XmlDocument();

        XSLTransformEngine transformEngine = new XSLTransformEngine();

        Transform transform = transformEngine.createTransform(XSLdoc);
        .
        .
        .
```

Next, I can transform the XML document into the result document's object this way:

```
import java.io.IOException;
        .
        .
        .
class xtjava
{
    public static void main(String[] args)
        throws IOException, SAXException, TransformException
    {

        XmlDocument XMLdoc = new XmlDocument().createXmlDocument(args[0]);
        XmlDocument XSLdoc = new XmlDocument().createXmlDocument(args[1]);
        XmlDocument newdoc = new XmlDocument();

        XSLTransformEngine transformEngine = new XSLTransformEngine();

        Transform transform = transformEngine.createTransform(XSLdoc);

        transform.transform(XMLdoc, newdoc);
        .
        .
        .
```

That completes the transformation. All that remains is to write the result document, `newdoc`, to disk, and I do that as follows with a `FileOutputStream` object:

Listing 10.10 **xtjava.java, Interfacing XT to Java**

```
import java.io.IOException;
import java.io.OutputStream;
import java.io.FileOutputStream;
import org.xml.sax.SAXException;
import com.sun.xml.tree.XmlDocument;
import com.jclark.xsl.dom.Transform;
import com.jclark.xsl.dom.TransformEngine;
import com.jclark.xsl.dom.TransformException;
import com.jclark.xsl.dom.XSLTransformEngine;

class xtjava
{
    public static void main(String[] args)
        throws IOException, SAXException, TransformException
    {

        XmlDocument XMLdoc = new XmlDocument().createXmlDocument(args[0]);
        XmlDocument XSLdoc = new XmlDocument().createXmlDocument(args[1]);
        XmlDocument newdoc = new XmlDocument();

        XSLTransformEngine transformEngine = new XSLTransformEngine();

        Transform transform = transformEngine.createTransform(XSLdoc);
```

```
        transform.transform(XMLdoc, newdoc);

        OutputStream out = new FileOutputStream(args[2]);
        newdoc.write(out);
        out.close();
    }
}
```

To run this example, you include xt.jar and xml.jar in the classpath:

```
C:\>set classpath=.;d:\xt\xt.jar;xml.jar
```

Then you compile xtjava.java with the Java compiler, javac, and run it as follows, supplying the URLs of the XML and XSL documents (you can also use file URLs, as you saw earlier in this chapter):

```
C:\>java xtjava http://www.starpowder.com/planets.xml
➥http://www.starpowder.com/planets.xsl planets.html
```

And that's all it takes.

Transforming XML to SQL-Based Databases

During any discussion of advanced XSLT topics, it's worthwhile to mention Saxon's SQL extension elements. Using Java Database Connectivity (JDBC), you can work with SQL-based databases. You've already seen XML to XML transformations, to HTML, to XHTML, to plain text, to RTF, to JavaScript, and so on in this book. Now you'll see an XML transformation to a SQL-based database.

Using Instant Saxon

Note that you cannot use the prebuilt Windows-only saxon.exe to connect to JDBC databases. You should run the Saxon Java class com.icl.saxon.StyleSheet instead, as I do at the end of this example.

In this example, I add the data in planets.xml to a Microsoft Access-style database, planets.mdb. If you want to follow along in this example, create this database file, creating four new text fields, named "Name", "Mass", "Radius", and "Day" in a table named "planets", and leaving the rest of the database file empty. In Windows, I'll register this database file as an ODBC source using the Data Sources (ODBC) icon in the control panel (if you're using Windows 2000, you'll find it in the Administrative Tools folder in the Control Panel), giving it the data source name "planets". When you run this example, it'll read the planetary data in planets.xml and add it to the database file, planets.mdb.

I use the Saxon <sql:connect> element to connect to this database using JDBC. The namespace prefix "sql" is defined this way in Saxon:

```
<xsl:stylesheet
    xmlns:sql="http://icl.com/saxon/extensions/com.icl.saxon.sql.SQLElementFactory"
    xmlns:xsl="http://www.w3.org/1999/XSL/Transform" version="1.1">
        .
        .
        .
```

To actually connect to the planets data source, you use the <sql:connect> extension element. That element has database, user, password, and driver attributes. For JDBC, you set the driver attribute to "sun.jdbc.odbc.JdbcOdbcDriver", the database attribute to the ODBC data source, "jdbc:odbc:planets", and the user and password attributes to a username and password needed to log in to the database. I don't need a username or password here, but I add placeholders for those parameters, because many database applications do require them:

```
<xsl:stylesheet
    xmlns:sql="http://icl.com/saxon/extensions/com.icl.saxon.sql.SQLElementFactory"
    xmlns:xsl="http://www.w3.org/1999/XSL/Transform" version="1.1">

    <xsl:param name="database" select="'jdbc:odbc:planets'"/>
    <xsl:param name="user"/>
    <xsl:param name="password"/>

    <xsl:template match="PLANETS">
        <sql:connect database="{$database}" user="{$user}" password="{$password}"
        driver="sun.jdbc.odbc.JdbcOdbcDriver" xsl:extension-element-prefixes="sql"/>
        <xsl:apply-templates select="PLANET"/>
    </xsl:template>
        .
        .
        .
```

At this point, then, I'm connected to the planets data source. I want to insert the data from each <PLANET> element into the database, so I construct a new template that matches <PLANET> elements and uses the Saxon <sql:insert> element to insert data into the planets table of the database:

```
<xsl:stylesheet
    xmlns:sql="http://icl.com/saxon/extensions/com.icl.saxon.sql.SQLElementFactory"
    xmlns:xsl="http://www.w3.org/1999/XSL/Transform" version="1.1">
```

```
        .
        .
        .
    <xsl:template match="PLANETS">
        <sql:connect database="{$database}" user="{$user}" password="{$password}"
        driver="sun.jdbc.odbc.JdbcOdbcDriver" xsl:extension-element-prefixes="sql"/>
        <xsl:apply-templates select="PLANET"/>
    </xsl:template>

    <xsl:template match="PLANET">
        <sql:insert table="planets" xsl:extension-element-prefixes="sql">
        .
        .
        .
        </sql:insert>
    </xsl:template>

</xsl:stylesheet>
```

The <sql:insert> element inserts a new record into the database. To specify the new data for the fields of this record, you use the <sql:column> element, setting the name attribute of this element to the name of the column in which the data is to be stored, and setting the select attribute to the data you want to store, as follows:

```
<xsl:stylesheet
    xmlns:sql="http://icl.com/saxon/extensions/com.icl.saxon.sql.SQLElementFactory"
    xmlns:xsl="http://www.w3.org/1999/XSL/Transform" version="1.1">
        .
        .
        .
    <xsl:template match="PLANET">
        <sql:insert table="planets" xsl:extension-element-prefixes="sql">
            <sql:column name="Name" select="NAME"/>
            <sql:column name="Mass" select="MASS"/>
            <sql:column name="Radius" select="RADIUS"/>
            <sql:column name="Day" select="DAY"/>
        </sql:insert>
    </xsl:template>

</xsl:stylesheet>
```

Ideally, this would be all you'd need, but with the most recent Access driver, Saxon doesn't appear to flush its data buffers at the end of the operation. This means that the data for the last planet in planets.xml, Earth, isn't sent to the database. To flush the data buffers, I call the <PLANET> template explicitly as a named template, this time using <sql:insert> with a dummy set of data:

Listing 10.11 **Working with a SQL-Based Database**

```
<xsl:stylesheet
    xmlns:sql="http://icl.com/saxon/extensions/com.icl.saxon.sql.SQLElementFactory"
    xmlns:xsl="http://www.w3.org/1999/XSL/Transform" version="1.1">

    <xsl:param name="database" select="'jdbc:odbc:planets'"/>
    <xsl:param name="user"/>
    <xsl:param name="password"/>

    <xsl:template match="PLANETS">
        <sql:connect database="{$database}" user="{$user}" password="{$password}"
        driver="sun.jdbc.odbc.JdbcOdbcDriver" xsl:extension-element-prefixes="sql"/>
        <xsl:apply-templates select="PLANET"/>
        <xsl:call-template name="writer"/>
    </xsl:template>

    <xsl:template match="PLANET" name="writer">
        <xsl:choose>
            <xsl:when test="NAME">
                <sql:insert table="planets" xsl:extension-element-prefixes="sql">
                    <sql:column name="Name" select="NAME"/>
                    <sql:column name="Mass" select="MASS"/>
                    <sql:column name="Radius" select="RADIUS"/>
                    <sql:column name="Day" select="DAY"/>
                </sql:insert>
            </xsl:when>
            <xsl:otherwise>
                <sql:insert table="planets" xsl:extension-element-prefixes="sql">
                    <sql:column name="Name" select="' '"/>
                    <sql:column name="Mass" select="' '"/>
                    <sql:column name="Radius" select="' '"/>
                    <sql:column name="Day" select="' '"/>
                </sql:insert>
            </xsl:otherwise>
        </xsl:choose>
    </xsl:template>

</xsl:stylesheet>
```

This stylesheet correctly adds three records to the planets.mdb database: one new record for each planet. As I mentioned, you can't use the pre-built saxon.exe executable file here; instead, you can use the Saxon Java class `com.icl.saxon.StyleSheet`. First, I set the `classpath` to include saxon.jar:

```
C:\>set classpath=.;c:\saxon\saxon.jar
```

Then I can pass `com.icl.saxon.StyleSheet` planets.xml and the XSL stylesheet you saw in Listing 10.11:

```
C:\>java com.icl.saxon.StyleSheet planets.xml saxonsql.xsl
```

And that's all it takes—the planetary data is inserted into planets.mdb. You can see the results of this stylesheet in Figure 10.4, where I've opened planets.mdb in Microsoft Access. Now we've seen an XML-to-SQL database transformation.

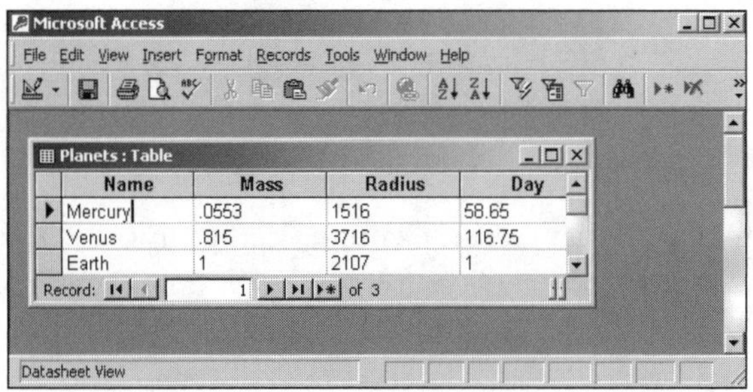

Figure 10.4 Using Saxon's SQL extensions.

Another aspect of XSLT for which you use programming is supporting XSLT on servers. To give you a taste of what's possible, I next transform planets.xml with planets.xsl using Microsoft's Active Server Pages (ASP), Sun's Java Server Pages (JSP), and Java servlets, all of which run on Web servers. They return the result document back to the user's browser.

There's no space here to cover how these technologies work in depth, but if you're unfamiliar with them and want more information, you can find the details online (as always, these URLs are subject to change):

- **ASP.** `http://msdn.microsoft.com/workshop/c-frame.htm#/workshop/server/Default.asp` (Microsoft's ASP tutorial and documentation)
- **JSP.** `http://java.sun.com/products/jsp/` (Sun's main JSP page)
- **Servlets.** `http://java.sun.com/products/servlet/` (Sun's main Servlet page)

Using XSLT with Active Server Pages

You run Active Server Pages on Microsoft Windows NT or 2000 servers, so I use Microsoft's MSXML processor on the server in this example to transform planets.xml, using planets.xsl, and return the result as an HTML document.

This is the same transformation you've now seen many times, creating an HTML table of planetary data, but this time, the transformation is done on a Web server and the user can then see that document when the server sends it. In the beginning of the ASP script, I set the MIME content-type of the result document to "text/html" so it will be treated as HTML:

```
<%@LANGUAGE="VBScript"%>

<%
    Response.ContentType = "text/html"
        .
        .
        .
```

Next, much as in the JavaScript examples earlier in this chapter, I create two MSXML document objects, one for the XML document and one for the XSL document:

```
<%@LANGUAGE="VBScript"%>

<%
    Response.ContentType = "text/html"

    Dim docXML
    Dim docXSL

    Set docXML = Server.CreateObject("MSXML2.DOMDocument.3.0")
    Set docXSL = Server.CreateObject("MSXML2.DOMDocument.3.0")
        .
        .
        .
```

Loading these documents on the server is much like loading them with JavaScript, except here you use the `Server` object's `MapPath` method to get the correct file paths. In this case, I place both planets.xml and planets.xsl in the same directory as the ASP script, so here's how I load these documents in:

```
<%@LANGUAGE="VBScript"%>

<%
    Response.ContentType = "text/html"

    Dim docXML
    Dim docXSL

    Set docXML = Server.CreateObject("MSXML2.DOMDocument.3.0")
```

```
    Set docXSL = Server.CreateObject("MSXML2.DOMDocument.3.0")

    docXML.ValidateOnParse = True
    docXSL.ValidateOnParse = True

    docXML.load Server.MapPath("planets.xml")
    docXSL.load Server.MapPath("planets.xsl")
        .
        .
        .
```

All that's left now is to use the `transformNode` method (as I did in JavaScript earlier) to perform the XSLT transformation and to display the results:

Listing 10.12 **Server-Based XSLT Using ASP**

```
<%@LANGUAGE="VBScript"%>

<%
    Response.ContentType = "text/html"

    Dim docXML
    Dim docXSL

    Set docXML = Server.CreateObject("MSXML2.DOMDocument.3.0")
    Set docXSL = Server.CreateObject("MSXML2.DOMDocument.3.0")

    docXML.ValidateOnParse = True
    docXSL.ValidateOnParse = True

    docXML.load Server.MapPath("planets.xml")
    docXSL.load Server.MapPath("planets.xsl")

    strOutput = docXML.transformNode(docXSL)

    Response.Write strOutput
%>
```

You can see the result of this ASP transformation in Figure 10.5. Now you've learned now to perform XSLT transformations on Web servers.

Here's one thing to note: Now that you're performing XSLT transformations on the server, you may want to think about optimizing your transformations depending on the client, because you wouldn't necessarily want to try to create the same display in a palmtop that you would in a desktop's browser. For example, you could customize the response from an ASP server script as follows, where I'm checking the server variable `http_user_agent`, to check whether the client is using the Internet Explorer:

```
<%@LANGUAGE="VBScript"%>

<%
Response.ContentType = "text/html"

If instr(request.servervariables("http_user_agent"), "MSIE") = 0 then
    Response.Write "Sorry, not optimized for your device."
    Response.End
End If
        .
        .
        .
```

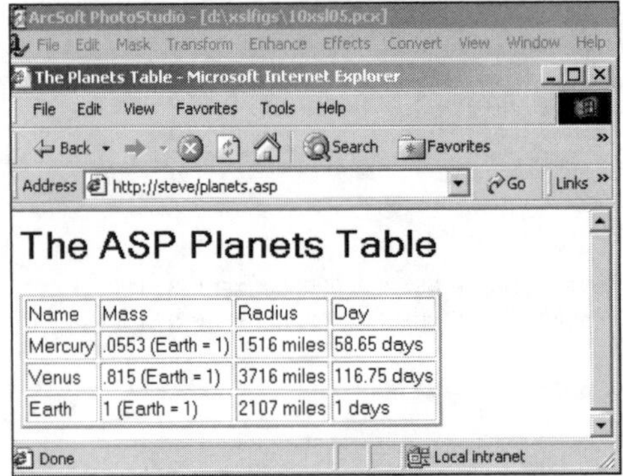

Figure 10.5 Using XSLT with ASP.

> **Separating Data and Presentation**
> One of the strongest recent trends is to separate data and the code you use for presenting that data. This example shows why that can be a good idea: You can have one set of data and transform it on the fly for various devices.

Using XSLT with Java Server Pages

I used Microsoft's MSXML processor with Active Server Pages, but Java Server Pages need not run on Windows server platforms, so I don't use MSXML with JSP. Instead, I use Xalan's Java API to perform the XSLT transformation and send the results to the client's browser.

For example, I can use Xalan to create planets.html as a temporary document on the server (this code assumes planets.xml and planets.xsl are in the same directory as the JSP script) this way:

```
<%@ page errorPage="error.jsp" language="java"
    contentType="text/html" import="org.apache.xalan.xslt.*;java.io.*" %>

    <%
        try
        {
            XSLTProcessor processor = XSLTProcessorFactory.getProcessor();
            processor.process(new XSLTInputSource("planets.xml"),
                new XSLTInputSource("planets.xsl"),
                new XSLTResultTarget("planets.html"));
        }
        catch(Exception e) {}
        .
        .
        .
```

Then all I have to do is to open that document and send it back to the client:

Listing 10.13 **Server-Based XSLT Using JSP**

```
<%@ page errorPage="error.jsp" language="java"
    contentType="text/html" import="org.apache.xalan.xslt.*;java.io.*" %>

    <%
        try
        {
            XSLTProcessor processor = XSLTProcessorFactory.getProcessor();
            processor.process(new XSLTInputSource("planets.xml"),
                new XSLTInputSource("planets.xsl"),
                new XSLTResultTarget("planets.html"));
        }
        catch(Exception e) {}

        FileReader filereader = new FileReader("planets.html");
        BufferedReader bufferedreader = new BufferedReader(filereader);
        String instring;

        while((instring = bufferedreader.readLine()) != null) { %>
            <%= instring %>
    <% }

    filereader.close();
    pw.close();

%>
```

That's all it takes. You can see the results of this JSP script in Figure 10.6.

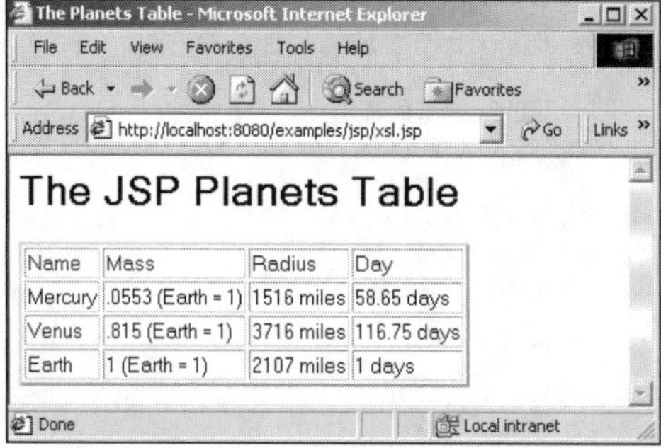

Figure 10.6 Using XSLT with JSP.

Using XSLT with Java Servlets

You can also use Java servlets to perform XSLT transformations on servers. Although many XSLT processors provide their own versions of servlets, I've found it much easier to simply use Xalan or other XSLT processors to perform the transformation myself and serve the result document back to the client.

In the following example, I use Xalan to transform planets.xml into the temporary file planets.html using planets.xsl in a servlet:

```
import java.net.*;
import java.sql.*;
import java.awt.*;
import java.awt.event.*;
import java.io.*;
import javax.servlet.*;
import org.apache.xalan.xslt.*;

public class xslservlet extends GenericServlet
{

    public void service(ServletRequest request, ServletResponse response)
        throws ServletException, IOException
    {
        try
        {
            XSLTProcessor processor = XSLTProcessorFactory.getProcessor();
            processor.process(new XSLTInputSource("planets.xml"),
                new XSLTInputSource("planets.xsl"),
                new XSLTResultTarget("planets.html"));
         }
         catch(Exception e) {}
        .
        .
        .
```

All that remains is to send the HTML document back to the client, which looks like this:

Listing 10.14 **Using Server-Based XSLT with Java Servlets**

```
import java.net.*;
import java.sql.*;
import java.awt.*;
import java.awt.event.*;
import java.io.*;
import javax.servlet.*;
import org.apache.xalan.xslt.*;

public class xslservlet extends GenericServlet
{

    public void service(ServletRequest request, ServletResponse response)
        throws ServletException, IOException
    {
        response.setContentType("text/html");

        PrintWriter pw = response.getWriter();

        try
        {
            XSLTProcessor processor = XSLTProcessorFactory.getProcessor();
            processor.process(new XSLTInputSource("planets.xml"),
                new XSLTInputSource("planets.xsl"),
                new XSLTResultTarget("planets.html"));
         }
         catch(Exception e) {}

        FileReader filereader = new FileReader("planets.html");
        BufferedReader bufferedreader = new BufferedReader(filereader);
        String instring;

        while((instring = bufferedreader.readLine()) != null) {
            pw.println(instring);
        }

        filereader.close();
        pw.close();
  }
}
```

That's all there is to it; you can see the result in Figure 10.7, which shows the HTML result as served from a servlet.

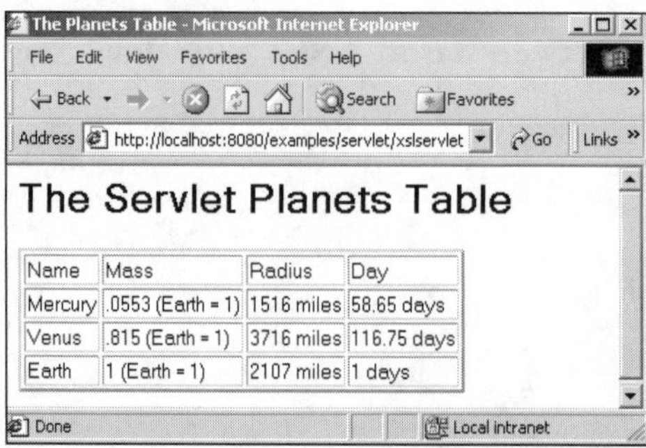

Figure 10.7 Using XSLT with Java servlets.

That's it for this chapter on using XSLT processor APIs in programming code. You've seen quite a bit here: how to interface to XSLT processor APIs using JavaScript and Java for the MSXML, Xalan, XT, Saxon, and Oracle XSLT processors, as well as examples of how to perform XSLT transformations on Web servers using ASP, JSP, and Java servlets.

The next chapter turns to what XSLT was originally created for—using it with XSL-FO.

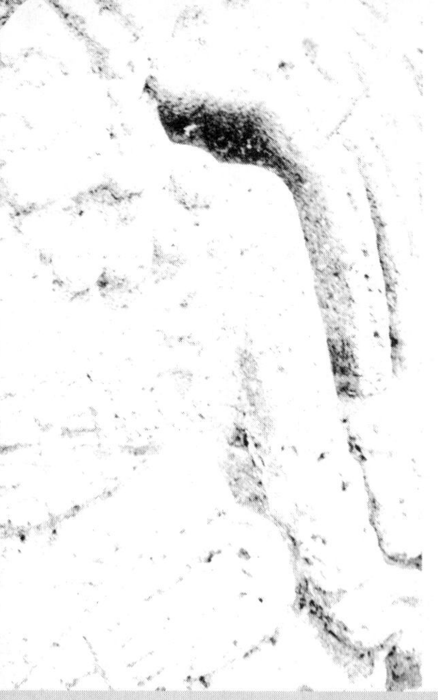

11 Using XSLT to Create XSL-FO Documents: Text and Tables

IN THIS BOOK, YOU'VE SEEN XSLT TRANSFORMATIONS from XML to XML, to HTML, to XHTML, to RTF, to plain text, to JavaScript, and even to SQL-based databases. In this and the next chapter, you're going to see a new transformation, the type that XSLT was created for: XML transformations to documents that use XSL formatting objects (XSL-FO documents).

This transformation was XSLT's original job. As you know, XSLT grew from the XSL specification to make it easier to work with formatting objects. Here, you'll see how to use XSLT to transform XML documents into those that use formatting objects. Note that XSL-FO is much larger than XSLT—I can provide only an introduction to the subject here.

XSL Formatting

As discussed in Chapter 1, XSLT and XSL-FO together make up the XSL specification. Currently, version 1.0 of that specification has candidate recommendation status, and you'll find the latest version at `www.w3.org/TR/xsl`.

The XSL-FO part of XSL enables you to format the exact appearance of a document, down to the last millimeter. For example, you can select what font to use, what font size, where on a page to position text, what its color should be, whether it should be underlined, and so on. In fact, using XSL-FO is much like creating RTF documents, with some extras—for example, you can create links in XSL-FO that enable you to navigate between documents.

As you can imagine, if you've ever seen the large number of codes RTF uses to format a document, XSL-FO is a complex and very large specification. (This is why XSLT was introduced to make it easier to work with.) So, there's only room for an introduction to the topic here. In fact, no software implements the entire specification yet, so relatively few people use XSL-FO beyond the what is covered in this and the next chapter. The following list includes some XSL-FO processors that are available:

- **fop**. `http://xml.apache.org/fop`. This popular processor converts XSL-FO to PDF. Developed by James Tauber at the Apache Software Foundation (`http://xml.apache.org/`).
- **PassiveTeX**. `http://users.ox.ac.uk/~rahtz/passivetex/`. This processor is actually a library of TeX macros that provides an environment for testing XSL-FO.
- **REXP**. `www.esng.dibe.unige.it/REXP`. This early version of an XSL-FO processor is based on fop. Creates PDF files.
- **Unicorn**. `www.unicorn-enterprises.com`. This processor (named UFO) is free and runs on Windows NT 4.0 and Windows 95.
- **XEP**. `www.renderx.com/FO2PDF.html`. () This processor, which used to be called FOP2PDF, converts XSL-FO documents to PDF format.
- **XSL Formatter**. `www.antennahouse.com/xslformatter.html`. An XSL-FO processor for Windows. A free evaluation version is available.

My personal favorite, and currently the most popular XSL-FO processor, is fop. I use the latest version of fop, version 0.17, in this and the next chapter. The Apache Software Foundation, the same group that creates Xalan, maintains the fop processor, which converts XSL-FO documents to Portable Data Format (PDF) documents, which you can view with the Adobe Acrobat PDF reader. You can get the Acrobat reader for free at `www.adobe.com/products/acrobat/readermain.html`. You can get the latest version of fop itself for free at `http://xml.apache.org/fop` (currently, you just click the download link in that page).

The fop processor works on XSL-FO documents, and in this and the next chapter, I use XSLT to transform XML documents to XSL-FO format and then use fop to convert XSL-FO documents to PDF format. (Using XSL-FO does *not* automatically mean creating PDF documents—there are other formats around—XSL-FO simply enables you to format data, and how that formatted data is presented is up to the application you're using). To work with XSL-FO, you have to understand the available XSL formatting objects.

The XSL-FO Formatting Objects

In XSLT documents, you use elements such as `<xsl:stylesheet>`, `<xsl:output>`, and so on:

```
<?xml version="1.0" encoding="UTF-8"?>
<xsl:stylesheet version="1.0"
xmlns:xsl="http://www.w3.org/1999/XSL/Transform">
    <xsl:output method="xml"/>
    <xsl:template match="*">
        <xsl:copy>
            <xsl:apply-templates/>
            .
            .
            .
```

An XSL-FO document is written in much the same way, but rather than use XSLT elements such as `<xsl:stylesheet>`, you use elements based on the XSL-FO formatting objects. There are 56 such formatting objects, such as the `root` object, which creates the root node of an XSL-FO document, or the `block` object, which creates a block region (a rectangular display area, much like the one an `<H1>` header creates in an HTML document).

XSL formatting objects have their own namespace, "http://www.w3.org/1999/XSL/Format", and the namespace prefix people use for that namespace is almost invariably `fo`, for formatting objects. (This convention was adopted because that's the namespace prefix used in the XSL specification.) To write XSL-FO documents, you use elements that correspond to the various XSL-FO objects, such as `<fo:root>` for the root element, `<fo:block>` to create a display block, and so on. For example, here's how you might start an XSL-FO document—note that I declare the "fo" namespace prefix to correspond to the XSL-FO namespace:

```
<?xml version="1.0" encoding="UTF-8"?>
<fo:root xmlns:fo="http://www.w3.org/1999/XSL/Format">

    <fo:layout-master-set>
        <fo:simple-page-master margin-right="20mm" margin-left="20mm"
            margin-bottom="10mm" margin-top="10mm" page-width="300mm"
            page-height="400mm" master-name="page">

            <fo:region-body margin-right="0mm" margin-left="0mm"
                margin-bottom="10mm" margin-top="0mm"/>
        .
        .
        .
```

Note that XSL-FO documents are XML documents, which means you can use standard XML comments, `<!-- like this one -->`, throughout. Note also that the elements `<fo:simple-page-master>` and `<fo:region-body>` have attributes such as `margin-right` and `page-height`. These attributes are called *properties* in XSL-FO, and there are a lot of them—about 240 as of this writing. For example, here's how I can create an XSL-FO block—a rectangular display area—that displays the text "Welcome to XSL formatting" in 36 point sans-serif font. I use the `<fo:block>` formatting object and the XSL-FO properties `font-family`, `line-height` (which specifies the height of the block), and `font-size` as follows:

```
<fo:block font-family="sans-serif" line-height="48pt" font-size="36pt">
    Welcome to XSL formatting
</fo:block>
```

In this section, I'll take a look at the XSL-FO objects, and in the next section, the XSL-FO properties that you can use with them. Using XSL-FO objects and properties, you can create XSL-FO documents, which are usually given the extension .fo. When you pass these documents to fop, it converts the document to .pdf format.

You can find all the XSL-FO formatting objects at `www.w3.org/TR/xsl/slice6.html`, along with a description of each. The following objects exist as of this writing, and you'll see many of them in action in this and the next chapter:

- `<fo:bidi-override>`. Overrides the default Unicode-bidirectionality algorithm direction. (This algorithm is used in mixed-language documents.)
- `<fo:block>`. Creates a display block, which is used for creating rectangular regions, such as you'd use for paragraphs, titles, headlines, figure and table captions, and so on.
- `<fo:block-container>`. Creates a container for blocks, which you can then position as you like in a document.
- `<fo:character>`. Represents a single character.
- `<fo:color-profile>`. Creates a color profile for a stylesheet, which you can then use with color functions (see `www.w3.org/TR/xsl/slice5.html#expr-color-functions` for more details).
- `<fo:conditional-page-master-reference>`. Specifies a page-master to be used when specified conditions are met.
- `<fo:declarations>`. Creates global declarations.
- `<fo:external-graphic>`. Adds a graphic to a document. (The graphics data resides outside the result document, but can be incorporated into PDF documents by processors like fop.)
- `<fo:float>`. Specifies that some content is formatted in a separate, floating area at the beginning of the page or placed to one side.

- `<fo:flow>`. Handles the text flow that is displayed in a document. Blocks an inline areas "flow" as they're placed in a document.
- `<fo:footnote>`. Specifies a footnote citation as well as the associated footnote.
- `<fo:footnote-body>`. Specifies the content of the footnote.
- `<fo:initial-property-set>`. Specifies the formatting properties for the initial line of a block.
- `<fo:inline>`. Creates an inline area. Inline areas are often used to format a specific part of the text in a block.
- `<fo:inline-container>`. Creates a container for inline objects, enabling you to handle them together.
- `<fo:instream-foreign-object>`. Used to insert an inline graphic or other object into a document.
- `<fo:layout-master-set>`. Specifies a wrapper for all the masters used in the document.
- `<fo:leader>`. Creates a row of a repeating character or pattern of characters that is used to separate two text formatting objects.
- `<fo:list-block>`. Creates a formatted list of the kind you'll see in the next chapter.
- `<fo:list-item>`. Specifies the label and the body of an item in a list.
- `<fo:list-item-body>`. Specifies the content of the body of an item in a list.
- `<fo:list-item-label>`. Specifies the content of the label of an item in a list.
- `<fo:marker>`. Used with `<fo:retrieve-marker>` to create headers or footers on the fly.
- `<fo:multi-case>`. Specifies objects that the parent `<fo:multi-switch>` can show or hide.
- `<fo:multi-properties>`. Enables you to switch between two or more property sets.
- `<fo:multi-property-set>`. Specifies an alternative set of properties.
- `<fo:multi-switch>`. Switches between two or more sub-trees of formatting objects.
- `<fo:multi-toggle>`. Used inside an `<fo:multi-case>` element to switch to another `<fo:multi-case>`.
- `<fo:page-number>`. Indicates the current page number.
- `<fo:page-number-citation>`. References the page number for the page containing a given formatting object.

- `<fo:page-sequence>`. Specifies how to create a sequence of pages within a document.
- `<fo:page-sequence-master>`. Contains sequences of page masters that are used to generate sequences of pages.
- `<fo:region-after>`. Indicates the region located after an `<fo:region-body>` region.
- `<fo:region-before>`. Indicates the region before a `<fo:region-body>` region.
- `<fo:region-body>`. Indicates the region in the center of an `<fo:simple-page-master>`.
- `<fo:region-end>`. Indicates the region at the end of a `<fo:region-body>` region.
- `<fo:region-start>`. Indicates the region starting a `<fo:region-body>` region.
- `<fo:repeatable-page-master-alternatives>`. Specifies repeated instances of a set of alternative page masters.
- `<fo:repeatable-page-master-reference>`. Indicates a sub-sequence of repeated instances of a single page-master.
- `<fo:retrieve-marker>`. Used with `<fo:marker>` to create headers or footers on the fly.
- `<fo:root>`. The document node of an XSL-formatted document.
- `<fo:simple-link>`. Specifies the start location in a simple link.
- `<fo:simple-page-master>`. Specifies the geometry of a page, which may be divided into up to five regions.
- `<fo:single-page-master-reference>`. Indicates a sub-sequence made up of a single instance of a single page-master.
- `<fo:static-content>`. Contains a sequence of formatting objects to be displayed in one region or repeated in regions on one or more pages in a page sequence. Most often used for repeating headers and footers.
- `<fo:table>`. Creates a table. Encloses elements such as `<fo:table-column>` and `<fo:table-body>`.
- `<fo:table-and-caption>`. Encloses the data and caption of a table.
- `<fo:table-body>`. Specifies the content of the table body. Encloses elements such as `<fo:table-row>`.
- `<fo:table-caption>`. Specifies block-level formatting objects, which hold the caption for a table.
- `<fo:table-cell>`. Places data in table cells.
- `<fo:table-column>`. Specifies characteristics for table cells that have the same column.

- `<fo:table-footer>`. Specifies the content of the table footer.
- `<fo:table-header>`. Specifies the content of the table header.
- `<fo:table-row>`. Connects table cells into rows. Contains `<fo:table-cell>` elements.
- `<fo:title>`. Specifies the title of a document.
- `<fo:wrapper>`. Specifies properties for a group of formatting objects.

Each of these elements also supports one or more XSL-FO *formatting properties.*

The XSL-FO Formatting Properties

You use the XSL-FO formatting properties to customize the actions of the formatting objects that were listed in the preceding section, and you use formatting properties as element attributes in XSL-FO documents. For example, here's how I use formatting properties to set the font family, font size, and font weight of text in a block:

```
<fo:block color="blue" font-family="Times"
    font-size="36pt" font-weight="bold">
    Hello from XSL-FO!
</fo:block>
```

You can find the complete list of XSL-FO properties and their descriptions at `www.w3.org/TR/xsl/slice7.html`. Many of the XSL-FO properties are inherited from the specification for cascading stylesheets, version 2, CSS2, which you can find at `www.w3.org/TR/REC-CSS2`.

The following list includes some of the more common XSL-FO properties. You'll find the complete list of properties (and it's a long one) in Appendix B. Here's the syntax used in this list, following the XSL-FO specification:

- <> indicates units for values (see Table 11.1), or properties (such as <color>) that have already been defined.
- | indicates alternatives, only one of which may be used.
- || indicates options, one or more of which must be used, in any order.
- [] indicates group statements, evaluated much like mathematical statements.
- * means the preceding term occurs zero or more times.
- + means the preceding term occurs one or more times.
- ? means the preceding term is optional.
- {} surrounds pairs of numbers giving the minimum and maximum number of times a term may occur (as in {1, 4}).

Many of the XSL-FO properties indicate a specific format for values that you may assign to them, such as `<color>` or `<angle>`, and you'll find those formats and their meanings in Table 11.1.

Table 11.1 **Formats in the XSL-FO Specification**

Format	Means
`<absolute-size>`	Absolute font sizes; may be xx-small, x-small, small, medium, large, x-large, xx-large.
`<angle>`	Angles; may be deg, grad, or rad.
`<border-style>`	A box's border; may be none, dotted, dashed, solid, double, groove, ridge, inset, or outset.
`<border-width>`	Sets the width of a border; may be thin, medium, thick, or an explicit length.
`<color>`	Color; may be specified with a predefined color value or RGB triplet color value as you'd use in HTML, such as "FFFFFF" for white.
`<country-language>`	Set to a `<language>` value (see `<language>`).
`<family-name>`	The name of a font family, such as Arial, Times New Roman, or Courier.
`<frequency>`	Frequency values; units may be Hz or KHz.
`<generic-family>`	Generic names for fonts that you use as a last resort if the browser can't find a specific font. Examples are serif (browser should choose a serif font), sans-serif (browser should choose a sans-serif family), and monospace (browser should choose a monospace font).
`<generic-voice>`	Aural voices; may be male, female, or child.
`<integer>`	Standard integer values.
`<keep>`	A context-dependant property you set to Auto for no keep-together constraints or Always for strict keep-together constraints. See the XSL specification for more information.
`<language>`	A language specifier that conforms to the RFC1766 specification (which you can find at `www.w3.org/TR/xsl/sliceD.html#RFC1766`).
`<length>`	Length; may start with a + or -, followed by a number, which may include a decimal point, followed by a unit identifier, which may be em (font size of the relevant font), ex (the x-height of the font), px (pixels as specified relative to the viewing device), pt (points, 1/72nds of an inch), in (inches), cm (centimeters), mm (millimeters), or pc (picas, 1/6th of an inch).

Format	Means
`<length-bp-ip-direction>`	Specifies the distance that separates adjacent cell borders in the row-stacking-direction. See www.w3.org/TR/xsl/slice7.html for more details.
`<length-conditional>`	A compound value specifying the width and any conditionality of the border for the before-edge. See www.w3.org/TR/xsl/slice7.html#pr-section for more details.
`<length-range>`	Specifies a length range, as defined in the XSL specification.
`<margin-width>`	Can be a `<length>`, `<percentage>`, or auto. How the auto value works is dependant on context; see www.w3.org/TR/REC-CSS2/visudet.html#Computing_widths_and_margins for more information.
`<number>`	A number; may include a sign and a decimal point.
`<padding-width>`	Set to a `<length>` value.
`<percentage>`	A number, which may include a sign, followed by a percentage sign (%).
`<relative-size>`	A font size relative to the parent element, may be either Larger or Smaller.
`<shape>`	Currently may only specify a rectangle, as in `rect(<top> <right> <bottom> <left>)`.
`<space>`	Specifies the minimum, optimum, and maximum values for a space. See www.w3.org/TR/xsl/slice4.html#spacecond for more information.
`<specific-voice>`	Specifies a specific voice. See www.w3.org/TR/REC-CSS2/aural.html#propdef-voice-family for more information.
`<time>`	Time units, specified as a number followed immediately by ms (for milliseconds) or s (for seconds).
`<uri-specification>`	Uniform Resource Indicator (URI); the Web address of a page element, such as an image.

Also, note that XSL-FO properties, like CSS2 properties, may be set to the value "inherit", which means the value of the property should be inherited from its parent element.

The following list includes the more common XSL-FO properties. For the complete list, refer to Appendix B.

- `absolute-position`. Specifies whether an item's position is absolute. Set to auto | absolute | fixed | inherit.
- `background`. A shorthand property for setting the individual background properties (background-color, background-image, background-repeat,

background-attachment and background-position) all at once. Set to [<background-color> || <background-image> || <background-repeat> || <background-attachment> || <background-position>]] | inherit.

- `background-attachment`. Specifies whether the background scrolls. Set to scroll | fixed | inherit.
- `background-color`. Specifies the background color of an element. Set to <color> | transparent | inherit.
- `background-image`. Specifies the background image of an element. Set to <uri-specification> | none | inherit.
- `background-repeat`. Specifies whether the background image is tiled, and if so, how. Set to repeat | repeat-x | repeat-y | no-repeat | inherit.
- `border`. A shorthand property for setting the same width, color, and style for all four borders (top, bottom, left, and right) of a box. Set to [<border-width> || <border-style> || <color>] | inherit.
- `border-after-color`. Specifies the color of the border on the after-edge of region. Set to <color> | inherit.
- `border-after-style`. Specifies the border style for the after edge. Set to <border-style> | inherit.
- `border-after-width`. Specifies the border width for the after edge. Set to <border-width> | <length-conditional> | inherit.
- `border-before-color`. Specifies the color of the border on a before edge. Set to <color> | inherit.
- `border-before-style`. Specifies the border style for a before edge. Set to <border-style> | inherit.
- `border-before-width`. Specifies the border width for a before edge. Set to <border-width> | <length-conditional> | inherit.
- `border-bottom`. A shorthand property for setting the width, style, and color of the bottom border of a block area or inline area. Set to [<border-top-width> || <border-style> || <color>] | inherit.
- `border-bottom-color`. Specifies the border color for a bottom edge. Set to <color> | inherit.
- `border-bottom-style`. Specifies the border style for a bottom edge. Set to <border-style> | inherit.
- `border-bottom-width`. Specifies the border width for a bottom edge. Set to <border-width> | inherit.
- `border-collapse`. Specifies a table's border model. Set to collapse | separate | inherit.

- `border-color`. Specifies the color of all four borders at once. Set to <color>{1,4} | transparent | inherit.
- `border-end-color`. Specifies the color of the border on an end edge. Set to <color> | inherit.
- `border-end-style`. Specifies the border style for an end edge. Set to <border-style> | inherit.
- `border-end-width`. Specifies the border width for an end edge. Set to <border-width> | <length-conditional> | inherit.
- `border-left`. A shorthand property for setting the width, style, and color of the left border all at once. Set to [<border-top-width> || <border-style> || <color>] | inherit.
- `border-left-color`. Specifies the border color for a left edge. Set to <color> | inherit.
- `border-left-style`. Specifies the border style for a left edge. Set to <border-style> | inherit.
- `border-left-width`. Specifies the border width for a left edge. Set to <border-width> | inherit.
- `border-right`. A shorthand property for setting the width, style, and color of a right border all at once. Set to [<border-top-width> || <border-style> || <color>] | inherit.
- `border-right-color`. Specifies the border color for a right edge. Set to <color> | inherit.
- `border-right-style`. Specifies the border style for a right edge. Set to <border-style> | inherit.
- `border-right-width`. Specifies the border width for a right edge. Set to <border-width> | inherit.
- `border-spacing`. Specifies the distance that separates adjacent cell borders. Set to <length> <length>? | inherit.
- `border-start-color`. Specifies the color of the border on a start edge. Set to <color>.
- `border-start-style`. Specifies the border style for the starting edge. Set to <border-style> | inherit.
- `border-start-width`. Specifies the border width for the starting edge. Set to <border-width> | <length-conditional> | inherit.
- `border-style`. Sets the style of the four borders. Set to <border-style>{1,4} | inherit.

- `border-top`. A shorthand property for setting the width, style, and color of the top border of a block area or inline area all at once. Set to [<border-top-width> || <border-style> || <color>] | inherit.
- `border-top-color`. Specifies the color of the border on a top edge. Set to <color> | inherit.
- `border-top-style`. Specifies the line style of a box's border (solid, double, dashed, and so on).
- `border-top-width`. Sets the width of the top border. Set to <border-width> | inherit.
- `border-width`. A shorthand property for setting `border-top-width`, `border-right-width`, `border-bottom-width`, and `border-left-width` all at once. Set to <border-width>{1,4} | inherit.
- `bottom`. Specifies how far a box's bottom content edge is offset above the bottom of the box's containing block. Set to <length> | <percentage> | auto | inherit.
- `character`. Specifies the Unicode character to be inserted. Set to <character>.
- `color`. Specifies the foreground color of an element's text. Set to <color> | inherit.
- `column-count`. Specifies the number of columns in a region. Set to <number> | inherit.
- `column-number`. Sets the column number for table cells. Set to <number>.
- `column-width`. Specifies the width of an object such as an external graphic. Set to auto | scale-to-fit | <length> | <percentage> | inherit.
- `float`. Specifies whether a box should float to the left, right, or not at all. Set to before | start | end | left | right | none | inherit.
- `flow-name`. Sets a flow's name. Set to <name>.
- `font`. A shorthand property for setting `font-style`, `font-variant`, `font-weight`, `font-size`, `line-height`, and `font-family` all at once. Set to [[<font-style> || <font-variant> || <font-weight>]? <font-size> [/ <line-height>]? <font-family>] | caption | icon | menu | message-box | small-caption | status-bar | inherit.
- `font-family`. Specifies a list of font family names and/or generic family names in order of preference. Set to [[<family-name> | <generic-family>],]* [<family-name> | <generic-family>] | inherit.
- `font-size`. Sets the font size. Set to <absolute-size> | <relative-size> | <length> | <percentage> | inherit.

- `font-style`. Sets the font's style. Set to normal | italic | oblique | backslant | inherit.
- `font-variant`. Selects bicameral fonts. Set to normal | small-caps | inherit
- `font-weight`. Sets the font weight. Set to normal | bold | bolder | lighter | 100 | 200 | 300 | 400 | 500 | 600 | 700 | 800 | 900 | inherit.
- `format`. An XSLT format. Set to <string>.
- `grouping-separator`. An XSLT format grouping separator. Set to <character>.
- `grouping-size`. The XSLT format grouping size. Set to <number>.
- `height`. Specifies the content height of boxes generated by block-level and replaced elements. Set to <length> | <percentage> | auto | inherit.
- `initial-page-number`. Sets the initial page number. Set to auto | auto-odd | auto-even | <number> | inherit.
- `left`. Specifies how far a box's left content edge is offset to the right of the left edge of a containing block. Set to: <length> | <percentage> | auto | inherit.
- `linefeed-treatment`. Specifies the treatment of linefeeds. Set to ignore | preserve | treat-as-space | treat-as-zero-width-space | inherit.
- `line-height`. Specifies the minimal height of each generated inline box. Set to normal | <length> | <number> | <percentage> | <space> | inherit.
- `margin`. A shorthand property for setting margin-top, margin-right, margin-bottom, and margin-left all at once. Set to <margin-width>{1,4} | inherit.
- `margin-bottom`. Sets the bottom margin of a box. Set to <margin-width> | inherit.
- `margin-left`. Sets the left margin of a box. Set to <margin-width> | inherit.
- `margin-right`. Sets the right margin of a box. Set to <margin-width> | inherit.
- `margin-top`. Sets the top margin of a box. Set to <margin-width> | inherit.
- `master-name`. Sets or selects a master. Set to <name>.
- `number-columns-spanned`. Sets the number of columns spanned by a table cell. Set to <number>.
- `number-rows-spanned`. Sets the number of rows spanned by a table cell. Set to <number>.
- `page-break-after`. Same as the CSS2 property of the same name. Set to auto | always | avoid | left | right | inherit.
- `page-break-before`. Same as the CSS2 property of the same name. Set to auto | always | avoid | left | right | inherit.

- `page-height`. Sets the page height. Set to auto | indefinite | <length> | inherit.
- `page-width`. Sets the page width. Set to auto | indefinite | <length> | inherit.
- `position`. Specifies the positioning scheme to be used. Set to static | relative | absolute | fixed | inherit.
- `relative-position`. Same as the CSS2 property of the same name. Set to static | relative | inherit.
- `right`. Specifies how far a content edge is offset to the left of the right edge of the containing block. Set to <length> | <percentage> | auto | inherit.
- `score-spaces`. Specifies whether the text-decoration property shall be applied to spaces. Set to true | false | inherit.
- `space-treatment`. Specifies the treatment of space and other whitespace characters except for linefeeds. Set to ignore | preserve | ignore-if-before-linefeed | ignore-if-after-linefeed | ignore-if-surrounding-linefeed | inherit.
- `span`. Specifies whether a block-level object should be placed in the current column or should span all columns of a multi-column region. Set to none | all | inherit.
- `src`. Specifies the URI reference that is to be used to locate an external resource. Set to <uri-specification> | inherit.
- `start-indent`. Specifies the distance from the start edge of the content rectangle of the containing reference area to the start edge of the content rectangle of that block area. Set to <length> | inherit.
- `starts-row`. Specifies whether this cell starts a row. Set to true | false.
- `text-align`. Specifies how inline content of a block is aligned. Set to start | center | end | justify | inside | outside | left | right | <string> | inherit.
- `text-decoration`. Specifies decorations that are added to the text of an element. Set to none | [[underline | no-underline] || [overline | no-overline] || [line-through | no-line-through] || [blink | no-blink]] | inherit.
- `text-indent`. Specifies the indentation of the first line of text in a block. Set to <length> | <percentage> | inherit.
- `text-shadow`. Specifies a comma-separated list of shadow effects to be applied to the text of the element. Set to none | [<color> || <length> <length> <length>? ,]* [<color> || <length> <length> <length>?] | inherit.

- `top`. Specifies how far a content edge is offset below the top edge of the containing block. Set to <length> | <percentage> | auto | inherit.
- `vertical-align`. Specifies vertical positioning. Set to baseline | middle | sub | super | text-top | text-bottom | <percentage> | <length> | top | bottom | inherit.
- `visibility`. Specifies whether the boxes generated by an element are rendered or not. Set to visible | hidden | collapse | inherit.
- `white-space`. Specifies how whitespace inside the element is handled. Set to normal | pre | nowrap | inherit.
- `white-space-collapse`. Specifies the treatment of consecutive whitespace. Set to false | true | inherit.
- `width`. Specifies the content width of boxes generated by block level and replaced elements. Set to <length> | <percentage> | auto | inherit.
- `wrap-option`. Specifies how line-wrapping of the formatting object is to be handled. Set to no-wrap | wrap | inherit.

Not all properties apply to all XSL-FO objects. I'll list which properties apply to the objects I'm using explicitly in this and the next chapter. Note also that no XSL-FO processor implements all these properties yet.

Now that you have had an overview of the structure of XSL-FO, it's time to put it to work. I do that by working through an example in detail now.

Formatting an XML Document

To see how XSL-FO can format XML data, I'll use planets.xml:

Listing 11.1 **planets.xml**

```
<?xml version="1.0"?>
<?xml-stylesheet type="text/xml" href="planets.xsl"?>
<PLANETS>

  <PLANET COLOR="RED">
    <NAME>Mercury</NAME>
    <MASS UNITS="(Earth = 1)">.0553</MASS>
    <DAY UNITS="days">58.65</DAY>
    <RADIUS UNITS="miles">1516</RADIUS>
    <DENSITY UNITS="(Earth = 1)">.983</DENSITY>
    <DISTANCE UNITS="million miles">43.4</DISTANCE><!--At perihelion-->
  </PLANET>

  <PLANET COLOR="WHITE">
    <NAME>Venus</NAME>
```

continues ▸

Listing 11.1 **Continued**

```
    <MASS UNITS="(Earth = 1)">.815</MASS>
    <DAY UNITS="days">116.75</DAY>
    <RADIUS UNITS="miles">3716</RADIUS>
    <DENSITY UNITS="(Earth = 1)">.943</DENSITY>
    <DISTANCE UNITS="million miles">66.8</DISTANCE><!--At perihelion-->
  </PLANET>

  <PLANET COLOR="BLUE">
    <NAME>Earth</NAME>
    <MASS UNITS="(Earth = 1)">1</MASS>
    <DAY UNITS="days">1</DAY>
    <RADIUS UNITS="miles">2107</RADIUS>
    <DENSITY UNITS="(Earth = 1)">1</DENSITY>
    <DISTANCE UNITS="million miles">128.4</DISTANCE><!--At perihelion-->
  </PLANET>

</PLANETS>
```

In this first example, I create an XSLT stylesheet to format planets.xml into planets.fo, which uses formatting objects to specify fonts, styles, and colors. Then I use the fop processor to convert planets.fo into planets.pdf, which you can see in Figure 11.1.

As you see in Figure 11.1, I use some text formatting in this first example: setting the font, underlining text, italicizing text, even setting text color. (Although you can't see it in Figure 11.1, the title, "The Planets Table", is bright blue.)

The first step in creating Figure 11.1 is to use an XSLT stylesheet to transform planets.xml to planets.fo.

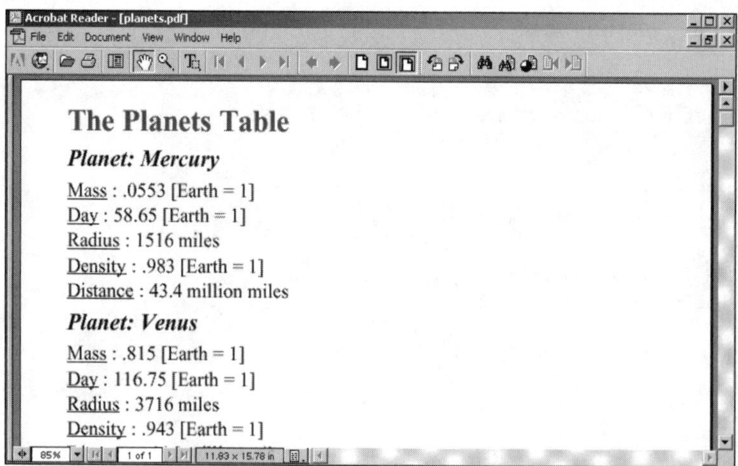

Figure 11.1 A PDF document created with formatting objects.

Using an XSLT Stylesheet to Transform to XSL-FO

In this chapter, I create the stylesheet I need to convert planets.xml into planets.fo. I construct this stylesheet step by step; for reference, here's what it is going to look like:

Listing 11.2 **planets.xsl**

```
<?xml version="1.0"?>
<xsl:stylesheet xmlns:xsl="http://www.w3.org/1999/XSL/Transform"
    xmlns:fo="http://www.w3.org/1999/XSL/Format"
    version="1.0">

    <xsl:template match="PLANETS">
        <fo:root xmlns:fo="http://www.w3.org/1999/XSL/Format">

            <fo:layout-master-set>
                <fo:simple-page-master master-name="page"
                    page-height="400mm" page-width="300mm"
                    margin-top="10mm" margin-bottom="10mm"
                    margin-left="20mm" margin-right="20mm">

                    <fo:region-body
                      margin-top="0mm" margin-bottom="10mm"
                      margin-left="0mm" margin-right="0mm"/>

                    <fo:region-after extent="10mm"/>
                </fo:simple-page-master>
             </fo:layout-master-set>

             <fo:page-sequence master-name="page">

                <fo:flow flow-name="xsl-region-body">
                    <fo:block font-weight="bold" font-size="36pt"
                        line-height="48pt" font-family="Times"
                        color="blue">
                        The Planets Table
                    </fo:block>
                    <xsl:apply-templates/>
                </fo:flow>
             </fo:page-sequence>

        </fo:root>
    </xsl:template>

    <xsl:template match="PLANET/NAME">
        <fo:block font-weight="bold" font-size="28pt"
            line-height="48pt" font-family="Times"
            font-style="italic">
            Planet:
            <xsl:apply-templates/>
```

continues ▸

Listing 11.2 **Continued**

```
        </fo:block>
    </xsl:template>

    <xsl:template match="PLANET/MASS">
        <fo:block font-size="24pt" line-height="32pt"
            font-family="Times">
            <fo:inline text-decoration="underline">
                Mass
            </fo:inline>:
            <xsl:apply-templates/>
            [Earth = 1]
        </fo:block>
    </xsl:template>

    <xsl:template match="PLANET/DAY">
        <fo:block font-size="24pt" line-height="32pt"
            font-family="Times">
            <fo:inline text-decoration="underline">
                Day
            </fo:inline>:
            <xsl:apply-templates/>
            [Earth = 1]
        </fo:block>
    </xsl:template>

    <xsl:template match="PLANET/RADIUS">
        <fo:block font-size="24pt" line-height="32pt"
            font-family="Times">
            <fo:inline text-decoration="underline">
                Radius
            </fo:inline>:
            <xsl:apply-templates/>
            miles
        </fo:block>
    </xsl:template>

    <xsl:template match="PLANET/DENSITY">
        <fo:block font-size="24pt" line-height="32pt"
            font-family="Times">
            <fo:inline text-decoration="underline">
                Density
            </fo:inline>:
            <xsl:apply-templates/>
            [Earth = 1]
        </fo:block>
    </xsl:template>

    <xsl:template match="PLANET/DISTANCE">
        <fo:block font-size="24pt" line-height="32pt"
```

```
            font-family="Times">
            <fo:inline text-decoration="underline">
                Distance
            </fo:inline>:
            <xsl:apply-templates/>
            million miles
        </fo:block>
    </xsl:template>

</xsl:stylesheet>
```

When you use this stylesheet to transform planets.xsl, you get planets.fo, which uses XSL-FO formatting objects to produce the display you saw in Figure 11.1. Here's what planets.fo looks like:

Listing 11.3 **planets.fo**

```
<?xml version="1.0" encoding="UTF-8"?>
<fo:root xmlns:fo="http://www.w3.org/1999/XSL/Format">

    <fo:layout-master-set>
        <fo:simple-page-master margin-right="20mm" margin-left="20mm"
            margin-bottom="10mm" margin-top="10mm" page-width="300mm"
            page-height="400mm" master-name="page">

            <fo:region-body margin-right="0mm" margin-left="0mm"
                margin-bottom="10mm" margin-top="0mm"/>

            <fo:region-after extent="10mm"/>

        </fo:simple-page-master>
    </fo:layout-master-set>

    <fo:page-sequence master-name="page">

        <fo:flow flow-name="xsl-region-body">

            <fo:block color="blue" font-family="Times"
                line-height="48pt" font-size="36pt" font-weight="bold">
                The Planets Table
            </fo:block>

            <fo:block font-style="italic" font-family="Times"
                line-height="48pt" font-size="28pt" font-weight="bold">
                Planet: Mercury
            </fo:block>

            <fo:block font-family="Times" line-height="32pt"
```

continues ▸

Listing 11.3 **Continued**

```
        font-size="24pt">
        <fo:inline text-decoration="underline">
            Mass
        </fo:inline>:
        .0553
        [Earth = 1]
    </fo:block>

    <fo:block font-family="Times" line-height="32pt"
        font-size="24pt">
        <fo:inline text-decoration="underline">
            Day
        </fo:inline>:
        58.65
        [Earth = 1]
    </fo:block>

    <fo:block font-family="Times" line-height="32pt"
        font-size="24pt">
        <fo:inline text-decoration="underline">
            Radius
        </fo:inline>:
        1516
        miles
    </fo:block>

    <fo:block font-family="Times" line-height="32pt"
        font-size="24pt">
        <fo:inline text-decoration="underline">
        Density
        </fo:inline>:
        .983
        [Earth = 1]
    </fo:block>

    <fo:block font-family="Times" line-height="32pt"
        font-size="24pt">
        <fo:inline text-decoration="underline">
            Distance
        </fo:inline>:
        43.4
        million miles
    </fo:block>

    <fo:block font-style="italic" font-family="Times"
        line-height="48pt"
        font-size="28pt" font-weight="bold">
        Planet:
        Venus
    </fo:block>
```

```
<fo:block font-family="Times" line-height="32pt"
    font-size="24pt">
    <fo:inline text-decoration="underline">
        Mass
    </fo:inline>:
    .815
    [Earth = 1]
</fo:block>

<fo:block font-family="Times" line-height="32pt"
    font-size="24pt">
    <fo:inline text-decoration="underline">
        Day
    </fo:inline>:
    116.75
    [Earth = 1]
</fo:block>

<fo:block font-family="Times" line-height="32pt"
    font-size="24pt">
    <fo:inline text-decoration="underline">
        Radius
    </fo:inline>:
    3716
    miles
</fo:block>

<fo:block font-family="Times" line-height="32pt"
    font-size="24pt">
    <fo:inline text-decoration="underline">
        Density
    </fo:inline>:
    .943
    [Earth = 1]
</fo:block>

<fo:block font-family="Times" line-height="32pt"
    font-size="24pt">
    <fo:inline text-decoration="underline">
        Distance
    </fo:inline>:
    66.8
    million miles
</fo:block>

<fo:block font-style="italic" font-family="Times"
    line-height="48pt"
    font-size="28pt" font-weight="bold">
    Planet:
    Earth
</fo:block>
```

continues ▸

Listing 11.3 **Continued**

```
            <fo:block font-family="Times" line-height="32pt"
                font-size="24pt">
                <fo:inline text-decoration="underline">
                    Mass
                </fo:inline>:
                1
                [Earth = 1]
            </fo:block>

            <fo:block font-family="Times" line-height="32pt"
                font-size="24pt">
                <fo:inline text-decoration="underline">
                    Day
                </fo:inline>:
                1
                [Earth = 1]
            </fo:block>

            <fo:block font-family="Times" line-height="32pt"
                font-size="24pt">
                <fo:inline text-decoration="underline">
                    Radius
                </fo:inline>:
                2107
                miles
            </fo:block>

            <fo:block font-family="Times" line-height="32pt"
                font-size="24pt">
                <fo:inline text-decoration="underline">
                    Density
                </fo:inline>:
                1
                [Earth = 1]
            </fo:block>

            <fo:block font-family="Times" line-height="32pt"
                font- size="24pt">
                <fo:inline text-decoration="underline">
                    Distance
                </fo:inline>:
                128.4
                million miles
            </fo:block>

        </fo:flow>

    </fo:page-sequence>

</fo:root>
```

To process planets.fo and create a formatted document, I'll use the Apache XML Project's fop. According to Apache:

> "FOP is the world's first print formatter driven by XSL formatting objects. It is a Java application that reads a formatting object tree and then turns it into a PDF document. The formatting object tree can be in the form of an XML document (output by an XSLT engine like XT or Xalan) or can be passed in memory as a DOM Document or (in the case of XT) SAX events."

I use fop 0.17, the current version as of this writing (new versions seem to come out just about monthly). You can get fop at `http://xml.apache.org/fop` for free. The fop download includes the three JAR files you'll need: fop.jar, w3c.jar, and xerces.jar, and all of them need to be in the `classpath` (add the correct paths to these JAR files as needed for your system), as follows:

```
C:\>set classpath=.;fop.jar;xerces.jar;w3c.jar
```

To convert planets.fo into planets.pdf, you can use the fop class `org.apache.fop.apps.CommandLine`, passing it the name of the input document, planets.fo, and the output document, planets.pdf, on the command line:

```
C:\>java org.apache.fop.apps.CommandLine planets.fo planets.pdf
```

And that's it; you can see the final result, planets.pdf, in the Adobe Acrobat reader if you refer back to Figure 11.1.

Now you've seen how the process works; it's time to get to the details and see how to create XSL-FO documents. To see this in detail, I'm going to take apart Listing 11.2, the XSLT stylesheet that creates planets.fo.

Writing XSL-FO Documents from Scratch

Note that it's not actually necessary to create an XSLT stylesheet to transform XSL documents to XSL-FO form. I could have written planets.fo in the form you see in Listing 11.3 from scratch—no XSLT stylesheet needed. However, for any but short XML documents, this is not usually a good idea. XSL-FO formatted documents become very long very quickly (compare the length of planets.xml to planets.fo), so you usually do use XSLT stylesheets to create XSL-FO documents (although some examples in the next chapter are short enough to be written using XSL-FO directly).

Creating the Document Root: *<fo:root>*

The first formatting element to cover is `<fo:root>`, the document node of any XSL-FO document. The document node of the formatting object document *must* be `<fo:root>`.

The children of the `<fo:root>` formatting object are a single `<fo:layout-master-set>` and a sequence of one or more `<fo:page-sequence>` elements.

The <fo:layout-master-set> formatting object holds all masters used in the document, which you use to specify how each page will actually be built. Each <fo:page-sequence> represents a sequence of pages formatted the way you want them. For example, each chapter of a book could be made up of its own page sequence, and you can give each sequence the same header and footer such as "Chapter 5: The Stranger Reappears".

As the first step in the XSLT stylesheet that transforms planets.xml, I match the document node in planets.xml, <PLANETS>, and replace it with an <fo:root> element that declares the "fo" namespace prefix:

```
<?xml version="1.0"?>
<xsl:stylesheet xmlns:xsl="http://www.w3.org/1999/XSL/Transform"
    xmlns:fo="http://www.w3.org/1999/XSL/Format"
    version="1.0">

    <xsl:template match="PLANETS">
        <fo:root xmlns:fo="http://www.w3.org/1999/XSL/Format">
            .
            .
            .
```

The <fo:root> element can contain both master set layouts and page sequences. I take a look at the <fo:layout-master-set object first.

Creating the Master Set Layout: *<fo:layout-master-set>*

You use *masters* to create templates for pages, page sequences, and regions. The <fo:layout-master-set> element contains all the masters used in the document, including page sequence masters, page masters, and region masters, which you apply to create page sequences, pages, and regions.

Page masters are templates for individual pages; page sequence masters are templates for sequences of pages; and region masters enable you to format specific regions in a page. In this example, I create a single page master using <fo:simple-page-master>.

You list the masters you want to use in the document in the <fo:layout-master-set> element, so I add that element to planets.xsl now:

```
<?xml version="1.0"?>
<xsl:stylesheet xmlns:xsl="http://www.w3.org/1999/XSL/Transform"
    xmlns:fo="http://www.w3.org/1999/XSL/Format"
    version="1.0">

    <xsl:template match="PLANETS">
        <fo:root xmlns:fo="http://www.w3.org/1999/XSL/Format">
```

```
        <fo:layout-master-set>
        .
        .
        .
        </fo:layout-master-set>
    .
    .
    .
```

This element contains the page master, as specified with an `<fo:simple-page-master>` element.

Creating a Page Master: *<fo:simple-page-master>*

As you can gather from its name, a page master is a template that is used to generate a page. A page master specifies the actual layout and geometry of a page. Each page master has a unique name, and you refer to it by that name when you want to use it.

In the current XSL specification, only one kind of page master is available, `<fo:simple-page-master>`, and I use that element to format pages here. You can use the following XSL-FO properties with the `<fo:simple-page-master>` object (see Appendix B for an explanation of these properties):

- Common margin properties for blocks: `margin-top`, `margin-bottom`, `margin-left`, `margin-right`, `space-before`, `space-after`, `start-indent`, `end-indent`
- `master-name`
- `page-height`
- `page-width`
- `reference-orientation`
- `writing-mode`

In the XSLT stylesheet I use on planets.xml, I give the simple page master the name "page" using the `master-name` property. That names the master, and when I want to create pages using this master, I refer to it by this name. I also specify the page dimensions and margins using page and margin properties as follows:

```
<?xml version="1.0"?>
<xsl:stylesheet xmlns:xsl="http://www.w3.org/1999/XSL/Transform"
    xmlns:fo="http://www.w3.org/1999/XSL/Format"
    version="1.0">

    <xsl:template match="PLANETS">
        <fo:root xmlns:fo="http://www.w3.org/1999/XSL/Format">

            <fo:layout-master-set>
```

```
            <fo:simple-page-master master-name="page"
                page-height="400mm" page-width="300mm"
                margin-top="10mm" margin-bottom="10mm"
                margin-left="20mm" margin-right="20mm">
                  .
                  .
                  .
    .
    .
    .
```

In addition to laying out the margins of a page, an `<fo:simple-page-master>` has children that specify one or more *regions* in the page, which enables you to customize the layout in detail.

Creating Regions

In version 1.0 of the XSL specification, page masters have five regions. The central region, which corresponds to body of the page, is called the *body region*. The top part of the page, the header, is called the *before region,* the bottom part of the page, the footer, is called the *after region*. In languages that read left to right, such as English, the left side of the page is called the *start region* and the right side is called the *end region*. In languages that read right to left, the start and end regions are reversed. The start and end regions are like sidebars that flank the body region.

The following XSL-FO elements correspond to these regions:

- `<fo:region-before>`
- `<fo:region-after>`
- `<fo:region-body>`
- `<fo:region-start>`
- `<fo:region-end>`

You can use these properties with the following elements:

- Common border, padding, and background properties: `background-attachment`, `background-color`, `background-image`, `background-repeat`, `background-position-horizontal`, `background-position-vertical`, `border-before-color`, `border-before-style`, `border-before-width`, `border-after-color`, `border-after-style`, `border-after-width`, `border-start-color`, `border-start-style`, `border-start-width`, `border-end-color`, `border-end-style`, `border-end-width`, `border-top-color`, `border-top-style`, `border-top-width`, `border-bottom-color`, `border-bottom-style`, `border-bottom-width`, `border-left-color`, `border-left-style`, border-left-width, border-right-color, border-right-style, border-right-width, padding-before, padding-after, padding-start, padding-end, padding-top, padding-bottom, padding-left, padding-right

- Common margin properties for blocks: margin-top, margin-bottom, margin-left, margin-right, space-before, space-after, start-indent, end-indent
- clip
- column-count
- column-gap
- display-align
- extent
- overflow
- region-name
- reference-orientation
- writing-mode

You can customize the regions of a page as you like, as in the XSLT stylesheet, where I set margins for the body region. The four outer regions (but not the body region) have an extent property that sets their size, and I use that here:

```
<?xml version="1.0"?>
<xsl:stylesheet xmlns:xsl="http://www.w3.org/1999/XSL/Transform"
    xmlns:fo="http://www.w3.org/1999/XSL/Format"
    version="1.0">

    <xsl:template match="PLANETS">
        <fo:root xmlns:fo="http://www.w3.org/1999/XSL/Format">

            <fo:layout-master-set>
                 <fo:simple-page-master master-name="page"
                     page-height="400mm" page-width="300mm"
                     margin-top="10mm" margin-bottom="10mm"
                     margin-left="20mm" margin-right="20mm">

                     <fo:region-body
                       margin-top="0mm" margin-bottom="10mm"
                       margin-left="0mm" margin-right="0mm"/>

                     <fo:region-after extent="10mm"/>
                 </fo:simple-page-master>
             </fo:layout-master-set>
    .
    .
    .
```

That completes the master I use in this document, the simple page master named "page", so that completes the `<fo:layout-master-set>` element as well.

In addition to the `<fo:layout-master-set>`, a formatting object document usually also contains one or more `<fo:page-sequence>` elements that define page sequences using the masters you define in the `<fo:layout-master-set>`, and I add a page sequence here.

Creating Page Sequences: *<fo:page-sequence>*

What's a page sequence? A page sequence is a run of pages that share the same characteristics, such as a chapter in a book, and you can format them in a similar way if you wish. The pages in a result document are actually created when the XSL-FO processor processes `<fo:page-sequence>` elements.

Each `<fo:page-sequence>` element refers to either an `<fo:page-sequence-master>` or a page master, and the actual layout of the pages is specified by those masters. You can get fairly involved here, creating sequences where the page number location alternates from side to side on the page, as when you're creating pages for a book.

The following properties apply to the `<fo:page-sequence>` object:

- `country`
- `format`
- `language`
- `letter-value`
- `grouping-separator`
- `grouping-size`
- `id`
- `initial-page-number`
- `force-page-count`
- `master-name`

In the current W3C XSL recommendation, you specify which page master you want to use for a page sequence with the `<fo:page-sequence>` element's `master-name` attribute. I named the simple page master I created "page", and I set that attribute to that name here:

```
 <?xml version="1.0"?>
<xsl:stylesheet xmlns:xsl="http://www.w3.org/1999/XSL/Transform"
    xmlns:fo="http://www.w3.org/1999/XSL/Format"
    version="1.0">
```

```
<xsl:template match="PLANETS">
    <fo:root xmlns:fo="http://www.w3.org/1999/XSL/Format">

        <fo:layout-master-set>
             <fo:simple-page-master master-name="page"
                 page-height="400mm" page-width="300mm"
                 margin-top="10mm" margin-bottom="10mm"
                 margin-left="20mm" margin-right="20mm">

                 <fo:region-body
                   margin-top="0mm" margin-bottom="10mm"
                   margin-left="0mm" margin-right="0mm"/>

                 <fo:region-after extent="10mm"/>
             </fo:simple-page-master>
         </fo:layout-master-set>

         <fo:page-sequence master-name="page">
            .
            .
            .
         </fo:page-sequence>
            .
            .
            .
```

That specifies what page master I want to use for a page sequence. Next, I have to specify the *content* of the page sequence. And the content of these pages comes from *flow* children of the `<fo:page-sequence`.

Creating Flows: *<fo:flows>*

Flow objects have that name because the text in them "flows" and is arranged to fit the page by the displaying software. The content of a page is handled with flow objects.

There are two kinds of flow objects: `<fo:static-content>` and `<fo:flow>`. An `<fo:static-content>` flow object holds content, such as the text that goes into headers and footers, that will be repeated on the pages of the page sequence (as you'll see in Chapter 12). The `<fo:flow>` flow object, on the other hand, holds the text itself that makes up the content of the document.

The following property applies `<fo:flow>`:

- `flow-name`

I use a `<fo:flow>` element to handle the text content of planets.xml. To make sure the text content of planets.xml is transformed into that flow, I use an `<xsl:apply-templates>` element:

```
<?xml version="1.0"?>
<xsl:stylesheet xmlns:xsl="http://www.w3.org/1999/XSL/Transform"
    xmlns:fo="http://www.w3.org/1999/XSL/Format"
    version="1.0">

    <xsl:template match="PLANETS">
        <fo:root xmlns:fo="http://www.w3.org/1999/XSL/Format">

            <fo:layout-master-set>
              .
              .
              .
            </fo:layout-master-set>

            <fo:page-sequence master-name="page">

                <fo:flow flow-name="xsl-region-body">
                    <xsl:apply-templates/>
                </fo:flow>
            </fo:page-sequence>
    .
    .
    .
```

That completes the <fo:page-sequence> element; I've specified a master to use for this sequence, and it provides the XSL-FO processor a way to format the content that is to go into the pages in the formatted document. Now that I've outlined the geometry of the pages I'm going to create, it's finally time to turn to the content of those pages. The first element that will actually display that content is <fo:block>.

Creating Block-Level Content: *<fo:block>*

Blocks are essential in XSL-FO; you use blocks in XSL-FO to create rectangular display areas set off from other display areas in a document. You can use the <fo:block> formatting object for formatting such items as paragraphs, titles, headlines, figure and table captions, and so on. Here's an example from the beginning of the chapter where I'm creating a block element and specifying various properties and the text in the block:

```
<fo:block font-family="Times" line-height="48pt" font-size="36pt">
    Welcome to XSL formatting.
</fo:block>
```

You can use the following properties with <fo:block>:

- Common accessibility properties: source-document, role
- Common aural properties: azimuth, cue-after, cue-before, elevation, pause-after, pause-before, pitch, pitch-range, play-during, richness,

speak, speak-header, speak-numeral, speak-punctuation, speech-rate, stress, voice-family, volume

- Common border, padding, and background properties: background-attachment, background-color, background-image, background-repeat, background-position-horizontal, background-position-vertical, border-before-color, border-before-style, border-before-width, border-after-color, border-after-style, border-after-width, border-start-color, border-start-style, border-start-width, border-end-color, border-end-style, border-end-width, border-top-color, border-top-style, border-top-width, border-bottom-color, border-bottom-style, border-bottom-width, border-left-color, border-left-style, border-left-width, border-right-color, border-right-style, border-right-width, padding-before, padding-after, padding-start, padding-end, padding-top, padding-bottom, padding-left, padding-right
- Common font properties: font-family, font-size, font-stretch, font-size-adjust, font-style, font-variant, font-weight
- Common hyphenation properties: country, language, script, hyphenate, hyphenation-character, hyphenation-push-character-count, hyphenation-remain-character-count
- Common margin properties for blocks: margin-top, margin-bottom, margin-left, margin-right, space-before, space-after, start-indent, end-indent
- break-after
- break-before
- color
- font-height-override-after
- font-height-override-before
- hyphenation-keep
- hyphenation-ladder-count
- id
- keep-together
- keep-with-next
- keep-with-previous
- last-line-end-indent
- linefeed-treatment
- line-height
- line-height-shift-adjustment
- line-stacking-strategy
- orphans

- relative-position
- space-treatment
- span
- text-align
- text-align-last
- text-indent
- visibility
- white-space-collapse
- widows
- wrap-option
- z-index

For example, I can add the title "The Planets Table" to the document by choosing Times font (currently, fop comes with the Times, Helvetica, Courier, Symbol, sans-serif, serif, and ZapfDingbats fonts built in), in the `font-family` property, 36-point font size by setting the `font-size` property, and boldface by setting the `font-weight` property to "bold". I set the height of the block with the `line-height` property and display the title in blue with the `color` property:

```
<?xml version="1.0"?>
<xsl:stylesheet xmlns:xsl="http://www.w3.org/1999/XSL/Transform"
    xmlns:fo="http://www.w3.org/1999/XSL/Format"
    version="1.0">

    <xsl:template match="PLANETS">
        <fo:root xmlns:fo="http://www.w3.org/1999/XSL/Format">

            <fo:layout-master-set>
            .
            .
            .
             </fo:layout-master-set>

             <fo:page-sequence master-name="page">

                 <fo:flow flow-name="xsl-region-body">
                     <fo:block font-weight="bold" font-size="36pt"
                         line-height="48pt" font-family="Times"
                         color="blue">
                         The Planets Table
                     </fo:block>
                     <xsl:apply-templates/>
```

```
                </fo:flow>
            </fo:page-sequence>
    .
    .
    .
```

That creates the title block you see at the top of the text in Figure 11.1. I can create similar blocks for each data item of each planet by using XSLT templates this way. Note also that I'm listing the name of each planet in italics by setting the font-style property to "italic", and I'm underlining other text by using the `text-decoration` property of `<fo:inline>` elements, which you'll see in the next chapter:

```
<?xml version="1.0"?>
<xsl:stylesheet xmlns:xsl="http://www.w3.org/1999/XSL/Transform"
    xmlns:fo="http://www.w3.org/1999/XSL/Format"
    version="1.0">

    <xsl:template match="PLANETS">
        <fo:root xmlns:fo="http://www.w3.org/1999/XSL/Format">

            <fo:layout-master-set>
            .
            .
            .
             </fo:layout-master-set>

             <fo:page-sequence master-name="page">
            .
            .
            .
             </fo:page-sequence>

        </fo:root>
    </xsl:template>

    <xsl:template match="PLANET/NAME">
        <fo:block font-weight="bold" font-size="28pt"
            line-height="48pt" font-family="Times"
            font-style="italic">
            Planet:
            <xsl:apply-templates/>
        </fo:block>
    </xsl:template>

    <xsl:template match="PLANET/MASS">
        <fo:block font-size="24pt" line-height="32pt"
            font-family="Times">
            <fo:inline text-decoration="underline">
```

```
            Mass
        </fo:inline>:
        <xsl:apply-templates/>
        [Earth = 1]
    </fo:block>
</xsl:template>
        .
        .
        .
</xsl:stylesheet>
```

And that's it. You've created your first XML to XSL-FO transformation, transforming planets.xml into planets.fo. The fop processor will create planets.pdf from planets.fo, and you can refer to Figure 11.1 to see the results.

This transformation formatted the data in planets.xml and displayed that data in blocks, one after the next. On the other hand, in earlier chapters you saw the planetary data in planets.xml displayed in a table. Can you do that in XSL-FO? No problem.

Creating Tables

Some of the most useful constructs you can format with XSL-FO are tables. A table in XSL-FO is much like one in HTML: a rectangular grid of rows and columns of cells. You can use nine formatting elements to create tables:

- `<fo:table-and-caption>`
- `<fo:table>`
- `<fo:table-column>`
- `<fo:table-caption>`
- `<fo:table-header>`
- `<fo:table-footer>`
- `<fo:table-body>`
- `<fo:table-row>`
- `<fo:table-cell>`

Creating tables in XSL-FO is similar to creating tables in HTML. You create an `<fo:table>` element to enclose the entire table, then format each column with an `<fo:table-column>` element. Next, create an `<fo:table-body>` element to specify the table's body. The `<fo:table-body>` element encloses all the `<fo:table-row>` elements, each of which creates a row in the table. Each `<fo:table-row>` element encloses the actual `<fo:table-cell>` elements that hold the table's cell-by-cell data.

The following example shows how this works. This XSLT stylesheet transforms planets.xml into an XSL-FO document that formats the planetary data in an XSL-FO-based table:

Listing 11.4 **tables.xsl**

```
<?xml version="1.0"?>
<xsl:stylesheet xmlns:xsl="http://www.w3.org/1999/XSL/Transform"
    xmlns:fo="http://www.w3.org/1999/XSL/Format"
    version="1.0">

    <xsl:template match="PLANETS">
        <fo:root xmlns:fo="http://www.w3.org/1999/XSL/Format">
            <fo:layout-master-set>
                 <fo:simple-page-master master-name="page"
                     page-height="400mm" page-width="300mm"
                     margin-top="10mm" margin-bottom="10mm"
                     margin-left="20mm" margin-right="20mm">

                     <fo:region-body
                       margin-top="0mm" margin-bottom="10mm"
                       margin-left="0mm" margin-right="0mm"/>

                     <fo:region-after extent="10mm"/>
                 </fo:simple-page-master>
             </fo:layout-master-set>

             <fo:page-sequence master-name="page">

                 <fo:flow flow-name="xsl-region-body">
                     <fo:table>

                         <fo:table-column column-width="30mm"/>
                         <fo:table-column column-width="30mm"/>
                         <fo:table-column column-width="30mm"/>
                         <fo:table-column column-width="30mm"/>
                         <fo:table-column column-width="30mm"/>
                         <fo:table-column column-width="30mm"/>

                         <fo:table-body>
                             <fo:table-row>
                                 <fo:table-cell border-width="0.5mm">
                                     <fo:block font-size="18pt"
                                         font-weight="bold">
                                         Name
                                     </fo:block>
                                 </fo:table-cell>

                                 <fo:table-cell border-width="0.5mm">
```

continues ▸

Listing 11.4 **Continued**

```
                                <fo:block font-size="18pt"
                                    font-weight="bold">
                                    Mass
                                </fo:block>
                            </fo:table-cell>

                            <fo:table-cell border-width="0.5mm">
                                <fo:block font-size="18pt"
                                    font-weight="bold">
                                    Day
                                </fo:block>
                            </fo:table-cell>

                            <fo:table-cell border-width="0.5mm">
                                <fo:block font-size="18pt"
                                    font-weight="bold">
                                    Radius
                                </fo:block>
                            </fo:table-cell>

                            <fo:table-cell border-width="0.5mm">
                                <fo:block font-size="18pt"
                                    font-weight="bold">
                                    Density
                                </fo:block>
                             </fo:table-cell>

                             <fo:table-cell border-width="0.5mm">
                                 <fo:block font-size="18pt"
                                     font-weight="bold">
                                     Distance
                                 </fo:block>
                             </fo:table-cell>
                        </fo:table-row>

                        <xsl:apply-templates/>

                    </fo:table-body>
                </fo:table>
            </fo:flow>
        </fo:page-sequence>
    </fo:root>
</xsl:template>

<xsl:template match="PLANET">
    <fo:table-row>
        <xsl:apply-templates/>
    </fo:table-row>
</xsl:template>
```

```
    <xsl:template match="NAME">
          <fo:table-cell border-width="0.5mm">
              <fo:block font-size="18pt">
                  <xsl:value-of select='.'/>
              </fo:block>
          </fo:table-cell>
    </xsl:template>

    <xsl:template match="MASS">
          <fo:table-cell border-width="0.5mm">
              <fo:block font-size="18pt">
                  <xsl:value-of select='.'/>
              </fo:block>
          </fo:table-cell>
    </xsl:template>

    <xsl:template match="DAY">
          <fo:table-cell border-width="0.5mm">
              <fo:block font-size="18pt">
                  <xsl:value-of select='.'/>
              </fo:block>
          </fo:table-cell>
    </xsl:template>

    <xsl:template match="RADIUS">
          <fo:table-cell border-width="0.5mm">
              <fo:block font-size="18pt">
                  <xsl:value-of select='.'/>
              </fo:block>
          </fo:table-cell>
    </xsl:template>

    <xsl:template match="DENSITY">
          <fo:table-cell border-width="0.5mm">
              <fo:block font-size="18pt">
                  <xsl:value-of select='.'/>
              </fo:block>
          </fo:table-cell>
    </xsl:template>

    <xsl:template match="DISTANCE">
          <fo:table-cell border-width="0.5mm">
              <fo:block font-size="18pt">
                  <xsl:value-of select='.'/>
              </fo:block>
          </fo:table-cell>
    </xsl:template>

</xsl:stylesheet>
```

Here's the result after you transform to an XSL-FO document, tables.fo:

Listing 11.5 **tables.fo**

```
<?xml version="1.0" encoding="UTF-8"?>
<fo:root xmlns:fo="http://www.w3.org/1999/XSL/Format">

    <fo:layout-master-set>
        <fo:simple-page-master margin-right="20mm" margin-left="20mm"
            margin-bottom="10mm" margin-top="10mm" page-width="300mm"
            page-height="400mm" master-name="page">

            <fo:region-body margin-right="0mm" margin-left="0mm"
                margin-bottom="10mm" margin-top="0mm"/>

            <fo:region-after extent="10mm"/>

        </fo:simple-page-master>
    </fo:layout-master-set>

    <fo:page-sequence master-name="page">

        <fo:flow flow-name="xsl-region-body">

            <fo:table>
                <fo:table-column column-width="30mm"/>
                <fo:table-column column-width="30mm"/>
                <fo:table-column column-width="30mm"/>
                <fo:table-column column-width="30mm"/>
                <fo:table-column column-width="30mm"/>
                <fo:table-column column-width="30mm"/>

                <fo:table-body>
                    <fo:table-row>
                        <fo:table-cell border-width="0.5mm">
                            <fo:block font-weight="bold" font-size="18pt">
                                Name
                            </fo:block>
                        </fo:table-cell>
                        <fo:table-cell border-width="0.5mm">
                            <fo:block font-weight="bold" font-size="18pt">
                                Mass
                            </fo:block>
                        </fo:table-cell>
                        <fo:table-cell border-width="0.5mm">
                            <fo:block font-weight="bold" font-size="18pt">
                                Day
                            </fo:block>
                        </fo:table-cell>
                        <fo:table-cell border-width="0.5mm">
                            <fo:block font-weight="bold" font-size="18pt">
```

```
                Radius
            </fo:block>
        </fo:table-cell>
            <fo:table-cell border-width="0.5mm">
                <fo:block font-weight="bold"
                    font-size="18pt">
                    Density
                </fo:block>
        </fo:table-cell>
        <fo:table-cell border-width="0.5mm">
            <fo:block font-weight="bold" font-size="18pt">
                Distance
            </fo:block>
        </fo:table-cell>
    </fo:table-row>

    <fo:table-row>
        <fo:table-cell border-width="0.5mm">
            <fo:block font-size="18pt">Mercury</fo:block>
        </fo:table-cell>
        <fo:table-cell border-width="0.5mm">
            <fo:block font-size="18pt">.0553</fo:block>
        </fo:table-cell>
        <fo:table-cell border-width="0.5mm">
            <fo:block font-size="18pt">58.65</fo:block>
        </fo:table-cell>
        <fo:table-cell border-width="0.5mm">
            <fo:block font-size="18pt">1516</fo:block>
        </fo:table-cell>
        <fo:table-cell border-width="0.5mm">
            <fo:block font-size="18pt">.983</fo:block>
        </fo:table-cell>
        <fo:table-cell border-width="0.5mm">
            <fo:block font-size="18pt">43.4</fo:block>
        </fo:table-cell>
    </fo:table-row>

    <fo:table-row>
        <fo:table-cell border-width="0.5mm">
            <fo:block font-size="18pt">Venus</fo:block>
        </fo:table-cell>
        <fo:table-cell border-width="0.5mm">
            <fo:block font-size="18pt">.815</fo:block>
        </fo:table-cell>
        <fo:table-cell border-width="0.5mm">
            <fo:block font-size="18pt">116.75</fo:block>
        </fo:table-cell>
        <fo:table-cell border-width="0.5mm">
            <fo:block font-size="18pt">3716</fo:block>
        </fo:table-cell>
        <fo:table-cell border-width="0.5mm">
```

continues ▸

Listing 11.5 **Continued**

```
                        <fo:block font-size="18pt">.943</fo:block>
                    </fo:table-cell>
                    <fo:table-cell border-width="0.5mm">
                        <fo:block font-size="18pt">66.8</fo:block>
                    </fo:table-cell>
                </fo:table-row>

                <fo:table-row>
                    <fo:table-cell border-width="0.5mm">
                        <fo:block font-size="18pt">Earth</fo:block>
                    </fo:table-cell>
                    <fo:table-cell border-width="0.5mm">
                        <fo:block font-size="18pt">1</fo:block>
                    </fo:table-cell>
                    <fo:table-cell border-width="0.5mm">
                        <fo:block font-size="18pt">1</fo:block>
                    </fo:table-cell>
                    <fo:table-cell border-width="0.5mm">
                        <fo:block font-size="18pt">2107</fo:block>
                    </fo:table-cell>
                    <fo:table-cell border-width="0.5mm">
                        <fo:block font-size="18pt">1</fo:block>
                    </fo:table-cell>
                    <fo:table-cell border-width="0.5mm">
                        <fo:block font-size="18pt">128.4</fo:block>
                    </fo:table-cell>
                </fo:table-row>
            </fo:table-body>
        </fo:table>
    </fo:flow>
  </fo:page-sequence>
</fo:root>
```

After running this document, tables.fo, through fop and creating tables.pdf, you can see the result in Figure 11.2. That's what an XSL-FO table looks like, although there are plenty of other options—you can set the background color cell by cell with the background-color property, for example. By default no border appears in these tables, but I've added one 0.5 mm thick with the `border-width` property. Note also that to set the font size of the text in each cell, I'm using a block inside each table cell:

```
<fo:table-cell border-width="0.5mm">
    <fo:block font-size="18pt">Earth</fo:block>
</fo:table-cell>
```

I'll take a look at the various elements you use to create tables now, starting with the big one, `<fo:table>`.

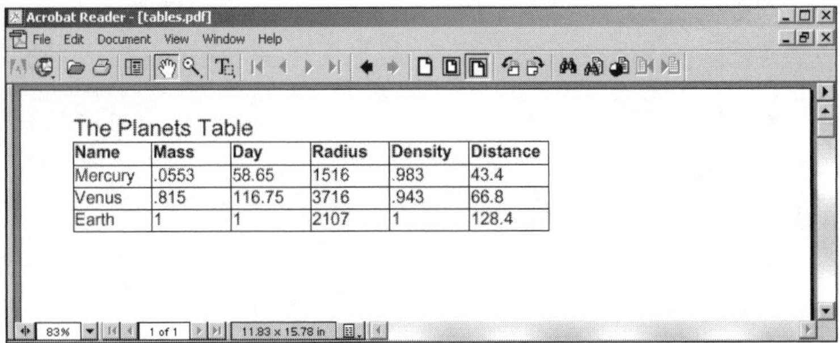

The Planets Table

Name	Mass	Day	Radius	Density	Distance
Mercury	.0553	58.65	1516	.983	43.4
Venus	.815	116.75	3716	.943	66.8
Earth	1	1	2107	1	128.4

Figure 11.2 An XSL-FO formatted table in Adobe Acrobat.

Creating Tables: *<fo:table>*

As you can guess from its name, you use the `<fo:table>` element to create a new table. The table itself consists of an optional header, an optional footer, and one or more table *bodies*. The actual table of cells, arranged into rows and columns, appears in the table body.

You can use the following properties with the `<fo:table>` element:

- Common accessibility properties: `source-document`, `role`
- Common aural properties: `azimuth`, `cue-after`, `cue-before`, `elevation`, `pause-after`, `pause-before`, `pitch`, `pitch-range`, `play-during`, `richness`, `speak`, `speak-header`, `speak-numeral`, `speak-punctuation`, `speech-rate`, `stress`, `voice-family`, `volume`
- Common border, padding, and background properties: `background-attachment`, `background-color`, `background-image`, `background-repeat`, `background-position-horizontal`, `background-position-vertical`, `border-before-color`, `border-before-style`, `border-before-width`, `border-after-color`, `border-after-style`, `border-after-width`, `border-start-color`, `border-start-style`, `border-start-width`, `border-end-color`, `border-end-style`, `border-end-width`, `border-top-color`, `border-top-style`, `border-top-width`, `border-bottom-color`, `border-bottom-style`, `border-bottom-width`, `border-left-color`, `border-left-style`, `border-left-width`, `border-right-color`, `border-right-style`, `border-right-width`, `padding-before`, `padding-after`, `padding-start`, `padding-end`, `padding-top`, `padding-bottom`, `padding-left`, `padding-right`
- Common margin properties: `margin-top`, `margin-bottom`, `margin-left`, `margin-right`, `space-before`, `space-after`, `start-indent`, `end-indent`
- `block-progression-dimension`
- `border-collapse`

- border-separation
- break-after
- break-before
- id
- inline-progression-dimension
- height
- keep-together
- keep-with-next
- keep-with-previous
- relative-position
- table-layout
- table-omit-footer-at-break
- table-omit-header-at-break
- width
- writing-mode

You can see that the table in Listing 11.5, tables.fo, starts with `<fo:table>`:

```
<fo:table>
        .
        .
        .
</fo:table>
```

The next step in creating a table is to specify the table columns, using `<fo:table-column>`.

Creating Table Columns: *<fo:table-column>*

You include one `<fo:table-column>` element for each column you want in the table. You can use this element to indicate characteristics that apply to table cells that have the same column. One of the most important properties here is the `column-width` property, which you use to set the width of each column.

You can use the following properties with the `<fo:table-column>` element:

- Common Border, padding, and background properties: `background-attachment`, `background-color`, `background-image`, `background-repeat`, `background-position-horizontal`, `background-position-vertical`, `border-before-color`, `border-before-style`, `border-before-width`, `border-after-color`, `border-after-style`, `border-after-width`, `border-start-color`, `border-start-style`, `border-`

start-width, border-end-color, border-end-style, border-end-width, border-top-color, border-top-style, border-top-width, border-bottom-color, border-bottom-style, border-bottom-width, border-left-color, border-left-style, border-left-width, border-right-color, border-right-style, border-right-width, padding-before, padding-after, padding-start, padding-end, padding-top, padding-bottom, padding-left, padding-right

- column-number
- column-width
- number-columns-repeated
- number-columns-spanned
- visibility

In tables.fo, I give each column the same width, 30mm, as follows:

```
<fo:table>
    <fo:table-column column-width="30mm"/>
    <fo:table-column column-width="30mm"/>
    <fo:table-column column-width="30mm"/>
    <fo:table-column column-width="30mm"/>
    <fo:table-column column-width="30mm"/>
    <fo:table-column column-width="30mm"/>
          .
          .
          .
</fo:table>
```

After specifying each column, you create the table's body.

Creating Table Bodies: *<fo:table-body>*

The table body holds the actual content of tables, and you create table bodies with `<fo:table-body>` elements. This element is the one that contains the actual `<fo:table-row>` elements, which in turn contain the `<fo:table-cell>` elements that hold the data for the table.

You can use the following properties with the `<fo:table-body` element:

- Common Border, padding, and background properties: background-attachment, background-color, background-image, background-repeat, background-position-horizontal, background-position-vertical, border-before-color, border-before-style, border-before-width, border-after-color, border-after-style, border-after-width, border-start-color, border-start-style, border-start-width, border-end-color, border-end-style, border-end-width, border-top-color, border-top-style, border-top-width, border-bottom-color, border-bottom-style, border-bottom-width, border-left-color, border-left-style, border-left-width, border-right-color, border-right-style, border-right-width, padding-before, padding-after, padding-start, padding-end, padding-top, padding-bottom, padding-left, padding-right

- id
- relative-position

As you can see in Listing 11.5, I use <fo:table-body> to create the table's body in tables.fo, as follows:

```
<fo:table>
    <fo:table-column column-width="30mm"/>
    <fo:table-column column-width="30mm"/>
    <fo:table-column column-width="30mm"/>
    <fo:table-column column-width="30mm"/>
    <fo:table-column column-width="30mm"/>
    <fo:table-column column-width="30mm"/>

    <fo:table-body>
        .
        .
        .
    </fo:table-body>
</fo:table>
```

After starting the table's body, you use one <fo:table-row> element for each row in the table.

Creating Table Rows: *<fo:table-row>*

Much as in HTML tables, you use the <fo:table-row> element to create rows in a table, and each row can contain table cells. As with HTML browsers, the XSL-FO processor determines the dimensions of the table by how many rows you've placed in the table.

You can use the following properties with the <fo:table-row> element:

- Common accessibility properties: source-document, role
- Common aural properties: azimuth, cue-after, cue-before, elevation, pause- after, pause-before, pitch, pitch-range, play-during, richness, speak, speak-header, speak-numeral, speak-punctuation, speech-rate, stress, voice-family, volume
- Common border, padding, and background properties: background-attachment, background-color, background-image, background-repeat, background-position-horizontal, background-position-vertical, border-before-color, border-before-style, border-before-width, border-after-color, border-

after-style, border-after-width, border-start-color, border-start-style, border-start-width, border-end-color, border-end-style, border-end-width, border-top-color, border-top-style, border-top-width, border-bottom-color, border-bottom-style, border-bottom-width, border-left-color, border-left-style, border-left-width, border-right-color, border-right-style, border-right-width, padding-before, padding-after, padding-start, padding-end, padding-top, padding-bottom, padding-left, padding-right

- block-progression-dimension
- break-after
- break-before
- id
- height
- keep-together
- keep-with-next
- keep-with-previous
- relative-position

I've added rows to the table in tables.fo with `<fo:table-row>` elements as follows:

```
<fo:table>
    <fo:table-column column-width="30mm"/>
    <fo:table-column column-width="30mm"/>
    <fo:table-column column-width="30mm"/>
    <fo:table-column column-width="30mm"/>
    <fo:table-column column-width="30mm"/>
    <fo:table-column column-width="30mm"/>

    <fo:table-body>
        <fo:table-row>
            .
            .
            .
        </fo:table-row>

        <fo:table-row>
            .
            .
            .
        </fo:table-row>
        .
        .
        .
    </fo:table-body>
</fo:table>
```

Having created the rows you want, you're ready to add the actual data in the table in its cells.

Creating Table Cells: *<fo:table-cell>*

Again matching table construction in HTML closely, you place data in a table's individual cells with the `<fo:table-cell>` element. Note that to specify the font and other characteristics of that content, you can enclose an `<fo:block>` element inside each `<fo:table-cell>` element. If you wish, you can connect a table cell with a particular table column using the `column-number` property, or even make a cell span multiple rows and columns, as in HTML tables.

You can use the following XSL-FO properties with the `<fo:table-cell>` element:

- Common accessibility properties: `source-document`, `role`
- Common aural properties: `azimuth`, `cue-after`, `cue-before`, `elevation`, `pause-after`, `pause-before`, `pitch`, `pitch-range`, `play-during`, `richness`, `speak`, `speak-header`, `speak-numeral`, `speak-punctuation`, `speech-rate`, `stress`, `voice-family`, `volume`
- Common border, padding, and background properties: `background-attachment`, `background-color`, `background-image`, `background-repeat`, `background-position-horizontal`, `background-position-vertical`, `border-before-color`, `border-before-style`, `border-before-width`, `border-after-color`, `border-after-style`, `border-after-width`, `border-start-color`, `border-start-style`, `border-start-width`, `border-end-color`, `border-end-style`, `border-end-width`, `border-top-color`, `border-top-style`, `border-top-width`, `border-bottom-color`, `border-bottom-style`, `border-bottom-width`, `border-left-color`, `border-left-style`, `border-left-width`, `border-right-color`, `border-right-style`, `border-right-width`, `padding-before`, `padding-after`, `padding-start`, `padding-end`, `padding-top`, `padding-bottom`, `padding-left`, `padding-right`
- `block-progression-dimension`
- `column-number`
- `display-align`
- `relative-align`
- `empty-cells`
- `ends-row`
- `height`

- id
- number-columns-spanned
- number-rows-spanned
- relative-position
- starts-row
- width

In tables.fo, I put both the labels for each column and table data in table cells this way:

```
<fo:table>
    <fo:table-column column-width="30mm"/>
    <fo:table-column column-width="30mm"/>
    <fo:table-column column-width="30mm"/>
    <fo:table-column column-width="30mm"/>
    <fo:table-column column-width="30mm"/>
    <fo:table-column column-width="30mm"/>

    <fo:table-body>
        <fo:table-row>
            <fo:table-cell border-width="0.5mm">
                <fo:block font-weight="bold" font-size="18pt">
                    Name
                </fo:block>
            </fo:table-cell>
            <fo:table-cell border-width="0.5mm">
                <fo:block font-weight="bold" font-size="18pt">
                </fo:block>
                    Mass
            </fo:table-cell>
            <fo:table-cell border-width="0.5mm">
                <fo:block font-weight="bold" font-size="18pt">
                    Day
                </fo:block>
            </fo:table-cell>
            <fo:table-cell border-width="0.5mm">
                <fo:block font-weight="bold" font-size="18pt">
                    Radius
                </fo:block>
            </fo:table-cell>
            <fo:table-cell border-width="0.5mm">
                <fo:block font-weight="bold" font-size="18pt">
                    Density
                </fo:block>
            </fo:table-cell>
            <fo:table-cell border-width="0.5mm">
```

```
                <fo:block font-weight="bold" font-size="18pt">
                    Distance
                </fo:block>
            </fo:table-cell>
        </fo:table-row>

        <fo:table-row>
            <fo:table-cell border-width="0.5mm">
                <fo:block font-size="18pt">Mercury</fo:block>
            </fo:table-cell>
            <fo:table-cell border-width="0.5mm">
                <fo:block font-size="18pt">.0553</fo:block>
            </fo:table-cell>
            <fo:table-cell border-width="0.5mm">
                <fo:block font-size="18pt">58.65</fo:block>
            </fo:table-cell>
            <fo:table-cell border-width="0.5mm">
                <fo:block font-size="18pt">1516</fo:block>
            </fo:table-cell>
            <fo:table-cell border-width="0.5mm">
                <fo:block font-size="18pt">.983</fo:block>
            </fo:table-cell>
            <fo:table-cell border-width="0.5mm">
                <fo:block font-size="18pt">43.4</fo:block>
            </fo:table-cell>
        </fo:table-row>
        .
        .
        .
    </fo:table-body>
</fo:table>
```

And that's it—the result appears in Figure 11.2, where you see the fully formatted table as created by the fop processor. Now you've learned to create tables with XSL formatting objects.

There's a lot more to XSL-FO, of course. The next chapter takes a look at working with lists, positioning, columns, page sequences, and more.

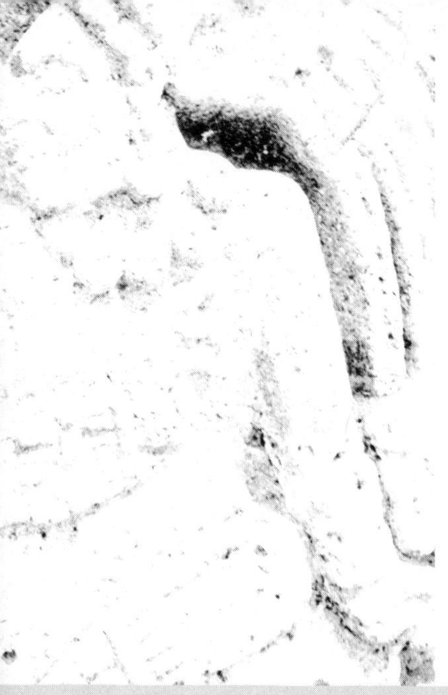

12
Using XSLT to Create XSL-FO Documents: Lists, Images, Columns, and Positioning

THIS CHAPTER CONTINUES WORKING WITH XSL-FO. It looks at handling lists, images, and columns, positioning of text, creating multiple-page sequences, and more. At the end of this chapter, you'll have a working knowledge of XSL-FO—at least the part of it that's implemented in today's software. I'll start this chapter with XSL-FO lists.

Creating XSL-FO Lists

As you saw in Chapter 11, XSL-FO tables work much as they do in HTML, and it turns out that lists do, too. Just as in HTML, an XSL list displays a vertical list of items. You use four XSL-FO elements to create lists:

- `<fo:list-block>`
- `<fo:list-item>`
- `<fo:list-item-label>`
- `<fo:list-item-body>`

You enclose the whole list in an `<fo:list-block>` element, and each item in the list in an `<fo:list-item>` element. To create a label for the list item, you use an `<fo:list-item-label>` element, and to insert the actual data for each list item, you use an `<fo:list-item-body>` element.

Here's an example, lists.xsl, that transforms planets.xml into XSL-FO list format, with each list item displaying the name of a planet:

Listing 12.1 **lists.xsl**

```
<?xml version='1.0'?>
<xsl:stylesheet xmlns:xsl="http://www.w3.org/1999/XSL/Transform"
    xmlns:fo="http://www.w3.org/1999/XSL/Format"
    version="1.0">

    <xsl:template match="PLANETS">
        <fo:root xmlns:fo="http://www.w3.org/1999/XSL/Format">

            <fo:layout-master-set>
                <fo:simple-page-master master-name="page"
                    page-height="400mm" page-width="300mm"
                    margin-top="10mm" margin-bottom="10mm"
                    margin-left="20mm" margin-right="20mm">

                    <fo:region-body
                        margin-top="0mm" margin-bottom="10mm"
                        margin-left="0mm" margin-right="0mm"/>

                    <fo:region-after extent="10mm"/>
                </fo:simple-page-master>
            </fo:layout-master-set>

            <fo:page-sequence master-name="page">

                <fo:flow flow-name="xsl-region-body">

                    <fo:block font-size="24pt">The Planets Table</fo:block>
                    <fo:list-block
                        provisional-distance-between-starts="15mm"
                        provisional-label-separation="5mm">

                        <xsl:apply-templates/>

                    </fo:list-block>
                </fo:flow>
            </fo:page-sequence>

        </fo:root>
    </xsl:template>

    <xsl:template match="PLANET">
        <fo:list-item line-height="20mm">
            <fo:list-item-label>
                <fo:block font-family="sans-serif"
                    font-size="36pt">
                    <xsl:number/>
                    <xsl:text>. </xsl:text>
```

```
                </fo:block>
            </fo:list-item-label>

            <xsl:apply-templates/>
        </fo:list-item>
    </xsl:template>

    <xsl:template match="NAME">
        <fo:list-item-body>
            <fo:block font-family="sans-serif"
                font-size="36pt">
                <xsl:value-of select='.'/>
            </fo:block>
        </fo:list-item-body>
    </xsl:template>

    <xsl:template match="MASS">
    </xsl:template>

    <xsl:template match="RADIUS">
    </xsl:template>

    <xsl:template match="DENSITY">
    </xsl:template>

    <xsl:template match="DAY">
    </xsl:template>

    <xsl:template match="DISTANCE">
    </xsl:template>

</xsl:stylesheet>
```

Here's the resulting XSL-FO document, lists.fo:

Listing 12.2 **lists.fo**

```
<?xml version="1.0" encoding="UTF-8"?>
<fo:root xmlns:fo="http://www.w3.org/1999/XSL/Format">

    <fo:layout-master-set>
        <fo:simple-page-master margin-right="20mm" margin-left="20mm"
            margin-bottom="10mm" margin-top="10mm" page-width="300mm"
            page-height="400mm" master-name="page">

            <fo:region-body margin-right="0mm" margin-left="0mm"
                margin-bottom="10mm" margin-top="0mm"/>

            <fo:region-after extent="10mm"/>

        </fo:simple-page-master>
```

continues ▸

Listing 12.2 **Continued**

```
    </fo:layout-master-set>

    <fo:page-sequence master-name="page">
        <fo:flow flow-name="xsl-region-body">

            <fo:block font-size="24pt">The Planets Table</fo:block>

            <fo:list-block provisional-label-separation="5mm"
                provisional-distance-between-starts="15mm">

                <fo:list-item line-height="20mm">
                    <fo:list-item-label>
                        <fo:block font-size="36pt"
                            font-family="sans-serif">1. </fo:block>
                    </fo:list-item-label>

                    <fo:list-item-body>
                        <fo:block font-size="36pt"
                            font-family="sans-serif">Mercury</fo:block>
                    </fo:list-item-body>
                </fo:list-item>

                <fo:list-item line-height="20mm">
                    <fo:list-item-label>
                        <fo:block font-size="36pt"
                            font-family="sans-serif">2. </fo:block>
                    </fo:list-item-label>

                    <fo:list-item-body>
                        <fo:block font-size="36pt"
                            font-family="sans-serif">Venus</fo:block>
                    </fo:list-item-body>
                </fo:list-item>

                <fo:list-item line-height="20mm">
                    <fo:list-item-label>
                        <fo:block font-size="36pt"
                            font-family="sans-serif">3. </fo:block>
                    </fo:list-item-label>

                    <fo:list-item-body>
                        <fo:block font-size="36pt"
                            font-family="sans-serif">Earth</fo:block>
                    </fo:list-item-body>
                </fo:list-item>

            </fo:list-block>
        </fo:flow>
    </fo:page-sequence>
</fo:root>
```

You can see the resulting PDF file in Adobe Acrobat in Figure 12.1, showing the list.

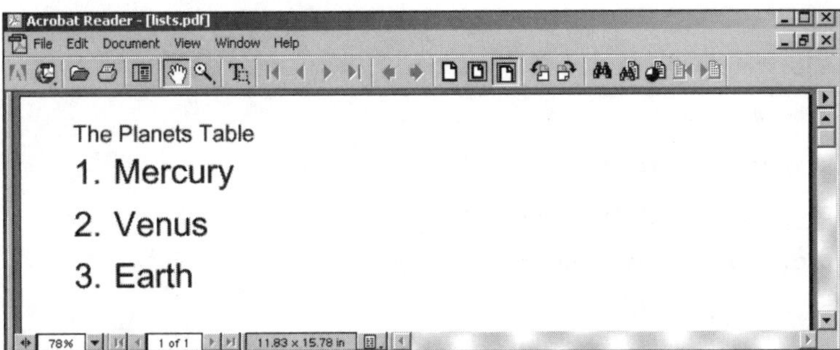

Figure 12.1 An XSL-FO formatted list in Adobe Acrobat.

It's time to take a look at the list formatting objects—and how lists.fo works—in more detail now.

Creating a List: *<fo:list-block>*

To start, you use the `<fo:list-block>` element to create an XSL-FO list; this object encloses the actual `<fo:list-item>` elements that contain the list data.

You can use the following properties with the `<fo:list-block>` element:

- Common accessibility properties: `source-document`, `role`
- Common aural properties: `azimuth`, `cue-after`, `cue-before`, `elevation`, `pause-after`, `pause-before`, `pitch`, `pitch-range`, `play-during`, `richness`, `speak`, `speak-header`, `speak-numeral`, `speak-punctuation`, `speech-rate`, `stress`, `voice-family`, `volume`
- Common border, padding, and background properties: `background-attachment`, `background-color`, `background-image`, `background-repeat`, `background-position-horizontal`, `background-position-vertical`, `border-before-color`, `border-before-style`, `border-before-width`, `border-after-color`, `border-after-style`, `border-after-width`, `border-start-color`, `border-start-style`, `border-start-width`, `border-end-color`, `border-end-style`, `border-end-width`, `border-top-color`, `border-top-style`, `border-top-width`, `border-bottom-color`, `border-bottom-style`, `border-bottom-width`, `border-left-color`, `border-left-style`, `border-left-width`, `border-right-color`, `border-right-style`, `border-right-width`, `padding-before`, `padding-after`, `padding-start`, `padding-end`, `padding-top`, `padding-bottom`, `padding-left`, `padding-right`
- Common margin properties: `margin-top`, `margin-bottom`, `margin-left`, `margin-right`, `space-before`, `space-after`, `start-indent`, `end-indent`

- `break-after`
- `break-before`
- `id`
- `keep-together`
- `keep-with-next`
- `keep-with-previous`
- `provisional-distance-between-starts`
- `provisional-label-separation`
- `relative-position`

Here's how the list in Listing 12.2, lists.fo, starts. In this case, I'm specifying values for the `provisional-distance-between-starts` property, which is the preferred distance between the starting indent of the list item's label and the starting indent of the list item's body, and the `provisional-label-separation` property, which is the preferred distance between the end of the list item's label (such as a bullet or a number) and the start of the list item's body:

```
<fo:list-block provisional-label-separation="5mm"
               provisional-distance-between-starts="15mm">
        .
        .
        .
        </fo:list-block>
```

Creating List Items: *<fo:list-item>*

Next, you use an `<fo:list-item>` element to contain the label and the body of an item in a list. There must be one of these elements for each item in the list.

You can use the following properties with the `<fo:list-item>` element:

- Common accessibility properties: `source-document`, `role`
- Common aural properties: `azimuth`, `cue-after`, `cue-before`, `elevation`, `pause-after`, `pause-before`, `pitch`, `pitch-range`, `play-during`, `richness`, `speak`, `speak-header`, `speak-numeral`, `speak-punctuation`, `speech-rate`, `stress`, `voice-family`, `volume`
- Common border, padding, and background properties: `background-attachment`, `background-color`, `background-image`, `background-repeat`, `background-position-horizontal`, `background-position-vertical`, `border-before-color`, `border-before-style`, `border-before-width`, `border-after-color`, `border-after-style`, `border-after-width`, `border-start-color`, `border-start-style`, `border-start-width`, `border-end-color`, `border-end-style`, `border-`

end-width, border-top-color, border-top-style, border-top-width, border-bottom-color, border-bottom-style, border-bottom-width, border-left-color, border-left-style, border-left-width, border-right-color, border-right-style, border-right-width, padding-before, padding-after, padding-start, padding-end, padding-top, padding-bottom, padding-left, padding-right

- Common margin properties: margin-top, margin-bottom, margin-left, margin-right, space-before, space-after, start-indent, end-indent
- break-after
- break-before
- id
- keep-together
- keep-with-next
- keep-with-previous
- relative-align
- relative-position

Here are the three <fo:list-item> elements in lists.fo:

```
<fo:list-block provisional-label-separation="5mm"
    provisional-distance-between-starts="15mm">

    <fo:list-item line-height="20mm">
    .
    .
    .
    </fo:list-item>

    <fo:list-item line-height="20mm">
    .
    .
    .
    </fo:list-item>

    <fo:list-item line-height="20mm">
    .
    .
    .
    </fo:list-item>

</fo:list-block>
```

Now it's time to create a label and add the data for each list item.

Creating List Item Labels: *<fo:list-item-label>*

To create a label for a list item, you use the `<fo:list-item-label>` element. You can use this element to enumerate or decorate the body of the list item.

You can use the following properties with the `fo:list-item-label` object:

- Common accessibility properties: `source-document`, `role`
- `id`
- `keep-together`

In lists.fo, I use `<fo:block>` elements to display the planet number as the list item's label (lists.xsl uses `<xsl:number>` to find that number and insert it into lists.fo):

```
<fo:list-block provisional-label-separation="5mm"
    provisional-distance-between-starts="15mm">

    <fo:list-item line-height="20mm">
        <fo:list-item-label>
            <fo:block font-size="36pt"
            font-family="sans-serif">
                1.
            </fo:block>
        </fo:list-item-label>
        .
        .
        .
    </fo:list-item>

    <fo:list-item line-height="20mm">
        <fo:list-item-label>
            <fo:block font-size="36pt"
                font-family="sans-serif">
                    2.
                </fo:block>
        </fo:list-item-label>
        .
        .
        .
    </fo:list-item>

    <fo:list-item line-height="20mm">
        <fo:list-item-label>
            <fo:block font-size="36pt"
                font-family="sans-serif">
                    3.
                </fo:block>
        </fo:list-item-label>
```

```
            .
            .
            .
        </fo:list-item>

    </fo:list-block>
```

All that's left is to add the actual data to display to this list.

Creating List Item Bodies: *<fo:list-item-body>*

You use the `<fo:list-item-body>` element to hold the actual body of a list item. Note that to format the item's body the way you want it, you can enclose an `<fo:block>` object in an `<fo:list-item-body>` element.

You can use the following properties with the `<fo:list-item-body>` object:

- Common accessibility properties: `source-document`, `role`
- `id`
- `keep-together`

Here are the `<fo:list-item-body>` elements in lists.fo, which hold the names of the planets:

```
    <fo:list-block provisional-label-separation="5mm"
        provisional-distance-between-starts="15mm">

        <fo:list-item line-height="20mm">
            <fo:list-item-label>
                <fo:block font-size="36pt"
                   font-family="sans-serif">
                      1.
                   </fo:block>
            </fo:list-item-label>

            <fo:list-item-body>
                <fo:block font-size="36pt"
                    font-family="sans-serif">
                    Mercury
                </fo:block>
            </fo:list-item-body>
        </fo:list-item>

        <fo:list-item line-height="20mm">
            <fo:list-item-label>
                <fo:block font-size="36pt"
                    font-family="sans-serif">
                    2.
                </fo:block>
            </fo:list-item-label>
```

```
            <fo:list-item-body>
                <fo:block font-size="36pt"
                    font-family="sans-serif">
                    Venus
                </fo:block>
            </fo:list-item-body>
        </fo:list-item>

        <fo:list-item line-height="20mm">
            <fo:list-item-label>
                <fo:block font-size="36pt"
                    font-family="sans-serif">
                        3.
                </fo:block>
            </fo:list-item-label>

            <fo:list-item-body>
                <fo:block font-size="36pt"
                    font-family="sans-serif">
                    Earth
                </fo:block>
            </fo:list-item-body>
        </fo:list-item>

    </fo:list-block>
```

That completes the list, which you saw in Figure 12.1. Working with lists is viable in XSL-FO, but personally I find myself using tables to display data or simple blocks. On the other hand, it's useful to know that lists are there if you want them.

Positioning Text with Block Containers: *<fo:block-container>*

XSL-FO processors are much like HTML browsers in one respect: They insert blocks into a page's "flow," which means those blocks can flow throughout the document, just as they would in an HTML browser. On the other hand, sometimes it's important to place items in a page at specific locations. And in XSL-FO, you can position items at absolute page coordinates, or at relative ones with respect to other items.

To show how this works, I use the `<fo:block-container>` element, which works as you'd expect: as a container for blocks. What makes this element useful is that block containers support absolute positioning properties, which blocks don't.

You can use the following properties with the `<fo:block-container>` element:

- Common absolute position properties: `absolute-position`, `top`, `right`, `bottom`, `left`
- Common border, padding, and background properties: `background-attachment`, `background-color`, `background-image`, `background-repeat`, `background-position-horizontal`, `background-position-vertical`, `border-before-color`, `border-before-style`, `border-before-width`, `border-after-color`, `border-after-style`, `border-after-width`, `border-start-color`, `border-start-style`, `border-start-width`, `border-end-color`, `border-end-style`, `border-end-width`, `border-top-color`, `border-top-style`, `border-top-width`, `border-bottom-color`, `border-bottom-style`, `border-bottom-width`, `border-left-color`, `border-left-style`, `border-left-width`, `border-right-color`, `border-right-style`, `border-right-width`, `padding-before`, `padding-after`, `padding-start`, `padding-end`, `padding-top`, `padding-bottom`, `padding-left`, `padding-right`
- Common margin properties for blocks: `margin-top`, `margin-bottom`, `margin-left`, `margin-right`, `space-before`, `space-after`, `start-indent`, `end-indent`
- `block-progression-dimension`
- `break-after`
- `break-before`
- `clip`
- `display-align`
- `height`
- `id`
- `inline-progression-dimension`
- `keep-together`
- `keep-with-next`
- `keep-with-previous`
- `overflow`
- `reference-orientation`
- `span`
- `width`
- `writing-mode`

In the following example, I'm using block containers as wrappers for blocks that I want to place at specific locations on the page:

Listing 12.3 **blockcontainer.fo**

```
<?xml version="1.0" encoding="UTF-8"?>
<fo:root xmlns:fo="http://www.w3.org/1999/XSL/Format">

    <fo:layout-master-set>
        <fo:simple-page-master margin-right="20mm" margin-left="20mm"
            margin-bottom="10mm" margin-top="10mm" page-width="300mm"
            page-height="400mm" master-name="page">

            <fo:region-body margin-right="0mm" margin-left="0mm"
                margin-bottom="10mm" margin-top="0mm"/>

            <fo:region-after extent="10mm"/>

        </fo:simple-page-master>
    </fo:layout-master-set>

    <fo:page-sequence master-name="page">
        <fo:flow flow-name="xsl-region-body">
            <fo:block-container height="4cm" width="12cm" top="0cm"
                left="0cm"
                position="absolute">
                <fo:block text-align="start" line-height="18pt"
                font-family="sans-serif" font-weight="bold" font-size="14pt">
                    Starpowder
                </fo:block>
                <fo:block text-align="start" line-height="18pt"
                    font-family="sans-serif"
                    font-size="14pt">
                    The Starpowder Building
                </fo:block>
                <fo:block text-align="start" line-height="18pt"
                    font-family="sans-serif"
                    font-size="14pt">
                    1 Starpowder Avenue
                </fo:block>
                <fo:block text-align="start" line-height="18pt"
                    font-family="sans-serif"
                    font-size="14pt">
                    New York, NY, 10011
                </fo:block>
            </fo:block-container>

            <fo:block-container height="1cm" width="6cm" top="0cm"
                left="14cm"
                position="absolute">
                <fo:block text-align="start" line-height="22pt"
                    font-family="sans-serif"
                    font-size="23pt">
```

```
        Invoice
    </fo:block>
</fo:block-container>

<fo:block-container border-color="black" border-style="solid"
    border-width="1pt" height="0.7cm" width="3.5cm" top="1.2cm"
    left="12.0cm" padding="2pt" position="absolute">
    <fo:block text-align="start" line-height="15pt"
        font-family="sans-serif"
        font-size="12pt">
        Date
    </fo:block>
</fo:block-container>

<fo:block-container border-color="black" border-style="solid"
    border-width="1pt" height="0.7cm" width="3.5cm" top="1.9cm"
    left="12.0cm" padding="2pt" position="absolute">
    <fo:block text-align="start" line-height="15pt"
        font-family="sans-serif" font-size="12pt">
        January 1, 2002
    </fo:block>
</fo:block-container>

<fo:block-container border-color="black" border-style="solid"
    border-width="1pt" height="0.7cm" width="3.5cm" top="1.2cm"
    left="15.5cm" padding="2pt" position="absolute">
    <fo:block text-align="start" line-height="15pt"
        font-family="sans-serif" font-size="12pt">
        Terms
    </fo:block>
</fo:block-container>

<fo:block-container border-color="black" border-style="solid"
   border-width="1pt" height="0.7cm" width="3.5cm" top="1.9cm"
   left="15.5cm" padding="2pt" position="absolute">
   <fo:block text-align="start" line-height="15pt"
      font-family="sans-serif" font-size="12pt">
      Immediate
   </fo:block>
</fo:block-container>

<fo:block-container border-color="black" border-style="solid"
    border-width="1pt" height="1.0cm" width="9cm" top="3cm"
    left="0cm" padding="2pt" position="absolute">
    <fo:block text-align="center" line-height="22pt"
        font-family="sans-serif" font-size="18pt">
        Description of Service
    </fo:block>
</fo:block-container>

<fo:block-container border-color="black" border-style="solid"
    border-width="1pt" height="4cm" width="9cm" top="4.0cm"
```

continues ▸

Listing 12.3 **Continued**

```
            left="0cm"
            padding="2pt" position="absolute">
            <fo:block text-align="start" line-height="15pt"
                font-family="sans-serif" font-size="12pt">
            </fo:block>
        </fo:block-container>

        <fo:block-container border-color="black" border-style="solid"
            border-width="1pt" height="1.0cm" width="9cm" top="3cm"
            left="10cm"
            padding="2pt" position="absolute">
            <fo:block text-align="center" line-height="22pt"
                font-family="sans-serif" font-size="18pt">
                Address for Payment
                </fo:block>
        </fo:block-container>

        <fo:block-container border-color="black" border-style="solid"
            border-width="1pt" height="4cm" width="9cm" top="4.0cm"
            left="10cm"
            padding="2pt" position="absolute">
            <fo:block text-align="start" line-height="15pt"
                font-family="sans-serif" font-size="12pt">
            </fo:block>
        </fo:block-container>

      </fo:flow>
   </fo:page-sequence>
</fo:root>
```

You can see the PDF document fop creates from blockcontainers.fo in Figure 12.2. As you see in that figure, I've positioned various blocks at various locations in that document. Some boxes must be positioned directly on top of others, so positioning is very important in this case.

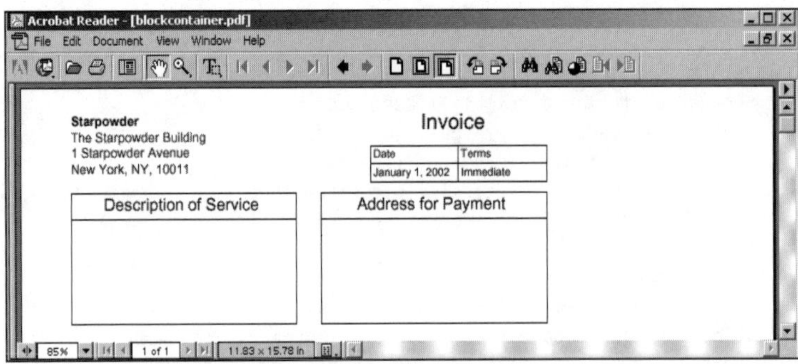

Figure 12.2 Using block containers.

In fact, it's easy to use block containers. For example, take a look at the "Description of Service" box in Figure 12.2. I create this box using two block containers, one holding the title, "Description of Service", and the other holding the blank box directly underneath. To create the title box, I use the `<fo:block-container>` element, specifying this box's dimensions with the `height` and `width` properties, and giving it a border with the `border-width` property. I also set its position on the page by setting the position property to "absolute" and using the left and top properties to position the top left corner of the box with respect to the top left corner of the page:

```
<fo:block-container border-color="black" border-style="solid"
    border-width="1pt" height="1.0cm" width="9cm" top="3cm"
    left="0cm" padding="2pt" position="absolute">
    .
    .
    .
</fo:block-container>
```

Now I can enclose a block with the title, "Description of Service", in it:

```
<fo:block-container border-color="black" border-style="solid"
    border-width="1pt" height="1.0cm" width="9cm" top="3cm"
    left="0cm" padding="2pt" position="absolute">
    <fo:block text-align="center" line-height="22pt"
        font-family="sans-serif"
        font-size="18pt">
        Description of Service
    </fo:block>
</fo:block-container>
```

Next, I position a blank box directly beneath the title box:

```
</fo:block-container>
<fo:block-container border-color="black" border-style="solid"
    border-width="1pt" height="1.0cm" width="9cm" top="3cm"
    left="0cm" padding="2pt" position="absolute">
    <fo:block text-align="center" line-height="22pt"
        font-family="sans-serif"
        font-size="18pt">
        Description of Service
    </fo:block>
</fo:block-container>

<fo:block-container border-color="black" border-style="solid"
    border-width="1pt" height="4cm" width="9cm" top="4.0cm"
    left="0cm"
    padding="2pt" position="absolute">
    <fo:block text-align="start" line-height="15pt"
    font-family="sans-serif"
    font-size="12pt">
```

```
            </fo:block>
        </fo:block-container>
```

And you can see the results in Figure 12.2. To me, this is one of the most useful aspects of XSL-FO: the ability it gives you to place items exactly where you want them. You can rely on the flow of objects as created by the XSL-FO processor, but sometimes you really want to place objects in a specific place, and now you can do it.

Inline-Level Formatting Objects

In addition to the block objects in XSL-FO, you can also create *inline* objects. An inline object represents part of a larger formatting region, such as a block; for example, it might represent a word or two in a block. Inline objects are usually used to format part of the text as that text follows the normal flow in the page. For example, you can make the first character in a paragraph larger, make the whole first line blue, insert page numbers, add images, and so on.

One reason you might create inline objects is to format parts of a block's text; for example, in Chapter 11, you saw the following use of the `text-decoration` property of `<fo:inline>` to underline text:

```
<xsl:template match="PLANET/MASS">
    <fo:block font-size="24pt" line-height="32pt"
        font-family="Times">
        <fo:inline text-decoration="underline">
            Mass
        </fo:inline>:
        <xsl:apply-templates/>
        [Earth = 1]
    </fo:block>
</xsl:template>
```

The following list includes the inline formatting elements:

- `<fo:bidi-override>`
- `<fo:character>`
- `<fo:initial-property-set>`
- `<fo:external-graphic>`
- `<fo:instream-foreign-object>`
- `<fo:inline>`
- `<fo:inline-container>`
- `<fo:leader>`
- `<fo:page-number>`
- `<fo:page-number-citation>`

I'll take a look at a few of the more common of these inline elements now, starting with `<fo:inline>` itself.

Creating Inline Regions: *<fo:inline>*

As you already saw in Chapter 11, you can use the `<fo:inline>` element to format a part of your text with a background, underline it, or enclose it with a border. This element lets you format an inline area, such as a few words in a block of text, almost as though it were a block itself.

You can use the following properties with `<fo:inline>`:

- Common accessibility properties: `source-document`, `role`
- Common aural properties: `azimuth`, `cue-after`, `cue-before`, `elevation`, `pause-after`, `pause-before`, `pitch`, `pitch-range`, `play-during`, `richness`, `speak`, `speak-header`, `speak-numeral`, `speak-punctuation`, `speech-rate`, `stress`, `voice-family`, `volume`
- Common border, padding, and background properties: `background-attachment`, `background-color`, `background-image`, `background-repeat`, `background-position-horizontal`, `background-position-vertical`, `border-before-color`, `border-before-style`, `border-before-width`, `border-after-color`, `border-after-style`, `border-after-width`, `border-start-color`, `border-start-style`, `border-start-width`, `border-end-color`, `border-end-style`, `border-end-width`, `border-top-color`, `border-top-style`, `border-top-width`, `border-bottom-color`, `border-bottom-style`, `border-bottom-width`, `border-left-color`, `border-left-style`, `border-left-width`, `border-right-color`, `border-right-style`, `border-right-width`, `padding-before`, `padding-after`, `padding-start`, `padding-end`, `padding-top`, `padding-bottom`, `padding-left`, `padding-right`
- Common font properties: `font-family`, `font-size`, `font-stretch`, `font-size-adjust`, `font-style`, `font-variant`, `font-weight`
- Common inline margin properties: `space-end`, `space-start`
- `alignment-adjust`
- `baseline-identifier`
- `baseline-shift`
- `color`
- `dominant-baseline`
- `id`
- `keep-together`
- `keep-with-next`
- `keep-with-previous`

- line-height
- line-height-shift-adjustment
- relative-position
- text-decoration
- visibility
- z-index

For example, you've already seen how to add an underline to a single word inside other text using the text-decoration property:

```
<xsl:template match="PLANET/MASS">
        <fo:block font-size="24pt" line-height="32pt"
            font-family="Times">
            <fo:inline text-decoration="underline">
                Mass
            </fo:inline>:
            <xsl:apply-templates/>
            [Earth = 1]
        </fo:block>
    </xsl:template>
```

You'll see more on how to use <fo:inline> when working with footnotes later in this chapter.

Handling Characters Individually: *<fo:character>*

As you can guess from its name, the <fo:character> object enables you to handle the characters in a document individually. One place to use <fo:character> is when you want to replace certain characters with other characters. In the following example, I match an element named <PASSWORD> and replace the characters in it with the character "*":

```
<xsl:template match="PASSWORD">
    <fo:character character="*">
        <xsl:value-of select="."/>
    </fo:character>
</xsl:template>
```

You can use the <fo:character> element to format individual characters, as in this case, which formats the characters in "Hello" using different colors:

```
<fo:character character="H" font-size="24pt" color="red"/>
<fo:character character="E" font-size="24pt" color="yellow"/>
<fo:character character="L" font-size="24pt" color="green"/>
<fo:character character="L" font-size="24pt" color="blue"/>
<fo:character character="O" font-size="24pt" color="orange"/>
```

You can use the following properties with <fo:character>:

- Common aural properties: azimuth, cue-after, cue-before, elevation, pause-after, pause-before, pitch, pitch-range, play-during, richness, speak, speak-header, speak-numeral, speak-punctuation, speech-rate, stress, voice-family, volume
- Common border, padding, and background properties: background-attachment, background-color, background-image, background-repeat, background-position-horizontal, background-position-vertical, border-before-color, border-before-style, border-before-width, border-after-color, border-after-style, border-after-width, border-start-color, border-start-style, border-start-width, border-end-color, border-end-style, border-end-width, border-top-color, border-top-style, border-top-width, border-bottom-color, border-bottom-style, border-bottom-width, border-left-color, border-left-style, border-left-width, border-right-color, border-right-style, border-right-width, padding-before, padding-after, padding-start, padding-end, padding-top, padding-bottom, padding-left, padding-right
- Common font properties: font-family, font-size, font-stretch, font-size-adjust, font-style, font-variant, font-weight
- Common hyphenation properties: country, language, script, hyphenate, hyphenation-character, hyphenation-push-character-count, hyphenation-remain-character-count
- Common inline margin properties: space-end, space-start
- alignment-adjust
- treat-as-word-space
- baseline-identifier
- baseline-shift
- character
- color
- dominant-baseline
- font-height-override-after
- font-height-override-before
- glyph-orientation-horizontal
- glyph-orientation-vertical
- id
- keep-with-next
- keep-with-previous

- letter-spacing
- line-height
- line-height-shift-adjustment
- relative-position
- score-spaces
- suppress-at-line-break
- text-decoration
- text-shadow
- text-transform
- word-spacing

Creating Page Numbers: *<fo:page-number>*

Another useful inline formatting object is <fo:page-number>. This element creates an inline area displaying the current page number. Here's an example:

```
<fo:block>
    You are now reading page <fo:page-number/>.
</fo:block>
```

You can use the following properties with <fo:page-number>:

- Common accessibility properties: source-document, role
- Common aural properties: azimuth, cue-after, cue-before, elevation, pause-after, pause-before, pitch, pitch-range, play-during, richness, speak, speak-header, speak-numeral, speak-punctuation, speech-rate, stress, voice-family, volume
- Common border, padding, and background properties: background-attachment, background-color, background-image, background-repeat, background-position-horizontal, background-position-vertical, border-before-color, border-before-style, border-before-width, border-after-color, border-after-style, border-after-width, border-start-color, border-start-style, border-start-width, border-end-color, border-end-style, border-end-width, border-top-color, border-top-style, border-top-width, border-bottom-color, border-bottom-style, border-bottom-width, border-left-color, border-left-style, border-left-width, border-right-color, border-right-style, border-right-width, padding-before, padding-after, padding-start, padding-end, padding-top, padding-bottom, padding-left, padding-right

- Common font properties: `font-family`, `font-size`, `font-stretch`, `font-size-adjust`, `font-style`, `font-variant`, `font-weight`
- Common inline margin properties: `space-end`, `space-start`
- `alignment-adjust`
- `baseline-identifier`
- `baseline-shift`
- `dominant-baseline`
- `id`
- `keep-with-next`
- `keep-with-previous`
- `letter-spacing`
- `line-height`
- `line-height-shift-adjustment`
- `relative-position`
- `score-spaces`
- `text-decoration`
- `text-shadow`
- `text-transform`
- `word-spacing`

You'll see an example using page numbers during the discussion of page sequences at the end of this chapter.

Inserting Graphics: *<fo:external-graphic>*

A popular element in XSL-FO formatting is `<fo:external-graphic>`, which you use to embed an image in a document.

You can use the following properties with `<fo:external-graphic>`:

- Common accessibility properties: `source-document`, `role`
- Common aural properties: `azimuth`, `cue-after`, `cue-before`, `elevation`, `pause-after`, `pause-before`, `pitch`, `pitch-range`, `play-during`, `richness`, `speak`, `speak-header`, `speak-numeral`, `speak-punctuation`, `speech-rate`, `stress`, `voice-family`, `volume`

- Common border, padding, and background properties: `background-attachment`, `background-color`, `background-image`, `background-repeat`, `background-position-horizontal`, `background-position-vertical`, `border-before-color`, `border-before-style`, `border-before-width`, `border-after-color`, `border-after-style`, `border-after-width`, `border-start-color`, `border-start-style`, `border-start-width`, `border-end-color`, `border-end-style`, `border-end-width`, `border-top-color`, `border-top-style`, `border-top-width`, `border-bottom-color`, `border-bottom-style`, `border-bottom-width`, `border-left-color`, `border-left-style`, `border-left-width`, `border-right-color`, `border-right-style`, `border-right-width`, `padding-before`, `padding-after`, `padding-start`, `padding-end`, `padding-top`, `padding-bottom`, `padding-left`, `padding-right`
- Common inline margin properties: `space-end`, `space-start`
- `alignment-adjust`
- `baseline-identifier`
- `baseline-shift`
- `block-progression-dimension`
- `content-height`
- `content-type`
- `content-width`
- `dominant-baseline`
- `height`
- `id`
- `inline-progression-dimension`
- `keep-with-next`
- `keep-with-previous`
- `line-height`
- `line-height-shift-adjustment`
- `relative-position`
- `overflow`
- `scaling`
- `scaling-method`
- `src`
- `width`

As in HTML, you can set the size of the image in the document; in XSL-FO, you use the `content-height`, `content-width`, and `scaling` properties, and if you don't set these properties, the image is displayed in its original size. The following example, graphics.fo, displays an image, xslfo.jpg, and a caption:

Listing 12.4 **graphics.fo**

```
<?xml version="1.0" encoding="UTF-8"?>
<fo:root xmlns:fo="http://www.w3.org/1999/XSL/Format">

    <fo:layout-master-set>
        <fo:simple-page-master margin-right="20mm"
            margin-left="20mm" margin-bottom="10mm"
            margin-top="10mm" page-width="300mm"
            page-height="400mm" master-name="page">

            <fo:region-body margin-right="0mm"
                margin-left="0mm" margin-bottom="10mm"
                margin-top="0mm"/>

         <fo:region-after extent="10mm"/>

        </fo:simple-page-master>
    </fo:layout-master-set>

    <fo:page-sequence master-name="page">
        <fo:flow flow-name="xsl-region-body">

            <fo:block space-after="12pt" font-weight="bold"
                font-size="36pt" text-align="center">
                Using Graphics
            </fo:block>

            <fo:block text-align="center">
                <fo:external-graphic src="file:xslfo.jpg"/>
            </fo:block>

            <fo:block space-before="10pt" text-align="center"
                font-size="24pt">
                An image embedded in a document.
            </fo:block>

        </fo:flow>
    </fo:page-sequence>
</fo:root>
```

You can see the PDF document created from graphics.fo in Figure 12.3.

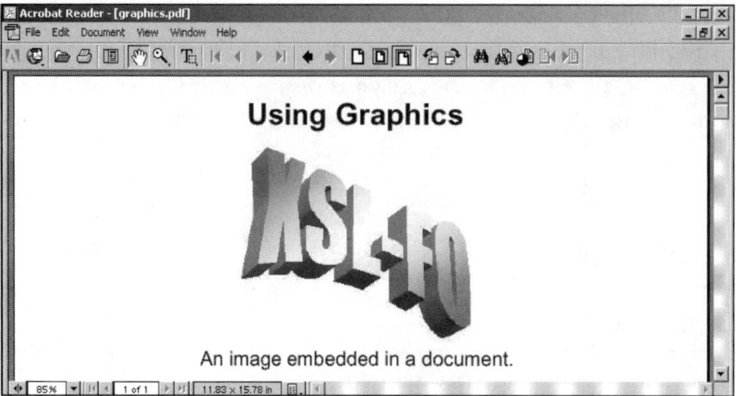

Figure 12.3 Displaying an image using formatting objects.

Actually inserting an image into the result document is easy if your software supports it. The fop processor now supports images (it didn't just a few versions ago), so you can use the `<fo:external-graphic>` element to insert the image this way:

```
<fo:block text-align="center">
    <fo:external-graphic src="file:xslfo.jpg"/>
</fo:block>
```

Formatting First Lines: *<fo:initial-property-set>*

You can use the `<fo:initial-property-set>` element to specify properties for and format the first line of a block. In the following example, I'm formatting the first line of a block in small caps using the `font-variant` property (which, incidentally, fop doesn't support):

```
<fo:block>
    <fo:initial-property-set font-variant="small-caps"/>
        This text will be displayed in the result document.
        The first line will be displayed using small caps.
</fo:block>
```

You can use the following properties with `<fo:initial-property-set>`:

- Common accessibility properties: `source-document`, `role`
- Common aural properties: `azimuth`, `cue-after`, `cue-before`, `elevation`, `pause-after`, `pause-before`, `pitch`, `pitch-range`, `play-during`, `richness`, `speak`, `speak-header`, `speak-numeral`, `speak-punctuation`, `speech-rate`, `stress`, `voice-family`, `volume`

- Common border, padding, and background properties: background-attachment, background-color, background-image, background-repeat, background-position-horizontal, background-position-vertical, border-before-color, border-before-style, border-before-width, border-after-color, border-after-style, border-after-width, border-start-color, border-start-style, border-start-width, border-end-color, border-end-style, border-end-width, border-top-color, border-top-style, border-top-width, border-bottom-color, border-bottom-style, border-bottom-width, border-left-color, border-left-style, border-left-width, border-right-color, border-right-style, border-right-width, padding-before, padding-after, padding-start, padding-end, padding-top, padding-bottom, padding-left, padding-right
- Common font properties: font-family, font-size, font-stretch, font-size-adjust, font-style, font-variant, font-weight
- color
- id
- letter-spacing
- line-height
- line-height-shift-adjustment
- relative-position
- score-spaces
- text-decoration
- text-shadow
- text-transform
- word-spacing

That completes this overview of the inline formatting objects; the next sections look at an *out-of-line* formatting object: footnotes.

Creating Footnotes: *<fo:footnote>* and *<fo:footnote-body>*

Footnotes are called "out-of-line" formatting objects because they add text at the bottom of the page. You create a footnote with the <fo:footnote> element, and the body text of the footnote with <fo:footnote-body>. Neither of these elements supports any properties in the current XSL-FO specification.

The following example, footnotes.fo, puts footnotes to work; in this case, I use two footnotes in the body of the document and add the text for those footnotes:

Listing 12.5 **footnotes.fo**

```
<?xml version="1.0" encoding="UTF-8"?>
<fo:root xmlns:fo="http://www.w3.org/1999/XSL/Format">

    <fo:layout-master-set>
        <fo:simple-page-master margin-right="20mm" margin-left="20mm"
            margin-bottom="10mm" margin-top="10mm" page-width="300mm"
            page-height="400mm" master-name="page">

            <fo:region-body margin-right="0mm" margin-left="0mm"
                margin-bottom="10mm" margin-top="0mm"/>

            <fo:region-after extent="10mm"/>

        </fo:simple-page-master>
    </fo:layout-master-set>

    <fo:page-sequence master-name="page">
        <fo:flow flow-name="xsl-region-body">

            <fo:block space-after="12pt" font-weight="bold"
                font-size="36pt" text-align="center">
                Using Footnotes
            </fo:block>

            <fo:block font-size="24pt">
                This
                <fo:footnote>
                    <fo:inline>footnote
                        <fo:inline font-size="16pt"
                        vertical-align="super">
                            1
                        </fo:inline>
                    </fo:inline>
                    <fo:footnote-body>
                        <fo:block>
                            1. Here's the first footnote's text.
                        </fo:block>
                    </fo:footnote-body>
                </fo:footnote>
                  refers to text at the bottom of this page.
            </fo:block>

            <fo:block font-size="24pt">
                This second
                <fo:footnote>
                    <fo:inline>footnote
```

```
                    <fo:inline font-size="16pt"
                    vertical-align="super">
                        2
                    </fo:inline>
                </fo:inline>
                <fo:footnote-body>
                    <fo:block>
                        2. And here's the second footnote's text.
                    </fo:block>
                </fo:footnote-body>
            </fo:footnote>
            also refers to text at the bottom of this page.
        </fo:block>

    </fo:flow>
  </fo:page-sequence>
</fo:root>
```

You can see text, complete with the footnote superscripts 1 and 2, in Figure 12.4.

And you can see the text for the two footnotes at the bottom of the same page in Figure 12.5.

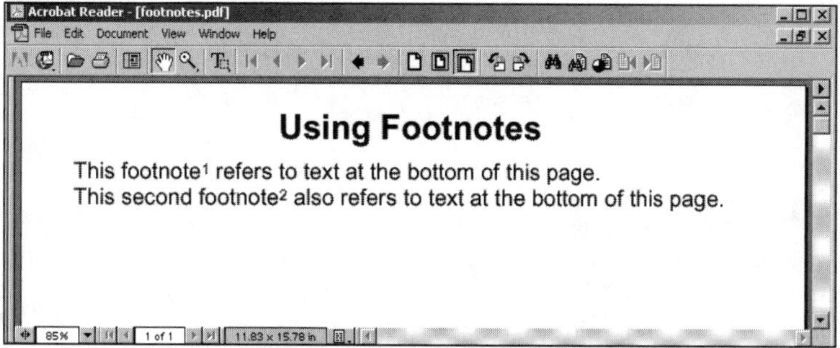

Figure 12.4 Text with footnotes.

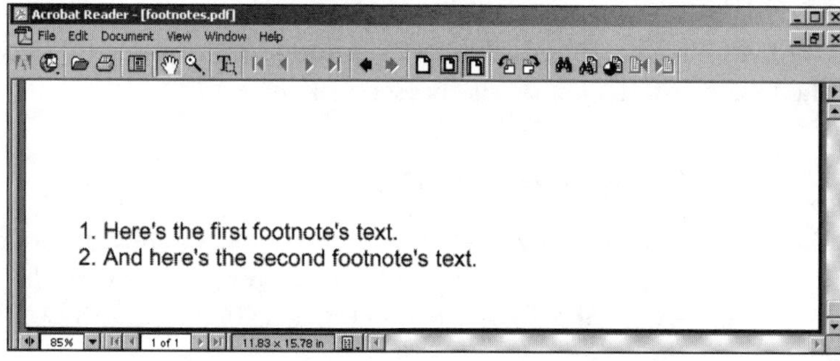

Figure 12.5 Footnote text at the bottom of a page.

To create footnoted text, you use the `<fo:footnote>` element. With the fop processor, you're responsible for adding the actual superscripted footnote number, such as 1 or 2, yourself. Here's how that looks in footnotes.fo, where I set an inline element's `vertical-align` property to "super" to create a superscript:

```
<fo:block font-size="24pt">
          This
          <fo:footnote>
              <fo:inline>footnote
                  <fo:inline font-size="16pt" vertical-align="super">1</fo:inline>
              </fo:inline>
              .
              .
              .
      </fo:block>
```

To create the footnote text that appears at the bottom of the page, you use an `<fo:footnote-body>` element inside the `<fo:footnote>` element. The fop processor does not number footnotes itself, so you're responsible for adding the footnote numbers, as follows:

```
<fo:block font-size="24pt">
    This
    <fo:footnote>
        <fo:inline>footnote
            <fo:inline font-size="16pt"
            vertical-align="super">
                1
            </fo:inline>
        </fo:inline>
        <fo:footnote-body>
            <fo:block>
                1. Here's the first footnote's text.
            </fo:block>
        </fo:footnote-body>
    </fo:footnote>
      refers to text at the bottom of this page.
</fo:block>
```

This XSL-FO produces both the first footnoted text you see in Figure 12.4 and the first footnote's text itself you see in Figure 12.5.

Creating Links: *<fo:basic-link>*

Another powerful aspect of XSL-FO is the ability to use *links* from document to document. This is currently supported in the fop processor with the XSL-FO `<fo:basic-link>` element, which acts much like a simple hyperlink.

You can use these properties with `<fo:basic-link>`:

- Common accessibility properties: source-document, role
- Common aural properties: azimuth, cue-after, cue-before, elevation, pause-after, pause-before, pitch, pitch-range, play-during, richness, speak, speak-header, speak-numeral, speak-punctuation, speech-rate, stress, voice-family, volume
- Common border, padding, and background properties: background-attachment, background-color, background-image, background-repeat, background-position-horizontal, background-position-vertical, border-before-color, border-before-style, border-before-width, border-after-color, border-after-style, border-after-width, border-start-color, border-start-style, border-start-width, border-end-color, border-end-style, border-end-width, border-top-color, border-top-style, border-top-width, border-bottom-color, border-bottom-style, border-bottom-width, border-left-color, border-left-style, border-left-width, border-right-color, border-right-style, border-right-width, padding-before, padding-after, padding-start, padding-end, padding-top, padding-bottom, padding-left, padding-right
- Common inline margin properties–inline: space-end, space-start
- Common relative position properties: top, right, bottom, left, relative-position
- alignment-adjust
- alignment-baseline
- baseline-shift
- destination-placement-offset
- dominant-baseline
- external-destination
- id
- indicate-destination
- internal-destination
- keep-together
- keep-with-next
- keep-with-previous
- line-height
- line-height-shift-adjustment
- show-destination

- `target-processing-context`
- `target-presentation-context`
- `target-stylesheet`

The following example, links.fo, includes a link to a PDF document created earlier in this chapter, graphics.pdf:

Listing 12.6 **links.fo**

```
<?xml version="1.0" encoding="UTF-8"?>
<fo:root xmlns:fo="http://www.w3.org/1999/XSL/Format">

    <fo:layout-master-set>
        <fo:simple-page-master margin-right="20mm" margin-left="20mm"
            margin-bottom="10mm" margin-top="10mm" page-width="300mm"
            page-height="400mm" master-name="page">

            <fo:region-body margin-right="0mm" margin-left="0mm"
                margin-bottom="10mm" margin-top="0mm"/>

            <fo:region-after extent="10mm"/>

        </fo:simple-page-master>
    </fo:layout-master-set>

    <fo:page-sequence master-name="page">
        <fo:flow flow-name="xsl-region-body">

            <fo:block space-after="12pt" font-weight="bold"
                font-size="36pt"
                text-align="center">
                Using Links
            </fo:block>

            <fo:block font-size="24pt">
                If you'd like to see some images, click
                <fo:basic-link external-destination="graphics.pdf">
                    <fo:inline text-decoration="underline">here</fo:inline>
                </fo:basic-link>.
            </fo:block>

        </fo:flow>
    </fo:page-sequence>
</fo:root>
```

You can see the PDF document built from links.fo in Figure 12.6. Note that I've explicitly underlined the link to make it appear more like a hyperlink. When you move the mouse cursor over the link in Adobe Acrobat, the cursor changes to the same one that browsers such as the Internet Explorer use for hyperlinks, as you see in Figure 12.6. When you click the link, Acrobat navigates to graphics.pdf (which you should place in the same directory as links.pdf for the purposes of this example), displaying that new document.

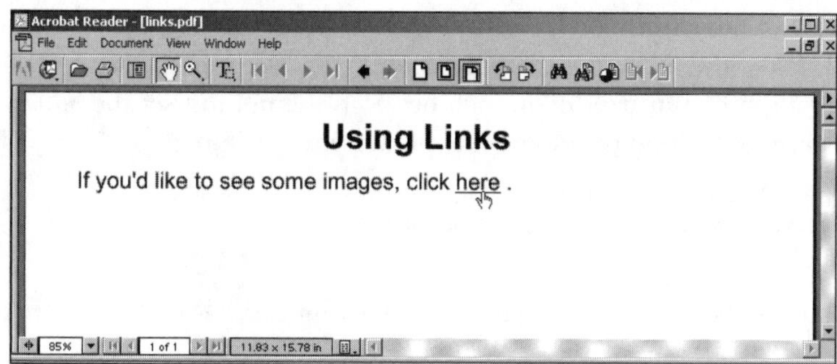

Figure 12.6 Supporting basic links with XSL-FO.

Creating the link is easy in this case; here, I'm just setting the `external-destination` property of the `<fo:basic-link>` element to "graphics.pdf":

```
<fo:block font-size="24pt">
        If you'd like to see some images, click
        <fo:basic-link external-destination="graphics.pdf">
        .
        .
        .
        </fo:basic-link>.
    </fo:block>
```

All that's left is to add some underlined text that the user can click to navigate to the new document. You don't need to make the text underlined, of course, but otherwise there's nothing to indicate that the text is a link, except that the mouse cursor changes when it moves over the text. You add the underlined text as follows:

```
<fo:block font-size="24pt">
        If you'd like to see some images, click
        <fo:basic-link external-destination="graphics.pdf">
            <fo:inline text-decoration="underline">here</fo:inline>
        </fo:basic-link>.
    </fo:block>
```

So far, the only implementations of XSL-FO links are basic ones, as shown in this example. However, if you're familiar with the XML specifications for XPointer and XLink, you should expect a great deal more sophistication in this area in the future.

Creating Columns

Another useful way of using XSL-FO to format text is to use *columns*. Creating columns is not difficult; all you have to do is to use the `column-count` and `column-gap` properties of the `<fo:region-body>` element and leave the rest up to the XSL-FO processor.

Look at the following example, columns.fo. To format text into two columns with a gap of a quarter of an inch between them, I just set the `column-count` property to "2" and the `column-gap` property to "0.25in":

```
<?xml version="1.0" encoding="utf-8"?>
<fo:root xmlns:fo="http://www.w3.org/1999/XSL/Format">

    <fo:layout-master-set>
        <fo:simple-page-master margin-right="20mm" margin-left="20mm"
            margin-bottom="10mm" margin-top="10mm" page-width="300mm"
            page-height="400mm" master-name="page">

            <fo:region-body margin-top="3cm" margin-bottom="2cm"
                column-count="2" column-gap="0.25in"/>

            <fo:region-before extent="3cm"/>
            <fo:region-after extent="2cm"/>

        </fo:simple-page-master>
    </fo:layout-master-set>
        .
        .
        .
```

All that's left is to add some sample text to display in the columns; note that I'm also using the `<fo:static-content>` element to create a header—more on `<fo:static-content>` in the following section:

Listing 12.7 **columns.fo**

```
<?xml version="1.0" encoding="utf-8"?>
<fo:root xmlns:fo="http://www.w3.org/1999/XSL/Format">

    <fo:layout-master-set>
        <fo:simple-page-master margin-right="20mm" margin-left="20mm"
            margin-bottom="10mm" margin-top="10mm" page-width="300mm"
            page-height="400mm" master-name="page">

            <fo:region-body margin-top="3cm" margin-bottom="2cm"
                column-count="2" column-gap="0.25in"/>

            <fo:region-before extent="3cm"/>
            <fo:region-after extent="2cm"/>
```

```
        </fo:simple-page-master>
    </fo:layout-master-set>

    <fo:page-sequence master-name="page">

        <fo:static-content flow-name="xsl-region-before">
            <fo:block text-align="center" font-size="36pt"
                font-family="sans-serif"
                line-height="48pt" >
                Creating Columns
            </fo:block>
        </fo:static-content>

        <fo:flow flow-name="xsl-region-body">
        <fo:block font-size="24pt" font-family="sans-serif" space-after="15pt">
                Sample Text. Sample Text. Sample Text. Sample Text. Sample Text.
                Sample Text. Sample Text. Sample Text. Sample Text. Sample Text.
                Sample Text. Sample Text. Sample Text. Sample Text. Sample Text.
                Sample Text. Sample Text. Sample Text. Sample Text. Sample Text.
                Sample Text. Sample Text. Sample Text. Sample Text. Sample Text.
                Sample Text. Sample Text. Sample Text. Sample Text. Sample Text.
                Sample Text. Sample Text. Sample Text. Sample Text. Sample Text.
                Sample Text. Sample Text. Sample Text. Sample Text. Sample Text.
                Sample Text. Sample Text. Sample Text. Sample Text. Sample Text.
                Sample Text. Sample Text. Sample Text. Sample Text. Sample Text.
                Sample Text. Sample Text. Sample Text. Sample Text. Sample Text.
                Sample Text. Sample Text. Sample Text. Sample Text. Sample Text.
                Sample Text. Sample Text. Sample Text. Sample Text. Sample Text.
                Sample Text. Sample Text. Sample Text. Sample Text. Sample Text.
                Sample Text. Sample Text. Sample Text. Sample Text. Sample Text.
                Sample Text. Sample Text. Sample Text. Sample Text. Sample Text.
                Sample Text. Sample Text. Sample Text. Sample Text. Sample Text.
                Sample Text. Sample Text. Sample Text. Sample Text. Sample Text.
                Sample Text. Sample Text. Sample Text. Sample Text. Sample Text.
                Sample Text. Sample Text. Sample Text. Sample Text. Sample Text.
                Sample Text. Sample Text. Sample Text. Sample Text. Sample Text.
                Sample Text. Sample Text. Sample Text. Sample Text. Sample Text.
                Sample Text. Sample Text. Sample Text. Sample Text. Sample Text.
                Sample Text. Sample Text. Sample Text. Sample Text. Sample Text.
                Sample Text. Sample Text. Sample Text. Sample Text. Sample Text.
                Sample Text. Sample Text. Sample Text. Sample Text. Sample Text.
                Sample Text. Sample Text. Sample Text. Sample Text. Sample Text.
            </fo:block>
        </fo:flow>
    </fo:page-sequence>
</fo:root>
```

You can see the results of this document, columns.pdf, in Figure 12.7.

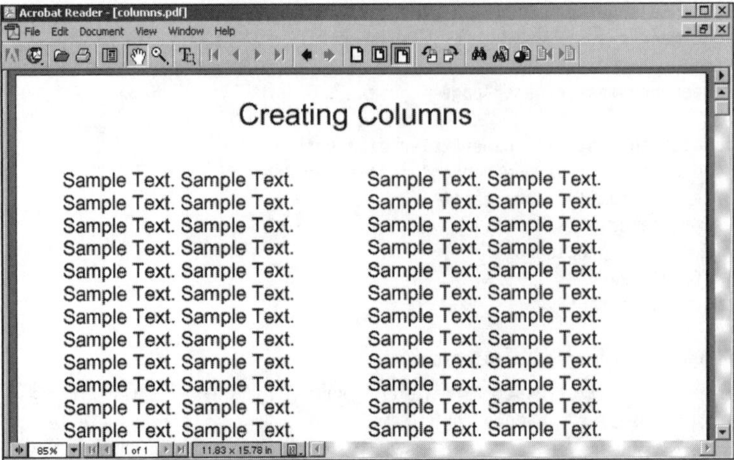

Figure 12.7 Creating columns using XSL-FO.

Page Sequences and Page Numbering

So far, I've used the same page master for all pages in these XSL-FO documents. If the content of a document fills more than one page, the XSL-FO processor uses the same page master for all subsequent pages.

However, you might want to use different page masters for different locations in your document. For example, you may want to format the first page differently from the subsequent pages. Using XSL-FO, you can do this.

Each `<fo:page-sequence>` element, which I've used in all XSL-FO examples, references either a page master *or* an `<fo:page-sequence-master>` element. Using the `<fo:page-sequence-master>` element, you can specify different page masters to use in a sequence.

The following example, pages.fo, shows how this works. In this case, I create one simple page master, "first", for the first page, starting the text part way down on the page by setting the `<fo:region-body>` element's `margin-top` property to "50mm":

```
<?xml version="1.0" encoding="utf-8"?>
<fo:root xmlns:fo="http://www.w3.org/1999/XSL/Format">

  <fo:layout-master-set>
        <fo:simple-page-master margin-right="20mm" margin-left="20mm"
            margin-bottom="10mm" margin-top="10mm" page-width="300mm"
            page-height="400mm" master-name="first">
```

```
        <fo:region-body margin-right="0mm" margin-left="0mm"
            margin-bottom="10mm" margin-top="50mm"/>

        <fo:region-after extent="10mm"/>
        <fo:region-before extent="10mm"/>

    </fo:simple-page-master>
    .
    .
    .
```

And I create a new page master, "rest", for all the other pages, starting the text on those pages near the top of the page by setting the `<fo:region-body>` element's `margin-top` property to "20mm":

```
<?xml version="1.0" encoding="utf-8"?>
<fo:root xmlns:fo="http://www.w3.org/1999/XSL/Format">

  <fo:layout-master-set>
        <fo:simple-page-master margin-right="20mm" margin-left="20mm"
            margin-bottom="10mm" margin-top="10mm" page-width="300mm"
            page-height="400mm" master-name="first">
            .
            .
            .
        </fo:simple-page-master>

        <fo:simple-page-master margin-right="25mm" margin-left="25mm"
            margin-bottom="15mm" margin-top="15mm" page-width="300mm"
            page-height="400mm" master-name="rest">

            <fo:region-body margin-right="0mm" margin-left="0mm"
                margin-bottom="10mm" margin-top="20mm"/>

            <fo:region-after extent="10mm"/>
            <fo:region-before extent="10mm"/>

        </fo:simple-page-master>
        .
        .
        .
```

To create a page sequence master that uses the simple page masters "first" and "rest", I use the `<fo:page-sequence-master>` element:

```
<?xml version="1.0" encoding="utf-8"?>
<fo:root xmlns:fo="http://www.w3.org/1999/XSL/Format">

  <fo:layout-master-set>
        <fo:simple-page-master margin-right="20mm" margin-left="20mm"
```

```
        margin-bottom="10mm" margin-top="10mm" page-width="300mm"
        page-height="400mm" master-name="first">
        .
        .
        .
    </fo:simple-page-master>

    <fo:simple-page-master margin-right="25mm" margin-left="25mm"
        margin-bottom="15mm" margin-top="15mm" page-width="300mm"
        page-height="400mm" master-name="rest">
        .
        .
        .
    </fo:simple-page-master>

    <fo:page-sequence-master master-name="sequence" >
        .
        .
        .
    </fo:page-sequence-master>

</fo:layout-master-set>
```

You can use this property with <fo:page-sequence-master>:

- master-name

In this case, I've just named the new page sequence "sequence". The type of page sequence master I'm creating here is a *repeatable page master*, and you use the <fo:repeatable-page-master-alternatives> element to specify the names of the page masters you want to use in the new sequence:

```
<fo:page-sequence-master master-name="sequence">
    <fo:repeatable-page-master-alternatives>
    .
    .
    .
    </fo:repeatable-page-master-alternatives>
</fo:page-sequence-master>
```

You can use this property with <fo:repeatable-page-master-alternatives> to indicate how many times you want the sequence to repeat:

- maximum-repeats

Finally, you specify the page masters that are to be used in this sequence master with the <fo:conditional-page-master-reference> element. This element references a page master with the master-name property, and that page master is used when a specified condition is met. To match the first page, you set the page-position property to "first", and to match the rest of the pages, you set page-position to "rest":

```
<fo:page-sequence-master master-name="sequence" >
    <fo:repeatable-page-master-alternatives>
<fo:conditional-page-master-reference master-name="first"
                page-position="first" />
            <fo:conditional-page-master-reference master-name="rest"
                page-position="rest" />
    </fo:repeatable-page-master-alternatives>
</fo:page-sequence-master>
```

You can use the following properties with <fo:conditional-page-master-reference>:

- master-name
- page-position
- odd-or-even
- blank-or-not-blank

Now when I create a page sequence with <fo:page-sequence>, I specify that the XSL-FO processor should use the sequence master, "sequence", that I just created by setting the <fo:page-sequence> element's master-name attribute:

```
<fo:page-sequence master-name="sequence">
    .
    .
    .
```

Now that I'm dealing with multiple pages, I want to also add page numbers to the pages in the document. The XSL-FO processor replaces the element <fo:page-number> with the current page number, so creating page numbering is no problem. To display the page number at the top of each page, I create a page header with the <fo:static-content> element.

There are two kinds of flow objects: <fo:static-content> and <fo:flow>. You've already seen how to use <fo:flow> to add pages to the flow of a document. You use the <fo:static-content> element to add headers and footers to document. You can use this property with <fo:static-content>:

- flow-name

To create a header, all I have to do is to place the <fo:static-content> element before the <fo:flow> element in the page sequence:

```
<fo:page-sequence master-name="sequence">
```

```
        <fo:static-content flow-name="xsl-region-before">
            <fo:block text-align="end"
                font-size="24pt"
                font-family="sans-serif"
                line-height="36pt" >
                Sample Document p. <fo:page-number/>
            </fo:block>
        </fo:static-content>

        <fo:flow flow-name="xsl-region-body">
        .
        .
        .
```

Setting the initial page number

To set the initial page number of a page sequence, you can use the <fo:page-sequence> element's initial-page-number property. This enables you, for example, to format chapters separately, starting each with the correct page number.

Finally, all that's left in pages.fo is to add some sample text to format so that the document contains more than one page; I color this filler text gray so it's not distracting:

Listing 12.8 **pages.fo**

```
<?xml version="1.0" encoding="utf-8"?>
<fo:root xmlns:fo="http://www.w3.org/1999/XSL/Format">

  <fo:layout-master-set>
        <fo:simple-page-master margin-right="20mm" margin-left="20mm"
            margin-bottom="10mm" margin-top="10mm" page-width="300mm"
            page-height="400mm" master-name="first">

            <fo:region-body margin-right="0mm" margin-left="0mm"
                margin-bottom="10mm" margin-top="50mm"/>

            <fo:region-after extent="10mm"/>
            <fo:region-before extent="10mm"/>

        </fo:simple-page-master>

        <fo:simple-page-master margin-right="25mm" margin-left="25mm"
            margin-bottom="15mm" margin-top="15mm" page-width="300mm"
            page-height="400mm" master-name="rest">

            <fo:region-body margin-right="0mm" margin-left="0mm"
                margin-bottom="10mm" margin-top="20mm"/>

            <fo:region-after extent="10mm"/>
            <fo:region-before extent="10mm"/>
```

```
    </fo:simple-page-master>

    <fo:page-sequence-master master-name="sequence" >
        <fo:repeatable-page-master-alternatives>
            <fo:conditional-page-master-reference master-name="first"
                page-position="first" />
            <fo:conditional-page-master-reference master-name="rest"
                page-position="rest" />
        </fo:repeatable-page-master-alternatives>
    </fo:page-sequence-master>

</fo:layout-master-set>

<fo:page-sequence master-name="sequence">

    <fo:static-content flow-name="xsl-region-before">
        <fo:block text-align="end"
            font-size="24pt"
            font-family="sans-serif"
            line-height="36pt" >
            Sample Document p. <fo:page-number/>
        </fo:block>
    </fo:static-content>

    <fo:flow flow-name="xsl-region-body">

        <fo:block font-size="36pt" font-family="Times"
            text-align="center"
            space-after="24pt">
            Sample Document
        </fo:block>
        <fo:block font-size="24pt" font-family="sans-serif" color="gray">
         Sample Text. Sample Text. Sample Text. Sample Text. Sample Text. Sample Text.
         Sample Text. Sample Text. Sample Text. Sample Text. Sample Text. Sample Text.
         Sample Text. Sample Text. Sample Text. Sample Text. Sample Text. Sample Text.
         Sample Text. Sample Text. Sample Text. Sample Text. Sample Text. Sample Text.
         Sample Text. Sample Text. Sample Text. Sample Text. Sample Text. Sample Text.
         Sample Text. Sample Text. Sample Text. Sample Text. Sample Text. Sample Text.
         Sample Text. Sample Text. Sample Text. Sample Text. Sample Text. Sample Text.
         Sample Text. Sample Text. Sample Text. Sample Text. Sample Text. Sample Text.
         Sample Text. Sample Text. Sample Text. Sample Text. Sample Text. Sample Text.
         Sample Text. Sample Text. Sample Text. Sample Text. Sample Text. Sample Text.
         Sample Text. Sample Text. Sample Text. Sample Text. Sample Text. Sample Text.
         Sample Text. Sample Text. Sample Text. Sample Text. Sample Text. Sample Text.
         Sample Text. Sample Text. Sample Text. Sample Text. Sample Text. Sample Text.
         Sample Text. Sample Text. Sample Text. Sample Text. Sample Text. Sample Text.
         Sample Text. Sample Text. Sample Text. Sample Text. Sample Text. Sample Text.
         Sample Text. Sample Text. Sample Text. Sample Text. Sample Text. Sample Text.
         Sample Text. Sample Text. Sample Text. Sample Text. Sample Text. Sample Text.
         Sample Text. Sample Text. Sample Text. Sample Text. Sample Text. Sample Text.
         Sample Text. Sample Text. Sample Text. Sample Text. Sample Text. Sample Text.
         Sample Text. Sample Text. Sample Text. Sample Text. Sample Text. Sample Text.
         Sample Text. Sample Text. Sample Text. Sample Text. Sample Text. Sample Text.
```

```
            Sample Text. Sample Text. Sample Text. Sample Text. Sample Text. Sample Text.
            Sample Text. Sample Text. Sample Text. Sample Text. Sample Text. Sample Text.
            Sample Text. Sample Text. Sample Text. Sample Text. Sample Text. Sample Text.
            Sample Text. Sample Text. Sample Text. Sample Text. Sample Text. Sample Text.
            Sample Text. Sample Text. Sample Text. Sample Text. Sample Text. Sample Text.
            Sample Text. Sample Text. Sample Text. Sample Text. Sample Text. Sample Text.
            Sample Text. Sample Text. Sample Text. Sample Text. Sample Text. Sample Text.
            Sample Text. Sample Text. Sample Text. Sample Text. Sample Text. Sample Text.
            Sample Text. Sample Text. Sample Text. Sample Text. Sample Text. Sample Text.
            Sample Text. Sample Text. Sample Text. Sample Text. Sample Text. Sample Text.
            Sample Text. Sample Text. Sample Text. Sample Text. Sample Text. Sample Text.
            Sample Text. Sample Text. Sample Text. Sample Text. Sample Text. Sample Text.
            Sample Text. Sample Text. Sample Text. Sample Text. Sample Text. Sample Text.
            Sample Text. Sample Text. Sample Text. Sample Text. Sample Text. Sample Text.
            Sample Text. Sample Text. Sample Text. Sample Text. Sample Text. Sample Text.
            Sample Text. Sample Text. Sample Text. Sample Text. Sample Text. Sample Text.
            Sample Text. Sample Text. Sample Text. Sample Text. Sample Text. Sample Text.
            Sample Text. Sample Text. Sample Text. Sample Text. Sample Text. Sample Text.
            Sample Text. Sample Text. Sample Text. Sample Text. Sample Text. Sample Text.
            Sample Text. Sample Text. Sample Text. Sample Text. Sample Text. Sample Text.
            Sample Text. Sample Text. Sample Text. Sample Text. Sample Text. Sample Text.
            Sample Text. Sample Text. Sample Text. Sample Text. Sample Text. Sample Text.
            Sample Text. Sample Text. Sample Text. Sample Text. Sample Text. Sample Text.
            Sample Text. Sample Text. Sample Text. Sample Text. Sample Text. Sample Text.
            Sample Text. Sample Text. Sample Text. Sample Text. Sample Text. Sample Text.
        </fo:block>

      </fo:flow>
    </fo:page-sequence>
</fo:root>
```

And that's it. You can see the first page created by pages.fo in Figure 12.8; as you can see in that figure, the text starts some distance down the first page.

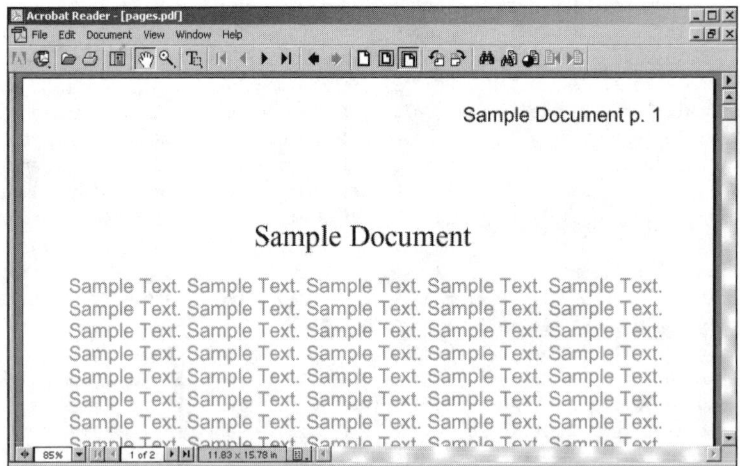

Figure 12.8 A first page as formatted with XSL-FO.

The text on the second page, on the other hand, starts near the top, as you see in Figure 12.9.

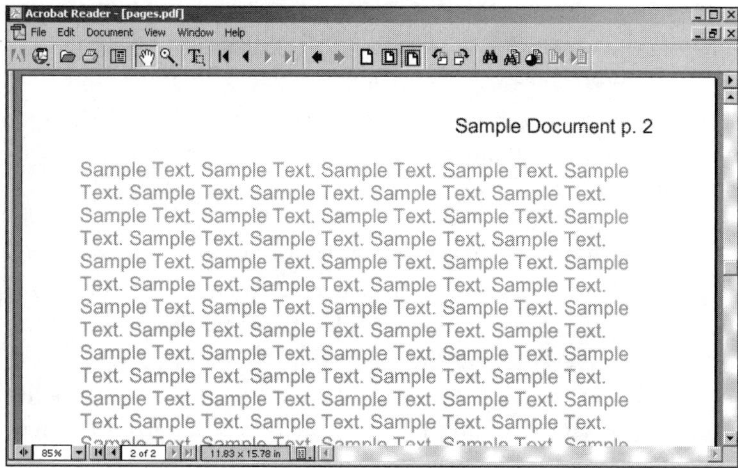

Figure 12.9 A second page as formatted with XSL-FO.

As you can see in Listing 12.8, I use a lot of lines that hold nothing but the words "Sample Text." in pages.fo to make sure there's enough text to create a multiple-page document. However, you don't actually need a lot of text to skip to the next page; you can also set the `<fo:block>` element's `break-after` property to "page", which causes the XSL-FO processor to skip to the next page after the current block:

```
<fo:flow flow-name="xsl-region-body">

  <fo:block font-size="36pt" font-family="Times" text-align="center"
  space-after="24pt">
  Sample Document
  </fo:block>

  <fo:block font-size="24pt" font-family="sans-serif" color="gray"
      break-after="page">
      Sample Text. Sample Text. Sample Text. Sample Text. Sample Text.
      Sample Text.
      Sample Text. Sample Text. Sample Text. Sample Text. Sample Text.
      Sample Text.
  </fo:block>

  <fo:block font-size="24pt" font-family="sans-serif" color="gray">
      Sample Text. Sample Text. Sample Text. Sample Text. Sample Text.
      Sample Text.
      Sample Text. Sample Text. Sample Text. Sample Text. Sample Text.
      Sample Text.
  </fo:block>

</fo:flow>
```

That's all it takes. Now the XSL-FO processor skips to the next page after the block. You can use the following properties and settings to create breaks:

- `break-after`. Specifies that the last area generated by formatting this formatting object shall be the last one placed in a particular context. Set to auto | column | page | even-page | odd-page | inherit.
- `break-before`. Specifies that the first area generated should be the first one placed in a specific context. Set to auto | column | page | even-page | odd-page | inherit.

Here's another example showing how to use page sequences. If you take a look at a book printed in Western languages such as English, German, or French, you see that even-numbered pages are typically on the left, and odd-numbered pages are on the right. You can format even and odd pages differently: for example, you can allow extra margin space near the book's binding, which means adding extra left-margin space for odd pages and extra right-margin space for even pages.

To implement that, you can use the `odd-or-even` attribute of the `<fo:conditional-page-master-reference>` element. You can set the `odd-or-even` attribute to "even" or "odd" to select even or odd pages respectively, as follows:

```
<?xml version="1.0" encoding="utf-8"?>
<fo:root xmlns:fo="http://www.w3.org/1999/XSL/Format">

    <fo:layout-master-set>
        <fo:simple-page-master margin-right="50mm" margin-left="20mm"
            margin-bottom="10mm" margin-top="10mm" page-width="300mm"
            page-height="400mm" master-name="leftpage">

            <fo:region-body margin-right="0mm" margin-left="0mm"
                margin-bottom="10mm" margin-top="50mm"/>

            <fo:region-after extent="10mm"/>
            <fo:region-before extent="10mm"/>

        </fo:simple-page-master>

        <fo:simple-page-master margin-right="20mm" margin-left="50mm"
            margin-bottom="10mm" margin-top="10mm" page-width="300mm"
            page-height="400mm" master-name="rightpage">

            <fo:region-body margin-right="0mm" margin-left="0mm"
                margin-bottom="10mm" margin-top="20mm"/>

            <fo:region-after extent="10mm"/>
```

```
        <fo:region-before extent="10mm"/>

    </fo:simple-page-master>

    <fo:page-sequence-master master-name="alternatingpages">
        <fo:repeatable-page-master-alternatives>
            <fo:conditional-page-master-reference master-name="rightpage"
                odd-or-even="odd" />
            <fo:conditional-page-master-reference master-name="leftpage"
                odd-or-even="even" />
        </fo:repeatable-page-master-alternatives>
    </fo:page-sequence-master>

</fo:layout-master-set>

<fo:page-sequence master-name="alternatingpages">
    .
    .
    .
```

That's all it takes. Now right-hand pages have extra left-margin space near the book's binding, and left-hand pages have extra right-margin space as well.

As you can see, there's a lot to the XSL-FO formatting objects, and as mentioned earlier, there's a lot more that this book doesn't have the space to cover. For more details, take a look at the W3C site, `www.w3.org/TR/xsl/`. Not many software packages can put formatting objects to work yet, although that's going to change in the future.

That's it for XSL-FO—and that's it for this book. You've seen all kinds of XSLT transformations here, from XML to XML, to HTML, to XHTML, to RTF, to plain text, to JavaScript, to SQL-based databases, and now to XSL-FO. You've seen all the available elements, attributes, and functions available in XSLT. And you've seen many working examples. All that remains is for you to put all this power to work for yourself. Best of luck to you in your XSLT work!

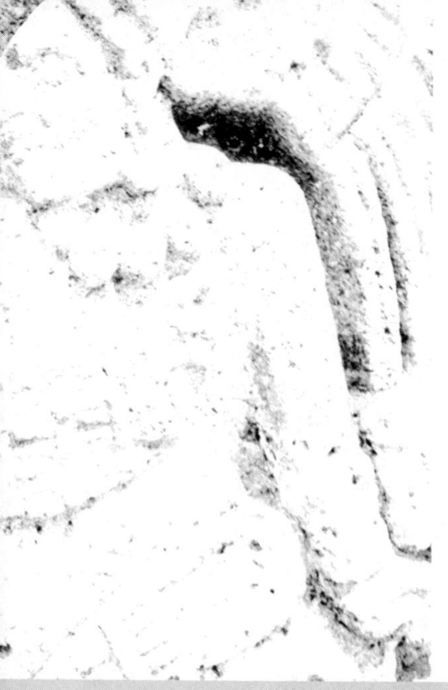

A
The XSLT DTD

THIS APPENDIX LISTS THE DTD FRAGMENT FOR XSLT 1.0 stylesheets, section C, in the W3C XSLT 1.0 recommendation at `www.w3.org/TR/xslt`. It lists the XSLT 1.0 elements and their attributes for reference.

W3C® DOCUMENT NOTICE AND LICENSE

Copyright © 1994-2000 World Wide Web Consortium, (Massachusetts Institute of Technology, Institut National de Recherche en Informatique et en Automatique, Keio University). All Rights Reserved.

`http://www.w3.org/Consortium/Legal/`

Public documents on the W3C site are provided by the copyright holders under the following license. The software or Document Type Definitions (DTDs) associated with W3C specifications are governed by the Software Notice. By using and/or copying this document, or the W3C document from which this statement is linked, you (the licensee) agree that you have read, understood, and will comply with the following terms and conditions:

Permission to use, copy, and distribute the contents of this document, or the W3C document from which this statement is linked, in any medium for any purpose and without fee or royalty is hereby granted, provided that you include the following on *ALL* copies of the document, or portions thereof, that you use:

A link or URL to the original W3C document.

The pre-existing copyright notice of the original author, or if it doesn't exist, a notice of the form: "Copyright © [$date-of-document] World Wide Web Consortium, (Massachusetts Institute of Technology, Institut National de Recherche en Informatique et en Automatique, Keio University). All Rights Reserved. http://www.w3.org/Consortium/Legal/" (Hypertext is preferred, but a textual representation is permitted.)

If it exists, the STATUS of the W3C document.

When space permits, inclusion of the full text of this **NOTICE** should be provided. We request that authorship attribution be provided in any software, documents, or other items or products that you create pursuant to the implementation of the contents of this document, or any portion thereof.

No right to create modifications or derivatives of W3C documents is granted pursuant to this license. However, if additional requirements (documented in the Copyright FAQ) are satisfied, the right to create modifications or derivatives is sometimes granted by the W3C to individuals complying with those requirements.

THIS DOCUMENT IS PROVIDED "AS IS," AND COPYRIGHT HOLDERS MAKE NO REPRESENTATIONS OR WARRANTIES, EXPRESS OR IMPLIED, INCLUDING, BUT NOT LIMITED TO, WARRANTIES OF MERCHANTABILITY, FITNESS FOR A PARTICULAR PURPOSE, NON-INFRINGEMENT, OR TITLE; THAT THE CONTENTS OF THE DOCUMENT ARE SUITABLE FOR ANY PURPOSE; NOR THAT THE IMPLEMENTATION OF SUCH CONTENTS WILL NOT INFRINGE ANY THIRD PARTY PATENTS, COPYRIGHTS, TRADEMARKS OR OTHER RIGHTS.

COPYRIGHT HOLDERS WILL NOT BE LIABLE FOR ANY DIRECT, INDIRECT, SPECIAL OR CONSEQUENTIAL DAMAGES ARISING OUT OF ANY USE OF THE DOCUMENT OR THE PERFORMANCE OR IMPLEMENTATION OF THE CONTENTS THEREOF.

The name and trademarks of copyright holders may NOT be used in advertising or publicity pertaining to this document or its contents without specific, written prior permission. Title to copyright in this document will at all times remain with copyright holders.

DTD Fragment for XSLT Stylesheets (Non-Normative)

NOTE: This DTD Fragment is not normative because XML 1.0 DTDs do not support XML Namespaces and thus cannot correctly describe the allowed structure of an XSLT stylesheet.

The following entity can be used to construct a DTD for XSLT stylesheets that create instances of a particular result DTD. Before referencing the entity, the stylesheet DTD must define a `result-elements` parameter entity listing the allowed result element types. For example:

```
<!ENTITY % result-elements "
  | fo:inline-sequence
  | fo:block
">
```

Such result elements should be declared to have `xsl:use-attribute-sets` and `xsl:extension-element-prefixes` attributes. The following entity declares the `result-element-atts` parameter for this purpose. The content that XSLT allows for result elements is the same as it allows for the XSLT elements that are declared in the following entity with a content model of `%template;`. The DTD may use a more restrictive content model than `%template;` to reflect the constraints of the result DTD.

The DTD may define the `non-xsl-top-level` parameter entity to allow additional top-level elements from namespaces other than the XSLT namespace.

The use of the `xsl:` prefix in this DTD does not imply that XSLT stylesheets are required to use this prefix. Any of the elements declared in this DTD may have attributes whose name starts with `xmlns:` or is equal to `xmlns` in addition to the attributes declared in this DTD.

```
<!ENTITY % char-instructions "
  | xsl:apply-templates
  | xsl:call-template
  | xsl:apply-imports
  | xsl:for-each
  | xsl:value-of
  | xsl:copy-of
  | xsl:number
  | xsl:choose
  | xsl:if
  | xsl:text
  | xsl:copy
```

```
  | xsl:variable
  | xsl:message
  | xsl:fallback
">

<!ENTITY % instructions "
  %char-instructions;
  | xsl:processing-instruction
  | xsl:comment
  | xsl:element
  | xsl:attribute
">

<!ENTITY % char-template "
 (#PCDATA
  %char-instructions;)*
">

<!ENTITY % template "
 (#PCDATA
  %instructions;
  %result-elements;)*
">

<!-- Used for the type of an attribute value that is a URI reference.-->
<!ENTITY % URI "CDATA">

<!-- Used for the type of an attribute value that is a pattern.-->
<!ENTITY % pattern "CDATA">

<!-- Used for the type of an attribute value that is an
     attribute value template.-->
<!ENTITY % avt "CDATA">

<!-- Used for the type of an attribute value that is a QName; the prefix
     gets expanded by the XSLT processor. -->
<!ENTITY % qname "NMTOKEN">

<!-- Like qname but a whitespace-separated list of QNames. -->
<!ENTITY % qnames "NMTOKENS">

<!-- Used for the type of an attribute value that is an expression.-->
<!ENTITY % expr "CDATA">

<!-- Used for the type of an attribute value that consists
     of a single character.-->
<!ENTITY % char "CDATA">

<!-- Used for the type of an attribute value that is a priority. -->
<!ENTITY % priority "NMTOKEN">

<!ENTITY % space-att "xml:space (default|preserve) #IMPLIED">
```

```
<!-- This may be overridden to customize the set of elements allowed
at the top-level. -->

<!ENTITY % non-xsl-top-level "">

<!ENTITY % top-level "
 (xsl:import*,
  (xsl:include
   | xsl:strip-space
   | xsl:preserve-space
   | xsl:output
   | xsl:key
   | xsl:decimal-format
   | xsl:attribute-set
   | xsl:variable
   | xsl:param
   | xsl:template
   | xsl:namespace-alias
  %non-xsl-top-level;)*)
">

<!ENTITY % top-level-atts '
  extension-element-prefixes CDATA #IMPLIED
  exclude-result-prefixes CDATA #IMPLIED
  id ID #IMPLIED
  version NMTOKEN #REQUIRED
  xmlns:xsl CDATA #FIXED "http://www.w3.org/1999/XSL/Transform"
  %space-att;
'>

<!-- This entity is defined for use in the ATTLIST declaration
for result elements. -->

<!ENTITY % result-element-atts '
  xsl:extension-element-prefixes CDATA #IMPLIED
  xsl:exclude-result-prefixes CDATA #IMPLIED
  xsl:use-attribute-sets %qnames; #IMPLIED
  xsl:version NMTOKEN #IMPLIED
'>

<!ELEMENT xsl:stylesheet %top-level;>
<!ATTLIST xsl:stylesheet %top-level-atts;>

<!ELEMENT xsl:transform %top-level;>
<!ATTLIST xsl:transform %top-level-atts;>

<!ELEMENT xsl:import EMPTY>
<!ATTLIST xsl:import href %URI; #REQUIRED>

<!ELEMENT xsl:include EMPTY>
<!ATTLIST xsl:include href %URI; #REQUIRED>
```

```
<!ELEMENT xsl:strip-space EMPTY>
<!ATTLIST xsl:strip-space elements CDATA #REQUIRED>

<!ELEMENT xsl:preserve-space EMPTY>
<!ATTLIST xsl:preserve-space elements CDATA #REQUIRED>

<!ELEMENT xsl:output EMPTY>
<!ATTLIST xsl:output
  method %qname; #IMPLIED
  version NMTOKEN #IMPLIED
  encoding CDATA #IMPLIED
  omit-xml-declaration (yes|no) #IMPLIED
  standalone (yes|no) #IMPLIED
  doctype-public CDATA #IMPLIED
  doctype-system CDATA #IMPLIED
  cdata-section-elements %qnames; #IMPLIED
  indent (yes|no) #IMPLIED
  media-type CDATA #IMPLIED
>

<!ELEMENT xsl:key EMPTY>
<!ATTLIST xsl:key
  name %qname; #REQUIRED
  match %pattern; #REQUIRED
  use %expr; #REQUIRED
>

<!ELEMENT xsl:decimal-format EMPTY>
<!ATTLIST xsl:decimal-format
  name %qname; #IMPLIED
  decimal-separator %char; "."
  grouping-separator %char; ","
  infinity CDATA "Infinity"
  minus-sign %char; "-"
  NaN CDATA "NaN"
  percent %char; "%"
  per-mille %char; "&#x2030;"
  zero-digit %char; "0"
  digit %char; "#"
  pattern-separator %char; ";"
>

<!ELEMENT xsl:namespace-alias EMPTY>
<!ATTLIST xsl:namespace-alias
  stylesheet-prefix CDATA #REQUIRED
  result-prefix CDATA #REQUIRED
>

<!ELEMENT xsl:template
 (#PCDATA
  %instructions;
  %result-elements;
  | xsl:param)*
>
```

```
<!ATTLIST xsl:template
  match %pattern; #IMPLIED
  name %qname; #IMPLIED
  priority %priority; #IMPLIED
  mode %qname; #IMPLIED
  %space-att;
>

<!ELEMENT xsl:value-of EMPTY>
<!ATTLIST xsl:value-of
  select %expr; #REQUIRED
  disable-output-escaping (yes|no) "no"
>

<!ELEMENT xsl:copy-of EMPTY>
<!ATTLIST xsl:copy-of select %expr; #REQUIRED>

<!ELEMENT xsl:number EMPTY>
<!ATTLIST xsl:number
   level (single|multiple|any) "single"
   count %pattern; #IMPLIED
   from %pattern; #IMPLIED
   value %expr; #IMPLIED
   format %avt; '1'
   lang %avt; #IMPLIED
   letter-value %avt; #IMPLIED
   grouping-separator %avt; #IMPLIED
   grouping-size %avt; #IMPLIED
>

<!ELEMENT xsl:apply-templates (xsl:sort|xsl:with-param)*>
<!ATTLIST xsl:apply-templates
  select %expr; "node()"
  mode %qname; #IMPLIED
>

<!ELEMENT xsl:apply-imports EMPTY>

<!-- xsl:sort cannot occur after any other elements or
any non-whitespace character -->

<!ELEMENT xsl:for-each
 (#PCDATA
  %instructions;
  %result-elements;
  | xsl:sort)*
>

<!ATTLIST xsl:for-each
  select %expr; #REQUIRED
  %space-att;
>
```

```
<!ELEMENT xsl:sort EMPTY>
<!ATTLIST xsl:sort
  select %expr; "."
  lang %avt; #IMPLIED
  data-type %avt; "text"
  order %avt; "ascending"
  case-order %avt; #IMPLIED
>

<!ELEMENT xsl:if %template;>
<!ATTLIST xsl:if
  test %expr; #REQUIRED
  %space-att;
>

<!ELEMENT xsl:choose (xsl:when+, xsl:otherwise?)>
<!ATTLIST xsl:choose %space-att;>

<!ELEMENT xsl:when %template;>
<!ATTLIST xsl:when
  test %expr; #REQUIRED
  %space-att;
>

<!ELEMENT xsl:otherwise %template;>
<!ATTLIST xsl:otherwise %space-att;>

<!ELEMENT xsl:attribute-set (xsl:attribute)*>
<!ATTLIST xsl:attribute-set
  name %qname; #REQUIRED
  use-attribute-sets %qnames; #IMPLIED
>

<!ELEMENT xsl:call-template (xsl:with-param)*>
<!ATTLIST xsl:call-template
  name %qname; #REQUIRED
>

<!ELEMENT xsl:with-param %template;>
<!ATTLIST xsl:with-param
  name %qname; #REQUIRED
  select %expr; #IMPLIED
>

<!ELEMENT xsl:variable %template;>
<!ATTLIST xsl:variable
  name %qname; #REQUIRED
  select %expr; #IMPLIED
>
```

```
<!ELEMENT xsl:param %template;>
<!ATTLIST xsl:param
  name %qname; #REQUIRED
  select %expr; #IMPLIED
>

<!ELEMENT xsl:text (#PCDATA)>
<!ATTLIST xsl:text
  disable-output-escaping (yes|no) "no"
>

<!ELEMENT xsl:processing-instruction %char-template;>
<!ATTLIST xsl:processing-instruction
  name %avt; #REQUIRED
  %space-att;
>

<!ELEMENT xsl:element %template;>
<!ATTLIST xsl:element
  name %avt; #REQUIRED
  namespace %avt; #IMPLIED
  use-attribute-sets %qnames; #IMPLIED
  %space-att;
>

<!ELEMENT xsl:attribute %char-template;>
<!ATTLIST xsl:attribute
  name %avt; #REQUIRED
  namespace %avt; #IMPLIED
  %space-att;
>

<!ELEMENT xsl:comment %char-template;>
<!ATTLIST xsl:comment %space-att;>

<!ELEMENT xsl:copy %template;>
<!ATTLIST xsl:copy
  %space-att;
  use-attribute-sets %qnames; #IMPLIED
>

<!ELEMENT xsl:message %template;>
<!ATTLIST xsl:message
  %space-att;
  terminate (yes|no) "no"
>

<!ELEMENT xsl:fallback %template;>
<!ATTLIST xsl:fallback %space-att;>
```

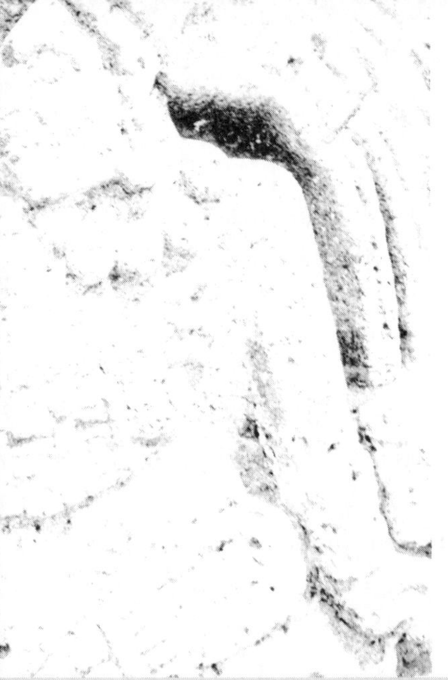

B
XSL-FO Formatting Properties

THIS APPENDIX LISTS ALL THE XSL-FO formatting properties in the XSL 1.0 specification. You can find more information on the XSL-FO properties at `www.w3.org/TR/xsl/slice7.html`. Many of the XSL-FO properties are inherited from the specification for Cascading Stylesheets version 2, CSS2, which you can find at `www.w3.org/TR/REC-CSS2`.

The following list includes the syntax used in this appendix, following the XSL-FO specification:

- <> Indicates units for values (see Table B.1) or properties (such as `<color>`) that have already been defined.
- | Indicates alternatives, only one of which may be used.
- || Indicates options, one or more of which must be used, in any order.
- [] Group statements evaluated much like mathematical statements.
- * Means the preceding term occurs zero or more times.
- + Means the preceding term occurs one or more times.
- ? Means the preceding term is optional.
- {} Surrounds pairs of numbers giving the minimum and maximum number of times a term may occur (as in {1, 4}).

Many of the XSL-FO properties indicate a specific format for values that you may assign to them, such as `<color>` or `<angle>`. You'll find the formats and their meanings in the following list.

- `<absolute-size>`. Absolute font sizes; may be xx-small, x-small, small, medium, large, x-large, xx-large.
- `<angle>`. Angles, may be deg, grad, or rad.
- `<border-style>`. A box's border; may be none, dotted, dashed, solid, double, groove, ridge, inset, or outset.
- `<border-width>`. Sets the width of a border; may be thin, medium, thick, or an explicit length.
- `<color>`. Color; may be specified with a predefined color value or RGB triplet color value.
- `<country-language>`. Set to a `<language>` value.
- `<family-name>`. The name of a font family, such as Arial, Times New Roman, or Courier.
- `<frequency>`. Frequency values; units may be Hz or KHz.
- `<generic-family>`. Generic names for fonts that you use as a last resort if the browser can't find a specific font. Examples are serif (browser should choose a serif font), sans-serif (browser should choose a sans-serif font), and monospace (browser should choose a monospace font).
- `<generic-voice>`. Aural voices; may be male, female, or child.
- `<integer>`. Standard integer values.
- `<keep>`. A `context-dependant` property you set to Auto for no keep-together constraints or Always for strict keep-together constraints. See the XSL specification for more information.
- `<language>`. A language specifier that conforms to the RFC1766 specification (which you can find at `www.w3.org/TR/xsl/sliceD.html#RFC1766`).
- `<length>`. Length; may start with a + or -, followed by a number, which may include a decimal point, followed by a unit identifier, which may be em (font size of the relevant font), ex (the x-height of the font), px (pixels as specified relative to the viewing device), pt (points, 1/72nds of an inch), in (inches), cm (centimeters), mm (millimeters), or pc (picas, 1/6th of an inch).
- `<length-bp-ip-direction>`. Specifies the distance that separates adjacent cell borders in the row-stacking-direction. See `www.w3.org/TR/xsl/slice7.html` for more details.

- `<length-conditional>`. A compound value specifying the width and any conditionality of the border for the before-edge. See `www.w3.org/TR/xsl/slice7.html#pr-section` for more details.
- `<length-range>`. Specifies a length range, as defined in the XSL specification.
- `<margin-width>`. Can be a `<length>`, `<percentage>`, or auto. How the auto value works is dependent on context; see `www.w3.org/TR/REC-CSS2/visudet.html#Computing_widths_and_margins` for more information.
- `<number>`. A number; may include a sign and a decimal point.
- `<padding-width>`. Set to a `<length>` value.
- `<percentage>`. A number, which may include a sign, followed by a percentage sign (%).
- `<relative-size>`. A font size relative to the parent element, may be either larger or smaller.
- `<shape>`. Currently may only specify a rectangle, as follows: `rect(<top> <right> <bottom> <left>)`.
- `<space>`. Specifies the minimum, optimum, and maximum values for a space. See `www.w3.org/TR/xsl/slice4.html#spacecond` for more information.
- `<specific-voice>`. Specifies a specific voice. See `www.w3.org/TR/REC-CSS2/aural.html#propdef-voice-family` for more information.
- `<time>`. Time units, specified as a number followed immediately by ms (for milliseconds) or s (for seconds).
- `<uri-specification>`. Uniform Resource Indicator (URI), which is the Web address of a page element, such as an image.

Also, note that XSL-FO properties, like CSS2 properties, may be set to the value "inherit", which means the value of the property should be inherited from its parent element.

The XSL-FO properties are as follows:

- `absolute-position`. Specifies whether an item's position is absolute. Set to auto | absolute | fixed | inherit.
- `active-state`. Specifies which of the `<fo:multi-property-sets>` are used to format child flow objects. Set to link | visited | active | hover | focus.
- `alignment-adjust`. Using this property, the position of the baseline identified by the "alignment-baseline" property can be adjusted. Set to auto | baseline | before-edge | text-before-edge | middle | central | after-edge | text-after-edge | ideographic | alphabetic | hanging | mathematical | <percentage> | <length> | inherit.

- `alignment-baseline`. Specifies how an object is aligned with respect to its parent. Set to auto | baseline | before-edge | text-before-edge | middle | central | after-edge | text-after-edge | ideographic | alphabetic | hanging | mathematical | inherit.
- `auto-restore`. Specifies whether the initial `<fo:multi-case>` should be restored when the `<fo:multi-switch>` gets hidden. Set to true | false.
- `azimuth`. Sets the azimuth for angles. Set to <angle> | [[left-side | far-left | left | center-left | center | center-right | right | far-right | right-side] || behind] | leftwards | rightwards | inherit.
- `background`. A shorthand property for setting the individual background properties (`background-color`, `background-image`, `background-repeat`, `background-attachment`, and `background-position`) all at once. Set to [<background-color> || <background-image> || <background-repeat> || <background-attachment> || <background-position>]] | inherit.
- `background-attachment`. Specifies whether the background scrolls or not. Set to scroll | fixed | inherit.
- `background-color`. Specifies the background color of an element. Set to <color> | transparent | inherit.
- `background-image`. Specifies the background image of an element. Set to <uri-specification> | none | inherit.
- `background-position`. Specifies the initial position of the background image. Set to [[<percentage> | <length>]{1,2} | [[top | center | bottom] || [left | center | right]]] | inherit.
- `background-position-horizontal`. Sets the background's horizontal position if a background image is specified. Set to <percentage> | <length> | left | center | right | inherit.
- `background-position-vertical`. Sets the background's vertical position if a background image is specified. Set to <percentage> | <length> | top | center | bottom | inherit.
- `background-repeat`. Specifies whether the background image is tiled, and if so, how. Set to repeat | repeat-x | repeat-y | no-repeat | inherit.
- `baseline-shift`. Repositions the baseline relative to the baseline of the parent. Set to baseline | sub | super | <percentage> | <length> | inherit.
- `blank-or-not-blank`. Forms part of a selection rule to determine whether the referenced page-master can be selected at this point in the page sequence. Set to blank | not-blank | any | inherit.
- `block-progression-dimension`. Same as the CSS2 property of the same name. Set to auto | <length> | <percentage> | <length-range> | inherit.

- `border`. A shorthand property for setting the same width, color, and style for all four borders (top, bottom, left, and right) of a box. Set to [<border-width> || <border-style> || <color>] | inherit.
- `border-after-color`. Specifies the color of the border on the after-edge of region. Set to <color> | inherit.
- `border-after-precedence`. Specifies the precedence of the border specification for the after border. Set to force | <integer> | inherit.
- `border-after-style`. Specifies the border style for the after edge. Set to <border-style> | inherit.
- `border-after-width`. Specifies the border width for the after edge. Set to <border-width> | <length-conditional> | inherit.
- `border-before-color`. Specifies the color of the border on a before edge. Set to <color> | inherit.
- `border-before-precedence`. Specifies the precedence of the border specification for the before border. Set to force | <integer> | inherit.
- `border-before-style`. Specifies the border style for a before edge. Set to <border-style> | inherit.
- `border-before-width`. Specifies the border width for a before edge. Set to <border-width> | <length-conditional> | inherit.
- `border-bottom`. A shorthand property for setting the width, style, and color of the bottom border of a block-area or inline-area. Set to [<border-top-width> || <border-style> || <color>] | inherit.
- `border-bottom-color`. Specifies the border color for a bottom edge. Set to <color> | inherit.
- `border-bottom-style`. Specifies the border style for a bottom edge. Set to <border-style> | inherit.
- `border-bottom-width`. Specifies the border width for a bottom edge. Set to <border-width> | inherit.
- `border-collapse`. Specifies a table's border model. Set to collapse | separate | inherit.
- `border-color`. Specifies the color of all four borders at once. Set to <color>{1,4} | transparent | inherit.
- `border-end-color`. Specifies the color of the border on an end edge. Set to <color> | inherit.
- `border-end-precedence`. Specifies the precedence of the border specification for the end border. Set to force | <integer> | inherit.

- `border-end-style`. Specifies the border style for an end edge. Set to <border-style> | inherit.
- `border-end-width`. Specifies the border width for an end edge. Set to <border-width> | <length-conditional> | inherit.
- `border-left`. A shorthand property for setting the width, style, and color of the left border all at once. Set to [<border-top-width> || <border-style> || <color>] | inherit.
- `border-left-color`. Specifies the border color for a left edge. Set to <color> | inherit.
- `border-left-style`. Specifies the border style for a left edge. Set to <border-style> | inherit.
- `border-left-width`. Specifies the border width for a left edge. Set to <border-width> | inherit.
- `border-right`. A shorthand property for setting the width, style, and color of a right border all at once. Set to [<border-top-width> || <border-style> || <color>] | inherit.
- `border-right-color`. Specifies the border color for a right edge. Set to <color> | inherit.
- `border-right-style`. Specifies the border style for a right edge. Set to <border-style> | inherit.
- `border-right-width`. Specifies the border width for a right edge. Set to <border-width> | inherit.
- `border-separation`. Sets the border separation between adjacent cells. Set to <length-bp-ip-direction> | inherit.
- `border-spacing`. Specifies the distance that separates adjacent cell borders. Set to <length> <length>? | inherit.
- `border-start-color`. Specifies the color of the border on a start edge. Set to <color> | inherit.
- `border-start-precedence`. Specifies the precedence of the border specification for the starting border. Set to force | <integer> | inherit.
- `border-start-style`. Specifies the border style for the starting edge. Set to <border-style> | inherit.
- `border-start-width`. Specifies the border width for the starting edge. Set to <border-width> | <length-conditional> | inherit.
- `border-style`. Sets the style of the four borders. Set to <border-style>{1,4} | inherit.

- `border-top`. A shorthand property for setting the width, style, and color of the top border of a block-area or inline-area all at once. Set to [<border-top-width> || <border-style> || <color>] | inherit.
- `border-top-color`. Specifies the color of the border on a top edge. Set to <color> | inherit.
- `border-top-style`. Specifies the line style of a box's border (solid, double, dashed, and so on).
- `border-top-width`. Sets the width of the top border. Set to <border-width> | inherit.
- `border-width`. A shorthand property for setting `border-top-width`, `border-right-width`, `border-bottom-width`, and `border-left-width` all at once. Set to <border-width>{1,4} | inherit.
- `bottom`. Specifies how far a box's bottom content edge is offset above the bottom of the box's containing block. Set to <length> | <percentage> | auto | inherit.
- `break-after`. Specifies that the last area generated shall be the last one placed in a particular context. Set to auto | column | page | even-page | odd-page | inherit.
- `break-before`. Specifies that the first area generated should be the first one placed in a specific context. Set to auto | column | page | even-page | odd-page | inherit.
- `caption-side`. Specifies the position of a caption. Set to before | after | start | end | top | bottom | left | right | inherit.
- `case-name`. Specifies a name for an `<fo:multi-case>` element. Set to <name>.
- `case-title`. Specifies a descriptive title for an `<fo:multi-case>` element. Set to <string>.
- `character`. Specifies the Unicode character to be inserted. Set to <character>.
- `clear`. Specifies which sides of an element's boxes may not be adjacent to an earlier floating box. Set to start | end | left | right | both | none | inherit.
- `clip`. Clips elements that have an "overflow" property with a value other than "visible". Set to <shape> | auto | inherit.
- `color`. Specifies the foreground color of an element's text. Set to <color> | inherit.
- `color-profile-name`. Specifies the name of a color-profile. Set to <name> | inherit.

- `column-count`. Specifies the number of columns in a region. Set to <number> | inherit.
- `column-gap`. Specifies the width of the separation between adjacent columns in a multi-column region. Set to <length> | <percentage> | inherit.
- `column-number`. Sets the column number for table cells. Set to <number>.
- `column-width`. Specifies the width of a column. Set to auto | scale-to-fit | <length> | <percentage> (7.25.9) – width of the column and no inherit.
- `content-height`. Specifies the height of an object such as an external graphic. Set to auto | scale-to-fit | <length> | <percentage> | inherit.
- `content-type`. This property specifies the content-type and may be used by a client to select how the data should be rendered. Set to <string> | auto.
- `content-width`. Specifies the width of an object such as an external graphic. Set to auto | scale-to-fit | <length> | <percentage> | inherit.
- `country`. Specifies the country to be used by the formatter in language- or locale-coupled services. Set to none | <country> | inherit.
- `cue`. Same as the CSS2 property of the same name. Set to <cue-before> || <cue-after> | inherit.
- `cue-after`. Same as the CSS2 property of the same name. Set to <uri-specification> | none | inherit.
- `cue-before`. Same as the CSS2 property of the same name. Set to <uri-specification> | none | inherit.
- `destination-placement-offset`. Specifies the distance from the top of the page to the innermost line-area that contains the first destination area. Set to <length>.
- `direction`. Specifies the base writing direction of text for the Unicode bidirectional algorithm. Set to ltr | rtl | inherit.
- `display-align`. Specifies the alignment of the areas that are the children of the reference area. Set to auto | before | center | after | inherit.
- `dominant-baseline`. Used to specify a scaled-baseline table. Set to auto | use-script | no-change | reset-size | ideographic | alphabetic | hanging | mathematical | inherit.
- `elevation`. Same as the CSS2 property of the same name. Set to <angle> | below | level | above | higher | lower | inherit.
- `empty-cells`. Controls the rendering of borders around cells that have no visible content. Set to show | hide | inherit.

- `end-indent`. Specifies the distance from the end edge of a block to the end edge of the containing reference area. Set to <length> | inherit.
- `ends-row`. Specifies whether this cell ends a row in a table row. Set to true | false.
- `extent`. Specifies the width of the region-start or region-end or the height of the region-before or region-after. Set to <length> | <percentage> | inherit.
- `external-destination`. Specifies the destination resource for an `<fo:basic-link>`. Set to <uri-specification>.
- `float`. Specifies whether a box should float to the left, right, or not at all. Set to before | start | end | left | right | none | inherit.
- `flow-name`. Sets a flow's name. Set to <name>.
- `font`. A shorthand property for setting `font-style`, `font-variant`, `font-weight`, `font-size`, `line-height`, and `font-family` all at once. Set to [[<font-style> || <font-variant> || <font-weight>]? <font-size> [/ <line-height>]? <font-family>] | caption | icon | menu | message-box | small-caption | status-bar | inherit.
- `font-family`. Specifies a list of font family names and/or generic family names in order of preference. Set to [[<family-name> | <generic-family>],]* [<family-name> | <generic-family>] | inherit.
- `font-size`. Sets the font size. Set to <absolute-size> | <relative-size> | <length> | <percentage> | inherit.
- `font-size-adjust`. Adjusts the font size for aspect ratio. Set to <number> | none | inherit.
- `font-selection-strategy`. Sets the strategy to be used to select a font. Set to auto | character-by-character | inherit (7.7.3).
- `font-stretch`. Selects a normal, condensed, or extended face from a font family. Set to normal | wider | narrower | ultra-condensed | extra-condensed | condensed | semi-condensed | semi-expanded | expanded | extra-expanded | ultra-expanded | inherit.
- `font-style`. Sets the font's style. Set to normal | italic | oblique | backslant | inherit.
- `font-variant`. Selects bicameral fonts. Set to normal | small-caps | inherit.
- `font-weight`. Sets the font weight. Set to normal | bold | bolder | lighter | 100 | 200 | 300 | 400 | 500 | 600 | 700 | 800 | 900 | inherit.

- `force-page-count`. Used to impose a constraint on the number of pages in a page sequence. Set to auto | even | odd | end-on-even | end-on-odd | no-force | inherit.
- `format`. An XSLT format. Set to <string>.
- `glyph-orientation-horizontal`. Specifies the orientation of glyphs; applied only to text written in a horizontal writing mode. Set to <angle>| inherit.
- `glyph-orientation-vertical`. Specifies the orientation of glyphs, applied only to text written in a vertical writing mode. Set to <angle> | inherit (7.26.3).
- `grouping-separator`. An XSLT format grouping separator. Set to <character>.
- `grouping-size`. The XSLT format grouping size. Set to <number>.
- `height`. Specifies the content height of boxes generated by block-level and replaced elements. Set to <length> | <percentage> | auto | inherit.
- `hyphenate`. Specifies whether hyphenation is allowed during line-breaking. Set to false | true | inherit.
- `hyphenation-character`. Specifies the Unicode character to be presented when a hyphenation break occurs. Set to <character> | inherit.
- `hyphenation-keep`. Specifies whether hyphenation can be performed on the last line that fits in a given area. Set to auto | column | page | inherit.
- `hyphenation-ladder-count`. Specifies a limit on the number of successive hyphenated line areas the formatter may generate in a block. Set to no-limit | <number> | inherit.
- `hyphenation-push-character-count`. Specifies a positive integer giving the minimum number of characters in a hyphenated word after the hyphenation character. Set to <number> | inherit.
- `hyphenation-remain-character-count`. Specifies a positive integer giving the minimum number of characters in a hyphenated word before the hyphenation character. Set to <number> | inherit.
- `id`. An identifier unique among all objects in the result tree with the same namespace. Set to <id>.
- `indicate-destination`. Specifies whether the destination should be indicated or not. Set to true | false.
- `initial-page-number`. Sets the initial page number. Set to auto | auto-odd | auto-even | <number> | inherit.
- `inline-progression-dimension`. Same as the CSS2 property of the same name. Set to auto | <length> | <percentage> | <length-range> | inherit.

- `internal-destination`. Specifies the destination flow object of an `<fo:basic-link>`. Set to empty string | <idref>.
- `keep-together`. Specifies what elements to keep together. Set to <keep> | inherit.
- `keep-with-next`. Specifies keep-with-next conditions on formatting objects. Set to <keep> | inherit.
- `keep-with-previous`. Specifies keep-with-previous conditions on formatting objects. Set to <keep> | inherit.
- `language`. Specifies the language to be used by the formatter. Set to none | <language> | inherit.
- `last-line-end-indent`. Specifies an indent to be applied to the end edge of the last line area in a block. Set to <length> | <percentage> | inherit.
- `leader-alignment`. Specifies leader alignment. Set to none | reference-area | page | inherit.
- `leader-length`. Sets the leader length. Set to <length-range> | inherit.
- `leader-pattern`. Sets the leader pattern. Set to space | rule | dots | use-content | inherit.
- `leader-pattern-width`. Sets the leader pattern width. Set to use-font-metrics | <length> | inherit.
- `left`. Specifies how far a box's left content edge is offset to the right of the left edge of a containing block. Set to <length> | <percentage> | auto | inherit.
- `letter-spacing`. Specifies spacing behavior between text characters. Set to normal | <length> | <space> | inherit.
- `letter-value`. Sets XSLT number to string conversion attributes. Set to auto | alphabetic | traditional.
- `linefeed-treatment`. Specifies the treatment of linefeeds. Set to ignore | preserve | treat-as-space | treat-as-zero-width-space | inherit.
- `line-height`. Specifies the minimal height of each generated inline box. Set to normal | <length> | <number> | <percentage> | <space> | inherit.
- `line-height-shift-adjustment`. Controls whether the line height is adjusted for content that has a baseline shift. Set to consider-shifts | disregard-shifts | inherit.
- `line-stacking-strategy`. Selects the strategy for positioning adjacent lines. Set to line-height | font-height | max-height | inherit.
- `margin`. A shorthand property for setting `margin-top`, `margin-right`, `margin-bottom`, and `margin-left` all at once. Set to <margin-width>{1,4} | inherit.

- `margin-bottom`. Sets the bottom margin of a box. Set to <margin-width> | inherit.
- `margin-left`. Sets the left margin of a box. Set to <margin-width> | inherit.
- `margin-right`. Sets the right margin of a box. Set to <margin-width> | inherit.
- `margin-top`. Sets the top margin of a box. Set to <margin-width> | inherit.
- `marker-class-name`. Specifies the `<fo:marker>` element as being in a group with others that have the same name, each of which can be retrieved by an `<fo:retrieve-marker>` element that has a "retrieve-class-name" property of the same value. Set to <name>.
- `master-name`. Sets or selects a master. Set to <name>.
- `max-height`. Sets the maximum height of a box. Set to <length> | <percentage> | none | inherit.
- `maximum-repeats`. Specifies the maximum number of pages in a sub-sequence of pages that may be generated by an `<fo:page-sequence>` that uses `<fo:repeatable-page-master-reference>` or `<fo:repeatable-page-master-alternatives>` elements. Set to <number> | no-limit | inherit.
- `max-width`. Sets the maximum width of a box. Set to <length> | <percentage> | none | inherit.
- `media-usage`. Specifies how the selected display medium is used to present the pages specified by the stylesheet. Set to auto | paginate | bounded-in-one-dimension | unbounded.
- `min-height`. Sets the minimum height of a box. Set to <length> | <percentage> | inherit.
- `min-width`. Sets the minimum width of a box. Set to <length> | <percentage> | inherit.
- `number-columns-repeated`. Specifies the repetition of a table-column specification. Set to <number>.
- `number-columns-spanned`. Sets the number of columns spanned by a table cell. Set to <number>.
- `number-rows-spanned`. Sets the number of rows spanned by a table cell. Set to <number>.
- `odd-or-even`. Used in a selection rule to determine whether the referenced page-master is eligible for selection at this point in the page sequence. Set to odd | even | any | inherit.

- `orphans`. Same as the CSS2 property of the same name. Set to <integer> | inherit.
- `overflow`. Specifies whether the content of a block element is clipped when it overflows. Set to visible | hidden | scroll | error-if-overflow | auto | inherit.
- `padding`. A shorthand property for setting `padding-top`, `padding-bottom`, `padding-left`, and `padding-right` properties all at once. Set to <padding-width>{1,4} | inherit.
- `padding-after`. Specifies the width of the padding on an after edge. Set to <padding-width> | <length-conditional> | inherit.
- `padding-before`. Specifies the width of the padding on a before edge. Set to <padding-width> | <length-conditional> | inherit.
- `padding-bottom`. Specifies the width of the padding on a bottom edge. Set to <padding-width> | inherit.
- `padding-end`. Specifies the width of the padding on an end edge. Set to <padding-width> | <length-conditional> | inherit.
- `padding-left`. Specifies the width of the padding on a left edge. Set to <padding-width> | inherit.
- `padding-right`. Specifies the width of the padding on a right edge. Set to <padding-width> | inherit.
- `padding-start`. Specifies the width of the padding on a start edge. Set to <padding-width> | <length-conditional> | inherit.
- `padding-top`. Specifies the width of the padding on a top edge. Set to <padding-width> | inherit.
- `page-break-after`. Same as the CSS2 property of the same name. Set to auto | always | avoid | left | right | inherit.
- `page-break-before`. Same as the CSS2 property of the same name. Set to auto | always | avoid | left | right | inherit.
- `page-break-inside`. Same as the CSS2 property of the same name. Set to auto | always | avoid | left | right | inherit.
- `page-height`. Sets the page height. Set to auto | indefinite | <length> | inherit.
- `page-position`. Used as part of a selection rule to determine whether the referenced page-master may be used at this point in the page sequence. Set to first | last | rest | any | inherit.
- `page-width`. Sets the page width. Set to auto | indefinite | <length> | inherit.

- `pause`. Same as the CSS2 property with the same name. Set to [<time> | <percentage>]{1,2} | inherit.
- `pause-after`. Same as the CSS2 property of the same name. Set to <time> | <percentage> | inherit.
- `pause-before`. Same as the CSS2 property of the same name. Set to <time> | <percentage> | inherit.
- `pitch`. Sets a sound's pitch. Set to <frequency> | x-low | low | medium | high | x-high | inherit.
- `pitch-range`. Sets a pitch's range. Set to <number> | inherit.
- `play-during`. Same as the CSS2 property of the same name. Set to <uri-specification> mix? repeat? | auto | none | inherit.
- `position`. Specifies the positioning scheme to be used. Set to static | relative | absolute | fixed | inherit.
- `precedence`. Specifies which region (that is, region-before, region-after, region-start, or region-end) takes precedence. Set to true | false | inherit.
- `provisional-distance-between-starts`. Specifies the provisional distance between the starting indent of a list item's label and the starting indent of the list item's body. Set to <length> | inherit.
- `provisional-label-separation`. Sets the distance between a list item label and the start of a list item body. Set to <length> | inherit.
- `reference-orientation`. Specifies the direction for the top of the current content rectangle. Set to 0 | 90 | 180 | 270 | -90 | -180 | -270 | inherit.
- `ref-id`. Reference to the object having the specified unique identifier. Set to <idref> | inherit.
- `region-name`. Identifies a region name. Set to xsl-region-body | xsl-region-start | xsl-region-end | xsl-region-before | xsl-region-after | xsl-before-float-separator | xsl-footnote-separator | <name>.
- `relative-align`. Specifies the alignment, in the block-progression-direction, between two or more areas. Set to before | baseline | inherit.
- `relative-position`. Same as the CSS2 property of the same name. Set to static | relative | inherit.
- `rendering-intent`. Specifies a color profile rendering intent other than the default. Set to auto | perceptual | relative-colorimetric | saturation | absolute-colorimetric | inherit.
- `retrieve-boundary`. Sets a retrieve boundary. Set to page | page-sequence | document.

- `retrieve-class-name`. Specifies that the `<fo:marker>` whose children are retrieved by the `<fo:retrieve-marker>` must have a `marker-class-name` property value that is the same as this property. Set to <name>.
- `retrieve-position`. Specifies the preference for which an `<fo:marker>` element's children should be retrieved by an `<fo:retrieve-marker>` element. Set to first-starting-within-page | first-including-carryover | last-starting-within-page | last-ending-within-page.
- `richness`. Sets a tone's richness. Set to <number> | inherit.
- `right`. Specifies how far a content edge is offset to the left of the right edge of the containing block. Set to <length> | <percentage> | auto | inherit.
- `role`. Specifies a hint for alternate renderers (such as aural readers) as to the role of the XML element that was used in this formatting object. Set to <string> | <uri-specification> | none | inherit.
- `rule-style`. Specifies the pattern of a rule. Set to none | dotted | dashed | solid | double | groove | ridge | inherit.
- `rule-thickness`. Specifies the overall thickness of a rule. Set to <length>.
- `scaling`. Specifies whether scaling needs to preserve the aspect ratio. Set to uniform | non-uniform | inherit.
- `scaling-method`. Specifies a preference to be used when formatting bitmapped graphics. Set to auto | integer-pixels | resample-any-method | inherit.
- `score-spaces`. Specifies whether the text-decoration property shall be applied to spaces. Set to true | false | inherit.
- `script`. Specifies the script to be used by the formatter in locale-coupled services. Set to none | auto | <script> | inherit.
- `show-destination`. Specifies where the destination resource should be displayed. Set to replace | new.
- `size`. Specifies the size and orientation of a page box. Set to <length>{1,2} | auto | landscape | portrait | inherit.
- `source-document`. Specifies a pointer back to the original XML document. Set to <uri-specification> [<uri-specification>]* | none | inherit.
- `space-after`. Specifies the value of the space-specifier for the space after the areas generated by this object. Set to <space> | inherit.
- `space-before`. Specifies the minimum, optimum, and maximum values for the space before any areas generated by this formatting object and the conditionality and precedence of this space. Set to <space> | inherit.
- `space-end`. Specifies the value of the space-specifier for the space after the areas generated by this formatting object. Set to <space> | inherit.

- `space-start`. Specifies the value of the space-specifier for the space before the areas generated by this formatting object. Set to <space> | inherit.
- `space-treatment`. Specifies the treatment of space and other whitespace characters except for linefeeds. Set to ignore | preserve | ignore-if-before-linefeed | ignore-if-after-linefeed | ignore-if-surrounding-linefeed | inherit.
- `span`. Specifies whether a block-level object should be placed in the current column or should span all columns of a multi-column region. Set to none | all | inherit.
- `speak`. Same as the CSS2 property of the same name. Set to normal | none | spell-out | inherit.
- `speak-header`. Specifies a header for the speak action. Set to once | always | inherit.
- `speak-numeral`. Same as the CSS2 property of the same name. Set to digits | continuous | inherit.
- `speak-punctuation`. Same as the CSS2 property of the same name. Set to code | none | inherit.
- `speech-rate`. Specifies the speech rate. Set to <number> | x-slow | slow | medium | fast | x-fast | faster | slower | inherit.
- `src`. Specifies the URI reference that should be used to locate an external resource such as an image or graphic. Set to <uri-specification> | inherit.
- `start-indent`. Specifies the distance from the start-edge of the content rectangle of the containing reference area to the start-edge of the content-rectangle of that block area. Set to <length> | inherit.
- `starting-state`. Specifies whether an `<fo:multi-case>` element can be initially displayed. Set to show | hide.
- `starts-row`. Specifies whether this cell starts a row. Set to true | false.
- `stress`. Sets aural stress. Set to <number> | inherit.
- `suppress-at-line-break`. Suppresses characters at line breaks. Set to auto | suppress | retain | inherit.
- `switch-to`. Specifies what `<fo:multi-case>` elements this `<fo:multi-toggle>` shall switch to. Set to xsl-preceding | xsl-following | xsl-any | <name> [<name>]*.
- `table-layout`. Specifies the algorithm used to lay out the table cells, rows, and columns. Set to auto | fixed | inherit.
- `table-omit-footer-at-break`. Specifies whether a table whose last area is not at the end of an area produced by the table should end with the content of the `<fo:table-footer>` formatting object. Set to true | false.

- `table-omit-header-at-break`. Specifies whether a table whose first area is not at the beginning of an area produced by the table should start with the content of the `<fo:table-header>` formatting object. Set to true | false.
- `target-presentation-context`. Sets the target presentation such as XML, XHTML, SVG. Set to use-target-processing-context | <uri-specification>.
- `target-processing-context`. Specifies the root of a virtual document that the processor should process if the external destination is a resource of a processed media type (for example, XML, SVG). Set to document-root | <uri-specification>.
- `target-stylesheet`. Specifies the stylesheet that shall be used for processing the resource. Set to use-normal-stylesheet | <uri-specification>.
- `text-align`. Specifies how inline content of a block is aligned. Set to start | center | end | justify | inside | outside | left | right | <string> | inherit.
- `text-align-last`. Specifies the alignment of the last line area in a block. Set to relative | start | center | end | justify | inside | outside | left | right | inherit.
- `text-altitude`. Specifies the "height" to be used for the ascent above the dominant baseline. Set to use-font-metrics | <length> | inherit.
- `text-decoration`. Specifies decorations that are added to the text of an element. Set to none | [[underline | no-underline] || [overline | no-overline] || [line-through | no-line-through] || [blink | no-blink]] | inherit.
- `text-depth`. Specifies the depth to be used for the descent below the baseline. Set to use-font-metrics | <length> | inherit.
- `text-indent`. Specifies the indentation of the first line of text in a block. Set to <length> | <percentage> | inherit.
- `text-shadow`. Specifies a comma-separated list of shadow effects to be applied to the text of the element. Set to none | [<color> || <length> <length> <length>? ,]* [<color> || <length> <length> <length>?] | inherit.
- `text-transform`. Specifies capitalization effects of an element's text. Set to capitalize | uppercase | lowercase | none | inherit.
- `top`. Specifies how far a content edge is offset below the top edge of the containing block. Set to <length> | <percentage> | auto | inherit.
- `treat-as-word-space`. Specifies whether a character shall be treated as a word-space or as a normal letter. Set to auto | true | false | inherit.
- `unicode-bidi`. Same as the CSS2 property of the same name. Set to normal | embed | bidi-override | inherit.

- `vertical-align`. Specifies vertical positioning. Set to baseline | middle | sub | super | text-top | text-bottom | <percentage> | <length> | top | bottom | inherit.
- `visibility`. Specifies whether the boxes generated by an element are rendered. Set to visible | hidden | collapse | inherit.
- `voice-family`. Sets the voice family. Set to [[<specific-voice> | <generic-voice>],]* [<specific-voice> | <generic-voice>] | inherit.
- `volume`. Sets aural volume. Set to <number> | <percentage> | silent | x-soft | soft | medium | loud | x-loud | inherit.
- `white-space`. Specifies how whitespace inside the element is handled. Set to normal | pre | nowrap | inherit.
- `white-space-collapse`. Specifies the treatment of consecutive white space. Set to false | true | inherit.
- `widows`. Specifies the minimum number of lines of a paragraph that must be left at the bottom of a page. Set to <integer> | inherit.
- `width`. Specifies the content width of boxes generated by block-level and replaced elements. Set to <length> | <percentage> | auto | inherit.
- `word-spacing`. Specifies spacing behavior between words. Set to normal | <length> | <space> | inherit.
- `wrap-option`. Specifies how line-wrapping of the formatting object is to be handled. Set to no-wrap | wrap | inherit.
- `writing-mode`. Sets the writing mode. Set to lr-tb | rl-tb | tb-rl | lr | rl | tb | inherit.
- `xml:lang`. Specifies the language and country to be used by the formatter. Set to <country-language> | inherit.
- `z-index`. Sets the stacking level of items. Set to auto | <integer> | inherit.

Index

A

B

C

D

E

F

G

H

I

J

M

N

O

Q-R

S

T

U

V

W

X

Y-Z

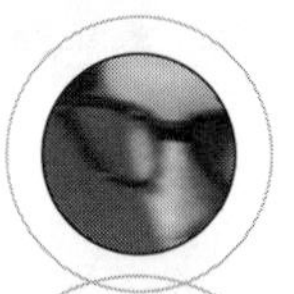

HOW TO CONTACT US

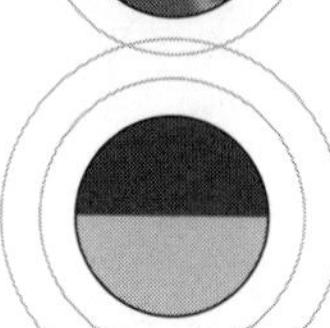

VISIT OUR WEB SITE

WWW.NEWRIDERS.COM

On our web site, you'll find information about our other books, authors, tables of contents, and book errata. You will also find information about book registration and how to purchase our books, both domestically and internationally.

EMAIL US

Contact us at: **nrfeedback@newriders.com**

- If you have comments or questions about this book
- To report errors that you have found in this book
- If you have a book proposal to submit or are interested in writing for New Riders
- If you are an expert in a computer topic or technology and are interested in being a technical editor who reviews manuscripts for technical accuracy

Contact us at: **nreducation@newriders.com**

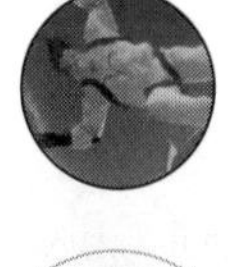

- If you are an instructor from an educational institution who wants to preview New Riders books for classroom use. Email should include your name, title, school, department, address, phone number, office days/hours, text in use, and enrollment, along with your request for desk/examination copies and/or additional information.

Contact us at: **nrmedia@newriders.com**

- If you are a member of the media who is interested in reviewing copies of New Riders books. Send your name, mailing address, and email address, along with the name of the publication or web site you work for.

BULK PURCHASES/CORPORATE SALES

If you are interested in buying 10 or more copies of a title or want to set up an account for your company to purchase directly from the publisher at a substantial discount, contact us at 800-382-3419 or email your contact information to `corpsales@pearsontechgroup.com`. A sales representative will contact you with more information.

WRITE TO US

New Riders Publishing
201 W. 103rd St.
Indianapolis, IN 46290-1097

CALL/FAX US

Toll-free (800) 571-5840
If outside U.S. (317) 581-3500
Ask for New Riders
FAX: (317) 581-4663

WWW.NEWRIDERS.COM

RELATED NEW RIDERS TITLES

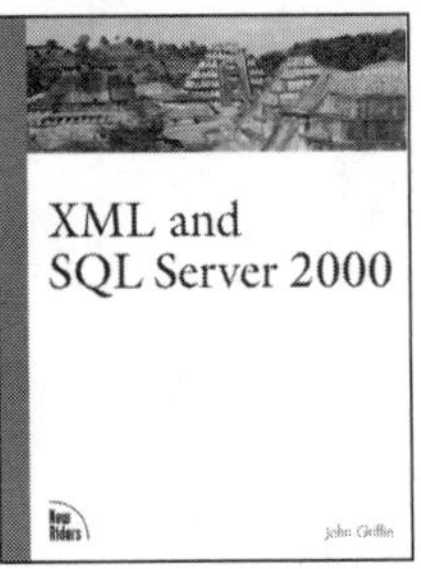

ISBN: 0735711127
400 pages
US $44.99

XML and SQL Server 2000

John Griffin

XML and SQL Server 2000 enables SQL developers to understand and work with XML, the preferred technology for integrating eBusiness systems. SQL Server 2000 has added several new features that SQL Server 7.0 never had that make working with and generating XML easier for the developer. *XML and SQL Server 2000* provides a comprehensive discussion of SQL Server 2000's XML capabilities.

ISBN: 073570970X
500 pages
US $44.99

PHP Functions Essential Reference

Graeme Merrall and
Landon Bradshaw

PHP Functions Essential Reference is a simple, clear, and authoritative function reference that clarifies and expands upon PHP's existing documentation. *PHP Functions Essential Reference* will help the reader write effective code that makes full use of the rich variety of functions available in PHP.

ISBN: 0735711178
300 pages
US $34.99

ebXML: The New Global Standard for Doing Business on the Internet

David Webber
Alan Kotok

To create an e-commerce initiative, managers need to understand that XML is the technology that will take them there. Companies understand that to achieve a successful Internet presence their company needs an e-commerce methodology implemented. Many department managers (the actual people who design, build, and execute the plan) don't know where to begin. *ebXML* will take them there.

ISBN: 073571052X
330 pages with CD-ROM
US $39.99

C++ XML

Fabio Arciniegas

The demand for robust solutions is at an all-time high. Developers and programmers are asking the question, "How do I get the power performance found with C++ integrated into my web applications?" Fabio Arciniegas knows how. He has created the best way to bring C++ to the web. Through development with XML and this book, he shares the secrets developers and programmers worldwide are searching for.

ISBN: 0735710201
1152 pages
US $49.99

Inside XML

Steven Holzner

Inside XML is a foundation book that covers both the Microsoft and non-Microsoft approach to XML programming. It covers in detail the hot aspects of XML, such as DTDs versus XML Schemas, CSS, XSL, XSLT, XLinks, XPointers, XHTML, RDF, CDF, parsing XML in Perl and Java, and much more.

ISBN: 0735710899
700 pages with CD-ROM
US $49.99

XML, XSLT, Java, and JSP: A Case Study in Developing a Web Application

Westy Rockwell

A practical, hands-on experience in building web applications based on XML and Java technologies, this book is unique because it teaches the technologies by using them to build a web chat project throughout the book. The project is explained in great detail, after the reader is shown how to get and install the necessary tools to be able to customize this project and build other web applications.

Colophon

The image on the cover of this book, captured by photographer Adalberto Rios Szala at the ancient ruins of Xochicalco, is a section of the detailed carvings that grace the four-sided base of the main temple at the site. Built during the eight and ninth centuries, Xochicalco was initially a site of religious importance. It would eventually serve as an important trading center, and later, as a defensive stronghold before the Spanish Conquest. The Xochicalco site is located near Cuernavaca, in the state of Morelos, Mexico. Xochicalco means "Place of Flowers."

This book was written and edited in Microsoft Word and laid out in QuarkXPress. The fonts used for the body text are Bembo and MCPdigital. It was printed on 50# Husky Offset Smooth paper at R.R. Donnelley & Sons in Crawfordsville, Indiana. Prepress consisted of PostScript computer-to-plate technology (filmless process). The Cover was printed at Moore Langen Printing in Terre Haute, Indiana, on Carolina, coated on one side.

QA 76.73 .X58 H65 2002
Holzner, Steven.
Inside XSLT